Black
Literature
in America

Black Literature in America

Houston A. Baker, Jr.
University of Virginia

McGraw-Hill Book Company

New York   St. Louis   San Francisco   Düsseldorf
Kuala Lumpur   London   Mexico   Montreal   New Delhi
Panama   Rio de Janeiro   Singapore   Sydney   Toronto

To Charlotte

This book was set in Modern 21 by Monotype Composition
Company, Inc., and printed on permanent paper and bound
by The Maple Press Company. The designer was Marsha
Cohen. The editors were Cheryl Kupper and Paula Henson.
Robert Fry was sponsor. Sally Ellyson supervised production.

Acknowledgments

Anonymous, "Ole Sis Goose" from *Coffee in the Gourd,* Austin, 1923, ed. J. Frank Dobie, University of Texas Press, and "Sheer Crops," from *Southwestern Lou,* Austin, 1931, ed. J. Frank Dobie, University of Texas Press. Used by permission of the Texas Folklore Society.

Anonymous, "Ballad of John Henry," from *John Henry, Tracking Down a Negro Legend* by Guy B. Johnson. University of North Carolina Press. Used by permission of the publisher.

James Baldwin, "Many Thousands Gone," from *Notes of a Native Son* by James Baldwin, copyright © 1951, 1955 by James Baldwin. Reprinted by permission of the Beacon Press.

Arna Bontemps, "Reconaissance," "Southern Mansion," "Nocturne at Bethesda," from *Personals,* copyright © 1963 by Arna Bontemps. "A Summer Tragedy," from *Best Short Stories by Negro Writers,* Little, Brown & Co., copyright © 1933 by Arna Bontemps. Reprinted by permission of Harold Ober Associates Incorporated.

Benjamin Brawley, "The Negro in American Fiction," from *The Negro in American Literature and Art,* 1918, Duffield and Company.

Gwendolyn Brooks, "The Second Sermon on the Warpland," from *In the Mecca* by Gwendolyn Brooks. Copyright © 1968 by Gwendolyn Brooks Blakely. "A Bronzeville Mother Loiters in Mississippi. Meanwhile, a Mississippi Mother Burns Bacon," from *The Bean Eaters* by Gwendolyn Brooks. Copyright © 1960 by Gwendolyn Brooks. Reprinted by permission of Harper & Row, Publishers.

Sterling A. Brown, "The American Race Problem as Reflected in American Literature," from *The Journal of Negro Education,* Vol. 8 (1939). Used by permission of the editors. "Sister Lou" and "Children of the Mississippi," from *Southern Road* by Sterling Brown, Arno Press, Inc. By permission of the author. "The Ballad of Stackalee," collected by Onah Spencer in *The Negro Caravan,* ed. Sterling Brown, Arthur Davis and Ulysses Lee.

Carl Carmer, "De Knee-high Man," from *Stars Fell on Alabama,* ed. Carl Carmer. The Literary Guild.

Charles W. Chesnutt, "The Bouquet," from *The Wife of His Youth,* University of Michigan Press.

Countee Cullen, "Heritage," "Yet Do I Marvel," "A Song of Praise," "Black Magdalens," and "Saturday's Child," from *On These I Stand* by Countee Cullen. Copyright 1925 by Harper & Brothers; renewed 1953 by Ida M. Cullen. Reprinted by permission of Harper & Row, Publishers.

Owen Dodson, "Rag Doll and Summer Birds," "Counterpoint," from *Powerful Long Ladder* by Owen Dodson, copyright 1946 by Owen Dodson. Reprinted with the permission of Farrar, Straus & Giroux, Inc.

Frederick Douglass, from *Narrative of the Life of Frederick Douglass, An American Slave, Written by Himself,* 1968, Arno Press, Inc.

W. E. B. Du Bois, "Of Mr. Booker T. Washington and Others," from *The Souls of Black Folk,* by W. E. B. Du Bois, Peter Smith, Publisher. "The Riddle of the Sphinx," from *Darkwater* by W. E. B. Du Bois, Harcourt, Brace & World, Inc. Used by the kind permission of Mrs. Shirley Graham Du Bois.

Paul Laurence Dunbar, "Philosophy," "Jealous," "Slow through the Dark," "Not They Who Soar," "When Malindy Sings," "Scamp," "Why Fades a Dream?" "We Wear the Mask," and "The Real Question," from *The Complete Poems of Paul Laurence Dunbar.* Reprinted by permission of Dodd, Mead & Company, Inc.

Ralph Ellison, "A Coupla Scalped Indians," from *New World Writing,* 1956, copyright © 1956 by Ralph Ellison. Reprinted by permission of William Morris Agency, Inc., on behalf of the author.

Mari Evans, "Status Symbol," and "I Am a Black Woman," copyright Mari Evans. Used by the kind permission of the author.

Rudolph Fisher, "The City of Refuge," from *Atlantic Monthly.* By permission of the publisher.

Hoyt Fuller, "The Role of the Negro Writer in an Era of Struggle." Used with the kind permission of the author.

Addison Gayle, "Cultural Strangulation: Black Literature and the White Aesthetic." Used by permission of Hoyt Fuller.

Robert Hayden, "A Ballad of Remembrance," "Tour 5," and "Middle Passage," from *Selected Poems* by Robert Hayden. Copyright © 1966 by Robert Hayden. Reprinted by permission of October House, Inc.

Langston Hughes, "Motherless Child," "Go Down, Moses," "The Virgin Mary Had a Baby Boy," "Oh Mary Don't You Weep," "Deep River," "Steal Away," "Good Morning Blues," "Southern Blues," "How Long Blues," from *The Book of Negro Folklore,* ed. Langston Hughes and Arna Bontemps, Dodd, Mead & Company, Inc. 1958. "Good Morning," "Same in Blues," and "Island," from *Montage of a Dream Deferred,* copyright 1951 by Langston Hughes. "Letter," from *Langston Hughes Reader,* copyright 1958 by Langston Hughes. "Brass Spitoons," from *Fine Clothes to the Jew,* copyright 1927 by Langston Hughes. Reprinted by permission of Harold Ober Associates. "The Negro Speaks of Rivers," "Dream Variations," "Troubled Woman," and "I, Too," copyright 1926 by Alfred A. Knopf, Inc., and renewed 1954 by Langston Hughes. "Silhouette," and "One-Way Ticket," copyright 1948 by Alfred A. Knopf, Inc. "Refuge in America," copyright 1943 by the Curtis Publishing Company. Reprinted from *Selected Poems* by Langston Hughes, by permission of Alfred A. Knopf, Inc. "Montmartre," from *Fields of Wonder,* copyright 1947 by Langston Hughes. "Undertow," from *The Panther and the Lash,"* copyright © 1967 by Arna Bontemps and George Houston Bass. "Jazzonia," from *The Weary Blues,* copyright 1926 by Alfred A. Knopf, Inc., and renewed 1954 by Langston Hughes. Reprinted by permission of Alfred A. Knopf, Inc.

Ted Joans, "The Ubiquitous Lions," and "In Homage to Heavy Loaded Trane, J.C.," from *Black Pow-wow* by Ted Joans. Copyright © 1969 by Ted Joans. Reprinted by permission of Hill & Wang, Inc.

James Weldon Johnson, "Preface to the First Edition," from *The Book of American Negro Poetry*, edited by James Weldon Johnson, copyright 1922, by Harcourt, Brace & World, Inc.; renewed, 1950, by Grace Johnson. Reprinted by permission of the publishers. "Go Down Death—a Funeral Sermon," from *God's Trombones* by James Weldon Johnson. Copyright 1927 by The Viking Press, Inc., renewed by Grace Nail Johnson. Reprinted by permission of The Viking Press, Inc. "O Black and Unknown Bards," and "The Black Mammy," from *Saint Peter Relates an Incident* by James Weldon Johnson. Copyright 1917 by James Weldon Johnson. All rights reserved. Reprinted by permission of The Viking Press, Inc.

Fenton Johnson, "Tired," and "The Scarlet Woman," from a collection of 42 W.P.A. poems. By permission of Arna Bontemps.

LeRoi Jones, "Preface to a Twenty Volume Suicide Note," from *Preface to a Twenty Volume Suicide Note,* by LeRoi Jones. Copyright © 1961 by LeRoi Jones. Reprinted by permission of Corinth Books. "I Substitute for the Dead Lecturer," and "The Politics of Rich Painters," from *The Dead Lecturer* by LeRoi Jones, Grove Press, 1964. Copyright © 1964 by LeRoi Jones. Reprinted by permission of The Sterling Lord Agency. "Black Art" and "Black People," from *Black Magic Poetry*. Copyright © 1969 by LeRoi Jones. Reprinted by permission of The Sterling Lord Agency.

William Melvin Kelley, "Cry for Me," from *Dancers on the Shore* by William Melvin Kelley. Copyright 1962 by Fawcett Publication, Inc. Reprinted by permission of Doubleday & Company, Inc.

John O. Killens, "God Bless America." Copyright © 1952, *The California Quarterly*. Reprinted by permission of International Famous Agency.

Etheridge Knight, "Hard Rock Returns to Prison from the Hospital for the Criminal Insane," "The Violent Space," and "It Was a Funky Deal," from *Poems from Prison* by Etheridge Knight. By permission of The Broadside Press.

Don L. Lee, "Introduction," "Back Again Home," from *Think Black*, third edition, 1969, Broadside Press. "A Poem for Black Minds," from *Black Pride*, 1968, Broadside Press. "Assassination," from *Don't Cry, Scream*, 1969, Broadside Press. All used by permission of Broadside Press.

Malcolm X, "1965," from *The Autobiography of Malcolm X,* by Malcolm X with the assistance of Alex Haley. Copyright © 1964 by Alex Haley and Malcolm X; renewed © 1965 by Alex Haley and Betty Shabazz. Reprinted by permission of Grove Press, Inc.

Paule Marshall, "Barbados," from *Soul Clap Hands and Sing*. Used by the kind permission of the author.

Julian Mayfield, "Into the Mainstream and Oblivion," from *The American Negro Writer and His Roots*, American Society for African Culture. Used by the kind permission of the author.

Claude McKay, "Home Thoughts," "If We Must Die," "The Lynching," "Tiger," "The Negro's Tragedy," "America," "The City's Love," "The Harlem Dancer," "Jasmine," from *Selected Poems of Claude McKay*, Twayne Publishers, Inc. By permission of the publisher.

Larry Neal, "Love Song in Middle Passage," and "Garvey's Ghost," from *Black Boogaloo (Notes on Black Liberation), Journal of Black Poetry*. Used by the kind permission of the poet.

Ann Petry, "Like a Winding Sheet," from *The Crisis*, 1945. Copyright © 1945 by The Crisis Publishing Company. Reprinted by permission of Russell & Volkening, Inc.

Dudley Randall, "Ballad of Birmingham," from *Poem Counterpoem*, and "Primitives," from *Cities Burning*. By permission of Broadside Press and the poet.

Jay Saunders Redding, "The Negro Writer and His Relationship to His Roots," from *The Negro Writer and His Roots*, American Society for African Culture. Used by the kind permission of the author.

Conrad Kent Rivers, "Four Sheets to the Wind and a One-Way Ticket to France, 1933," and "Africa," from *These Black Bodies and This Sunburnt Face*, Free Lance Poets and Prose Workshop, Inc. By permission of the publisher.

Melvin Tolson, "Dark Symphony," from *Rendezvous with America* by Melvin Tolson. Copyright 1944 by Dodd, Mead & Company, Inc. Reprinted by permission of the publisher. "Psi," from *Harlem Gallery* by Melvin Tolson, copyright by Twayne Publishers, Inc. Reprinted by permission of the publisher.

Jean Toomer, "Avey," "Georgia Dusk," "Song of the Sun," and "Storm Ending," from *Cane*, by Jean Toomer. Copyright 1951 by Jean Toomer. By permission of Liveright, Publishers, New York.

David Walker, "Article II Our Wretchedness in Consequence of Ignorance," from *David Walker's Appeal to the Coloured Citizens of the World*, edited and with an introduction by Charles M. Wiltse. Copyright © 1965 by Hill & Wang, Inc. Reprinted by permission of Hill & Wang, Inc.

Margaret Walker, "For My People," from *For My People* by Margaret Walker. Copyright © 1942 by Yale University Press. By permission of the publisher.

Booker T. Washington, "The Atlanta Exposition Address," from *Up from Slavery*, by Booker T. Washington. Reprinted by permission of Doubleday & Company, Inc.

John A. Williams, "Son in the Afternoon," from *The Angry Black*, 1966, Cooper Square. By permission of the poet.

Richard Wright, "Bright and Morning Star," and "The Ethics of Living Jim Crow," from *Uncle Tom's Children*, by Richard Wright. Copyright, 1938 by Richard Wright; renewed 1966 by Ellen Wright. Reprinted by permission of Harper & Row, Publishers.

Contents

Preface

Black American literature has just begun to receive the attention it has so long deserved. Issues that should have been raised long ago are being debated; the question of who constitutes a major black American author is now being posed, and thoughtful critics are beginning to establish boundaries on the origins and high points of black American literature. This sense of a beginning creates an ideal atmosphere in which to edit an anthology of black American literature: the public is receptive, the presses are eager, and the interest is high. But this sense of a beginning also creates certain responsibilities for the editor. If boundaries have not been firmly established and major authors have not been finally decided, the editor cannot work with the same sense of assurance that the editor of an anthology in British or white American literature so easily assumes. Voluminous scholarship accompanies the body of British and white American literature, and the editor can usually arrive at an acceptable point of view with some degree of ease. The editor of an anthology in black American literature finds himself in a somewhat different situation.

His responsibility is to decide whether he will evaluate and select his materials in accord with generally accepted critical standards alone or whether he will attempt to evaluate and select his materials on a broader basis—a basis that encompasses existing critical standards and goes on to include standards that are indigenous to black American literature. The broader basis seems the more feasible since black American literature has just started to receive widescale scholarly treatment and no one can be absolutely certain what standards are applicable in dealing with the literature. Existing standards are fine as far as they go, but they cannot serve as the sole criteria for determining the worthy or unworthy in a body of literature that was largely ignored when the standards were being formulated. For example, the degree of wit, tension, and ambiguity that a literary work contains may help to determine its merit, but if a black American author produced that work, the elements of black folklore that it contains may be equally important in determining the work's merit. Moreover, while sociohistorical factors may play only a minor role in determining the merit of some literary works, sociohistorical factors take on the utmost significance in evaluating black American literature. Structural, new-critical, or architechtonic standards alone cannot serve as the basis for selecting materials for an anthology of black American literature, and the responsibility to determine what further standards are necessary rests upon the editor alone.

I have already hinted at the standards that have been applied in bringing together the present selection of black literature in America.

The vast and accomplished body of black American folklore remains in view throughout the work because it seems to me that black American literature, like all other bodies of literature, develops from a folkloristic base and constantly manifests its dependence on the folk base in its conscious works of literature. I have also stressed sociohistorical concerns throughout the work since black American literature—like the black American himself—is to a large extent a social product. I am aware that my choice of standards reflects a single point of view concerning black American literature, and I am aware that any single point of view has its limitations. Some black American authors of merit do not appear in the present work, as some aspects of black American literature do not. But the old addage still obtains that it is as impossible to include everything as it is to please everybody. I can only hope that the present work will serve to introduce those who have not experienced it to the beauty of black literature, that it will be of service to those who know and love the literature, and that it will help to elucidate or at least to make inroads on some of the manifold problem areas that confront the critic, the instructor, and the student of black literature at the present time.

The task of explaining or prefacing the work would not be complete if I neglected to mention those who have helped and guided me along the way toward finding standards and editing this work. Arna Bontemps was extremely kind throughout all stages of my work; without his encouragement and assistance I would still be wandering in dark mazes. J. Saunders Redding provided a very helpful critique of the overall plan for the anthology and was kind enough to suggest some authors who would fit the design of the work. Ernest Kaiser lent his outstanding bibliographical knowledge and his encouragement to my task, and Arthur Davis was more than generous when called on for assistance. The staff members of the Beinecke and the Schomburg libraries were extremely cooperative; my typist, Mrs. Olga De Pascale, was efficient and longsuffering; Hoyt Fuller and Dudley Randall supplied needed information. Finally I must thank my English 52 class at Yale University for honestly reflecting on some of the ideas presented in this work, and I must thank my wife, Charlotte, for helping to bring these ideas to life.

Houston A. Baker, Jr.

I
Black
American
Literature:
An Overview

An overview of black or Negro American literature has to have at its base a definition of the black or Negro American, and statements made by both Richard Wright and Ralph Ellison can be of help in arriving at such a definition. For after speaking of several black writers in his essay "The Literature of the Negro in the United States," Wright says: "Truly, you must now know that the word Negro in America means something not racial or biological, but something purely social, something made in the United States."[1] And in *Shadow and Act*, Ralph Ellison says:

It is not skin color which makes a Negro American but cultural heritage as shaped by the American experience, the social and political predicament; a sharing of that "concord of sensibilities" which the group expresses through historical circumstances and through which it has come to constitute a subdivision of the larger American culture. Being a Negro American has to do with the memory of slavery and the hope for emancipation and the betrayal by allies and the revenge and contempt inflicted by our former masters after the Reconstruction, and the myths, both Northern and Southern, which are propagated in justification of that betrayal. It involves, too, a special attitude toward the waves of immigrants who have come later and passed us by.[2]

A recognition of the black American as "something purely social," as a product of a "cultural heritage as shaped by the American experience, the social and political predicament," is a necessity for a full understanding of the literature of the black man in the United States. For just as the black American is—perhaps to a greater extent than any other American—a social product, so the literature of the black American is—perhaps to a greater extent than any other body of literature—most fully understood in terms of a sociohistorical framework. A critical approach which aims at a just overview of black literature, therefore, cannot slight sociohistorical factors. As a case in point we can see how an attention to these factors aids in an explanation of the absence of black American literature of merit before the end of the nineteenth and the beginning of the twentieth century.

Arriving in America in chains, the black man was systematically and legally robbed of his humanity. As early as the seventeenth century "black codes" were in effect to check the threat which miscegenation and an increasing black population offered to the white majority; and when the founding fathers signed the basic social document undergirding the newly emergent United States, there were three provisions in that document which denied the black man's humanity. First it was provided that the foreign slave trade was to continue for two decades after the signing of the Constitution. Second, the Constitution stated that fugitive slaves apprehended in free states were to be returned to their masters. And third, the Constitution stated that in matters of apportionment and taxation the black American was to be counted as three-fifths of a man. The often-stated dichotomy

---

[1] Richard Wright, "The Literature of the Negro in the United States," *White Man Listen!*, Doubleday, New York, 1964, p. 80.

[2] Ralph Ellison, "The World and the Jug," *Shadow and Act*, Random House, New York, 1966, p. 136.

between American social ideals and American social action, therefore, is not as much of a dichotomy as it may appear. Slavery was, after all, written into the Constitution. The fact that slavery appeared to be a dying institution in 1787, however, helps to make understandable the actions of the founding fathers.

But the ironies of history are ever at work, and the growth of the textile industry in England and America as well as the invention of the cotton gin in 1793 gave new life to a dying institution. American slavery not only became profitable, but one of the most profitable institutions in the entire Western world. Cotton rapidly became the most important agricultural product of the American South, and by 1860 three-fourths of all black agricultural workers in the United States were engaged in its cultivation.[3]

Given this brief history, it is easy to see why no black American literature of merit was produced during the first 280 years of the black man's history in the United States. The man legally set apart by black codes, the man defined by his environment as three-fifths of a man, the man forced to work entirely for the profit of others from sunrise to sunset hardly had time to turn his attention to the conscious creation of works of art. Though "black and unknown bards" did emerge, poems and novels of merit were beyond the pale of such an experience. And here one must stress the words *of merit* for even when the situation of the black American was at its worst, several black authors, due to their unique circumstances, were able to produce works of literature.

Thus we find Phillis Wheatley's *Poems on Various Subjects, Religious and Moral* appearing in 1773, and before Phillis Wheatley there were the pious poems of the slave Jupiter Hammon. In the early nineteenth century, we find the work of another slave, George Moses Horton, who wrote love lyrics for the students of Chapel Hill, North Carolina, and published two volumes of poetry. And there was James M. Whitfield, one of the first nonslave black poets, whose name joins a number of others in the early and middle nineteenth century. In fiction we have the works of William Wells Brown, Frank Webb, Martin Delany, and Frances Harper as examples of early, conscious literary creation by black Americans. As Sterling Brown tells us in *Negro Poetry and Drama*, therefore:

The record of conscious literary artists among Negroes thus goes as far back as America's colonial period. Antebellum Negroes, both slave and free, wanted to be poets, read and studied as widely as circumstances permitted, and wrote down their thoughts in the forms approved by the times.[4]

But, as Brown and a host of others (notably James Weldon Johnson in the preface to *The Book of American Negro Poetry*) have pointed out, we must also see that the work of these early writers is of little literary value; it shows poor craftsmanship and a servile imitation of accepted models in both theme and

[3] Benjamin Quarles, *The Negro in the Making of America*, Macmillan, New York, 1968, p. 63.

[4] Sterling Brown, *Negro Poetry and Drama*, Atheneum, New York, 1969, p. 12.

content. Moreover, these early works failed in a greater sense, for they failed to honestly reflect the experience of the black man in America. These early, conscious literary artists were so intent on the just imitation of their models, so intent upon duplicating the poetic diction and pious concerns of white authors that they failed to portray the condition, fears, and aspirations of suffering humanity; they lacked, that is to say, the stuff of which great literature is made.

It was left for another body of black expression to reflect with honesty and originality the experiences of the majority of black Americans. This body of expression consists of the black work songs, ballads, folk rhymes, folk tales, and, preeminently, the black spirituals. Here, in this body of folk expression, we find the humor, pathos, aspiration, and tragedy which characterized the early life of the black man in America. The black man's protest against slavery finds expression in spirituals like "Mary, Don't You Weep" and "Let My People Go"; his sense of alienation and homelessness is reflected in the haunting chords of "Sometimes I Feel Like a Motherless Child." "A Laugh That Meant Freedom" and "How Buck Won His Freedom" evince the humor and subtle rebellion of the clever slave. And the anguish of the man driven to death by inhuman competition and an industrial-capitalist society is consummately revealed by "John Henry." Finally, the hope for a better life in another world beyond this temporal existence finds expression in "When the Saints Go Marching In." In black folk expression, therefore, we find an accurate reflection of the sociohistorical conditions surrounding the early history of the black American. The forms are original, and the content is that of the greatest literature.

The two streams of black expression—conscious literary expression and folk expression—moved along almost entirely separate courses until the last of the nineteenth and the beginning of the twentieth century. In the one hundred or so slave narratives produced by black Americans we find some crossover; Frederick Douglass's *Narrative,* for example, might well be labeled a "conscious, literary autobiography," and Arna Bontemps has pointed out that while the narratives are folk products, they still constitute a genre of black literature that has influenced the work of more recent black authors.[5] For the most part, the two streams of black expression remain separate. In the work of Paul Laurence Dunbar and Charles Chesnutt, however, the two streams of black expression draw together. Both Dunbar and Chesnutt wrote around the turn of the century, and both were conscious literary artists who made use of the folk experiences of the black American. In poems like "The Party," "The Spelling Bee," "The Real Question," and "Philosophy," Dunbar managed to capture both the humor and the pathos of the folk experience, and he did so in verse that was true to the black man's distinctive idiom. Like Dunbar, Charles Chesnutt made full use of the black American folk experience in his 1899 volume of short stories, *The Conjure Woman.* Dunbar, whose cause was championed by William Dean Howells, is

---

[5] Arna Bontemps, *Great Slave Narratives,* Beacon Press, Boston, 1969, p. x.

usually accorded the title of the first black American poet of distinction; and Chesnutt, whose short stories enjoyed wide popularity in *The Atlantic,* is usually considered the first black American fiction writer of distinction.

Both Dunbar and Chesnutt, however, were surrounded by difficulty; both were victims of what Saunders Redding has called cultural and psychological dualism.[6] Just as both writers, because of their backgrounds, were set apart from the cultural mainstream by whites, so both were internally torn by the question of writing honestly and not being read or accepted by a white audience, or writing falsely and being read and accepted. Dunbar laments this plight in his poem "The Poet" when he says:

> He sang of love when earth was young,
> And Love, itself, was in his lays.
> But ah, the world, it turned to praise
> A jingle in a broken tongue.[7]

The white majority, in other words, was unwilling to have its stereotypes of the black American as a happy child of nature broken by the honest and forthright words of black writers. Both Dunbar and Chesnutt, therefore, donned the mask, and the pain of the experience was recorded by Dunbar:

> We smile, but, O great Christ our cries
> To thee from tortured souls arise.
> We sing, but oh the clay is vile
> Beneath our feet, and long the mile;
> But let the world dream otherwise,
> We wear the mask![8]

By 1906, Dunbar was dead; Charles Chesnutt had become silent; and America at large had grown indifferent to black literature.

Once again historical factors are of importance, for they help to explain the plight of Dunbar and Chesnutt and the indifference of America to both the black man and to his literature. That which primarily helps to explain the reaction to Dunbar and Chesnutt is the growth of Jim Crow codes throughout the nation. In *The Strange Career of Jim Crow,*[9] C. Vann Woodward tells us that Jim Crow legislation proliferated in America toward the turn of the century. The Supreme Court, the federal government, and state and local legislatures were busy piling up prohibitive laws which turned the ever-present hostility toward the

---

[6] Saunders Redding, "The Negro Writer and American Literature," in Herbert Hill (ed.), *Anger, and Beyond: The Negro Writer in the United States,* Harper & Row, New York, 1968, pp. 1–2.

[7] Paul Laurence Dunbar, *The Complete Poems of Paul Laurence Dunbar,* Dodd, Mead & Company, New York, 1968, p. 191.

[8] *Ibid.,* p. 71.

[9] C. Vann Woodward, *The Strange Career of Jim Crow,* Oxford University Press, New York, 1968, pp. 67–109.

black American into open aggression around the turn of the century. Added to this growth of Jim Crow legislation were America's imperialistic advances against the colored peoples of the Pacific and the Carribean in 1898. The American experience in the Pacific and the Carribean made the myth of "the white man's burden" an essential element in the American *Weltanschauung*. Scholars, journalists, and politicians (who might have been more liberal) all had a stake now in perpetuating the myth of white supremacy, and most became devoted to the stereotypes of the black American which found their most ardent champions in the South. Northern liberal opinion, which had been a restraining factor before and during the Civil War, had been on the decline since the Hayes-Tilden compromise of 1876, and America's imperialistic adventures caused it to decline even faster. Added to these factors was, ironically, the philosophy of the chief leader and spokesman for black Americans, Booker Taliafero Washington. Washington, one of the strongest and most influential leaders ever to emerge among black Americans, helped to reinforce the stereotypes set forth by the whites. He assured his white patrons and friends that the best thing for black Americans was hard work, an education in the trades, and a life of service to the community. Social integration, Washington assured white America, was as much an anathema to him and his followers as it was to the country at large. Washington's philosophy was best expressed in one of the classic works of black literature, *Up from Slavery*, published in 1901. A number of sociohistorical factors, therefore, militated against the growth of black literature around the turn of the century, and an understanding of the plight of both Paul Laurence Dunbar and Charles Chesnutt is aided by a knowledge of these factors.

There was one work published around the turn of the century, however, which stood apart from the work of either Dunbar or Chesnutt. That work, which appeared in 1903, was W. E. B. Du Bois's *The Souls of Black Folk*. In both content and form, Du Bois's collection of essays belongs to a later period; it was by all standards a prophetic work, a harbinger of things to come. That America at large and black Americans in particular did not respond favorably to Du Bois's forthright and scathingly honest work is explained by the same historical factors which determined the fate of Dunbar and Chesnutt. White America was not ready to hear from the pen of a young, militant black American that the problem of the twentieth century was the problem of "the color line." Nor was America ready to respond favorably to Du Bois's scrupulously accurate portrayal of the hypocrisy, hostility, and brutality of white America toward black America. The black leadership, moreover, under the banner of Booker T. Washington, was willing to accord but little notice to a young man who thought that black Americans had as much right in the opera house as in the factory, and as much right to handle Aeschylus as an awl. Du Bois's work, in short, did not receive nearly the praise it deserved.

But Du Bois could justifiably have given the answer of the professor who when asked why he was always on the wave of the future responded, "Because I create the wave." Du Bois's work, both literary and social, truly created the wave of the future. For in the years between 1900 and the early 1920s, we can see the decline of those sociohistorical restrictions which brought about the fate of Dunbar and Chesnutt, and accompanying their decline, we can see a growth in the type of attitude which Du Bois projected in *The Souls of Black Folk*. Both of these trends resulted in a different type of black literature: literature of great merit, militancy, and race-pride. James Weldon Johnson's *The Autobiography of an Ex-Colored Man* (1912) constitutes an example of literature of the highest merit. In this well-written, realistic, and highly entertaining novel, Johnson followed the picaresque adventures of a young mulatto through turn-of-the-century Europe and America. In his 1917 volume of poetry, *Fifty Years,* Johnson provided a number of examples of militant black writing like the poem "To America," and in the following lines from "Fifty Years," the title poem, we get a strong sense of race-pride:

> Courage! Look out, beyond, and see
> The far horizon's beckoning span!
> Faith in your God-known destiny!
> We are a part of some great plan.[10]

This feeling of race-pride can also be seen in Benjamin Brawley's fine critical work *The Negro in Literature and Art* (1910), which celebrated the multiple achievements of black artists in America. Du Bois's militancy was continued in both literature and social action; for in his 1911 novel, *The Quest of the Silver Fleece,* he exposed the inequities of the capitalistic system in the cotton kingdom, and in 1909 he was active in the establishment of the National Association for the Advancement of Colored People. Out of the NAACP came the journal *Crisis* edited by Du Bois, and in this journal appeared the works of young black writers of merit, writers filled with racial pride and sharing Du Bois's anti-Washingtonian views on the race problem. During the years between 1900 and the early 1920s, Carter G. Woodson was also at work, engaged in historical studies destined to give the black American a sense of pride in his history. Woodson founded the Association for the Study of Negro Life in 1915, and in the following year he brought out the first issue of the *Journal of Negro History*. In the years prior to the twenties, militant black journalism also gained impetus due to the efforts of William Monroe Trotter and Robert S. Abbott.

These efforts by black writers, journalists, and scholars, of course, cannot be divorced from the social climate of America as a whole. The educational opportunities for black Americans were increasing, and as a result there was an increasing number of college-educated black men to fill the ranks of a Du Boisian Talented Tenth. In addition, the great migration of black Americans to thriving urban centers put more black men in contact with both American opportunities

---

[10] James Weldon Johnson, *Fifty Years and Other Poems,* Cornhill, Boston, 1917, p. 4.

and the American dream. As a result, black Americans reached out toward greater social, economic, and political opportunity. This migration was accelerated by the outbreak of World War I, because war industries demanded war workers, and black Americans gladly left the South to fill this role. The urban black American, the militant black American, the race-proud black American—all have their genesis in the years between 1900 and the early 1920s. But the highest literary manifestations of these black Americans did not come until the twenties.

The ferment of those years between the beginning of the twentieth century and the 1920s reached its culmination in a movement that has been variously labeled "The Harlem Renaissance," "The New Negro Movement," and "The Awakening of the Twenties." As all these terms imply, what happened among black Americans in the twenties embodied a rebirth, a bursting forth of the black American spirit that seemed to be *sui generis*. The race-pride, concern for the history of "the race," and militancy over the condition of black people found expression in some of the finest works ever produced by black American writers. For between 1922 and 1929, the year which marks the beginning of the Great Depression, the works of Claude McKay, Jean Toomer, Countee Cullen, Alain Locke, and Langston Hughes went a long way toward destroying the myth of the "Old Negro," and proved decisively that opportunity and race-pride could put black American writers on a par with (if not above) the best of their white contemporaries.

The themes employed by the writers of the twenties were to a large extent those which had characterized the years immediately prior to the Harlem Renaissance, but with this difference: the dialect tradition, the stereotypes, the donning of masks of any sort was deemed an anathema by the writers of the twenties. As Alain Locke, one of the most influential figures of the movement, stated it:

Uncle Tom and Sambo have passed on, and even the "Colonel" and "George" play barnstorm roles from which they escape with relief when the public spotlight is off. The popular melodrama has about played itself out, and it is time to scrap the fictions, garret the bogeys and settle down to a realistic facing of facts.[11]

The most patently obvious fact was that here in the twenties were writers that any body of literature would be proud to rank among its own.

Claude McKay's mastery of the sonnet is a thing of beauty, and in one of his most finely wrought and often-quoted pieces, we can see that beauty at work:

> If we must die, let it not be like hogs
> Hunted and penned in an inglorious spot,
> While round us bark the mad and hungry dogs,
> Making their mock at our accursed lot.

[11] Alain Locke, "The New Negro," in Alain Locke (ed.), *The New Negro*, Albert & Charles Boni, New York, 1968, p. 5.

> If we must die, oh, let us nobly die,
> So that our precious blood may not be shed
> In vain; then even the monsters we defy
> Shall be constrained to honor us though dead!
> Oh, Kinsmen! We must meet the common foe!
> Though far outnumbered, let us show us brave,
> And for their thousand blows deal one death-blow!
> What though before us lies the open grave?
> Like men we'll face the murderous, cowardly pack,
> Pressed to the wall, dying, but fighting back![12]

There is no need to belabor the fine sense of craftsmanship here, the sure sense of rhyme, and the lyrical intensity. This sonnet is not one of those gems "of purest ray serene" found among the dross; McKay's entire canon sparkles with equally impressive works.

Two other poets of note who emerged from the Harlem Renaissance were Countee Cullen and Langston Hughes. Cullen worked for the most part in romantic verse forms somewhat overwrought in their "sweetness" and poetic diction, but in more than one instance he managed to express with poignancy what it meant to be a black American. Such an instance is provided by his poem "Incident":

> Once riding in old Baltimore,
>   Heart-filled, head-filled with glee,
> I saw a Baltimorean
>   Keep looking straight at me.
>
> Now I was eight and very small
>   And he was no whit bigger
> And so I smiled, but he poked out
>   His tongue and called me, "Nigger."
>
> I saw the whole of Baltimore
>   From May until December:
> Of all the things that happened there
>   That's all that I remember.[13]

This poem, characterized by a biting irony and a sure dramatic sense, added to "Yet Do I Marvel" was enough to assure Cullen's fame. The same might be said of one of Langston Hughes's early poems, "The Negro Speaks of Rivers" dedicated to W. E. B. Du Bois:

> I've known rivers:
> I've known rivers ancient as the world and older than the flow of
>   human blood in human veins.

[12] Claude McKay, *Selected Poems of Claude McKay*, Bookman Associates, New York, 1953, p. 36.

[13] Countee Cullen, *Color*, Harper & Brothers, New York, 1925, p. 15.

My soul has grown deep like the rivers.

I bathed in the Euphrates when dawns were young.
I built my hut near the Congo and it lulled me to sleep.
I looked upon the Nile and raised pyramids above it.
I heard the singing of the Mississippi when Abe Lincoln went down
    to New Orleans, and I've seen its muddy bosom turn all golden
    in the sunset.

I've known rivers:
Ancient, dusky rivers.

My soul has grown deep like the rivers.[14]

The pride in the history of black people is unmistakable here, and the flowing, soft lines charged with meaning capture in a Whitmanesque manner that river of time that has been the black man's history in America. Unlike Cullen, Hughes chose to work in the idiom of the black American, and in a number of his poems we find the rhythms and that special knowledge which characterize black American folk expression. Hughes's canon is so extensive and his range is so great that it would be impossible to do him justice in the brief review given here. Other poems which show both his range and technical virtuosity, however, include "I, Too," "Montmarte," "Refugee in America," and "Brass Spitoons." In addition to writing poetry, Hughes, like Cullen, made notable contributions to the field of drama, and both his novel *Not without Laughter* and his collection of short stories *The Ways of White Folk* show a good deal of talent in prose.

Hughes's foremost (or most widely known) prose works, however, are the "simple" stories which deal with the experiences and viewpoints of the urban black American—viewpoints and experiences which come from the mind and mouth of the memorable Harlem figure, Jesse B. Simple. Hughes's treatment of the urban black American in both poetry and prose is but one manifestation of the concern for low-life city characters which Edward Margolies[15] has seen as one of the most salient factors of the Harlem Renaissance. Claude McKay's *Home to Harlem* is a typical product of this concern for the lower strata of the city. Rudolph Fisher's short stories "City of Refuge," "Ringtail," and "Blades of Steel" (all of which appeared in *The Atlantic* during the twenties and showed great technical merit) touch on this same concern for poor black city dwellers in America.

One of the foremost literary products of the Harlem Renaissance, however, did not take black American urban life as its theme; instead, it explored the mystery, emotion, and hysteria of the black man's experience in the rural South. In *Cane* (1923), a collection of short fiction, poetry, and drama, Jean Toomer explored the hidden depths of the black American experience and produced a

[14] Langston Hughes, *The Weary Blues*, Alfred Knopf, New York, 1926, p. 51.

[15] Edward Margolies, *Native Sons, a Critical Study of Twentieth-century Negro American Authors*, J. B. Lippincott, New York, 1969, pp. 30–1.

mysterious brand of Southern psychological realism that has been matched only in the best work of William Faulkner. "Fern," one of the best short stories in Toomer's volume, is a fine illustration of the author's sense of psychological realism. The sensual, tempting heroine of the story is much more than an indolent Southern woman; she encompasses, indeed symbolizes, the life of that Georgia Pike by which she sits staring at the world with haunting eyes. The temptations and promises presented by Fern's body are symbolic of the temptations and promises held out by the road of life (the Georgia Pike) which stretches before the rural black American, and the frustration experienced by men in their affairs with Fern is symbolic of the frustration of the life journey. Men are willing to give their all, but the result is simply frustration, haunting memory, and hysteria. Toomer's unique handling of the symbolic heroine and significant detail can be seen in several other stories in *Cane*, notably in "Becky" and "Avey."

The author's fine portrayal of the trials of the psyche and his keen sense of rhythm were not confined to prose, however, for in *Cane* we find excellent poems which display the same distinctive craftsmanship. "Storm Ending" offers a case in point:

> Thunder blossoms gorgeously above our heads,
> Great, hollow, bell-like flowers,
> Rumbling in the wind,
> Stretching clappers to strike our ears . . .
> Full-lipped flowers
> Bitten by the sun
> Bleeding rain
> Dripping rain like golden honey—
> And the sweet earth flying from the thunder.[16]

From this poem there emerges a strong sense of time and place which characterize the whole of *Cane*, for even when Toomer deals with the life of the urban black American in his volume, he still presents the rhythms and psychological factors that condition life in the land of sugar cane, a land populated by the "sons of Cain."

The fine craftsmanship of Jean Toomer in fiction was matched by the technical virtuosity of another black writer—a writer, in fact, who emerged as the chief critic of the movement. Alain Locke's *The New Negro* (1925) contains several fine statements of the ideals of the Harlem Renaissance, and these statements, written in a lucid prose style, are charged with careful social and aesthetic analyses. Locke was virtually the father of the New Negro literary movement, and he stated the attitude of the majority of black Americans in 1925 when he said:

By shedding the old chrysalis of the Negro problem we are achieving something like a spiritual emancipation. Until recently, lacking self-understanding, we have been

---

[16] Jean Toomer, *Cane*, Harper & Row, New York, 1969, p. 90.

almost as much of a problem to ourselves as we still are to others. But the decade that found us with a problem has left us with only a task. The multitude perhaps feels as yet only a strange relief and a new vague urge, but the thinking few know that in the reaction the vital inner grip of prejudice has been broken.[17]

This statement from *The New Negro* offers only one example of Locke's keen analysis and lucid prose, for in the same essay he touches on all the most salient characteristics of the Harlem Renaissance. He speaks, for example, of the new sense of an African past which found its expression in the Garvey movement of the twenties, and he sees the problems of the urban black American as the most pressing ones of the future. The last two characteristics of the Harlem Renaissance —a concern with the African past of the black American and a concern with the urban black American—are but two of the factors which connect the Harlem Renaissance in a very real sense with the more recent renaissance of black writers in the fifties and sixties.

The outpouring, the bursting forth of a new black American spirit, the flowering of literary genius that was the Harlem Renaissance, however, was destined to be short lived. When the stock market crashed in 1929, the white patrons who had supported black writers, the fun-lovers who had come to Harlem in search of that bizarre world portrayed by Carl Van Vechten's *Nigger Heaven,* the restless escapists of the Jazz Age who had sought some elan vital through association with the black American, and the black American himself, writers and nonwriters alike—all turned from art and the high life of the twenties to grapple with the basic problem of the depression years, survival. The output of black literature, however, was not halted by the Depression, and in some ways it may have been aided by the great social crisis. A statement by Arna Bontemps helps to explain this paradox:

Well, the Depression had sent the Harlem writers scurrying. But I think it more than compensated for this damage by the opportunities it provided for the next wave of literary expression by Negroes. Many old and defeated writers, like the poet Fenton Johnson, wandered into the Writers' Project of the WPA. But the project also drew the likes of Richard Wright, Ralph Ellison, Frank Yerby, Roi Ottley, Willard Motley and several others, and began to create an environment in which the Negro writer could at last stretch himself full length.[18]

To a large extent, the experimentation begun by black authors in the twenties continued into the next decade, and the audience for literature about black Americans had increased considerably by the thirties. This increased audience was partially the result of the work of writers like Carl Van Vechten, Dubose Hayward, Eugene O'Neill, Paul Green, and Sherwood Anderson. All these writers had dealt with the black American experience in a less than stereotyped manner,

---

[17] Locke, p. 4.

[18] Arna Bontemps, "Reflections on Richard Wright: A Symposium on an Exiled Native Son," *Anger, and Beyond,* p. 202.

and the portrayal of a black man as something other than a stock character was becoming much more common in American letters.

Given the increased audience and the aid of the Writers' Project of the WPA (Works Progress Administration), an author like Arna Bontemps could continue an illustrious career during the thirties, and Richard Wright could begin his career as one of America's most distinguished authors. In addition, the thirties saw the publication of Sterling Brown's beautiful volume of verse, *Southern Road* (1932), and the appearance of his invaluable critical work, *The Negro in American Fiction* (1937).

It is the three years immediately following the publication of Brown's critical work, however, which mark a high point in black American writing. In 1938, Richard Wright's *Uncle Tom's Children* was published, and for perhaps the first time in fifteen years (since Toomer's *Cane*) the condition of the black American, the violence, the oppression, and the attendant warping of the spirit were portrayed in enthralling fiction. In the five short stories of this volume, Wright showed a mastery of style and a dramatic sense far superior to that of most of his black contemporaries and predecessors and on a par with that of his most talented white contemporaries. The violence and the terrible effects of prejudice are perhaps nowhere more skillfully set forth than in the first story of the volume, "Big Boy Leaves Home." In this story it is not simply the violence of the white man which militates against the black man; there is a sense of cosmic violence seen in coiling snakes, enraged roosters, snarling dogs, and threatening storms. In the last story of the volume, "Bright and Morning Star," Wright portrays this same sense of violence while at the same time he captures the sense of hope which many black Americans felt as a result of the work of the Communist Party in the twenties and thirties.

Two years after the publication of *Uncle Tom's Children*, *Native Son* appeared, and Richard Wright's reputation was established. Here, in one of the finest novels ever produced in America, Wright mercilessly set forth a portrait of one of America's most "native" sons, Bigger Thomas. Bigger Thomas is an archetypal black American, a figure both pulsatingly human and at the same instant "bigger" than the individual case. Bigger's plight, brought on by prejudice and racist societal attitudes, is universal in scope; and Wright's handling of dialogue, mood, and description insured the universal literary appeal of his first novel. The protest in Wright's novel was not a new element in black American literature, but the unflinching realism, the technical mastery, and the magnificent dramatic sense marked *Native Son* as perhaps the highest point of black literary expression in the novel achieved before the fifties. Moreover, Wright's handling of the Communist ideology in the novel constitutes perhaps the finest literary expression of what Communism and the rising of a new proletariat meant to the black American of the thirties.

Wright's reputation was further enhanced by the 1945 publication of *Black Boy*, which was both a factual autobiography and a spiritual record of the black

American people. In his autobiography, Wright scrupulously and skillfully analyzed the American racial dilemma through the lenses of self-experience. And the significance of Wright's achievement was recognized by no less an artist than Ralph Ellison who recorded his reaction to the book in "Richard Wright's Blues."[19] Ellison stated that Wright's book captured the essentials of the black man's experience in America, and he felt that it did so in a blues form, a form, that is, which constituted "an autobiographical chronicle of personal catastrophe expressed lyrically."

Despite his domination of the forties, however, Wright was not the only black author of merit to come out of that decade. In poetry we find the works of Owen Dodson, Robert Hayden, Melvin Tolson, and Gwendolyn Brooks; and in fiction we may find the works of James Baldwin, Ann Petry, and Ralph Ellison. Most of these writers were products of the postwar years, and their work is marked by certain characteristics that Richard Wright pointed out in his essay "The Literature of the Negro in the United States." Wright stated that the works of the postwar writers were characterized by "a sharp loss of lyricism, a drastic reduction of the racial content, a rise in preoccupation with urban themes and subject matter both in the novel and the poem." While one might question parts of this statement, one is forced to recognize its essential validity. Lyricism in the old, highflown style of poetic diction and "sweetness" is largely absent from the verse of Dodson, Hayden, and Brooks. The new poets tended to work more in imagistic terms, stressing a concreteness of detail and a sparseness of language. A stanza from Robert Hayden's "A Ballad of Remembrance" serves to illustrate:

> Quadroon mermaids, Afro angels, black saints
> balanced upon the switchblades of that air
> and sang. Tight streets unfolding to the eye
> like fans of corrosion and elegiac lace
> crackled with their singing: Shadow of time. Shadow
>   of blood.[20]

This *is* a long way from the more burdened lyricism of—say—Fenton Johnson or Countee Cullen. Dodson's *Powerful Long Ladder* (1946), Hayden's *Heart-Shape in the Dust* (1940) and *The Lion and the Archer* (1948), and Brooks's *A Street in Bronzeville* (1948) all contain examples of verse of high quality written in a style which differs greatly from the more lyrical cadences of earlier black American poets.

In regard to Wright's point about "a drastic reduction of the racial content," we can only say that racial content as it had existed before Wright and in the work of Wright may have been reduced, but racial content of another sort was present to replace it. In the early stories of Ellison and Petry, racial content still

[19] Ellison, *Shadow and Act*, pp. 89–104.

[20] From Robert Hayden, *Selected Poems*, October House, New York, 1966, p. 39. Hayden's poem originally appeared in his volume, *The Lion and the Archer*.

carries all before it, but there is a broader scope involved in these stories. The black characters have become more complex human beings than those portrayed in the work of, for example, Zora Neale Hurston and Rudolph Fisher. The concerns of the characters portrayed by Ralph Ellison, Chester Himes, and Ann Petry are those of a complex, industrial, American society. And the same might be said of the characters encountered in the early work of James Baldwin.

The third part of Wright's statement is the only one that can be taken at its face value, for surely there was (there had been since the turn of the century) an increasing "preoccupation with urban themes and subject matter" in the postwar years. The elements that Wright noted as characteristic of postwar black writing, therefore, provide a helpful index toward understanding that work which preceded the most recent decades of black expression. For the elements which characterized black American literature in the latter years of the forties are to a large extent the same elements that have characterized black writing in the fifties and sixties. The appearance of these elements is to some extent explained by sociohistorical factors that are still at work on the black American literature of the present.

The epoch between 1945 and 1971 is so close upon us that it would be impossible to set forth with any degree of finality the historical patterns that have conditioned the black literature of this period. Nonetheless, certain factors have without a doubt had an effect on the works of black authors. One of the most important of these factors was the emergence of America as a world leader from World War II; following the war, the world was suddenly stretched between the Communist East and the Democratic West. In order for America to capture the loyalty of the undeclared colored masses of the world, it had to set its racial house in order; therefore, greater opportunities were extended to the black American. And as more opportunities became available, black Americans began to demand full citizenship and equality under the law. Supreme Court decisions, the sit-in movement, the emergence of a more militant leadership along with more militant strategies among black leaders—all these have played a role in making the black American more truly an American citizen.

The American racial revolution, however, is only one aspect of a larger American social revolution which had its genesis in World War II and is as contemporary as the present. As the average age level of the American population has decreased (and the average educational level has increased), the old verities and ancient foundations of moral authority have steadily crumbled. American concepts of race, sex, education, religion, and even stimulation have been held up to the scrutiny of scholarly thinkers, active protesters, and militant fighters. And out of this change has come an increasingly complex literature, appealing (partially due to the great increase in the average educational level of the American population) to a broader and more complex audience. And (again due to educational and other opportunities) this broader and more complex audience represents a merger of the formerly disjunct black and white audiences.

The primary results of the American social revolution in terms of the black American have been an increased diversity, an increased complexity, and an increased "Americanization." And as the diversity, complexity, and Americanization of black America has increased, the literature of the black American has followed suit. In addition, the new reading public that resulted from this stratification, this movement into the mainstream by black Americans, insured black writers the opportunity to deal with their experiences honestly and forthrightly. Ralph Ellison's *Invisible Man* (1952), offers an ample illustration.

Ellison's novel is written in the picaresque tradition, and it goes far beyond strictly racial themes. *Invisible Man* is, in fact, an American odyssey which captures the whole of the American experience and reflects an employment of the best American literary traditions. The protagonist is not only a black man, but also a complex American searching for the reality of existence in a technological society characterized by swift change. Ellison's protagonist is perhaps the best example of the multifaceted, complex, Americanized black character who resulted in part from the historical factors that we touched on above; and the acclaim which *Invisible Man* has received offers more than ample evidence of the broader and more complex audience available to the black writer.

Other works of the fifties by black writers show the same diversity and complexity that confronts us in Ellison's novel. James Baldwin's *Go Tell It on the Mountain* (1952), for example, is far more than the chronicle of the experiences of a single black boy in a Harlem environment. The novel is a *Bildungsroman* (a novel recording the development of a young man) of universal appeal, and it speaks eloquently of the terrors and hopes of youth as a whole, while at the same time it portrays the very special terror of being young and black in America. John O. Killens's 1954 work, *Youngblood*, captures some of this same hope and terror in a fine and lucid prose style, and Killens's first novel is but another example of that Americanization and diversification—that movement into the mainstream—which characterized black American literature during a great part of the fifties. Arthur Davis, in "Integration and Race Literature,"[21] admirably demonstrates how the movement of the black American into the mainstream has affected black American literature; Davis points to works like *Savage Holiday* (Richard Wright), *Anger at Innocence* (William Gardner Smith), and *Country Place* (Ann Petry) as examples of novels by black writers that employ a white main character, and he singles out novels like *The Outsider* (Richard Wright) and *Third Generation* (Chester Himes) as examples of works by black authors that show a distinct shift from the protest tradition and a strict concentration on racial themes and characters. Davis concludes by saying:

Summing up then, I think we can safely say that the leaven of integration is very much at work. It has forced the Negro creative artist to play down his most

[21] Arthur P. Davis, "Integration and Race Literature," *The American Negro Writer and His Roots*, American Society of African Culture, New York, 1960.

cherished tradition; it has made him abandon, at least on occasion, the Negro character and background; and it has possibly helped to silence a few of the older writers now living.[22]

This movement into the mainstream was not destined to continue throughout the sixties, however, for the historical factors conditioning the experiences of the black American took a turn for the worst in the early years of that decade. The more forcefully voiced demands of black Americans were met in the early sixties by violence on one hand and indifference and apathy on the other, and American mass media projected this violence, indifference, and apathy into the households of black families across the nation. Marshall McCluhan must here be given his due, for perhaps there was never a more widely publicized struggle than that of the black American in the early sixties, and the touch (the massage) of the mass media was one of the most influential factors in bringing about a widescale shift in tactics in the black man's struggle in America. Both the philosophies and the strategies of black leaders became more militant, and the literature of the black American reflected this increased militancy. Events and the literature reflecting them, therefore, had taken that turn which Richard Wright prophecied in the essay quoted earlier. For after speaking of the broadening of black expression which characterized the late forties and early fifties, Wright says: "If the expression of the American Negro should take a sharp turn toward strictly racial themes, then you will know by that token that we are suffering our old and ancient agonies at the hands of our white American neighbors."

"A sharp turn toward strictly racial themes" is surely one of the foremost characteristics of black literature from Baldwin's *Another Country* (1963) to the most recent work of LeRoi Jones. Once again in black American literature we witness a surge of militancy, race-pride, and pride in the history of the black people like that which characterized the Harlem Renaissance of the twenties. Things African have gained a new respect among black Americans due to the emergence in the fifties and sixties of a host of independent African states and due to the growing disaffection of black Americans with all things American. The new sense of race-pride has been reflected in modes of speech, dress, and action; and the sense of pride in the history of black people has found expression in the demands for books, courses, and mass-media programs that deal justly with the history of the black American. There is an essential difference, however, between the literary philosophies of the earlier Harlem Renaissance and those of the current outpouring of the black American spirit. The writers of the twenties, as Alain Locke pointed out, were interested in shedding their chrysalises in order to merge into the mainstream of American life. Today's writers, however, are engaged in an attempt to construct a chrysalis of blackness, a distinctive covering which will set them apart and enable them to grasp the essence of the black American's reality.

[22] *Ibid.*, p. 39.

LeRoi Jones, one of the most talented black writers of the sixties, has expressed this antimainstream aesthetic in his essays, poems, and dramas; and an increasing number of talented young black authors seem to be following Jones's lead. The prevalent attitude in the black American literature of this particular historical moment seems to be that expressed by Julian Mayfield's notable essay: an increasing number of black writers seem to feel that to move into the mainstream is to move into oblivion. The works of LeRoi Jones constitute the finest literary results of this revolutionary aesthetic. Jones's poems dislocate, they force language into new meanings in a truly Eliotian fashion, and his dramas—notably *Dutchman* and *The Slave*—show a fine technical control and a sometimes startling sense of idiomatic rhythms.

It is with these all-too-brief remarks on Jones that this overview of black American literature proposes to halt—despite the fact that Jones's work does not bring us to the doorstep of this very day in the history of black American literature. Although surely we can say that Jones's craftsmanship, command of language, and range have not been transcended by a more recent black American author.

II
Black
Folklore

It is impossible to obtain an understanding of black American literature
without some knowledge of black folklore, for black literary artists from Paul
Laurence Dunbar to LeRoi Jones have made use of its values, forms, and techniques. Dunbar, the first black American poet of distinction, was essentially a
folk poet who employed the lore of the agrarian folk experience in a beautifully
lyrical style; Jones, the foremost of today's black and angry writers, has employed blues forms and blues values in a number of his works, and his *Blues
People* is one of the most enthralling works yet written on a single aspect of the
black folk experience. To mention other black writers who have employed aspects
of the black folklore tradition would be to mention almost every writer in the
black American literary tradition, and of the finest work of one of today's most
accomplished novelists we can surely say "here is God's plenty." The trickster,
the blues, the subversion, the fused strength, the badman hero—all are present
in Ralph Ellison's *Invisible Man*.

The black American literary tradition begins with the "existing monuments"
that constitute "an ideal order"; it begins also with a knowledge of "the group"
that provided all the "maturing and value" for the black writer. It is black folklore that provides our first view of the existing monuments and tells us about the
group in which the talented black writer has his genesis. The genres of black folklore are the same as those seen in other lores, but the reflected experience is
unique. Since the black American, as Richard Wright pointed out, is a "social
product," something made in America, the folk expression of the black American
is composed of elements from many lores that come together to reflect a unique
folk experience. The slave experience of the black American stands apart in history, and the urban experience of the black American is no less unique. We thus
see a different type of folk hero, a different type of music, and a different type
of religious experience in black folklore.

Within the "trickster" animal-tale genre ("Sheer Crops" and "Why
Br'Gator's Hide Is So Horny"), for example, we not only have the etiological, or
explanatory, component, but also a certain psychical component. The trickster
animal (like the slave in the "John Cycle"—"Swapping Dreams") comes to represent the slave himself and his wish-fulfillment victories over that "peculiar institution" which nourished black Americans. In a ballad like "John Henry," we have
not only the work hero, but also the new industrial hero, the man who pits his
strength against an awesome technology. In "Stackalee" we have more than the
typical badman hero; we also have the hero of lower-eschelon, black-urban
existence, the man willing to use any means necessary to obtain his ends.

And if we can say that the black folk hero is somewhat unique, surely we
can say the same of black folk music. The spirituals, for example, constitute what
is perhaps the most pervasive indigenous body of American music, and their
complexity captures innumerable phases of the black folk experience. We have
sorrow, joy, subversion, apocalyptic concerns, and otherworldliness in the immortal sacred songs of black Americans. The secular songs of the black American
folk deal with work experiences on chain gangs, levees, and the nation's water-

ways; they also express the essence of the black folk experience in the blues form. The blues, as Ellison has pointed out, record the endurance in the face of tragedy and the transcendence of tragedy by lyricism that are prototypal of the black American experience.

In black religious lore we have the traditional fabliaux, or humorous religious tales, about the preacher, but we also have the original and powerful sermons ("The Wounds of Jesus") and testimonials like "God Struck Me Dead." In the sermons and testimonials, we witness a startling body of imagery, and we are presented with a personal, affable, and powerful God who looks after his "chosen people" and provides hope for the future. The sermons and testimonials of black folklore constitute some of the finest poetry of belief ever written, and the influence of black religious lore can certainly be seen in works like James Weldon Johnson's *God's Trombones* and James Baldwin's *Go Tell It on the Mountain*.

Black American folklore, therefore, provides a base for the black literary tradition as a whole. The questions that Johnson posed in apostrophe to "black and unknown bards of long ago" are questions that are being posed by critics today in regard to all black American writers:

> O black and unknown bards of long ago,
> How came your lips to touch the sacred fire?
> How, in your darkness, did you come to know
> The power and beauty of the minstrel's lyre?

A consideration of black folklore provides many of the answers.

REFERENCES

Abrahams, Roger: "The Changing Concept of the Negro Hero," *The Golden Log*, Mody C. Boatright, Wilson M. Hudson, and Allen Maxwell (eds.), Southern Methodist University Press, Dallas, 1962, pp. 119–134.

Bontemps, Arna, and Langston Hughes (eds.): *The Book of Negro Folklore*, Dodd, Mead, New York, 1969.

Botkin, B. A.: *Lay My Burden Down: A Folk History of Slavery*, University of Chicago Press, Chicago, 1945.

Brewer, J. Mason: *American Negro Folklore*, Quadrangle Books, Chicago, 1968.

————: *The Word on the Brazos*, University of Texas Press, Austin, 1953.

Courlander, Harold: *Negro Folk Music, U.S.A.*, Columbia University Press, New York, 1963.

Cuney-Hare, Maud: *Negro Musicians and Their Music*, Associated Publishers, Washington, D.C., 1936.

Dorson, Richard M.: *Negro Folktales in Michigan*, Harvard University Press, Cambridge, 1956.

Harris, Joel Chandler: *Uncle Remus, His Songs and Sayings*, Houghton Mifflin, New York, 1880.

Hurston, Zora Neale: *Mules and Men,* J. B. Lippincott, Philadelphia, 1935.

Jackson, Bruce (ed.): *The Negro and His Folklore in the Nineteenth-century Periodical,* University of Texas Press, Austin, 1967.

Johnson, James Weldon: *The Book of American Negro Spirituals,* Viking Press, New York, 1969.

Krehbiel, H. E.: *Afro-American Folksongs,* G. Schirmer, New York, 1914.

Puckett, Newbell Niles: *Folk Beliefs of the Southern Negro,* University of North Carolina Press, Chapel Hill, 1926.

Weldon, Fred O., Jr.: "Negro Folktale Heroes," *And Horns on the Toads,* Mody C. Boatright, Wilson M. Hudson, and Allen Maxwell (eds.), Southern Methodist University Press, Dallas, 1959, pp. 170–189.

Wilgus, D. K.: "The Negro-White Spirituals," *Anglo-American Folksong Scholarship Since 1898,* Rutgers University Press, New Brunswick, 1959.

Sheer Crops

Br'er Bear en Br'er Rabbit dey wuz farmers. Br'er Bear he has acres en acres uf good bottom land, en Br'er Rabbit has des' er small sandy-land farm. Br'er Bear wuz allus er "raisin' Cain" wid his neighbors, but Br'er Rabbit was er most engenerally raisin' chillun.

After while Br'er Rabbit's boys 'gun to git grown, en Br'er Rabbit 'lows he's gwine to have to git more land if he makes buckle en tongue meet.

So he goes ober to Br'er Bear's house, he did, en he say, sez he, "Mo'nin', Br'er Bear. I craves ter rent yer bottom field nex' year."

Br'er Bear he hum en he haw, en den he sez, "I don't spec I kin 'commodate yer, Br'er Rabbit, but I moughten consider hit, bein's hit's yer."

"How does you rent yer land, Br'er Bear?"

"Well," said Br'er Bear, "I takes der top of de crop fer my sheer, en yer takes de rest fer yer sheer."

Br'er Rabbit thinks erbout it rale hard, en he sez, "All right, Br'er Bear, I took it; we goes ter plowin' ober dare nex' week."

Den Br'er Bear goes back in der house des' er-laughin'. He sho is tickled ez to how he hez done put one by ole Br'er Rabbit dat time.

Well, 'long in May Br'er Rabbit done sont his oldest son to tell Br'er Bear to come down to the field to see erbout dat are sheer crop. Br'er Bear he comes er-pacin' down to de field en Br'er Rabbit wuz er-leanin' on de fence.

"Mo'nin', Br'er Bear. See what er fine crop we hez got. You is to hab de tops fer yer sheer. Whare is you gwine to put 'em? I wants ter git' em off so I kin dig my 'taters."

Br'er Bear wuz sho hot. But he done made dat trade wid Br'er Rabbit, en he had to stick to hit. So he went off all huffed up, en didn't even tell Br'er Rabbit what to do wid de vines. But Br'er Rabbit perceeded to dig his 'taters.

'Long in de fall Br'er Rabbit lows he's gwine to see Br'er Bear ergin en try to rent der bottom field. So he goes down to Br'er Bear's house en after passin' de time of day en other pleasant sociabilities, he sez, sez he, "Br'er Bear, how erbout rentin' der bottom field nex' year? Is yer gwine ter rent hit to me ergin?''

Br'er Bear say, he did, "You cheat me out uf my eyes las' year, Br'er Rabbit. I don't think I kin let yer hab it dis year."

Den Br'er Rabbit scratch his head er long time, en he say, "Oh, now, Br'er Bear, yer know I ain't cheated yer. Yer jes' cheat yerself. Yer made de trade yerself en I done tuck yer at yer word. Yer sed yer wanted der tops fer yer sheer, en I gib um ter yer, didn't I? Now yer jes' think hit all ober ergin and see if yer can't make er new deal fer yerself."

Den Br'er Bear said, "Well, I rents to yer only on dese perditions: dat yer hab all de tops fer yer sheer en I hab all de rest fer my sheer."

Br'er Rabbit he twis' en he turn en he sez, "All right, Br'er Bear, I'se got ter hab more land fer my boys. I'll tuck hit. We go to plowin' in dare right erway."

Den Br'er Bear he amble back into de house. He wuz shore he'd made er good trade dat time.

Way 'long in nex' June Br'er Rabbit done sont his boy down to Br'er Bear's house ergin, to tell him to come down ter de field ter see erbout his rent. When he got dare, Br'er Rabbit say, he did:

"Mo'nin', Br'er Bear. See what er fine crop we hez got? I specks hit will make forty bushels to der acre. I'se gwine ter put my oats on der market. What duz yer want me ter do wid yer straw?"

Br'er Bear sho wuz mad, but hit wa'nt no use. He done saw whar Br'er Rabbit had'im. So he lies low en 'lows to hisself how he's gwine to git eben wid Br'er Rabbit yit. So he smile en say, "Oh, der crop is all right, Br'er Rabbit. Jes' stack my straw anywheres around dare. Dat's all right."

Den Br'er Bear smile en he say, "What erbout nex' year, Br'er Rabbit? Is yer cravin' ter rent dis field ergin?"

"I ain't er-doin nothin' else but wantin' ter rent hit, Br'er Bear," sez Br'er Rabbit.

"All right, all right, yer kin rent her ergin. But dis time I'se gwine ter hab der tops fer my sheer, en I'se gwine ter hab de bottoms fer my sheer too."

Br'er Rabbit wuz stumped. He didn't know whatter do nex'. But he finally managed to ask, "Br'er Bear, ef yer gits der tops en der bottoms fer yer sheer, what will I git fer my sheer?"

Den ole Br'er Bear laff en say, "Well yer would git de middles."

Br'er Rabbit he worry en he fret, he plead en he argy, but hit do no good.

Br'er Bear sez, "Take hit er leave hit," en jes' stand pat.

Br'er Rabbit took hit.

Way 'long nex' summer old Br'er Bear 'cided he would go down to der bottom field en see erbout dat dare sheer crop he had wid Br'er Rabbit. While he wuz er-passin' through de woods on hiz way, he sez to himself, he did:

"De fust year I rents to de ole Rabbit, I makes de tops my sheer, en ole Rabbit planted 'taters; so I gits nothin' but vines. Den I rents ergin, en der

Rabbit is to hab de tops, en I de bottoms, en ole Rabbit plants oats; so I gits nothin' but de straw. But I sho is got dat ole Rabbit dis time. I gits both de tops en de bottoms, en de ole Rabbit gits only de middles. I'se bound ter git' im dis time."

Jes' den de old Bear come ter de field. He stopped. He look at hit. He shet up his fist. He cuss en he say, "Dat derned little scoundrel! He done went en planted dat fiel' in corn."

Ole Sis Goose

Ole Sis Goose wus er-sailin' on de lake, and ole Br'er Fox wus hid in de weeds. By um by ole Sis Goose swum up close to der bank and ole Br'er Fox lept out an cotched her.

"O yes, ole Sis Goose, I'se got yer now, you'se been er-sailin' on der lake er long time, en I'se got yer now. I'se gwine to break yer neck en pick yer bones."

"Hole on der', Br'er Fox, hold on, I'se got jes' as much right to swim in der lake as you has ter lie in der weeds. Hit's des' as much my lake es hit is yours, and we is gwine to take dis matter to der cotehouse and see if you has any right to break my neck and pick my bones."

And so dey went to cote, and when dey got dere, de sheriff, he wus er fox, en de judge, he wus er fox, and der tourneys, dey wus fox, en all de jurymen, dey was foxes, too.

En dey tried ole Sis Goose, en dey 'victed her and dey 'scuted her, and dey picked her bones.

Now, my chilluns, listen to me, when all de folks in de cotehouse is foxes, and you is des' er common goose, der ain't gwine to be much jestice for you pore cullud folks.

De Knee-high Man

"De Knee-high man lived by de swamp. He wuz alwez a-wantin' to be big 'stead of little. He sez to hisself: 'I is gwinter ax de biggest thing in dis neighborhood how I kin git sizable.' So he goes to see Mr. Horse. He ax him: 'Mr. Horse, I come to git you to tell me how to git big like you is.'

Mr. Horse, he say: 'You eat a whole lot of corn and den you run round and round and round, till you ben about twenty miles and atter a while you big as me.'

So de knee-high man, he done all Mr. Horse tole him. An' de corn make his stomach hurt, and runnin' make his legs hurt and de trying make his mind hurt. And he gits littler and littler. Den de knee-high man he set in his house and study how come Mr. Horse ain't help him none. And he say to hisself: 'I is gwinter go see Brer Bull.'

So he go to see Brer Bull and he say: 'Brer Bull, I come to ax you to tell me how to git big like you is.'

And Brer Bull, he say: 'You eat a whole lot o' grass and den you bellow and bellow and fust thing you know you gits big like I is.'

And de knee-high man he done all Brer Bull tole him. And de grass make his stomach hurt, and de bellowing make his neck hurt and de thinking make his mind hurt. And he git littler and littler. Den de knee-high man he set in his house and he stidy how come Brer Bull ain't done him no good. Atter wile, he hear ole Mr. Hoot Owl way in de swamp preachin' dat de bad peoples is sure gwinter have de bad luck.

Den de knee-high man he say to hisself: 'I gwinter ax Mr. Hoot Owl how I kin git to be sizable,' and he go to see Mr. Hoot Owl.

And Mr. Hoot Owl say: 'What for you want to be big?' and de knee-high man say: 'I wants to be big so when I gits a fight, I ken whup.'

And Mr. Hoot Owl say: 'Anybody ever try to pick a scrap wid you?'

De knee-high man he say naw. And Mr. Hoot Owl say: 'Well den, you ain't got no cause to fight, and you ain't got no cause to be mo' sizable 'an you is.'

De knee-high man says: 'But I wants to be big so I kin see a fur ways.' Mr. Hoot Owl, he say: 'Can't you climb a tree and see a fur ways when you is clim' to de top?'

De knee-high man, he say: 'Yes.' Den Mr. Hoot Owl say: 'You ain't got no cause to be bigger in de body, but you sho' is got cause to be bigger in de BRAIN.' "

Why Br' Gator's Hide Is So Horny

One time Br' Alligator's back used to be smooth an' white as a catfish-skin, so dat when he come out o' de water, an' lie down for sleep in de sun-hot on de mudbank, he shine like a piece o' silber. He been mighty proud o' he hide, an' mighty pleased wid heself nohow.

He an' his wife an' he fambly lib down in de ribber at de edge o' de rice fiel'. Dem hab plenty o' fish to nyam for dem bittle, an' nebber bodder wid none o' de creeter what been on de lan', lessn dem bog in de mud by de ribber-side, or fall in de water. Dem projeck roun' down in de bottom o' de ditch an' canal, an' eben if dey aint so smart, dem mek out alright. An' ebery year God sen', dey hab a gang o' chillen, so dey house is full-up widout axin' in no company. An' de whole dit an' bilin' been dat satisfy wid deyself dat dey t'ink dey ain' nobody quite like 'em. An' dey aint hab no notion how true dat is!

Well, suh, one hot day in de fall Br' Gator been res' heself 'pontop de rice-fiel' bank, a-lettin' de sun soak into dat bright back o' hisn, when along come Br' Rabbit.

Now Br' Rabbit ain' got a bit o' use for Br' Gator, but he stop all de same for pass de time o' day an' hab a little compersation wid him, 'cause Br' Rabbit too lub compersation! Rather dan keep he mout' shut he will eben gone out o' he way for talk, if tis only wid one o' dem ridic'lous creeter dat ain' know no better dan to lib in de water.

"Howdy, Br' Alligator. How is Sis' Alligator, an' all de young Alligator mekin' out?"

Br' Gator ain't bodder to speak to Br' Rabbit at de fus' goin' off. Seem like he ain' care what no other creeter t'ink 'bout him, nor how dey git 'long dey-self. But after while he fix he cat-eye on Br' Rabbit, an' tell-him say, "Please Gawd, I like you to know dat dey gits on fine! But taint no wonder dat dem chillen is smart, an' purty, an' rais' right, 'cause dey lib in de ribber. I swear-to-Gawd I can't see how oonuh (you) mek out, a-libin' up 'pon-top o' dat dry, drafty lan'. An' you, an' all de udder creeter dat ain' fitten to lib in de water, seems to spen' all o' you' time a-skirmishin' roun', till you must' be wore out 'fore de day is half done!"

Br' Rabbit is bex wid Br' Gator for bein' so set in he notions, till he had a-mind to tell him what he t'ink o' dat kind o' talk, but he been jis' so bex dat he lay low, an' 'tend like Br' Gator's is speakin' de truth. He sigh an' he shake he head, an' say bery mou'nful-like, "Mebbe so. We sho' is been seein' a heap o' trouble!"

"Who dat, you talk 'bout, Br' Rabbit—Trouble?"

Br' Rabbit s'pose dat Br' Gator mus' be jokin' him, 'cause he 'member too good 'bout dat trouble Br' Gator had wid Br' Dog. "How, Br' Alligator! You aint nebber hear o' Trouble?"

Br' Gator shake he head. "No. I nebber yeddy 'bout him, needer seen him. How he is stan'?"

Br' Rabbit ain't b'liebe he ears. "Oh, cry out, Br' Alligator! Old as you is, an' ain' nebber seed Trouble yit?"

"I tell you, Br' Rabbit, I ain' nebber know nothin' 'bout dis here Trouble. How is Trouble look?"

Br' Rabbit scratch he head. He figger if Br' Gator been so stupid, an' so satisfy wid heself an' he own t'ing, an' so ridic'lous an' onmannersable 'bout all dat lib on de lan', dat now here is he chance for learn Br' Gator he right place. An' Br' Rabbit is so mischiebous dat he scheme 'bout he he goin' to hab de mos' fun out o' Br' Gator.

"I dunno dat I kin 'xactly tell you how Trouble stan'. But mebbe you'd like for see him?"

"Sho' 'nough, Br' Rabbit, I like bery much for see him."

"O' cose I kin show him to you, Br' Alligator, but I dunno dat I is a-goin' to. Mebbe you aint like him so good."

"Go'long, boy! I ain' scare' o' dat. I jis' want to see him. If I don' like him, dat ain' goin' to be no matter to me."

"I is purty busy jis' now," Br' Rabbit 'tend.

"Do, Br' Rabbit! You gots time for a lot o' no-count t'ing, an' after all, tis Me what ax you—don't forget dat!"

"Sho! O' cose. How kin I forgit dat!" Br' Rabbit mock him, only Br' Gator ain' nebber see dat Br' Rabbit mean mischief. "But I gots to fix me house, an' Sis' Rabbit is poly, an' de chillen gotta be 'tend to, an'—"

"Tchk! All dat'll tek care o' itself!" An' Br' Alligator 'suade an' beg, an' beg an' 'suade, till at las' Br' Rabbit 'gree to show him Trouble.

"Meet me in dis same place soon as de jew dry up offn de grass nex' Saturday. Dat been a good day. Trouble mebbe hab some time off come Sunday." An' Br' Rabbit bid him good mawnin', an' gone 'long.

Come Saturday, Br' Gator git up befo' day-clean in de mornin', an' start for fix heself.

Sis' Alligator wake up, an' ax, "Whe' you gwine?"

Br' Gator aint crack he teet' at she, but gone 'long fixin' heself.

Dat jis' set Sis' Alligator for bodder him. "Whe' is you gwine?" she ax again. An' she squestion an' she squestion, till after sich a lengt' o' time Br' Gator see dat de 'oman is jis' boun' for know.

He gi' up at las'. "I is goin' out wid Br' Rabbit."

"Whe' is you goin' to?"

Br' Alligator mek a long mout', an' try for pay no mo' 'tention.

But Sis' Alligator know de ways for git roun' dat fellah! An' after such anudder length o' time, Br' Alligator tell she: "I is goin' for see Trouble."

"What Trouble is?"

"How I know? Dat's what I goin' for see."

"Kin I go 'long?" ax Sis' Alligator.

He say no, but after talk an' 'suade, an' talk an' 'suade, at las' Br' Alligator say, short-patience-like, "All right, you kin come 'long."

So she start for fix sheself. What wid all de talkin' an' goin' on, all de leetle alligators wake up by dis time. Dem look at dey pappy, an' dey mammy, fixin' deyself an' gittin' ready to gone out, an' dem run to Br' Gator an' ax him, "Whe' you gwine, Pappy?"

"None o' yo' business!"

Dem run den to Sis' Alligator, an' all cry out, one after anudder, "How! Where is you goin', Mammy?"

But all Sis' Alligator say is, "Git 'way, an' let me 'lone."

Den dey run to dey Pa, an' tease, "Pappy, Mammy say you is for tell we where you is goin'."

Br' Gator is bex but he see taint no use to try for hold back. "I go for see Trouble."

"Pappy! Kin we go? Kin we go?" An' dem chillen all jump up an' down, an' holler, an' beg him.

Br' Gator tell 'em, "No!"

So dem run to dey Ma, an' ax, "Mammy, kin we go?"

An' dey Ma tell-'em-say, "If you' Pa say you kin go, den you kin go."

So back dem gone at dey Pa. "Ma say we kin go if you jis' let we!"

By dis time Br' Gator is plumb wore out, so he say, "Well, den, yes! You kin go. But fix you'self nice an' purty. An' act mannersable, now! You is to show Br' Rabbit how much better water-chillen behave dan woods-chillen!"

Dem run for fix deyself nice, an' turreckly dey is all dress up for gone out. Dey hab on dey bes', wid mud on dey head, an' marsh on dey back, an' moonshine on dey tails, an' dey t'ink dat dey jis' look fine.

'Bout dis time Br' Gator look out de do', an' see dat de jew is mos' off de grass. He call he wife an' he chillen, "Come on!"

An' dem come a-crowdin', an' all gone out on de rice fiel' bank to wait on Br' Rabbit.

Dey aint been there long, 'for here come Br' Rabbit, a-smokin' he pipe. When he git up wid dem, he been s'prise to see what a hebby haul he is mek—de whole dart fambly. He laugh to hisself, but he ain' say nothin' but jus' say, "Howdy," to Br' Gator an' he wife. An' he tell 'em, "How nice de chillen is all a-lookin'!" But all de time he say to heself, "Do Lord! Dis is a oagly gang o' people. An' how mean dey clo'es is! Dat "oman is a po' buckra hussy, for true."

Br' Gator aint eben 'pologize to him for fetch sich a crowd. All he say is, "Dey all beg me so dat I hab to giv in, an' let 'em come along."

Br' Rabbit say, "Plenty o' room for all. Hope you will all enjoy yo'self."

"T'enky!" dey all tell him. An' de chillen all been dat glad dat Br' Rabbit ain' sen' 'em home dey all dance 'bout wid joy.

Dey look so comical, a-histin' dey nose an' dey tail, till Br' Rabbit mos' laugh in dey face. But 'stid o' dat he squinch up he eyebrow an' look at he watch, an' say, "Time to gone 'long, I reckin."

So dem all start down de rice fiel' bank, Br' Rabbit an' Br' Gator leadin' off, wid Sis' Alligator walkin' behin' to mek de leetle Alligator behave deyself'. But dey wouldn't hardlly mind she—dey played 'long, or dawdled, or fit, till dey 'most set her 'stracted.

Br' Rabbit lead dem up through a patch o' woods till he git to a ol' fiel' all growed up full o' broom-grass an' briar! De grass stan' so t'ick you hardly kin see roun' in it an' tis dry as tinder, an' yaller like de pure gol'. De path dem tek gone spang through de fiel', an' twas a big fiel' too. Br' Rabbit lead, an' after a while dem git to de middle o' de fiel', an' den he stop.

Br' Rabbit tek he pipe out he mout', an' he clap he han' to he ear, an' mek out like he listen. Seem like he hear somet'ing. "Sh! Sh!" he tell de chillen.

Sis' Alligator say, "Sh! Sh! Or I'll lick de tar out o' you!"

After Br' Rabbit listen some mo', he shout out, "Who dat a-callin' Br' Rabbit?"

Den he mek out like he yeddy somet'in' mo', an' yell back, "Yes. Tis me. What you want wid me?"

He clap he han' to he ear again, an' den he say, "I is comin' right now." An'
he turn to Br' Gator an' tell him, "Ax you' pardon, but somebody is callin' me
'way a minute on a business. Please for 'scuse me. An' wait right whe' you is till
I kin git back."

"We goin' to stay right here," Br' Gator promise.

Br' Rabbit mek him a low bow, an' run 'long de path, out o' sight. Dat
'ceitful debbil gone till he git to de edge o' de woods, an' set heself down an'
snigger to heself like he was tastin' de fun before he started it. Den he gone to
business.

He smell de wind an' look which way it is drivin'. Den he pull a handful
o' dat long, dry broom-grass, an' he knock out de hot coal from he pipe on it,
an' he blow till de grass catch fire good. Den he run long de edge o' de fiel' wid
de fire, an' set de fiel' roun' an' roun'. When he is done dat, he git up on a safe
high stump whe' he kin se good, an' he set down an' wait.

All dis time de Alligator been down in de middle o' de fiel'. Dey been tired
wid walkin' so far, an' mighty satisfy wid res' deyself awhile.

Sis' Alligator been jus' de kind dat like for know jis' what she is goin' for
see, an' she pester an' bodder Br' Gator wid w'ich-an'-w'y talk, "W'ich way is we
gwine for find Trouble? Whyn you mek Br' Rabbit tell you mo' 'bout dis t'ing
you is a-lookin' for? How long we got to wait?"

He aint mek she no answer, but jus' set still an' grunt ebery now an' den.

Once in awhile Sis' Alligator call to de chillen dat been aprojeckin' aroun',
"Stop dat rookus!"

An' dey set, an' dey set.

De fire burn an' burn. At last de wind catch it an' it flared up high, an' de
spark an' flame flew up, 'way up, in de element. One o' de leetle Alligator see dat.
An' he holler out, "Look-a'-dere! Look-a-dere!"

But jis den he Ma ax he Pa another squestion, an' she hesh de chillen right
short.

But all de turrah res' o' dem little Alligators look de way dey bubbuh
(brother) p'int, an' dey sing out too, "Look-a'-dere!"

An' one get a notion an' he holler out, "Mus' be dat is Trouble."

An' Sis' Alligator turn an' look, an' she squizzit Br' Gator, "Look, Pa! Is dat
Trouble for true?"

Br' Gator been so ignorant he ain' know. He lib in water an' mud, an' he
aint ebber see fire till now, but he ain' feel easy in he mind. "Reckin mebbe Br'
Rabbit git los' or somepn?" he ax Sis' Alligator, widout answer de squestion.

Den one o' de chillen sing out, "Trouble is pretty!"

An' wid dat, all o' de brats h'ist dey tail an' dey voice, an' holler. "Trouble
is pretty! Trouble is pretty! Trouble is pretty!"

Br' Gator say, "If dat is Trouble, he sho' nough is pretty! De chile speak de
trut'." An' he an' he wife set a-gogglin' dey big eye up in de element, watchin'
de fire come on, an' dey kind o' forgit all 'bout Br' Rabbit. An' all de chillen

goggle dey eye too, same as dey Ma an' Pa, an' keep still, as if dey ben 'fraid dat dey might scare Trouble away.

At las' a hot spark lan' right on one o' dem leetle Alligator' back. An' he squall, an' cry out, "Trouble hurt! O'hey! O'hey! O'hey!"

He Ma fetch him a smack in de jaw an' tell him to mind he manners an' shut up, an' look how pretty Trouble is. But jus' as she done so, a hebby spark light on she, an' burn she too bad. An' she start for jump 'bout, an' holler.

"'Tis true Trouble hurt! Trouble hurt for true? O'hey! O'hey! O'hey!" An' dey 'member quick who dey is forgit! "Br' Rabbit! Br' Rabbit! We don't want to see no mo' o' Trouble, Br' Rabbit! Oh, Br' Rabbit!"

Well, my frien', 'bout dat time de spark begin for sweeten de whole lot o' dem. Dey is dat put to it dey don't know whaffor do. An' dey run 'bout an' run 'bout, dis way an' dat way, for git out; but eberywhere dem turn is de fire. An' dey holler out, an' holler out, "Br' Rabbit, whe' is you? Call to Trouble, Br' Rabbit! Come for we! Ooh, Br' Rabbit!"

But Br' Rabbit ain' come, an' he ain' say nothin'. An' mighty soon de fire git so close on dem Gator', dat dey can't hol' dey groun' no longer. Dey quit callin' on Br' Rabbit, an' jis' git ready for breck t'rough de best dey kin.

Dey ain' got no notion o' nothin' lef' in dey head but Git Home!

Sis' Alligator holler, "Chillen, foller you' Pa."

An' right t'rough de scorchin' fire dey bus', Sis' Alligator a-herdin' dem. Dey don't walk so fas' ebery day, but dis been a special day, wid dat hot fire a-blisterin' an' a-frizzlin' 'em, an' dey gone a-runnin'. After dey git t'rough dey ain' slow up. Dey gone past Br' Rabbit just a-scuttlin'! An' dey look dat comical till Br' Rabbit most fall off de stump, he laugh so hard.

"Ki, Br' Alligator!" he shout, "I reckin you is seen Trouble now! Git 'long back in de water, where you belong. An' don't nebber, no mo', hunt Trouble!"

But dem Gator been too busy runnin' to stop to argue wid him.

Dem aint stop till dey git spang to de rice fiel' bank an' jump in de ribber. An' dey is still so hot from de fire when dey gone overboard an' de water hit dem, it gone "Swiish-sssssssssh-sh!" An' de pure steam rise up like a cloud.

Dey aint come out again de lib-long day, nor dat night needer; but when next dey git a chance to look upon one anudder dey find dat de fire work on dem so bad dat dey white skin is just as black an' crinkly as a burnt log o' wood, an' rough as a libe-oak bark. Dat family done git swinged for bein' so fool. An' from dat day to dis Gator hab a horny hide.

How Buck Won His Freedom

Buck was the shrewdest slave on the big Washington plantation. He could steal things almost in front of his master's eyes without being detected. Finally, after having had his chickens and pigs stolen until he was sick, Master Harry Washington called Buck to him one day and said, "Buck, how do you manage to steal without getting caught?"

"Dat's easy, Massa," replied Buck, "dat's easy. Ah kin steal yo' clo'es right tonight, wid you a-guardin' 'em."

"No, no," said the master, "you may be a slick thief, but you can't do that. I will make a proposition to you: If you steal my suit of clothes tonight, I will give you your freedom, and if you fail to steal them, then you will stop stealing my chickens."

"Aw right, Massa, aw right," Buck agreed. "Dat's uh go."

That night about nine o'clock the master called his wife into the bedroom, got his Sunday suit of clothes, laid it out on the table, and told his wife about the proposition he had made with Buck. He got on one side of the table and had his wife get on the other side, and they waited. Pretty soon, through a window that was open, the master heard the mules and horses in the stable lot running as if some one were after them.

"Here, wife," said he, "you take this gun and keep an eye on this suit. I'm going to see what's the matter with those animals."

Buck, who had been out to the horse lot and started the stampede to attract the master's attention, now approached the open window. He was a good mimic, and in tones that sounded like his master's he called out, "Ol'lady, ol'lady, ol'lady, you better hand me that suit. That damn thief might steal it while I'm gone."

The master's wife thinking that it was her husband asking for his suit, took it from the table and handed it out the window to Buck. This is how Buck won his freedom.

Swapping Dreams

Master Jim Turner, an unusually good-natured master, had a fondness for telling long stories woven out of what he claimed to be his dreams, and especially did he like to "swap" dreams with Ike, a witty slave who was a house servant. Every morning he would set Ike to telling about what he had dreamed the night before. It always seemed, however, that the master could tell the best dream tale, and Ike had to admit that he was beaten most of the time.

One morning, when Ike entered the master's room to clean it, he found the master just preparing to get out of bed. "Ike," he said, "I certainly did have a strange dream last night."

"Sez yuh did, Massa, sez yuh did?" answered Ike. "Lemme hyeah it."

"All right," replied the master. "It was like this: I dreamed I went to Nigger Heaven last night, and saw there a lot of garbage, some old torn-down houses, a few old broken-down, rotten fences, the muddiest, sloppiest streets I ever saw, and a big bunch of ragged, dirty Negroes walking around."

"Umph, umph, Massa," said Ike, "yuh sho' musta et de same t'ing Ah did las' night, 'case Ah dreamed Ah went up ter de white man's paradise, an' de streets wuz all ob gol' an' silvah, and dey wuz lots o' milk an' honey dere, an' putty pearly gates, but dey wuzn't uh soul in de whole place."

A Laugh That Meant Freedom

There were some slaves who had a reputation for keeping out of work because of their wit and humor. These slaves kept their masters laughing most of the time, and were able, if not to keep from working altogether, at least to draw the lighter tasks.

Nehemiah was a clever slave, and no master who had owned him had ever been able to keep him at work, or succeeded in getting him to do heavy work. He would always have some funny story to tell or some humorous remark to make in response to the master's question or scolding. Because of this faculty for avoiding work, Nehemiah was constantly being transferred from one master to another. As soon as an owner found out that Nehemiah was outwitting him, he sold Nehemiah to some other slaveholder. One day David Wharton, known as the most cruel slave master in Southwest Texas, heard about him.

"I bet I can make that rascal work," said David Wharton, and he went to Nehemiah's master and bargained to buy him.

The morning of the first day after his purchase, David Wharton walked over to where Nehemiah was standing and said, "Now you are going to work, you understand. You are going to pick four hundred pounds of cotton today."

"Wal, Massa, dat's aw right," answered Nehemiah, "but ef Ah meks you laff, won' yuh lemme off fo' terday?"

"Well," said David Wharton, who had never been known to laugh, "if you make me laugh, I won't only let you off for today, but I'll give you your freedom."

"Ah decla', Boss," said Nehemiah, "yuh sho' is uh goodlookin' man."

"I am sorry I can't say the same thing about you," retorted David Wharton.

"Oh, yes, Boss, yuh could," Nehemiah laughed out, "yuh could, if yuh tole ez big uh lie ez Ah did."

David Wharton could not help laughing at this; he laughed before he thought. Nehemiah got his freedom.

The Wounds of Jesus

Our theme this morning is the wounds of Jesus. When the father shall ast, "What are these wounds in thine hand?" He shall answer, "Those are they with which I was wounded in the house of my friends." Zach. 13:6.

We read in the 53rd Chapter of Isaiah where He was wounded for our trans-
gressions and bruised for our iniquities, and the apostle Peter affirms that His
blood was spilt from before the foundation of the world.

I have seen gamblers wounded. I have seen desperadoes wounded; thieves
and robbers and every other kind of characters, law-breakers and each one had
a reason for his wounds. Some of them was unthoughtful, and some for being
overbearing, and some by the doctor's knife, but all wounds disfigures a person.

Jesus was not unthoughtful. He was not overbearing. He was never a bully.
He was never sick. He was never a criminal before the law and yet He was
wounded. Now, a man usually gets wounded in the midst of his enemies, but this
man was wounded, says the text, in the house of His friends. It is not your
enemies that harm you all the time. Watch that close friend. Every believer in
Christ is considered His friend, and every sin we commit is a wound to Jesus.
The blues we play in our homes is a club to beat up Jesus, and these social card
parties.

> Jesus have always loved us from the foundation of the world
> When God
> Stood out on the apex of His power
> Before the hammers of creation
> Fell upon the anvils of Time and hammered out the ribs of the
>   earth
> Before He made any ropes
> By the breath of fire
> And set the boundaries of the ocean by the gravity of His power
> When God said, Ha!
> Let us make man
> And the elders upon the altar cried, ha!
> If you make man, Ha!
> Father!! Ha-aa
> I am the teeth of time
> That comprehended de dust of de earth
> And weighed de hills in scales
> That painted de rainbow dat marks de end of de parting storm
> Measured de seas in de holler of my hand
> That held de elements in a unbroken chain of controllment.
> Make man, ha!
> If he sin I will redeem him
> I'll break de chasm of hell
> Where de fire's never quenched
> I'll go into de grave
> Where de worm never dies, Ah!

So God A'mighty, Ha!
Got His stuff together
He dipped some water out of de mighty deep
He got Him a handful of dirt
From de foundation sills of de earth
He seized a thimble full of breath
From de drums of de wind, ha!
God, my master!
Now I'm ready to make man
Aa-aah!
Who shall I make him after? Ha!
Worlds within worlds begin to wheel and roll
De Sun, Ah!
Gethered up de fiery skirts of her garments
and wheeled around de throne, Ah!
Saying, Ah, make man after me, ha!
God gazed upon the sun
And sent her back to her blood-red socket
And shook His head, ha!
De Moon, ha!
Grabbed up de reins of de tides.
And dragged a thousand seas behind her
As she walked around de throne
Ah-h, please make man after me
But God said "NO"!
I'll make man in my own image, ha!
I'll put him in de garden
And Jesus said, ha!
And if he sin,
I'll go his bond before yo' mighty throne
Ah, He was yo' friend
He made us all, ha!
Delegates to de judgment convention
Ah!
Faith hasn't got no eyes, but she' long-legged
But take de spy-glass of Faith
And look into dat upper room
When you are alone to yourself
When yo' heart is burnt with fire, ha!
When de blood is lopin' thru yo' veins
Like de iron monasters (monsters) on de rail
Look into dat upper chamber, ha!
We notice at de supper table

As we gazed upon his friends, ha!
His eyes flowin' wid tears, ha! He said
"My soul is exceedingly sorrowful unto death, ha!
For this night, ha!
One of you shall betray me, ha!
It were not a Roman officer, ha!
It were not a centurion
But one of you
Who I have chosen my bosom friend
That sops in the dish with me shall betray me."
I want to draw a parable.
I see Jesus
Leaving heben with all of His grandeur
Dis-robin' Hisself of His matchless honor
Yielding up de scepter of revolvin' worlds
Clothing Hisself in de garment of humanity
Coming into de world to rescue His friends.
Two thousand years have went by on their rusty ankles
But with the eye of Faith, I can see Him
Look down from His high towers of elevation
I can hear Him when He walks the golden streets
I can hear 'em ring under His footsteps
Sol me-e-e, Sol do
Sol me-e-e, Sol do
I can see Him step out upon the rim bones of nothing
Crying I am de way
De truth and de light
Ah!
God A'mighty!
I see Him grab de throttle
Of de well ordered train of mercy
I see kingdoms crush and crumble
Whilst de archangels held de winds in de corner chambers
I see Him arrive on dis earth
And walk de streets thirty and three years
Oh-h-hhh!
I see Him walking beside de sea of Galilee wid His disciples
This declaration gendered on His lips
"Let us go on to the other side"
God A'mighty!
Dey entered de boat
Wid their oarus (oars) stuck in de back
Sails unfurled to de evenin' breeze

And de ship was now sailin'
As she reached de center of de lake
Jesus was sleep on a pillow in de rear of de boat
And de dynamic powers of nature became disturbed
And de mad winds broke de heads of de Western drums
And fell down on de lake of Galilee
And buried themselves behind de gallopin' waves
And de white-caps marbilized themselves like an army
And walked out like soldiers goin' to battle
And de zig-zag lightning
Licked out her fiery tongue
And de flying clouds
Threw their wings in the channels of the deep
And bedded de waters like a road-plow
And faced de current of de chargin' billows
And de terrific bolts of thunder—they bust in de clouds
And de ship begin to reel and rock
God A'mighty!
And one of de disciples called Jesus
"Master!! Carest Thou not that we perish?"
And He arose
And de storm was in its pitch
And de lightnin' played on His raiments as
        He stood on the prow of the boat
And placed His foot upon the neck of the storm
And spoke to the howlin' winds
And de sea fell at His feet like a marble floor
And de thunders went back in their vault
Then He set down on de rim of de ship
And took de hooks of His power
And lifted de billows in His lap
And rocked de winds to sleep on His arm
And said, "Peace, be still."
And de Bible says there was a calm.
I can see Him wid de eye of faith.
When He went from Pilate's house
Wid the crown of seventy-two wounds upon His head
I can see Him as He mounted Calvary and hung upon de cross for
        our sins.
I can see-eee-ee
De mountains fall to their rocky knees when He cried
"My God, my God! Why hast Thou forsaken me?"
The mountains fell to their rocky knees and trembled like a beast
From the stroke of the master's axe

One angel took the flinches of God's eternal power
And bled the veins of the earth
One angel that stood at the gate with a flaming sword
Was so well pleased with his power
Until he pierced the moon with his sword
And she ran down in blood
And de sun
Batted her fiery eyes and put on her judgment robe
And laid down in de cradle of eternity
And rocked herself into sleep and slumber
He died until the great belt in the wheel of time
And de geological strata fell aloose
And a thousand angels rushed to de canopy of heben
With flamin' swords in their hands
And placed their feet upon blue ether's bosom, and looked back
    at de dazzlin' throne
And de arc angels had veiled their faces
And de throne was draped in mornin'
And de orchestra had struck silence for the space of half an hour
Angels had lifted their harps to de weepin' willows
And God had looked off to-wards immensity
And blazin' worlds fell of His teeth
And about that time Jesus groaned on de cross, and
Dropped His head in the locks of His shoulder and said, "It is
    finished, it is finished."
And then de chambers of hell exploded
And de damnable spirits
Come up from de Sodomistic world and rushed into de smoky
    camps of eternal night,
And cried, "Woe! Woe! Woe!"
And then de Centurion cried out,
"Surely this is the Son of God."
And about dat time
De angel of Justice unsheathed his flamin' sword and ripped de
    veil of de temple
And de High Priest vacated his office
And then de sacrificial energy penetrated de mighty strata
And quickened de bones of de prophets
And they arose from their graves and walked about in de streets
    of Jerusalem
I heard de whistle of de damnation train
Dat pulled out from Garden of Eden loaded wid cargo goin' to
    hell
Ran at break-neck speed all de way thru de law

All de way thru de prophetic age
All de way thru de reign of Kings and judges—
Plowed her way thru de Jurdan
And on her way to Calvary, when she blew for de switch
Jesus stood out on her track like a rough-backed mountain
And she threw her cow-catcher in His side and His blood ditched
    de train
He died for our sins.
Wounded in the house of His friends.
That's where I got off de damnation train
And dat's where you must get off, ha!
For in dat mor-ornin', ha!
When we shall all be delegates, ha!
To dat Judgment Convention
When de two trains of Time shall meet on de trestle
And wreck de burning axles of de unformed ether
And de mountains shall skip like lambs
When Jesus shall place one foot on de neck of de sea, ha!
One foot on dry land, ah
When his chariot wheels shall be running hub-deep in fire
He shall take His friends thru the open bosom of an unclouded
    sky
And place in their hands de "hosanna" fan
And they shall stand 'round and 'round his beautific throne
And praise His name forever,
                                        Amen.

God Struck Me Dead

I have always been a sheep. I was never a goat. I was created and cut out and born in the world for Heaven. Even before God freed my soul and told me to go I never was hell-scared. I just never did feel that my soul was made to burn in hell.

God started on me when I wasn't but ten years old. I was sick with the fever and He called me and said, "You are ten years old." I didn't know how old I was but later on I asked my older sister and she told me that I was ten years old when I had the fever.

As I grew up I used to frolic a lot and was considered a good dancer but I never took much interest in such things. I just went many times to please my friends and, later on, my husband. What I loved more than all else was to go to church.

I used to pray then. I pray now and just tell God to take me and do His will for He knows the every secret of my heart. He knows what we stand most in need of before we ask for it and if we trust Him, He will give us what we ought to have in due season. Some people pray and call on God as if they think He is ignorant of their needs or else asleep. But God is a time-God. I know this for He told me so. I remember one morning I was on my way home with a bundle of clothes to wash—it was after my husband had died—I felt awfully burdened down and so I commenced to talk to God. It looked like I was having such a hard time. Everybody seemed to be getting along well but poor me. I told Him so. I said, "Lord, it looks like You come to everybody's house but mine. I never bother my neighbors or cause any disturbance. I have lived as it is becoming a poor widow woman to live and yet, Lord, it looks like I have a harder time than anybody." When I said this something told me to turn around and look. I put my bundle down and looked towards the east part of the world. A voice spoke to me as plain as day but it was inward and said, "I am a time-God working after the counsel of my own will. In due time I will bring all things to you. Remember and cause your heart to sing."

When God struck me dead with His power I was living on 14th Avenue. It was the year of the Centennial. I was in my house alone and I declare unto you when His power struck me I died. I fell out on the floor on my back. I could neither speak nor move for my tongue stuck to the roof of my mouth; my jaws were locked and my limbs were stiff.

In my vision I saw hell and the devil. I was crawling along a high brick wall, it seems, and it looked like I would fall into a dark roaring pit. I looked away to the east and saw Jesus. He was standing in snow—the prettiest, whitest snow I have ever seen. I said, "Lord, I can't go for that snow is too deep and cold. He commanded me the third time before I would go. I stepped out in it but it didn't seem a bit cold nor did my feet sink into it. We travelled on east in a little narrow path and came to something that looked like a grape-arbor and the snow was hanging down like icicles. But it was so pretty and white that it didn't look like snow. He told me to take some of it and eat but I said, "Lord, it is too cold." He commanded me three times before I would eat any of it. I took some and tasted it and it was the best-tasting snow I ever put into my mouth.

The Father, the Son and the Holy Ghost led me on to glory. I saw God sitting in a big arm-chair. Everything seemed to be made of white stones and pearls. God didn't seem to pay me any attention. He just sat looking into space. I saw the Lamb's book of life and my name written in it. A voice spoke to me and said, "Whosoever my Son sets free is free indeed. I give you a through ticket from hell to Heaven. Go into yonder world and be not afraid, neither be dismayed for you are an elect child and ready for the fold." But when He commanded me to go I was stubborn and didn't want to leave. He said, "My little one, I have commanded you and you shall obey."

I saw, while I was still in the spirit, myself going to my neighbors and to the church telling them what God had done for me. When I came to this world I arose shouting and went carrying the good news. I didn't do like the Lord told me though for I was still in doubt and I wanted to make sure. Because of my disobedience He threw a great affliction on me. I got awfully sick and my limbs were all swollen so that I could hardly walk. I began to have more faith then and put more trust in God. He put this affliction on me because it was hard for me to believe. But I just didn't want to be a hypocrite and go around hollering and not knowing what I was talking and shouting about. I told God this in my prayer and He answered me saying, "My little one, my grace is sufficient. Behold I have commanded you to go and you shall go."

When I was ready to be baptized I asked God to do two things. It had been raining for days and on the morning of my baptism it was still raining. I said, "Lord, if You are satisfied with me and pleased with what I have told the people, cause the sun to shine this evening when I go to the river." Bless your soul, when we went to the river, it looked like I had never seen the sun shine as bright. It stayed out about two hours and then it clouded up again and rained some more.

The other thing I asked God was that I might feel the spirit when I went down to the river. And I declare unto you, my soul caught on fire. From the minute I stepped in the carriage to go to the river. I had been hobbling around on a stick but I threw it away and forgot that I was ever a cripple.

Later the misery came back and I asked God to heal me. The spirit directed me to get some peach-tree leaves and beat them up and put them about my limbs. I did this and in a day or two that swelling left me and I haven't been bothered since. More than this, I don't remember ever paying out but $3.00 for doctor's bills in my life either for myself, my children or my grandchildren. Dr. Jesus tells me what to do.

Motherless Child

Sometimes I feel like a motherless child,
Sometimes I feel like a motherless child,
Sometimes I feel like a motherless child,
A long ways from home,
A long ways from home.

Sometimes I feel like I'm almost gone,
Sometimes I feel like I'm almost gone,
Sometimes I feel like I'm almost gone,
A long ways from home,
A long ways from home.

Sometimes I feel like a feather in the air,
Sometimes I feel like a feather in the air,
Sometimes I feel like a feather in the air,
And I spread my wings and I fly,

I spread my wings and I fly.

Go Down, Moses

Go down, Moses,
Way down in Egyptland
Tell old Pharaoh
To let my people go.

When Israel was in Egyptland
Let my people go
Oppressed so hard they could not stand
Let my people go.

Go down, Moses,
Way down in Egyptland
Tell old Pharaoh
"Let my people go."

"Thus saith the Lord," bold Moses said,
"Let my people go;
If not I'll smite your first-born dead
Let my people go."

Go down, Moses,
Way down in Egyptland,
Tell old Pharaoh,
"Let my people go!"

The Virgin Mary Had a Baby Boy

The Virgin Mary had a baby boy,
The Virgin Mary had a baby boy,
The Virgin Mary had a baby boy,
And they said His name was Jesus.
He come from the glory,
He come from the glorious kingdom!
Oh, yes, believer!
He come from the glory,
He come from the glorious kingdom!

Oh Mary, Don't You Weep

Oh Mary, don't you weep, don't you moan,
Oh Mary, don't you weep, don't you moan,

Pharaoh's army got drownded,
Oh Mary, don't you weep.

One of dese mornings, bright and fair,
Take my wings and cleave de air,
Pharaoh's army got drownded,
Oh Mary, don't you weep.

One of dese mornings, five o'clock,
Dis ole world gonna reel and rock,
Pharaoh's army got drownded,
Oh Mary, don't you weep.

Oh Mary, don't you weep, don't you moan,
Oh Mary, don't you weep, don't you moan,
Pharaoh's army got drownded,
Oh Mary, don't you weep.

Deep River

Deep river, my home is over Jordan,
Deep river, Lord; I want to cross over into camp ground.

O, don't you want to go to that gospel feast,
That promised land where all is peace?

Deep river, my home is over Jordan,
Deep river, Lord; I want to cross over into camp ground.

Steal Away

Steal away, steal away, steal away to Jesus,
Steal away, steal away home,
I ain't got long to stay here.

My Lord, He calls me,
He calls me by the thunder,
The trumpet sounds within-a my soul,
I ain't got long to stay here.

Steal away, steal away, steal away to Jesus,
Steal away, steal away home,
I ain't got long to stay here.

Green trees a-bending,
Po' sinner stands a-trembling
The trumpet sounds within-a my soul,
I ain't got long to stay here.

Steal away, steal away, steal away to Jesus,
Steal away, steal away home,
I ain't got long to stay here.

John Henry

Some say he's from Georgia,
Some say he's from Alabam,
But it's wrote on the rock at the Big Ben Tunnel,
John Henry's a East Virginia Man,
John Henry's a East Virginia Man.

John Henry he could hammah,
He could whistle, he could sing,
He went to the mountain early in the mornin'
To hear his hammah ring,
To hear his hammah ring.

John Henry went to the section boss,
Says the section boss what kin you do?
Says I can line a track, I kin histe a jack,
I kin pick and shovel, too,
I kin pick and shovel, too.

John Henry went to the tunnel
And they put him in lead to drive,
The rock was so tall and John Henry so small
That he laid down his hammah and he cried,
That he laid down his hammah and he cried.

The steam drill was on the right han' side,
John Henry was on the left,
Says before I let this steam drill beat me down,
I'll hammah myself to death,
I'll hammah myself to death.

Oh the cap'n said to John Henry,
I bleeve this mountain's sinkin' in.

John Henry said to the cap'n, Oh my!
Tain't nothin' but my hammah suckin' wind,
Tain't nothin' but my hammah suckin' wind.

John Henry had a pretty liddle wife,
She come all dressed in blue.
And the last words she said to him,
John Henry I been true to you,
John Henry I been true to you.

John Henry was on the mountain,
The mountain was so high,
He called to his pretty liddle wife,
Said Ah kin almos' touch the sky,
Said Ah kin almos' touch the sky.

Who gonna shoe yoh pretty liddle feet,
Who gonna glove yoh han',
Who gonna kiss yoh rosy cheeks,
An' who gonna be yoh man,
An' who gonna be yoh man?

Papa gonna shoe my pretty liddle feet,
Mama gonna glove my han',
Sistah gonna kiss my rosy cheeks,
An' I ain't gonna have no man,
An' I ain't gonna have no man.

Then John Henry he did hammah,
He did make his hammah soun',
Says now one more lick fore quittin' time,
An' I'll beat this steam drill down,
An' I'll beat this steam drill down.

The hammah that John Henry swung,
It weighed over nine poun',
He broke a rib in his left han' side,
And his intrels fell on the groun',
And his intrels fell on the groun'.

All the women in the West
That heard of John Henry's death,
Stood in the rain, flagged the east bound train,

Goin' where John Henry dropped dead,
Goin' where John Henry dropped dead.

They took John Henry to the White House,
And buried him in the san',
And every locomotive come roarin' by,
Says there lays that steel drivin' man,
Says there lays that steel drivin' man.

Stackalee

It was in the year of eighteen hundred and sixty-one
In St. Louis on Market Street where Stackalee was born.
Everybody's talkin about Stackalee.
It was on one cold and frosty night
When Stackalee and Billy Lyons had one awful fight,
Stackalee got his gun. Boy, he got it fast!
He shot poor Billy through and through;
Bullet broke a lookin glass.
Lord, O Lord, O Lord!
Stackalee shot Billy once; his body fell to the floor.
He cried out, Oh, please, Stack, please don't shoot me no more.

The White Elephant Barrel House was wrecked that night;
Gutters full of beer and whiskey; it was an awful sight.
Jewelry and rings of the purest solid gold
Scattered over the dance and gamblin hall.
The can-can dancers they rushed for the door
When Billy cried, Oh, please, Stack, don't shoot me no more.
Have mercy, Billy groaned, Oh, please spare my life;

Stack says, God bless your children, damn your wife!
You stold my magic Stetson; I'm gonna steal your life.
But, says Billy, I always treated you like a man.
'Tain't nothin to that old Stetson but the greasy band.
He shot poor Billy once, he shot him twice,
And the third time Billy pleaded, please go tell my wife.
Yes, Stackalee, the gambler, everybody knowed his name;
Made his livin hollerin high, low, jack and the game.

Meantime the sergeant strapped on his big forty-five,
Says now we'll bring in this bad man, dead or alive.
And brass-buttoned policemen tall dressed in blue

Came down the sidewalk marchin two by two.
Sent for the wagon and it hurried and come
Loaded with pistols and a big gatlin gun.
At midnight on that stormy night there came an awful wail
Billy Lyons and a graveyard ghost outside the city jail.
Jailer, jailer, says Stack, I can't sleep,
For around my bedside poor Billy Lyons still creeps.
He comes in shape of a lion with a blue steel in his hand,
For he knows I'll stand and fight if he comes in shape of man.
Stackalee went to sleep that night by the city clock bell,
Dreaming the devil had come all the way up from hell.
Red devil was sayin, you better hunt your hole;
I've hurried here from hell just to get your soul.

Stackalee told him yes, maybe you're right,
But I'll give even you one hell of a fight.
When they got into the scuffle, I heard the devil shout,
Come and get this bad man before he puts my fire out.
The next time I seed the devil he was scramblin up the wall,
Yellin, come and get this bad man fore he mops up with us all.

II

Then here come Stack's woman runnin, says, daddy, I love you
    true;
See what beer, whiskey, and smokin hop has brought you to.
But before I'll let you lay in there, I'll put my life in pawn.
She hurried and got Stackalee out on a five thousand dollar bond.
Stackalee said, ain't but one thing that grieves my mind,
When they take me away, babe, I leave you behind.
But the woman he really loved was a voodoo queen
From Creole French market, way down in New Orleans.
He laid down at home that night, took a good night's rest,
Arrived in court at nine o'clock to hear the coroner's inquest.
Crowds jammed the sidewalk, far as you could see,
Tryin to get a good look at tough Stackalee.
Over the cold, dead body Stackalee he did bend,
Then he turned and faced those twelve jury men.
The judge says, Stackalee, I would spare your life,
But I know you're a bad man; I can see it in your red eyes.
The jury heard the witnesses, and they didn't say no more;
They crowded into the jury room, and the messenger closed the
    door.

The jury came to agreement, the clerk he wrote it down,
And everybody was whisperin, he's penitentiary bound.
When the jury walked out, Stackalee didn't budge,
They wrapped the verdic and passed it to the judge.
Judge looked over his glasses, says, Mr. Bad Man Stackalee,
The jury finds you guilty of murder in the first degree.
Now the trial's come to an end, how the folks gave cheers;
Bad Stackalee was sent down to Jefferson pen for seventy-five
    years.

Now late at night you can hear him in his cell,
Arguin with the devil to keep from goin to hell.
And the other convicts whisper, whatcha know about that?
Gonna burn in hell forever over an old Stetson hat!
Everybody's talkin bout Stackalee.
That bad man, Stackalee!

Good Morning Blues

Good mornin', blues,
Blues, how do you do?
Good mornin', blues,
Blues, how do you do?
Good morning, how are you?

I laid down last night,
Turning from side to side;
Yes, I was turning from side to side,
I was not sick,
I was just dissatisfied.

When I got up this mornin',
Blues walking round my bed;
Yes, the blues walkin' round my bed,
I went to eat my breakfast,
The blues was all in my bread.

I sent for you yesterday baby,
Here you come a walking today;
Yes, here you come a walking today,
Got your mouth wide open,
You don't know what to say.

Good mornin', blues,
Blues, how do you do?
Yes, blues, how do you do?
I'm doing all right,
Good morning, how are you?

Southern Blues

House catch on fire
And ain't no water around,
If your house catch on fire,
Ain't no water around,
Throw yourself out the window,
Let it burn on down.

I went to the gypsy
To have my fortune told,
I went to the gypsy
To have my fortune told,
She said, "Dog-gone you, girlie,
Dog-gone your hard-luck soul!"

I turned around and
Went to that gypsy next door.
I turned around and
Went to that gypsy next door.
She said, "You can get a man
Anywhere you go."

Let me be your ragdoll
Until your china comes.
Let me be your ragdoll
Until your china comes.
If he keeps me ragged,
He's got to rag it some.

How Long Blues

How long, baby, how long
Has that even' train been gone?
How long? How long? I say, How long?
Standin' at the station watchin' my baby leave town,

Sure am disgusted—for where could she be gone—
For how long? How long? I say, how long?

I can hear the whistle blowin' but I cannot see no train
And deep down in my heart I got an ache and pain
For how long? How long? I say, how long?

Sometimes I feel so disgusted and I feel so blue
That I hardly know what in this world it's best to do
For how long, how long, how long?

If I could holler like I was a mountain jack
I'd go up on the mountain and call my baby back.
For how long, how long, how long?

If some day she's gonna be sorry that she done me wrong
Baby, it will be too late then—for I'll be gone
For so long, so long, so long!

My mind get's to rattling, I feel so bad
Thinkin' 'bout the bad luck that I have had
For so long, so long, so long.

How long? Baby, how long?
Baby, how long?
How long?

III
Up
from
Slavery

In one of the finest images in his *Narrative of the Life of Frederick Douglass* (1845), Frederick Douglass captured the essential dialectic of the first six decades of nineteenth-century America. Most black men (and many white) would have agreed with the alternatives that Douglass set forth when he said:

On the one hand, there stood slavery, a stern reality, glaring frightfully upon us,— its robes already crimsoned with the blood of millions, and even now feasting greedily upon our own flesh. On the other hand, away back in the dim distance, under the flickering light of the north star, behind some craggy hill or snow-covered mountain stood a doubtful freedom—half frozen—beckoning us to come and share her hospitality.

Before Douglass, David Walker had set forth the same dichotomy in his *Appeal to the Coloured Citizens of the World* written in 1829. Walker and Douglass both shared the concerns of one of the most idealistic movements in nineteenth-century England and America; both were abolitionists to the core, and in the *Appeal* and the *Narrative,* we find the two poles of the abolitionist movement.

Men are still debating whether the proper title for the abolitionists is "fanatic" or "reformer," and the works of Walker and Douglass give us some clues about the origin of the debate. Walker was essentially a pamphleteer in his work, and he assumed the role of impassioned preacher, militant revolutionary, and American radical in order to show that American slavery was the most opprobrious slave system that had ever existed. Walker went on to counsel his brothers in bondage to throw off their shackles and rise up against their white oppressors. His advice to the "Christian" slaveholders was to repent before an avenging God sent his fiery wrath upon them. Walker was a zealous champion of black liberation, and his *Appeal* stands in the forefront of a tradition of militant abolitionism. Walker clearly belongs on the John Brown side of the abolitionist movement; if any black American was fanatically intent on the liberation of his brothers, it was David Walker. His appeal is charged with heated phrases, burning denunciations, and pyrotechnic exclamations, and the printing techniques that he employed drive home his points with a vengeance. Walker is, in many respects, the father of "the Negro revolt."

Frederick Douglass's *Narrative* is a fit illustration of the adage, "the style is the man." The realism, humor, and objectivity of Douglass's work are diametrically opposed to the impassioned prose of Walker's *Appeal*. Douglass too championed the immediate liberation of the black man in America, but his primary objective was to convince unbelievers that he had indeed been a slave; his critics felt that a man of Douglass's distinction could not possibly have suffered under slavery. The focus of his *Narrative,* therefore, is on the man himself, and the verisimilitude of the work carries us right into the heart of the slave environment. We witness the brutality, the degradation, and the hypocrisy of an inefficient system of forced labor through the eyes of a narrator who possesses a remarkably ironic sense of humor. Douglass's quips and understatement heighten the effectiveness of his work, and when we finish the *Narrative,* we feel as though we truly understand the author. The work is in fact a *Bildungsroman,* and its appeal to the reason and the "higher sympathies" of the reader place it in the "reform" tradition of the abolitionist movement. Douglass's work, however, transcends the category of a "slave narrative"; it is a self-conscious, skillfully finished work of literature—an autobiography of the first order. If this is the type of work Arna Bontemps had in mind when he said that most of our recent black novelists owe a debt to the slave narratives, we can surely understand why the black novel in the twentieth century has made such an outstanding contribution to literature.

Both Douglass and Walker looked to the folk tradition in their work, Walker by assuming the role of the impassioned preacher, and Douglass in his detailing of the agrarian black folk environment and in his employment of folk humor. Moreover, both writers expressed the *Zeitgeist,* or spirit, of the age in which they lived, for both shared the concerns of the reformers and idealists of their day. The most important role of Douglass and Walker, however, was that of prophet; they both looked forward to the day of total liberation which they knew must come for the black American if America was to survive. And both writers set forth the methods that have been employed in the black American's struggle for freedom. One of the most important methods to both men was education—that process of developing mind, skill, and character. Walker stated his belief in education in his own inimitable and fervent fashion when he said:

I pray that the Lord may undeceive my ignorant brethren, and permit them to throw away pretensions, and seek after the substance of learning. I would crawl on my hands and knees through mud and mire, to the feet of a learned man, where I would sit and humbly supplicate him to instil into me, that which neither devils nor tyrants could remove, only with my life—for coloured people to acquire learning in this country makes tyrants quake and tremble on their sandy foundation.

It was left for Booker T. Washington to insure the education of thousands of black men in America in such a manner that there would be little quaking or trembling. And the outstanding *Up from Slavery* (1901) is a chronicle of the Washingtonian educational philosophy and the growth of the institution where that philosophy was inculcated. Washington had an enduring faith in education as a process of inculcating both skill and character, and a host of Tuskegee graduates went forth as proof of Washington's faith. Today the founder of Tuskegee, and the most influential leader of black Americans between 1895 and 1915, is looked upon with an extremely skeptical eye; but Washington was, above all, a product of his age. In *Up from Slavery* we witness the same faith in self-help, "merit," and institutions that characterized both Britain and America during the age of Washington. Life reduces itself in Washington's work, therefore, to a pursuit of cleanliness, virtue, and industrial skill; and the method of obtaining all these is the institution. Tuskegee virtually comes to life in Washington's work, and institutions dominate his text. We witness Washington's movement from a condition of slavery to a position as a recipient of a Harvard honorary degree, and throughout the work, the author presents himself as the "humblest man alive." Washington's perspective was a narrow one, and his myopia led him to compromise some of the most fundamental rights of the black American. The demands of black people were minimized to a clean, well-lighted place where one could learn a skill or make a dollar or two while growing in character. In his Atlanta address, we witness Washington's philosophy at its best; this was perhaps his clearest statement of his ideals. Yet we cannot completely condemn Washington or simply write him out of the records in Orwellian fashion; after all, his accomplishments would have been great in any age or country; that he accomplished what he did in a militantly racist, late nineteenth- and early twentieth-century America was just short of miraculous.

W. E. B. Du Bois, one of the first black men of "culture," was strongly in favor of writing Washington out of the records. Du Bois felt that the vision of the black American should not only encompass freedom, but also the best that had been thought and said in the world. Indeed, before freedom could become a reality, Du Bois felt that there had to be a class of black Americans composed of the Talented Tenth, a minority made up of "black college-bred men." The college-bred men of culture would act as the leaders of the depressed "black masses." Du Bois was thus against any narrowing of perspectives that would cause the black American to demand less than total equality; the intellectual way was through a broad vista where classical texts, great literature, and German writers and philosophers bestowed messages of value. The university, and not the trade or industrial school, was the means toward liberation for Du Bois, and he led the attack of the black intellectuals on the Washingtonian point of view. The author of *The Souls of Black Folk*, however, cannot be forced into a confining category of "culture"; Du Bois was a man of "race" in every sense of the word. In *The Souls of Black Folk* we find race-pride and race-consciousness in abundance. Black leaders like Alexander Crummell are championed; black institutions like the church are praised in ringing tones; and the legacy from the folk tradition, the "sorrow songs," are portrayed in all of their glory by means of Du Bois's refined and perfected style. Du Bois thus looks before and after and pines, in his own magnificent fashion, for that which is not; he follows Douglass, Walker, and Washington in his concern for the liberation of the black American and in his concern for education as a means toward liberation. Moreover, Du Bois makes copious use of the folk tradition in *The Souls of Black Folk* and in his early novels. Du Bois's most notable role, however, is as the father of a militant, intellectual, race-conscious brand of black literature that was to find its finest expression in the Harlem Renaissance of the twenties. Du Bois clearly marks a transition from folk expression and slave narratives to conscious literary artistry that reflects a "cultured" point of view and a proud militancy.

REFERENCES

Aptheker, Herbert: *"One Continual Cry": David Walker's Appeal to the Colored Citizens of the World (1829–1830): Its Setting and Its Meaning,* Humanities Press, New York, 1965.

Bontemps, Arna: *Frederick Douglass: Slave, Fighter, Freeman,* Alfred Knopf, New York, 1959.

———: "Introduction," *Great Slave Narratives,* Beacon Press, Boston, 1969.

Broderick, Francis L.: *W. E. B. Du Bois, Negro Leader in a Time of Crisis,* Stanford University Press, Stanford, 1959.

Foner, Philip: *Frederick Douglass, a Biography,* Citadel Press, New York, 1964.

———: *The Life and Writings of Frederick Douglass,* International Publishers, New New York, 1950–1955. [4 Vols.]

Hawkins, Hugh: *Booker T. Washington and His Critics,* D. C. Heath, Boston, 1962.

Meier, August: *Negro Thought in America, 1880–1915; Racial Ideologies in the Age of Booker T. Washington,* University of Michigan Press, Ann Arbor, 1963.

Quarles, Benjamin: *Frederick Douglass,* Associated Publishers, Washington, 1948.

Rudwick, Elliott M.: *W. E. B. Du Bois; A Study in Minority Group Leadership,* University of Pennsylvania Press, Philadelphia, 1960.

———: *W. E. B. Du Bois, Propagandist of the Negro Protest,* Atheneum, New York, 1969.

Spencer, Samuel R.: *Booker T. Washington and the Negro's Place in American Life,* Little, Brown, Boston, 1955.

Thornbrough, Emma Lou: *Booker T. Washington,* Prentice-Hall, Englewood Cliffs, 1969.

David Walker (1785-1830)

Article II   Our Wretchedness in Consequence of Ignorance

From Appeal to the Coloured Citizens of the World

Ignorance, my brethren, is a mist, low down into the very dark and almost impenetrable abyss in which, our fathers for many centuries have been plunged. The Christians, and enlightened of Europe, and some of Asia, seeing the ignorance and consequent degradation of our fathers, instead of trying to enlighten them, by teaching them that religion and light with which God had blessed them, they have plunged them into wretchedness ten thousand times more intolerable, than if they had left them entirely to the Lord, and to add to their miseries, deep down into which they have plunged them tell them, that they are an *inferior* and *distinct race* of beings, which they will be glad enough to recall and swallow by and by. Fortune and misfortune, two inseparable companions, lay rolled up in the wheel of events, which have from the creation of the world, and will continue to take place among men until God shall dash worlds together.

When we take a retrospective view of the arts and sciences—the wise legislators—the Pyramids, and other magnificent buildings—the turning of the channel of the river Nile, by the sons of Africa or of Ham, among whom learning originated, and was carried thence into Greece, where it was improved upon and refined. Thence among the Romans, and all over the then enlightened parts of the world, and it has been enlightening the dark and benighted minds of men from then, down to this day. I say, when I view retrospectively, the renown of that once mighty people, the children of our great progenitor I am indeed cheered. Yea further, when I view that mighty son of Africa, HANNIBAL, one of the greatest generals of antiquity, who defeated and cut off so many thousands of the white Romans or murderers, and who carried his victorious arms, to the very gate of Rome, and I give it as my candid opinion, that had Carthage been well united and had given him good support, he would have carried that cruel and barbarous city by storm. But they were dis-united, as the coloured people are now, in the United States of America, the reason our natural enemies are enabled to keep their feet on our throats.

Beloved brethren—here let me tell you, and believe it, that the Lord our God, as true as he sits on his throne in heaven, and as true as our Saviour died to redeem the world, will give you a Hannibal, and when the Lord shall have raised him up, and given him to you for your possession, O my suffering brethren! remember the divisions and consequent sufferings of *Carthage* and of *Hayti*. Read the history particularly of Hayti, and see how they were butchered by the whites, and do you take warning. The person whom God shall give you, give him your support and let him go his length, and behold in him the salvation of your God. God will indeed, deliver you through him from your deplorable and wretched condition under the Christians of America. I charge you this day before my God to lay no obstacle in his way, but let him go.

The whites want slaves, and want us for their slaves, but some of them will curse the day they ever saw us. As true as the sun ever shone in its meridian splendor, my colour will root some of them out of the very face of the earth. They shall have enough of making slaves of, and butchering, and murdering us in the manner which they have. No doubt some may say that I write with a bad spirit, and that I being a black, wish these things to occur. Whether I write with a bad or a good spirit, I say if these things do not occur in their proper time, it is because the world in which we live does not exist, and we are deceived with regard to its existence.—It is immaterial however to me, who believe, or who refuse—though I should like to see the whites repent peradventure God may have mercy on them, some however, have gone so far that their cup must be filled.

But what need have I to refer to antiquity, when Hayti, the glory of the blacks and terror of tyrants, is enough to convince the most avaricious and stupid of wretches—which is at this time, and I am sorry to say it, plagued with that scourge of nations, the Catholic religion; but I hope and pray God that she may yet rid herself of it, and adopt in its stead the Protestant faith; also, I hope that she may keep peace within her borders and be united, keeping a strict look out for tyrants, for if they get the least chance to injure her, they will avail themselves of it, as true as the Lord lives in heaven. But one thing which gives me joy is, that they are men who would be cut off to a man, before they would yield to the combined forces of the whole world—in fact, if the whole world was combined against them, it could not do any thing with them, unless the Lord delivers them up.

Ignorance and treachery one against the other—a grovelling servile and abject submission to the lash of tyrants, we see plainly, my brethren, are not the natural elements of the blacks, as the Americans try to make us believe; but these are misfortunes which God has suffered our fathers to be enveloped in for many ages, no doubt in consequence of their disobedience to their Maker, and which do, indeed, reign at this time among us, almost to the destruction of all other principles: for I must truly say, that ignorance, the mother of treachery and deceit, gnaws into our very vitals. Ignorance, as it now exists among us, produces a state of things, Oh my Lord! too horrible to present to the world. Any man who is curious to see the full force of ignorance developed among the coloured people of the United States of America, has only to go into the southern and western states of this confederacy, where, if he is not a tyrant, but has the feelings of a human being, who can feel for a fellow creature, he may see enough to make his very heart bleed! He may see there, a son take his mother, who bore almost the pains of death to give him birth, and by the command of a tyrant, strip her as naked as she came into the world, and apply the cow-hide to her, until she falls a victim to death in the road! He may see a husband take his dear wife, not unfrequently in a pregnant state, and perhaps far advanced, and beat her for an unmerciful wretch, until his infant falls a lifeless lump at her feet! Can the Americans escape God Almighty? If they do, can he be to us a God of Justice? God is just, and I know it—for he has convinced me to my satisfaction—I cannot doubt him. My observer may see fathers beating their sons, mothers their daughters, and children their parents, all to pacify the passions of unrelenting tyrants. He may also, see them telling news and lies, making mischief one upon another. These are some of the productions of ignorance, which he will see practised among my dear brethren, who are held in unjust slavery and wretchedness, by avaricious and unmerciful tyrants, to whom, and their hellish deeds, I would suffer my life to be taken before I would submit. And when my curious observer comes to take notice of those who are said to be free, (which assertion I deny) and who are making some frivolous pretentions to common sense, he will see that branch of ignorance among the slaves assuming a more cunning and deceitful course of procedure.—He may see some of my brethren in league with tyrants, selling their own brethren into *hell upon earth*, not dissimilar to the exhibitions in Africa, but in a more secret, servile and abject manner. Oh

Heaven! I am full! ! ! I can hardly move my pen! ! ! ! and as I expect some will try to put me to death, to strike terror into others, and to obliterate from their minds the notion of freedom, so as to keep my brethren the more secure in wretchedness, where they will be permitted to stay but a short time (whether tyrants believe it or not)—I shall give the world a development of facts, which are already witnessed in the courts of heaven. My observer may see some of those ignorant and treacherous creatures (coloured people) sneaking about in the large cities, endeavouring to find out all strange coloured people, where they work and where they reside, asking them questions, and trying to ascertain whether they are runaways or not, telling them, at the same time, that they always have been, are, and always will be, friends to their brethren; and, perhaps, that they themselves are absconders, and a thousand such treacherous lies to get the better information of the more ignorant! ! ! There have been and are at this day in Boston, New-York, Philadelphia, and Baltimore, coloured men, who are in league with tyrants, and who receive a great portion of their daily bread, of the moneys which they acquire from the blood and tears of their more miserable brethren, whom they scandalously delivered into the hands of our *natural enemies! ! ! ! !*

To show the force of degraded ignorance and deceit among us some farther, I will give here an extract from a paragraph, which may be found in the Columbian Centinel of this city, for September 9, 1829, on the first page of which, the curious may find an article, headed

"Affray and Murder."
"Portsmounth, (Ohio) Aug. 22, 1829.

"A most shocking outrage was committed in Kentucky, about eight miles from this place, on 14th inst. A negro driver, by the name of Gordon, who had purchased in Maryland about sixty negroes, was taking them, assisted by an associate named Allen, and the wagoner who conveyed the baggage, to the Mississippi. The men were hand-cuffed and chained together, in the usual manner for driving those poor wretches, while the women and children were suffered to proceed without incumbrance. It appears that, by means of a file the negroes, unobserved, had succeeded in separating the iron which bound their hands, in such a way as to be able to throw them off at any moment. About 8 o'clock in the morning, while proceeding on the state road leading from Greenup to Vanceburg, two of them dropped their shackles and commenced a fight, when the wagoner (Petit) rushed in with his whip to compel them to desist. At this moment, every negro was found to be perfectly at liberty; and one of them seizing a club, gave Petit a violent blow on the head, and laid him dead at his feet; and Allen, who came to his assistance, met a similar fate, from the contents of a pistol fired by another of the gang. Gordon was then attacked, seized and held by one of the negroes, whilst another fired twice at him with a pistol, the ball of which each time grazed his head, but not proving effectual, he was beaten with clubs, and left for dead. They then commenced pillaging the wagon, and with an axe split open the trunk of Gordon, and rifled it of the money, about $2,400. Sixteen of the negroes then took to the woods; Gordon, in the mean time, not being materially injured, was enabled, by the assistance of one of the women, to mount his horse and flee; pursued, however, by one of the gang on another horse, with a drawn pistol; fortunately he escaped with his life barely, arriving at a plantation, as the negro came in sight; who then turned about and retreated.

"The neighbourhood was immediately rallied, and a hot pursuit given—which, we understand, has resulted in the capture of the whole gang and the recovery of the greatest part of the money. Seven of the negro men and one woman, it is said were engaged in the murders, and will be brought to trial at the next court in Greenups-burg."

Here my brethren, I want you to notice particularly in the above article, the *ignorant* and *deceitful actions* of this coloured woman. I beg you to view it candidly, as for ETERNITY ! ! ! ! Here a *notorious wretch*, with two other con-federates had SIXTY of them in a gang, driving them like *brutes*—the men all in chains and hand-cuffs, and by the help of God they got their chains and hand-cuffs thrown off, and caught two of the wretches and put them to death, and beat the other until they thought he was dead, and left him for dead; however, he deceived them, and rising from the ground, this *servile woman* helped him upon his horse, and he made his escape. Brethren, what do you think of this? Was it the natural *fine feelings* of this woman, to save such a wretch alive? I know that the blacks, take them half enlightened and ignorant, are more humane and merci-ful than the most enlightened and refined European that can be found in all the earth. Let no one say that I assert this because I am prejudiced on the side of my colour, and against the whites or Europeans. For what I write, I do it candidly, for my God and the good of both parties: Natural observations have taught me these things; there is a solemn awe in the hearts of the blacks, as it respects *murdering* men:* whereas the whites, (though they are great cowards) where they have the advantage, or think that there are any prospects of getting it, they murder all before them, in order to subject men to wretchedness and degradation under them. This is the natural result of pride and avarice. But I declare, the actions of this black woman are really insupportable. For my own part, I cannot think it was any thing but servile deceit, combined with the most gross ignorance: for we must remember that *humanity, kindness* and the *fear of the Lord,* does not consist in protecting *devils.* Here is a set of wretches, who had SIXTY of them in a gang, driving them around the country like *brutes,* to dig up gold and silver for them, (which they will get enough of yet.) Should the lives of such creatures be spared? Are God and Mammon in league? What has the Lord to do with a gang of desperate wretches, who go *sneaking about the country like robbers*—light upon his people wherever they can get a chance, binding them with chains and hand-cuffs, beat and murder them as they would *rattle-snakes?* Are they not the Lord's enemies? Ought they not to be destroyed? Any person who will save such wretches from destruction, is fighting against the Lord, and will receive his just recompense. The black men acted like *blockheads.* Why did they not make sure of the wretch? He would have made sure of them, if he could. It is just the way with black men—eight white men can frighten fifty of them; whereas, if you can only get courage into the blacks, I do declare it, that one good black man can put to death six white men; and I give it as a fact,

_____
* Which is the reason the whites take the advantage of us.

let twelve black men get well armed for battle, and they will kill and put to flight fifty whites.—The reason is, the blacks, once you get them started, they glory in death. The whites have had us under them for more than three centuries, murdering, and treating us like brutes; and, as Mr. Jefferson wisely said, they have never *found us out*—they do not know, indeed, that there is an unconquerable disposition in the breasts of the blacks, which, when it is fully awakened and put in motion, will be subdued, only with the destruction of the animal existence. Get the blacks started, and if you do not have a gang of tigers and lions to deal with, I am a deceiver of the blacks and of the whites. How sixty of them could let that wretch escape unkilled, I cannot conceive—they will have to suffer as much for the two whom, they secured, as if they had put one hundred to death: if you commence, make sure work—do not trifle, for they will not trifle with you—they want us for their slaves, and think nothing of murdering us in order to subject us to that wretched condition—therefore, if there is an *attempt* made by us, kill or be killed. Now, I ask you, had you not rather be killed than to be a slave to a tyrant, who takes the life of your mother, wife, and dear little children? Look upon your mother, wife and children, and answer God Almighty; and believe this, that it is no more harm for you to kill a man, who is trying to kill you, than it is for you to take a drink of water when thirsty; in fact, the man who will stand still and let another murder him, is worse than an infidel, and, if he has common sense, ought not to be pitied. The actions of this deceitful and ignorant coloured woman, in saving the life of a desperate wretch, whose avaricious and cruel object was to drive her, and her companions in miseries, through the country like cattle, to make his fortune on their carcasses, are but too much like that of thousands of our brethren in these states: if any thing is whispered by one, which has any allusion to the melioration of their dreadful condition, they run and tell tyrants, that they may be enabled to keep them the longer in wretchedness and miseries. Oh! coloured people of these United States, I ask you, in the name of that God who made us, have we, in consequence of oppression, nearly lost the spirit of man, and, in no very trifling degree, adopted that of brutes? Do you answer, no?—I ask you, then, what set of men can you point me to, in all the world, who are so abjectly employed by their oppressors, as we are by our *natural enemies?* How can, Oh! how can those enemies but say that we and our children are not of the HUMAN FAMILY, but were made by our Creator to be an inheritance to them and theirs for ever? How can the slaveholders but say that they can bribe the best coloured person in the country, to sell his brethren for a trifling sum of money, and take that atrocity to confirm them in their avaricious opinion, that we were made to be slaves to them and their children? How could Mr. Jefferson but say, "I advance it therefore as a suspicion only, that the blacks, whether originally a distinct race, or made distinct by time and circumstances, are *inferior* to the whites in the endowments both of body and mind?"—"It," says he, "is not against experience to suppose, that different species of the same genius, or varieties of the same species, may possess different qualifications." [Here, my brethren, listen to him.] ☞ "Will not a lover of natural history, then, one who views the gradations in all the races of *animals* with the eye of philosophy, excuse an effort to keep those in the department of MAN as *distinct* as nature has formed them?"—I hope you will try to find out the meaning of this verse—its widest sense and all its bearings: whether you do or not, remember the whites do. This very verse, brethren, having emanated from Mr. Jefferson, a much greater philosopher the world never afforded, has in truth injured us more, and has been as great a barrier to our emancipation as any thing that has ever been advanced against us. I hope you will not let it pass unnoticed. He goes on further, and says: "This *unfortunate* difference of colour, and *perhaps* of *faculty*, is a powerful obstacle to the emancipation of these people. Many of their advocates, while they wish to vindicate the liberty of human nature are anxious also to preserve its *dignity* and *beauty*. Some of these, embarrassed by the question, 'What further is to be done with them?' join themselves in opposition with those who are actuated by sordid avarice only." Now I ask you candidly, my suffering brethren in time, who are candidates for the eternal worlds, how could Mr. Jefferson but have given the world these remarks respecting us, when we are so submissive to them, and so much servile deceit prevail among ourselves—when we so *meanly* submit to their murderous lashes, to which neither the Indians nor any other people under Heaven would submit? No, they would die to a man, before they would suffer such things from men who are no better than themselves, and *perhaps not so good*. Yes, how can our friends but be embarrassed, as Mr. Jefferson says, by the question, "What further is to be done with these people?" For while they are working for our emancipation, we are, by our treachery, wickedness and deceit, working against ourselves and our children—helping ours, and the enemies of God, to keep us and our deal little children in their infernal chains of slavery! ! ! Indeed, our friends cannot but relapse and join themselves "with those who are actuated by *sordid avarice* only! ! ! !" For my own part, I am glad Mr. Jefferson has advanced his positions for your sake; for you will either have to contradict or confirm him by your own actions, and not by what our friends have said or done for us; for those things are other men's labours, and do not satisfy the Americans, who are waiting for us to prove to them ourselves, that we are MEN, before they will be willing to admit the fact; for I pledge you my sacred word of honour, that Mr. Jefferson's remarks respecting us, have sunk deep into the hearts of millions of the whites, and never will be removed this side of eternity.—For how can they, when we are confirming him every day, by our *groveling submissions* and *treachery?* I aver, that when I look over these United States of America, and the world, and see the ignorant deceptions and consequent wretchedness of my brethren, I am brought oftimes solemnly to a stand, and in the midst of my reflections I exclaim to my God, "Lord didst thou make us to be slaves to our brethren, the whites?" But when I reflect that God is just, and that millions of my wretched brethren would meet death with glory—yea, more, would plunge into the very mouths of cannons

and be torn into particles as minute as the atoms which compose the elements
of the earth, in preference to a mean submission to the lash of tyrants, I am with
streaming eyes, compelled to shrink back into nothingness before my Maker, and
exclaim again, thy will be done, O Lord God Almighty.

Men of colour, who are also of sense, for you particularly is my APPEAL
designed. Our more ignorant brethren are not able to penetrate its value. I call
upon you therefore to cast your eyes upon the wretchedness of your brethren,
and to do your utmost to enlighten them—*go to work and enlighten your brethren!*—Let the Lord see you doing what you can to rescue them and yourselves
from degradation. Do any of you say that you and your family are free and
happy, and what have you to do with the wretched slaves and other people? So
can I say, for I enjoy as much freedom as any of you, if I am not quite as well
off as the best of you. Look into our freedom and happiness, and see of what
kind they are composed! ! They are of the very lowest kind—they are the very
dregs!—they are the most servile and abject kind, that ever a people was in
possession of! If any of you wish to know how FREE you are, let one of you start
and go through the southern and western States of this country, and unless you
travel as a slave to a white man (a servant is a *slave* to the man whom he serves)
or have your free papers, (which if you are not careful they will get from you)
if they do not take you up and put you in jail, and if you cannot give good
evidence of your freedom, sell you into eternal slavery, I am not a living man: or
any man of colour, immaterial who he is, or where he came from, if he is not
the fourth from the negro race! ! (as we are called) the white Christians of
America will serve him the same they will sink him into wretchedness and degradation for ever while he lives. And yet some of you have the hardihood to say
that you are free and happy! May God have mercy on your freedom and happiness! ! I met a coloured man in the street a short time since, with a string of
boots on his shoulders; we fell into conversation, and in course of which, I said
to him, what a miserable set of people we are! He asked, why?—Said I, we are
so subjected under the whites, that we cannot obtain the comforts of life, but by
cleaning their boots and shoes, old clothes, waiting on them, shaving them &c.
Said he, (with the boots on his shoulders) "I am completely happy! ! ! I never
want to live any better or happier than when I can get a plenty of boots and
shoes to clean! ! !" Oh! how can those who are actuated by avarice only, but
think, that our Creator made us to be an inheritance to them for ever, when they
see that our greatest glory is centered in such mean and low objects? Understand
me, brethren, I do not mean to speak against the occupations by which we acquire enough and sometimes scarcely that, to render ourselves and families comfortable through life. I am subjected to the same inconvenience, as you all.—My
objections are, to our *glorying* and being *happy* in such low employments; for if
we are men, we ought to be thankful to the Lord for the past, and for the future.
Be looking forward with thankful hearts to higher attainments than *wielding the
razor* and *cleaning boots and shoes.* The man whose aspirations are not *above,*
and even *below* these, is indeed, ignorant and wretched enough. I advanced it

therefore to you, not as a *problematical,* but as an unshaken and for ever immovable *fact,* that your full glory and happiness, as well as all other coloured people under Heaven, shall never be fully consummated, but with the *entire emancipation of your enslaved brethren all over the world.* You may therefore, go to work and do what you can to rescue, or join in with tyrants to oppress them and yourselves, until the Lord shall come upon you all like a thief in the night. For I believe it is the will of the Lord that our greatest happiness shall consist in working for the salvation of our whole body. When this is accomplished a burst of glory will shine upon you, which will indeed astonish you and the world. Do any of you say this never will be done? I assure you that God will accomplish it—if nothing else will answer, he will hurl tyrants and devils into *atoms* and make way for his people. But O my brethren! I say unto you again, you must go to work and prepare the way of the Lord.

There is a great work for you to do, as trifling as some of you may think of it. You have to prove to the Americans and the world, that we are MEN, and not *brutes,* as we have been represented, and by millions treated. Remember, to let the aim of your labours among your brethren, and particularly the youths, be the dissemination of education and religion.* It is lamentable, that many of our children go to school, from four until they are eight or ten, and sometimes fifteen years of age, and leave school knowing but a little more about the grammar of their language than a horse does about handling a musket—and not a few of them are really so ignorant, that they are unable to answer a person correctly, general questions in geography, and to hear them read, would only be to disgust a man who has a taste for reading; which, to do well, as trifling as it may appear to some, (to the ignorant in particular) is a great part of learning. Some few of them, may make out to scribble tolerably well, over a half sheet of paper, which I believe has hitherto been a powerful obstacle in our way, to keep us from acquiring knowledge. An ignorant father, who knows no more than what nature has taught him, together with what little he acquires by the senses of hearing and seeing, finding his son able to write a neat hand, sets it down for granted that he has as good learning as any body; the young, ignorant gump, hearing his father or mother, who perhaps may be ten times more ignorant, in point of literature, than himself, extolling his learning, struts about, in the full assurance, that his attainments in literature are sufficient to take him through the world, when, in fact, he has scarcely any learning at all! ! ! !

I promiscuously fell in conversation once, with an elderly coloured man on the topics of education, and of the great prevalency of ignorance among us: Said he, "I know that our people are very ignorant but my son has a good educa-

---

* Never mind what the ignorant ones among us may say, many of whom when you speak to them for their good, and try to enlighten their minds, laugh at you, and perhaps tell you plump to your face, that they want no instruction from you or any other Niger, and all such aggravating language. Now if you are a man of understanding and sound sense, I conjure you in the name of the Lord, and of all that is good, to impute their actions to ignorance, and wink at their follies, and do your very best to get around them some way or other, for remember they are your brethren ; and I declare to you that it is for your interests to teach and enlighten them.

tion: I spent a great deal of money on his education: he can write as well as any white man, and I assure you that no one can fool him," &c. Said I, what else can your son do, besides writing a good hand? Can he post a set of books in a mercantile manner? Can he write a neat piece of composition in prose or in verse? To these interrogations he answered in the negative. Said I, did your son learn, while he was at school, the width and depth of English Grammar? To which he also replied in the negative, telling me his son did not learn those things. Your son, said I, then, has hardly any learning at all—he is almost as ignorant, and more so, than many of those who never went to school one day in all their lives. My friend got a little put out, and so walking off, said that his son could write as well as any white man. Most of the coloured people, when they speak of the education of one among us who can write a neat hand, and who perhaps knows nothing but to scribble and puff pretty fair on a small scrap of paper, immaterial whether his words are grammatical, or spelt correctly, or not; if it only looks beautiful, they say he has as good an education as any white man— he can write as well as any white man, &c. The poor, ignorant creature, hearing, this, he is ashamed, forever after, to let any person see him humbling himself to another for knowledge but going about trying to deceive those who are more ignorant than himself, he at last falls an ignorant victim to death in wretched- ness. I pray that the Lord may undeceive by ignorant brethren, and permit them to throw away pretensions, and seek after the substance of learning. I would crawl on my hands and knees through mud and mire, to the feet of a learned man, where I would sit and humbly supplicate him to instil into me, that which neither devils nor tyrants could remove, only with my life—for coloured people to acquire learning in this country, makes tyrants quake and tremble on their sandy foundation. Why, what is the matter? Why, they know that their infernal deeds of cruelty will be made known to the world. Do you suppose one man of good sense and learning would submit himself, his father, mother, wife and chil- dren, to be slaves to a wretched man like himself, who, instead of compensating him for his labours, chains, hand-cuffs and beats him and family almost to death, leaving life enough in them, however, to work for, and call him master? No! no! he would cut his devilish throat from ear to ear, and well do slave-holders know it. The bare name of educating the coloured people, scares our cruel oppressors almost to death. But if they do not have enough to be frightened for yet, it will be, because they can always keep us ignorant, and because God approbates their cruelties, with which they have been for centuries murdering us. The whites shall have enough of the blacks, yet, as true as God sits on his throne in Heaven.

Some of our brethren are so very full of learning, that you cannot mention any thing to them which they do not know better than yourself! !—nothing is strange to them! !—they knew every thing years ago!—if any thing should be mentioned in company where they are, immaterial how important it is respecting us or the world, if they had not divulged it; they make light of it, and affect to have known it long before it was mentioned and try to make all in the room, or wherever you may be, believe that your conversation is nothing! !—not worth hearing! All this is the result of ignorance and ill-breeding; for a man of good-breeding, sense and penetration, if he had heard a subject told twenty times over, and should happen to be in company where one should commence telling it again, he would wait with patience on its narrator, and see if he would tell it as it was told in his presence before—paying the most strict attention to what is said, to see if any more light will be thrown on the subject: for all men are not gifted alike in telling, or even hearing the most simple narration. These ignorant, vicious, and wretched men, contribute almost as much injury to our body as tyrants themselves, by doing so much for the promotion of ignorance amongst us; for they, making such pretensions to knowledge, such of our youth as are seeking after knowledge, and can get access to them, take them as criterions to go by, who will lead them into a channel, where, unless the Lord blesses them with the privilege of seeing their folly, they will be irretrievably lost forever, while in time! ! !

I must close this article by relating the very heart-rending fact, that I have examined school-boys and young men of colour in different parts of the country, in the most simple parts of Murray's English Grammar, and not more than one in thirty was able to give a correct answer to my interrogations. If any one contradicts me, let him step out of his door into the streets of Boston, New-York, Philadelphia, or Baltimore, (no use to mention any other, for the Christians are too charitable further south or west!)—I say, let him who disputes me, step out of his door into the streets of either of these four cities, and promiscuously collect one hundred school-boys, or young men of colour, *who have been to school,* and who are considered by the coloured people to have received an excellent education, because, perhaps, some of them can write a good hand, but who, notwithstanding their neat writing, may be almost as ignorant, in comparison, as a horse.—And, I say it, he will hardly find (in this enlightened day, and in the midst of this *charitable* people) five in one hundred, who, are able to correct the false grammar of their language.—The cause of this almost universal ignorance among us, I appeal to our schoolmasters to declare. Here is a fact, which I this very minute take from the mouth of a young coloured man, who has been to school in this state (Massachusetts) nearly nine years, and who knows grammar this day, *nearly* as well as he did the day he first entered the school-house, under a white master. This young man says: "My master would never allow me to study grammar." I asked him, why? "The school committee," said he "forbid the coloured children learning grammar—they would not allow any but the white children to study grammar." It is a notorious fact, that the major part of the white Americans, have, ever since we have been among them, tried to keep us ignorant, and make us believe that God made us and our children to be slaves to them and theirs. *Oh! my God, have mercy on Christian Americans! ! !*

Frederick Douglass (1817-1895)

Chapter X

From Narrative of the Life of Frederick Douglass, an American Slave, Written by Himself

I left Master Thomas's house, and went to live with Mr. Covey, on the 1st of January, 1833. I was now, for the first time in my life, a field hand. In my new employment, I found myself even more awkward than a country boy appeared to be in a large city. I had been at my new home but one week before Mr. Covey gave me a very severe whipping, cutting my back, causing the blood to run, and raising ridges on my flesh as large as my little finger. The details of this affair are as follows: Mr. Covey sent me, very early in the morning of one of our coldest days in the month of January, to the woods, to get a load of wood. He gave me a team of unbroken oxen. He told me which was the in-hand ox, and which the off-hand one. He then tied the end of a large rope around the horns of the in-hand ox, and gave me the other end of it, and told me, if the oxen started to run, that I must hold on upon the rope. I had never driven oxen before, and of course I was very awkward. I, however, succeeded in getting to the edge of the woods with little difficulty; but I had got a very few rods into the woods, when the oxen took fright, and started full tilt, carrying the cart against trees, and over stumps, in the most frightful manner. I expected every moment that my brains would be dashed out against the trees. After running thus for a considerable distance, they finally upset the cart, dashing it with great force against a tree, and threw themselves into a dense thicket. How I escaped death, I do not know. There I was, entirely alone, in a thick wood, in a place new to me. My cart was upset and shattered, my oxen were entangled among the young trees, and there was none to help me. After a long spell of effort, I succeeded in getting my cart righted, my oxen disentangled, and again yoked to the cart. I now proceeded with my team to the place where I had, the day before, been chopping wood, and loaded my cart pretty heavily, thinking in this way to tame my oxen. I then proceeded on my way home. I had now consumed one half of the day. I got out of the woods safely, and now felt out of danger. I stopped my oxen to open the woods gate; and just as I did so, before I could get hold of my ox-rope, the oxen again started, rushed through the gate, catching it between the wheel and the body of the cart, tearing it to pieces, and coming within a few inches of crushing me against the gate-post. Thus twice, in one short day, I escaped death by the merest chance. On my return, I told Mr. Covey what had happened, and how it happened. He ordered me to return to the woods again immediately. I did so, and he followed on after me. Just as I got into the woods, he came up and told me to stop my cart, and that he would teach me how to trifle away my time, and break gates. He then went to a large gum-tree, and with his axe cut three large switches, and, after trimming them up neatly with his pocketknife, he ordered me to take off my clothes. I made him no answer, but stood with my clothes on. He repeated his order. I still made him no answer, nor did I move to strip myself. Upon this he rushed at me with the fierceness of a tiger, tore off my clothes, and lashed me till he had worn out his switches, cutting me so savagely as to leave the marks visible for a long time. This whipping was the first of a number just like it, and for similar offences.

I lived with Mr. Covey one year. During the first six months, of that year, scarce a week passed without his whipping me. I was seldom free from a sore back. My awkwardness was almost always his excuse for whipping me. We were worked fully up to the point of endurance. Long before day we were up, our horses fed, and by the first approach of day we were off to the field with our hoes and ploughing teams. Mr. Covey gave us enough to eat, but scarce time to eat it. We were often less than five minutes taking our meals. We were often in the field from the first approach of day till its last lingering ray had left us; and at saving-fodder time, midnight often caught us in the field binding blades.

Covey would be out with us. The way he used to stand it, was this. He would spend the most of his afternoons in bed. He would then come out fresh in the evening, ready to urge us on with his words, example, and frequently with the whip. Mr. Covey was one of the few slaveholders who could and did work with his hands. He was a hard-working man. He knew by himself just what a man or a boy could do. There was no deceiving him. His work went on in his absence almost as well as in his presence; and he had the faculty of making us feel that he was ever present with us. This he did by surprising us. He seldom approached the spot where we were at work openly, if he could do it secretly. He always aimed at taking us by surprise. Such was his cunning, that we used to call him, among ourselves, "the snake." When we were at work in the corn-field, he would sometimes crawl on his hands and knees to avoid detection, and all at once he would rise nearly in our midst, and scream out, "Ha, ha! Come, come! Dash on, dash on!" This being his mode of attack, it was never safe to stop a single minute. His comings were like a thief in the night. He appeared to us as being ever at hand. He was under every tree, behind every stump, in every bush, and at every window, on the plantation. He would sometimes mount his horse, as if bound to St. Michael's, a distance of seven miles, and in half an hour afterwards you would see him coiled up in the corner of the wood-fence, watching every motion of the slaves. He would, for this purpose, leave his horse tied up in the woods. Again, he would sometimes walk up to us, and give us orders as though he was upon the point of starting on a long journey, turn his back upon us, and make as though he was going to the house to get ready; and, before he would get half way thither, he would turn short and crawl into a fence-corner, or behind some tree, and there watch us till the going down of the sun.

Mr. Covey's *forte* consisted in his power to deceive. His life was devoted to planning and perpetrating the grossest deceptions. Every thing he possessed in the shape of learning or religion, he made conform to his disposition to deceive. He seemed to think himself equal to deceiving the Almighty. He would make a short prayer in the morning, and a long prayer at night; and, strange as it may seem, few men would at times appear more devotional than he. The exercises of his family devotions were always commenced with singing; and, as he was a very poor singer himself, the duty of raising the hymn generally came upon me. He would read his hymn, and nod at me to commence. I would at times do so; at others, I would not. My noncompliance would almost always produce much confusion. To show himself independent of me, he would start and stagger through with his hymn in the most discordant manner. In this state of mind, he prayed with more than ordinary spirit. Poor man! such was his disposition, and success at deceiving, I do verily believe that he sometimes deceived himself into the solemn belief, that he was a sincere worshipper of the most high God; and this, too, at a time when he may be said to have been guilty of compelling his woman slave to commit the sin of adultery. The facts in the case are these: Mr. Covey was a poor man; he was just commencing in life; he was only able to buy one slave; and, shocking as is the fact, he bought her, as he said, for *a breeder*. This woman was named Caroline. Mr. Covey bought her from Mr. Thomas Lowe, about six miles from St. Michael's. She was a large, able-bodied woman, about twenty years old. She had already given birth to one child, which proved her to be just what he wanted. After buying her, he hired a married man of Mr. Samuel Harrison, to live with him one year; and him he used to fasten up with her every night! The result was, that, at the end of the year, the miserable woman gave birth to twins. At this result Mr. Covey seemed to be highly pleased, both with the man and the wretched woman. Such was his joy, and that of his wife, that nothing they could do for Caroline during her confinement was too good, or too hard, to be done. The children were regarded as being quite an addition to his wealth.

If at any one time of my life more than another, I was made to drink the bitterest dregs of slavery, that time was during the first six months of my stay with Mr. Covey. We were worked in all weathers. It was never too hot or too cold; it could never rain, blow, hail, or snow, too hard for us to work in the field. Work, work, work, was scarcely more the order of the day than of the night. The longest days were too short for him, and the shortest nights too long for him. I was somewhat unmanageable when I first went there, but a few months of this discipline tamed me. Mr. Covey succeeded in breaking me. I was broken in body, soul, and spirit. My natural elasticity was crushed, my intellect languished, the disposition to read departed, the cheerful spark that lingered about my eye died; the dark night of slavery closed in upon me; and behold a man transformed into a brute!

Sunday was my only leisure time. I spent this in a sort of beast-like stupor, between sleep and wake, under some large tree. At times I would rise up, a flash of energetic freedom would dart through my soul, accompanied with a faint beam of hope, that flickered for a moment, and then vanished. I sank down again, mourning over my wretched condition. I was sometimes prompted to take my life, and that of Covey, but was prevented by a combination of hope and fear. My sufferings on this plantation seem now like a dream rather than a stern reality.

Our house stood within a few rods of the Chesapeake Bay, whose broad bosom was ever white with sails from every quarter of the habitable globe. Those beautiful vessels, robed in purest white, so delightful to the eye of freemen, were to me so many shrouded ghosts, to terrify and torment me with thoughts of my wretched condition. I have often, in the deep stillness of a summer's Sabbath, stood all alone upon the lofty banks of that noble bay, and traced, with saddened heart and tearful eye, the countless number of sails moving off to the mighty ocean. The sight of these always affected me powerfully. My thoughts would compel utterance; and there, with no audience but the Almighty, I would pour out my soul's complaint, in my rude way, with an apostrophe to the moving multitude of ships:—

"You are loosed from your moorings, and are free; I am fast in my chains, and am a slave! You move merrily before the gentle gale, and I sadly before the bloody whip! You are freedom's swift-winged angels, that fly round the world; I am confined in bands of iron! O that I were free! O, that I were on one of your gallant decks, and under your protecting wing! Alas! betwixt me and you, the turbid waters roll. Go on, go on. O that I could also go! Could I but swim! If I could fly! O, why was I born a man, of whom to make a brute! The glad ship is gone; she hides in the dim distance. I am left in the hottest hell of un-ending slavery. O God, save me! God, deliver me! Let me be free! Is there any God? Why am I a slave? I will run away. I will not stand it. Get caught, or get clear, I'll try it. I had as well die with ague as the fever. I have only one life to lose. I had as well be killed running as die standing. Only think of it; one hundred miles straight north, and I am free! Try it? Yes! God helping me, I will. It cannot be that I shall live and die a slave. I will take to the water. This very bay shall yet bear me into freedom. The steamboats steered in a north-east course from North Point. I will do the same; and when I get to the head of the bay, I will turn my canoe adrift, and walk straight through Delaware into Pennsyl-vania. When I get there, I shall not be required to have a pass; I can travel without being disturbed. Let but the first opportunity offer, and, come what will, I am off. Meanwhile, I will try to bear up under the yoke. I am not the only slave in the world. Why should I fret? I can bear as much as any of them. Besides, I am but a boy, and all boys are bound to some one. It may be that my misery in slavery will only increase my happiness when I get free. There is a better day coming."

Thus I used to think, and thus I used to speak to myself; goaded almost to madness at one moment, and at the next reconciling myself to my wretched lot.

I have already intimated that my condition was much worse, during the first six months of my stay at Mr. Covey's, than in the last six. The circumstances leading to the change in Mr. Covey's course toward me form an epoch in my humble history. You have seen how a man was made a slave; you shall see how a slave was made a man. On one of the hottest days of the month of August, 1833, Bill Smith, William Hughes, a slave named Eli, and myself, were engaged in fanning wheat. Hughes was clearing the fanned wheat from before the fan. Eli was turning, Smith was feeding, and I was carrying wheat to the fan. The work was simple, requiring strength rather than intellect; yet, to one entirely unused to such work, it came very hard. About three o'clock of that day, I broke down; my strength failed me; I was seized with a violent aching of the head, attended with extreme dizziness; I trembled in every limb. Finding what was coming, I nerved myself up, feeling it would never do to stop work. I stood as long as I could stagger to the hopper with grain. When I could stand no longer, I fell, and felt as if held down by an immense weight. The fan of course stopped; every one had his own work to do; and no one could do the work of the other, and have his own go on at the same time.

Mr. Covey was at the house, about one hundred yards from the treading-yard where we were fanning. On hearing the fan stop, he left immediately, and came to the spot where we were. He hastily inquired what the matter was. Bill answered that I was sick, and there was no one to bring wheat to the fan. I had by this time crawled away under the side of the post and rail-fence by which the yard was enclosed, hoping to find relief by getting out of the sun. He then asked where I was. He was told by one of the hands. He came to the spot, and, after looking at me awhile, asked me what was the matter. I told him as well as I could, for I scarce had strength to speak. He then gave me a savage kick in the side, and told me to get up. I tried to do so, but fell back in the attempt. He gave me another kick, and again told me to rise. I again tried, and succeeded in gaining my feet; but, stooping to get the tub with which I was feeding the fan, I again staggered and fell. While down in this situation, Mr. Covey took up the hickory slat with which Hughes had been striking off the half-bushel measure, and with it gave me a heavy blow upon the head, making a large wound, and the blood ran freely; and with this again told me to get up. I made no effort to comply, having now made up my mind to let him do his worst. In a short time after receiving this blow, my head grew better. Mr. Covey had now left me to my fate. At this moment I resolved, for the first time, to go to my master, enter a complaint, and ask his protection. In order to do this, I must that afternoon walk seven miles; and this, under the circumstances, was truly a severe undertaking. I was exceedingly feeble; made so as much by the kicks and blows which I received, as by the severe fit of sickness to which I had been subjected. I, however, watched my chance, while Covey was looking in an opposite direction, and started for St. Michael's: I succeeded in getting a considerable distance on my way to the woods, when Covey discovered me, and called after me to come back, threatening what he would do if I did not come. I disregarded both his calls and his threats, and made my way to the woods as fast as my feeble state would allow; and thinking I might be overhauled by him if I kept the road, I walked through the woods, keeping far enough from the road to avoid detection, and near enough to prevent losing my way. I had not gone far before my little strength again failed me. I could go no farther. I fell down, and lay for a considerable time. The blood was yet oozing from the wound on my head. For a time I thought I should bleed to death; and think now that I should have done so, but that the blood so matted my hair as to stop the wound. After lying there about three quarters of an hour, I nerved myself up again, and started on my way, through bogs and briers, barefooted and bareheaded, tearing my feet sometimes at nearly every step; and after a journey of about seven miles, occupying some five hours to perform it, I arrived at master's store. I then presented an appearance enough to affect any but a heart of iron. From the crown of my head to my feet, I was covered with blood. My hair was all clotted with dust and blood; my shirt was stiff with blood. My legs and feet were torn in sundry places with briers and thorns, and were also covered with blood. I suppose I looked like a man who had escaped a den of wild beasts, and barely escaped them. In this state I appeared before my master, humbly entreating him to interpose his authority for my protection. I told him all the circumstances as well as I could, and it seemed, as I spoke, at time to affect him. He would then walk the floor, and seek to justify Covey by saying he expected I deserved it. He asked me what I wanted. I told him, to let me get a new home; that as sure as I lived with Mr. Covey again, I should live with but to die with him; that Covey would surely kill me; he was in a fair way for it. Master Thomas ridiculed the idea that there was any danger of Mr. Covey's killing me, and said that he knew Mr. Covey, that he was a good man, and that he could not think of taking me from him; that, should he do so, he would lose the whole year's wages; that I belonged to Mr. Covey for one year, and that I must go back to him, come what might; and that I must not trouble him with any more stories, or that he would himself *get hold of me*. After threatening me thus, he gave me a very large dose of salts, telling me that I might remain in St. Michael's that night, (it being quite late,) but that I must be off back to Mr. Covey's early in the morning; and that if I did not, he would *get hold of me*, which meant that he would whip me. I remained all night, and, according to his orders, I started off to Covey's in the morning, (Saturday morning,) wearied in body and broken in spirit. I got no supper that night, or breakfast that morning. I reached Covey's about nine o'clock; and just as I was getting over the fence that divided Mrs. Kemp's fields from ours, out ran Covey with his cowskin, to give me another whipping. Before he could reach me, I succeeded in getting to the cornfield; and as the corn was very high, it afforded me the means of hiding. He seemed very angry, and searched for me a long time. My behavior was altogether unaccountable. He finally gave up the chase, thinking, I suppose, that I must come home for something to eat; he would give himself no further trouble in looking for me. I spent that day mostly in the woods, having the alternative before me,—to go home and be whipped to death, or stay in the woods and be starved to death. That night, I fell in with Sandy Jenkins, a slave with whom I was somewhat acquainted. Sandy had a free wife who lived about four miles from Mr. Covey's; and it being Saturday, he was on his way to see her. I told him my circumstances, and he very kindly invited me to go home with him. I went home with him, and talked this whole matter over, and got his advice as to what course it was best for me to pursue. I found Sandy an old adviser. He told me, with great solemnity, I must go back to Covey; but that before I went, I must go with him into another part of the woods, where there was a certain *root*, which, if I would take some of it with me, carrying it *always on my right side*, would render it impossible for Mr. Covey, or any other white man, to whip me. He said he had carried it for years; and since he had done so, he had never received a blow, and never expected to while he carried it. I at first rejected the idea, that the simple carrying of a root in my pocket would have any such effect as he had said, and was not disposed to take it; but Sandy impressed the necessity with much earnestness, telling me it could do no harm, if it did no good. To please him, I at length took the root, and, according to his direction, carried it upon my right side. This was Sunday morning. I immediately started for home; and upon entering the yard gate, out came Mr. Covey on his way to meeting. He spoke to me very kindly, bade me drive the pigs from a lot near by, and passed on towards the church. Now, this singular conduct of Mr. Covey really made me begin to think that there was something in the *root* which Sandy had given me; and had it been on any other day than Sunday, I could have attributed the conduct to no other cause than the influence of that root; and as it was, I was half inclined to think the *root* to be something more than I at first had taken it to be. All went well till Monday morning. On this morning, the virtue of the *root* was fully tested. Long before daylight, I was called to go and rub, curry, and feed, the horses. I obeyed, and was glad to obey. But whilst thus engaged, whilst in the act of throwing down some blades from the loft, Mr. Covey entered the stable with a long rope; and just as I was half out of the loft, he caught hold of my legs, and was about tying me. As soon as I found what he was up to, I gave a sudden spring, and as I did so, he holding to my legs, I was brought sprawling on the stable floor. Mr. Covey seemed now to think he had me, and could do what he pleased; but at this moment—from whence came the spirit I don't know—I resolved to fight; and, suiting my action to the resolution, I seized Covey hard by the throat; and as I did so, I rose. He held on to me, and I to him. My resistance was so entirely unexpected, that Covey seemed taken all aback. He trembled like a leaf. This gave me assurance, and I held him uneasy, causing the blood to run where I touched him with the ends of my fingers. Mr. Covey soon called out to Hughes for help. Hughes came, and, while Covey held me, attempted to tie my right hand. While he was in the act of doing so, I watched my chance, and gave him a heavy kick close under the ribs. This kick fairly sickened Hughes, so that he left me in the hands of Mr. Covey. This kick had the effect of not only weakening Hughes, but Covey also. When he saw Hughes bending over with pain, his courage quailed. He asked me if I meant to persist in my resistance. I told him I did, come what might; that he had used me like a brute for six months, and that I was determined to be used so no longer. With that, he strove to drag me to a stick that was lying just out of the stable door. He meant to knock me down. But just as he was leaning over to get the stick, I seized him with both hands by his collar, and brought him by a sudden snatch to the ground. By this time, Bill came. Covey called upon him for assistance. Bill wanted to know what he could do. Covey said, "Take hold of him, take hold of him!" Bill said his master hired him out to work, and not to help to whip me; so he left Covey and myself to fight our own battle out. We were at it for nearly two hours. Covey at length let me go, puffing and blowing at a great rate, saying that if I had not resisted, he would not have whipped me half so much. The truth was, that he had not whipped me at all. I considered him as getting entirely the worst end of the bargain; for he had drawn no blood from me, but I had from him. The whole six months afterwards, that I spent with Mr. Covey, he never laid the weight of his finger upon me in anger. He would occasionally say, he didn't want to get hold of me again. "No," thought I, "you need not; for you will come off worse than you did before."

This battle with Mr. Covey was the turning-point in my career as a slave. It rekindled the few expiring embers of freedom, and revived within me a sense of my own manhood. It recalled the departed self-confidence, and inspired me again with a determination to be free. The gratification afforded by the triumph was a full compensation for whatever else might follow, even death itself. He only can understand the deep satisfaction which I experienced, who has himself repelled by force the bloody arm of slavery. I felt as I never felt before. It was a glorious resurrection, from the tomb of slavery, to the heaven of freedom. My long-crushed spirit rose, cowardice departed, bold defiance took its place; and I now resolved that, however long I might remain a slave in form, the day had passed forever when I could be a slave in fact. I did not hesitate to let it be known of me, that the white man who expected to succeed in whipping, must also succeed in killing me.

From this time I was never again what might be called fairly whipped, though I remained a slave four years afterwards. I had several fights, but was never whipped.

It was for a long time a matter of surprise to me why Mr. Covey did not immediately have me taken by the constable to the whipping-post, and there regularly whipped for the crime of raising my hand against a white man in defence of myself. And the only explanation I can now think of does not entirely satisfy me; but such as it is, I will give it. Mr. Covey enjoyed the most unbounded reputation for being a first-rate overseer and negro-breaker. It was of considerable importance to him. That reputation was at stake; and had he sent me—a boy about sixteen years old—to the public whipping-post, his reputation would have been lost; so, to save his reputation, he suffered me to go unpunished.

My term of actual service to Mr. Edward Covey ended on Christmas day, 1833. The days between Christmas and New Year's day are allowed as holidays; and, accordingly, we were not required to perform any labor, more than to feed and take care of the stock. This time we regarded as our own, by the grace of our masters; and we therefore used or abused it nearly as we pleased. Those of us who had families at a distance, were generally allowed to spend the whole six days in their society. This time, however, was spent in various ways. The staid, sober, thinking and industrious ones of our number would employ themselves in making corn-brooms, mats, horse-collars, and baskets; and another class of us would spend the time in hunting opossums, hares, and coons. But by far the larger part engaged in such sports and merriments as playing ball, wrestling, running foot-races, fiddling, dancing, and drinking whisky; and this latter mode of spending the time was by far the most agreeable to the feelings of our masters. A slave who would work during the holidays was considered by our masters as scarcely deserving them. He was regarded as one who rejected the favor of his master. It was deemed a disgrace not to get drunk at Christmas; and he was regarded as lazy indeed, who had not provided himself with the necessary means, during the year, to get whisky enough to last him through Christmas.

From what I know of the effect of these holidays upon the slave, I believe them to be among the most effective means in the hands of the slaveholder in keeping down the spirit of insurrection. Were the slaveholders at once to abandon this practice, I have not the slightest doubt it would lead to an immediate insurrection among the slaves. These holidays serve as conductors, or safety-valves, to carry off the rebellious spirit of enslaved humanity. But for these, the slave would be forced up to the wildest desperation; and woe betide the slaveholder, the day he ventures to remove or hinder the operation of those conductors! I warn him that, in such an event, a spirit will go forth in their midst, more to be dreaded than the most appalling earthquake.

The holidays are part and parcel of the gross fraud, wrong, and inhumanity of slavery. They are professedly a custom established by the benevolence of the slaveholders; but I undertake to say, it is the result of selfishness, and one of the grossest frauds committed upon the down-trodden slave. They do not give the slaves this time because they would not like to have their work during its continuance, but because they know it would be unsafe to deprive them of it. This will be seen by the fact, that the slaveholders like to have their slaves spend those days just in such a manner as to make them as glad of their ending as of their beginning. Their object seems to be, to disgust their slaves with freedom, by plunging them into the lowest depths of dissipation. For instance, the slaveholders not only like to see the slave drink of his own accord, but will adopt various plans to make him drunk. One plan is, to make bets on their slaves, as to who can drink the most whisky without getting drunk; and in this way they succeed in getting whole multitudes to drink to excess. Thus, when the slave asks for virtuous freedom, the cunning slaveholder, knowing his ignorance, cheats him with a dose of vicious dissipation, artfully labelled with the name of liberty. The most of us used to drink it down, and the result was just what might be supposed: many of us were led to think that there was little to choose between liberty and slavery. We felt, and very properly too, that we had almost as well be slaves to man as to rum. So, when the holidays ended, we staggered up from the filth of our wallowing, took a long breath, and marched to the field,—feeling, upon the whole, rather glad to go, from what our master had deceived us into a belief was freedom, back to the arms of slavery.

I have said that this mode of treatment is a part of the whole system of fraud and inhumanity of slavery. It is so. The mode here adopted to disgust the slave with freedom, by allowing him to see only the abuse of it, is carried out in other things. For instance, a slave loves molasses; he steals some. His master, in many cases, goes off to town, and buys a large quantity; he returns, takes his whip, and commands the slave to eat the molasses, until the poor fellow is made sick at the very mention of it. The same mode is sometimes adopted to make the slaves refrain from asking for more food than their regular allowance. A slave runs through his allowance, and applies for more. His master is enraged at him; but, not willing to send him off without food, gives him more than is necessary, and compels him to eat it within a given time. Then, if he complains that he cannot eat it, he is said to be satisfied neither full nor fasting, and is whipped for being hard to please! I have an abundance of such illustrations of the same principle, drawn from my own observation, but think the cases I have cited sufficient. The practice is a very common one.

On the first of January, 1834, I left Mr. Covey, and went to live with Mr. William Freeland, who lived about three miles from St. Michael's. I soon found Mr. Freeland a very different man from Mr. Covey. Though not rich, he was what would be called an educated southern gentleman. Mr. Covey, as I have shown, was a well-trained negro-breaker and slavedriver. The former (slaveholder though he was) seemed to possess some regard for honor, some reverence for justice, and some respect for humanity. The latter seemed totally insensible to all such sentiments. Mr. Freeland had many of the faults peculiar to slaveholders, such as being very passionate and fretful; but I must do him the justice to say, that he was exceedingly free from those degrading vices to which Mr. Covey was constantly addicted. The one was open and frank, and we always knew where to find him. The other was a most artful deceiver, and could be understood only by such as were skillful enough to detect his cunningly-devised frauds. Another advantage I gained in my new master was, he made no pretensions to, or profession of, religion; and this, in my opinion, was truly a great advantage. I assert most unhesitatingly, that the religion of the south is a mere covering for the most horrid crimes,—a justifier of the most appalling barbarity,—a sanctifier of the most hateful frauds,—and a dark shelter under, which the darkest, foulest, grossest, and most infernal deeds of slaveholders find the strongest protection. Were I to be again reduced to the chains of slavery, next to that enslavement, I should regard being the slave of a religious master the greatest calamity that could befall me. For of all slaveholders with whom I have ever met, religious slaveholders are the worst. I have ever found them the meanest and basest, the

most cruel and cowardly, of all others. It was my unhappy lot not only to belong
to a religious slaveholder, but to live in a community of such religionists. Very
near Mr. Freeland lived the Rev. Daniel Weeden, and in the same neighborhood
lived the Rev. Rigby Hopkins. These were members and ministers in the Re-
formed Methodist Church. Mr. Weeden owned, among others, a woman slave,
whose name I have forgotten. This woman's back, for weeks, was kept literally
raw, made so by the lash of this merciless, *religious* wretch. He used to hire
hands. His maxim was, Behave well or behave ill, it is the duty of a master
occasionally to whip a slave, to remind him of his master's authority. Such was
his theory, and such his practice.

Mr. Hopkins was even worse than Mr. Weeden. His chief boast was his
ability to manage slaves. The peculiar feature of his government was that of
whipping slaves in advance of deserving it. He always managed to have one or
more of his slaves to whip every Monday morning. He did this to alarm their
fears, and strike terror into those who escaped. His plan was to whip for the
smallest offences, to prevent the commission of large ones. Mr. Hopkins could
always find some excuse for whipping a slave. It would astonish one, unaccus-
tomed to a slaveholding life, to see with what wonderful ease a slaveholder can
find things, of which to make occasion to whip a slave. A mere look, word, or
motion,—a mistake, accident, or want of power,—are all matters for which a
slave may be whipped at any time. Does a slave look dissatisfied? It is said, he
has the devil in him, and it must be whipped out. Does he speak loudly when
spoken to by his master? Then he is getting high-minded, and should be taken
down a button-hole lower. Does he forget to pull off his hat at the approach of
a white person? Then he is wanting in reverence, and should be whipped for it.
Does he ever venture to vindicate his conduct, when censured for it? Then he is
guilty of impudence,—one of the greatest crimes of which a slave can be guilty.
Does he ever venture to suggest a different mode of doing things from that
pointed out by his master? He is indeed presumptuous, and getting above himself; and nothing less than a flogging will do for him. Does he, while ploughing,
break a plough,—or, while hoeing, break a hoe? It is owing to his carelessness,
and for it a slave must always be whipped. Mr. Hopkins could always find something of this sort to justify the use of the lash, and he seldom failed to embrace
such opportunities. There was not a man in the whole county, with whom the
slaves who had the getting their own home, would not prefer to live, rather than
with this Rev. Mr. Hopkins. And yet there was not a man any where round, who
made higher professions of religion, or was more active in revivals,—more atten-
tive to the class, love-feast, prayer and preaching meetings, or more devotional in
his family,—that prayed earlier, later, louder, and longer,—than this same
reverend slave-driver, Rigby Hopkins.

But to return to Mr. Freeland, and to my experience while in his employment. He, like Mr. Covey, gave us enough to eat; but, unlike Mr. Covey, he also
gave us sufficient time to take our meals. He worked us hard, but always between

sunrise and sunset. He required a good deal of work to be done, but gave us good tools with which to work. His farm was large, but he employed hands enough to work it, and with ease, compared with many of his neighbors. My treatment, while in his employment, was heavenly, compared with what I experienced at the hands of Mr. Edward Covey.

Mr. Freeland was himself the owner of but two slaves. Their names were Henry Harris and John Harris. The rest of his hands he hired. These consisted of myself, Sandy Jenkins,* and Handy Caldwell. Henry and John were quite intelligent, and in a very little while after I went there, I succeeded in creating in them a strong desire to learn how to read. This desire soon sprang up in the others also. They very soon mustered up some old spelling-books, and nothing would do but that I must keep a Sabbath school. I agreed to do so, and accordingly devoted my Sundays to teaching these my loved fellow-slaves how to read. Neither of them knew his letters when I went there. Some of the slaves of the neighboring farms found what was going on, and also availed themselves of this little opportunity to learn to read. It was understood, among all who came, that there must be as little display about it as possible. It was necessary to keep our religious masters at St. Michael's unacquainted with the fact, that, instead of spending the Sabbath in wrestling, boxing, and drinking whisky, we were trying to learn how to read the will of God; for they had much rather see us engaged in those degrading sports, than to see us behaving like intellectual, moral, and accountable beings. My blood boils as I think of the bloody manner in which Messrs. Wright Fairbanks and Garrison West, both class-leaders, in connection with many others, rushed in upon us with sticks and stones, and broke up our virtuous little Sabbath school, at St. Michael's—all calling themselves Christians! humble followers of the Lord Jesus Christ! But I am again digressing.

I held my Sabbath school at the house of a free colored man, whose name I deem it imprudent to mention; for should it be known, it might embarrass him greatly, though the crime of holding the school was committed ten years ago. I had at one time over forty scholars, and those of the right sort, ardently desiring to learn. They were of all ages, though mostly men and women. I look back to those Sundays with an amount of pleasure not to be expressed. They were great days to my soul. The work of instructing my dear fellow-slaves was the sweetest engagement with which I was ever blessed. We loved each other, and to leave them at the close of the Sabbath was a severe cross indeed. When I think that these precious souls are to-day shut up in the prison-house of slavery, my feelings overcome me, and I am almost ready to ask, "Does a righteous God govern the universe? and for what does he hold the thunders in his right hand, if not to smite the oppressor, and deliver the spoiled out of the hand of the spoiler?"

---

* This is the same man who gave me the roots to prevent my being whipped by Mr. Covey. He was "a clever soul." We used frequently to talk about the fight with Covey, and as often as we did so, he would claim my success as the result of the roots which he gave me. This superstition is very common among the more ignorant slaves. A slave seldom dies but that his death is attributed to trickery.

These dear souls came not to Sabbath school because it was popular to do so, nor did I teach them because it was reputable to be thus engaged. Every moment they spent in that school, they were liable to be taken up, and given thirty-nine lashes. They came because they wished to learn. Their minds had been starved by their cruel masters. They had been shut up in mental darkness. I taught them, because it was the delight of my soul to be doing something that looked like bettering the condition of my race. I kept up my school nearly the whole year I lived with Mr. Freeland; and, beside my Sabbath school, I devoted three evenings in the week, during the winter, to teaching the slaves at home. And I have the happiness to know, that several of those who came to Sabbath school learned how to read; and that one, at least, is now free through my agency.

The year passed off smoothly. It seemed only about half as long as the year which preceded it. I went through it without receiving a single blow. I will give Mr. Freeland the credit of being the best master I ever had, *till I became my own master*. For the ease with which I passed the year, I was, however, somewhat indebted to the society of my fellow-slaves. They were noble souls; they not only possessed loving hearts, but brave ones. We were linked and interlinked with each other. I loved them with a love stronger than any thing I have experienced since. It is sometimes said that we slaves do not love and confide in each other. In answer to this assertion, I can say, I never loved any or confided in any people more than my fellow-slaves, and especially those with whom I lived at Mr. Freeland's. I believe we would have died for each other. We never undertook to do any thing, of any importance, without a mutual consultation. We never moved separately. We were one; and as much so by our tempers and dispositions, as by the mutual hardships to which we were necessarily subjected by our condition as slaves.

At the close of the year 1834, Mr. Freeland again hired me of my master, for the year 1835. But, by this time, I began to want to live *upon free land* as well as *with Freeland;* and I was no longer content, therefore, to live with him or any other slaveholder. I began, with the commencement of the year, to prepare myself for a final struggle, which should decide my fate one way or the other. My tendency was upward. I was fast approaching manhood, and year after year had passed, and I was still a slave. These thoughts roused me—I must do something. I therefore resolved that 1835 should not pass without witnessing an attempt, on my part, to secure my liberty. But I was not willing to cherish this determination alone. My fellow-slaves were dear to me. I was anxious to have them participate with me in this, my life-giving determination. I therefore, though with great prudence, commenced early to ascertain their views and feelings in regard to their condition, and to imbue their minds with thoughts of freedom. I bent myself to devising ways and means for our escape, and meanwhile strove, on all fitting occasions, to impress them with the gross fraud and inhumanity of slavery. I went first to Henry, next to John, then to the others. I found, in them all, warm hearts and noble spirits. They were ready to hear, and ready to act when a feasible plan should be proposed. This was what I wanted. I talked to them of our want of manhood, if we submitted to our enslavement without at least one noble effort to be free. We met often, and consulted frequently, and told our hopes and fears, recounted the difficulties, real and imagined, which we should be called on to meet. At times we were almost disposed to give up, and try to content ourselves with our wretched lot; at others, we were firm and unbending in our determination to go. Whenever we suggested any plan, there was shrinking—the odds were fearful. Our path was beset with the greatest obstacles; and if we succeeded in gaining the end of it, our right to be free was yet questionable—we were yet liable to be returned to bondage. We could see no spot, this side of the ocean, where we could be free. We knew nothing about Canada. Our knowledge of the north did not extend farther than New York; and to go there, and be forever harassed with the frightful liability of being returned to slavery—with the certainty of being treated tenfold worse than before—the thought was truly a horrible one, and one which it was not easy to overcome. The case sometimes stood thus: At every gate through which we were to pass, we saw a watchman—at every ferry a guard—on every bridge a sentinel—and in every wood a patrol. We were hemmed in upon every side. Here were the difficulties, real or imagined—the good to be sought, and the evil to be shunned. On the one hand, there stood slavery, a stern reality, glaring frightfully upon us,—its robes already crimsoned with the blood of millions, and even now feasting itself greedily upon our own flesh. On the other hand, away back in the dim distance, under the flickering light of the north star, behind some craggy hill or snow-covered mountain, stood a doubtful freedom—half frozen—beckoning us to come and share its hospitality. This in itself was sometimes enough to stagger us; but when we permitted ourselves to survey the road, we were frequently appalled. Upon either side we saw grim death, assuming the most horrid shapes. Now it was starvation, causing us to eat our own flesh;—now we were contending with the waves, and were drowned;—now we were overtaken, and torn to pieces by the fangs of the terrible bloodhound. We were stung by scorpions, chased by wild beasts, bitten by snakes, and finally, after having nearly reached the desired spot,—after swimming rivers, encountering wild beasts, sleeping in the woods, suffering hunger and nakedness,—we were overtaken by our pursuers, and, in our resistance, we were shot dead upon the spot! I say, this picture sometimes appalled us, and made us

> "rather bear those ills we had,
> Than fly to others, that we knew not of."

In coming to a fixed determination to run away, we did more than Patrick Henry, when he resolved upon liberty or death. With us it was a doubtful liberty at most, and almost certain death if we failed. For my part, I should prefer death to hopeless bondage.

Sandy, one of our number, gave up the notion, but still encouraged us. Our company then consisted of Henry Harris, John Harris, Henry Bailey, Charles Roberts, and myself. Henry Bailey was my uncle, and belonged to my master. Charles married my aunt: he belonged to my master's father-in-law, Mr. William Hamilton.

The plan we finally concluded upon was, to get a large canoe belonging to Mr. Hamilton, and upon the Saturday night previous to Easter holidays, paddle directly up the Chesapeake Bay. On our arrival at the head of the bay, a distance of seventy or eighty miles from where we lived, it was our purpose to turn our canoe adrift, and follow the guidance of the north star till we got beyond the limits of Maryland. Our reason for taking the water route was, that we were less liable to be suspected as runaways; we hoped to be regarded as fishermen; whereas, if we should take the land route, we should be subjected to interruptions of almost every kind. Any one having a white face, and being so disposed, could stop us, and subject us to examination.

The week before our intended start, I wrote several protections, one for each of us. As well as I can remember, they were in the following words, to wit:—

"This is to certify that I, the undersigned, have given the bearer, my servant, full liberty to go to Baltimore, and spend the Easter holidays. Written with mine own hand, &c., 1835.

"*William Hamilton,*
"Near St. Michael's, in Talbot county, Maryland."

We were not going to Baltimore; but, in going up the bay, we went toward Baltimore, and these protections were only intended to protect us while on the bay.

As the time drew near for our departure, our anxiety became more and more intense. It was truly a matter of life and death with us. The strength of our determination was about to be fully tested. At this time, I was very active in explaining every difficulty, removing every doubt, dispelling every fear, and inspiring all with the firmness indispensable to success in our undertaking; assuring them that half was gained the instant we made the move; we had talked long enough; we were now ready to move; if not now, we never should be; and if we did not intend to move now, we had as well fold our arms, sit down, and acknowledge ourselves fit only to be slaves. This, none of us were prepared to acknowledge. Every man stood firm; and at our last meeting, we pledged ourselves afresh, in the most solemn manner, that, at the time appointed, we would certainly start in pursuit of freedom. This was in the middle of the week, at the end of which we were to be off. We went, as usual, to our several fields of labor, but with bosoms highly agitated with thoughts of our truly hazardous undertaking. We tried to conceal our feelings as much as possible; and I think we succeeded very well.

After a painful waiting, the Saturday morning, whose night was to witness our departure, came. I hailed it with joy, bring what sadness it might. Friday night was a sleepless one for me. I probably felt more anxious than the rest, because I was, by common consent, at the head of the whole affair. The responsibility of success or failure lay heavily upon me. The glory of the one, and the confusion of the other, were alike mine. The first two hours of that morning were such as I never experienced before, and hope never to again. Early in the morning, we went, as usual, to the field. We were spreading manure; and all at once, while thus engaged, I was overwhelmed with an indescribable feeling, in the fulness of which I turned to Sandy, who was near by, and said, "We are betrayed!" "Well," said he, "that thought has this moment struck me." We said no more. I was never more certain of any thing.

The horn was blown as usual, and we went up from the field to the house for breakfast. I went for the form, more than for want of any thing to eat that morning. Just as I got to the house, in looking out at the lane gate, I saw four white men, with two colored men. The white men were on horseback, and the colored ones were walking behind, as if tied. I watched them a few moments till they got up to our lane gate. Here they halted, and tied the colored men to the gatepost. I was not yet certain as to what the matter was. In a few moments, in rode Mr. Hamilton, with a speed betokening great excitement. He came to the door, and inquired if Master William was in. He was told he was at the barn. Mr. Hamilton, without dismounting, rode up to the barn with extraordinary speed. In a few moments, he and Mr. Freeland returned to the house. By this time, the three constables rode up, and in great haste dismounted, tied their horses, and met Master William and Mr. Hamilton returning from the barn; and after talking awhile, they all walked up to the kitchen door. There was no one in the kitchen but myself and John. Henry and Sandy were up at the barn. Mr. Freeland put his head in at the door, and called me by name, saying, there were some gentlemen at the door who wished to see me. I stepped to the door, and inquired what they wanted. They at once seized me, and, without giving me any satisfaction, tied me—lashing my hands closely together. I insisted upon knowing what the matter was. They at length said, that they had learned I had been in a "scrape," and that I was to be examined before my master; and if their information proved false, I should not be hurt.

In a few moments, they succeeded in tying John. They then turned to Henry, who had by this time returned, and commanded him to cross his hands. "I won't!" said Henry, in a firm tone, indicating his readiness to meet the consequences of his refusal. "Won't you?" said Tom Graham, the constable. "No, I won't!" said Henry, in a still stronger tone. With this, two of the constables pulled out their shining pistols, and swore, by their Creator, that they would make him cross his hands or kill him. Each cocked his pistol, and, with fingers on the trigger, walked up to Henry, saying, at the same time, if he did not cross his hands, they would blow his damned heart out. "Shoot me, shoot me!" said

Henry; "you can't kill me but once. Shoot, shoot,—and be damned! *I won't be tied!*" This he said in a tone of loud defiance; and at the same time, with a motion as quick as lightning, he with one single stroke dashed the pistols from the hand of each constable. As he did this, all hands fell upon him, and, after beating him some time, they finally overpowered him, and got him tied.

During the scuffle, I managed, I know not how, to get my pass out, and, without being discovered, put it into the fire. We were all now tied; and just as we were to leave for Easton jail, Betsy Freeland, mother of William Freeland, came to the door with her hands full of biscuits, and divided them between Henry and John. She then delivered herself of a speech, to the following effect:— addressing herself to me, she said, *"You devil! You yellow devil!* it was you that put it into the heads of Henry and John to run away. But for you, you long-legged mulatto devil! Henry nor John would never have thought of such a thing." I made no reply, and was immediately hurried off towards St. Michael's. Just a moment previous to the scuffle with Henry, Mr. Hamilton suggested the propriety of making a search for the protections which he had understood Frederick had written for himself and the rest. But, just at the moment he was about carrying his proposal into effect, his aid was needed in helping to tie Henry; and the excitement attending the scuffle caused them either to forget, or to deem it unsafe, under the circumstances, to search. So we were not yet convicted of the intention to run away.

When we got about half way to St. Michael's, while the constables having us in charge were looking ahead, Henry inquired of me what he should do with his pass. I told him to eat it with his biscuit, and own nothing; and we passed the word around, *"Own nothing;"* and *"Own nothing!"* said we all. Our confidence in each other was unshaken. We were resolved to succeed or fail together, after the calamity had befallen us as much as before. We were now prepared for any thing. We were to be dragged that morning fifteen miles behind horses, and then to be placed in the Easton jail. When we reached St. Michael's, we underwent a sort of examination. We all denied that we ever intended to run away. We did this more to bring out the evidence against us, than from any hope of getting clear of being sold; for, as I have said, we were ready for that. The fact was, we cared but little where we went, so we went together. Our greatest concern was about separation. We dreaded that more than any thing this side of death. We found the evidence against us to be the testimony of one person; our master would not tell who it was; but we came to a unanimous decision among ourselves as to who their informant was. We were sent off to the jail at Easton. When we got there, we were delivered up to the sheriff, Mr. Joseph Graham, and by him placed in jail. Henry, John, and myself, were placed in one room together— Charles, and Henry Bailey, in another. Their object in separating us was to hinder concert.

We had been in jail scarcely twenty minutes, when a swarm of slave traders, and agents for slave traders, flocked into jail to look at us, and to ascertain if we were for sale. Such a set of beings I never saw before! I felt myself surrounded by so many fiends from perdition. A band of pirates never looked more like their father, the devil. They laughed and grinned over us, saying, "Ah, my boys! we have got you, haven't we?" And after taunting us in various ways, they one by one went into an examination of us, with intent to ascertain our value. They would impudently ask us if we would not like to have them for our masters. We would make them no answer, and leave them to find out as best they could. Then they would curse and swear at us, telling us that they could take the devil out of us in a very little while, if we were only in their hands.

While in jail, we found ourselves in much more comfortable quarters than we expected when we went there. We did not get much to eat, nor that which was very good; but we had a good clean room, from the windows of which we could see what was going on in the street, which was very much better than though we had been placed in one of the dark, damp cells. Upon the whole, we got along very well, so far as the jail and its keeper were concerned. Immediately after the holidays were over, contrary to all our expectations, Mr. Hamilton and Mr. Freeland came up to Easton, and took Charles, the two Henrys, and John, out of jail, and carried them home, leaving me alone. I regarded this separation as a final one. It caused me more pain than any thing else in the whole transaction. I was ready for any thing rather than separation. I supposed that they had consulted together, and had decided that, as I was the whole cause of the intention of the others to run away, it was hard to make the innocent suffer with the guilty; and that they had, therefore, concluded to take the others home, and sell me, as a warning to the others that remained. It is due to the noble Henry to say, he seemed almost as reluctant at leaving the prison as at leaving home to come to the prison. But we knew we should, in all probability, be separated, if we were sold; and since he was in their hands, he concluded to go peaceably home.

I was now left to my fate. I was all alone, and within the walls of a stone prison. But a few days before, and I was full of hope. I expected to have been safe in a land of freedom; but now I was covered with gloom, sunk down to the utmost despair. I thought the possibility of freedom was gone. I was kept in this way about one week, at the end of which, Captain Auld, my master, to my surprise and utter astonishment, came up, and took me out, with the intention of sending me, with a gentleman of his acquaintance, into Alabama. But, from some cause or other, he did not send me to Alabama, but concluded to send me back to Baltimore, to live again with his brother Hugh, and to learn a trade.

Thus, after an absence of three years and one month, I was once more permitted to return to my old home at Baltimore. My master sent me away, because there existed against me a very great prejudice in the community, and he feared I might be killed.

In a few weeks after I went to Baltimore, Master Hugh hired me to Mr. William Gardner, an extensive ship-builder, on Fell's Point. I was put there to learn how to calk. It, however, proved a very unfavorable place for the accomplishment of this object. Mr. Gardner was engaged that spring in building two large man-of-war brigs, professedly for the Mexican government. The vessels were to be launched in the July of that year, and in failure thereof, Mr. Gardner was to lose a considerable sum; so that when I entered, all was hurry. There was no time to learn any thing. Every man had to do that which he knew how to do. In entering the shipyard, my orders from Mr. Gardner were, to do whatever the carpenters commanded me to do. This was placing me at the beck and call of about seventy-five men. I was to regard all these as masters. Their word was to be my law. My situation was a most trying one. At times I needed a dozen pair of hands. I was called a dozen ways in the space of a single minute. Three or four voices would strike my ear at the same moment. It was—"Fred., come help me to cant this timber here."—"Fred., come carry this timber yonder."—"Fred., bring that roller here."—"Fred., go get a fresh can of water."—"Fred., come help me saw off the end of this timber."—"Fred., go quick, and get the crowbar."—"Fred., hold on the end of this fall."—"Fred., go to the blacksmith's shop, and get a new punch."—"Hurra, Fred.! run and bring me a cold chisel."—"I say, Fred., bear a hand, and get up a fire as quick as lightning under that steambox."—"Halloo, nigger! come, turn this grindstone."—"Come, come! move, move! and bowse this timber forward."—"I say, darky, blast your eyes, why don't you heat up some pitch?"—"Halloo! halloo! halloo!" (Three voices at the same time.) "Come here!—Go there!—Hold on where you are! Damn you, if you move, I'll knock your brains out!"

This was my school for eight months; and I might have remained there longer, but for a most horrid fight I had with four of the white apprentices, in which my left eye was nearly knocked out, and I was horribly mangled in other respects. The facts in the case were these: Until a very little while after I went there, white and black ship-carpenters worked side by side, and no one seemed to see any impropriety in it. All hands seemed to be very well satisfied. Many of the black carpenters were freemen. Things seemed to be going on very well. All at once, the white carpenters knocked off, and said they would not work with free colored workmen. Their reason for this, as alleged, was, that if free colored carpenters were encouraged, they would soon take the trade into their own hands, and poor white men would be thrown out of employment. They therefore felt called upon at once to put a stop to it. And, taking advantage of Mr. Gardner's necessities, they broke off, swearing they would work no longer, unless he would discharge his black carpenters. Now, though this did not extend to me in form, it did reach me in fact. My fellow-apprentices very soon began to feel it degrading to them to work with me. They began to put on airs, and talk about the "niggers" taking the country, saying we all ought to be killed; and, being encouraged by the journeymen, they commenced making my condition as hard as they could, by hectoring me around, and sometimes striking me. I, of course, kept the vow I made after the fight with Mr. Covey, and struck back again, regardless of consequences; and while I kept them from combining, I succeeded very well; for I could whip the whole of them, taking them separately. They, however, at length combined, and came upon me, armed with sticks, stones, and heavy handspikes. One came in front with a half brick. There was one at each side of me, and one behind me. While I was attending to those in front, and on either side, the one behind ran up with the handspike, and struck me a heavy blow upon the head. It stunned me. I fell, and with this they all ran upon me, and fell to beating me with their fists. I let them lay on for a while, gathering strength. In an instant, I gave a sudden surge, and rose to my hands and knees. Just as I did that, one of their number gave me, with his heavy boot, a powerful kick in the left eye. My eyeball seemed to have burst. When they saw my eye closed, and badly swollen, they left me. With this I seized the handspike, and for a time pursued them. But here the carpenters interfered, and I thought I might as well give it up. It was impossible to stand my hand against so many. All this took place in sight of not less than fifty white ship-carpenters, and not one interposed a friendly word; but some cried, "Kill the damned nigger! Kill him! kill him! He struck a white person." I found my only chance for life was in flight. I succeeded in getting away without an additional blow, and barely so; for to strike a white man is death by Lynch law,—and that was the law in Mr. Gardner's ship-yard; nor is there much of any other out of Mr. Gardner's ship-yard.

I went directly home, and told the story of my wrongs to Master Hugh; and I am happy to say of him, irreligious as he was, his conduct was heavenly, compared with that of his brother Thomas under similar circumstances. He listened attentively to my narration of the circumstances leading to the savage outrage, and gave many proofs of his strong indignation at it. The heart of my once overkind mistress was again melted into pity. My puffed-out eye and blood-covered face moved her to tears. She took a chair by me, washed the blood from my face, and, with a mother's tenderness, bound up my head, covering the wounded eye with a lean piece of fresh beef. It was almost compensation for my suffering to witness, once more, a manifestation of kindness from this, my once affectionate old mistress. Master Hugh was very much enraged. He gave expression to his feelings by pouring out curses upon the heads of those who did the deed. As soon as I got a little the better of my bruises, he took me with him to Esquire Watson's, on Bond Street, to see what could be done about the matter. Mr. Watson inquired who saw the assault committed. Master Hugh told him it was done in Mr. Gardner's ship-yard, at midday, where there were a large company of men at work. "As to that," he said, "the deed was done, and there was no question as to who did it." His answer was, he could do nothing in the case, unless some white man would come forward and testify. He could issue no warrant on my word. If I had been killed in the presence of a thousand colored people, their testimony combined would have been insufficient to have arrested one of the murderers. Master Hugh, for once, was compelled to say this state of things was too bad. Of course, it was impossible to get any white man to volunteer his testimony in my behalf, and against the white young men. Even those who may have sympathized with me were not prepared to do this. It required a degree of courage unknown to them to do so; for just at that time, the slightest manifestation of humanity toward a colored person was denounced as abolitionism, and that name subjected its bearer to frightful liabilities. The watchwords of the bloody-minded in that region, and in those days, were, "Damn the abolitionists!" and "Damn the niggers!" There was nothing done, and probably nothing would have been done if I had been killed. Such was, and such remains, the state of things in the Christian city of Baltimore.

Master Hugh, finding he could get no redress, refused to let me go back again to Mr. Gardner. He kept me himself, and his wife dressed my wound till I was again restored to health. He then took me into the ship-yard of which he was foreman, in the employment of Mr. Walter Price. There I was immediately set to calking, and very soon learned the art of using my mallet and irons. In the course of one year from the time I left Mr. Gardner's, I was able to command the highest wages given to the most experienced calkers. I was now of some importance to my master. I was bringing him from six to seven dollars per week. I sometimes brought him nine dollars per week: my wages were a dollar and a half a day. After learning how to calk, I sought my own employment, made my own contracts, and collected the money which I earned. My pathway became much more smooth than before; my condition was now much more comfortable. When I could get no calking to do, I did nothing. During these leisure times, those old notions about freedom would steal over me again. When in Mr. Gardner's employment, I was kept in such a perpetual whirl of excitement, I could think of nothing, scarcely, but my life; and in thinking of my life, I almost forgot my liberty. I have observed this in my experience of slavery,—that whenever my condition was improved, instead of its increasing my contentment, it only increased my desire to be free, and set me to thinking of plans to gain my freedom. I have found that, to make a contented slave, it is necessary to make a thoughtless one. It is necessary to darken his moral and mental vision, and, as far as possible, to annihilate the power of reason. He must be able to detect no inconsistencies in slavery; he must be made to feel that slavery is right; and he can be brought to that only when he ceases to be a man.

I was now getting, as I have said, one dollar and fifty cents per day. I contracted for it; I earned it; it was paid to me; it was rightfully my own; yet, upon each returning Saturday night, I was compelled to deliver every cent of that money to Master Hugh. And why? Not because he earned it,—not because he had any hand in earning it,—not because I owed it to him,—nor because he possessed the slightest shadow of a right to it; but solely because he had the power to compel me to give it up. The right of the grim-visaged pirate upon the high seas is exactly the same.

Booker T. Washington (1856-1915)

Chapter XIV   The Atlanta Exposition Address

From Up from Slavery

The Atlanta Exposition, at which I had been asked to make an address as a representative of the Negro race, as stated in the last chapter, was opened with a short address from Governor Bullock. After other interesting exercises, including an invocation from Bishop Nelson, of Georgia, a dedicatory ode by Albert Howell, Jr., and addresses by the President of the Exposition and Mrs. Joseph Thompson, the President of the Woman's Board, Governor Bullock introduced me with the words, "We have with us to-day a representative of Negro enterprise and Negro civilization."

When I arose to speak, there was considerable cheering, especially from the coloured people. As I remember it now, the thing that was uppermost in my mind was the desire to say something that would cement the friendship of the races and bring about hearty coöperation between them. So far as my outward surroundings were concerned, the only thing that I recall distinctly now is that when I got up, I saw thousands of eyes looking intently into my face. The following is the address which I delivered:—

Mr. President and Gentlemen of the Board of Directors and Citizens.

One-third of the population of the South is of the Negro race. No enterprise seeking the material, civil, or moral welfare of this section can disregard this element of our population and reach the highest success. I but convey to you, Mr. President and Directors, the sentiment of the masses of my race when I say that in no way have the value and manhood of the American Negro been more fittingly and generously recognized than by the managers of this magnificent Exposition at every stage of its progress. It is a recognition that will do more to cement the friendship of the two races than any occurrence since the dawn of our freedom.

Not only this, but the opportunity here afforded will awaken among us a new era of industrial progress. Ignorant and inexperienced, it is not strange that in the first years of our new life we began at the top instead of at the bottom; that a seat in Congress or the state legislature was more sought than real estate or industrial skill; that the political convention of stump speaking had more attractions than starting a dairy farm or truck garden.

A ship lost at sea for many days suddenly sighted a friendly vessel. From the mast of the unfortunate vessel was seen a signal, "Water, water; we die of thirst!" The answer from the friendly vessel at once came back, "Cast down your bucket where you are." A second time the signal, "Water, water; send us water!" ran up from the distressed vessel, and was answered, "Cast down your bucket where you are." And a third and fourth signal for water was answered, "Cast down your bucket where you are." The captain of the distressed vessel, at last heeding the injunction, cast down his bucket, and it came up full of fresh, sparkling water from the mouth of the Amazon River. To those of my race who depend on bettering their condition in a foreign land or who underestimate the importance of cultivating friendly relations with the Southern white man, who is their next-door neighbour, I would say: "Cast down your bucket where you are"—cast it down in making friends in every manly way of the people of all races by whom we are surrounded.

Cast it down in agriculture, mechanics, in commerce, in domestic service, and in the professions. And in this connection it is well to bear in mind that whatever other sins the South may be called to bear, when it comes to business, pure and simple, it is in the South that the Negro is given a man's chance in the commercial world, and in nothing is this Exposition more eloquent than in emphasizing this chance. Our greatest danger is that in the great leap from slavery to freedom we may overlook the fact that the masses of us are to live by the productions of our hands, and fail to keep in mind that we shall prosper in proportion as we learn to dignify and glorify common labour and put brains and skill into the common occupations of life; shall prosper in proportion as we learn to draw the line between the superficial and the substantial, the ornamental gewgaws of life and the useful. No race can prosper till it learns that there is as much dignity in tilling a field as in writing a poem. It is at the bottom of life we must begin, and not at the top. Nor should we permit our grievances to overshadow our opportunities.

To those of the white race who look to the incoming of those of foreign birth and strange tongue and habits for the prosperity of the South, were I permitted I would repeat what I say to my own race, "Cast down your bucket where you are." Cast it down among the eight millions of Negroes whose habits you know, whose fidelity and love you have tested in days when to have proved treacherous meant the ruin of your firesides. Cast down your bucket among these people who have, without strikes and labour wars, tilled your fields, cleared your forests, builded your railroads and cities, and brought forth treasures from the bowels of the earth, and helped make possible this magnificent representation of the progress of the South. Casting down your bucket among my people, helping and encouraging them as you are doing on these grounds, and to education of head, hand, and heart, you will find that they will buy your surplus land, make blossom the waste places in your fields, and run your factories. While doing this, you can be sure in the future, as in the past, that you and your families will be surrounded by the most patient, faithful, law-abiding, and unresentful people that the world has seen. As we have proved our loyalty to you in the past, in nursing your children, watching by the sickbed of your mothers and fathers, and often following them with tear-dimmed eyes to their graves, so in the future, in our humble way, we shall stand by you with a devotion that no foreigner can approach, ready to lay down our lives, if need be, in defence of yours, interlacing our industrial, commercial, civil, and religious life with yours in a way that shall make the interests of both races one. In all things that are purely social we can be as separate as the fingers, yet one as the hand in all things essential to mutual progress.

There is no defence or security for any of us except in the highest intelligence and development of all. If anywhere there are efforts tending to curtail the fullest growth of the Negro, let these efforts be turned into stimulating, encouraging, and making him the most useful and intelligent citizen. Effort or means so invested will pay a thousand per cent interest. These efforts will be twice blessed—"blessing him that gives and him that takes."

There is no escape through law of man or God from the inevitable:—

> The laws of changeless justice bind
>   Oppressor with oppressed;
> And close as sin and suffering joined
>   We march to fate abreast.

Nearly sixteen millions of hands will aid you in pulling the load upward, or they will pull against you the load downward. We shall constitute one-third and more of the ignorance and crime of the South, or one-third its intelligence and progress; we shall contribute one-third to the business and industrial prosperity of the South, or we shall prove a veritable body of death, stagnating, depressing, retarding every effort to advance the body politic.

Gentlemen of the Exposition, as we present to you our humble effort at an exhibition of our progress, you must not expect overmuch. Starting thirty years ago with ownership here and there in a few quilts and pumpkins and chickens (gathered from miscellaneous sources), remember the path that has led from these to the inventions and production of agricultural implements, buggies, steam-engines, newspapers, books, statuary, carving, paintings, the management of drug-stores and banks, has not been trodden without contact with thorns and thistles. While we take pride in what we exhibit as a result of our independent efforts, we do not for a moment forget that our part in this exhibition would fall far short of your expectations but for the constant help that has come to our educational life, not only from the Southern states, but especially from Northern philanthropists, who have made their gifts a constant stream of blessing and encouragement.

The wisest among my race understand that the agitation of questions of social equality is the extremest folly, and that progress in the enjoyment of all the privileges that will come to us must be the result of severe and constant struggle rather than of artificial forcing. No race that has anything to contribute to the markets of the world is long in any degree ostracized. It is important and right that all privileges of the law be ours, but it is vastly more important that we be prepared for the exercises of these privileges. The opportunity to earn a dollar in a factory just now is worth infinitely more than the opportunity to spend a dollar in an opera-house.

In conclusion, may I repeat that nothing in thirty years has given us more hope and encouragement, and drawn us so near to you of the white race, as this opportunity offered by the Exposition; and here bending, as it were, over the altar that represents the results of the struggles of your race and mine, both starting practically empty-handed three decades ago. I pledge that in your effort to work out the great and intricate problem which God has laid at the doors of the South, you shall have at all times the patient, sympathetic help of my race; only let this be constantly in mind, that, while from representations in these buildings of the product of field, of forest, of mine, of factory, letters, and art, much good will come, yet far above and beyond material benefits will be that higher good, that, let us pray God, will come, in a blotting out of sectional differences and racial animosities and suspicions, in a determination to administer absolute justice, in a willing obedience among all classes to the mandates of law. This, then, coupled with our material prosperity, will bring into our beloved South a new heaven and a new earth.

The first thing that I remember, after I had finished speaking, was that Governor Bullock rushed across the platform and took me by the hand, and that others did the same. I received so many and such hearty congratulations that I found it difficult to get out of the building. I did not appreciate to any degree, however, the impression which my address seemed to have made, until the next morning, when I went into the business part of the city. As soon as I was recognized, I was surprised to find myself pointed out and surrounded by a crowd of men who wished to shake hands with me. This was kept up on every street on to which I went, to an extent which embarrassed me so much that I went back to my boarding-place. The next morning I returned to Tuskegee. At the station in Atlanta, and at almost all of the stations at which the train stopped between that city and Tuskegee, I found a crowd of people anxious to shake hands with me.

The papers in all parts of the United States published the address in full, and for months afterward there were complimentary editorial references to it. Mr. Clark Howell, the editor of the Atlanta *Constitution*, telegraphed to a New

York paper, among other words, the following, "I do not exaggerate when I say that Professor Booker T. Washington's address yesterday was one of the most notable speeches, both as to character and as to the warmth of its reception, ever delivered to a Southern audience. The address was a revelation. The whole speech is a platform upon which blacks and whites can stand with full justice to each other."

The Boston *Transcript* said editorially: "The speech of Booker T. Washington at the Atlanta Exposition, this week, seems to have dwarfed all the other proceedings and the Exposition itself. The sensation that it has caused in the press has never been equalled."

I very soon began receiving all kinds of propositions from lecture bureaus, and editors of magazines and papers, to take the lecture platform, and to write articles. One lecture bureau offered me fifty thousand dollars, or two hundred dollars a night and expenses, if I would place my services at its disposal for a given period. To all these communications I replied that my life-work was at Tuskegee; and that whenever I spoke it must be in the interests of the Tuskegee school and my race, and that I would enter into no arrangements that seemed to place a mere commercial value upon my services.

Some days after its delivery I sent a copy of my address to the President of the United States, the Hon. Grover Cleveland. I received from him the following autographed reply:—

Gray Gables, Buzzard's Bay, Mass.,
October 6, 1895.

Booker T. Washington, Esq.:

My Dear Sir: I thank you for sending me a copy of your address delivered at the Atlanta Exposition.

I thank you with much enthusiasm for making the address. I have read it with intense interest, and I think the Exposition would be fully justified if it did not do more than furnish the opportunity for its delivery. Your words cannot fail to delight and encourage all who wish well for your race; and if our coloured fellow-citizens do not from your utterances gather new hope and form new determinations to gain every valuable advantage offered them by their citizenship, it will be strange indeed.

Yours very truly,
Grover Cleveland.

Later I met Mr. Cleveland, for the first time, when, as President, he visited the Atlanta Exposition. At the request of myself and others he consented to spend an hour in the Negro Building, for the purpose of inspecting the Negro exhibit and of giving the coloured people in attendance an opportunity to shake hands with him. As soon as I met Mr. Cleveland I became impressed with his simplicity, greatness, and rugged honesty. I have met him many times since then, both at public functions and at his private residence in Princeton, and the more

I see of him the more I admire him. When he visited the Negro Building in Atlanta he seemed to give himself up wholly, for that hour, to the coloured people. He seemed to be as careful to shake hands with some old coloured "auntie" clad partially in rags, and to take as much pleasure in doing so, as if he were greeting some millionaire. Many of the coloured people took advantage of the occasion to get him to write his name in a book or on a slip of paper. He was as careful and patient in doing this as if he were putting his signature to some great state document.

Mr. Cleveland has not only shown his friendship for me in many personal ways, but has always consented to do anything I have asked of him for our school. This he has done, whether it was to make a personal donation or to use his influence in securing the donations of others. Judging from my personal acquaintance with Mr. Cleveland, I do not believe that he is conscious of possessing any colour prejudice. He is too great for that. In my contact with people I find that, as a rule, it is only the little, narrow people who live for themselves, who never read good books, who do not travel, who never open up their souls in a way to permit them to come into contact with other souls—with the great outside world. No man whose vision is bounded by colour can come into contact with what is highest and best in the world. In meeting men, in many places, I have found that the happiest people are those who do the most for others; the most miserable are those who do the least. I have also found that few things, if any, are capable of making one so blind and narrow as race prejudice. I often say to our students, in the course of my talks to them on Sunday evenings in the chapel, that the longer I live and the more experience I have of the world, the more I am convinced that, after all, the one thing that is most worth living for— and dying for, if need be—is the opportunity of making some one else more happy and more useful.

The coloured people and the coloured newspapers at first seemed to be greatly pleased with the character of my Atlanta address, as well as with its reception. But after the first burst of enthusiasm began to die away, and the coloured people began reading the speech in cold type, some of them seemed to feel that they had been hypnotized. They seemed to feel that I had been too liberal in my remarks toward the Southern whites, and that I had not spoken out strongly enough for what they termed the "rights" of the race. For a while there was a reaction, so far as a certain element of my own race was concerned, but later these reactionary ones seemed to have been won over to my way of believing and acting.

While speaking of changes in public sentiment, I recall that about ten years after the school at Tuskegee was established, I had an experience that I shall never forget. Dr. Lyman Abbott, then the pastor of Plymouth Church, and also editor of the *Outlook* (then the *Christian Union*), asked me to write a letter for his paper giving my opinion of the exact condition, mental and moral, of the coloured ministers in the South, as based upon my observations. I wrote the letter, giving the exact facts as I conceived them to be. The picture painted was a rather black one—or, since I am black, shall I say "white"? It could not be otherwise with a race but a few years out of slavery, a race which had not had time or opportunity to produce a competent ministry.

What I said soon reached every Negro minister in the country, I think, and the letters of condemnation which I received from them were not few. I think that for a year after the publication of this article every association and every conference or religious body of any kind, of my race, that met, did not fail before adjourning to pass a resolution condemning me, or calling upon me to retract or modify what I had said. Many of these organizations went so far in their resolutions as to advise parents to cease sending their children to Tuskegee. One association even appointed a "missionary" whose duty it was to warn the people against sending their children to Tuskegee. This missionary had a son in the school, and I noticed that, whatever the "missionary" might have said or done with regard to others, he was careful not to take his son away from the institution. Many of the coloured papers, especially those that were the organs of religious bodies, joined in the general chorus of condemnation or demands for retraction.

During the whole time of the excitement, and through all the criticism, I did not utter a word of explanation or retraction. I knew that I was right, and that time and the sober second thought of the people would vindicate me. It was not long before the bishops and other church leaders began to make a careful investigation of the conditions of the ministry, and they found out that I was right. In fact, the oldest and most influential bishop in one branch of the Methodist Church said that my words were far too mild. Very soon public sentiment began making itself felt, in demanding a purifying of the ministry. While this is not yet complete by any means, I think I may say, without egotism, and I have been told by many of our most influential ministers, that my words had much to do with starting a demand for the placing of a higher type of men in the pulpit. I have had the satisfaction of having many who once condemned me thank me heartily for my frank words.

The change of the attitude of the Negro ministry, so far as regards myself, is so complete that at the present time I have no warmer friends among any class than I have among the clergymen. The improvement in the character and life of the Negro ministers is one of the most gratifying evidences of the progress of the race. My experience with them, as well as other events in my life, convinced me that the thing to do, when one feels sure that he has said or done the right thing, and is condemned, is to stand still and keep quiet. If he is right, time will show it.

In the midst of the discussion which was going on concerning my Atlanta speech, I received the letter which I give below, from Dr. Gilman, the President of Johns Hopkins University, who had been made chairman of the judges of award in connection with the Atlanta Exposition:—

Johns Hopkins University, Baltimore,
President's Office, September 30, 1895.

DEAR MR. WASHINGTON: Would it be agreeable to you to be one of the Judges of Award in the Department of Education at Atlanta? If so, I shall be glad to place your name upon the list. A line by telegraph will be welcomed.

Yours very truly,

D. C. Gilman.

I think I was even more surprised to receive this invitation than I had been to receive the invitation to speak at the opening of the Exposition. It was to be a part of my duty, as one of the jurors, to pass not only upon the exhibits of the coloured schools, but also upon those of the white schools. I accepted the position, and spent a month in Atlanta in performance of the duties which it entailed. The board of jurors was a large one, consisting in all of sixty members. It was about equally divided between Southern white people and Northern white people. Among them were college presidents, leading scientists and men of letters, and specialists in many subjects. When the group of jurors to which I was assigned met for organization, Mr. Thomas Nelson Page, who was one of the number, moved that I be made secretary of that division, and the motion was unanimously adopted. Nearly half of our division were Southern people. In performing my duties in the inspection of the exhibits of white schools I was in every case treated with respect, and at the close of our labours I parted from my associates with regret.

I am often asked to express myself more freely than I do upon the political condition and the political future of my race. These recollections of my experience in Atlanta give me the opportunity to do so briefly. My own belief is, although I have never before said so in so many words, that the time will come when the Negro in the South will be accorded all the political rights which his ability, character, and material possessions entitle him to. I think, though, that the opportunity to freely exercise such political rights will not come in any large degree through outside or artificial forcing, but will be accorded to the Negro by the Southern white people themselves, and that they will protect him in the exercise of those rights. Just as soon as the South gets over the old feeling that it is being forced by "foreigners," or "aliens," to do something which it does not want to do, I believe that the change in the direction that I have indicated is going to begin. In fact, there are indications that it is already beginning in a slight degree.

Let me illustrate my meaning. Suppose that some months before the opening of the Atlanta Exposition there had been a general demand from the press and public platform outside the South that a Negro be given a place on the opening programme, and that a Negro be placed upon the board of jurors of award. Would any such recognition of the race have taken place? I do not think so. The Atlanta officials went as far as they did because they felt it to be a pleasure, as well as a duty, to reward what they considered merit in the Negro race. Say what we will, there is something in human nature which we cannot blot out, which makes one man, in the end, recognize and reward merit in another, regardless of colour or race.

I believe it is the duty of the Negro—as the greater part of the race is already doing—to deport himself modestly in regard to political claims, depending upon the slow but sure influences that proceed from the possession of property, intelligence, and high character for the full recognition of his political rights. I think that the according of the full exercise of political rights is going to be a matter of natural, slow growth, not an over-night, gourd-vine affair. I do not believe that the Negro should cease voting, for a man cannot learn the exercise of self-government by ceasing to vote any more than a boy can learn to swim by keeping out of the water, but I do believe that in his voting he should more and more be influenced by those of intelligence and character who are his next-door neighbours.

I know coloured men who, through the encouragement, help, and advice of Southern white people, have accumulated thousands of dollars' worth of property, but who, at the same time, would never think of going to those same persons for advice concerning the casting of their ballots. This, it seems to me, is unwise and unreasonable, and should cease. In saying this I do not mean that the Negro should truckle, or not vote from principle, for the instant he ceases to vote from principle he loses the confidence and respect of the Southern white man even.

I do not believe that any state should make a law that permits an ignorant and poverty-stricken white man to vote, and prevents a black man in the same condition from voting. Such a law is not only unjust, but it will react, as all unjust laws do, in time; for the effect of such a law is to encourage the Negro to secure education and property, and at the same time it encourages the white man to remain in ignorance and poverty. I believe that in time, through the operation of intelligence and friendly race relations, all cheating at the ballot box in the South will cease. It will become apparent that the white man who begins by cheating a Negro out of his ballot soon learns to cheat a white man out of his, and that the man who does this ends his career of dishonesty by the theft of property or by some equally serious crime. In my opinion, the time will come when the South will encourage all of its citizens to vote. It will see that it pays better, from every standpoint, to have healthy, vigorous life than to have that political stagnation which always results when one-half of the population has no share and no interest in the Government.

As a rule, I believe in universal, free suffrage, but I believe that in the South we are confronted with peculiar conditions that justify the protection of the ballot in many of the states, for a while at least, either by an educational test, a property test, or by both combined; but whatever tests are required, they should be made to apply with equal and exact justice to both races.

W. E. B. Du Bois (1868-1963)

Chapter III   Of Mr. Booker T. Washington and Others

From The Souls of Black Folk

From birth till death enslaved; in word, in deed, unmanned!

Hereditary bondsmen! Know ye not
Who would be free themselves must strike the blow?

                                                          Byron.

Easily the most striking thing in the history of the American Negro since 1876 is the ascendancy of Mr. Booker T. Washington. It began at the time when war memories and ideals were rapidly passing; a day of astonishing commercial development was dawning; a sense of doubt and hesitation overtook the freedmen's sons,—then it was that his leading began. Mr. Washington came, with a single definite programme, at the psychological moment when the nation was a little ashamed of having bestowed so much sentiment on Negroes, and was concentrating its energies on Dollars. His programme of industrial education, conciliation of the South, and submission and silence as to civil and political rights, was not wholly original; the Free Negroes from 1830 up to wartime had striven to build industrial schools, and the American Missionary Association had from the first taught various trades; and Price and others had sought a way of honorable alliance with the best of the Southerners. But Mr. Washington first indissolubly linked these things; he put enthusiasm, unlimited energy, and perfect faith into this programme, and changed it from a by-path into a veritable Way of Life.

And the tale of the methods by which he did this is a fascinating study of human life.

It startled the nation to hear a Negro advocating such a programme after many decades of bitter complaint; it startled and won the applause of the South, it interested and won the admiration of the North; and after a confused murmur of protest, it silenced if it did not convert the Negroes themselves.

To gain the sympathy and coöperation of the various elements comprising the white South was Mr. Washington's first task; and this, at the time Tuskegee was founded, seemed, for a black man, well-nigh impossible. And yet ten years later it was done in the word spoken at Atlanta: "In all things purely social we can be as separate as the five fingers, and yet one as the hand in all things essential to mutual progress." This "Atlanta Compromise" is by all odds the most notable thing in Mr. Washington's career. The South interpreted it in different ways: the radicals received it as a complete surrender of the demand for civil and political equality; the conservatives, as a generously conceived working basis for mutual understanding. So both approved it, and to-day its author is certainly the most distinguished Southerner since Jefferson Davis, and the one with the largest personal following.

Next to this achievement comes Mr. Washington's work in gaining place and consideration in the North. Others less shrewd and tactful had formerly essayed to sit on these two stools and had fallen between them; but as Mr. Washington knew the heart of the South from birth and training, so by singular insight he intuitively grasped the spirit of the age which was dominating the North. And so thoroughly did he learn the speech and thought of triumphant commercialism, and the ideals of material prosperity, that the picture of a lone black boy poring over a French grammar amid the weeds and dirt of a neglected home soon seemed to him the acme of absurdities. One wonders what Socrates and St. Francis of Assisi would say to this.

And yet this very singleness of vision and thorough oneness with his age is a mark of the successful man. It is as though Nature must needs make men narrow in order to give them force. So Mr. Washington's cult has gained unquestioning followers, his work has wonderfully prospered, his friends are legion, and his enemies are confounded. To-day he stands as the one recognized spokesman of his ten million fellows, and one of the most notable figures in a nation of seventy millions. One hesitates, therefore, to criticise a life which, beginning with so little, has done so much. And yet the time is come when one may speak in all sincerity and utter courtesy of the mistakes and shortcomings of Mr. Washington's career, as well as of his triumphs, without being thought captious or envious, and without forgetting that it is easier to do ill than well in the world.

The criticism that has hitherto met Mr. Washington has not always been of this broad character. In the South especially has he had to walk warily to avoid the harshest judgments,—and naturally so, for he is dealing with the one subject of deepest sensitiveness to that section. Twice—once when at the Chicago celebration of the Spanish-American War he alluded to the color-prejudice that is "eating away the vitals of the South," and once when he dined with President Roosevelt—has the resulting Southern criticism been violent enough to threaten seriously his popularity. In the North the feeling has several times forced itself into words, that Mr. Washington's counsels of submission overlooked certain elements of true manhood, and that his educational programme was unnecessarily narrow. Usually, however, such criticism has not found open expression, although, too, the spiritual sons of the Abolitionists have not been prepared to acknowledge that the schools founded before Tuskegee, by men of broad ideals and self-sacrificing spirit, were wholly failures or worthy of ridicule. While, then, criticism has not failed to follow Mr. Washington, yet the prevailing public opinion of the land has been but too willing to deliver the solution of a wearisome problem into his hands, and say, "If that is all you and your race ask, take it."

Among his own people, however, Mr. Washington has encountered the strongest and most lasting opposition, amounting at times to bitterness, and even to-day continuing strong and insistent even though largely silenced in outward expression by the public opinion of the nation. Some of this opposition is, of course, mere envy; the disappointment of displaced demagogues and the spite of narrow minds. But aside from this, there is among educated and thoughtful colored men in all parts of the land a feeling of deep regret, sorrow, and apprehension at the wide currency and ascendancy which some of Mr. Washington's theories have gained. These same men admire his sincerity of purpose, and are willing to forgive much to honest endeavor which is doing something worth the doing. They coöperate with Mr. Washington as far as they conscientiously can; and, indeed, it is no ordinary tribute to this man's tact and power that, steering as he must between so many diverse interests and opinions, he so largely retains the respect of all.

But the hushing of the criticism of honest opponents is a dangerous thing. It leads some of the best of the critics to unfortunate silence and paralysis of effort, and others to burst into speech so passionately and intemperately as to lose listeners. Honest and earnest criticism from those whose interests are most nearly touched,—criticism of writers by readers, of government by those governed, of leaders by those led,—this is the soul of democracy and the safeguard of modern society. If the best of the American Negroes receive by outer pressure a leader whom they had not recognized before, manifestly there is here a certain palpable gain. Yet there is also irreparable loss,—a loss of that peculiarly valuable education which a group receives when by search and criticism it finds and commissions its own leaders. The way in which this is done is at once the most elementary and the nicest problem of social growth. History is but the record of such group-leadership; and yet how infinitely changeful is its type and character! And of all types and kinds, what can be more instructive than the leadership of a group within a group?—that curious double movement where real progress may be negative and actual advance be relative retrogression. All this is the social student's inspiration and despair.

Now in the past the American Negro has had instructive experience in the choosing of group leaders, founding thus a peculiar dynasty which in the light of present conditions is worth while studying. When sticks and stones and beasts form the sole environment of a people, their attitude is largely one of determined opposition to and conquest of natural forces. But when to earth and brute is added an environment of men and ideas, then the attitude of the imprisoned group may take three main forms,—a feeling of revolt and revenge; an attempt to adjust all thought and action to the will of the greater group; or, finally, a determined effort at self-realization and self-development despite environing opinion. The influence of all of these attitudes at various times can be traced in the history of the American Negro, and in the evolution of his successive leaders.

Before 1750, while the fire of African freedom still burned in the veins of the slaves, there was in all leadership or attempted leadership but the one motive of revolt and revenge,—typified in the terrible Maroons, the Danish blacks, and Cato of Stono, and veiling all the Americas in fear of insurrection. The liberalizing tendencies of the latter half of the eighteenth century brought, along with kindlier relations between black and white, thoughts of ultimate adjustment and assimilation. Such aspiration was especially voiced in the earnest songs of Phyllis, in the martyrdom of Attucks, the fighting of Salem and Poor, the intellectual accomplishments of Banneker and Derham, and the political demands of the Cuffes.

Stern financial and social stress after the war cooled much of the previous humanitarian ardor. The disappointment and impatience of the Negroes at the persistence of slavery and serfdom voiced itself in two movements. The slaves in the South, aroused undoubtedly by vague rumors of the Haitian revolt, made three fierce attempts at insurrection,—in 1800 under Gabriel in Virginia, in 1822 under Vesey in Carolina, and in 1831 again in Virginia under the terrible Nat Turner. In the Free States, on the other hand, a new and curious attempt at self-development was made. In Philadelphia and New York color-prescription led to a withdrawal of Negro communicants from white churches and the formation of a peculiar socio-religious institution among the Negroes known as the African Church,—an organization still living and controlling in its various branches over a million of men.

Walker's wild appeal against the trend of the times showed how the world was changing after the coming of the cotton-gin. By 1830 slavery seemed hopelessly fastened on the South, and the slaves thoroughly cowed into submission. The free Negroes of the North, inspired by the mulatto immigrants from the West Indies, began to change the basis of their demands; they recognized the slavery of slaves, but insisted that they themselves were freemen, and sought assimilation and amalgamation with the nation on the same terms with other men. Thus, Forten and Purvis of Philadelphia, Shad of Wilmington, Du Bois of New Haven, Barbadoes of Boston, and others, strove singly and together as men, they said, not as slaves; as "people of color," not as "Negroes." The trend of the times, however, refused them recognition save in individual and exceptional cases, considered them as one with all the despised blacks, and they soon found themselves striving to keep even the rights they formerly had of voting and working and moving as freemen. Schemers of migration and colonization arose among them; but these they refused to entertain, and they eventually turned to the Abolition movement as a final refuge.

Here, led by Remond, Nell, Wells-Brown, and Douglass, a new period of self-assertion and self-development dawned. To be sure, ultimate freedom and assimilation was the ideal before the leaders, but the assertion of the manhood rights of the Negro by himself was the main reliance, and John Brown's raid was the extreme of its logic. After the war and emancipation, the great form of Frederick Douglass, the greatest of American Negro leaders, still led the host. Self-assertion, especially in political lines, was the main programme, and behind Douglass came Elliot, Bruce, and Langston, and the Reconstruction politicians, and, less conspicuous but of greater social significance Alexander Crummell and Bishop Daniel Payne.

Then came the Revolution of 1876, the suppression of the Negro votes, the changing and shifting of ideals, and the seeking of new lights in the great night. Douglass, in his old age, still bravely stood for the ideals of his early manhood,—ultimate assimilation *through* self-assertion, and on no other terms. For a time Price arose as a new leader, destined, it seemed, not to give up, but to re-state the old ideals in a form less repugnant to the white South. But he passed away in his prime. Then came the new leader. Nearly all the former ones had become leaders by the silent suffrage of their fellows, had sought to lead their own people alone, and were usually, save Douglass, little known outside their race. But Booker T. Washington arose as essentially the leader not of one race but of two, —a compromiser between the South, the North, and the Negro. Naturally the Negroes resented, at first bitterly, signs of compromise which surrendered their civil and political rights, even though this was to be exchanged for larger chances of economic development. The rich and dominating North, however, was not only weary of the race problem, but was investing largely in Southern enterprises, and welcomed any method of peaceful coöperation. Thus, by national opinion, the Negroes began to recognize Mr. Washington's leadership; and the voice of criticism was hushed.

Mr. Washington represents in Negro thought the old attitude of adjustment and submission; but adjustment at such a peculiar time as to make his programme unique. This is an age of unusual economic development, and Mr. Washington's programme naturally takes an economic cast, becoming a gospel of Work and Money to such an extent as apparently almost completely to overshadow the higher aims of life. Moreover, this is an age when the more advanced races are coming in closer contact with the less developed races, and the race-feeling is therefore intensified; and Mr. Washington's programme practically accepts the alleged inferiority of the Negro races. Again, in our own land, the reaction from the sentiment of war time has given impetus to race-prejudice against Negroes, and Mr. Washington withdraws many of the high demands of Negroes as men and American citizens. In other periods of intensified prejudice all the Negro's tendency to self-assertion has been called forth; at this period a policy of submission is advocated. In the history of nearly all other races and peoples the doctrine preached at such crises has been that manly self-respect is worth more than lands and houses, and that a people who voluntarily surrender such respect, or cease striving for it, are not worth civilizing.

In answer to this, it has been claimed that the Negro can survive only through submission. Mr. Washington distinctly asks that black people give up, at least for the present, three things,—

First, political power,

Second, insistence on civil rights,

Third, higher education of Negro youth,—

and concentrate all their energies on industrial education, the accumulation of wealth, and the conciliation of the South. This policy has been courageously and insistently advocated for over fifteen years, and has been triumphant for perhaps ten years. As a result of this tender of the palm-branch, what has been the return? In these years there have occurred:

1. The disfranchisement of the Negro.
2. The legal creation of a distinct status of civil inferiority for the Negro.
3. The steady withdrawal of aid from institutions for the higher training of the Negro.

These movements are not, to be sure, direct results of Mr. Washington's teachings; but his propaganda has, without a shadow of doubt, helped their speedier accomplishment. The question then comes: Is it possible, and probable, that nine millions of men can make effective progress in economic lines if they are deprived of political rights, made a servile caste, and allowed only the most meagre chance for developing their exceptional men? If history and reason give any distinct answer to these questions, it is an emphatic *No*. And Mr. Washington thus faces the triple paradox of his career:

1. He is striving nobly to make Negro artisans business men and property-owners; but it is utterly impossible, under modern competitive methods, for workingmen and property-owners to defend their rights and exist without the right of suffrage.
2. He insists on thrift and self-respect, but at the same time counsels a silent submission to civic inferiority such as is bound to sap the manhood of any race in the long run.
3. He advocates common-school and industrial training, and depreciates institutions of higher learning; but neither the Negro common-schools, nor Tuskegee itself, could remain open a day were it not for teachers trained in Negro colleges, or trained by their graduates.

This triple paradox in Mr. Washington's position is the object of criticism by two classes of colored Americans. One class is spiritually descended from Toussaint the Savior, through Gabriel, Vesey, and Turner, and they represent the attitude of revolt and revenge; they hate the white South blindly and distrust the white race generally, and so far as they agree on definite action, think that the Negro's only hope lies in emigration beyond the borders of the United States. And yet, by the irony of fate, nothing has more effectually made this programme seem hopeless than the recent course of the United States toward weaker and darker peoples in the West Indies, Hawaii, and the Philippines,—for where in the world may we go and be safe from lying and brute force?

The other class of Negroes who cannot agree with Mr. Washington has hitherto said little aloud. They deprecate the sight of scattered counsels, of internal disagreement; and especially they dislike making their just criticism of a useful and earnest man an excuse for a general discharge of venom from smallminded opponents. Nevertheless, the questions involved are so fundamental and serious that is is difficult to see how men like the Grimkes, Kelly Miller, J. W. E. Bowen, and other representatives of this group, can much longer be silent. Such men feel in conscience bound to ask of this nation three things:

1. The right to vote.
2. Civic equality.
3. The education of youth according to ability.

They acknowledge Mr. Washington's invaluable service in counselling patience and courtesy in such demands; they do not ask that ignorant black men vote when ignorant whites are debarred, or that any reasonable restrictions in the suffrage should not be applied; they know that the low social level of the mass of the race is responsible for much discrimination against it, but they also know, and the nation knows, that relentless color-prejudice is more often a cause than a result of the Negro's degradation; they seek the abatement of this relic of barbarism, and not its systematic encouragement and pampering by all agencies of social power from the Associated Press to the Church of Christ. They advocate, with Mr. Washington, a broad system of Negro common schools supplemented by thorough industrial training; but they are surprised that a man of Mr. Washington's insight cannot see that no such educational system ever has rested or can rest on any other basis than that of the well-equipped college and university, and they insist that there is a demand for a few such institutions throughout the South to train the best of the Negro youth as teachers, professional men, and leaders.

This group of men honor Mr. Washington for his attitude of conciliation toward the white South; they accept the "Atlanta Compromise" in its broadest interpretation; they recognize, with him, many signs of promise, many men of high purpose and fair judgment, in this section; they know that no easy task has been laid upon a region already tottering under heavy burdens. But, nevertheless, they insist that the way to truth and right lies in straightforward honesty, not in indiscriminate flattery; in praising those of the South who do well and criticising uncompromisingly those who do ill; in taking advantage of the opportunities at hand and urging their fellows to do the same, but at the same time in remembering that only a firm adherence to their higher ideals and aspirations will ever keep those ideals within the realm of possibility. They do not expect that the free right to vote, to enjoy civic rights, and to be educated, will come in a moment; they do not expect to see the bias and prejudices of years disappear at the blast of a trumpet; but they are absolutely certain that the way for a people to gain their reasonable rights is not by voluntarily throwing them away and insisting that they do not want them; that the way for a people to gain respect is not by continually belittling and ridiculing themselves; that, on the contrary, Negroes must insist continually, in season and out of season, that voting is necessary to modern manhood, that color discrimination is barbarism, and that black boys need education as well as white boys.

In failing thus to state plainly and unequivocally the legitimate demands of their people, even at the cost of opposing an honored leader, the thinking classes of American Negroes would shirk a heavy responsibility,—a responsibility to themselves, a responsibility to the struggling masses, a responsibility to the darker races of men whose future depends so largely on this American experiment, but especially a responsibility to this nation,—this common Fatherland. It is wrong to encourage a man or a people in evil-doing; it is wrong to aid and abet a national crime simply because it is unpopular not to do so. The growing spirit of kindliness and reconciliation between the North and South after the frightful difference of a generation ago ought to be a source of deep congratulation to all, and especially to those whose mistreatment caused the war; but if that reconciliation is to be marked by the industrial slavery and civic death of those same black men, with permanent legislation into a position of inferiority, then those black men, if they are really men, are called upon by every consideration of patriotism and loyalty to oppose such a course by all civilized methods, even though such opposition involves disagreement with Mr. Booker T. Washington. We have no right to sit silently by while the inevitable seeds are sown for a harvest of disaster to our children, black and white.

First, it is the duty of black men to judge the South discriminatingly. The present generation of Southerners are not responsible for the past, and they should not be blindly hated or blamed for it. Furthermore, to no class is the indiscriminate endorsement of the recent course of the South toward Negroes more nauseating than to the best thought of the South. The South is not "solid"; it is a land in the ferment of social change, wherein forces of all kinds are fighting for supremacy; and to praise the ill the South is to-day perpetrating is just as wrong as to condemn the good. Discriminating and broad-minded criticism is what the South needs,—needs it for the sake of her own white sons and daughters, and for the insurance of robust, healthy mental and moral development.

To-day even the attitude of the Southern whites toward the blacks is not, as so many assume, in all cases the same; the ignorant Southerner hates the Negro, the workingmen fear his competition, the money-makers wish to use him as a laborer, some of the educated see a menace in his upward development, while others—usually the sons of the masters—wish to help him to rise. National opinion has enabled this last class to maintain the Negro common schools, and to protect the Negro partially in property, life, and limb. Through the pressure of the money-makers, the Negro is in danger of being reduced to semi-slavery, especially in the country districts; the workingmen, and those of the educated who fear the Negro, have united to disfranchise him, and some have urged his deportation; while the passions of the ignorant are easily aroused to lynch and abuse any black man. To praise this intricate whirl of thought and prejudice is nonsense; to inveigh indiscriminately against "the South" is unjust; but to use the same breath in praising Governor Aycock, exposing Senator Morgan, arguing with Mr. Thomas Nelson Page, and denouncing Senator Ben Tillman, is not only sane, but the imperative duty of thinking black men.

It would be unjust to Mr. Washington not to acknowledge that in several instances he has opposed movements in the South which were unjust to the Negro; he sent memorials to the Louisiana and Alabama constitutional conventions, he has spoken against lynching, and in other ways has openly or silently set his influence against sinister schemes and unfortunate happenings. Notwithstanding this, it is equally true to assert that on the whole the distinct impression left by Mr. Washington's propaganda is, first, that the South is justified in its present attitude toward the Negro because of the Negro's degradation; secondly, that the prime cause of the Negro's failure to rise more quickly is his wrong education in the past; and, thirdly, that his future rise depends primarily on his own efforts. Each of these propositions is a dangerous half-truth. The supplementary truths must never be lost sight of: first, slavery and race-prejudice are potent if not sufficient causes of the Negro's position; second, industrial and common-school training were necessarily slow in planting because they had to await the black teachers trained by higher institutions,—it being extremely doubtful if any essentially different development was possible, and certainly a Tuskegee was unthinkable before 1880; and, third, while it is a great truth to say that the Negro must strive and strive mightily to help himself, it is equally true that unless his striving be not simply seconded, but rather aroused and encouraged, by the initiative of the richer and wiser environing group, he cannot hope for great success.

In his failure to realize and impress this last point, Mr. Washington is especially to be criticised. His doctrine has tended to make the whites, North and South, shift the burden of the Negro problem to the Negro's shoulders and stand aside as critical and rather pessimistic spectators; when in fact the burden belongs to the nation, and the hands of none of us are clean if we bend not our energies to righting these great wrongs.

The South ought to be led, by candid and honest criticism, to assert her better self and do her full duty to the race she has cruelly wronged and is still wronging. The North—her co-partner in guilt—cannot salve her conscience by plastering it with gold. We cannot settle this problem by diplomacy and suaveness, by "policy" alone. If worse comes to worst, can the moral fibre of this country survive the slow throttling and murder of nine millions of men?

The black men of America have a duty to perform, a duty stern and delicate,—a forward movement to oppose a part of the work of their greatest leader. So far as Mr. Washington preaches Thrift, Patience, and Industrial Training for the masses, we must hold up his hands and strive with him, rejoicing in his honors and glorying in the strength of this Joshua called of God and of man to lead the headless host. But so far as Mr. Washington apologizes for injustice, North or South, does not rightly value the privilege and duty of voting, belittles the emasculating effects of caste distinctions, and opposes the higher training and ambition of our brighter minds,—so far as he, the South, or the Nation, does this,—we must unceasingly and firmly oppose them. By every civilized and peaceful method we must strive for the rights which the world accords to men, clinging unwaveringly to those great words which the sons of the Fathers would fain forget: "We hold these truths to be self-evident: That all men are created equal; that they are endowed by their Creator with certain unalienable rights; that among these are life, liberty, and the pursuit of happiness."

IV Early Poetry, Fiction, and Criticism

The epoch that saw the rise of Paul Laurence Dunbar, Charles Chesnutt, Benjamin Brawley, W. E. B. Du Bois, and James Weldon Johnson was not a peaceful time shot through with nostalgia and infinite progress. For the black American the battles raged on many fronts. There was the quest for education as black denominational schools began to appear in increasing numbers; there was the fight against the racist policies of the Woodrow Wilson administration; and there was the turmoil, effort, and agony of World War I. The black American, however, did stride forward in the first two decades of the twentieth century, and black literature, as Benjamin Brawley pointed out, reached a mature stage.

The most notable black literary figure during the early years of the century was, without a doubt, Paul Laurence Dunbar. Dunbar's poetry enjoyed widespread popularity, and it received the acclaim of William Dean Howells, the foremost critic in turn-of-the-century America. Writing in both dialect and standard literary English, Dunbar managed to capture the humor, pathos, and aspiration of a struggling people. Moreover, he was able to express in a number of poems the great optimism that pervaded the dawning of a new century. Though the poet is often criticized for his "artificiality" and "romantic nostalgia" (after the school of Joel Chandler Harris and Thomas Nelson Page), an objective look at Dunbar's canon is enough to refute some of the charges leveled against him. Dunbar is often too rhetorical, but in a poem like "Ships That Pass in the Night," or in an effort like "Not They Who Soar," we can see standard literary English brought to a point of high lyrical intensity and far short of the realms of bombast. Again, in a poem like "Dawn," we can see Dunbar at his simplistic, mythologizing best; the poem is beautiful without being artificial or overly saccharine. A great number of poems that Dunbar wrote in standard literary English deserve more praise than they have received, and this is particularly true if we regard the state of American poetry as a whole during the age of Dunbar.

It is as a folk poet, however, that Dunbar stands out; and surely it is impossible to write off America's first outstanding black poet as a simple imitator of the dialect tradition, a man who wrote in antebellum language with antebellum values. While it is true that in a poem like "Chrismus on the Plantation" Dunbar showed black southerners preferring the plantation to the world, it is also true that in poems like "The Party," "The Spelling Bee," and "When the Colored Band Comes Marching Down the Street" Dunbar managed to capture the communal love, humor, strength, and devotion that unite black people. And in a poem like "Scamp," Dunbar captures childhood in its essence, no matter what the age or the country. Moreover, in "When Malindy Sings" the poet raises the black American's gift of song to a cosmic and etherealized plane; Malindy's singing and the voice of God, or that which is ultimately spiritual, become one. If Dunbar turned irony on his own people, it was an overwhelming irony of love. The poet may have aspired toward the white stars, but he managed to capture the folk and the concerns of the soil in his journeying. And the militant and tortured voice of protest is heard in poems like "Philosophy," "The Real Question," and "We Wear the Mask." Dunbar, to a greater extent than any of his poetic contemporaries, was able to capture the restlessness, humor, joy, and pain of a people on the move. His optimism may have been unwarranted, and he may have fallen into the great American trap of sentimentality more than once, but his efforts in both verse and prose were often successes on an elevated scale.

Success was also the measure of Charles Chesnutt, the first black American fiction writer of distinction. Chesnutt was the first black American to have short fiction accepted by *The Atlantic,* and his first two volumes of short stories reveal a masterful craftsman at work. Chesnutt's stories offer a blend of folk realism, humor, irony, and satire; and it is difficult to find a Chesnutt story that one can unequivocally label as "bad." It is quite easy to denote a number of his stories that are unqualified successes. "The Goophered Grapevine," "The Bouquet," and "A Matter of Principle" would stand well in any company. Chesnutt possessed a good deal of Swiftian objectivity, and in his prose he turned his barbs toward black and white alike. While he denounced with scathing irony the school of Harris, Page, and others, he was also able to turn his satirical humor upon the foibles and pretensions of the "blue vein" societies among his own people. Chesnutt's novels tend to be overly polemical, but in his short stories he handles language, symbol, and wit with consummate skill.

The work of W. E. B. Du Bois—both literary and social—took on new meaning in an age that saw the rebirth of the Ku Klux Klan and the swelling of its membership to the millions. In 1905, Du Bois, along with William Monroe Trotter, had launched the Niagara Movement designed to bring about the equality of the black American. The Niagara Movement passed rather ineffectively from the scene, but in its place there grew the National Association for the Advancement of Colored People. With Du Bois at the helm of its chief organ, *Crisis,* the association moved into a leadership position in the black American's struggle. While editor of *Crisis,* Du Bois published his resonantly bitter poem "The Sphinx" and the angry and militant effort titled "A Litany at Atlanta" along with several other notable efforts that were to appear in *Darkwater* (1920). Du Bois's creative talents also found outlet in a number of fine essays and in his novel *The Quest of the Silver Fleece* (1911).

As an editor, Du Bois gave the public the prose works of Jessie Fauset, Charles Chesnutt, and Benjamin Brawley as well as the poetry of Fenton Johnson, James Weldon Johnson, Stanley Braithewaite, and Georgia Douglas Johnson. Three of these notable names in the black literary tradition stand out for our consideration: two of the Johnsons and Benjamin Brawley. Fenton Johnson produced four volumes of poetry during his lifetime, and while he did not capture the folk tradition with any degree of skill in his dialect poems, he did manage to express a new mood of militancy and despair in several of his poems in standard literary English. James Weldon Johnson was an incomparably better poet than Fenton Johnson, and in two of the poems from his 1917 volume, *Fifty Years,* he manifests the new sense of pride that the black American was beginning to show;

"O Black and Unknown Bards" and "The Black Mammy" are finely wrought expressions of race-consciousness and pride. And in his novel, *The Autobiography of an Ex-Colored Man* (1912), James Weldon Johnson managed to capture the pains of the black American's ambivalent position behind "the Veil." In Benjamin Brawley's *The Negro in Literature and Art in the United States* (1910, rev. 1918, rev. 1929), we see another expression of the black American's new consciousness of his contributions to the world. Brawley deals with the black American's creative genius in its many forms, and he comes down hard on those who would deny the black man's outstanding role in the history of American arts and letters.

The first two decades of the twentieth century, therefore, mark the coming of age of black American literature; the creative and critical works produced by black writers in the early years of the century offer a number of examples of skilled craftsmanship, telling analysis, and surpassing beauty. Dunbar, Chesnutt, and Johnson, along with a number of other black writers, partook of the spirit of their age; they stretched forth toward a new world in a new century, and their contributions—in both theme and technique—provided an adequate foundation of conscious literary expression for the growth of black literature in the twentieth century.

REFERENCES

Brawley, Benjamin: *Paul Laurence Dunbar, Poet of His People,* University of North Carolina Press, Chapel Hill, 1936.
————: *The Negro in Literature and Art in the United States,* Duffield and Company, New York, 1918. (Contains chapters on Dunbar, Chesnutt, and Du Bois and critical material on James Weldon Johnson.)
Brown, Sterling: *Negro Poetry and Drama,* Atheneum, New York, 1969.
————: *The Negro in American Fiction,* Atheneum, New York, 1969.
Chesnutt, Helen M.: *Charles Waddell Chesnutt: Pioneer of the Color Line,* University of North Carolina Press, Chapel Hill, 1952.
Cunningham, Virginia: *Paul Laurence Dunbar and His Song,* Dodd, Mead and Company, New York, 1947.
Lawson, Victor: *Dunbar Critically Examined,* Associated Publishers, Washington, D. C., 1941.
Loggins, Vernon: *The Negro Author and His Development in America,* Columbia University Press, New York, 1931.
Redding, J. Saunders: *To Make a Poet Black,* University of North Carolina Press, Chapel Hill, 1939.
Tate, Ernest Cater: *The Social Implications of the Writings and the Career of James Weldon Johnson,* The American Press, New York, 1968.
Terry, Ellen: *Young Jim: the Early Years of James Weldon Johnson,* Dodd, Mead and Company, New York, 1967.
Thorpe, Earl Endris: *Negro Historians in the United States,* Fraternal Press, Baton Rouge, 1958. (pp. 38–40 deal with Brawley.)

Paul Laurence Dunbar

Philosophy

I been t'inkin' 'bout de preachah; whut he said de othah night,
  'Bout hit bein' people's dooty, fu' to keep dey faces bright;
How one ought to live so pleasant dat ouah tempah never riles,
  Meetin' evahbody roun' us wid ouah very nicest smiles.

Dat 's all right, I ain't a-sputin' not a t'ing dat soun's lak fac',
  But you don't ketch folks a-grinnin' wid a misery in de back;
An' you don't fin' dem a-smilin' w'en dey's hongry ez kin be,
  Leastways, dat 's how human natur' allus seems to 'pear to me.

We is mos' all putty likely fu' to have our little cares,
  An' I think we 'se doin' fus' rate w'en we jes' go long and bears,
Widout breakin' up ouah faces in a sickly so't o' grin,
  W'en we knows dat in ouah innards we is p'intly mad ez sin.

Oh dey 's times fu' bein' pleasant an' fu' goin' smilin' roun',
  'Cause I don't believe in people allus totin' roun' a frown,
But it 's easy 'nough to titter w'en de stew is smokin' hot,
  But hit 's mighty ha'd to giggle w'en dey 's nuffin' in de pot.

Jealous

Hyeah come Cæsar Higgins,
Don't he think he 's fine?
Look at dem new riggin's
Ain't he tryin' to shine?
Got a standin' collar
An' a stove-pipe hat,
I 'll jes' bet a dollar
Some one gin him dat.

Don't one o' you mention,
Nothin' 'bout his cloes,
Don't pay no attention,
Er let on you knows
Dat he 's got 'em on him,
Why, 't 'll mek him sick,
Jes go on an' sco'n him,
My, ain't dis a trick!

Look hyeah, whut 's he doin'
Lookin' t' othah way?
Dat ere move 's a new one,
Some one call him, "Say!"
Can't you see no pusson—
Puttin' on you' airs,
Sakes alive, you 's wuss'n
Dese hyeah millionaires.

Need n't git so flighty,
Case you got dat suit.
Dem cloes ain't so mighty,—
Second hand to boot,
I 's a-tryin' to spite you!
Full of jealousy!
Look hyeah, man, I'll fight you,
Don't you fool wid me!

Slow through the Dark

Slow moves the pageant of a climbing race;
    Their footsteps drag far, far below the height,
    And, unprevailing by their utmost might,
Seem faltering downward from each hard won place.
No strange, swift-sprung exception we; we trace
    A devious way thro' dim, uncertain light,—
    Our hope, through the long vistaed years, a sight
Of that our Captain's soul sees face to face.
    Who, faithless, faltering that the road is steep,
Now raiseth up his drear insistent cry?
    Who stoppeth here to spend a while in sleep
Or curseth that the storm obscures the sky?
    Heed not the darkness round you, dull and deep;
The clouds grow thickest when the summit's nigh.

Not They Who Soar

Not they who soar, but they who plod
Their rugged way, unhelped, to God
Are heroes; they who higher fare,
And, flying, fan the upper air,
Miss all the toil that hugs the sod.

'Tis they whose backs have felt the rod,
Whose feet have pressed the path unshod,
May smile upon defeated care,
    Not they who soar.

High up there are no thorns to prod,
Nor boulders lurking 'neath the clod
To turn the keenness of the share,
For flight is ever free and rare;
But heroes they the soil who've trod,
    Not they who soar!

When Malindy Sings

G'way an' quit dat noise, Miss Lucy—
    Put dat music book away;
What 's de use to keep on tryin'?
    Ef you practise twell you 're gray,
You cain't sta't no notes a-flyin'
    Lak de ones dat rants and rings
F'om de kitchen to be big woods
    When Malindy sings.

You ain't got de nachel o'gans
    Fu' to make de soun' come right,
You ain't got de tu'ns an' twistin's
    Fu' to make it sweet an' light.
Tell you one thing now, Miss Lucy,
    An' I'm tellin' you fu' true,
When hit comes to raal right singin',
    'T ain't no easy thing to do.

Easy 'nough fu' folks to hollah,
    Lookin' at de lines an' dots,
When dey ain't no one kin sence it,
    An' de chune comes in, in spots;
But fu' real melojous music,
    Dat jes' strikes yo' hea't and clings,
Jes' you stan' an' listen wif me
    When Malindy sings.

Ain't you nevah hyeahd Malindy?
    Blessed soul, tek up de cross!

Look hyeah, ain't you jokin', honey?
  Well, you don't know whut you los'.
Y' ought to hyeah dat gal a-wa'blin',
  Robins, la'ks, an' all dem things,
Heish dey moufs an' hides dey faces
  When Malindy sings.

Fiddlin' man jes' stop his fiddlin',
  Lay his fiddle on de she'f;
Mockin'-bird quit tryin' to whistle,
  'Cause he jes' so shamed hisse'f.
Folks a-playin' on de banjo
  Draps dey fingahs on de strings—
Bless yo' soul—fu'gits to move em,
  When Malindy sings.

She jes' spreads huh mouf and hollahs,
  "Come to Jesus," twell you hyeah
Sinnahs' tremblin' steps and voices,
  Timid-lak a-drawin' neah;
Den she tu'ns to "Rock of Ages,"
  Simply to de cross she clings,
An' you fin' yo' teahs a-drappin'
  When Malindy sings.

Who dat says dat humble praises
  Wif de Master nevah counts?
Heish yo' mouf, I hyeah dat music,
  Ez hit rises up an' mounts—
Floatin' by de hills an' valleys,
  Way above dis buryin' sod,
Ez hit makes its way in glory
  To de very gates of God!

Oh, hit 's sweetah dan de music
  Of an edicated band;
An' hit 's dearah dan de battle's
  Song o' triumph in de lan'.
It seems holier dan evenin'
  When de solemn chu'ch bell rings,
Ez I sit an' ca'mly listen
  While Malindy sings.

Towsah, stop dat ba'kin', hyeah me!
 Mandy, mek dat chile keep still;
Don't you hyeah de echoes callin'
 F'om de valley to de hill?
Let me listen, I can hyeah it,
 Th'oo de bresh of angels' wings,
Sof' an' sweet, "Swing Low, Sweet Chariot,"
 Ez Malindy sings.

Scamp

Ain't it nice to have a mammy
 W'en you kin' o' tiahed out
Wid a-playin' in de meddah,
 An' a-runnin' roun' about
Till hit's made you mighty hongry,
 An' yo' nose hit gits to know
What de smell means dat 's a-comin'
 F'om de open cabin do'?
  She wash yo' face,
  An' mek yo' place,
 You's hongry as a tramp;
Den hit's eat you suppah right away,
 You sta'vin' little scamp.

W'en you's full o' braid an' bacon,
 An' dey ain't no mo' to eat,
An' de lasses dat's a-stickin'
 On yo' face ta'se kin' o' sweet,
Don' you t'ink hit's kin' o' pleasin'
 Fu' to have som'body neah
Dat'll wipe yo' han's an' kiss you
 Fo' dey lif' you f'om you' cheah?
  To smile so sweet,
  An' wash yo' feet,
 An' leave 'em co'l an' damp;
Den hit's come let me undress you, now
 You lazy little scamp.

Don' yo' eyes git awful heavy,
 An' yo' lip git awful slack,

Ain't dey som'p'n' kin' o' weaknin'
  In de backbone of yo' back?
Don' yo' knees feel kin' o' trimbly,
  An' yo' head go bobbin' roun',
W'en you says yo' "Now I lay me,"
  An' is sno'in on de "down"?
    She kiss yo' nose,
    She kiss yo' toes,
  An' den tu'n out de lamp,
Den hit's creep into yo' trunnel baid,
  You sleepy little scamp.

Why Fades a Dream?

Why fades a dream?
  An iridescent ray
Flecked in between the tryst
  Of night and day.
  Why fades a dream?—
Of consciousness the shade
Wrought out by lack of light and made
  Upon life's stream.
  Why fades a dream?

That thought may thrive,
  So fades the fleshless dream;
Lest men should learn to trust
  The things that seem.
  So fades a dream,
That living thought may grow
And like a waxing star-beam glow
  Upon life's stream—
  So fades a dream.

We Wear the Mask

We wear the mask that grins and lies,
It hides our cheeks and shades our eyes,—
This debt we pay to human guile;
With torn and bleeding hearts we smile,
And mouth with myriad subtleties.

Why should the world be overwise,
In counting all our tears and sighs?
Nay, let them only see us, while
　　We wear the mask.

We smile, but, O great Christ, our cries
To thee from tortured souls arise.
We sing, but oh the clay is vile
Beneath our feet, and long the mile;
But let the world dream otherwise,
　　We wear the mask!

The Real Question

Folks is talkin' 'bout de money, 'bout de silvah an' de gold;
All de time de season 's changin' an' de days is gittin' cold.
An' dey 's wond'rin' 'bout de metals, whethah we'll have one er
　　two.
While de price o' coal is risin' an' dey 's two months' rent dat 's
　　due.

Some folks says dat gold 's de only money dat is wuff de name,
Den de othahs rise an' tell 'em dat dey ought to be ashame,
An' dat silvah is de only thing to save us f'om de powah
Of de gold-bug ragin' 'roun' an' seekin' who he may devowah.

Well, you folks kin keep on shoutin' wif yo' gold er silvah cry,
But I tell you people hams is sceerce an' fowls is roostin' high.
An' hit ain't de so't o' money dat is pesterin' my min',
But de question I want answehed 's how to get at any kin'!

Charles W. Chesnutt (1858-1932)

The Bouquet

Mary Myrover's friends were somewhat surprised when she began to teach a
colored school. Miss Myrover's friends are mentioned here, because nowhere
more than in a Southern town is public opinion a force which cannot be lightly

contravened. Public opinion, however, did not oppose Miss Myrover's teaching colored children; in fact, all the colored public schools in town—and there were several—were taught by white teachers, and had been so taught since the State had undertaken to provide free public instruction for all children within its boundaries. Previous to that time, there had been a Freedman's Bureau school and a Presbyterian missionary school, but these had been withdrawn when the need for them became less pressing. The colored people of the town had been for some time agitating their right to teach their own schools, but as yet the claim had not been conceded.

The reason Miss Myrover's course created some surprise was not, therefore, the fact that a Southern white woman should teach a colored school; it lay in the fact that up to this time no woman of just her quality had taken up such work. Most of the teachers of colored schools were not of those who had constituted the aristocracy of the old régime; they might be said rather to represent the new order of things, in which labor was in time to become honorable, and men were, after a somewhat longer time, to depend, for their place in society, upon themselves rather than upon their ancestors. Mary Myrover belonged to one of the proudest of the old families. Her ancestors had been people of distinction in Virginia before a collateral branch of the main stock had settled in North Carolina. Before the war, they had been able to live up to their pedigree; but the war brought sad changes. Miss Myrover's father—the Colonel Myrover who led a gallant but desperate charge at Vicksburg—had fallen on the battlefield, and his tomb in the white cemetery was a shrine for the family. On the Confederate Memorial Day, no other grave was so profusely decorated with flowers, and, in the oration pronounced, the name of Colonel Myrover was always used to illustrate the highest type of patriotic devotion and self-sacrifice. Miss Myrover's brother, too, had fallen in the conflict; but his bones lay in some unknown trench, with those of a thousand others who had fallen on the same field. Ay, more, her lover, who had hoped to come home in the full tide of victory and claim his bride as a reward for gallantry, had shared the fate of her father and brother. When the war was over, the remnant of the family found itself involved in the common ruin,—more deeply involved, indeed, than some others; for Colonel Myrover had believed in the ultimate triumph of his cause, and had invested most of his wealth in Confederate bonds, which were now only so much waste paper.

There had been a little left. Mrs. Myrover was thrifty, and had laid by a few hundred dollars, which she kept in the house to meet unforeseen contingencies. There remained, too, their home, with an ample garden and a well-stocked orchard, besides a considerable tract of country land, partly cleared, but productive of very little revenue.

With their shrunken resources, Miss Myrover and her mother were able to hold up their heads without embarrassment for some years after the close of the war. But when things were adjusted to the changed conditions, and the stream of life began to flow more vigorously in the new channels, they saw themselves in danger of dropping behind, unless in some way they could add to their meagre income. Miss Myrover looked over the field of employment, never very wide for women in the South, and found it occupied. The only available position she could be supposed prepared to fill, and which she could take without distinct loss of caste, was that of a teacher, and there was no vacancy except in one of the colored schools. Even teaching was a doubtful experiment; it was not what she would have preferred, but it was the best that could be done.

"I don't like it, Mary," said her mother. "It's a long step from owning such people to teaching them. What do they need with education? It will only make them unfit for work."

"They're free now, mother, and perhaps they'll work better if they're taught something. Besides, it's only a business arrangement, and doesn't involve any closer contact than we have with our servants."

"Well, I should say not!" sniffed the old lady. "Not one of them will ever dare to presume on your position to take any liberties with us. *I'll* see to that."

Miss Myrover began her work as a teacher in the autumn, at the opening of the school year. It was a novel experience at first. Though there had always been negro servants in the house, and though on the streets colored people were more numerous than those of her own race, and though she was so familiar with their dialect that she might almost be said to speak it, barring certain characteristic grammatical inaccuracies, she had never been brought in personal contact with so many of them at once as when she confronted the fifty or sixty faces—of colors ranging from a white almost as clear as her own to the darkest livery of the sun—which were gathered in the schoolroom on the morning when she began her duties. Some of the inherited prejudice of her caste, too, made itself felt, though she tried to repress any outward sign of it; and she could perceive that the children were not altogether responsive; they, likewise, were not entirely free from antagonism. The work was unfamiliar to her. She was not physically very strong, and at the close of the first day went home with a splitting headache. If she could have resigned then and there without causing comment or annoyance to others, she would have felt it a privilege to do so. But a night's rest banished her headache and improved her spirits, and the next morning she went to her work with renewed vigor, fortified by the experience of the first day.

Miss Myrover's second day was more satisfactory. She had some natural talent for organization, though hitherto unaware of it, and in the course of the day she got her classes formed and lessons under way. In a week or two she began to classify her pupils in her own mind, as bright or stupid, mischievous or well behaved, lazy or industrious, as the case might be, and to regulate her discipline accordingly. That she had come of a long line of ancestors who had exercised authority and mastership was perhaps not without its effect upon her character, and enabled her more readily to maintain good order in the school. When she was fairly broken in, she found the work rather to her liking, and derived much pleasure from such success as she achieved as a teacher.

It was natural that she should be more attracted to some of her pupils than to others. Perhaps her favorite—or, rather, the one she liked best, for she was too fair and just for conscious favoritism—was Sophy Tucker. Just the ground for the teacher's liking for Sophy might not at first be apparent. The girl was far from the whitest of Miss Myrover's pupils; in fact, she was one of the darker ones. She was not the brightest in intellect, though she always tried to learn her lessons. She was not the best dressed, for her mother was a poor widow, who went out washing and scrubbing for a living. Perhaps the real tie between them was Sophy's intense devotion to the teacher. It had manifested itself almost from the first day of the school, in the rapt look of admiration Miss Myrover always saw on the little black face turned toward her. In it there was nothing of envy, nothing of regret; nothing but worship for the beautiful white lady—she was not especially handsome, but to Sophy her beauty was almost divine—who had come to teach her. If Miss Myrover dropped a book, Sophy was the first to spring and pick it up; if she wished a chair moved, Sophy seemed to anticipate her wish; and so of all the numberless little services that can be rendered in a schoolroom.

Miss Myrover was fond of flowers, and liked to have them about her. The children soon learned of this taste of hers, and kept the vases on her desk filled with blossoms during their season. Sophy was perhaps the most active in providing them. If she could not get garden flowers, she would make excursions to the woods in the early morning, and bring in great dew-laden bunches of bay, or jasmine, or some other fragrant forest flower which she knew the teacher loved.

"When I die, Sophy," Miss Myrover said to the child one day, "I want to be covered with roses. And when they bury me, I'm sure I shall rest better if my grave is banked with flowers, and roses are planted at my head and at my feet."

Miss Myrover was at first amused at Sophy's devotion; but when she grew more accustomed to it, she found it rather to her liking. It had a sort of flavor of the old régime, and she felt, when she bestowed her kindly notice upon her little black attendant, some of the feudal condescension of the mistress toward the slave. She was kind to Sophy, and permitted her to play the rôle she had assumed, which caused sometimes a little jealousy among the other girls. Once she gave Sophy a yellow ribbon which she took from her own hair. The child carried it home, and cherished it as a priceless treasure, to be worn only on the greatest occasions.

Sophy had a rival in her attachment to the teacher, but the rivalry was altogether friendly. Miss Myrover had a little dog, a white spaniel, answering to the name of Prince. Prince was a dog of high degree, and would have very little to do with the children of the school; he made an exception, however, in the case of Sophy, whose devotion for his mistress he seemed to comprehend. He was a clever dog, and could fetch and carry, sit up on his haunches, extend his paw to shake hands, and possessed several other canine accomplishments. He was very fond of his mistress, and always, unless shut up at home, accompanied her to school, where he spent most of his time lying under the teacher's desk, or, in cold weather, by the stove, except when he would go out now and then and chase an imaginary rabbit round the yard, presumably for exercise.

At school Sophy and Prince vied with each other in their attentions to Miss Myrover. But when school was over, Prince went away with her, and Sophy stayed behind; for Miss Myrover was white and Sophy was black, which they both understood perfectly well. Miss Myrover taught the colored children, but she could not be seen with them in public. If they occasionally met her on the street, they did not expect her to speak to them, unless she happened to be alone and no other white person was in sight. If any of the children felt slighted, she was not aware of it, for she intended no slight; she had not been brought up to speak to negroes on the street, and she could not act differently from other people. And though she was a woman of sentiment and capable of deep feeling, her training had been such that she hardly expected to find in those of darker hue than herself the same susceptibility—varying in degree, perhaps, but yet the same in kind—that gave to her own life the alternations of feeling that made it most worth living.

Once Miss Myrover wished to carry home a parcel of books. She had the bundle in her hand when Sophy came up.

"Lemme tote yo' bundle fer yer, Miss Ma'y?" she asked eagerly. "I'm gwine yo' way."

"Thank you, Sophy," was the reply. "I'll be glad if you will."

Sophy followed the teacher at a respectful distance. When they reached Miss Myrover's home, Sophy carried the bundle to the doorstep, where Miss Myrover took it and thanked her.

Mrs. Myrover came out on the piazza as Sophy was moving away. She said, in the child's hearing, and perhaps with the intention that she should hear: "Mary, I wish you wouldn't let those little darkeys follow you to the house. I don't want them in the yard. I should think you'd have enough of them all day."

"Very well, mother," replied her daughter. "I won't bring any more of them. The child was only doing me a favor."

Mrs. Myrover was an invalid, and opposition or irritation of any kind brought on nervous paroxysms that made her miserable, and made life a burden to the rest of the household, so that Mary seldom crossed her whims. She did not bring Sophy to the house again, nor did Sophy again offer her services as porter.

One day in spring Sophy brought her teacher a bouquet of yellow roses.

"Dey come off'n my own bush, Miss Ma'y," she said proudly, "an' I did n' let nobody e'se pull 'em, but saved 'em all fer you, 'cause I know you likes roses so much. I 'm gwine bring 'em all ter you as long as dey las'."

"Thank you, Sophy," said the teacher; "you are a very good girl."

For another year Mary Myrover taught the colored school, and did excellent service. The children made rapid progress under her tuition, and learned to love her well; for they saw and appreciated, as well as children could, her fidelity to a trust that she might have slighted, as some others did, without much fear of criticism. Toward the end of her second year she sickened, and after a brief illness died.

Old Mrs. Myrover was inconsolable. She ascribed her daughter's death to her labors as teacher of negro children. Just how the color of the pupils had produced the fatal effects she did not stop to explain. But she was too old, and had suffered too deeply from the war, in body and mind and estate, ever to reconcile herself to the changed order of things following the return of peace; and, with an unsound yet perfectly explainable logic, she visited some of her displeasure upon those who had profited most, though passively, by her losses.

"I always feared something would happen to Mary," she said. "It seemed unnatural for her to be wearing herself out teaching little negroes who ought to have been working for her. But the world has hardly been a fit place to live in since the war, and when I follow her, as I must before long, I shall not be sorry to go."

She gave strict orders that no colored people should be admitted to the house. Some of her friends heard of this, and remonstrated. They knew the teacher was loved by the pupils, and felt that sincere respect from the humble would be a worthy tribute to the proudest. But Mrs. Myrover was obdurate.

"They had my daughter when she was alive," she said, "and they've killed her. But she's mine now, and I won't have them come near her. I don't want one of them at the funeral or anywhere around."

For a month before Miss Myrover's death Sophy had been watching her rosebush—the one that bore the yellow roses—for the first buds of spring, and, when these appeared, had awaited impatiently their gradual unfolding. But not until her teacher's death had they become full-blown roses. When Miss Myrover died, Sophy determined to pluck the roses and lay them on her coffin. Perhaps, she thought, they might even put them in her hand or on her breast. For Sophy remembered Miss Myrover's thanks and praise when she had brought her the yellow roses the spring before.

On the morning of the day set for the funeral, Sophy washed her face until it shone, combed and brushed her hair with painful conscientiousness, put on her best frock, plucked her yellow roses, and, tying them with the treasured ribbon her teacher had given her, set out for Miss Myrover's home.

She went round to the side gate—the house stood on a corner—and stole up the path to the kitchen. A colored woman, whom she did not know, came to the door.

"W'at yer want, chile?" she inquired.

"Kin I see Miss Ma'y?" asked Sophy timidly.

"I don't know, honey. Ole Miss Myrover say she don't want no cullud folks roun' de house endyoin' dis fun'al. I'll look an' see if she 's roun' de front room, whar de co'pse is. You sed down heah an' keep still, an' ef she 's upstairs maybe

I kin git yer in dere a minute. Ef I can't, I kin put yo' bokay 'mongs' de res', whar she won't know nuthin' erbout it."

A moment after she had gone, there was a step in the hall, and old Mrs. Myrover came into the kitchen.

"Dinah!" she said in a peevish tone; "Dinah!"

Receiving no answer, Mrs. Myrover peered around the kitchen, and caught sight of Sophy.

"What are you doing here?" she demanded.

"I—I 'm-m waitin' ter see de cook, ma'am," stammered Sophy.

"The cook isn't here now. I don't know where she is. Besides, my daughter is to be buried to-day, and I won't have any one visiting the servants until the funeral is over. Come back some other day, or see the cook at her own home in the evening."

She stood waiting for the child to go, and under the keen glance of her eyes Sophy, feeling as though she had been caught in some disgraceful act, hurried down the walk and out of the gate, with her bouquet in her hand.

"Dinah," said Mrs. Myrover, when the cook came back, "I don't want any strange people admitted here to-day. The house will be full of our friends, and we have no room for others."

"Yas 'm," said the cook. She understood perfectly what her mistress meant; and what the cook thought about her mistress was a matter of no consequence.

The funeral services were held at St. Paul's Episcopal Church, where the Myrovers had always worshiped. Quite a number of Miss Myrover's pupils went to the church to attend the services. The building was not a large one. There was a small gallery at the rear, to which colored people were admitted, if they chose to come, at ordinary services; and those who wished to be present at the funeral supposed that the usual custom would prevail. They were therefore surprised, when they went to the side entrance, by which colored people gained access to the gallery stairs, to be met by an usher who barred their passage.

"I'm sorry," he said, "but I have had orders to admit no one until the friends of the family have all been seated. If you wish to wait until the white people have all gone in, and there's any room left, you may be able to get into the back part of the gallery. Of course I can't tell yet whether there'll be any room or not."

Now the statement of the usher was a very reasonable one; but, strange to say, none of the colored people chose to remain except Sophy. She still hoped to use her floral offering for its destined end, in some way, though she did not know just how. She waited in the yard until the church was filled with white people, and a number who could not gain admittance were standing about the doors. Then she went round to the side of the church, and, depositing her bouquet carefully on an old mossy gravestone, climbed up on the projecting sill of a window near the chancel. The window was of stained glass, of somewhat ancient make. The church was old, had indeed been built in colonial times, and the stained glass had been brought from England. The design of the window showed Jesus blessing little children. Time had dealt gently with the window, but just at the feet of the figure of Jesus a small triangular piece of glass had been broken out. To this aperture Sophy applied her eyes, and through it saw and heard what she could of the services within.

Before the chancel, on trestles draped in black, stood the sombre casket in which lay all that was mortal of her dear teacher. The top of the casket was covered with flowers; and lying stretched out underneath it she saw Miss Myrover's little white dog, Prince. He had followed the body to the church, and, slipping in unnoticed among the mourners, had taken his place, from which no one had the heart to remove him.

The white-robed rector read the solemn service for the dead, and then delivered a brief address, in which he dwelt upon the uncertainty of life, and, to the believer, the certain blessedness of eternity. He spoke of Miss Myrover's kindly spirit, and, as an illustration of her love and self-sacrifice for others, referred to her labors as a teacher of the poor ignorant negroes who had been placed in their midst by an all-wise Providence, and whom it was their duty to guide and direct in the station in which God had put them. Then the organ pealed, a prayer was said, and the long cortége moved from the church to the cemetery, about half a mile away, where the body was to be interred.

When the services were over, Sophy sprang down from her perch, and, taking her flowers, followed the procession. She did not walk with the rest, but at a proper and respectful distance from the last mourner. No one noticed the little black girl with the bunch of yellow flowers, or thought of her as interested in the funeral.

The cortége reached the cemetery and filed slowly through the gate; but Sophy stood outside, looking at a small sign in white letters on black background:—

"**Notice.** This cemetery is for white people only. Others please keep out."

Sophy, thanks to Miss Myrover's painstaking instruction, could read this sign very distinctly. In fact, she had often read it before. For Sophy was a child who loved beauty, in a blind, groping sort of way, and had sometimes stood by the fence of the cemetery and looked through at the green mounds and shaded walks and blooming flowers within, and wished that she might walk among them. She knew, too, that the little sign on the gate, though so courteously worded, was no mere formality; for she had heard how a colored man, who had wandered into the cemetery on a hot night and fallen asleep on the flat top of a tomb, had been arrested as a vagrant and fined five dollars, which he had worked out on the streets, with a ball-and-chain attachment, at twenty-five cents a day. Since that time the cemetery gate had been locked at night.

So Sophy stayed outside, and looked through the fence. Her poor bouquet had begun to droop by this time, and the yellow ribbon had lost some of its freshness. Sophy could see the rector standing by the grave, the mourners gathered round; she could faintly distinguish the solemn words with which ashes were committed to ashes, and dust to dust. She heard the hollow thud of the earth falling on the coffin; and she leaned against the iron fence, sobbing softly, until the grave was filled and rounded off, and the wreaths and other floral pieces were disposed upon it. When the mourners began to move toward the gate, Sophy walked slowly down the street, in a direction opposite to that taken by most of the people who came out.

When they had all gone away, and the sexton had come out and locked the gate behind him, Sophy crept back. Her roses were faded now, and from some of them the petals had fallen. She stood there irresolute, loath to leave with her heart's desire unsatisfied, when, as her eyes sought again the teacher's last resting-place, she saw lying beside the new-made grave what looked like a small bundle of white wool. Sophy's eyes lighted up with a sudden glow.

"Prince! Here, Prince!" she called.

The little dog rose, and trotted down to the gate. Sophy pushed the poor bouquet between the iron bars. "Take that ter Miss Ma'y, Prince," she said, "that's a good doggie."

The dog wagged his tail intelligently, took the bouquet carefully in his mouth, carried it to his mistress's grave, and laid it among the other flowers. The bunch of roses was so small that from where she stood Sophy could see only a dash of yellow against the white background of the mass of flowers.

When Prince had performed his mission he turned his eyes toward Sophy inquiringly, and when she gave him a nod of approval lay down and resumed his watch by the graveside. Sophy looked at him a moment with a feeling very much like envy, and then turned and moved slowly away.

Fenton Johnson (1886-1958)

Tired

I am tired of work; I am tired of building up somebody else's
    civilization.

Let us take a rest, M'Lissy Jane.

I will go down to the Last Chance Saloon, drink a gallon or two of
    gin, shoot a game or two of dice and sleep the rest of the
    night on one of Mike's barrels.

You will let the old shanty go to rot, the white people's clothes turn to dust, and the Calvary Baptist Church sink to the bottomless pit.

You will spend your days forgetting you married me and your nights hunting the warm gin Mike serves the ladies in the rear of the Last Chance Saloon.

Throw the children into the river; civilization has given us too many. It is better to die than it is to grow up and find out that you are colored.

Pluck the stars out of the heavens. The stars mark our destiny. The stars marked my destiny.

I am tired of civilization.

The Scarlet Woman

Once I was good like the Virgin Mary and the Minister's wife.

My father worked for Mr. Pullman and white people's tips; but he died two days after his insurance expired.

I had nothing, so I had to go to work.

All the stock I had was a white girl's education and a face that enchanted the men of both races.

Starvation danced with me.

So when Big Lizzie, who kept a house for white men, came to me with tales of fortune that I could reap from the sale of my virtue I bowed my head to Vice.

Now I can drink more gin than any man for miles around.

Gin is better than all the water in Lethe.

W. E. B. Du Bois (1868-1963)

The Riddle of the Sphinx

Dark daughter of the lotus leaves that watch the Southern Sea!
Wan spirit of a prisoned soul a-panting to be free!
    The muttered music of thy streams, the whisper of the deep,
    Have kissed each other in God's name and kissed a world to sleep.

The will of the world is a whistling wind, sweeping a cloud-swept
    sky,
And not from the East and not from the West knelled that soul-
    waking cry,
    But out of the South,—the sad, black South—it screamed from
      the top of the sky,
      Crying: "Awake, O ancient race!" Wailing, "O woman, arise!"
And crying and sighing and crying again as a voice in the mid-
    night cries,—
But the burden of white men bore her back and the white world
    stifled her sighs.

The white world's vermin and filth:
      All the dirt of London,
      All the scum of New York;
      Valiant spoilers of women
      And conquerors of unarmed men;
      Shameless breeders of bastards,
      Drunk with the greed of gold,
      Baiting their blood-stained hooks
      With cant for the souls of the simple;
      Bearing the white man's burden
      Of liquor and lust and lies!
Unthankful we wince in the East,
Unthankful we wail from the westward,
Unthankfully thankful, we curse,
In the unworn wastes of the wild:
      I hate them, Oh!
      I hate them well,
      I hate them, Christ!
      As I hate hell!
      If I were God,
      I'd sound their knell
      This day!
Who raised the fools to their glory,
But black men of Egypt and Ind,
Ethiopia's sons of the evening,
Indians and yellow Chinese,
Arabian children of morning,
And mongrels of Rome and Greece?
      Ah, well!
And they that raised the boasters

Shall drag them down again,—
Down with the theft of their thieving
And murder and mocking of men;
Down with their barter of women
And laying and lying of creeds;
Down with their cheating of childhood
And drunken orgies of war,—
    down
      down
        deep down,
Till the devil's strength be shorn,
Till some dim, darker David, a-hoeing of his corn,
And married maiden, mother of God,
Bid the black Christ be born!
Then shall our burden be manhood,
Be it yellow or black or white;
And poverty and justice and sorrow,
The humble and simple and strong
Shall sing with the sons of morning
And daughters of even-song:
Black mother of the iron hills that ward the blazing sea,
Wild spirit of a storm-swept soul, a-struggling to be free,
Where 'neath the bloody finger-marks thy riven bosom quakes,
Thicken the thunders of God's Voice and lo! a world awakes!

Benjamin Brawley (1882-1939)

The Negro in American Fiction

From The Negro in Literature and Art

Ever since Sydney Smith sneered at American books a hundred years ago, honest critics have asked themselves if the literature of the United States was not really open to the charge of provincialism. Within the last year or two the argument has been very much revived; and an English critic, Mr. Edward Garnett, writing in *The Atlantic Monthly*, has pointed out that with our predigested ideas and made-to-order fiction we not only discourage individual genius, but make it possible for the multitude to think only such thoughts as have passed through a sieve. Our most popular novelists, and sometimes our most respectable writers, see only the sensation that is uppermost for the moment in the mind of the crowd—divorce, graft, tainted meat or money—and they proceed to cut the cloth of their fiction accordingly. Mr. Owen Wister, a "regular practitioner" of the novelist's art, in substance admitting the weight of these charges, lays the blame on our crass democracy which utterly refuses to do its own thinking and which is satisfied only with the tinsel and gewgaws and hobbyhorses of literature. And no theme has suffered so much from the coarseness of the mob-spirit in literature as that of the Negro.

As a matter of fact, the Negro in his problems and strivings offers to American writers the greatest opportunity that could possibly be given to them to-day. It is commonly agreed that only one other large question, that of the relations of capital and labor, is of as much interest to the American public; and even this great issue fails to possess quite the appeal offered by the Negro from the social standpoint. One can only imagine what a Victor Hugo, detached and philosophical, would have done with such a theme in a novel. When we see what actually has been done—how often in the guise of fiction a writer has preached a sermon or shouted a political creed, or vented his spleen—we are not exactly proud of the art of novel-writing as it has been developed in the United States of America. Here was opportunity for tragedy, for comedy, for the subtle portrayal of all the relations of man with his fellow man, for faith and hope and love and sorrow. And yet, with the Civil War fifty years in the distance, not one novel or one short story of the first rank has found its inspiration in this great theme. Instead of such work we have consistently had traditional tales, political tracts, and lurid melodramas.

Let us see who have approached the theme, and just what they have done with it, for the present leaving out of account all efforts put forth by Negro writers themselves.

The names of four exponents of Southern life come at once to mind—George W. Cable, Joel Chandler Harris, Thomas Nelson Page, and Thomas Dixon; and at once, in their outlook and method of work, the first two become separate from the last two. Cable and Harris have looked toward the past, and have embalmed vanished or vanishing types. Mr. Page and Mr. Dixon, with their thought on the present (though for the most part they portray the recent past), have used the novel as a vehicle for political propaganda.

It was in 1879 that "Old Creole Days" evidenced the advent of a new force in American literature; and on the basis of this work, and of "The Grandissimes" which followed, Mr. Cable at once took his place as the foremost portrayer of life in old New Orleans. By birth, by temperament, and by training he was thoroughly fitted for the task to which he set himself. His mother was from New England, his father of the stock of colonial Virginia; and the stern Puritanism of the North was mellowed by the gentler influences of the South. Moreover, from his long apprenticeship in newspaper work in New Orleans he had received abundantly the knowledge and training necessary for his work. Setting himself

to a study of the Negro of the old régime, he made a specialty of the famous—
and infamous—quadroon society of Louisiana of the third and fourth decades of
the last century. And excellent as was his work, turning his face to the past in
manner as well as in matter, from the very first he raised the question pro-
pounded by this paper. In his earliest volume there was a story entitled " 'Tite
Poulette," the heroine of which was a girl amazingly fair, the supposed daughter
of one Madame John. A young Dutchman fell in love with 'Tite Poulette, championed her cause at all times, suffered a beating and stabbing for her, and was by
her nursed back to life and love. In the midst of his perplexity about joining
himself to a member of another race, came the word from Madame John that
the girl was not her daughter, but the child of yellow fever patients whom she
had nursed until they died, leaving their infant in her care. Immediately upon
the publication of this story, the author received a letter from a young woman
who had actually lived in very much the same situation as that portrayed in
" 'Tite Poulette," telling him that his story was not true to life and that he
knew it was not, for Madame John really *was* the mother of the heroine. Accepting the criticism, Mr. Cable set about the composition of "Madame Delphine,"
in which the situation is somewhat similar, but in which at the end the mother
tamely makes a confession to a priest. What is the trouble? The artist is so bound
by circumstances and hemmed in by tradition that he simply has not the courage
to launch out into the deep and work out his human problems for himself. Take
a representative portrait from "The Grandissimes":

Clemence had come through ages of African savagery, through fires that do not
refine, but that blunt and blast and blacken and char; starvation, gluttony, drunkenness, thirst, drowning, nakedness, dirt, fetichism, debauchery, slaughter, pestilence,
and the rest—she was their heiress; they left her the cinders of human feelings.
...She had had children of assorted colors—had one with her now, the black boy
that brought the basil to Joseph; the others were here and there, some in the
Grandissime households or field-gangs, some elsewhere within occasional sight, some
dead, some not accounted for. Husbands—like the Samaritan woman's. We know
she was a constant singer and laugher.

Very brilliant of course; and yet Clemence is a relic, not a prophecy.

Still more of a relic is Uncle Remus. For decades now, this charming old
Negro has been held up to the children of the South as the perfect expression
of the beauty of life in the glorious times "befo' de wah," when every Southern
gentleman was suckled at the bosom of a "black mammy." Why should we not
occasionally attempt to paint the Negro of the new day—intelligent, ambitious,
thrifty, manly? Perhaps he is not so poetic; but certainly the human element
is greater.

To the school of Cable and Harris belong also of course Miss Grace King and
Mrs. Ruth McEnery Stuart, a thoroughly representative piece of work being
Mrs. Stuart's "Uncle 'Riah's Christmas Eve." Other more popular writers of the
day, Miss Mary Johnston and Miss Ellen Glasgow for instance, attempt no

special analysis of the Negro. They simply take him for granted as an institution that always has existed and always will exist, as a hewer of wood and drawer of water, from the first flush of creation to the sounding of the trump of doom.

But more serious is the tone when we come to Thomas Nelson Page and Thomas Dixon. We might tarry for a few minutes with Mr. Page to listen to more such tales as those of Uncle Remus; but we must turn to living issues. Times have changed. The grandson of Uncle Remus does not feel that he must stand with his hat in his hand when he is in our presence, and he even presumes to help us in the running of our government. This will never do; so in "Red Rock" and "The Leopard's Spots" it must be shown that he should never have been allowed to vote anyway, and those honorable gentlemen in the Congress of the United States in the year 1865 did not know at all what they were about. Though we are given the characters and setting of a novel, the real business is to show that the Negro has been the "sentimental pet" of the nation all too long. By all means let us have an innocent white girl, a burly Negro, and a burning at the stake, or the story would be incomplete.

We have the same thing in "The Clansman," a "drama of fierce revenge." But here we are concerned very largely with the blackening of a man's character. Stoneman (Thaddeus Stevens very thinly disguised) is himself the whole Congress of the United States. He is a gambler, and "spends a part of almost every night at Hall & Pemberton's Faro Place on Pennsylvania Avenue." He is hysterical, "drunk with the joy of a triumphant vengeance." "The South is conquered soil," he says to the President (a mere figure-head, by the way), "I mean to blot it from the map." Further: "It is but the justice and wisdom of heaven that the Negro shall rule the land of his bondage. It is the only solution of the race problem. Wait until I put a ballot in the hand of every Negro, and a bayonet at the breast of every white man from the James to the Rio Grande." Stoneman, moreover, has a mistress, a mulatto woman, a "yellow vampire" who dominates him completely. "Senators, representatives, politicians of low and high degree, artists, correspondents, foreign ministers, and cabinet officers hurried to acknowledge their fealty to the uncrowned king, and hail the strange brown woman who held the keys of his house as the first lady of the land." This, let us remember, was for some months the best-selling book in the United States. A slightly altered version of it has very recently commanded such prices as were never before paid for seats at a moving-picture entertainment; and with "The Traitor" and "The Southerner" it represents our most popular treatment of the gravest social question in American life! "The Clansman" is to American literature exactly what a Louisiana mob is to American democracy. Only too frequently, of course, the mob represents us all too well.

Turning from the longer works of fiction to the short story, I have been interested to see how the matter has been dealt with here. For purposes of comparison I have selected from ten representative periodicals as many distinct stories, no one of which was published more than ten years ago; and as these are in almost every case those stories that first strike the eye in a periodical index, we may assume that they are thoroughly typical. The ten are: "Shadow," by Harry Stillwell Edwards, in the *Century* (December, 1906); "Callum's Co'tin': A Plantation Idyl," by Frank H. Sweet, in the *Craftsman* (March, 1907); "His Excellency the Governor," by L. M. Cooke, in *Putnam's* (February, 1908); "The Black Drop," by Margaret Deland in *Collier's Weekly* (May 2 and 9, 1908); "Jungle Blood," by Elmore Elliott Peake, in *McClure's* (September, 1908); "The Race-Rioter," by Harris Merton Lyon, in the *American* (February, 1910); "Shadow," by Grace MacGowan Cooke and Alice MacGowan, in *Everybody's* (March, 1910); "Abram's Freedom," by Edna Turpin, in the *Atlantic* (September, 1912); "A Hypothetical Case," by Norman Duncan, in *Harper's* (June, 1915); and "The Chalk Game," by L. B. Yates, in the *Saturday Evening Post* (June 5, 1915). For high standards of fiction I think we may safely say that, all in all, the periodicals here mentioned are representative of the best that America has to offer. In some cases the story cited is the only one on the Negro question that a magazine has published within the decade.

"Shadow" (in the *Century*) is the story of a Negro convict who for a robbery committed at the age of fourteen was sentenced to twenty years of hard labor in the mines of Alabama. An accident disabled him, however, and prevented his doing the regular work for the full period of his imprisonment. At twenty he was a hostler, looking forward in despair to the fourteen years of confinement still waiting for him. But the three little girls of the prison commissioner visit the prison. Shadow performs many little acts of kindness for them, and their hearts go out to him. They storm the governor and the judge for his pardon, and present the Negro with his freedom as a Christmas gift. The story is not long, but it strikes a note of genuine pathos.

"Callum's Co'tin'" is concerned with a hardworking Negro, a blacksmith, nearly forty, who goes courting the girl who called at his shop to get a trinket mended for her mistress. At first he makes himself ridiculous by his finery; later he makes the mistake of coming to a crowd of merrymakers in his working clothes. More and more, however, he storms the heart of the girl, who eventually capitulates. From the standpoint simply of craftsmanship, the story is an excellent piece of work.

"His Excellency the Governor" deals with the custom on Southern plantations of having, in imitation of the white people, a Negro "governor" whose duty it was to settle minor disputes. At the death of old Uncle Caleb, who for years had held this position of responsibility, his son Jubal should have been the next in order. He was likely to be superseded, however, by loud-mouthed Sambo, though urged to assert himself by Maria, his wife, an old house-servant who had no desire whatever to be defeated for the place of honor among the women by Sue, a former field-hand. At the meeting where all was to be decided, however, Jubal with the aid of his fiddle completely confounded his rival and won. There are some excellent touches in the story; but, on the whole, the composition is hardly more than fair in literary quality.

"The Black Drop," throughout which we see the hand of an experienced writer, analyzes the heart of a white boy who is in love with a girl who is almost white, and who when the test confronts him suffers the tradition that binds him to get the better of his heart. "But you will still believe that I love you?" he asks, ill at ease as they separate. "No, of course I can not believe that," replies the girl.

"Jungle Blood" is the story of a simple-minded, simple-hearted Negro of gigantic size who in a moment of fury kills his pretty wife and the white man who has seduced her. The tone of the whole may be gleaned from the description of Moss Harper's father: "An old darky sat drowsing on the stoop. There was something ape-like about his long arms, his flat, wide-nostriled nose, and the mat of gray wool which crept down his forehead to within two inches of his eyebrows."

"The Race-Rioter" sets forth the stand of a brave young sheriff to protect his prisoner, a Negro boy, accused of the assault and murder of a little white girl. Hank Egge tries by every possible subterfuge to defeat the plans of a lynching party, and finally dies riddled with bullets as he is defending his prisoner. The story is especially remarkable for the strong and sympathetic characterization of such contrasting figures as young Egge and old Dikeson, the father of the dead girl.

"Shadow" (in *Everybody's*) is a story that depends for its force very largely upon incident. It studies the friendship of a white boy, Ranny, and a black boy, Shadow, a relationship that is opposed by both the Northern white mother and the ambitious and independent Negro mother. In a fight, Shad breaks a collar-bone for Ranny; later he saves him from drowning. In the face of Ranny's white friends, all the harsher side of the problem is seen; and yet the human element is strong beneath it all. The story, not without considerable merit as it is, would have been infinitely stronger if the friendship of the two boys had been pitched on a higher plane. As it is, Shad is very much like a dog following his master.

"Abram's Freedom" is at the same time one of the most clever and one of the most provoking stories with which we have to deal. It is a perfect example of how one may walk directly up to the light and then deliberately turn his back upon it. The story is set just before the Civil War. It deals with the love of the slave Abram for a free young woman, Emmeline. "All his life he had heard and used the phrase 'free nigger' as a term of contempt. What, then, was this vague feeling, not definite enough yet to be a wish or even a longing?" So far, so good. Emmeline inspires within her lover the highest ideals of manhood, and he becomes a hostler in a livery-stable, paying to his master so much a year for his freedom. Then comes the astounding and forced conclusion. At the very moment when, after years of effort, Emmeline has helped her husband to gain his freedom (and when all the slaves are free as a matter of fact by virtue of the Emancipation Proclamation), Emmeline, whose husband has special reason to be grateful to his former master, says to the lady of the house: "Me an' Abram ain't got nothin' to do in dis worl' but to wait on you an' master."

In "A Hypothetical Case" we again see the hand of a master-craftsman. Is a white boy justified in shooting a Negro who has offended him? The white father is not quite at ease, quibbles a good deal, but finally says Yes. The story, however, makes it clear that the Negro did not strike the boy. He was a hermit living on the Florida coast and perfectly abased when he met Mercer and his two companions. When the three boys pursued him and finally overtook him, the Negro simply held the hands of Mercer until the boy had recovered his temper. Mercer in his rage really struck himself.

"The Chalk Game" is the story of a little Negro jockey who wins a race in Louisville only to be drugged and robbed by some "flashlight" Negroes who send him to Chicago. There he recovers his fortunes by giving to a group of gamblers the correct "tip" on another race, and he makes his way back to Louisville much richer by his visit. Throughout the story emphasis is placed upon the superstitious element in the Negro race, an element readily considered by men who believe in luck.

Of these ten stories, only five strike out with even the slightest degree of independence. "Shadow" (in the *Century*) is not a powerful piece of work, but it is written in tender and beautiful spirit. "The Black Drop" is a bold handling of a strong situation. "The Race-Rioter" also rings true, and in spite of the tragedy there is optimism in this story of a man who is not afraid to do his duty. "Shadow" (in *Everybody's*) awakens all sorts of discussion, but at least attempts to deal honestly with a situation that might arise in any neighborhood at any time. "A Hypothetical Case" is the most tense and independent story in the list.

On the other hand, "Callum's Co'tin'" and "His Excellency the Governor," bright comedy though they are, belong, after all, to the school of Uncle Remus. "Jungle Blood" and "The Chalk Game" belong to the class that always regards the Negro as an animal, a minor, a plaything—but never as a man. "Abram's Freedom," exceedingly well written for two-thirds of the way, falls down hopelessly at the end. Many old Negroes after the Civil War preferred to remain with their former masters; but certainly no young woman of the type of Emmeline would sell her birthright for a mess of pottage.

Just there is the point. That the Negro is ever to be taken seriously is incomprehensible to some people. It is the story of "The Man that Laughs" over again. The more Gwynplaine protests, the more outlandish he becomes to the House of Lords.

We are simply asking that those writers of fiction who deal with the Negro shall be thoroughly honest with themselves, and not remain forever content to embalm old types and work over outworn ideas. Rather should they sift the present and forecast the future. But of course the editors must be considered. The editors must give their readers what the readers want; and when we consider the populace, of course we have to reckon with the mob. And the mob does not find anything very attractive about a Negro who is intelligent, cultured, manly, and who does not smile. It will be observed that in no one of the ten stories above mentioned, not even in one of the five remarked most favorably, is there a Negro of this type. Yet he is obliged to come. America has yet to reckon with him. The day of Uncle Remus as well as of Uncle Tom is over.

Even now, however, there are signs of better things. Such an artist as Mr. Howells, for instance, has once or twice dealt with the problem in excellent spirit. Then there is the work of the Negro writers themselves. The numerous attempts in fiction made by them have most frequently been open to the charge of crassness already considered; but Paul Laurence Dunbar, Charles W. Chesnutt, and W. E. Burghardt DuBois have risen above the crowd. Mr. Dunbar, of course, was better in poetry than in prose. Such a short story as "Jimsella," however, exhibited considerable technique. "The Uncalled" used a living topic treated with only partial success. But for the most part, Mr. Dunbar's work looked toward the past. Somewhat stronger in prose is Mr. Chesnutt. "The Marrow of Tradition" is not much more than a political tract, and "The Colonel's Dream" contains a good deal of preaching; but "The House Behind the Cedars" is a real novel. Among his short stories, "The Bouquet" may be remarked for technical excellence, and "The Wife of His Youth" for a situation of unusual power. Dr. DuBois's "The Quest of the Silver Fleece" contains at least one strong dramatic situation, that in which Bles probes the heart of Zora; but the author is a sociologist and essayist rather than a novelist. The grand epic of the race is yet to be produced.

Some day we shall work out the problems of our great country. Some day we shall not have a state government set at defiance, and the massacre of Ludlow. Some day our little children will not slave in mines and mills, but will have some chance at the glory of God's creation; and some day the Negro will cease to be a problem and become a human being. Then, in truth, we shall have the Promised Land. But until that day comes let those who mold our ideals and set the standards of our art in fiction at least be honest with themselves and independent. Ignorance we may for a time forgive; but a man has only himself to blame if he insists on not seeing the sunrise in the new day.

James Weldon Johnson (1871-1938)

The Black Mammy

O whitened head entwined in turban gay,
O kind black face, O crude, but tender hand,
O foster-mother in whose arms there lay
The race whose sons are masters of the land!

It was thine arms that sheltered in their fold,
It was thine eyes that followed through the length
Of infant days these sons. In times of old
It was thy breast that nourished them to strength.

So often hast thou to thy bosom pressed
The golden head, the face and brow of snow;
So often has it 'gainst thy broad, dark breast
Lain, set off like a quickened cameo.
Thou simple soul, as cuddling down that babe
With thy sweet croon, so plaintive and so wild,
Came ne'er the thought to thee, swift like a stab,
That it some day might crush thy own black child?

O Black and Unknown Bards

O black and unknown bards of long ago,
How came your lips to touch the sacred fire?
How, in your darkness, did you come to know
The power and beauty of the minstrel's lyre?
Who first from midst his bonds lifted his eyes?
Who first from out the still watch, lone and long,
Feeling the ancient faith of prophets rise
Within his dark-kept soul, burst into song?

Heart of what slave poured out such melody
As "Steal Away to Jesus"? On its strains
His spirit must have nightly floated free,
Though still about his hands he felt his chains.
Who heard great "Jordan roll"? Whose starward eye
Saw chariot "swing low"? And who was he
That breathed that comforting, melodic sigh,
"Nobody Knows de Trouble I See"?

What merely living clod, what captive thing,
Could up toward God through all its darkness grope,
And find within its deadened heart to sing
These songs of sorrow, love, and faith, and hope?
How did it catch that subtle undertone,
That note in music heard not with the ears?
How sound the elusive reed so seldom blown,
Which stirs the soul or melts the heart to tears?

Not that great German master in his dream
Of harmonies that thundered amongst the stars
At the creation, ever heard a theme
Nobler than "Go Down, Moses." Mark its bars,
How like a mighty trumpet-call they stir
The blood. Such are the notes that men have sung
Going to valorous deeds; such tones there were
That helped make history when Time was young.

There is a wide, wide wonder in it all,
That from degraded rest and servile toil
The fiery spirit of the seer should call
These simple children of the sun and soil.
O black slave singers, gone, forgot, unfamed,
You—you alone, of all the long, long line
Of those who've sung untaught, unknown, unnamed,
Have stretched out upward, seeking the divine.

You sang not deeds of heroes or of kings;
No chant of bloody war, no exulting pæan
Of arms-won triumphs; but your humble strings
You touched in chord with music empyrean.
You sang far better than you knew; the songs
That for your listeners' hungry hearts sufficed
Still live—but more than this to you belongs:
You sang a race from wood and stone to Christ.

V
The
Renaissance
of the
Twenties

The twenties roared with the high life, sported raccoon coats, drank bathtub gin, danced to tunes of the Jazz Age, and quested for life after the devastating deaths of World War I. Some sophisticated and talented men of the age, some poets and writers, had peered into the heart of darkness; they had seen Mr. Kurtz's vision of horror, and they sought means of expressing that horror and means of transcending the normal flux of life in a rebirth of the spirit. Hemingway, Faulkner, Eliot, Williams, Pound—all are names associated with the twenties; and each of these writers engaged in experimentation in literature and undertook a quest for new forms and new meanings in life as a whole. After the sentimental romanticism of the Edwardian Age, after the devastation and death of World War I, therefore, we have a "rebirth" of literature and a flourishing of life in the twenties. And the black American was very much a part of the flourishing life and the literary culture of the twenties.

Motivated by the flames of East St. Louis, enraged by the hangings at Houston, and inspired by the "Red Summer" of 1919, Claude McKay wrote the well-known sonnet "If We Must Die." And yearning for a type of Bergsonian essence beneath the prosaic flow of life, Jean Toomer produced the mystical and brilliant *Cane*. Countee Cullen became a celebrated poet in his junior year at New York University when *Color* appeared, and by 1927, Langston Hughes, one of America's finest poets, had published two volumes of outstanding poetry— *The Weary Blues* and *Fine Clothes to the Jew*. Black Americans thus assumed vanguard roles in the literary output of the twenties, and on the social scene, Charles S. Johnson, W. E. B. Du Bois, and James Weldon Johnson were waging an incessant battle for new forms and new meanings in American life as a whole, forms and meanings that would make freedom, justice, and democracy (the aim of the late War) realities in the lives of black Americans.

The center for the social and literary activity of the black American during the twenties was Harlem, that dusky sash across Manhattan which had first been a site for Dutch farms, and later an exclusive white residential area. The great migrations of the first two decades of the twentieth century brought vast numbers of black Americans to urban areas, and restrictive housing codes and stringent Jim Crow legislation forced most of the black population of any city to live in one section. In New York it was Harlem, and the lure of the American "city of light" brought some of the most talented black Americans in the country to Harlem in the 1920s. The fact that black American musicians, artists, poets, and novelists grouped together in Harlem is no more surprising than the fact that noted British artists group together in certain sections of London and noted white American artists group together in a number of New York residential areas. The influence of the Harlem writers was so great during the twenties, however, that the entire black literary movement of the period has often been called the "Harlem Renaissance."

The term *renaissance* may be somewhat of a misnomer, since the writers of the twenties simply built on the conscious, literary foundations that had been laid by the black writers of former decades. What we witness is more a distinct maturation: during the decade between 1920 and 1930 black American artists discovered new forms and reached new peaks in artistic expression. On the other hand, we also witness a casting out of many of the cherished formulas of bygone eras; the dialect tradition is scathingly repudiated, and the guidelines for a "New Negro" are set forth in some of the finest prose and poetry ever written by black Americans. And to a great extent, the folk were left behind as black Phi Beta Kappas, Guggenheim recipients, and cosmopolitan travellers became the spokesmen of black Americans. Many of the writers of the renaissance had studied at predominantly white universities, and some of the foremost leaders of the renaissance were determined that a new image of the black American as a man of culture, cleanliness, intellect, and overall respectability should result from the efforts of the twenties. The somewhat risque novels of Claude McKay were thus thorns in many sides; W. E. B. Du Bois and James Weldon Johnson, for example, spoke in derogatory terms of McKay's works, which showed the low-life black American, the migratory down-and-outer who loved his fine brown women and his straight gin.

Countee Cullen, who is often denoted as the "poet laureate" of the Harlem Renaissance, surely fits the middle-class image. Cullen was educated at New York University and at Harvard University, and much of his effort was directed toward proving the black American's "universality." Cullen's ideal poet was John Keats, and some of his most mellifluous verses are totally devoid of racial themes and images. But the "poet laureate" was also struck by the irony of his own situation and the paradox of his own assertions. The irony and paradox find consummate expression in the poem "Yet Do I Marvel," the final couplet of which—"Yet do I marvel at this curious thing:/To make a poet black, and bid him sing!"—is perhaps the most frequently quoted set of lines written during the Harlem Renaissance. And in "Heritage," Cullen once again gave witness to the fact that a writer cannot escape his fundamental life experiences; the poem is but one expression of the atavistic yearnings for Africa that found their readiest outlet during the twenties in Marcus Garvey's Universal Negro Improvement Association. While the bulk of Cullen's work is nonracial in theme, poems like "Yet Do I Marvel," "Heritage," "Black Magdalens," and "Incident" stand as proof that most of a writer's best works are constituted by his imaginative reflections on his basic life experiences, which, in the case of Cullen, were black American life experiences.

Another accomplished poet of the Harlem Renaissance, Claude McKay, unlike Cullen, did not try to escape his blackness in the least degree. McKay's career began with the writing of verse in West Indian dialect, and after his travels in America, he took pen in hand and produced some of the finest sonnets that have ever been written in America. Each of McKay's sonnets is a drama in itself, and the rigid form seems like a thin wall holding back the angry content that would explode in the face of Americans who perpetuate injustice and brutality. In "Tiger," "Lynching," and "If We Must Die," McKay captures the bitterness and pain of centuries, and he expresses the new militant stand of the black American who laid down the gauntlet in the twenties. But the angry poet was also capable of beautiful description, exoticism, and vibrant nostalgia within the sonnet form, and it is difficult to believe that McKay's range could span from "If We Must Die" to "Jasmine," "Harlem Dancer," and "Home Thoughts."

Langston Hughes was an even more versatile poet, for his canon moves from the atavistic "The Negro Speaks of Rivers" through the blues-filled "Troubled Woman" and "Jazzonia" to the impressionistic "Montmarte" and the militant "Undertow." Hughes was one of the writers of the Harlem Renaissance who seldom averted his eyes from the black folk who surrounded him. Aided by Carl Van Vechten, wooed by other white patrons, and praised by Vachel Lindsay, Hughes kept his eyes and his feet on his own people's ground. Thus he was one of the finest folk poets since Paul Laurence Dunbar, and most of his poems ring with folk rhythms and folk themes. The title of his first volume, *The Weary Blues* (1926), is a testament to Hughes's concern for the folk, and in poems like "I, Too," "One-way Ticket," "Silhouette," and "Refugee in America," Hughes captured the pain and joy of the black American experience in brilliant poetry.

Brilliant is a word that can also be used in any discussion of Jean Toomer's *Cane*, James Weldon Johnson's "Preface" to the *Book of American Negro Poetry* (1922), or Alain Locke's "The New Negro" from the larger volume of the same title. Toomer was at the head of a long line of accomplished prose-fiction writers who made their debut in the twenties. The output of fiction during the decade of the Harlem Renaissance was greater than the output of poetry, and Wallace Thurman, Nella Larsen, Eric Walrond, Walter White, Jessie Fauset, and Rudolph Fisher were all products of the twenties. Just as Fisher's "City of Refuge" and other short stories dealing with the new urban masses stand at the top of the form for the short story, so Toomer's *Cane* stands in the foremost rank of the black American novel of the twenties. Toomer's realism, mysticism, and beautiful style antedate Faulkner's better fiction, and the short section entitled "Avey" is one of the finest pieces in *Cane*.

The prose of James Weldon Johnson and that of Alain Locke is no less telling than that of Rudolph Fisher and Jean Toomer; Johnson and Locke, however, where concerned with accurate and concise criticism rather than the composition of fiction. Both men sought to analyze the place of the black artist in the American scheme of things, and both were dedicated to a just portrayal of the significant contributions that black American artists had made to American culture as a whole. In his "Preface," Johnson touched on all aspects of the black American's creative genius, and in "The New Negro," Locke provided the manifesto of the Harlem Renaissance. Johnson's preface to the *Book of American Negro Spirituals* (1925) and his introductory remarks to the *Second Book of*

American Negro Spirituals (1926) are also invaluable; and as the editor of the Harlem number of the *Survey Graphic* (1925) and *The New Negro* (1925), an outgrowth of the magazine issue, Locke acted as a sort of spiritual father for the Renaissance.

The Harlem Renaissance, however, is too complex a phenomenon to be captured in a single view, and a selection of even the best products of the movement cannot do it full justice. Aspects of the Renaissance like the growth of the blues through the efforts of Bessie Smith and Ethel Waters, the growth of jazz in the hands of Duke Ellington and Louis Armstrong, the flourishing of a back-to-Africa movement under the generalship of Marcus Garvey, and the rising of the ire and protest of the black American under the guidance of the Urban League and the NAACP—all these must surely be mentioned. And certainly it is worth mentioning that the journalistic organs of both the NAACP and the Urban League— *Crisis* and *Opportunity* respectively—opened both their pages and their coffers to aspiring black artists by sponsoring annual literary contests for cash prizes. Black Americans in increasing numbers were becoming aware of the value of fine artistic, musical, and literary expression, and the audience available to the black artist was becoming larger as white authors like Carl Van Vechten, DuBose Heyward, Eugene O'Neill, and Paul Green turned their attention to a less stereotyped picture of black Americans and made the world take note. Moreover, black Americans themselves were providing an increasingly large audience as more black men took advantage of the available educational opportunities and moved into a sort of Du Boisian Talented Tenth. And both the black writer and his black audience were becoming more cosmopolitan as increasing numbers of black Americans travelled to Europe, Russia, and the East. On a European trip in 1926, Countee Cullen saw Alain Locke, Arthur Fauset, and Mercer Cook, and later, Cullen and Eric Walrond were to share an apartment in Paris. Hughes and McKay spent time in Russia, and Toomer studied Gurdjieff's mysticism in France.

Given the complexity of the Harlem Renaissance, it is perhaps too simplistic to say that it "ended" with the stock market crash of 1929 and the onset of the Great Depression; the efforts of the artists mentioned here and the efforts of musicians like William Grant Still, illustrators like Aaron Douglas, and folklorists like Zora Neal Hurston constituted an advanced stage of black expression that was not cast into darkness by the shadow of the Depression. The spirit and the concerns of the Harlem Renaissance continued into the following decade, and major renaissance artists continued to produce noteworthy works. And perhaps the penultimate results of that outbreak of the black American spirit and that maturation of the black American literary tradition that took place in the twenties are to be seen in our own day; surely the black American artists of today have in many cases sought their models, themes, and heroes among the artistic rolls of the twenties.

REFERENCES

Bontemps, Arna: "The Harlem Renaissance," *Saturday Review,* March 22, 1947.

———: "Harlem in the '20's," *Opportunity,* vol. LXIII, 1966.

———: "The Negro Renaissance: Jean Toomer and the Harlem Writers of the 1920's" *Anger, and Beyond,* Herbert Hill (ed.), Harper and Row, New York, 1969, pp. 20–36.

Brawley, Benjamin: *The Negro Genius,* Dodd, Mead and Company, New York, 1937.

Bronz, Stephen H.: *Roots of Negro Racial Consciousness, The 1920's: Three Harlem Renaissance Authors,* Libra, New York, 1964.

Clarke, John Henrik (ed.): *Harlem: A Community in Transition,* Citadel Press, New York, 1964.

Dickinson, Donald C.: *A Bio-bibliography of Langston Hughes, 1902–1967,* Archon Books, Hamden, Conn., 1967.

Emanuel, James A.: *Langston Hughes,* Twayne Publishers, New York, 1967.

Ferguson, Blanche E.: *Countee Cullen and the Negro Renaissance,* Dodd, Mead and Company, New York, 1966.

Johnson, James Weldon: *Black Manhattan,* Alfred Knopf, New York, 1930.

Locke, Alain: *Four Negro Poets,* Simon and Schuster, New York, 1927. [McKay, Toomer, Cullen, and Hughes.]

Munson, Gorham B.: "The Significance of Jean Toomer," *Opportunity,* vol. III, 1925.

Redding, J. Saunders: "Emergence of the New Negro," *To Make a Poet Black,* University of North Carolina Press, Chapel Hill, 1939, pp. 93–125.

Alain Locke (1886-1954)

The New Negro

From The New Negro

In the last decade something beyond the watch and guard of statistics has happened in the life of the American Negro and the three norns who have traditionally presided over the Negro problem have a changeling in their laps. The Sociologist, the Philanthropist, the Race-leader are not unaware of the New Negro, but they are at a loss to account for him. He simply cannot be swathed in their formulæ. For the younger generation is vibrant with a new psychology; the new spirit is awake in the masses, and under the very eyes of the professional observers is transforming what has been a perennial problem into the progressive phases of contemporary Negro life.

Could such a metamorphosis have taken place as suddenly as it has appeared to? The answer is no; not because the New Negro is not here, but because the Old Negro had long become more of a myth than a man. The Old Negro, we must remember, was a creature of moral debate and historical controversy. His has been a stock figure perpetuated as an historical fiction partly in innocent sentimentalism, partly in deliberate reactionism. The Negro himself has contributed his share to this through a sort of protective social mimicry forced upon him by the adverse circumstances of dependence. So for generations in the mind of America, the Negro has been more of a formula than a human being—a something to be argued about, condemned or defended, to be "kept down," or "in his place," or "helped up," to be worried with or worried over, harassed or patronized, a social bogey or a social burden. The thinking Negro even has been induced to share this same general attitude, to focus his attention on controversial issues, to see himself in the distorted perspective of a social problem. His shadow, so to speak, has been more real to him than his personality. Through having had to appeal from the unjust stereotypes of his oppressors and traducers to those of his liberators, friends and benefactors he has had to subscribe to the traditional positions from which his case has been viewed. Little true social or self-understanding has or could come from such a situation.

But while the minds of most of us, black and white, have thus burrowed in the trenches of the Civil War and Reconstruction, the actual march of development has simply flanked these positions, necessitating a sudden reorientation of view. We have not been watching in the right direction; set North and South on a sectional axis, we have not noticed the East till the sun has us blinking.

Recall how suddenly the Negro spirituals revealed themselves; suppressed for generations under the stereotypes of Wesleyan hymn harmony, secretive, half-ashamed, until the courage of being natural brought them out—and behold, there was folk-music. Similarly the mind of the Negro seems suddenly to have slipped from under the tyranny of social intimidation and to be shaking off the psychology of imitation and implied inferiority. By shedding the old chrysalis of the Negro problem we are achieving something like a spiritual emancipation. Until recently, lacking self-understanding, we have been almost as much of a problem to ourselves as we still are to others. But the decade that found us with a problem has left us with only a task. The multitude perhaps feels as yet only a strange relief and a new vague urge, but the thinking few know that in the reaction the vital inner grip of prejudice has been broken.

With this renewed self-respect and self-dependence, the life of the Negro community is bound to enter a new dynamic phase, the buoyancy from within compensating for whatever pressure there may be of conditions from without. The migrant masses, shifting from countryside to city, hurdle several generations of experience at a leap, but more important, the same thing happens spiritually in the life-attitudes and self-expression of the Young Negro, in his poetry, his art, his education and his new outlook, with the additional advantage, of course, of the poise and greater certainty of knowing what it is all about. From this comes the promise and warrant of a new leadership. As one of them has discerningly put it:

> We have tomorrow
> Bright before us
> Like a flame.
>
> Yesterday, a night-gone thing
> A sun-down name.
>
> And dawn today
> Broad arch above the road we came.
> We march!

This is what, even more than any "most creditable record of fifty years of freedom," requires that the Negro of to-day be seen through other than the dusty spectacles of past controversy. The day of "aunties," "uncles" and "mammies" is equally gone. Uncle Tom and Sambo have passed on, and even the "Colonel" and "George" play barnstorm rôles from which they escape with relief when the public spotlight is off. The popular melodrama has about played itself out, and it is time to scrap the fictions, garret the bogeys and settle down to a realistic facing of facts.

First we must observe some of the changes which since the traditional lines of opinion were drawn have rendered these quite obsolete. A main change has been, of course, that shifting of the Negro population which has made the Negro problem no longer exclusively or even predominantly Southern. Why should our minds remain sectionalized, when the problem itself no longer is? Then the trend of migration has not only been toward the North and the Central Midwest, but city-ward and to the great centers of industry—the problems of adjustment are new, practical, local and not peculiarly racial. Rather they are an integral part of the large industrial and social problems of our present-day democracy. And finally, with the Negro rapidly in process of class differentiation, if it ever was warrantable to regard and treat the Negro *en masse* it is becoming with every day less possible, more unjust and more ridiculous.

In the very process of being transplanted, the Negro is becoming transformed.

The tide of Negro migration, northward and city-ward, is not to be fully explained as a blind flood started by the demands of war industry coupled with the shutting off of foreign migration, or by the pressure of poor crops coupled with increased social terrorism in certain sections of the South and Southwest. Neither labor demand, the bollweevil nor the Ku Klux Klan is a basic factor, however contributory any or all of them may have been. The wash and rush of this human tide on the beach line of the northern city centers is to be explained primarily in terms of a new vision of opportunity, of social and economic freedom, of a spirit to seize, even in the face of an extortionate and heavy toll, a chance for the improvement of conditions. With each successive wave of it, the movement of the Negro becomes more and more a mass movement toward the larger and the more democratic chance—in the Negro's case a deliberate flight not only from countryside to city, but from medieval America to modern.

Take Harlem as an instance of this. Here in Manhattan is not merely the largest Negro community in the world, but the first concentration in history of so many diverse elements of Negro life. It has attracted the African, the West Indian, the Negro American; has brought together the Negro of the North and the Negro of the South; the man from the city and the man from the town and village; the peasant, the student, the business man, the professional man, artist, poet, musician, adventurer and worker, preacher and criminal, exploiter and social outcast. Each group has come with its own separate motives and for its own special ends, but their greatest experience has been the finding of one another. Proscription and prejudice have thrown these dissimilar elements into a common area of contact and interaction. Within this area, race sympathy and unity have determined a further fusing of sentiment and experience. So what began in terms of segregation becomes more and more, as its elements mix and react, the laboratory of a great race-welding. Hitherto, it must be admitted that American Negroes have been a race more in name than in fact, or to be exact, more in sentiment than in experience. The chief bond between them has been that of a common condition rather than a common consciousness; a problem in common rather than a life in common. In Harlem, Negro life is seizing upon its first chances for group expression and self-determination. It is—or promises at least to be—a race capital. That is why our comparison is taken with those nascent centers of folk-expression and self-determination which are playing a creative part in the world to-day. Without pretense to their political significance, Harlem has the same rôle to play for the New Negro as Dublin has had for the New Ireland or Prague for the New Czechoslovakia.

Harlem, I grant you, isn't typical—but it is significant, it is prophetic. No sane observer, however sympathetic to the new trend, would contend that the great masses are articulate as yet, but they stir, they move, they are more than physically restless. The challenge of the new intellectuals among them is clear enough—the "race radicals" and realists who have broken with the old epoch of philanthropic guidance, sentimental appeal and protest. But are we after all only reading into the stirrings of a sleeping giant the dreams of an agitator? The answer is in the migrating peasant. It is the "man farthest down" who is most active in getting up. One of the most characteristic symptoms of this is the professional man, himself migrating to recapture his constituency after a vain effort to maintain in some Southern corner what for years back seemed an established living and clientele. The clergyman following his errant flock, the physician or lawyer trailing his clients, supply the true clues. In a real sense it is the rank and file who are leading, and the leaders who are following. A transformed and transforming psychology permeates the masses.

When the racial leaders of twenty years ago spoke of developing race-pride and stimulating race-consciousness, and of the desirability of race solidarity, they could not in any accurate degree have anticipated the abrupt feeling that has surged up and now pervades the awakened centers. Some of the recognized Negro leaders and a powerful section of white opinion identified with "race work" of the older order have indeed attempted to discount this feeling as a "passing phase," an attack of "race nerves" so to speak, an "aftermath of the war," and the like. It has not abated, however, if we are to gauge by the present tone and temper of the Negro press, or by the shift in popular support from the officially recognized and orthodox spokesmen to those of the independent, popular, and often radical type who are unmistakable symptoms of a new order. It is a social disservice to blunt the fact that the Negro of the Northern centers has reached a stage where tutelage, even of the most interested and well-intentioned sort, must give place to new relationships, where positive self-direction must be reckoned with in ever increasing measure. The American mind must reckon with a fundamentally changed Negro.

The Negro too, for his part, has idols of the tribe to smash. If on the one hand the white man has erred in making the Negro appear to be that which would excuse or extenuate his treatment of him, the Negro, in turn, has too often unnecessarily excused himself because of the way he has been treated. The intelligent Negro of to-day is resolved not to make discrimination an extenuation for his shortcomings in performance, individual or collective; he is trying to hold himself at par, neither inflated by sentimental allowances nor depreciated by current social discounts. For this he must know himself and be known for precisely what he is, and for that reason he welcomes the new scientific rather than the old sentimental interest. Sentimental interest in the Negro has ebbed. We used to lament this as the falling off of our friends; now we rejoice and pray to be delivered both from self-pity and condescension. The mind of each racial group has had a bitter weaning, apathy or hatred on one side matching disillusionment or resentment on the other; but they face each other to-day with the possibility at least of entirely new mutual attitudes.

It does not follow that if the Negro were better known, he would be better liked or better treated. But mutual understanding is basic for any subsequent coöperation and adjustment. The effort toward this will at least have the effect of remedying in large part what has been the most unsatisfactory feature of our present stage of race relationships in America, namely the fact that the more intelligent and representative elements of the two race groups have at so many points got quite out of vital touch with one another.

The fiction is that the life of the races is separate, and increasingly so. The fact is that they have touched too closely at the unfavorable and too lightly at the favorable levels.

While inter-racial councils have sprung up in the South, drawing on forward elements of both races, in the Northern cities manual laborers may brush elbows in their everyday work, but the community and business leaders have experienced no such interplay or far too little of it. These segments must achieve contact or the race situation in America becomes desperate. Fortunately this is happening. There is a growing realization that in social effort the co-operative basis must supplant long-distance philanthropy, and that the only safeguard for mass relations in the future must be provided in the carefully maintained contacts of the enlightened minorities of both race groups. In the intellectual realm a renewed and keen curiosity is replacing the recent apathy; the Negro is being carefully studied, not just talked about and discussed. In art and letters, instead of being wholly caricatured, he is being seriously portrayed and painted.

To all of this the New Negro is keenly responsive as an augury of a new democracy in American culture. He is contributing his share to the new social understanding. But the desire to be understood would never in itself have been sufficient to have opened so completely the protectively closed portals of the thinking Negro's mind. There is still too much possibility of being snubbed or patronized for that. It was rather the necessity for fuller, truer self-expression, the realization of the unwisdom of allowing social discrimination to segregate him mentally, and a counter-attitude to cramp and fetter his own living—and so the "spite-wall" that the intellectuals built over the "color-line" has happily been taken down. Much of this reopening of intellectual contacts has centered in New York and has been richly fruitful not merely in the enlarging of personal experience, but in the definite enrichment of American art and letters and in the clarifying of our common vision of the social tasks ahead.

The particular significance in the re-establishment of contact between the more advanced and representative classes is that it promises to offset some of the unfavorable reactions of the past, or at least to re-surface race contacts somewhat for the future. Subtly the conditions that are molding a New Negro are molding a new American attitude.

However, this new phase of things is delicate; it will call for less charity but more justice; less help, but infinitely closer understanding. This is indeed a critical stage of race relationships because of the likelihood, if the new temper is not understood, of engendering sharp group antagonism and a second crop of more calculated prejudice. In some quarters, it has already done so. Having weaned the Negro, public opinion cannot continue to paternalize. The Negro to-day is inevitably moving forward under the control largely of his own objectives. What are these objectives? Those of his outer life are happily already well and finally formulated, for they are none other than the ideals of American institutions and democracy. Those of his inner life are yet in process of formation, for the new psychology at present is more of a consensus of feeling than of opinion, of attitude rather than of program. Still some points seem to have crystallized.

Up to the present one may adequately describe the Negro's "inner objectives" as an attempt to repair a damaged group psychology and reshape a warped social perspective. Their realization has required a new mentality for the American Negro. And as it matures we begin to see its effects; at first, negative, iconoclastic, and then positive and constructive. In this new group psychology we note the lapse of sentimental appeal, then the development of a more positive self-respect and self-reliance; the repudiation of social dependence, and then the gradual recovery from hyper-sensitiveness and "touchy" nerves, the repudiation of the double standard of judgment with its special philanthropic allowances and then the sturdier desire for objective and scientific appraisal; and finally the rise from social disillusionment to race pride, from the sense of social debt to the responsibilities of social contribution, and offsetting the necessary working and common-sense acceptance of restricted conditions, the belief in ultimate esteem and recognition. Therefore the Negro to-day wishes to be known for what he is, even in his faults and shortcomings, and scorns a craven and precarious survival at the price of seeming to be what he is not. He resents being spoken of as a social ward or minor, even by his own, and to being regarded a chronic patient for the sociological clinic, the sick man of American Democracy. For the same reasons, he himself is through with those social nostrums and panaceas, the so-called "solutions" of his "problem," with which he and the country have been so liberally dosed in the past. Religion, freedom, education, money—in turn, he has ardently hoped for and peculiarly trusted these things; he still believes in them, but not in blind trust that they alone will solve his life-problem.

Each generation, however, will have its creed, and that of the present is the belief in the efficacy of collective effort, in race co-operation. This deep feeling of race is at present the mainspring of Negro life. It seems to be the outcome of the reaction to proscription and prejudice; an attempt, fairly successful on the whole, to convert a defensive into an offensive position, a handicap into an incentive. It is radical in tone, but not in purpose and only the most stupid forms of opposition, misunderstanding or persecution could make it otherwise. Of course, the thinking Negro has shifted a little toward the left with the world-trend, and there is an increasing group who affiliate with radical and liberal movements. But fundamentally for the present the Negro is radical on race matters, conservative on others, in other words, a "forced radical," a social protestant rather than a genuine radical. Yet under further pressure and injustice iconoclastic thought and motives will inevitably increase. Harlem's quixotic radicalisms call for their ounce of democracy to-day lest to-morrow they be beyond cure.

The Negro mind reaches out as yet to nothing but American wants, American ideas. But this forced attempt to build his Americanism on race values is a unique social experiment, and its ultimate success is impossible except through the fullest sharing of American culture and institutions. There should be no delusion about this. American nerves in sections unstrung with race hysteria are often fed the opiate that the trend of Negro advance is wholly separatist, and that the effect of its operation will be to encyst the Negro as a benign foreign body in the body politic. This cannot be—even if it were desirable. The racialism of the Negro is no limitation or reservation with respect to American life; it is only a constructive effort to build the obstructions in the stream of his progress into an efficient dam of social energy and power. Democracy itself is obstructed and stagnated to the extent that any of its channels are closed. Indeed they cannot be selectively closed. So the choice is not between one way for the Negro and another way for the rest, but between American institutions frustrated on the one hand and American ideals progressively fulfilled and realized on the other.

There is, of course, a warrantably comfortable feeling in being on the right side of the country's professed ideals. We realize that we cannot be undone without America's undoing. It is within the gamut of this attitude that the thinking Negro faces America, but with variations of mood that are if anything more significant than the attitude itself. Sometimes we have it taken with the defiant ironic challenge of McKay:

> Mine is the future grinding down to-day
> Like a great landslip moving to the sea,
> Bearing its freight of débris far away
> Where the green hungry waters restlessly
> Heave mammoth pyramids, and break and roar
> Their eerie challenge to the crumbling shore.

Sometimes, perhaps more frequently as yet, it is taken in the fervent and almost filial appeal and counsel of Weldon Johnson's:

> O Southland, dear Southland!
> Then why do you still cling
> To an idle age and a musty page,
> To a dead and useless thing?

But between defiance and appeal, midway almost between cynicism and hope, the prevailing mind stands in the mood of the same author's *To America*, an attitude of sober query and stoical challenge:

> How would you have us, as we are?
> Or sinking 'neath the load we bear,
> Our eyes fixed forward on a star,
> Or gazing empty at despair?
>
> Rising or falling? Men or things?
> With dragging pace or footsteps fleet?
> Strong, willing sinews in your wings,
> Or tightening chains about your feet?

More and more, however, an intelligent realization of the great discrepancy between the American social creed and the American social practice forces upon the Negro the taking of the moral advantage that is his. Only the steadying and sobering effect of a truly characteristic gentleness of spirit prevents the rapid rise of a definite cynicism and counter-hate and a defiant superiority feeling. Human as this reaction would be, the majority still deprecate its advent, and would gladly see it forestalled by the speedy amelioration of its causes. We wish our race pride to be a healthier, more positive achievement than a feeling based upon a realization of the shortcomings of others. But all paths toward the attainment of a sound social attitude have been difficult; only a relatively few enlightened minds have been able as the phrase puts it "to rise above" prejudice. The ordinary man has had until recently only a hard choice between the alternatives of supine and humiliating submission and stimulating but hurtful counter-prejudice. Fortunately from some inner, desperate resourcefulness has recently sprung up the simple expedient of fighting prejudice by mental passive resistance, in other words by trying to ignore it. For the few, this manna may perhaps be effective, but the masses cannot thrive upon it.

Fortunately there are constructive channels opening out into which the balked social feelings of the American Negro can flow freely.

Without them there would be much more pressure and danger than there is. These compensating interests are racial but in a new and enlarged way. One is the consciousness of acting as the advance-guard of the African peoples in their contact with Twentieth Century civilization; the other, the sense of a mission of rehabilitating the race in world esteem from that loss of prestige for which the fate and conditions of slavery have so largely been responsible. Harlem, as we shall see, is the center of both these movements; she is the home of the Negro's "Zionism." The pulse of the Negro world has begun to beat in Harlem. A Negro newspaper carrying news material in English, French and Spanish, gathered from all quarters of America, the West Indies and Africa has maintained itself in Harlem for over five years. Two important magazines, both edited from New York, maintain their news and circulation consistently on a cosmopolitan scale. Under American auspices and backing, three pan-African congresses have been held abroad for the discussion of common interests, colonial questions and the future co-operative development of Africa. In terms of the race question as a world problem, the Negro mind has leapt, so to speak, upon the parapets of prejudice and extended its cramped horizons. In so doing it has linked up with the growing group consciousness of the dark-peoples and is gradually learning their common interests. As one of our writers has recently put it: "It is imperative that we understand the white world in its relations to the non-white world." As with the Jew, persecution is making the Negro international.

As a world phenomenon this wider race consciousness is a different thing from the much asserted rising tide of color. Its inevitable causes are not of our making. The consequences are not necessarily damaging to the best interests of civilization. Whether it actually brings into being new Armadas of conflict or argosies of cultural exchange and enlightenment can only be decided by the attitude of the dominant races in an era of critical change. With the American Negro, his new internationalism is primarily an effort to recapture contact with the scattered peoples of African derivation. Garveyism may be a transient, if spectacular, phenomenon, but the possible rôle of the American Negro in the future development of Africa is one of the most constructive and universally helpful missions that any modern people can lay claim to.

Constructive participation in such causes cannot help giving the Negro valuable group incentives, as well as increased prestigé at home and abroad. Our greatest rehabilitation may possibly come through such channels, but for the present, more immediate hope rests in the revaluation by white and black alike of the Negro in terms of his artistic endowments and cultural contributions, past and prospective. It must be increasingly recognized that the Negro has already made very substantial contributions, not only in his folk-art, music especially, which has always found appreciation, but in larger, though humbler and less acknowledged ways. For generations the Negro has been the peasant matrix of that section of America which has most undervalued him, and here he has contributed not only materially in labor and in social patience, but spiritually as well. The South has unconsciously absorbed the gift of his folk-temperament. In less than half a generation it will be easier to recognize this, but the fact remains that a leaven of humor, sentiment, imagination and tropic nonchalance has gone into the making of the South from a humble, unacknowledged source. A second crop of the Negro's gifts promises still more largely. He now becomes a conscious contributor and lays aside the status of a beneficiary and ward for that of a collaborator and participant in American civilization. The great social gain in this is the releasing of our talented group from the arid fields of controversy and debate to the productive fields of creative expression. The especially cultural recognition they win should in turn prove the key to that revaluation of the Negro which must precede or accompany any considerable further betterment of race relationships. But whatever the general effect, the present generation will have added the motives of self-expression and spiritual development to the old and still unfinished task of making material headway and progress. No one who understandingly faces the situation with its substantial accomplishment or views the new scene with its still more abundant promise can be entirely without hope. And certainly, if in our lifetime the Negro should not be able to celebrate his full initiation into American democracy, he can at least, on the warrant of these things, celebrate the attainment of a significant and satisfying new phase of group development, and with it a spiritual Coming of Age.

Countee Cullen (1903-1946)

Yet Do I Marvel

I doubt not God is good, well-meaning, kind,
And did He stoop to quibble could tell why
The little buried mole continues blind,
Why flesh that mirrors Him must some day die,

Make plain the reason tortured Tantalus
Is baited by the fickle fruit, declare
If merely brute caprice dooms Sisyphus
To struggle up a never-ending stair.
Inscrutable His ways are, and immune
To catechism by a mind too strewn
With petty cares to slightly understand
What awful brain compels His awful hand.
Yet do I marvel at this curious thing:
To make a poet black, and bid him sing!

Heritage

(For Harold Jackman)

What is Africa to me:
Copper sun or scarlet sea,
Jungle star or jungle track,
Strong bronzed men, or regal black
Women from whose loins I sprang
When the birds of Eden sang?
One three centuries removed
From the scenes his fathers loved,
Spicy grove, cinnamon tree,
What is Africa to me?

So I lie, who all day long
Want no sound except the song
Sung by wild barbaric birds
Goading massive jungle herds,
Juggernauts of flesh that pass
Trampling tall defiant grass
Where young forest lovers lie,
Plighting troth beneath the sky.
So I lie, who always hear,
Though I cram against my ear
Both my thumbs, and keep them there,
Great drums throbbing through the air.
So I lie, whose fount of pride,
Dear distress, and joy allied,
Is my somber flesh and skin,
With the dark blood dammed within
Like great pulsing tides of wine

That, I fear, must burst the fine
Channels of the chafing net
Where they surge and foam and fret.

Africa? A book one thumbs
Listlessly, till slumber comes.
Unremembered are her bats
Circling through the night, her cats
Crouching in the river reeds,
Stalking gentle flesh that feeds
By the river brink; no more
Does the bugle-throated roar
Cry that monarch claws have leapt
From the scabbards where they slept.
Silver snakes that once a year
Doff the lovely coats you wear,
Seek no covert in your fear
Lest a mortal eye should see;
What's your nakedness to me?
Here no leprous flowers rear
Fierce corollas in the air;
Here no bodies sleek and wet,
Dripping mingled rain and sweat,
Tread the savage measures of
Jungle boys and girls in love.
What is last year's snow to me,
Last year's anything? The tree
Budding yearly must forget
How its past arose or set—
Bough and blossom, flower, fruit,
Even what shy bird with mute
Wonder at her travail there,
Meekly labored in its hair.
One three centuries removed
From the scenes his fathers loved,
Spicy grove, cinnamon tree,
What is Africa to me?

So I lie, who find no peace
Night or day, no slight release
From the unremittant beat
Made by cruel padded feet
Walking through my body's street.

Up and down they go, and back,
Treading out a jungle track.
So I lie, who never quite
Safely sleep from rain at night—
I can never rest at all
When the rain begins to fall;
Like a soul gone mad with pain
I must match its weird refrain;
Ever must I twist and squirm,
Writhing like a baited worm,
While its primal measures drip
Through my body, crying, "Strip!
Doff this new exuberance.
Come and dance the Lover's Dance!"
In an old remembered way
Rain works on me night and day.

Quaint, outlandish heathen gods
Black men fashion out of rods,
Clay, and brittle bits of stone,
In a likeness like their own,
My conversion came high-priced;
I belong to Jesus Christ,
Preacher of humility;
Heathen gods are naught to me.

Father, Son, and Holy Ghost,
So I make an idle boast;
Jesus of the twice-turned cheek,
Lamb of God, although I speak
With my mouth thus, in my heart
Do I play a double part.
Ever at Thy glowing altar
Must my heart grow sick and falter,
Wishing He I served were black,
Thinking then it would not lack
Precedent of pain to guide it,
Let who would or might deride it;
Surely then this flesh would know
Yours had borne a kindred woe.
Lord, I fashion dark gods, too,
Daring even to give You
Dark despairing features where,
Crowned with dark rebellious hair,

Patience wavers just so much as
Mortal grief compels, while touches
Quick and hot, of anger, rise
To smitten cheek and weary eyes.
Lord, forgive me if my need
Sometimes shapes a human creed.
All day long and all night through,
One thing only must I do:
Quench my pride and cool my blood,
Lest I perish in the flood.
Lest a hidden ember set
Timber that I thought was wet
Burning like the dryest flax,
Melting like the merest wax,
Lest the grave restore its dead.
Not yet has my heart or head
In the least way realized
They and I are civilized.

Saturday's Child

Some are teethed on a silver spoon,
    With the stars strung for a rattle;
I cut my teeth as the black raccoon—
    For implements of battle.

Some are swaddled in silk and down,
    And heralded by a star;
They swathed my limbs in a sackcloth gown
    On a night that was black as tar.

For some, godfather and goddame
    The opulent fairies be;
Dame Poverty gave me my name,
    And Pain godfathered me.

For I was born on Saturday—
    "Bad time for planting a seed,"
Was all my father had to say,
    And, "One mouth more to feed."

Death cut the strings that gave me life,
    And handed me to Sorrow,

The only kind of middle wife
  My folks could beg or borrow.

Black Magdalens

These have no Christ to spit and stoop
  To write upon the sand,
Inviting him that has not sinned
  To raise the first rude hand.

And if he came they could not buy
  Rich ointment for his feet,
The body's sale scarce yields enough
  To let the body eat.

The chaste clean ladies pass them by
  And draw their skirts aside,
But Magdalens have a ready laugh;
  They wrap their wounds in pride.

They fare full ill since Christ forsook
  The cross to mount a throne,
And Virtue still is stooping down
  To cast the first hard stone.

A Song of Praise

(For one who praised his lady's being fair.)

You have not heard my love's dark throat,
  Slow-fluting like a reed,
Release the perfect golden note
  She caged there for my need.

Her walk is like the replica
  Of some barbaric dance
Wherein the soul of Africa
  Is winged with arrogance.

And yet so light she steps across
  The ways her sure feet pass,
She does not dent the smoothest moss
  Or bend the thinnest grass.

My love is dark as yours is fair,
　Yet lovelier I hold her
Than listless maids with pallid hair,
　And blood that's thin and colder.

You-proud-and-to-be-pitied one,
　Gaze on her and despair;
Then seal your lips until the sun
　Discovers one as fair.

Jean Toomer (1894-1967)

Avey

From Cane

For a long while she was nothing more to me than one of those skirted beings whom boys at a certain age disdain to play with. Just how I came to love her, timidly, and with secret blushes, I do not know. But that I did was brought home to me one night, the first night that Ned wore his long pants. Us fellers were seated on the curb before an apartment house where she had gone in. The young trees had not outgrown their boxes then. V Street was lined with them. When our legs grew cramped and stiff from the cold of the stone, we'd stand around a box and whittle it. I like to think now that there was a hidden purpose in the way we hacked them with our knives. I like to feel that something deep in me responded to the trees, the young trees that whinnied like colts impatient to be let free. . . On the particular night I have in mind, we were waiting for the top-floor light to go out. We wanted to see Avey leave the flat. This night she stayed longer than usual and gave us a chance to complete the plans of how we were going to stone and beat that feller on the top floor out of town. Ned especially had it in for him. He was about to throw a brick up at the window when at last the room went dark. Some minutes passed. Then Avey, as unconcerned as if she had been paying an old-maid aunt a visit, came out. I don't remember what she had on, and all that sort of thing. But I do know that I turned hot as bare pavements in the summertime at Ned's boast: "Hell, bet I could get her too if you little niggers weren't always spying and crabbing everything." I didnt say a word to him. It wasnt my way then. I just stood there like the others, and something like a fuse burned up inside of me. She never noticed us, but swung along lazy and easy as anything. We sauntered to the corner and watched her till her door banged to. Ned repeated what he'd said. I didnt seem to care. Sitting around old Mush-Head's bread box, the discussion began. "Hang if I can see how she gets away with it," Doc started. Ned knew, of course. There was nothing he didnt know when it came to women. He dilated on the emotional needs of girls. Said they werent much different from men in that respect. And concluded with the solemn avowal: "It does em good." None of us liked Ned much. We all talked dirt; but it was the way he said it. And then too, a couple of the fellers had sisters and had caught Ned playing with them. But there was no disputing the superiority of his smutty wisdom. Bubs Sanborn, whose mother was friendly with Avey's, had overhead the old ladies talking. "Avey's mother's ont her," he said. We thought that only natural and began to guess at what would happen. Some one said she'd marry that feller on the top floor. Ned called that a lie because Avey was going to marry nobody but him. We had our doubts about that, but we did agree that she'd soon leave school and marry some one. The gang broke up, and I went home, picturing myself as married.

Nothing I did seemed able to change Avey's indifference to me. I played basket-ball, and when I'd make a long clean shot she'd clap with the others, louder than they, I thought. I'd meet her on the street, and there'd be no difference in the way she said hello. She never took the trouble to call me by my name. On the days for drill, I'd let my voice down a tone and call for a complicated maneuver when I saw her coming. She'd smile appreciation, but it was an impersonal smile, never for me. It was on a summer excursion down to Riverview that she first seemed to take me into account. The day had been spent riding merry-go-rounds, scenic-railways, and shoot-the-chutes. We had been in swimming and we had danced. I was a crack swimmer then. She didnt know how. I held her up and showed her how to kick her legs and draw her arms. Of course she didnt learn in one day, but she thanked me for bothering with her. I was also somewhat of a dancer. And I had already noticed that love can start on a dance floor. We danced. But though I held her tightly in my arms, she was way away. That college feller who lived on the top floor was somewhere making money for the next year. I imagined that she was thinking, wishing for him. Ned was along. He treated her until his money gave out. She went with another feller. Ned got sore. One by one the boys' money gave out. She left them. And they got sore. Every one of them but me got sore. This is the reason, I guess, why I had her to myself on the top deck of the *Jane Mosely* that night as we puffed up the Potomac, coming home. The moon was brilliant. The air was sweet like clover. And every now and then, a salt tang, a stale drift of sea-weed. It was not my mind's fault if it went romancing. I should have taken her in my arms the minute we were stowed in that old lifeboat. I dallied, dreaming. She took me in hers. And I could feel by the touch of it that it wasnt a man-to-woman love. It made me restless. I felt chagrined. I didnt know what it was, but I did know that I couldnt handle it. She ran her fingers through my hair and kissed my forehead. I itched to break through her tenderness to passion. I wanted her to take me in her arms as I knew she had that college feller. I wanted her to love me passionately as she did him. I gave her one burning kiss. Then she laid me in her lap as if I were a child. Helpless. I got sore when she started to hum a lullaby. She wouldnt let me go. I talked. I knew damned well that I could beat her at that. Her eyes were soft and misty, the curves of her lips were wistful, and her smile seemed indulgent of the irrelevance of my remarks. I gave up at last and let her love me, silently, in her own way. The moon was brilliant. The air was sweet like clover, and every now and then, a salt tang, a stale drift of sea-weed. . .

The next time I came close to her was the following summer at Harpers Ferry. We were sitting on a flat projecting rock they give the name of Lover's Leap. Some one is supposed to have jumped off it. The river is about six hundred feet beneath. A railroad track runs up the valley and curves out of sight where part of the mountain rock had to be blasted away to make room for it. The engines of this valley have a whistle, the echoes of which sound like iterated gasps and sobs. I always think of them as crude music from the soul of Avey. We sat there holding hands. Our palms were soft and warm against each other. Our fingers were not tight. She would not let them be. She would not let me twist them. I wanted to talk. To explain what I meant to her. Avey was as silent as those great trees whose tops we looked down upon. She has always been like that. At least, to me. I had the notion that if I really wanted to, I could do with her just what I pleased. Like one can strip a tree. I did kiss her. I even let my hands cup her breasts. When I was through, she'd seek my hand and hold it till my pulse cooled down. Evening after evening we sat there. I tried to get her to talk about that college feller. She never would. There was no set time to go home. None of my family had come down. And as for hers, she didnt give a hang about them. The general gossips could hardly say more than they had. The boarding-house porch was always deserted when we returned. No one saw us enter, so the time was set conveniently for scandal. This worried me a little, for I thought it might keep Avey from getting an appointment in the schools. She didnt care. She had finished normal school. They could give her a job if they wanted to. As time went on, her indifference to things began to pique me; I was ambitious. I left the Ferry earlier than she did. I was going off to college. The more I thought of it, the more I resented, yes, hell, thats what it was, her downright laziness. Sloppy indolence. There was no excuse for a healthy girl taking life so easy. Hell! she was no better than a cow. I was certain that she was a cow when I felt an udder in a Wisconsin stock-judging class. Among those energetic Swedes, or whatever they are, I decided to forget her. For two years I thought I did. When I'd come home for the summer she'd be away. And before she returned, I'd be gone. We never wrote; she was too damned lazy for that. But what a bluff I put up about forgetting her. The girls up that way, at least the ones I knew, havent got the stuff: they dont know how to love. Giving themselves completely was tame beside just the holding of Avey's hand. One day I received a note from her. The writing, I decided, was slovenly. She wrote on a torn bit of note-book paper. The envelope had a faint perfume that I remembered. A single line told me she had lost her school and was going away. I comforted myself with the reflection that shame held no pain for one so indolent as she. Nevertheless, I left Wisconsin that year for good. Washington had seemingly forgotten her. I hunted Ned. Between curses, I caught his opinion of her. She was no better than a whore. I saw her mother on the street. The same old pinch-beck, jerky-gaited creature that I'd always known.

Perhaps five years passed. The business of hunting a job or something or other had bruised my vanity so that I could recognize it. I felt old. Avey and my real relation to her, I thought I came to know. I wanted to see her. I had been told that she was in New York. As I had no money, I hiked and bummed my way there. I got work in a ship-yard and walked the streets at night, hoping to meet her. Failing in this, I saved enough to pay my fare back home. One evening in early June, just at the time when dusk is most lovely on the eastern horizon, I saw Avey, indolent as ever, leaning on the arm of a man, strolling under the recently lit arc-lights of U Street. She had almost passed before she recognized me. She showed no surprise. The puff over her eyes had grown heavier. The eyes themselves were still sleepy-large, and beautiful. I had almost concluded—indifferent. "You look older," was what she said. I wanted to convince her that I was, so I asked her to walk with me. The man whom she was with, and whom she never took the trouble to introduce, at a nod from her, hailed a taxi, and drove away. That gave me a notion of what she had been used to. Her dress was of some fine, costly stuff. I suggested the park, and then added that the grass might stain her skirt. Let it get stained, she said, for where it came from there are others.

I have a spot in Soldier's Home to which I always go when I want the simple beauty of another's soul. Robins spring about the lawn all day. They leave their footprints in the grass. I imagine that the grass at night smells sweet and fresh because of them. The ground is high. Washington lies below. Its light spreads like a blush against the darkened sky. Against the soft dusk sky of Washington. And when the wind is from the South, soil of my homeland falls like a fertile shower upon the lean streets of the city. Upon my hill in Soldier's Home. I know the policeman who watches the place of nights. When I go there alone, I talk to him. I tell him I come there to find the truth that people bury in their hearts. I tell him that I do not come there with a girl to do the thing he's paid to watch out for. I look deep in his eyes when I say these things, and he believes me. He comes over to see who it is on the grass. I say hello to him. He greets me in the same way and goes off searching for other black splotches upon the lawn. Avey and I went there. A band in one of the buildings a fair distance off was playing a march. I wished they would stop. Their playing was like a tin spoon in one's mouth. I wanted the Howard Glee Club to sing "Deep River," from the road. To sing "Deep River, Deep River," from the road. . . Other than the first comments, Avey had been silent. I started to hum a folk-tune. She slipped her hand in mine. Pillowed her head as best she could upon my arm. Kissed the hand that she was holding and listened, or so I thought, to what I had to say. I traced my development from the early days up to the present time, the phase in which I could understand her. I described her own nature and temperament. Told how they needed a larger life for their expression. How incapable Washington was of understanding that need. How it could not meet it. I pointed out that in lieu of proper channels, her emotions had overflowed into paths that dissipated them. I talked, beautifully I thought, about an art that would be born, an art that would open the way for women the likes of her. I asked her to hope, and build up an inner life against the coming of that day. I recited some of my own things to her. I sang, with a strange quiver in my voice, a promise-song. And then I began to wonder why her hand had not once returned a single pressure. My old-time feeling about her laziness came back. I spoke sharply. My policeman friend passed by. I said hello to him. As he went away, I began to visualize certain possibilities. An immediate and urgent passion swept over me. Then I looked at Avey. Her heavy eyes were closed. Her breathing was as faint and regular as a child's in slumber. My passion died. I was afraid to move lest I disturb her. Hours and hours, I guess it was, she lay there. My body grew numb. I shivered. I coughed. I wanted to get up and whittle at the boxes of young trees. I withdrew my hand. I raised her head to waken her. She did not stir. I got up and walked around. I found my policeman friend and talked to him. We both came up, and bent over her. He said it would be all right for her to stay there just so long as she got away before the workmen came at dawn. A blanket was borrowed from a neighbor house. I sat beside her through the night. I saw the dawn steal over Washington. The Capitol dome looked like a gray ghost ship drifting in from sea. Avey's face was pale, and her eyes were heavy. She did not have the gray crimson-splashed beauty of the dawn. I hated to wake her. Orphan-woman. . .

Georgia Dusk

From Cane

The sky, lazily disdaining to pursue
    The setting sun, too indolent to hold
    A lengthened tournament for flashing gold,
Passively darkens for night's barbecue,

A feast of moon and men and barking hounds,
    An orgy for some genius of the South
    With blood-hot eyes and cane-lipped scented mouth,
Surprised in making folk-songs from soul sounds.

The sawmill blows its whistle, buzz-saws stop,
    And silence breaks the bud of knoll and hill,
    Soft settling pollen where plowed lands fulfill
Their early promise of a bumper crop.

Smoke from the pyramidal sawdust pile
  Curls up, blue ghosts of trees, tarrying low
  Where only chips and stumps are left to show
The solid proof of former domicile.

Meanwhile, the men, with vestiges of pomp,
  Race memories of king and caravan,
  High-priests, an ostrich, and a juju-man,
Go singing through the footpaths of the swamp.

Their voices rise . . the pine trees are guitars,
  Strumming, pine-needles fall like sheets of rain . .
  Their voices rise . . the chorus of the cane
Is caroling a vesper to the stars. .

O singers, resinous and soft your songs
  Above the sacred whisper of the pines,
  Give virgin lips to cornfield concubines,
Bring dreams of Christ to dusky cane-lipped throngs.

Song of the Son

From Cane

Pour O pour that parting soul in song,
O pour it in the sawdust glow of night,
Into the velvet pine-smoke air to-night,
And let the valley carry it along.
And let the valley carry it along.

O land and soil, red soil and sweet-gum tree,
So scant of grass, so profligate of pines,
Now just before an epoch's sun declines
Thy son, in time, I have returned to thee,
Thy son, I have in time returned to thee.

In time, for though the sun is setting on
A song-lit race of slaves, it has not set;
Though late, O soil, it is not too late yet
To catch thy plaintive soul, leaving, soon gone,
Leaving, to catch thy plaintive soul soon gone.

O Negro slaves, dark purple ripened plums,
Squeezed, and bursting in the pine-wood air,

Passing, before they stripped the old tree bare
One plum was saved for me, one seed becomes

An everlasting song, a singing tree,
Caroling softly souls of slavery,
What they were, and what they are to me,
Caroling softly souls of slavery.

Storm Ending

From Cane

Thunder blossoms gorgeously above our heads,
Great, hollow, bell-like flowers,
Rumbling in the wind,
Stretching clappers to strike our ears . .
Full-lipped flowers
Bitten by the sun
Bleeding rain
Dripping rain like golden honey—
And the sweet earth flying from the thunder.

Claude McKay (1889-1948)

If We Must Die

If we must die, let it not be like hogs
Hunted and penned in an inglorious spot,
While round us bark the mad and hungry dogs,
Making their mock at our accursed lot.
If we must die, O let us nobly die,
So that our precious blood may not be shed
In vain; then even the monsters we defy
Shall be constrained to honor us though dead!
O kinsmen! we must meet the common foe!
Though far outnumbered let us show us brave,
And for their thousand blows deal one deathblow!
What though before us lies the open grave?
Like men we'll face the murderous, cowardly pack,
Pressed to the wall, dying, but fighting back!

The Lynching

His Spirit in smoke ascended to high heaven.
His father, by the cruelest way of pain,
Had bidden him to his bosom once again;
The awful sin remained still unforgiven.
All night a bright and solitary star
(Perchance the one that ever guided him,
Yet gave him up at last to Fate's wild whim)
Hung pitifully o'er the swinging char.
Day dawned, and soon the mixed crowds came to view
The ghastly body swaying in the sun.
The women thronged to look, but never a one
Showed sorrow in her eyes of steely blue.

And little lads, lynchers that were to be,
Danced round the dreadful thing in fiendish glee.

America

Although she feeds me bread of bitterness,
And sinks into my throat her tiger's tooth,
Stealing my breath of life, I will confess
I love this cultured hell that tests my youth!
Her vigor flows like tides into my blood,
Giving me strength erect against her hate.
Her bigness sweeps my being like a flood.
Yet as a rebel fronts a king in state,
I stand within her walls with not a shred
Of terror, malice, not a word of jeer.
Darkly I gaze into the days ahead,
And see her might and granite wonders there,
Beneath the touch of Time's unerring hand,
Like priceless treasures sinking in the sand.

The City's Love

For one brief golden moment rare like wine,
The gracious city swept across the line;
Oblivious of the color of my skin,
Forgetting that I was an alien guest,
She bent to me, my hostile heart to win,
Caught me in passion to her pillowy breast.
The great, proud city, seized with a strange love,
Bowed down for one flame hour my pride to prove.

The Harlem Dancer

Applauding youths laughed with young prostitutes
And watched her perfect, half-clothed body sway;
Her voice was like the sound of blended flutes
Blown by black players upon a picnic day.
She sang and danced on gracefully and calm,
The light gauze hanging loose about her form;
To me she seemed a proudly-swaying palm
Grown lovelier for passing through a storm.
Upon her swarthy neck black shiny curls·
Luxuriant fell; and tossing coins in praise,
The wine-flushed, bold-eyed boys, and even the girls,
Devoured her shape with eager, passionate gaze;
But looking at her falsely-smiling face,
I knew her self was not in that strange place.

The Negro's Tragedy

It is the Negro's tragedy I feel
Which binds me like a heavy iron chain,
It is the Negro's wounds I want to heal
Because I know the keenness of his pain.
Only a thorn-crowned Negro and no white
Can penetrate into the Negro's ken,
Or feel the thickness of the shroud of night
Which hides and buries him from other men.

So what I write is urged out of my blood.
There is no white man who could write my book,
Though many think their story should be told
Of what the Negro people ought to brook.
Our statesmen roam the world to set things right.
This Negro laughs and prays to God for Light!

Jasmine

Your scent is in the room.
Swiftly it overwhelms and conquers me!
Jasmine, night jasmine, perfect of perfume,
Heavy with dew before the dawn of day!
Your face was in the mirror. I could see
You smile and vanish suddenly away,
Leaving behind the vestige of a tear.
Sad suffering face, from parting grown so dear!

Night jasmine cannot bloom in this cold place;
Without the street is wet and weird with snow;
The cold nude trees are tossing to and fro;
Too stormy is the night for your fond face;
For your low voice too loud the wind's mad roar.
But oh, your scent is here—jasmines that grow
Luxuriant, clustered round your cottage door!

Home Thoughts

Oh something just now must be happening there!
That suddenly and quiveringly here,
Amid the city's noises, I must think
Of mangoes leaning to the river's brink,
And dexterous Davie climbing high above,
The gold fruits ebon-speckled to remove,
And toss them quickly in the tangled mass
Of wis-wis twisted round the guinea grass.
And Cyril coming through the bramble-track
A prize bunch of bananas on his back;
And Georgie—none could ever dive like him—
Throwing his scanty clothes off for a swim;
And schoolboys, from Bridge-tunnel going home,
Watching the waters downward dash and foam.
This is no daytime dream, there's something in it,
Oh something's happening there this very minute!

Tiger

The white man is a tiger at my throat,
Drinking my blood as my life ebbs away,
And muttering that his terrible striped coat
Is Freedom's and portends the Light of Day.
Oh white man, you may suck up all my blood
And throw my carcass into potter's field,
But never will I say with you that mud
Is bread for Negroes! Never will I yield.

Europe and Africa and Asia wait
The touted New Deal of the New World's hand!
New systems will be built on race and hate,
The Eagle and the Dollar will command.
Oh Lord! My body, and my heart too, break—
The tiger in his strength his thirst must slake!

Rudolph Fisher (1897-1934)

The City of Refuge

I

Confronted suddenly by daylight, King Solomon Gillis stood dazed and blinking. The railroad station, the long, white-walled corridor, the impassible slot-machine, the terrifying subway train—he felt as if he had been caught up in the jaws of a steam-shovel, jammed together with other helpless lumps of dirt, swept blindly along for a time, and at last abruptly dumped.

There had been strange and terrible sounds: 'New York! Penn Terminal—all change!' 'Pohter, hyer, pohter, suh?' Shuffle of a thousand soles, clatter of a thousand heels, innumerable echoes. Cracking rifle-shots—no, snapping turnstiles. 'Put a nickel in!' 'Harlem? Sure. This side—next train.' Distant thunder, nearing. The screeching onslaught of the fiery hosts of hell, headlong, breath-taking. Car doors rattling, sliding, banging open. 'Say, wha' d'ye think this is, a baggage car?' Heat, oppression, suffocation—eternity—'Hundred 'n turdy-fif' next!' More turnstiles. Jonah emerging from the whale.

Clean air, blue sky, bright sunlight.

Gillis set down his tan-cardboard extension-case and wiped his black, shining brow. Then slowly, spreadingly, he grinned at what he saw: Negroes at every turn; up and down Lenox Avenue, up and down One Hundred and Thirty-Fifth Street; big, lanky Negroes, short, squat Negroes; black ones, brown ones, yellow ones; men standing idle on the curb, women, bundle-laden, trudging reluctantly homeward, children rattle-trapping about the sidewalks; here and there a white face drifting along, but Negroes predominantly, overwhelmingly everywhere. There was assuredly no doubt of his whereabouts. This was Negro Harlem.

Back in North Carolina Gillis had shot a white man and, with the aid of prayer and an automobile, probably escaped a lynching. Carefully avoiding the railroads, he had reached Washington in safety. For his car a Southwest bootlegger had given him a hundred dollars and directions to Harlem; and so he had come to Harlem.

Ever since a traveling preacher had first told him of the place, King Solomon Gillis had longed to come to Harlem. The Uggams were always talking about it; one of their boys had gone to France in the draft and, returning, had never got any nearer home than Harlem. And there were occasional 'colored' newspapers from New York: newspapers that mentioned Negroes without comment, but always spoke of a white person as 'So-and-so, white.' That was the point. In Harlem, black was white. You had rights that could not be denied you; you had privileges, protected by law. And you had money. Everybody in Harlem had money. It was a land of plenty. Why, had not Mouse Uggam sent back as much as fifty dollars at a time to his people in Waxhaw?

The shooting, therefore, simply catalyzed whatever sluggish mental reaction had been already directing King Solomon's fortunes toward Harlem. The land of plenty was more than that now: it was also the city of refuge.

Casting about for direction, the tall newcomer's glance caught inevitably on the most conspicuous thing in sight, a magnificent figure in blue that stood in the middle of the crossing and blew a whistle and waved great white-gloved hands. The Southern Negro's eyes opened wide; his mouth opened wider. If the inside of New York had mystified him, the outside was amazing him. For there stood a handsome, brass-buttoned giant directing the heaviest traffic Gillis had ever seen; halting unnumbered tons of automobiles and trucks and wagons and pushcarts and street-cars; holding them at bay with one hand while he swept similar tons peremptorily on with the other; ruling the wide crossing with supreme self-assurance; and he, too, was a Negro!

Yet most of the vehicles that leaped or crouched at his bidding carried white passengers. One of these overdrove bounds a few feet and Gillis heard the officer's shrill whistle and gruff reproof, saw the driver's face turn red and his car draw back like a threatened pup. It was beyond belief—impossible. Black might be white, but it could n't be that white!

'Done died an' woke up in Heaven,' thought King Solomon, watching, fascinated; and after a while, as if the wonder of it were too great to believe simply by seeing, 'Cullud policemans!' he said, half aloud; then repeated over and over, with greater and greater conviction, 'Even got cullud policemans—even got cullud—'

'Where y' want to go, big boy?'

Gillis turned. A little, sharp-faced yellow man was addressing him.

'Saw you was a stranger. Thought maybe I could help y' out.'

King Solomon located and gratefully extended a slip of paper. 'Wha' dis hyeh at, please, suh?'

The other studied it a moment, pushing back his hat and scratching his head. The hat was a tall-crowned, unindented brown felt; the head was brown patent-leather, its glistening brush-back flawless save for a suspicious crimpiness near the clean-grazed edges.

'See that second corner? Turn to the left when you get there. Number forty-five 's about halfway the block.'

'Thank y', suh.'

'You from—Massachusetts?'

'No, suh, Nawth Ca'lina.'

'Is 'at so? You look like a Northerner. Be with us long?'

'Till I die,' grinned the flattered King Solomon.

'Stoppin' there?'

'Reckon I is. Man in Washin'ton 'lowed I'd find lodgin' at dis ad-dress.'

'Good enough. If y' don't, maybe I can fix y' up. Harlem's pretty crowded. This is me.' He proffered a card.

'Thank y', suh,' said Gillis, and put the card in his pocket.

The little yellow man watched him plod flat-footedly on down the street, long awkward legs never quite straightened, shouldered extension-case bending him sidewise, wonder upon wonder halting or turning him about. Presently, as he proceeded, a pair of bright-green stockings caught and held his attention. Tony, the storekeeper, was crossing the sidewalk with a bushel basket of apples. There was a collision; the apples rolled; Tony exploded; King Solomon apologized. The little yellow man laughed shortly, took out a notebook, and put down the address he had seen on King Solomon's slip of paper.

'Guess you 're the shine I been waitin' for,' he surmised.

As Gillis, approaching his destination, stopped to rest, a haunting notion grew into an insistent idea. 'Dat li'l yaller nigger was a sho' 'nuff gen'man to show me de road. Seem lak I knowed him befo'—' He pondered. That receding brow, that sharp-ridged, spreading nose, that tight upper lip over the two big front teeth, that chinless jaw— He fumbled hurriedly for the card he had not looked at and eagerly made out the name.

'Mouse Uggam, sho' 'nuff! Well, dog-gone!'

II

Uggam sought out Tom Edwards, once a Pullman porter, now prosperous proprietor of a cabaret, and told him:—

'Chief, I got him: a baby jess in from the land o' cotton and so dumb he thinks ante bellum 's an old woman.'

'Where 'd you find him?'

'Where you find all the jay birds when they first hit Harlem—at the subway entrance. This one come up the stairs, batted his eyes once or twice, an' froze to the spot—with his mouth open. Sure sign he 's from 'way down behind the sun an' ripe f' the pluckin'.'

Edwards grinned a gold-studded, fat-jowled grin. 'Gave him the usual line, I suppose?'

'Did n't miss. An' he fell like a ton o' bricks. 'Course I've got him spotted, but damn 'f I know jess how to switch 'em on to him.'

'Get him a job around a store somewhere. Make out you 're befriendin' him. Get his confidence.'

'Sounds good. Ought to be easy. He 's from my state. Maybe I know him or some of his people.'

'Make out you do, anyhow. Then tell him some fairy tale that 'll switch your trade to him. The cops 'll follow the trade. We could even let Froggy flop into some dumb white cop's hands and "confess" where he got it. See?'

'Chief, you got a head, no lie.'

'Don't lose no time. And remember, hereafter, it 's better to sacrifice a little than to get squealed on. Never refuse a customer. Give him a little credit. Humor him along till you can get rid of him safe. You don't know what that guy that

died may have said; you don't know who 's on to you now. And if they get you—
I don't know you.'

'They won't get *me*,' said Uggam.

King Solomon Gillis sat meditating in a room half the size of his hencoop
back home, with a single window opening into an airshaft.

An airshaft: cabbage and chitterlings cooking; liver and onions sizzling,
sputtering; three player-pianos out-plunking each other; a man and woman calling each other vile things; a sick, neglected baby wailing; a phonograph broad-
casting blues; dishes clacking; a girl crying heartbrokenly; waste noises,
waste odors of a score of families, seeking issue through a common channel;
pollution from bottom to top—a sewer of sounds and smells.

Contemplating this, King Solomon grinned and breathed, 'Dog-gone!' A little
later, still gazing into the sewer, he grinned again. 'Green stockin's,' he said;
'loud green!' The sewer gradually grew darker. A window lighted up opposite,
revealing a woman in camisole and petticoat, arranging her hair. King Solomon,
staring vacantly, shook his head and grinned yet again. 'Even got cullud policemans!' he mumbled softly.

III

Uggam leaned out of the room's one window and spat maliciously into the
dinginess of the airshaft. 'Damn glad you got him,' he commented, as Gillis
finished his story. 'They's a thousand shines in Harlem would change places with
you in a minute jess f' the honor of killin' a cracker.'

'But I did n't go to do it. 'T was a accident.'

'That 's the only part to keep secret.'

'Know whut dey done? Dey killed five o' Mose Joplin's hawses 'fo he lef'. Put
groun' glass in de feed-trough. Sam Cheevers come up on three of 'em one night
pizenin' his well. Bleesom beat Crinshaw out o' sixty acres o' lan' an' a year's
crops. Dass jess how 't is. Soon 's a nigger make a li'l sump'n he better git to
leavin'. An' 'fo long ev'ybody 's goin' be lef'!'

'Hope to hell they don't all come here.'

The doorbell of the apartment rang. A crescendo of footfalls in the hallway
culminated in a sharp rap on Gillis's door. Gillis jumped. Nobody but a policeman would rap like that. Maybe the landlady had been listening and had called
in the law. It came again, loud, quick, angry. King Solomon prayed that the
policeman would be a Negro.

Uggam stepped over and opened the door. King Solomon's apprehensive eyes
saw framed therein, instead of a gigantic officer, calling for him, a little blot of
a creature, quite black against even the darkness of the hallway, except for a
dirty, wide-striped silk shirt, collarless, with the sleeves rolled up.

'Ah hahve bill fo' Mr. Gillis.' A high, strongly accented Jamaican voice, with
its characteristic singsong intonation, interrupted King Solmon's sigh of relief.

'Bill? Bill fo' me? What kin' o' bill?'

'Wan bushel appels. T'ree seventy-fife.'

'Apples? I ain' bought no apples.' He took the paper and read aloud, laboriously, 'Antonio Gabrielli to K. S. Gillis, Doctor—'

'Mr. Gabrielli say, you not pays him, he send policemon.'

'What I had to do wid 'is apples?'

'You bumps into him yesterday, no? Scatter appels everywhere—on de sidewalk, in de gutter. Kids pick up an' run away. Others all spoil. So you pays.'

Gillis appealed to Uggam. 'How 'bout it, Mouse?'

'He 's a damn liar. Tony picked up most of 'em; I seen him. Lemme look at that bill—Tony never wrote this thing. This baby's jess playin' you for a sucker.'

'Ain' had no apples, ain' payin' fo' none,' announced King Solomon, thus prompted. 'Did n't have to come to Harlem to git cheated. Plenty o' dat right wha' I come fum.'

But the West Indian warmly insisted. 'You cahn't do daht, mon. Whaht you t'ink, 'ey? Dis mon loose 'is appels an' 'is money too?'

'What diff'ence it make to you, nigger?'

'Who you call nigger, mon? Ah hahve you understahn'—'

'Oh, well, white folks, den. What all you got t' do wid dis hyeh, anyhow?'

'Mr. Gabrielli send me to collect bill!'

'How I know dat?'

'Do Ah not bring bill? You t'ink Ah steal t'ree dollar, 'ey?'

'Three dollars an' sebenty-fi' cent,' corrected Gillis. 'Nuther thing: wha' you ever see me befo'? How you know dis is me?'

'Ah see you, sure. Ah help Mr. Gabrielli in de store. When you knocks down de baskette appels, Ah see. Ah follow you. Ah know you comes in dis house.'

'Oh, you does? An' how come you know my name an' flat an' room so good? How come dat?'

'Ah fin' out. Sometime Ah brings up here vegetables from de store.'

'Humph! Mus' be workin' on shares.'

'You pays, 'ey? You pays me or de policemon?'

'Wait a minute,' broke in Uggam, who had been thoughtfully contemplating the bill. 'Now listen, big shorty. You haul hips on back to Tony. We got your menu all right'—he waved the bill—'but we don't eat your kind o' cookin', see?'

The West Indian flared. 'Whaht it is to you, 'ey? You can not mind your own business? Ah hahve not spik to you!'

'No, brother. But this is my friend, an' I 'll be john-browned if there 's a monkey-chaser in Harlem can gyp him if I know it, see? Bes' thing f' you to do is catch air, toot sweet.'

Sensing frustration, the little islander demanded the bill back. Uggam figured he could use the bill himself, maybe. The West Indian hotly persisted; he even menaced. Uggam pocketed the paper and invited him to take it. Wisely enough, the caller preferred to catch air.

When he had gone, King Solomon sought words of thanks.

'Bottle it,' said Uggam. 'The point is this: I figger you got a job.'

'Job? No I ain't! Wha' at?'

'When you show Tony this bill, he'll hit the roof and fire that monk.'

'What ef he do?'

'Then you up 'n ask f' the job. He 'll be too grateful to refuse. I know Tony some, an' I' ll be there to put in a good word. See?'

King Solomon considered this. 'Sho' needs a job, but ain' after stealin' none.'

'Stealin'? 'T would n't be stealin'. Stealin' 's what that damn monkey-chaser tried to do from you. This would be doin' Tony a favor an' gettin' y'self out o' the barrel. What 's the hold-back?'

'What make you keep callin' him monkey-chaser?'

'West Indian. That's another thing. Any time y' can knife a monk, do it. They 's too damn many of 'em here. They 're an achin' pain.'

'Jess de way white folks feels 'bout niggers.'

'Damn that. How 'bout it? Y' want the job?'

'Hm—well—I 'd ruther be a policeman.'

'Policeman?' Uggam gasped.

'M-hm. Dass all I wants to be, a policeman, so I kin police all de white folks right plumb in jail!'

Uggam said seriously, 'Well, y' might work up to that. But it takes time. An' y've got to eat while y're waitin'.' He paused to let this penetrate. 'Now, how 'bout this job at Tony's in the meantime? I should think y'd jump at it.'

King Solomon was persuaded.

'Hm—well—reckon I does,' he said slowly.

'Now y're tootin'!' Uggam's two big front teeth popped out in a grin of genuine pleasure. 'Come on. Let 's go.'

IV

Spitting blood and crying with rage, the West Indian scrambled to his feet. For a moment he stood in front of the store gesticulating furiously and jabbering shrill threats and unintelligible curses. Then abruptly he stopped and took himself off.

King Solomon Gillis, mildly puzzled, watched him from Tony's doorway. 'I jess give him a li'l shove,' he said to himself, 'an' he roll' clean 'cross de sidewalk.' And a little later, disgustedly, 'Monkey-chaser!' he grunted, and went back to his sweeping.

'Well, big boy, how y' comin' on?'

Gillis dropped his broom. 'Hay-o, Mouse. Wha' you been las' two-three days?'

'Oh, around. Gettin' on all right here? Had any trouble?'

'Deed I ain't—'ceptin' jess now I had to throw 'at li'l jigger out.'

'Who? The monk?'

'M-hm. He sho' Lawd doan like me in his job. Look like he think I stole it from him, stiddy him tryin' to steal from me. Had to push him down sho' 'nuff 'fo I could git rid of 'im. Den he run off talkin' Wes' Indi'man an' shakin' his fis' at me.'

'Ferget it.' Uggam glanced about. 'Where 's Tony?'

'Boss man? He be back direckly.'

'Listen—like to make two or three bucks a day extra?'

'Huh?'

'Two or three dollars a day more 'n what you 're gettin' already?'

'Ain' I near 'nuff in jail now?'

'Listen.' King Solomon listened. Uggam had n't been in France for nothing. Fact was, in France he 'd learned about some valuable French medicine. He 'd brought some back with him,—little white pills,—and while in Harlem had found a certain druggist who knew what they were and could supply all he could use. Now there were any number of people who would buy and pay well for as much of this French medicine as Uggam could get. It was good for what ailed them, and they did n't know how to get it except through him. But he had no store in which to set up an agency and hence no single place where his customers could go to get what they wanted. If he had, he could sell three or four times as much as he did.

King Solomon was in a position to help him now, same as he had helped King Solomon. He would leave a dozen packages of the medicine—just small envelopes that could all be carried in a coat pocket—with King Solomon every day. Then he could simply send his customers to King Solomon at Tony's store. They 'd make some trifling purchase, slip him a certain coupon which Uggam had given them, and King Solomon would wrap the little envelope of medicine with their purchase. Must n't let Tony catch on, because he might object, and then the whole scheme would go gaflooey. Of course it would n't really be hurting Tony any. Would n't it increase the number of his customers?

Finally, at the end of each day, Uggam would meet King Solomon some place and give him a quarter for each coupon he held. There 'd be at least ten or twelve a day—two and a half or three dollars plumb extra! Eighteen or twenty dollars a week!

'Dog-gone!' breathed Gillis.

'Does Tony ever leave you heer alone?'

'M-hm. Jess started dis mawnin'. Doan nobody much come round 'tween ten an' twelve, so he done took to doin' his buyin' right 'long 'bout dat time. Nobody hyeh but me fo' 'n hour or so.'

'Good. I' ll try to get my folks to come 'round here mostly while Tony's out, see?'

'I doan miss.'

'Sure y' get the idea, now?' Uggam carefully explained it all again. By the time he had finished, King Solomon was wallowing in gratitude.

'Mouse, you sho' is been a friend to me. Why, 'f 't had n' been fo' you—'

'Bottle it,' said Uggam. 'I 'll be round to your room to-night with enough stuff for to-morrer, see? Be sure 'n be there.'

'Won't be nowha' else.'

'An' remember, this is all jess between you 'n me.'

'Nobody else but,' vowed King Solomon.

Uggam grinned to himself as he went on his way. 'Dumb Oscar! Wonder how much can we make before the cops nab him? French medicine—Hmph!'

V

Tony Gabrielli, an oblate Neapolitan of enormous equator, wabbled heavily out of his store and settled himself over a soap box.

Usually Tony enjoyed sitting out front thus in the evening, when his helper had gone home and his trade was slackest. He liked to watch the little Gabriellis playing over the sidewalk with the little Levys and Johnsons; the trios and quartettes of brightly dressed, dark-skinned girls merrily out for a stroll; the slovenly gaited, darker men, who eyed them up and down and commented to each other with an unsupressed 'Hot damn!' or 'Oh no, now!'

But to-night Tony was troubled. Something was wrong in the store; something was different since the arrival of King Solomon Gillis. The new man had seemed to prove himself honest and trustworthy, it was true. Tony had tested him, as he always tested a new man, by apparently leaving him alone in charge for two or three mornings. As a matter of fact, the new man was never under more vigilant observation than during these two or three mornings. Tony's store was a modification of the front rooms of his flat and was in direct communication with it by way of a glass-windowed door in the rear. Tony always managed to get back into his flat via the side-street entrance and watch the new man through this unobtrusive glass-windowed door. If anything excited his suspicion, like unwarranted interest in the cash register, he walked unexpectedly out of this door to surprise the offender in the act. Thereafter he would have no more such trouble. But he had not succeeded in seeing King Solomon steal even an apple.

What he had observed, however, was that the number of customers that came into the store during the morning's slack hour had pronouncedly increased in the last few days. Before, there had been three or four. Now there were twelve or fifteen. The mysterious thing about it was that their purchases totaled little more than those of the original three or four.

Yesterday and to-day Tony had elected to be in the store at the time when, on the other days, he had been out. But Gillis had not been over-charging or short-changing; for when Tony waited on the customers himself—strange faces all—he found that they bought something like a yeast cake or a five-cent loaf of bread. It was puzzling. Why should strangers leave their own neighborhoods and repeatedly come to him for a yeast cake or a loaf of bread? They were not new neighbors. New neighbors would have bought more variously and extensively and at different times of day. Living near by, they would have come in, the men often in shirtsleeves and slippers, the women in kimonos, with boudoir caps covering their lumpy heads. They would have sent in strange children for things like yeast cakes and loaves of bread. And why did not some of them come in at night when the new helper was off duty?

As for accosting Gillis on suspicion, Tony was too wise for that. Patronage had a queer way of shifting itself in Harlem. You lost your temper and let slip a single '*nègre.*' A week later you sold your business.

Spread over his soap box, with his pudgy hands clasped on his preposterous paunch, Tony sat and wondered. Two men came up, conspicuous for no other reason than that they were white. They displayed extreme nervousness, looking about as if afraid of being seen; and when one of them spoke to Tony it was in a husky, toneless, blowing voice, like the sound of a dirty phonograph record.

'Are you Antonio Gabrielli?'

'Yes, sure.' Strange behavior for such lusty-looking fellows. He who had spoken unsmilingly winked first one eye then the other, and indicated by a gesture of his head that they should enter the store. His companion looked cautiously up and down the Avenue, while Tony, wondering what ailed them, rolled to his feet and puffingly led the way.

Inside, the spokesman snuffled, gave his shoulder a queer little hunch, and asked, 'Can you fix us up, buddy?' The other glanced restlessly about the place as if he were constantly hearing unaccountable noises.

Tony thought he understood clearly now. 'Booze, 'ey?' he smiled. 'Sorry— I no got.'

'Booze? Hell, no!' The voice dwindled to a throaty whisper. 'Dope. Coke, milk, dice—anything. Name your price. Got to have it.'

'Dope?' Tony was entirely at a loss. 'What 's a dis, dope?'

'Aw, lay off, brother. We 're in on this. Here.' He handed Tony a piece of paper. 'Froggy gave us a coupon. Come on. You can't go wrong.'

'I no got,' insisted the perplexed Tony; nor could he be budged on that point.

Quite suddenly the manner of both men changed. 'All right,' said the first angrily, in a voice as robust as his body. 'All right, you 're clever, You no got. Well, you will get. You 'll get twenty years!'

'Twenty year? Whadda you talk?'

'Wait a minute, Mac,' said the second caller. 'Maybe the wop 's on the level. Look here, Tony, we 're officers, see? Policemen.' He produced a badge. 'A couple of weeks ago a guy was brought in dying for the want of a shot, see? Dope—he needed some dope—like this—in his arm. See? Well, we tried to make him tell us where he 'd been getting it, but he was too weak. He croaked next day. Evidently he had n't had money enough to buy any more.

'Well, this morning a little nigger that goes by the name of Froggy was brought into the precinct pretty well doped up. When he finally came to, he swore he got the stuff here at your store. Of course, we 've just been trying to trick you into giving yourself away, but you don't bite. Now what 's your game? Know anything about this?'

Tony understood. 'I dunno,' he said slowly; and then his own problem, whose contemplation his callers had interrupted, occurred to him. 'Sure!' he exclaimed. 'Wait. Maybeso I know somet'ing.'

'All right. Spill it.'

'I got a new man, work-a for me.' And he told them what he had noted since King Solomon Gillis came.

'Sounds interesting. Where is this guy?'

'Here in da store—all day.'

'Be here to-morrow?'

'Sure. All day.'

'All right. We'll drop in to-morrow and give him the eye. Maybe he 's our man.'

'Sure. Come ten o'clock. I show you,' promised Tony.

VI

Even the oldest and rattiest cabarets in Harlem have sense of shame enough to hide themselves under the ground—for instance, Edwards's. To get into Edwards's you casually enter a dimly lighted corner saloon, apparently—only apparently—a subdued memory of brighter days. What was once the family entrance is now a side entrance for ladies. Supporting yourself against close walls, you crouchingly descend a narrow, twisted staircase until, with a final turn, you find yourself in a glaring, long, low basement. In a moment your eyes become accustomed to the haze of tobacco smoke. You see men and women seated at wire-legged, white-topped tables, which are covered with half-empty bottles and glasses; you trace the slow-jazz accompaniment you heard as you came down the stairs to a pianist, a cornetist, and a drummer on a little platform at the far end of the room. There is a cleared space from the foot of the stairs, where you are standing, to the platform where this orchestra is mounted, and in it a tall brown girl is swaying from side to side and rhythmically proclaiming that she has the world in a jug and the stopper in her hand. Behind a counter at your left sits a fat, bald, tea-colored Negro, and you wonder if this is Edwards—Edwards, who stands in with the police, with the political bosses, with the importers of wines and worse. A white-vested waiter hustles you to a seat and takes your order. The song's tempo changes to a quicker; the drum and the cornet rip out a fanfare, almost drowning the piano; the girl catches up her dress and begins to dance. . . .

Gillis's wondering eyes had been roaming about. They stopped.

'Look, Mouse!' he whispered. 'Look a-yonder!'

'Look at what?'

'Dog-gone if it ain' de self-same gal!'

'Wha' d' ye mean, self-same girl?'

'Over yonder, wi' de green stockin's. Dass de gal made me knock over dem apples fust day I come to town. 'Member? Been wishin' I could see her ev'y sence.'

'What for?' Uggam wondered.

King Solomon grew confidential. 'Ain' but two things in dis world, Mouse, I really wants. One is to be a policeman. Been wantin' dat ev'y sence I seen dat cullud traffic-cop dat day. Other is to git myse'f a gal lak dat one over yonder!'

'You 'll do it,' laughed Uggam, 'if you live long enough.'

'Who dat wid her?'

'How 'n hell do I know?'

'He cullud?'

'Don't look like it. Why? What of it?'

'Hm—nuthin'—'

'How many coupons y' got to-night?'

'Ten.' King Solomon handed them over.

'Y' ought to 've slipt 'em to me under the table, but it 's all right now, long as we got this table to ourselves. Here 's y' medicine for to-morrer.'

'Wha'?'

'Reach under the table.'

Gillis secured and pocketed the medicine.

'An' here 's two-fifty for a good day's work.' Uggam passed the money over. Perhaps he grew careless; certainly the passing this time was above the table, in plain sight.

'Thanks, Mouse.'

Two white men had been watching Gillis and Uggam from a table near by. In the tumult of merriment that rewarded the entertainer's most recent and daring effort, one of these men, with a word to the other, came over and took the vacant chair beside Gillis.

'Is your name Gillis?'

' 'T ain' nuthin' else.'

Uggam's eyes narrowed.

The white man showed King Solomon a police officer's badge.

'You 're wanted for dope-peddling. Will you come along without trouble?'

'Fo' what?'

'Violation of the narcotic law—dope-selling.'

'Who—me?'

'Come on, now, lay off that stuff. I saw what happened just now myself.' He addressed Uggam. 'Do you know this fellow?'

'Nope. Never saw him before tonight.'

'Did n't I just see him sell you something?'

'Guess you did. We happened to be sittin' here at the same table and got to talkin'. After a while I says I can't seem to sleep nights, so he offers me sump'n he says 'll make me sleep, all right. I don't know what it is, but he says he uses it himself an' I offers to pay him what it cost him. That 's how I come to take it. Guess he 's got more in his pocket there now.'

The detective reached deftly into the coat pocket of the dumfounded King Solomon and withdrew a packet of envelopes. He tore off a corner of one, emptied a half-dozen tiny white tablets into his palm, and sneered triumphantly. 'You 'll make a good witness,' he told Uggam.

The entertainer was issuing an ultimatum to all sweet mammas who dared to monkey round her loving man. Her audience was absorbed and delighted, with the exception of one couple—the girl with the green stockings and her escort. They sat directly in the line of vision of King Solomon's wide eyes, which, in the calamity that had descended upon him, for the moment saw nothing.

'Are you coming without trouble?'

Mouse Uggam, his friend. Harlem. Land of plenty. City of refuge—city of refuge. If you live long enough—

Consciousness of what was happening between the pair across the room suddenly broke through Gillis's daze like flame through smoke. The man was trying to kiss the girl and she was resisting. Gillis jumped up. The detective, taking the act for an attempt at escape, jumped with him and was quick enough to intercept him. The second officer came at once to his fellow's aid, blowing his whistle several times as he came.

People overturned chairs getting out of the way, but nobody ran for the door. It was an old crowd. A fight was a treat; and the tall Negro could fight.

'Judas Priest!'

'Did you see that?'

'Damn!'

White—both white. Five of Mose Joplin's horses. Poisoning a well. A year's crops. Green stockings—white—white—

'That 's the time, papa!'

'Do it, big boy!'

'Good night!'

Uggam watched tensely, with one eye on the door. The second cop had blown for help—

Downing one of the detectives a third time and turning to grapple again with the other, Gillis found himself face to face with a uniformed black policeman.

He stopped as if stunned. For a moment he simply stared. Into his mind swept his own words like a forgotten song, suddenly recalled:—

'Cullud policemans!'

The officer stood ready, awaiting his rush.

'Even—got—cullud—policemans—'

Very slowly King Solomon's arms relaxed; very slowly he stood erect; and the grin that came over his features had something exultant about it.

James Weldon Johnson (1871-1938)

From Preface to the First Edition

From The Book of American Negro Poetry

. . . The American Negro has accomplished something in pure literature. The list of those who have done so would be surprising both by its length and the excellence of the achievements. One of the great books written in this country since the Civil War is the work of a colored man, *The Souls of Black Folk*, by W. E. B. Du Bois.

Such a list begins with Phillis Wheatley. In 1761 a slave ship landed a cargo of slaves in Boston. Among them was a little girl seven or eight years of age. She attracted the attention of John Wheatley, a wealthy gentleman of Boston, who purchased her as a servant for his wife. Mrs. Wheatley was a benevolent woman. She noticed the girl's quick mind and determined to give her opportunity for its development. Twelve years later Phillis published a volume of poems. The book was brought out in London, where Phillis was for several months an object of great curiosity and attention.

Phillis Wheatley has never been given her rightful place in American literature. By some sort of conspiracy she is kept out of most of the books, especially the text-books on literature used in the schools. Of course, she is not a *great* American poet—and in her day there were no great American poets—but she is an important American poet. Her importance, if for no other reason, rests on the fact that, save one, she is the first in order of time of all the women poets of America. And she is among the first of all American poets to issue a volume.

It seems strange that the books generally give space to a mention of Urian Oakes, President of Harvard College, and to quotations from the crude and lengthy elegy which he published in 1667; and print examples from the execrable versified version of the Psalms made by the New England divines, and yet deny a place to Phillis Wheatley.

Here are the opening lines from the elegy by Oakes, which is quoted from in most of the books on American literature:

> Reader, I am no poet, but I grieve.
> Behold here what that passion can do,
> That forced a verse without Apollo's leave,
> And whether the learned sisters would or no.

There was no need for Urian to admit what his handiwork declared. But this from the versified Psalms is still worse, yet it is found in the books:

> The Lord's song sing can we? being
> in stranger's land, then let

lose her skill my right hand if I
Jerusalem forget.

Anne Bradstreet preceded Phillis Wheatley by a little over twenty years.
She published her volume of poems, *The Tenth Muse,* in 1750. Let us strike a
comparison between the two. Anne Bradstreet was a wealthy, cultivated Puritan
girl, the daughter of Thomas Dudley, Governor of Bay Colony. Phillis, as we
know, was a Negro slave girl born in Africa. Let us take them both at their
best and in the same vein. The following stanza is from Anne's poem entitled
"Contemplation":

> While musing thus with contemplation fed,
> And thousand fancies buzzing in my brain,
> The sweet tongued Philomel percht o'er my head,
> And chanted forth a most melodious strain,
> Which rapt me so with wonder and delight,
> I judged my hearing better than my sight,
> And wisht me wings with her awhile to take my flight.

And the following is from Phillis' poem entitled "Imagination":

> Imagination! who can sing thy force?
> Or who describe the swiftness of thy course?
> Soaring through air to find the bright abode,
> Th' empyreal palace of the thundering God,
> We on thy pinions can surpass the wind,
> And leave the rolling universe behind.
> From star to star the mental optics rove,
> Measure the skies, and range the realms above;
> There in one view we grasp the mighty whole,
> Or with new worlds amaze th' unbounded soul.

We do not think the black woman suffers much by comparison with the
white. Thomas Jefferson said of Phillis: "Religion has produced a Phillis
Wheatley, but it could not produce a poet; her poems are beneath contempt." It
is quite likely that Jefferson's criticism was directed more against religion than
against Phillis' poetry. On the other hand, General George Washington wrote
her with his own hand a letter in which he thanked her for a poem which she
had dedicated to him. He later received her with marked courtesy at his camp
at Cambridge.

It appears certain that Phillis was the first person to apply to George
Washington the phrase, "First in peace." The phrase occurs in her poem addressed to "His Excellency, General George Washington," written in 1775. The
encomium, "First in war, first in peace, first in the hearts of his countrymen,"
was originally used in the resolutions presented to Congress on the death of
Washington, December, 1799.

Phillis Wheatley's poetry is the poetry of the Eighteenth Century. She wrote when Pope and Gray were supreme; it is easy to see that Pope was her model. Had she come under the influence of Wordsworth, Byron or Keats or Shelley, she would have done greater work. As it is, her work must not be judged by the work and standards of a later day, but by the work and standards of her own day and her own contemporaries. By this method of criticism she stands out as one of the important characters in the making of American literature, without any allowances for her sex or her antecedents.

According to *A Bibliographical Checklist of American Negro Poetry*, compiled by Mr. Arthur A. Schomburg, more than one hundred Negroes in the United States have published volumes of poetry ranging in size from pamphlets to books of from one hundred to three hundred pages. About thirty of these writers fill in the gap between Phillis Wheatley and Paul Laurence Dunbar. Just here it is of interest to note that a Negro wrote and published a poem before Phillis Wheatley arrived in this country from Africa. He was Jupiter Hammon, a slave belonging to a Mr. Lloyd of Queens-Village, Long Island. In 1760 Hammon published a poem, eighty-eight lines in length, entitled "An Evening Thought, Salvation by Christ, with Penettential Cries." In 1788 he published "An Address to Miss Phillis Wheatley, Ethiopian Poetess in Boston, who came from Africa at eight years of age, and soon became acquainted with the Gospel of Jesus Christ." These two poems do not include all that Hammon wrote.

The poets between Phillis Wheatley and Dunbar must be considered more in the light of what they attempted than of what they accomplished. Many of them showed marked talent, but barely a half dozen of them demonstrated even mediocre mastery of technique in the use of poetic material and forms. And yet there are several names that deserve mention. George M. Horton, Frances E. Harper, James M. Bell and Alberry A. Whitman, all merit consideration when due allowances are made for their limitations in education, training and general culture. The limitations of Horton were greater than those of either of the others; he was born a slave in North Carolina in 1797, and as a young man began to compose poetry without being able to write it down. Later he received some instruction from professors of the University of North Carolina, at which institution he was employed as a janitor. He published a volume of poems, *The Hope of Liberty*, in 1829.

Mrs. Harper, Bell, and Whitman would stand out if only for the reason that each of them attempted sustained work. Mrs. Harper published her first volume of poems in 1854, but later she published "Moses, a Story of the Nile," a poem which ran to 52 closely printed pages. Bell in 1864 published a poem of 28 pages in celebration of President Lincoln's Emancipation Proclamation. In 1870 he published a poem of 32 pages in celebration of the ratification of the Fifteenth Amendment to the Constitution. Whitman published his first volume of poems, a book of 253 pages, in 1877; but in 1884 he published "The Rape of Florida," an epic poem written in four cantos and done in the Spenserian stanza, and which ran to 97 closely printed pages. The poetry of both Mrs. Harper and of Whitman had a large degree of popularity; one of Mrs. Harper's books went through more than twenty editions.

Of these four poets, it is Whitman who reveals not only the greatest imagination but also the more skillful workmanship. His lyric power at its best may be judged from the following stanza from the "Rape of Florida":

> "Come now, my love, the moon is on the lake;
> Upon the waters is my light canoe;
> Come with me, love, and gladsome oars shall make
> A music on the parting wave for you.
> Come o'er the waters deep and dark and blue;
> Come where the lilies in the marge have sprung,
> Come with me, love, for Oh, my love is true!"
> This is the song that on the lake was sung,
> The boatman sang it when his heart was young.

Some idea of Whitman's capacity for dramatic narration may be gained from the following lines taken from "Not a Man, and Yet a Man," a poem of even greater length than "The Rape of Florida."

> A flash of steely lightning from his hand,
> Strikes down the groaning leader of the band;
> Divides his startled comrades, and again
> Descending, leaves fair Dora's captors slain.
> Her, seizing then within a strong embrace,
> Out in the dark he wheels his flying pace;

> He speaks not, but with stalwart tenderness
> Her swelling bosom firm to his doth press;
> Springs like a stag that flees the eager hound,
> And like a whirlwind rustles o'er the ground.
> Her locks swim in disheveled wildness o'er
> His shoulders, streaming to his waist and more;
> While on and on, strong as a rolling flood,
> His sweeping footsteps part the silent wood.

It is curious and interesting to trace the growth of individuality and race consciousness in this group of poets. Jupiter Hammon's verses were almost entirely religious exhortations. Only very seldom does Phillis Wheatley sound a native note. Four times in single lines she refers to herself as "Afric's muse." In a poem of admonition addressed to the students at the "University of Cambridge in New England" she refers to herself as follows:

> Ye blooming plants of human race divine,
> An Ethiop tells you 'tis your greatest foe.

But one looks in vain for some outburst or even complaint against the bondage of her people, for some agonizing cry about her native land. In two poems she refers definitely to Africa as her home, but in each instance there seems to be under the sentiment of the lines a feeling of almost smug contentment at her own escape therefrom. In the poem, "On Being Brought from Africa to America," she says:

> 'Twas mercy brought me from my pagan land,
> Taught my benighted soul to understand
> That there's a God and there's a Saviour too;
> Once I redemption neither sought nor knew.
> Some view our sable race with scornful eye—
> "Their color is a diabolic dye."
> Remember, Christians, Negroes black as Cain,
> May be refined, and join th' angelic train.

In the poem addressed to the Earl of Dartmouth, she speaks of freedom and makes a reference to the parents from whom she was taken as a child, a reference which cannot but strike the reader as rather unimpassioned:

> Should you, my lord, while you peruse my song,
> Wonder from whence my love of Freedom sprung,
> Whence flow these wishes for the common good,
> By feeling hearts alone best understood;
> I, young in life, my seeming cruel fate
> Was snatch'd from Afric's fancy'd happy seat;
> What pangs excruciating must molest,
> What sorrows labor in my parent's breast?
> Steel'd was that soul and by no misery mov'd
> That from a father seiz'd his babe belov'd;
> Such, such my case. And can I then but pray
> Others may never feel tyrannic sway?

The bulk of Phillis Wheatley's work consists of poems addressed to people of prominence. Her book was dedicated to the Countess of Huntington, at whose house she spent the greater part of her time while in England. On his repeal of the Stamp Act, she wrote a poem to King George III, whom she saw later; another poem she wrote to the Earl of Dartmouth, whom she knew. A number of her verses were addressed to other persons of distinction. Indeed, it is apparent that Phillis was far from being a democrat. She was far from being a democrat not only in her social ideas but also in her political ideas; unless a religious meaning is given to the closing lines of her ode to General Washington, she was a decided royalist:

> A crown, a mansion, and a throne that shine
> With gold unfading, Washington! be thine.

Nevertheless, she was an ardent patriot. Her ode to General Washington (1775), her spirited poem, "On Major General Lee" (1776), and her poem, "Liberty and Peace," written in celebration of the close of the war, reveal not only strong patriotic feeling but an understanding of the issues at stake. In her poem, "On Major General Lee," she makes her hero reply thus to the taunts of the British commander into whose hands he has been delivered through treachery:

> O arrogance of tongue!
> And wild ambition, ever prone to wrong!
> Believ'st thou, chief, that armies such as thine
> Can stretch in dust that heaven-defended line?
> In vain allies may swarm from distant lands,
> And demons aid in formidable bands.
> Great as thou art, thou shun'st the field of fame,
> Disgrace to Britain and the British name!
> When offer'd combat by the noble foe
> (Foe to misrule) why did the sword forego
> The easy conquest of the rebel-land?
> Perhaps TOO easy for thy martial hand.
> What various causes to the field invite!
> For plunder YOU, and we for freedom fight;
> Her cause divine with generous ardor fires,
> And every bosom glows as she inspires!
> Already thousands of your troops have fled
> To the drear mansions of the silent dead:
> Columbia, too, beholds with streaming eyes
> Her heroes fall—'tis freedom's sacrifice!
> So wills the power who with convulsive storms
> Shakes impious realms, and nature's face deforms;
> Yet those brave troops, innum'rous as the sands,
> One soul inspires, one General Chief commands;
> Find in your train of boasted heroes, one
> To match the praise of Godlike Washington.
> Thrice happy Chief in whom the virtues join,
> And heaven taught prudence speaks the man divine.

What Phillis Wheatley failed to achieve is due in no small degree to her education and environment. Her mind was steeped in the classics; her verses are filled with classical and mythological allusions. She knew Ovid thoroughly and was familiar with other Latin authors. She must have known Alexander Pope by heart. And, too, she was reared and sheltered in a wealthy and cultured family, —a wealthy and cultured Boston family; she never had the opportunity to learn life; she never found out her own true relation to life and to her surroundings. And it should not be forgotten that she was only about thirty years old when she died. The impulsion or the compulsion that might have driven her genius off the worn paths, out on a journey of exploration, Phillis Wheatley never received. But, whatever her limitations, she merits more than America has accorded her.

Horton, who was born three years after Phillis Wheatley's death, expressed in all of his poetry strong complaint at his condition of slavery and a deep longing for freedom. The following verses are typical of his style and his ability:

> Alas! and am I born for this,
>   To wear this slavish chain?
> Deprived of all created bliss,
>   Through hardship, toil, and pain?
>
> Come, Liberty! thou cheerful sound,
>   Roll through my ravished ears;
> Come, let my grief in joys be drowned,
>   And drive away my fears.

In Mrs. Harper we find something more than the complaint and the longing of Horton. We find an expression of a sense of wrong and injustice. The following stanzas are from a poem addressed to the white women of America:

> You can sigh o'er the sad-eyed Armenian
>   Who weeps in her desolate home.
> You can mourn o'er the exile of Russia
>   From kindred and friends doomed to roam.
>
> But hark! from our Southland are floating
>   Sobs of anguish, murmurs of pain;
> And women heart-stricken are weeping
>   O'er their tortured and slain.
>
> Have ye not, oh, my favored sisters,
>   Just a plea, a prayer or a tear
> For mothers who dwell 'neath the shadows
>   Of agony, hatred and fear?
>
> Weep not, oh, my well sheltered sisters,
>   Weep not for the Negro alone,
> But weep for your sons who must gather
>   The crops which their fathers have sown.

Whitman, in the midst of "The Rape of Florida," a poem in which he related the taking of the State of Florida from the Seminoles, stops and discusses the race question. He discusses it in many other poems; and he discusses it from many different angles. In Whitman we find not only an expression of a sense of wrong and injustice, but we hear a note of faith and a note also of defiance. For example, in the opening to Canto II of "The Rape of Florida":

> Greatness by nature cannot be entailed;
> It is an office ending with the man,—
> Sage, hero, Saviour, tho' the Sire be hailed,

The son may reach obscurity in the van:
Sublime achievements know no patent plan,
Man's immortality's a book with seals,
And none but God shall open—none else can—
But opened, it the mystery reveals,—
Manhood's conquest of man to heaven's respect appeals.

Is manhood less because man's face is black?
Let thunders of the loosened seals reply!
Who shall the rider's restive steed turn back?
Or who withstand the arrows he lets fly
Between the mountains of eternity?
Genius ride forth! Thou gift and torch of heav'n!
The mastery is kindled in thine eye;
To conquest ride! thy bow of strength is giv'n—
The trampled hordes of caste before three shall be driv'n!

'Tis hard to judge if hatred of one's race,
By those who deem themselves superior-born,
Be worse than that quiescence in disgrace,
Which only merits—and should only—scorn.
Oh, let me see the Negro night and morn,
Pressing and fighting in, for place and power!
All earth is place—all time th' auspicious hour,
While heaven leans forth to look, oh, will he quail or cower?

Ah! I abhor his protest and complaint!
His pious looks and patience I despise!
He can't evade the test, disguised as saint;
The manly voice of freedom bids him rise,
And shake himself before Philistine eyes!
And, like a lion roused, no sooner than
A foe dare come, play all his energies,
And court the fray with fury if he can;
For hell itself respects a fearless, manly man.

It may be said that none of these poets strike a deep native strain or sound a distinctly original note, either in matter or form. That is true; but the same thing may be said of all the American poets down to the writers of the present generation, with the exception of Poe and Walt Whitman. The thing in which these black poets are mostly excelled by their contemporaries is mere technique.

Paul Laurence Dunbar stands out as the first poet from the Negro race in the United States to show a combined mastery over poetic material and poetic technique, to reveal innate literary distinction in what he wrote, and to maintain a high level of performance. He was the first to rise to a height from which he could take a perspective view of his own race. He was the first to see objectively its humor, its superstitions, its shortcomings; the first to feel sympathetically its heart-wounds, its yearnings, its aspirations, and to voice them all in a purely literary form.

Dunbar's fame rests chiefly on his poems in Negro dialect. This appraisal of him is, no doubt, fair; for in these dialect poems he not only carried his art to the highest point of perfection, but he made a contribution to American literature unlike what any one else had made, a contribution which, perhaps, no one else could have made. Of course, Negro dialect poetry was written before Dunbar wrote, most of it by white writers; but the fact stands out that Dunbar was the first to use it as a medium for the true interpretation of Negro character and psychology. And yet, dialect poetry does not constitute the whole or even the bulk of Dunbar's work. In addition to a large number of poems of a very high order done in literary English, he was the author of four novels and several volumes of short stories.

Indeed, Dunbar did not begin his career as a writer of dialect. I may be pardoned for introducing here a bit of reminiscence. My personal friendship with Paul Dunbar began before he had achieved recognition, and continued to be close until his death. When I first met him he had published a thin volume, *Oak and Ivy*, which was being sold chiefly through his own efforts. *Oak and Ivy* showed no distinctive Negro influence, but rather the influence of James Whitcomb Riley. At this time Paul and I were together every day for several months. He talked to me a great deal about his hopes and ambitions. In these talks he revealed that he had reached a realization of the possibilities of poetry in the dialect, together with a recognition of the fact that it offered the surest way by which he could get a hearing. Often he said to me: "I've got to write dialect poetry; it's the only way I can get them to listen to me." I was with Dunbar at the beginning of what proved to be his last illness. He said to me then: "I have not grown. I am writing the same things I wrote ten years ago, and am writing them no better." His self-accusation was not fully true; he had grown, and he had gained a surer control of his art, but he had not accomplished the greater things of which he was constantly dreaming; the public had held him to the things for which it had accorded him recognition. If Dunbar had lived he would have achieved some of those dreams, but even while he talked so dejectedly to me he seemed to feel that he was not to live. He died when he was only thirty-three.

It has a bearing on this entire subject to note that Dunbar was of unmixed Negro blood; so, as the greatest figure in literature which the colored race in the United States has produced, he stands as an example at once refuting and confounding those who wish to believe that whatever extraordinary ability an Aframerican shows is due to an admixture of white blood.

As a man, Dunbar was kind and tender. In conversation he was brilliant and polished. His voice was his chief charm, and was a great element in his success as a reader of his own works. In his actions he was impulsive as a child, sometimes even erratic; indeed, his intimate friends almost looked upon him as a spoiled boy. He was always delicate in health. Temperamentally, he belonged to that class of poets who Taine says are vessels too weak to contain the spirit of poetry, the poets whom poetry kills, the Byrons, the Burnses, the De Mussets, the Poes.

To whom may he be compared, this boy who scribbled his early verses while he ran an elevator, whose youth was a battle against poverty, and who, in spite of almost insurmountable obstacles, rose to success? A comparison between him and Burns is not unfitting. The similarity between many phases of their lives is remarkable, and their works are not incommensurable. Burns took the strong dialect of his people and made it classic; Dunbar took the humble speech of his people and in it wrought music.

.   .   .

It may be surprising to many to see how little of the poetry being written by Negro poets today is being written in Negro dialect. The newer Negro poets show a tendency to discard dialect; much of the subject-matter which went into the making of traditional dialect poetry, 'possums, watermelons, etc., they have discarded altogether, at least, as poetic material. This tendency will, no doubt, be regretted by the majority of white readers; and, indeed, it would be a distinct loss if the American Negro poets threw away this quaint and musical folk speech as a medium of expression. And yet, after all, these poets are working through a problem not realized by the reader, and, perhaps, by many of these poets themselves not realized consciously. They are trying to break away from, not Negro dialect itself, but the limitations on Negro dialect imposed by the fixing effects of long convention.

The Negro in the United States has achieved or been placed in a certain artistic niche. When he is thought of artistically, it is as a happy-go-lucky, singing, shuffling, banjo-picking being or as a more or less pathetic figure. The picture of him is in a log cabin amid fields of cotton or along the levees. Negro dialect is naturally and by long association the exact instrument for voicing this phase of Negro life; and by that very exactness it is an instrument with but two full stops, humor and pathos. So even when he confines himself to purely racial themes, the Aframerican poet realizes that there are phases of Negro life in the United States which cannot be treated in the dialect either adequately or artistically. Take, for example, the phases rising out of life in Harlem, that most wonderful Negro city in the world. I do not deny that a Negro in a log cabin is more picturesque than a Negro in a Harlem flat, but the Negro in the Harlem flat is here, and he is but part of a group growing everywhere in the country, a group whose ideals are becoming increasingly more vital than those of the traditionally artistic group, even if its members are less picturesque.

What the colored poet in the United States needs to do is something like what Synge did for the Irish; he needs to find a form that will express the racial spirit by symbols from within rather than by symbols from without, such as the mere mutilation of English spelling and pronunciation. He needs a form that is freer and larger than dialect, but which will still hold the racial flavor;

a form expressing the imagery, the idioms, the peculiar turns of thought, and the distinctive humor and pathos, too, of the Negro, but which will also be capable of voicing the deepest and highest emotions and aspirations, and allow of the widest range of subjects and the widest scope of treatment.

Negro dialect is at present a medium that is not capable of giving expression to the varied conditions of Negro life in America, and much less is it capable of giving the fullest interpretation of Negro character and psychology. This is no indictment against the dialect as dialect, but against the mold of convention in which Negro dialect in the United States has been set. In time these conventions may become lost, and the colored poet in the United States may sit down to write in dialect without feeling that his first line will put the general reader in a frame of mind which demands that the poem be humorous or pathetic. In the meantime, there is no reason why these poets should not continue to do the beautiful things that can be done, and done best, in the dialect.

In stating the need for Aframerican poets in the United States to work out a new and distinctive form of expression I do not wish to be understood to hold any theory that they should limit themselves to Negro poetry, to racial themes; the sooner they are able to write *American* poetry spontaneously, the better. Nevertheless, I believe that the richest contribution the Negro poet can make to the American literature of the future will be the fusion into it of his own individual artistic gifts.

Go Down Death—a Funeral Sermon

From God's Trombones

Weep not, weep not,
She is not dead;
She's resting in the bosom of Jesus.
Heart-broken husband—weep no more;
Grief-stricken son—weep no more;
Left-lonesome daughter—weep no more;
She's only just gone home.

Day before yesterday morning,
God was looking down from his great, high heaven,
Looking down on all his children,
And his eye fell on Sister Caroline,
Tossing on her bed of pain.
And God's big heart was touched with pity,
With the everlasting pity.

And God sat back on his throne,
And he commanded that tall, bright angel standing at his right
      hand:
Call me Death!
And that tall, bright angel cried in a voice
That broke like a clap of thunder:
Call Death!—Call Death!
And the echo sounded down the streets of heaven
Till it reached away back to that shadowy place,
Where Death waits with his pale, white horses.

And Death heard the summons,
And he leaped on his fastest horse,
Pale as a sheet in the moonlight.
Up the golden street Death galloped,
And the hoofs of his horse struck fire from the gold,
But they didn't make no sound.
Up Death rode to the Great White Throne,
And waited for God's command.

And God said: Go down, Death, go down,
Go down to Savannah, Georgia,
Down in Yamacraw,
And find Sister Caroline.
She's borne the burden and heat of the day,
She's labored long in my vineyard,
And she's tired—
She's weary—
Go down, Death, and bring her to me.

And Death didn't say a word,
But he loosed the reins on his pale, white horse,
And he clamped the spurs to his bloodless sides,
And out and down he rode,
Through heaven's pearly gates,
Past suns and moons and stars;
On Death rode,
And the foam from his horse was like a comet in the sky;
On Death rode,
Leaving the lightning's flash behind;
Straight on down he came.

While we were watching round her bed,
She turned her eyes and looked away,

She saw what we couldn't see;
She saw Old Death. She saw Old Death
Coming like a falling star.
But Death didn't frighten Sister Caroline;
He looked to her like a welcome friend.
And she whispered to us: I'm going home,
And she smiled and closed her eyes.

And Death took her up like a baby,
And she lay in his icy arms,
But she didn't feel no chill.
And Death began to ride again—
Up beyond the evening star,
Out beyond the morning star,
Into the glittering light of glory,
On to the Great White Throne.

And there he laid Sister Caroline
On the loving breast of Jesus.
And Jesus took his own hand and wiped away her tears,
And he smoothed the furrows from her face,
And the angels sang a little song,
And Jesus rocked her in his arms,
And kept a-saying: Take your rest,
Take your rest, take your rest.

Weep not—weep not,
She is not dead;
She's resting in the bosom of Jesus.

Langston (James Mercer) Hughes (1902-1967)

The Negro Speaks of Rivers

I've known rivers:
I've known rivers ancient as the world and older than the flow of
    human blood in human veins.

My soul has grown deep like the rivers.

I bathed in the Euphrates when dawns were young.
I built my hut near the Congo and it lulled me to sleep.
I looked upon the Nile and raised the pyramids above it.
I heard the singing of the Mississippi when Abe Lincoln went
    down to New Orleans, and I've seen its muddy bosom turn
    all golden in the sunset.

I've known rivers:
Ancient, dusky rivers.

My soul has grown deep like the rivers.

Refugee in America

There are words like *Freedom*
Sweet and wonderful to say.
On my heart-strings freedom sings
All day everyday.

There are words like *Liberty*
That almost make me cry.
If you had known what I knew
You would know why.

I, Too

I, too, sing America.

I am the darker brother.
They send me to eat in the kitchen
When company comes,
But I laugh,
And eat well,
And grow strong.

Tomorrow,
Ill be at the table
When company comes.
Nobody'll dare
Say to me,

"Eat in the kitchen,"
Then.

Besides,
They'll see how beautiful I am
And be ashamed—

I, too, am America.

Troubled Woman

She stands
In the quiet darkness,
This troubled woman
Bowed by
Weariness and pain
Like an
Autumn flower
In the frozen rain,
Like a
Wind-blown autumn flower
That never lifts its head
Again.

Silhouette

Southern gentle lady,
Do not swoon.
They've just hung a black man
In the dark of the moon.

They've hung a black man
To a roadside tree
In the dark of the moon
For the world to see
How Dixie protects
Its white womanhood.

Southern gentle lady,
  Be good!
  Be good!

Dream Variations

To fling my arms wide
In some place of the sun,
To whirl and to dance
Till the white day is done.
Then rest at cool evening
Beneath a tall tree
While night comes on gently,
    Dark like me—
That is my dream!

To fling my arms wide
In the face of the sun,
Dance! Whirl! Whirl!
Till the quick day is done.
Rest at pale evening . . .
A tall, slim tree . . .
Night coming tenderly
    Black like me.

One-way Ticket

I pick up my life
And take it with me
And I put it down in
Chicago, Detroit,
Buffalo, Scranton,
Any place that is
North and East—
And not Dixie.

I pick up my life
And take it on the train
To Los Angeles, Bakersfield,
Seattle, Oakland, Salt Lake,
Any place that is
North and West—
And not South.

I am fed up
With Jim Crow laws,
People who are cruel
And afraid,
Who lynch and run,

Who are scared of me
And me of them.

I pick up my life
And take it away
On a one-way ticket—
Gone up North,
Gone out West,
Gone!

Brass Spitoons

Clean the spitoons, boy.
   Detroit,
   Chicago,
   Atlantic City,
   Palm Beach.
Clean the spitoons.
The steam in hotel kitchens,
And the smoke in hotel lobbies,
And the slime in hotel spitoons:
Part of my life.
   Hey, boy!
   A nickel,
   A dime,
   A dollar,
Two dollars a day.
   Hey, boy!
   A nickel,
   A dime,
   A dollar,
   Two dollars
Buys shoes for the baby.
House rent to pay.
Gin on Saturday,
Church on Sunday.
   My God!
Babies and gin and church
and women and Sunday
all mixed up with dimes and
dollars and clean spitoons
and house rent to pay.
   Hey, boy!

A bright bowl of brass is beautiful to the Lord.
Bright polished brass like the cymbals
Of King David's dancers,
Like the wine cups of Solomon.
   Hey, boy!
A clean spitoon on the altar of the Lord.
A clean bright spitoon all newly polished,—
At least I can offer that.
   Com' mere, boy!

Jazzonia

Oh, silver tree!
Oh, shining rivers of the soul!

In a Harlem cabaret
Six long-headed jazzers play.
A dancing girl whose eyes are bold
Lifts high a dress of silken gold.
Oh, singing tree!
Oh, shining rivers of the soul!

Were Eve's eyes
In the first garden
Just a bit too bold?
Was Cleopatra gorgeous
In a gown of gold?

Oh, shining tree!
Oh, silver rivers of the soul!

In a whirling cabaret
Six long-headed jazzers play.

Montmartre

   Pigalle:

   A neon rose

In a champagne bottle.

   At dawn

   The petals

   Fall.

Good Morning

From Montage of a Dream Deferred

Good morning, daddy!
I was born here, he said,
watched Harlem grow
until colored folks spread
from river to river
across the middle of Manhattan
out of Penn Station
dark tenth of a nation,
planes from Puerto Rico,
and holds of boats, chico,
up from Cuba Haiti Jamaica,
in busses marked NEW YORK
from Georgia Florida Louisiana
to Harlem Brooklyn the Bronx
but most of all to Harlem
dusky sash across Manhattan
I've seen them come dark
   wondering
   wide-eyed
   dreaming
out of Penn Station—
but the trains are late.
The gates open—
but there're bars
at each gate.

   What happens
   to a dream deferred?

Daddy, ain't you heard?

Same In Blues

From Montage of a Dream Deferred

I said to my baby,
Baby, take it slow.
I can't, she said, I can't!
I got to go!

There's a certain
amount of traveling
in a dream deferred.

Lulu said to Leonard,
I want a diamond ring.
Leonard said to Lulu,
You won't get a goddamn thing!

A certain
amount of nothing
in a dream deferred.

Daddy, daddy, daddy,
All I want is you.
You can have me, baby—
but my lovin' days is through.

A certain
amount of impotence
in a dream deferred.

Three parties
On my party line—
But that third party,
Lord, ain't mine!

There's liable
to be confusion
in a dream deferred.

From river to river,
Uptown and down,
There's liable to be confusion
when a dream gets kicked around.

Letter

From Montage of a Dream Deferred

Dear Mama,
Time I pay rent and get my food
and laundry I don't have much left

but here is five dollars for you
to show you I still appreciates you.
My girl-friend send her love and say
she hopes to lay eyes on you sometime in life.
Mama, it has been raining cats and dogs up
here. Well, that is all so I will close.
                Your son baby
                      Respectably as ever,
                          Joe

Island

From Montage of a Dream Deferred

Between two rivers,
North of the park,
Like darker rivers
The streets are dark.

Black and white,
Gold and brown—
Chocolate-custard
Pie of a town.

Dream within a dream,
Our dream deferred.

Good morning, daddy!

Ain't you heard?

Undertow

The solid citizens
Of the country club set,
Caught between
Selma and Peking,
Feel the rug of dividends,
Bathmats of pride,
Even soggy country club
Pink paper towels
Dropped on the MEN'S ROOM floor

Slipping out from under them
Like waves of sea
Between Selma, Peking,
Westchester
And me.

VI
The
Thirties
and
Forties

The hopes and dreams of the twenties fluttered down slowly; the gramo-
phones ground to a halt, and society grew melancholy as the Depression settled
over America. The easy life became a battle to make ends meet, and the search
for the bizarre and the exotic became a search for means of survival. In Harlem,
the capitol of the New Negro Renaissance, 60 percent of the population was on
relief and another 20 percent was supported by federal jobs in the 1930s. The
writers and artists who had congregated in the black metropolis of New York
were scattered over the country, and their white patrons, friends, and publishers
found that they had larger causes to champion than black American letters. The
story of the depression years is the story of an ailing capitalism. And the decline
of capitalism meant the absence of jobs, the increase of discrimination, the height-
ening of discontent, and the growth of racial tension and mass frustration. In
March of 1935, the black enclave that had served as a cultural center in the
twenties was transformed overnight into a place of darkness and confusion as a
riot swept over Harlem. Hopelessness finding its outlet in violence: this was the
essence of the 1935 riot.

Three years before the Harlem riot, however, the "bringer of hope and light"
had stepped into the nation's highest office, and in 1933, the New Deal had
officially begun. Franklin D. Roosevelt served as the charismatic godfather of
capitalism, bringing it out of the slough of despond. His New Deal was devoted
to the creation of jobs, the rectification of social wrongs, the stabilization of the
nation's economy, and the uplifting of America's "forgotten man." What this
meant, in terms of real social and material gains for the black American, is still
being debated. Mrs. Mary Bethune has expressed the view that Roosevelt was
a reincarnated Lincoln, a true friend to the black American. Allan Morrison, on
the other hand, has viewed Roosevelt as a cautious, politic, and meticulous leader
who had no clear policy toward the black American and who sacrificed the pressing needs of the black American to a "higher good." Wherever the truth about
Roosevelt may lie, one thing is certain: he was in a large measure responsible for
the continuance and growth of the black American literary tradition during the
thirties. The New Deal created a number of federal relief agencies, and the most
important one for black artists was the Work Projects Administration. The
Federal Writers' Projects were outstanding components of the WPA, and a host
of black American writers received jobs, salaries, and opportunities to produce
fine literary works in these federal projects. Arna Bontemps has pointed out that
not only the older writers, but also promising young talents like Richard Wright,
Ralph Ellison, Roi Ottley, and Willard Mottley found their way to Federal
Writers' Projects in various areas of the country. Ironically, then, in the midst
of one of the greatest depressions the world has ever witnessed, black writers
found an environment in which they could work according to their will and
receive mete compensation for their labors.

While the position of black writers was symptomatic of improving race relations in America, the black American still had a plethora of grievances to air.

Segregation still characterized the South; lynching was still a common practice (and Roosevelt refused to support an antilynching bill in order to retain the support of southern Democrats); discrimination in hiring and employment practices was widespread; federal relief money was not always distributed on an equal basis among white and minority groups; poll taxes and absurd registration examinations were a way of life for black southerners; professional athletics remained closed to black Americans throughout the thirties; and "Jim Crow" was a ubiquitous figure in all parts of the North and South during the thirties. Despite Roosevelt's protestations, therefore, it seems that the black American—particularly the ghetto dweller and the tenant farmer—remained a "forgotten man." Black writers were not slow to point out the neglected position of the black American.

Arna Bontemps, for example, captured the poverty, depression, and hopelessness of the southern tenant farmer in his short story "A Summer Tragedy." The season in which the tragedy occurs is significant: in the juvescence of the American year (in the renaissance of the economy that marked the New Deal and subsequent years), the black southerner remains poor, maimed, sightless, and without hope. The journey over a barren landscape and into death is all too symbolic of the plight of the tenant farmer from the Reconstruction period to the present day. Bontemps, though noted for his prose, also produced several poems that delineated the condition of the black American. The author who won both the *Crisis* poetry prize and Alexander Pushkin awards during the twenties seems at his best in poems like "Reconaissance," "Southern Mansion," and "Nocturne at Bethesda."

Sterling Brown, another black writer of the thirties, also dealt with the plight of the black southerner. Brown's 1932 volume of poetry, *Southern Road,* is in the best tradition of Dunbar and Hughes; throughout the work we are presented with black folk themes handled in beautifully lyrical folk forms. Brown employs the rhythms of the early folk songs, the stoicism of the blues, and the humor of the early folktales in an attempt to capture the struggle and frustration that characterize the black man's road in the South. "Sister Lou," which captures the same idiosyncrasies of idiom and communal feeling seen in Dunbar, is one of Brown's finest efforts, and "Children of the Mississippi" follows close behind. The skill revealed in Brown's poems is more than matched by the skill manifested in his critical works. *Negro Poetry and Drama* and *The Negro in American Fiction* detail with consummate skill the contributions of a "forgotten race" to American culture. And one of the best examples of Brown's accomplishments as a critic is his article "The American Race Problem as Reflected in American Literature" (1938).

Despite the plight of less fortunate black Americans, however, the American *Weltanschauung* of the thirties and forties stressed egalitarianism and internationalism. Alain Locke stated that this liberal and egalitarian spirit forced white authors to take a more accurate measure of the black man. The work begun by writers like Heyward, O'Neill, and Green in the twenties was continued in the thirties and forties by writers like Thomas Wolfe, Sherwood Anderson, William Faulkner, and Erskine Caldwell. Each of these writers sought to present a realistic picture of the black American, and a "new realism," one which captured both the smiling face of life and its more naturalistic visage, characterized American poetry and fiction during the years between 1930 and 1945. The black American was not often caricatured or slandered by white writers, and with increasing educational and employment opportunities, the black American moved steadily into the mainstream of American life. The ideal of black Americans became total equality through integration.

This broader spirit, this turning outward from the myopia of things strictly racial, can be seen in the early work of a number of black poets who came out of the thirties and forties. Melvin Tolson, for example, wrote poetry that combined the best American poetic techniques with broadly humanistic themes. "Old Man Michael" and "The Mountain Climber" reflect struggles and hopes that are universal in scope, and "Dark Symphony" concludes with a vision of black Americans advancing into the mainstream of American life. Margaret Walker's "For My People" is much like Tolson's "Dark Symphony." While the poem addresses itself to a specific racial group, it still portrays the movement of that group on a broad American vista. Robert Hayden and Owen Dodson, in their early verse, were more outspoken than the early Tolson and Walker; but both Dodson and Hayden strove for a metaphysical tension and a universality of theme. Dodson's "Counterpoint," which chronicles the terrors of World War II, and Hayden's "A Ballad of Remembrance" seem fit illustrations of the artist's struggle to reconcile opposites and reach universality. It is not difficult, therefore, to pinpoint the mainstream leanings of black poets during the thirties and forties; in all fairness, however, one must note that the later work of all four of the poets mentioned here reflects a different spirit. All of them have spoken out in recent decades in militant voices charged with black realism. Tolson's "Psi" from *Harlem Gallery* takes a realistic and brilliantly crafted look at the trials of the black artist; Margaret Walker's *Jubilee* deals realistically, in black terms, with the plight and the history of black Americans. Hayden's incredible "Middle Passage," "Witch Doctor," and "Runagate Runagate" speak in thrilling language to a black psyche; and Dodson's libretto on the death of Medgar Evers is a beautiful and stirring work.

One of the bequests of the thirties and forties to later decades was a spirit of black militancy, a spirit that Richard M. Dalfiume has traced to the war years. During these years, black Americans began a militant campaign for equality that has continued into our own day. The March on Washington Movement led by A. Philip Randolph was one example of this new spirit; the Harlem riot in 1943 was another manifestation, and all over the land young black Americans prepared to take up the cudgels of resistance and revolt. An increasingly sociological outlook led to indisputable conclusions about the sordid conditions surrounding a forgotten people, and black writers were not the least of those to speak out against America's treatment of the black man. In 1938, Richard Wright gained national recognition by publishing *Uncle Tom's Children,* a collection of short stories that dealt in realistic and bitter terms with the condition of the black American. In "Bright and Morning Star," Wright displayed remarkable skill in the delineation of violence and anguish; but a note of hope breathes through the story as the Communist star rises, portending salvation for the black American. Wright's sociological vision continued to unfold in one of the best novels produced during the forties—*Native Son* (1940). Like the muckrakers and other protest novelists of his age, Wright depicted a deplorable social environment and the dire ramifications to which it led. Bigger Thomas, like Sinclair's Jurgis Rudkus, Dreisser's Clyde Griffiths, and Farrell's Studs Lonigan, is an American victim; Bigger falls prey to the social forces that militate against him, and the only hope in the novel is offered by a Communist vision of the future. Wright's novel thus shared the concerns of American fiction as a whole while it dealt in uncompromising terms with the condition of the black American.

And Ann Petry was in the best tradition of Wright, of sociological fiction, and of militant activism in her short stories of the forties. In "Like a Winding Sheet," Mrs. Petry works in a realistic tradition to show the deathlike pressures that hem in the black worker in America. The pressures result in violence, and Mrs. Petry did not flinch from the portrayal of violence. For, in her novel *The Street* (1946), Mrs. Petry set forth in telling fashion the violence of the urban streets and the effects that it produced on Americans forced to reside in the most depressed areas of the city.

Richard Wright and Ann Petry present but two examples of the voluble protest launched by black Americans in the forties, and their voices, along with those of their fellow black Americans, were to be recognized and heeded by Roosevelt's successor, Harry Truman. America had moved into a position of economic and political leadership by the end of World War II, and Truman set out in 1945 to purge the American house of injustice and inequality. A civil rights' commission, the end of discrimination in the armed services, and the enforcement of fair employment regulations—these were a few of the achievements of the Truman era. Black Americans who had begun their advance into the mainstream in the twenties and thirties demanded more recognition and opportunity in the forties, and they received both during the Truman years. The works of black American writers of the thirties and forties reveal the various social concerns of the two decades, and they accurately reflect the major trends of thought that characterized black and white America in depression and war. The works of Bontemps, Brown, Wright, and others, however, are vastly more than documentation; the works of the black writers of the thirties and forties reveal the themes, techniques, and magnificent literary craftsmanship that have characterized the black American creative tradition from its earliest years. And the writers and works of the thirties and forties provided adequate models for the black literary artists of our most recent decades; Baldwin, Ellison, and Gwendolyn Brooks, for example, —three of today's most talented black authors—served their apprenticeships in the early years of Hayden, Tolson, and Wright.

REFERENCES

Bone, Robert A.: *The Negro Novel in America,* Yale University Press, New Haven, 1958, pp. 109–172.

Butcher, Margaret J.: *The Negro in American Culture,* Alfred Knopf, New York, 1956.

Cruse, Harold: *The Crisis of the Negro Intellectual,* William Morrow, New York, 1967, pp. 115–189.

Gray, Yohma: *An American Metaphor: The Novels of Richard Wright,* New Haven, 1967. (Thesis, Yale University, University Microfilms, Ann Arbor, Michigan.)

Kaiser, Ernest: "The Literature of Harlem," *Harlem: A Community in Transition,* John Henrik Clarke (ed.), Citadel Press, New York, 1965, pp. 26–41. (Sections on the literature of the depression and war years.)

Locke, Alain: "Harlem: Dark Weather Vane," *Survey Graphic,* August, 1936.

———: "The Negro in American Literature," *New World Writing,* New American Library of World Literature, New York, 1952, pp. 18–33.

McKay, Claude: *Harlem: A Negro Metropolis,* E. P. Dutton & Co., New York, 1940.

Margolis, Edward: *Native Sons,* J. B. Lippincott, New York, 1969, pp. 21–46.

———: *The Art of Richard Wright,* Southern Illinois University Press, Carbondale, 1969.

Sternsher, Bernard (ed.): *The Negro in Depression and War, Prelude to Revolution, 1930–1945,* Quadrangle Books, Chicago, 1969. (Contains extremely helpful articles by Leslie Fishel, W. E. B. Du Bois, Mary Bethune, Allan Morrison, Richard Dalfiume, and others.)

Webb, Constance: *Richard Wright, a Biography,* G. P. Putnam, New York, 1968.

Arna Bontemps (1902-   )

A Summer Tragedy

Old Jeff Patton, the black share farmer, fumbled with his bow tie. His fingers trembled and the high, stiff collar pinched his throat. A fellow loses his hand for such vanities after thirty or forty years of simple life. Once a year, or maybe twice if there's a wedding among his kinfolks, he may spruce up; but generally fancy clothes do nothing but adorn the wall of the big room and feed the moths. That had been Jeff Patton's experience. He had not worn his stiff-bosomed shirt more than a dozen times in all his married life. His swallow-tailed coat lay on the bed beside him, freshly brushed and pressed, but it was as full of holes as the overalls in which he worked on weekdays. The moths had used it badly. Jeff twisted his mouth into a hideous toothless grimace as he contended with the obstinate bow. He stamped his good foot and decided to give up the struggle.

"Jennie," he called.

"What's that, Jeff?" His wife's shrunken voice came out of the adjoining room like an echo. It was hardly bigger than a whisper.

"I reckon you'll have to he'p me wid this heah bow tie, baby," he said meekly. "Dog if I can hitch it up."

Her answer was not strong enough to reach him, but presently the old woman came to the door, feeling her way with a stick. She had a wasted, dead-leaf appearance. Her body, as scrawny and gnarled as a string bean, seemed less than nothing in the ocean of frayed and faded petticoats that surrounded her. These hung an inch or two above the tops of her heavy unlaced shoes and showed little grotesque piles where the stockings had fallen down from her negligible legs.

"You oughta could do a heap mo' wid a thing like that'n me—beingst as you got yo' good sight."

"Looks like I oughta could," he admitted. "But ma fingers is gone democrat on me. I get all mixed up in the looking glass an' can't tell wicha way to twist the devilish thing."

Jennie sat on the side of the bed and old Jeff Patton got down on one knee while she tied the bow knot. It was a slow and painful ordeal for each of them in this position. Jeff's bones cracked, his knee ached, and it was only after a half dozen attempts that Jennie worked a semblance of a bow into the tie.

"I got to dress maself now," the old woman whispered. "These is ma old shoes an' stockings, and I ain't so much as unwrapped ma dress."

"Well, don't worry 'bout me no mo', baby," Jeff said. "That 'bout finishes me. All I gotta do now is slip on that old coat 'n ves' an' I'll be fixed to leave."

Jennie disappeared again through the dim passage into the shed room. Being blind was no handicap to her in that black hole. Jeff heard the cane placed against the wall beside the door and knew that his wife was on easy ground. He put on his coat, took a battered top hat from the bed post and hobbled to the front door. He was ready to travel. As soon as Jennie could get on her Sunday shoes and her old black silk dress, they would start.

Outside the tiny log house, the day was warm and mellow with sunshine. A host of wasps were humming with busy excitement in the trunk of a dead sycamore. Gray squirrels were searching through the grass for hickory nuts and blue jays were in the trees, hopping from branch to branch. Pine woods stretched away to the left like a black sea. Among them were scattered scores of log houses like Jeff's, houses of black share farmers. Cows and pigs wandered freely among the trees. There was no danger of loss. Each farmer knew his own stock and knew his neighbor's as well as he knew his neighbor's children.

Down the slope to the right were the cultivated acres on which the colored folks worked. They extended to the river, more than two miles away, and they were today green with the unmade cotton crop. A tiny thread of a road, which passed directly in front of Jeff's place, ran through these green fields like a pencil mark.

Jeff, standing outside the door, with his absurd hat in his left hand, surveyed the wide scene tenderly. He had been forty-five years on these acres. He loved them with the unexplained affection that others have for the countries to which they belong.

The sun was hot on his head, his collar still pinched his throat, and the Sunday clothes were intolerably hot. Jeff transferred the hat to his right hand and began fanning with it. Suddenly the whisper that was Jennie's voice came out of the shed room.

"You can bring the car round front whilst you's waitin'," it said feebly. There was a tired pause; then it added, "I'll soon be fixed to go."

"A'right, baby," Jeff answered. "I'll get it in a minute."

But he didn't move. A thought struck him that made his mouth fall open. The mention of the car brought to his mind, with new intensity, the trip he and Jennie were about to take. Fear came into his eyes; excitement took his breath. Lord, Jesus!

"Jeff. . . . O Jeff," the old woman's whisper called.

He awakened with a jolt. "Hunh, baby?"

"What you doin'?"

"Nuthin. Jes studyin'. I jes been turnin' things round 'n round in ma mind."

"You could be gettin' the car," she said.

"Oh yes, right away, baby."

He started round to the shed, limping heavily on his bad leg. There were three frizzly chickens in the yard. All his other chickens had been killed or stolen recently. But the frizzly chickens had been saved somehow. That was fortunate indeed, for these curious creatures had a way of devouring "poison" from the yard and in that way protecting against conjure and black luck and spells. But even the frizzly chickens seemed now to be in a stupor. Jeff thought they had some ailment; he expected all three of them to die shortly.

The shed in which the old T-model Ford stood was only a grass roof held up by four corner poles. It had been built by tremulous hands at a time when the little rattletrap car had been regarded as a peculiar treasure. And, miraculously, despite wind and downpour, it still stood.

Jeff adjusted the crank and put his weight upon it. The engine came to life with a sputter and bang that rattled the old car from radiator to tail light. Jeff hopped into the seat and put his foot on the accelerator. The sputtering and banging increased. The rattling became more violent. That was good. It was good banging, good sputtering and rattling, and it meant that the aged car was still in running condition. She could be depended on for this trip.

Again Jeff's thought halted as if paralyzed. The suggestion of the trip fell into the machinery of his mind like a wrench. He felt dazed and weak. He swung the car out into the yard, made a half turn and drove around to the front door. When he took his hands off the wheel, he noticed that he was trembling violently. He cut off the motor and climbed to the ground to wait for Jennie.

A few minutes later she was at the window, her voice rattling against the pane like a broken shutter.

"I'm ready, Jeff."

He did not answer, but limped into the house and took her by the arm. He led her slowly through the big room, down the step and across the yard.

"You reckon I'd oughta lock the do'?" he asked softly.

They stopped and Jennie weighed the question. Finally she shook her head. "Ne' mind the do'," she said. "I don't see no cause to lock up things."

"You right," Jeff agreed. "No cause to lock up."

Jeff opened the door and helped his wife into the car. A quick shudder passed over him. Jesus! Again he trembled.

"How come you shaking so?" Jennie whispered.

"I don't know," he said.

"You mus' be scairt, Jeff."

"No, baby, I ain't scairt."

He slammed the door after her and went around to crank up again. The motor started easily. Jeff wished that it had not been so responsive. He would have liked a few more minutes in which to turn things around in his head. As it was, with Jennie chiding him about being afraid, he had to keep going. He swung the car into the little pencil-mark road and started off toward the river, driving very slowly, very cautiously.

Chugging across the green countryside, the small battered Ford seemed tiny indeed. Jeff felt a familiar excitement, a thrill, as they came down the first slope to the immense levels on which the cotton was growing. He could not help reflecting that the crops were good. He knew what that meant, too; he had made forty-five of them with his own hands. It was true that he had worn out nearly a dozen mules, but that was the fault of old man Stevenson, the owner of the land. Major Stevenson had the odd notion that one mule was all a share farmer needed to work a thirty-acre plot. It was an expensive notion, the way it killed mules from overwork, but the old man held to it. Jeff thought it killed a good many share farmers as well as mules, but he had no sympathy for them. He had always been strong, and he had been taught to have no patience with weakness in men. Women or children might be tolerated if they were puny, but a weak man was a curse. Of course, his own children—

Jeff's thought halted there. He and Jennie never mentioned their dead children any more. And naturally, he did not wish to dwell upon them in his mind. Before he knew it, some remark would slip out of his mouth and that would make Jennie feel blue. Perhaps she would cry. A woman like Jennie could not easily throw off the grief that comes from losing five grown children within two years. Even Jeff was still staggered by the blow. His memory had not been much good recently. He frequently talked to himself. And, although he had kept it a secret, he knew that his courage had left him. He was terrified by the least unfamiliar sound at night. He was reluctant to venture far from home in the daytime. And that habit of trembling when he felt fearful was now far beyond his control. Sometimes he became afraid and trembled without knowing what had frightened him. The feeling would just come over him like a chill.

The car rattled slowly over the dusty road. Jennie sat erect and silent with a little absurd hat pinned to her hair. Her useless eyes seemed very large, very white in their deep sockets. Suddenly Jeff heard her voice, and he inclined his head to catch the words.

"Is we passed Delia Moore's house yet?" she asked.

"Not yet," he said.

"You must be drivin' mighty slow, Jeff."

"We just as well take our time, baby."

There was a pause. A little puff of steam was coming out of the radiator of the car. Heat wavered above the hood. Delia Moore's house was nearly half a mile away. After a moment Jennie spoke again.

"You ain't really scairt, is you, Jeff?"

"Nah, baby, I ain't scairt."

"You know how we agreed—we gotta keep on goin'."

Jewels of perspiration appeared on Jeff's forehead. His eyes rounded, blinked, became fixed on the road.

"I don't know," he said with a shiver, "I reckon it's the only thing to do."

"Hm."

A flock of guinea fowls, pecking in the road, were scattered by the passing car. Some of them took to their wings; others hid under bushes. A blue jay, swaying on a leafy twig, was annoying a roadside squirrel. Jeff held an even speed till he came near Delia's place. Then he slowed down noticeably.

Delia's house was really no house at all, but an abandoned store building converted into a dwelling. It sat near a crossroads, beneath a single black cedar tree. There Delia, a cattish old creature of Jennie's age, lived alone. She had been there more years than anybody could remember, and long ago had won the disfavor of such women as Jennie. For in her young days Delia had been gayer, yellower and saucier than seemed proper in those parts. Her ways with menfolks had been dark and suspicious. And the fact that she had had as many husbands as children did not help her reputation.

"Yonder's old Delia," Jeff said as they passed.

"What she doin'?"

"Jes sittin' in the do'," he said.

"She see us?"

"Hm," Jeff said. "Musta did."

That relieved Jennie. It strengthened her to know that her old enemy had seen her pass in her best clothes. That would give the old she-devil something to chew her gums and fret about, Jennie thought. Wouldn't she have a fit if she didn't find out? Old evil Delia! This would be just the thing for her. It would pay her back for being so evil. It would also pay her, Jennie thought, for the way she used to grin at Jeff—long ago when her teeth were good.

The road became smooth and red, and Jeff could tell by the smell of the air that they were nearing the river. He could see the rise where the road turned and ran along parallel to the stream. The car chugged on monotonously. After a long silent spell, Jennie leaned against Jeff and spoke.

"How many bale o' cotton you think we got standin'?" she said.

Jeff wrinkled his forehead as he calculated.

" 'Bout twenty-five, I reckon."

"How many you make las' year?"

"Twenty-eight," he said. "How come you ask that?"

"I's jes thinkin'," Jennie said quietly.

"It don't make a speck o' difference though," Jeff reflected. "If we get much or if we get little, we still gonna be in debt to old man Stevenson when he gets through counting up agin us. It's took us a long time to learn that."

Jennie was not listening to these words. She had fallen into a trance-like meditation. Her lips twitched. She chewed her gums and rubbed her gnarled hands nervously. Suddenly, she leaned forward, buried her face in the nervous hands and burst into tears. She cried aloud in a dry cracked voice that suggested the rattle of fodder on dead stalks. She cried aloud like a child, for she had never learned to suppress a genuine sob. Her slight old frame shook heavily and seemed hardly able to sustain such violent grief.

"What's the matter, baby?" Jeff asked awkwardly. "Why you cryin' like all that?"

"I's jes thinkin'," she said.

"So you the one what's scairt now, hunh?"

"I ain't scairt, Jeff. I's jes thinkin' 'bout leavin' eve'thing like this—eve'thing we been used to. It's right sad-like."

Jeff did not answer, and presently Jennie buried her face again and cried.

The sun was almost overhead. It beat down furiously on the dusty wagon-path road, on the parched roadside grass and the tiny battered car. Jeff's hands, gripping the wheel, became wet with perspiration; his forehead sparkled. Jeff's lips parted. His mouth shaped a hideous grimace. His face suggested the face of a man being burned. But the torture passed and his expression softened again.

"You mustn't cry, baby," he said to his wife. "We gotta be strong. We can't break down."

Jennie waited a few seconds, then said, "You reckon we oughta do it, Jeff? You reckon we oughta go 'head an' do it, really?"

Jeff's voice choked; his eyes blurred. He was terrified to hear Jennie say the thing that had been in his mind all morning. She had egged him on when he had wanted more than anything in the world to wait, to reconsider, to think things over a little longer. Now she was getting cold feet. Actually, there was no need of thinking the question through again. It would only end in making the same painful decision once more. Jeff knew that. There was no need of fooling around longer.

"We jes as well to do like we planned," he said. "They ain't nothin' else for us now—it's the bes' thing."

Jeff thought of the handicaps, the near impossibility, of making another crop with his leg bothering him more and more each week. Then there was always the chance that he would have another stroke, like the one that had made him lame. Another one might kill him. The least it could do would be to leave him helpless. Jeff gasped—Lord, Jesus! He could not bear to think of being helpless, like a baby, on Jennie's hands. Frail, blind Jennie.

The little pounding motor of the car worked harder and harder. The puff of steam from the cracked radiator became larger. Jeff realized that they were climbing a little rise. A moment later the road turned abruptly and he looked down upon the face of the river.

"Jeff."

"Hunh?"

"Is that the water I hear?"

"Hm. Tha's it."

"Well, which way you goin' now?"

"Down this-a way," he said. "The road runs 'long 'side o' the water a lil piece."

She waited a while calmly. Then she said, "Drive faster."

"A'right, baby," Jeff said.

The water roared in the bed of the river. It was fifty or sixty feet below the level of the road. Between the road and the water there was a long smooth slope, sharply inclined. The slope was dry, the clay hardened by prolonged summer heat. The water below, roaring in a narrow channel, was noisy and wild.

"Jeff."

"Hunh?"

"How far you goin'?"

"Jes a lil piece down the road."

"You ain't scairt is you, Jeff?"

"Nah, baby," he said trembling. "I ain't scairt."

"Remember how we planned it, Jeff. We gotta do it like we said. Brave-like."

"Hm."

Jeff's brain darkened. Things suddenly seemed unreal, like figures in a dream. Thoughts swam in his mind foolishly, hysterically, like little blind fish in a pool within a dense cave. They rushed, crossed one another, jostled, collided, retreated and rushed again. Jeff soon became dizzy. He shuddered violently and turned to his wife.

"Jennie, I can't do it. I can't." His voice broke pitifully.

She did not appear to be listening. All the grief had gone from her face. She sat erect, her unseeing eyes wide open, strained and frightful. Her glossy black skin had become dull. She seemed as thin, as sharp and bony, as a starved bird. Now, having suffered and endured the sadness of tearing herself away from beloved things, she showed no anguish. She was absorbed with her own thoughts, and she didn't even hear Jeff's voice shouting in her ear.

Jeff said nothing more. For an instant there was light in his cavernous brain. The great chamber was, for less than a second, peopled by characters he knew and loved. They were simple, healthy creatures, and they behaved in a manner that he could understand. They had quality. But since he had already taken leave of them long ago, the remembrance did not break his heart again. Young Jeff Patton was among them, the Jeff Patton of fifty years ago who went down to New Orleans with a crowd of country boys to the Mardi Gras doings. The gay young crowd, boys with candy-striped shirts and rouged-brown girls in noisy silks, was like a picture in his head. Yet it did not make him sad. On that very trip Slim Burns had killed Joe Beasley—the crowd had been broken up. Since then Jeff Patton's world had been the Greenbriar Plantation. If there had been other Mardi Gras carnivals, he had not heard of them. Since then there had been no time; the years had fallen on him like waves. Now he was old, worn out. Another paralytic stroke (like the one he had already suffered) would put him on his back for keeps. In that condition, with a frail blind woman to look after him, he would be worse off than if he were dead.

Suddenly Jeff's hands became steady. He actually felt brave. He slowed down the motor of the car and carefully pulled off the road. Below, the water of the stream boomed, a soft thunder in the deep channel. Jeff ran the car onto the clay slope, pointed it directly toward the stream and put his foot heavily on the accelerator. The little car leaped furiously down the steep incline toward the water. The movement was nearly as swift and direct as a fall. The two old black folks, sitting quietly side by side, showed no excitement. In another instant the car hit the water and dropped immediately out of sight.

A little later it lodged in the mud of a shallow place. One wheel of the crushed and upturned little Ford became visible above the rushing water.

Nocturne at Bethesda

I thought I saw an angel flying low,
I thought I saw the flicker of a wing
Above the mulberry trees; but not again.
Bethesda sleeps. This ancient pool that healed
A host of bearded Jews does not awake.

This pool that once the angels troubled does not move.
No angel stirs it now, no Saviour comes
With healing in His hands to rise the sick
And bid the lame man leap upon the ground.

The golden days are gone. Why do we wait
So long upon the marble steps, blood
Falling from our open wounds? and why
Do our black faces search the empty sky?
Is there something we have forgotten? some precious thing
We have lost, wandering in strange lands?

There was a day, I remember now,
I beat my breast and cried, "Wash me, God,
Wash me with a wave of wind upon
The barley; O quiet One, draw near, draw near!
Walk upon the hills with lovely feet
And in the waterfall stand and speak.

"Dip white hands in the lily pool and mourn
Upon the harps still hanging in the trees
Near Babylon along the river's edge,
But oh, remember me, I pray, before
The summer goes and rose leaves lose their red."

The old terror takes my heart, the fear
Of quiet waters and of faint twilights.
There will be better days when I am gone
And healing pools where I cannot be healed.
Fragrant stars will gleam forever and ever
Above the place where I lie desolate.

Yet I hope, still I long to live.
And if there can be returning after death
I shall come back. But it will not be here;
If you want me you must search for me
Beneath the palms of Africa. Or if
I am not there then you may call to me
Across the shining dunes, perhaps I shall
Be following a desert caravan.

I may pass through centuries of death
With quiet eyes, but I'll remember still
A jungle tree with burning scarlet birds.
There is something I have forgotten, some precious thing.
I shall be seeking ornaments of ivory,
I shall be dying for a jungle fruit.

You do not hear, Bethesda.
O still green water in a stagnant pool!
Love abandoned you and me alike.
There was a day you held a rich full moon
Upon your heart and listened to the words
Of men now dead and saw the angels fly.
There is a simple story on your face;

Years have wrinkled you. I know, Bethesda!
You are sad. It is the same with me.

Southern Mansion

Poplars are standing there still as death
And ghosts of dead men
Meet their ladies walking
Two by two beneath the shade
And standing on the marble steps.

There is a sound of music echoing
Through the open door
And in the field there is
Another sound tinkling in the cotton:
Chains of bondmen dragging on the ground.

The years go back with an iron clank,
A hand is on the gate,
A dry leaf trembles on the wall.
Ghosts are walking.
They have broken roses down
And poplars stand there still as death.

Reconnaissance

After the cloud embankments,
The lamentation of wind,
And the starry descent into time,
We came to the flashing waters and shaded our eyes
From the glare.

Alone with the shore and the harbor,
The stems of the cocoanut trees,

The fronds of silence and hushed music,
We cried for the new revelation
And waited for miracles to rise.

Where elements touch and merge,
Where shadows swoon like outcasts on the sand
And the tired moment waits, its courage gone—
There were we

In latitudes where storms are born.

Sterling A. Brown (1901-   )

Sister Lou

Honey
When de man
Calls out de las' train
You're gonna ride,
Tell him howdy.

Gather up yo' basket
An' yo' knittin' an' yo' things,
An' go on up an' visit
Wid frien' Jesus fo' a spell.

Show Marfa
How to make yo' greengrape jellies,
An' give po' Lazarus
A passel of them Golden Biscuits.

Scald some meal
Fo' some rightdown good spoonbread
Fo' li'l box-plunkin' David.

An' sit aroun'
An' tell them Hebrew Chillen
All yo' stories. . . .

Honey
Don't be feared of them pearly gates,
Don't go 'round to de back,
No mo' dataway⁻
Not evah no mo'.

Let Michael tote yo' burden
An' yo' pocketbook an' evah thing
'Cept yo' Bible,
While Gabriel blows somp'n
Solemn but loudsome
On dat horn of his'n.

Honey
Go Straight on to de Big House,
An' speak to yo' God
Widout no fear an' tremblin'.

Then sit down
An' pass de time of day awhile.

Give a good talkin' to
To yo' favorite 'postle Peter,
An' rub the po' head
Of mixed-up Judas,
An' joke awhile wid Jonah.

Then, when you gits de chance,
Always rememberin' yo' raisin',
Let 'em know youse tired
Jest a mite tired.

Jesus will find yo' bed fo' you
Won't no servant evah bother wid yo' room.
Jesus will lead you
To a room wid windows
Openin' on cherry trees an' plum trees
Bloomin' everlastin'.

An' dat will be yours
Fo' keeps.

Den take yo' time. . . .
Honey, take yo' bressed time.

Children of the Mississippi

These know fear; for all their singing
As the moon thrust her tip above dark woods,
Tuning their voices to the summer night,
These folk knew even then the hints of fear.
For all their loafing on the levee,
Unperturbedly spendthrift of time,
Greeting the big boat swinging the curve
"Do it, Mister Pilot! Do it, Big Boy!"
Beneath their dark laughter
Roaring like a flood roars, swung into a spillway,
There rolled even then a strong undertow
Of fear.

Now, intimately
These folk know fear.
They have seen
Blackwater creeping, slow-footed Fate,
Implacably, unceasingly
Over their bottomlands, over their cornshocks,
Past highwater marks, past wildest conjecture,
Black water creeping before their eyes,
Rolling while they toss in startled half sleep.

> *De Lord tole Norah*
> *Dat de flood was due,*
> *Norah listened to de Lord*
> *An' got his stock on board,*
> *Wish dat de Lord*
> *Had tole us too.*

These folks know grief.
They have seen
Black water gurgling, lapping, roaring,
Take their lives' earnings, roll off their paltry
Fixtures of home, things as dear as old hearthgods.
These have known death
Surprising, rapacious of cattle, of children,
Creeping with the black water
Secretly, unceasingly.

> *Death pick out new ways*
> *Now fo' to come to us,*

Black water creepin'
White folk is sleepin',
Death on de black water
Ugly an' treacherous.

These, for all their vaunted faith, know doubt.
These know no Ararat;
No arc of promise bedecking blue skies;
No dove, betokening calm;
No fondled favor towards new beginnings.
These know
Promise of baked lands, burnt as in brickkilns,
Cracked uglily, crinkled crust at the seedtime,
Rotten with stench, watched over by vultures,
Promise of winter, bleak and unpitying,
No buoyant hoping now, only dank memories
Bitter as the waters, bracken as the waters
Black and unceasing as hostile waters.

Winter a-comin'
Leaner dan ever,
What we done done to you
Makes you do lak you do?
How we done harmed you
Black-hearted river?

These folk know fear, now, as a bosom crony;
Children, stepchildren
Of the Mississippi. . . .

The American Race Problem
as Reflected in American Literature

From The Journal of Negro Education

Introduction

In "Calling America," the special number of the *Survey Graphic* which sprang
from American concern with the plight of minorities in Europe, William Allan
Neilson writes:

The greatest of the minority problems in the United States concerns *the Negro,*
involving as it does some 10 per cent of our population....It would be flagrant
hypocrisy to pretend that the position of the Negro in the United States is in har-

mony with the principles of democracy and equality of opportunity to which we habitually pay lip service.[1]

W. E. B. DuBois considered that the problem of the twentieth century is the problem of the color line. In a blither spirit a historian of Reconstruction assures the readers of *The Road to Reunion* that "The Negro Problem Always Ye Have With You." An alarmist "scientist" titled his book on the Negro *America's Greatest Problem*. American literature seems to second the warnings and the assurance: the problems attendant upon the presence of the Negro in America have engaged the attention of writers from the earliest years of our national literature.

It is the purpose of this essay to trace what American writers have said about "the Negro problem." Difficult of precise definition, and therefore not defined here, "the Negro problem" is recognizable enough for such a purpose.

This essay will be confined chiefly to creative literature in which poets, dramatists and fiction writers attempt to reflect the "Negro Problem." The voluminous literature on "the problem" under which library shelves sag has been made use of only to show how influential the ethnologists, psychologists, sociologists, theologians, and historians have been upon the creative artists, who admitted that they were writing fiction.

The essay is divided chronologically into three periods: (1) the antebellum, (2) reconstruction to the turn of the century, and (3) the twentieth century.

Kelly Miller in one of his aphorisms states that "The Negro must get along, get white, or get out." Creative artists have agreed with these as solutions. They see "the problem" or "problems" differently, however. For instance, proslavery authors see the Negro as failing to get along when he was discontented as a slave, or free in the North; antislavery authors when he was treated as a chattel; most Negro authors when he is denied citizenship. The problems then are of two sorts: the problem that the Negro's presence caused those who believed in a white America, *i.e.*, the problem of the Negro to whites; and the problems that the Negro has met with in America, *i.e.*, the problem of America to Negroes.

It is not a purpose of this paper to discuss the question of propaganda in literature, or to evaluate the points of view expressed, although evaluations have not been avoided. This is one of the most controversial subjects in American literature. If one is a good American, it is very difficult to enter this ring where such a rousing battle royal is going on without once raising his arm and letting fly.

The Ante-Bellum Period

American readers had abundant opportunity to learn of the gravity of the problem of slavery from the reports of English travelers such as Charles Dickens,

[1] William Allan Neilson, " 'Minorities' In Our *Midst*," *Survey Graphic* (Calling America), 28:102, 103, F 1939.

Harriet Martineau, and J. S. Buckingham, and of Northerners such as Frederick Law Olmsted. But such testimony could be dismissed as British or Yankee prejudice. Often too realistic for comfort, the analysis of slavery as an injury to Negroes and a cause of general Southern backwardness, was shunted aside.

Creative artists stated the same conclusions in more emotionally stirring forms. Richard Hildreth, an American historian, was the first to use the novel for antislavery opinions. Published in 1836 as the memoirs of an educated slave, his work was enlarged after the great success of *Uncle Tom's Cabin* and renamed *The White Slave* (1852). Considering the pastoral picture of slavery to be largely mythical, Hildreth, like so many of his followers, stressed the slave's basic humanity, introduced Negro runaways, "maroons," insurrectionists; and described with realistic detail the callousness of the domestic slave-trade, the inevitable miscegenation and the brutalities. In the latter section of the book, Hildreth permits his characters to debate slavery at length. One enlightened slave-owner is a mild colonizationist:

The late president Jefferson . . . [remarked] that we hold the slaves like a wolf by the ear, whom it is neither safe to hold nor to let go. . . . It seems to me that we whites are the wolf, and the unfortunate negroes the lamb . . . whom, if we only had the will, we might let go without any sort of danger. Why can't we allow freedom to the negroes as well as to the Irish or the Germans? But with the inveterate prejudices of our people . . . [they] would be all up in arms at the very idea of it. The more low, brutal, and degraded a white man is, the more strenuously does he insist on the natural superiority of the white man, and the more he is shocked at the idea of allowing freedom to the "niggers." Our colonization system yields to this invincible feeling.[2]

Hildreth does not disguise his belief that colonization is a visionary solution, that Negroes if set free would prosper, and that the whites more than the Negroes need to be readied for the emancipation of the latter. He tells approvingly of a planter's scheme for freeing his Negroes and setting them up on a plantation in a free state.

The antislavery literary crusade took its start from people whose sense of human dignity was shocked by the idea of men and women being held as property. Transcendentalists like Theodore Parker and Thoreau, Quakers like Whittier and Thomas Garrett, agitators like Garrison and Theodore Weld saw slavery as a curse, in Longfellow's words as "a blind Samson in the temple of our liberties." They wanted the curse removed, the Samson throttled. Attack upon the evil was the pressing task for many of the poets and novelists, and they were not perturbed about what would follow its abolition. Happy endings were fashioned for their heroes and heroines: the octoroon Camilla marries her Northern white rescuer; the white slave Archie Moore at last finds his lost wife and sails for England; broken families are happily united in Canada.

[2] Richard Hildreth, *The White Slave*. Boston: Tappan and Whittemore, 1852, p. 273.

Fugitive slaves, like Frederick Douglass, William Wells Brown, Lewis and Milton Clarke in their autobiographies, and Harriet Tubman, Josiah Henson, and William and Ellen Craft in their dictated narratives told chiefly of the practical, immediate problems of food, clothing and lodging, of avoiding the slave-buyer, of staying out of the ill graces of the driver, the overseer or the slave-breaker, of finding trustworthy mates to dare an escape, of guarding against treacherous slaves, of dodging the patrol, of checkmating the slave-hunters and kidnappers. With such problems solved, it is no wonder that the spirit of much of their writing was that of the fellow who, spirited away by Harriet Tubman to Canada, threw himself upon free soil and shouted his thanks to God that he was free at last. Some of the noted fugitives, especially Douglass, turned their thoughts to the new set of problems, but most of the autobiographies of ex-slaves close with jubilees.

Some of the novelists, however, although deploring slavery, viewed with distrust the presence in America of free Negroes. Some were like Hildreth in fearing race prejudice; others, believing the Negro to have his peculiarities, could not visualize two races living side by side in harmony. This second attitude goes far back: in one of the earliest antislavery pamphlets, *The Selling of Joseph*, Judge Sewall writes:

Few can endure to hear of a Negro's being made free; and indeed they can seldom use their freedom well; yet their continual aspiring after their forbidden Liberty, renders them Unwilling Servants. And there is such a disparity in their Conditions, Color & Hair, that they can never embody with us, and grow up into orderly Families, to the Peopling of the Land: but still remain in our Body Politick as a kind of extravasat blood.[3]

In *The Spy* Cooper expresses both hope for gradual emancipation and anxiety over the increasing class of free Negroes, vagrants "without principles and attachments."[4] Melville includes antislavery passages in *Mardi* (1849), but convinced that tampering with the peculiar institution will cause secession and revolt, he concludes gloomily that "Time must befriend these thralls!"

At the time of *Uncle Tom's Cabin* (1851) Harriet Beecher Stowe was perplexed about the future of the free Negro. George Harris' reunion with Eliza in Canada is not unadulterated bliss. His future course is a quandary. He decides that "passing for white" would be disloyal to his mother's race and that his individual fight in America for abolition would be ineffectual. In Africa, however, he dreams that a republic, a nation of his people, is rising that will

roll the tide of civilization and Christianity along its shores, and plant there mighty republics, that growing with the rapidity of tropical vegetation, shall be for all coming ages.

---

[3] Samuel Sewall, *The Selling of Joseph* in Warfel, Gabriel, and Williams, *The American Mind*, p. 64.

[4] James Fenimore Cooper, *The Spy*. New York: Charles Scribner's Sons, 1931, p. 44.

He knows that colonization has been used to retard emancipation, but there is a "God above all man's schemes" who will use it to found a Negro nation. The Negro has rights to be allowed in America, "equal rights . . . as the Irishman, the German, the Swede," and the added claim of "an injured race for reparation." But George does not want those rights.

I want a country, a nation of my own. I think that the African race has peculiarities yet to be unfolded in the light of civilization and Christianity, which, if not the same with those of the Anglo-Saxon, may prove to be morally, of even a higher type.[5]

In *Dred,* her second antislavery novel, Mrs. Stowe does not dispatch her Negro heroes and heroines to Africa, but leaves them in Canada. Like Harriet Tubman, Mrs. Stowe seems to believe that after the Fugitive Slave Bill fugitives can be safe only near the defending paws of the British lion.

Mrs. Stowe believes that the African race (her militant and intelligent heroes and heroines are almost always nearly white) has its peculiarities (generally of a higher moral caliber than the Anglo-Saxon's). She pleads for humane treatment of Negroes in the North in order to enable them to attain the "moral and intellectual maturity" requisite for missionary service in Africa. Influenced by Mrs. Stowe, H. L. Hosmer's *Adela, The Octoroon* after describing the misery of Mississippi slaves and of Northern free Negroes, shows Liberia to be a happy land of opportunity.

When Frederick Douglass opposed colonization as "an old enemy of the colored people in this country,"[6] he expressed the animus of the outright abolitionists, who, like Garrison, assaulted caste as well as slavery. But Douglass' scornful addition that "almost every respectable man belongs to it by direct membership or by affinity," was true of some antislavery writers. During the Civil War, the *Saturday Review* in England commented upon the strange illusion

that any respectable party or body of Northerners honestly propose to put the negro on a perfect level with white men . . . neither sober American citizens . . . nor sober Englishmen who have visited . . . The West Indies, will give the slightest adhesion to a principle which makes the negro the social equal of the white man, and encourages the dusky pets of the platform to aspire to a matrimonial alliance with white women.[7]

Besides men like Benjamin Lundy and Joshua Coffin who opposed slavery because of its wrong to Negroes, there were other Southern writers who opposed it as working injury to nonslaveholding whites. J. J. Flournoy, convinced that

---

[5] Harriet Beecher Stowe, *Uncle Tom's Cabin.* New York: The Macmillan Company, 1928, p. 417.

[6] Frederick Douglass, "Speech in Faneuil Hall," June 8, 1849, in Woodson, Carter G., *Negro Orators and Their Orations.* Washington: The Associated Publishers 1925, p. 178.

[7] Cedric Dover, *Know This of Race.* London: Secker and Warburg, 1939, p. 97.

Negroes were "constitutionally ignorant and uncouth, malicious when in power [written in 1836], and proud without beauty—blasphemous and full of obloquy" and therefore "not fit to associate with the whites" founded a sect called "The Efficient and Instantaneous Expulsion Association of Philosophic and Fearless Patriots."[8] Nearly twenty years later, Hinton Rowan Helper developed Flournoy's ideas. Protesting his dislike for Negroes, he still believed that slavery was a great wrong, and that the system of logic that justified it, merely because "Nature had been pleased to do a trifle more for the Caucasian race than for the African," was "antagonistic to the spirit of democracy." Helper produced "expulsion" as the only stay of the impending ruin.[9]

Many non-slaveholders agreed with Helper, but his book was judged to be as incendiary as *The Liberator,* and the poets and novelists strung along with the master class. They countered Helper's strictures on the waste of slavery with paeans about its blessings to planters and slaves, with the latter chief beneficiaries. They agreed with Helper, however, that Negroes—if free—should be ejected from the paradise.

Proslavery authors found biological warrant for their beliefs in the work of savants whom Helper characterized as "ethnographical oligarchs." The Negro's "different bodily formation" was one of the ways by which Providence assured his political condition. *The Bible Defense of Slavery* established that the Negro was the natural born slave in such ways as citing the great length and width of his foot, "the extraordinary protrusion of the heel backward, placing the leg nearly in the middle of the foot in many instances"; the skin where the "Divine hand" has placed "myriads of little cups of pellucid water mingled with the capillary vessels" to throw off the sun's rays and avert sunstroke.[10]

A later book embodying many of the scientific justifications of slavery was *White Supremacy and Negro Subordination* or *The Negro, A Subordinate Race and (So-Called) Slavery Its Normal Condition.* To its author, C. J. H. Van Evrie, M.D.:

The beard symbolizes our highest conceptions of manhood—it is the outward evidence ... of complete growth, mental as well as physical—of strength, wisdom and manly grace.[11]

But the Negro cannot raise a beard, being capable at his best of only "a little tuft on the chin and sometimes on the upper lip, . . . nothing that can be confounded with a beard." He goes on:

---

[8] William Sumner Jenkins, *Pro-Slavery Thought in the Old South.* Chapel Hill: University of North Carolina Press, 1935, pp. 92–93.

[9] Hinton Rowan Helper, *The Impending Crisis of the South.* New York: A. B. Burdick, 1860, p. 184.

[10] Josiah Priest, Bible Defense of Slavery. Glasgow, Ky.: W. S. Brown, 1851, p. 51.

[11] C. J. Van Evrie, *White Supremacy and Negro Subordination.* New York: Van Evrie, Horton & Co., 1870, p. 102.

The negro, lowest in the scale, presents an almost absolute resemblance to each other [sic]....Except where wide differences of age exist they are all alike, and even in size rarely depart from that standard uniformity that nature has stamped upon the race. The entire external surface, as well as his interior organism, differs radically from the Caucasian. His muscles, the form of the limbs, his feet, hands, pelvis, skeleton, all the organs of locomotion are...radically different from the Caucasian.[12]

The Negro's beardlessness, uniformity, and the other biological differences do more than doom him to subordination. They likewise are reasons why "Music is to the Negro an impossible art, and therefore such a thing as a Negro singer is unknown" and why a correctly proportioned brain "could no more be born of a Negress than an elephant could be!"[13]

Theological warrant for slavery could be quite as fantastic. When Ham laughed at his father's drunkenness and disarray, he and all of his descendants were doomed to perpetual servitude. "Cursed be Canaan; a servent of servants shall he be unto his brethren." For the Fugitive Slave Bill divine sanction could be derived from God's commanding the runaway Hagar to return to her mistress Sarah (Genesis XVI:9). So ran some of the biblical arguments.

It was to the biological, psychological, and theological sanctions that the creative authors turned rather than to the more hard-headed political economy which held that slavery has its *raison d'être* in the need for "sordid, servile, laborious beings" to perform "sordid, servile, laborious offices." J. P. Kennedy's *Swallow Barn* (1832) praised slavery as a beneficent guardianship for an "essentially parasitical race" noted for "intellectual feebleness." William Grayson in a long poem, *The Hireling and the Slave* (1856), described the life of the slaves as "unassailed by care," full of "blessings claimed in fabled states alone." Slavery was the design of Providence to transfer the Negro from bestiality to "celestial light." The hero in Caroline Lee Hentz's *The Planter's Northern Bride* cribs arguments from *The Bible Defense of Slavery* to prove the Negro to be divinely ordained to pick his cotton:

In the first place, his skull has a hardness and thickness greater than our own, which defy the arrowy sunbeams of the South. Then his skin...secretes a far greater quantity of moisture, which like dew, throws back the heat absorbed by us. I could mention many more peculiarities which prove his adaptedness to the situation he occupies....The mountains and the valleys proclaim it.[14]

The fantasies of the scientists and the theologues were dressed up in sentimentality and melodrama by the romancers. They made slavery, according to a Southern critic, into an "unbroken Mardi Gras." But they admitted that a few problems existed. There were serpents in this Eden: abolitionists sneaking about

[12] *Ibid.*, p. 106.

[13] *Ibid.*, p. 130.

[14] Caroline Lee Hentz, *The Planter's Northern Bride.* Philadelphia: Perry & McMillan, 1854, II, p. 4.

stirring discontent, short-sighted Southerners who would teach Negroes to read and write, and fractious Negroes who resented what was for their best good.

Thus Kennedy regarded the interference of abolitionists as "an unwarrantable and mischievous design to do us injury," sometimes resented "to the point of involving the innocent Negro in the rigor which it provokes."[15] W. J. Smith in *Life at the South* or *Uncle Tom's Cabin As It Is* shows an abolitionist worming his way into the confidence of honest, unspoiled Negroes and changing their happy lives. *A Yankee Slave Dealer* has an abolitionist foolishly trying to decoy satisfied Negroes; Mrs. Hentz's *The Planter's Northern Bride* has a Dickensian villain preaching liberty and causing an abortive revolt.

Vigilance could of course lessen the impact of the abolitionists. Much graver to proslavery authors was the increasing class of the free Negroes, some runaways; some manumitted as natural children of white fathers, or as reward for services; some who by hiring themselves out, scraping and hoarding had saved enough money to buy their own bodies. These, not the safely stowed slaves, constituted the Negro problem to slaveowners and their literary men.

W. J. Grayson gave classic form to the Southerners' concept of the free Negro in the North:

> There in suburban dens and human sties,
> In foul excesses sunk, the Negro lies;
> A moral pestilence to taint and stain,
> His life a curse, his death a social gain,
> ... with each successive year,
> In drunken want his numbers disappear.[16]

William Thompson in a book of burlesque travels in the North, loses his tone of burlesque in writing of the Northern free Negroes. He can only pity the "pore, miserable, sickly looking creaters . . . diseased and bloated up like frogs—[in a condition] to which the philanthropists . . . wants to bring the happy black people of the South." Uncle Tom, in *Life at the South* finds labor for hire in Canada to be harder than slavery in Virginia, and discovers Negroes frozen to death in snowstorms in Buffalo. Crissy in *The Planter's Northern Bride* runs away from unfeeling Northerners to get back to the freedom of the plantation— a sort of Underground Railroad in reverse. The consensus is expressed by Uncle Robin in John W. Page's *Uncle Robin in His Cabin:* "Dis, sir, is no country for free black men: Africa de only place for he, sir."

Proslavery authors sometimes caught up with the spirit of their age and suspected that slavery could not be permanent. W. L. G. Smith writes in the Preface to *Life at the South:*

---

[15] J. P. Kennedy. *Swallow Barn.* New York: G. P. Putnam's Sons, 1895 (reprint) p. 453.

[16] W. J. Grayson, *The Hireling and the Slave,* Charleston, S.C.: McCarter & Co., 1856, p. 69.

The day will yet come when the descendants of Ham will be gathered in the land of their ancestors, and Liberia, in God's own good time, will take its position among the independent states of the world.

W. J. Grayson waxes poetic at the prospect of the Negro (no longer necessary for the development of the South) returning to Africa on missionary duty now instead of agricultural:

> To Africa, their fatherland, they go,
> Law, industry, instruction to bestow:
> To pour, from Western skies, religious light,
> Drive from each hill or vale its pagan rite,
> Teach brutal hordes a nobler life to plan,
> And change, at last, the savage to the man.[17]

This was to take place, however, "In God's own good time."

Reconstruction and After

The Emancipation Proclamation ended one phase of the Negro problem, but only aggravated others. Abraham Lincoln illustrates the indecision that plagued so many humanitarians. In his campaigning for office Lincoln had disclaimed any purpose to introduce political and social equality between the races. "There is a physical difference between the two, which in my judgment, will forever forbid their living together in perfect equality." Lincoln's earlier sponsorship of colonization had resulted in an attempt to settle a cargo of freedmen on the Island of Vache in the West Indies. That ill-fated experiment taught him the futility of colonization, but he was not to live long enough to see the results of his other plans for the freedmen.

Walt Whitman, as contradictory as usual, turned upon the freedmen with surprising invective:

As if we had not strained the voting … caliber of American democracy to the utmost for the last fifty years with the millions of ignorant foreigners, we have now infused a powerful percentage of blacks, with about as much intellectual caliber (in the mass) as so many baboons.[18]

Whitman described a parade of freedmen in Washington as "very disgusting and alarming in some respects," the jubilant Negroes looking "like so many wild brutes let loose."[19]

---

[17] W. J. Grayson, *op. cit.*, p. 73.

[18] V. F. Calverton, *The Liberation of American Literature.* New York: Charles Scribner's Sons, 1932, p. 296.

[19] Newton Arvin, *Whitman.* New York: The Macmillan Co., 1938, p. 32.

Lincoln's perplexity and Whitman's disgust were prevalent among Northern writers who had been humanitarians toward the slave. Few retained the staunchness of such equalitarians as Garrison, Stevens, and Sumner. One honorable exception was David Ross Locke, who, under the pen-name Petroleum V. Nasby, attacked copper-heads and "dough-faces," laid the bogey of Negro domination, caricatured Southern chivalry, and ridiculed the superstition that the Negro out of slavery would perish like a fish out of water. But another humorist, Marietta Holly, after describing the horrors of the Klan in *Aunt Samantha on the Race Problem*, could counsel colonization as the only solution, even as late as 1892. Another Northerner in the South, Constance Fenimore Woolson, was shocked by the hopelessness of doing anything for the freedmen, and reserved her pity for the suffering master class.

With reconciliation the watchword of many Northerners, the South seized the opportunity to glorify its lost cause, and to persuade the North to leave the Negro problem in Southern hands. This campaign started almost with Appomattox. J. H. Van Evrie republished his book at the close of the Civil War with such prefatory remarks:

We will return to the Constitution and the "Union as it was"; and every man, and woman too in this broad land must accept the simple but stupendous truth of white supremacy and negro subordination, or consent to have it forced on them by years of social anarchy, horror, and misery![20]

His book was intended to prove that what was called slavery was not slavery at all, "but a natural relation of the races." Whenever the two races "are in juxtaposition, the normal condition of the Negro . . . is to be guided and controlled socially and politically by the white race."[21]

Literary artists, with superior skill, sold Van Evie's ideas in a more sophisticated, convincing version to the North which, wearied after the long war, was ready to forget, forgive and concede. Their contrivance was simple. Slavery was to be shown as not slavery at all, but a happy state best suited for an inferior, childish but lovable race. In this normal condition, the Negro was to be shown thriving. Then came his emancipation, which the better class of Negroes did not want, and which few could understand or profit by. Freedom meant anarchy. Only by restoring control (euphemism for tenant farming, sharecropping, black codes, enforced labor, segregation and all the other ills of the new slavery) could equilibrium in the South, so important to the nation, be achieved.

Thomas Nelson Page is the chief of these glorifiers of the Old South and alarmists about the New. His old relicts of slavery, Charley McCarthys in blackface, breathe forth sighs for the vanished days when Negroes were happy: "Dem

[20] J. H. Van Evrie. *op. cit.* VI.

[21] *Ibid.*, VIII.

wuz good old times, marster—de bes' Sam ever see!" Reconstruction showed servants corrupted by scalawags, carpetbaggers, Yankee soldiers and school-marms: faithful housedogs injected with hydrophobia. *In Ole Virginia* is a plaintive cry for the lost heaven; *Red Rock* is a turgid description of the new hell. When the "new issue" Negroes, struggling for schooling and for property, do not enrage Page, they succeed in making him laugh as *Pastime Stories* (1899) indicates. An old Negro, approved by Page (he softens his attacks when dealing with decrepit graybeards whose days of menace are over) says:

You knows de way to de spring and de wood pile, and de mill, an' when you gits a little bigger I's gwine to show you de way to de hoe-handle, an' de cawn furrer, an' dats all de geog-aphy a nigger's got to know.

Joel Chandler Harris has his pet, Uncle Remus, likewise scornful of "nigger 'book-larnin' '":

Hits de ruinashun er dis country....Put a spellin' book in a nigger's hans', en right den an' dar' you loozes a plow-hand. I kin take a bar'l stave an' fling mo' sense inter a nigger in one minnit dan all de schoolhouses betwixt dis en de state er Midgigin.

Harris was fundamentally of greater decency than Page, but he still has his mouthpiece Uncle Remus speaking too often the social policy of white Georgians rather than of his own people.

The author who most strongly urged that the Negro be kept "in his place" was Thomas Dixon, whose fiction embodied the creed of the Ku Klux Klan. Dixon makes use of one old trick of the racialist: he equates political equality with sexual license. The argument runs crudely: keep the Negro from the ballot-box, keep him underpaid and uneducated, or else the purity of white woman-hood is threatened.

As far back as the Lincoln-Douglas debates, Lincoln was taunted with sponsoring intermarriage when he urged merely that the Negro has "the right to eat the bread which his own hands have earned. . . . Judge Douglas infers that because I do not want a Negro woman for a slave, that I must want her for my wife." In the Reconstruction, intermarriage was dragged out in a more sinister guise. The pat response to assertion of Negro rights became "Would you want your daughter [sister, kinfolks, as the case might warrant] to marry a Negro?" For this, Thomas Dixon and his school are largely responsible. The only Negroes for whom Dixon has any respect are those who dislike Yankees, worship their old masters and mistresses, and prefer slavery. The Negroes engaged in politics are uniformly vicious. The height of their ambition seems to be to make love to a white woman. Negro soldiers abduct white brides; Negro half-wits assault white children. Dixon revels in describing rape. The Ku Klux Klan, the Red Shirts, and other vigilante groups indulge in terroristic activity not for economic or political advantage but to preserve white chastity. A whole school of authors, dreading amalgamation (a bit belatedly) followed Dixon's lead.

Lafcadio Hearn, as fascinated by Negroes as Dixon was repelled, nevertheless expressed one article of the Reconstruction creed. Where Dixon, in company with many others, believed social and political equality would enable a minority to engulf a majority, Hearn foresaw Negro extinction. Freedom would be destruction for "the poor, child-like people":

Dependent like the ivy, he [the Negro] needs some strong oak-like friend to cling to. His support has been cut from him, and his life must wither in its prostrate helplessness.[22]

Certain Southern writers like George Washington Cable and Mark Twain were sympathetic to the struggles of the freedmen. But Cable's best creative work, where it deals with the tragic injustice of the Negro's lot, is set in the antebellum past and chiefly concerns the abuses of the *Code Noïr* and the women of mixed blood. Cable does connect the problems of the old South and the new by pointed asides, and he protests current abuses. At the price of ostracism he condemned the convict lease system and the silence of the South on the general indecency of race relations. But this protest was conveyed in polemical essays, not in fiction. Mark Twain, perfectly aware of America's sorry defaulting of its debt to the Negro, still did not reveal this awareness in creative work.

Albion Tourgee, a Northerner who became part of North Carolina's Reconstruction government, used fiction for propaganda purposes. He showed what his contemporaries refused to touch: the slow but steady progress of the freedmen in education, manliness, social awareness, self-sufficiency; the terrorism of the secret orders; the fraud and violence resorted to in order to reduce freedmen to serfs. He felt that he was waging a futile fight, not because of the unreadiness of the freedman but because of the solidifying South. The titles of his best-known books indicate his doubt; they are *A Fool's Errand* and *Bricks Without Straw*.

Negro writers, however, took up the challenge that Tourgee had spoken. Charles Waddell Chesnutt in his fiction included many of the problems of the color line: the problem of the "half-caste" heroine (overemployed even by this time); of the professional man, hampered by prejudice from performing his best service; of the double standard of morality; of convict labor; of mob violence. Chesnutt handled as well problems within the race which later Negroes have shunted aside: the problem of intraracial color prejudice, of the cleavage between the classes and the masses; of treacherous "hat-in-hand" tactics. Cresnutt wrote melodramatically, but his social understanding should not be underestimated.

Dunbar, Chesnutt's contemporary, was more conciliatory. His dialect poetry

---

[22] Lafcadio Hearn, *Letters from the Raven*. New York: A. and C. Boni 1930, p. 168.

was often of the plantation tradition idealizing slavery, or was gently pastoral. His protest was confined to his standard English poems, and those, since they inclined to the romantic school, were inexplicit on the causes for protest. In his fiction, especially *The Sport of the Gods*, Dunbar occasionally confronted problems, but in general he elected to portray the less disturbing aspects of Negro life.

The Twentieth Century

Many of the Negro writers of the early twentieth century preserved their trust in conciliatory tactics, in appeals to the Christianity of white America. Some counselled that no wrong this side of heaven was too great to be forgiven since "Christ washed the feet of Judas," or that "Vengeance is Jehovah's own. . . . Let us live like loving men," or that

> The heart of the world is beating
> With the love that was born of God.

Leslie Pinckney Hill in "Self Determination (The Philosophy of the American Negro)" enumerates "four benedictions which the meek unto the proud are privileged to speak": refusal to hate, philosophic mirth, idealism, and unwavering loyalty. There were others who spoke of the wrongs guardedly, abstractly: "We wear the mask"; "We ask for peace"; "At the Closed Gate of Justice": "To be a Negro in a day like this, demands forgiveness . . . rare patience . . . strange loyalty."

> Alas! Lord God, what evil have we done?

This poetry is melancholy with the self-pity of the "talented tenth," but it goes no farther in protest. The dialect poets aimed at farce or sweet bucolics.

But there were some who, disillusioned at the results gained by forbearance, realized that if the struggle for equal rights was to be a long pull, there was even less need to postpone the starting. Novelists, angered at the scorn and hatred of Page and Dixon, retaliated in kind. In their counter-propaganda Negroes were generally faultless victims of white villains, who were generally "poor whites." The heroines were beautiful maidens, the heroes intelligent, militant race-leaders: "As to color he was black, but even those prejudiced as to color forgot that prejudice when they gazed upon this ebony-like Apollo."[23] One novelist had no patience with the school of Booker Washington: "What are houses, land and money to men who are women?"[24]

---

[23] Sutton Griggs, *Unfettered*. Nashville, Tenn.: Orion Publishing Co., 1902, p. 71.

[24] J. W. Grant, *Out of the Darkness*. Nashville, Tenn.: National Baptist Publishing Board, 1909, p. 19.

W. E. B. DuBois recognized the importance of creative writing as a vehicle for propaganda. He made effective use of many types: chants and short stories denouncing prejudice and mob violence, satires of the shams of democracy, essays combining scholarly research with the emotions of an embittered participant. His first novel, *The Quest of the Silver Fleece*, melodramatic and idealized, was crowded with informed discussions of the "problem"; his second novel *The Dark Princess* shares the preoccupation, presenting mordant and convincing realism in the sections dealing with America.

Early poems of James Weldon Johnson presented his deliberation on the "problem"; asserting the Negro's right to be in America because of his service and achievement; expressing faith in God's will; posing the question "To America": "How would you have us. . . . Men or things":

> Strong, willing sinews in your wings?
> Or tightening chains about your feet?[25]

Johnson's novel *The Autobiography of an Ex-Colored Man* (1912) was the first by a Negro to deal with the dilemmas of the mulatto who, finally beaten by prejudice and lack of opportunity, decides to "pass" for white. Like Chesnutt and DuBois, Johnson reveals many aspects of the problem, subordinating character and action to its exposition.

Most white writers of the early years of the century followed Page and Dixon, urging that the extension of civil rights to Negroes was equivalent to producing a "mongrel race" in America, or else, satisfied that the Negro problem had been safely handled, viewed Negro life jocularly. John McNeill, for instance, in a poem called "Mr. Nigger" comforted his addressee that he should no longer fear expatriation, since minstrel shows, politicians, planters and lynching mobs depended upon him. The poem is intended to be amusing. More honest writers, realists aware of the tragic uneasiness of American life, occasionally wrote of Negroes in a different vein: Upton Sinclair shows Negro strike-breakers in *The Jungle* (1905) and Stephen Crane and Dreiser recorded brutalities. Mary White Ovington continued the abolitionist tradition in *The Shadow* (1920).

After the War to Make the World Safe for Democracy, Negroes began to write more defiant challenges and more ironic appraisals of America. Fenton Johnson might have produced a parallel to *The Spoon River Anthology*, had he continued delineation of what he started in "Tired" and "The Scarlet Woman." Johnson found brooding defeatism instead of gayety and optimism on the other side of the tracks. Claude McKay's poetry protested "the bread of bitterness" America fed him, and described the Harlem streetwalkers, the workers lost in a city of stone and steel, the menials trying to forget their unhappiness in gin and

---

[25] James Weldon Johnson, *Fifty Years and Other Poems*. Boston: The Cornhill Publishing Co., 1917, p. 5.

carousing, the lynching mobs. His best known poem "If We Must Die" was a rallying cry in the epidemic of riots during the post-war years.

Although some of McKay's characters talk lengthily of race, McKay's fiction was like so much of the Harlem school. Written during a "boom period" of culture, the Harlem novels generally showed a life free of perplexities graver than boy getting girl. Wallace Thurman's *Blacker the Berry* (1929) approached an intraracial problem generally shied away from: the predicament of the darker woman in upper-class "society." But Thurman showed little depth in characterizing his heroine. He probably shared the flippancy of many of the literati whom he described, not without caricature, in *Infants of the Spring* (1932). These were riding a crest, and Harlem to them—a small, select circle—seemed to be a Mecca of gay abandon. These younger "intellectuals" of the Harlem province, if we are to believe Thurman and their own confessions, sent in repeated orders for the gin of existence and let the bitters go. Others—Rudolph Fisher, George Schuyler, and Countee Cullen—intelligently aware and quite concerned about the Negro's predicament, still wrote good-natured "spoofs" of what they called professional race-men and their organizations.

But the carelessness of the hedonist and the lighter touch of the satirist were not the chief fashions in fiction. Some Negro novelists felt that wonders would be accomplished by revealing to white America that Negroes had a cultivated middle class—that "we aren't all alike." Many saw lynching as the most flagrant wrong to be attacked. Walter White's *Fire in the Flint* is the classic example of the lynching novel: two upstanding ambitious Negroes become victims of mob violence, the first for avenging an insult to his sister, and the second for attending a white patient, which is interpreted as assault. As long as lynching remains the sole American crime protected by filibustering congressmen it is likely that it will be written of by American artists. But many writers isolate lynching as the chief problem of Negroes and, without much knowledge and understanding of the South, handle it in a stereotyped, unconvincing manner.

Another problem unduly emphasized was that of the "passing" heroine, the octoroon of long standing in American literature. Contemporary white writers still celebrate her misery: "It must be unbearable to have to live on that side of the barrier," they say from their side. "I won't be black," says their octoroon, marked with what Artemus Ward jokingly calls the "brand of Kane." Negro novelists insist upon the octoroon's unhappiness when she "passed" from her people, whose gifts are warm humanity and philosophic mirth. Both sets of interpreters made more of her problems than they seem to deserve. Graver problems, even concerning the mulatto, awaited and await interpretation.

For the statements of these, especially in the South (a section not written of by young Negro writers as much as one might expect) one must resort frequently to southern white novelists. The better known, like Julia Peterkin and DuBose Heyward, while writing with sympathy of their characters, deal little with social and economic hardships, showing tragedies caused by fate, or if made by man, springing from the violence of a primitive folk. As Irvin Cobb has said: "Ef you wants to perduse a piece showing a lot of niggers gittin' skinned, let it be another nigger w'ich skins em . . . an' whatever else you does don't mess wid no race problem."[26]

But all Southern writers have not heeded Cobb's injunction. E. C. L. Adam's *Nigger to Nigger* (1928) is one of the sharpest indictments of Southern race relations. A chorus of unfooled folk Negroes speak their minds on the travesty of Southern justice, the fraud and violence with which white "supremacy" is maintained, the daily insults, the high hurdles in the Negro's way to minimum decency of living. The dialogue discussing the Ben Bess Case, where a Negro was jailed for thirteen years on the trumped up charges of a trollop is worth far more than pretentious propaganda. *Nigger to Nigger* is a remarkable book to have been written by a white Southerner. Paul Green's *In Abraham's Bosom* courage-ously recorded the struggle of a Negro for schools for his people against the fear and hostility of whites and the fear and inertia of Negroes. T. S. Stribling, trac-ing both the white and Negro branches of a Southern family, is likewise con-vincing in his portrayal of callous brutality, sanctioned by Southern custom. Erskine Caldwell in his short stories—"Kneel to the Rising Sun" is probably the most effective in this regard—shows the Negro to be an exploited serf, only nominally free, a catspaw for sadistic landlords and their minions. "Niggers will git killt," says his Tobacco Road philosopher. Grace Lumpkin in *A Sign for Cain* (1935), Theodore Strauss in *Night at Hogwallow* (1937) and other left wing writers see the Negro problem now as a challenge to democracy. Like the best of the old abolitionists, they stress the basic humanity of the Negro. They are more interested in his problems as a member of the working class than as a member of a race. Sympathetic in recording his struggles, his aspirations, and his tragedies, they have told valuable truths about him, and incidentally have gained stature as artists.

The picture would be false, however, if certain white authors who differ from the liberals and radicals were omitted. There are strange survivals today of the attitudes and proposals of the antebellum and Reconstruction periods. Vachel Lindsay's vision of the "Congo creeping through the black," is coupled with his vision of a Congo paradise with "sacred capitals, temples clean":

> 'Twas a land transfigured, 'twas a new creation
> Oh, a singing wind swept the Negro nation.[27]

Donald Davidson, distrusting so many things—industrialism, democracy, etc.— warns the Negro, now "perhaps unfortunately . . . no longer a child":

---

[26] Irvin Cobb, *Jeff Poindexter, Colored*. New York: George H. Doran Co., 1922, p. 138.

[27] Vachel Lindsay, "The Congo (A Study of the Negro Race)" in Untermeyer, Louis, *Modern American Poetry*. New York: Harcourt Brace & Co., 1930, p. 317.

> There is the wall
> Between us, anciently erected. Once
> It might have been crossed, men say. But now I cannot
> Forget that I was master, and you can hardly
> Forget that you were slave. . . .
> Let us not bruise our foreheads on the wall.[28]

Others continue the plaint of the feebleness of the Negro, without the guidance of the Southern white, in the perplexed modern world. These characterize the North as proslavery authors did, as the graveyard for the Negro, deploring factors as diverse as Harlem, schooling, factory work, voting, etc., as murderous of the finest qualities of the race. They mourn as Page did for the departed old Negro, pitying what one author has called "the helplessness of a simple jungle-folk . . . set down in the life of cities and expected to be men."[29]

Younger Negro artists consider their people not "helpless simple jungle-folk," but an exploited American minority. Unlike earlier race-apologists who expressed the injuries to heroes of the "talented tenth," these social realists are interested in the submerged nine-tenths. Langston Hughes catches the spirit of the elevator boy "climbing up a mountain of yessirs," hears the tragic undercurrent in the minstrel man's laughter. The little boy in *Not Without Laughter* is turned away from the carnival on Children's Day with: "I told you little darkies this wasn't your party." Hughes believes that some day the Negro will no longer "eat in the kitchen" and he trusts to working-class unity to bring this about. His *Ways of White Folks* is an ironic series of short stories showing race prejudice in many of its guises.

George Lee's *River George* is the first novel by a Negro to deal specifically with the evils of sharecropping. Frank Marshall Davis writes vigorous poems of American hypocrisy, and lashes out as well against the sham, the striving and the cowardice to be found in Negro life. Richard Wright in *Uncle Tom's Children* has conveyed with brilliant effectiveness several of the problems of the Southern Negro. His stories are all violent, but they show convincingly how precarious the Negro's hold is upon life and happiness. Self defense in an accidental quarrel, the protection of one's home, the organization of a hunger march, all are due cause for the mob to punish or kill. And the paralyzed fear that Wright shows creeping over the Negro community is eloquent illustration of what life in America means to far too many Negroes.

Not many Negro writers have followed Art for Art's sake. Even so since there are few Negro writers, many problems remain untouched. Especially is this true of intraracial problems. Since the race is so frequently on the defensive, counter-propaganda seems to be called for. Too often the problem is simplified: victimized Negro versus villainous white. Writers analyzing complexities within

[28] Donald Davidson, *The Tall Men*. New York: Houghton Mifflin Co., 1927, p. 39.

[29] Eleanor Mercein Kelly, "Monkey Notions," in Williams, Blanch Colton, *O. Henry Prize Stories of 1927*. Garden City: Doubleday Doran & Co. 1927. p. 207.

the race, stating disagreeable truths, and satirists of what could well be satirized are accused of treason. Social realism is a new literary force, and like other important contemporary trends has made incomplete impression on Negro writers. Of the numerous books on Harlem, for instance, there is not one even attempting to do what Michael Gold did in *Jews Without Money* or Farrell did in the Studs Lonigan trilogy. Problems of the Negro middle-class, Northern and Southern, and of the working-class are abundant. The field, except in well-ploughed patches, has barely been scratched. Certainly it has received only the first turning over.

Conclusion

From the earliest, American creative writers have recorded the Negro problem. Many wrote protesting his enslavement, some believing that with emancipation the problem would be solved. Others were humanitarian towards the slave, but believed that the free Negro had no place in America and should be colonized. Southern antislavery writers agreed that free Negroes belonged in Africa. Proslavery authors saw no problem if Negroes were left under "beneficent guardianship" suited to their peculiar endowment. The only problematical Negroes were free Negroes; these they intended to keep at a minimum. When slavery should end, and some authors foresaw this eventuality "in God's good time," Negroes were to be sent back to carry to benighted Africans the torch lighted in American bondage.

In Reconstruction, some writers—the minority—described the wrongs heaped upon the freedmen and, following equalitarians like Stevens and Sumner, wished to see the Negro integrated in America as a citizen. The majority of white authors who dealt with the Negro were Southerners who dictated national conciliation upon Southern terms. The Negro problem to these was keeping the Negro in his place, which was away from the ballot box, the schoolroom, and the real estate office. The Negro's problem to these was keeping alive, since the Southern white man's beneficent guardianship had been removed.

In the twentieth century, creative artists have become more and more the defenders of democracy. Realism, recording life as it is in America, has revealed much that is tragically out-of-joint. Realistic observation has developed into social protest. The treatment of the Negro problem, or problems, reflects this major interest of American literature. American treatment of the Negro is now seen to be one of the greatest challenges to democracy. Negro writers, becoming more and more articulate and socially aware, are joining in the depiction of the problems faced by Negroes. Writing from the inside, they are often powerfully persuasive. But they are still very few to harvest the wide field. Nevertheless, even though few, if they believe that literature has social pertinence, that it should interpret what the artist knows most fully, and should help to effect changes that he desires most deeply, they should be challenged by the opportunities that wait.

Melvin Tolson (1898-1966)

Dark Symphony

I   *Allegro Moderato*

Black Crispus Attucks taught
    Us how to die
Before white Patrick Henry's bugle breath
Uttered the vertical
    Transmitting cry:
"Yea, give me liberty or give me death."

Waifs of the auction block,
    Men black and strong
The juggernauts of despotism withstood,
Loin-girt with faith that worms
    Equate the wrong
And dust is purged to create brotherhood.

No Banquo's ghost can rise
    Against us now,
Aver we hobnailed Man beneath the brute,
Squeezed down the thorns of greed
    On Labor's brow,
Garroted lands and carted off the loot.

II   *Lento Grave*

The centuries-old pathos in our voices
Saddens the great white world,
And the wizardry of our dusky rhythms
Conjures up shadow-shapes of ante-bellum years:

Black slaves singing *One More River to Cross*
In the torture tombs of slave-ships,
Black slaves singing *Steal Away to Jesus*
In jungle swamps,
Black slaves singing *The Crucifixion*
In slave-pens at midnight,
Black slaves singing *Swing Low, Sweet Chariot*
In cabins of death,
Black slaves singing *Go Down, Moses*
In the canebrakes of the Southern Pharaohs.

III   *Andante Sostenuto*

They tell us to forget
The Golgotha we tread . . .
We who are scourged with hate,
A price upon our head.
They who have shackled us
Require of us a song,
They who have wasted us
Bid us condone the wrong.

They tell us to forget
Democracy is spurned.
They tell us to forget
The Bill of Rights is burned.
Three hundred years we slaved,
We slave and suffer yet:
Though flesh and bone rebel,
They tell us to forget!

Oh, how can we forget
Our human rights denied?
Oh, how can we forget
Our manhood crucified?
When Justice is profaned
And plea with curse is met,
When Freedom's gates are barred,
Oh, how can we forget?

IV   *Tempo Primo*

The New Negro strides upon the continent
In seven-league boots . . .
The New Negro
Who sprang from the vigor-stout loins
Of Nat Turner, gallows-martyr for Freedom,
Of Joseph Cinquez, Black Moses of the Amistad Mutiny,
Of Frederick Douglass, oracle of the Catholic Man,
Of Sojourner Truth, eye and ear of Lincoln's legions,
Of Harriet Tubman, Saint Bernard of the Underground Railroad.

The New Negro
Breaks the icons of his detractors,

Wipes out the conspiracy of silence,
Speaks to *his* America:
"My history-moulding ancestors
Planted the first crops of wheat on these shores,
Built ships to conquer the seven seas,
Erected the Cotton Empire,
Flung railroads across a hemisphere,
Disemboweled the earth's iron and coal,
Tunneled the mountains and bridged rivers,
Harvested the grain and hewed forests,
Sentineled the Thirteen Colonies,
Unfurled Old Glory at the North Pole,
Fought a hundred battles for the Republic."

The New Negro:
His giant hands fling murals upon high chambers,
His drama teaches a world to laugh and weep,
His music leads continents captive,
His voice thunders the Brotherhood of Labor,
His science creates seven wonders,
His Republic of Letters challenges the Negro-baiters.

The New Negro,
Hard-muscled, Fascist-hating, Democracy-ensouled,
Strides in seven-league boots
Along the Highway of Today
Toward the Promised Land of Tomorrow!

V Larghetto

　　None in the Land can say
　　To us black men Today:
You send the tractors on their bloody path,
And create Okies for *The Grapes of Wrath*.
You breed the slum that breeds a *Native Son*
To damn the good earth Pilgrim Fathers won.

None in the Land can say
To us black men Today:
You dupe the poor with rags-to-riches tales,
And leave the workers empty dinner pails.
You stuff the ballot box, and honest men
Are muzzled by your demagogic din.

None in the Land can say
To us black men Today:
You smash stock markets with your coined blitzkriegs,
And make a hundred million guinea pigs.
You counterfeit our Christianity,
And bring contempt upon Democracy.

None in the Land can say
To us black men Today:
You prowl when citizens are fast asleep,
And hatch Fifth Column plots to blast the deep
Foundations of the State and leave the Land
A vast Sahara with a Fascist brand.

VI   *Tempo di Marcia*

Out of abysses of Illiteracy,
Through labyrinths of Lies,
Across waste lands of Disease . . .
We advance!

Out of dead-ends of Poverty,
Through wildernesses of Superstition,
Across barricades of Jim Crowism . . .
We advance!

With the Peoples of the World . . .
We advance!

PSI

Black Boy,
let me get up from the white man's Table of Fifty Sounds
in the kitchen; let me gather the crumbs and cracklings
of this autobio-fragment,
before the curtain with the skull and bones descends.

Many a *t* in the ms.
I've left without a cross,
many an *i* without a dot.
A dusky Lot
with a third degree and a second wind and a seventh turn
of pitch-and-toss,

my psyche escaped the Sodom of Gylt
and the Big White Boss.

Black Boy,
you stand before your heritage,
naked and agape;
cheated like a mockingbird
pecking at a Zuexian grape,
pressed like an awl to do
duty as a screw-
driver, you
ask the American Dilemma in you:
"If the trying plane
of Demos fail,
what will the trowel
of Uncle Tom avail?"

Black Boy,
in this race, at this time, in this place,
to be a Negro artist is to be
a flower of the gods, whose growth
is dwarfed at an early stage—
a Brazilian owl moth,
a giant among his own in an acreage
dark with the darkman's designs,
where the milieu moves back downward like the sloth.

Black Boy,
true—you
have not
dined and wined
(*ignoti nulla cupido*)
in the El Dorado of aeried Art,
for unreasoned reasons;
and your artists, not so lucky as the Buteo,
find themselves without a
skyscape sanctuary
in the
season of seasons:
in contempt of the contemptible,
refuse the herb of grace, the rue
of Job's comforter;
take no

lie-tea in lieu
of Broken Orange Pekoe.
Doctor Nkomo said: *"What* is he who smacks
his lips when dewrot eats away the golden grain
of self-respect exposed like flax
to the rigors of sun and rain?"

Black Boy,
every culture,
every caste,
every people,
every class,
facing the barbarians
with lips hubris-curled,
believes its death rattle omens
the *Dies Irae* of the world.

Black Boy,
summon Boas and Dephino,
Blumenbach and Koelreuter,
from their posts
around the gravestone of Bilbo,
who, with cancer in his mouth,
orated until he quaked the magnolias of the South,
while the pocketbooks of his weeping black serfs
shriveled in the drouth;
summon the ghosts
of scholars with rams' horns from Jericho
and facies in letters from Jerusalem,
so
we may ask them:
"What is a Negro?"

Black Boy,
what's in a people's name that wries the brain
like the neck of a barley bird?
Can sounding brass create
an ecotype with a word?

Black Boy,
beware of the thin-bladed mercy
stroke, for one drop of Negro blood
(V. *The Black Act of the F.F.V.*)

opens the flood-
gates of the rising tide of color
and jettisons
the D. A. R. in the Heraclitean flux
with Uncle Tom and
Crispus Attucks.
The Black Belt White,
painstaking as a bedbug in
a tenant farmer's truckle bed,
rabbit-punched old Darrow
because
he quoted Darwin's sacred laws
(instead of the Lord God Almighty's)
and gabbled that the Catarrhine ape
(the C from a Canada goose nobody knows)
appears,
after X's of years,
in the vestigial shape
of the Nordic's thin lips, his aquiline nose,
his straight hair,
orangutanish on legs and chest and head.
Doctor Nkomo, a votary of touch-and-go,
who can stand the gaff
of Negrophobes and, like Aramis,
parry a thrust with a laugh,
said:

"In spite of the pig in the python's coils,
in spite of Blake's lamb in the jaws of the tiger,
Nature is kind, even in the raw: she toils
. . . aeons and aeons and aeons . . .
gives the African a fleecy canopy
to protect the seven faculties of the brain
from the burning convex lens of the sun;
she foils
whiteness
(without disdain)
to bless the African
(as Herodotus marvels)
with the birthright of a burnt skin for work or fun;
she roils
the Aryan
(as his eye and ear repose)

to give the African an accommodation nose
that cools the drying-up air;
she entangles the epidermis in broils
that keep the African's body free from lice-infested hair.
As man to man,
the Logos is
Nature is on the square
with the African.
If a black man circles the rim
of the Great White World, he will find
(even if Adamness has made him half blind)
the bitter waters of Marah *and*
the fresh fountains of Elim."

Although his transition
was a far cry
from Shakespeare to Sardou,
the old Africanist's byplay gave
no soothing feverfew
to the Dogs in the Zulu Club;
said he:
"A Hardyesque artistry
of circumstance
divides the Whites and Blacks in life,
like the bodies of the dead
eaten by vultures
in a Tower of Silence.
Let, then, the man with a maggot in his head
lean . . . lean . . . lean
on race or caste or class,
for the wingless worms of blowflies shall grub,
dry and clean,
the stinking skeletons of these,
when the face of the macabre weather-
cock turns to the torrid wind of misanthropy;
and later their bones shall be swept together
(like the Parsees')
in the Sepulchre of Anonymity."

A Zulu Wit cleared away his unsunned
mood with dark laughter;
but I sensed the thoughts of Doctor Nkomo

pacing nervously to and fro
like Asscher's, after
he'd cleaved the giant Cullinan Diamond.

Black Boy,
the vineyard is the fittest place
in which to booze (with Omar) and study
soil and time and integrity—
the telltale triad of grape and race.
Palates that can read the italics
of *salt* and *sugar* know
a grapevine
transplanted from Bordeaux
to Pleasant Valley
cannot give grapes that make a Bordeaux wine.
Like the sons of the lone mother of dead empires,
who boasted their ancestors,
page after page—
wines are peacocky
in their vintage and their age,
disdaining the dark ways of those engaging
in the profits
of chemical aging.
When the bluebirds sing
their perennial anthem
a capriccio, in the Spring,
the sap begins to move up the stem
of the vine, and the wine in the bed of the deep
cask stirs in its winter sleep.
Its bouquet
comes with the years, dry or wet;
so the connoisseurs say:
"The history of the wine
is repeated by the vine."

Black Boy,
beware of wine labels,
for the Republic does not guarantee
what the phrase "Château Bottled" means—
the estate, the proprietor, the quality.
This ignominy will baffle you, Black Boy,
because the white man's law

has raked your butt many a time
with fang and claw.
Beware of the waiter who wraps
a napkin around your Clos Saint Thierry,
if Chance takes you into high-hat places
open to all creeds and races
born to be or not to be.
Beware of the pop
of a champagne cork:
like the flatted fifth and octave jump in Bebop,
it is theatrical
in Vicksburg or New York.
Beware of the champagne cork
that does not swell up like your ma when she had you—*that*
comes out flat,
because the bottle of wine
is dead . . . dead
like Uncle Tom and the Jim Crow Sign.
Beware . . . yet
your dreams in the Great White World
shall be unthrottled
by pigmented and unpigmented lionhearts,
for we know *without no*
every people, by and by, produces its "Château Bottled."

White Boy,
as regards the ethnic origin
of Black Boy and me,
the *What* in Socrates' *"Tò tí?"*
is for the musk-ox habitat of anthropologists;
but there is another question,
dangerous as a moutaba tick,
secreted in the house
of every Anglo-Saxon sophist and hick:

Who is a Negro?
(I am a White in deah ole Norfolk.)
Who is a White?
(I am a Negro in little old New York.)
Since my mongrelization is invisible
and my Negroness a state of mind conjured up
by Stereotypus, I am a chameleon

on *that* side of the Mason-Dixon
that a white man's conscience
is not on.
My skin is as white
as a Roman's toga when he sought an office on the sly;
my hair is as blond
as xanthein;
my eyes are as blue
as the hawk's-eye.
At the Olympian powwow of curators,
when I revealed my Negroness,
my peers became shocked like virgins in a house
where satyrs tattooed on female thighs heralds of success.

White Boy,
counterfeit scholars have used
the newest brush-on Satinlac,
to make our ethnic identity
crystal clear for the lowest IQ
in every mansion and in every shack.
Therefore,
according to the myth that Negrophobes bequeath
to the Lost Gray Cause, since Black Boy is the color
of betel-stained teeth,
he and I
(from ocular proof
that cannot goof)
belong to races
whose dust-of-the-earth progenitors
the Lord God Almighty created
of different bloods,
in antipodal places.
However,
even the F. F. V. pate
is aware that laws defining a Negro
blackjack each other with*in* and with*out* a state.
The Great White World, White Boy, leaves you in a sweat
like a pitcher with three runners on the bases;
and, like Kant, you seldom get
your grammar straight—yet,
you are the wick that absorbs the oil in my lamp,
in all kinds of weather;

and we are teeth in the pitch wheel
that work together.

White Boy,
when I hear the word *Negro* defined,
why does it bring to mind
the chef, the gourmand, the belly-god,
the disease of kings, the culinary art
in alien lands, Black Mammy in a Dixie big house,
and the dietitian's chart?
Now, look at Black Boy scratch his head!
It's a stereotypic gesture of Uncle Tom,
a learned Gentleman of Color said
in his monumental tome,
The *Etiquette of the New Negro,*
which,
the publishers say,
by the way,
should be in every black man's home.

The Negro is a dish in the white man's kitchen—
a potpourri,
an ola-podrida,
a mixie-maxie,
a hotchpotch of lineal ingredients;
with UN guests at his table,
the host finds himself a Hamlet on the spot,
for, in spite of his catholic pose,
the Negro dish is a dish nobody knows:
to some . . . tasty,
like an exotic condiment—
to others . . . unsavory
and inelegant.

White Boy,
the Negro dish is a mix
like . . . and *un*like
pimiento brisque, chop suey,
eggs à la Goldenrod, and eggaroni;
tongue-and-corn casserole, mulligan stew,
baked fillets of halibut, and cheese fondue;
macaroni milanaise, egg-milk shake,
mullagatawny soup, and sour-milk cake.

Just as the Chinese lack
an ideogram for "to be,"
our lexicon has no definition
for an ethnic amalgam like Black Boy and me.

Behold a Gordian knot without
the *beau geste* of an Alexander's sword!
Water, O Modern Mariner, water, everywhere,
unfit for *vitro di trina* glass
or the old-oaken-bucket's gourd!

For dark hymens on the auction block,
the lord of the mansion knew the macabre score:
not a dog moved his tongue,
not a lamb lost a drop of blood to protect a door.
O
Xenos of Xanthos,
what midnight-to-dawn lecheries,
in cabin and big house,
produced these brown hybrids and yellow motleys?

White Boy,
Buchenwald is a melismatic song
whose single syllable is sung to blues notes
to dark wayfarers who listen for the gong
at the crack of doom along
. . . that Lonesome Road . . .
before they travel on.

A Pelagian with the *raison d'être* of a Negro,
I cannot say I have outwitted dread,
for I am conscious of the noiseless tread
of the Yazoo tiger's ball-like pads behind me
in the dark
as I trudge ahead,
up and up . . . that Lonesome Road . . . up and up.

In a Vision in a Dream,
from the frigid seaport of the proud Xanthochroid,
the good ship *Défineznegro*
sailed fine, under an unabridged moon,
to reach the archipelago
Nigeridentité.
In the Strait of Octoroon,

off black Scylla,
after the typhoon Phobos, out of the Stereotypus Sea,
had rived her hull and sail to a T,
the *Défineznegro* sank the rock
and disappeared in the abyss
(*Vanitas vanitatum!*)
of white Charybdis.

Robert Hayden (1913-   )

A Ballad of Remembrance

Quadroon mermaids, Afro angels, black saints
balanced upon the switchblades of that air
and sang. Tight streets unfolding to the eye
like fans of corrosion and elegiac lace
crackled with their singing: Shadow of time. Shadow of blood.

Shadow, echoed the Zulu king, dangling
from a cluster of balloons. Blood,
whined the gun-metal priestess, floating
over the courtyard where dead men diced.

What will you have? she inquired, the sallow vendeuse
of prepared tarnishes and jokes of nacre and ormolu,
what but those gleamings, oldrose graces,
manners like scented gloves? Contrived ghosts
rapped to metronome clack of lavalieres.

Contrived illuminations riding a threat
of river, masked Negroes wearing chameleon
satins gaudy now as a fortuneteller's
dream of disaster, lighted the crazy flopping
dance of love and hate among joys, rejections.

Accommodate, muttered the Zulu king,
toad on a throne of glaucous poison jewels.
Love, chimed the saints and the angels and the mermaids.
Hate, shrieked the gun-metal priestess
from her spiked bellcollar curved like a fleur-de-lis:

As well have a talon as a finger, a muzzle as a mouth,
as well have a hollow as a heart. And she pinwheeled
away in coruscations of laughter, scattering
those others before her like foil stars.

But the dance continued—now among metaphorical
doors, coffee cups floating poised
hysterias, decors of illusion; now among
mazurka dolls offering death's-heads
of cocaine roses and real violets.

Then you arrived, meditative, ironic,
richly human; and your presence was shore where I rested
released from the hoodoo of that dance, where I spoke
with my true voice again.

And therefore this is not only a ballad of remembrance
for the down-South arcane city with death
in its jaws like gold teeth and archaic cusswords;
not only a token for the troubled generous friends
held in the fists of that schizoid city like flowers,
but also, Mark Van Doren,
a poem of remembrance, a gift, a souvenir for you.

Tour 5

The road winds down through autumn hills
in blazonry of farewell scarlet
and recessional gold,
past cedar groves, through static villages
whose names are all that's left
of Choctaw, Chickasaw.

We stop a moment in a town
watched over by Confederate sentinels,
buy gas and ask directions of a rawboned man
whose eyes revile us as the enemy.

Shrill gorgon silence breathes behind
his taut civility
and in the ever-tautening air,
dark for us despite its Indian summer glow.
We drive on, following the route
of highwaymen and phantoms,

Of slaves and armies.
Children, wordless and remote,
wave at us from kindling porches.
And now the land is flat for miles,
the landscape lush, metallic, flayed,
its brightness harsh as bloodstained swords.

Middle Passage

I.

Jesús, Estrella, Esperanza, Mercy:

> Sails flashing to the wind like weapons,
> sharks following the moans the fever and the dying;
> horror the corposant and compass rose.

Middle Passage:
        voyage through death
                to life upon these shores.

> "10 April 1800—
> Blacks rebellious. Crew uneasy. Our linguist says
> their moaning is a prayer for death,
> ours and their own. Some try to starve themselves.
> Lost three this morning leaped with crazy laughter
> to the waiting sharks, sang as they went under."

Desire, Adventure, Tartar, Ann:

> Standing to America, bringing home
> black gold, black ivory, black seed.

> *Deep in the festering hold thy father lies,*
> *of his bones New England pews are made,*
> *those are altar lights that were his eyes.*

Jesus Saviour Pilot Me
Over Life's Tempestuous Sea

> We pray that Thou wilt grant, O Lord,
> safe passage to our vessels bringing
> heathen souls unto Thy chastening.

Jesus Saviour

"8 bells. I cannot sleep, for I am sick
with fear, but writing eases fear a little
since still my eyes can see these words take shape
upon the page & so I write, as one
would turn to exorcism. 4 days scudding,
but now the sea is calm again. Misfortune
follows in our wake like sharks (our grinning
tutelary gods). Which one of us
has killed an albatross? A plague among
our blacks—Ophthalmia: blindness—& we
have jettisoned the blind to no avail.
It spreads, the terrifying sickness spreads.
Its claws have scratched sight from the Capt.'s eyes
& there is blindness in the fo'c'sle
& we must sail 3 weeks before we come
to port."

What port awaits us, Davy Jones'
or home? I've heard of slavers drifting, drifting,
playthings of wind and storm and chance, their crews
gone blind, the jungle hatred
crawling up on deck.

Thou Who Walked On Galilee

"Deponent further sayeth *The Bella J*
left the Guinea Coast
with cargo of five hundred blacks and odd
for the barracoons of Florida:

"That there was hardly room 'tween-decks for half
the sweltering cattle stowed spoon-fashion there;
that some went mad of thirst and tore their flesh
and sucked the blood:

"That Crew and Captain lusted with the comeliest
of the savage girls kept naked in the cabins;
that there was one they called The Guinea Rose
and they cast lots and fought to lie with her:

"That when the Bo's'n piped all hands, the flames
spreading from starboard already were beyond

control, the negroes howling and their chains
entangled with the flames:

"That the burning blacks could not be reached,
that the Crew abandoned ship,
leaving their shrieking negresses behind,
that the Captain perished drunken with the wenches:

"Further Deponent sayeth not."

Pilot Oh Pilot Me

II.

Aye, lad, and I have seen those factories,
Gambia, Rio Pongo, Calabar;
have watched the artful mongos baiting traps
of war wherein the victor and the vanquished

Were caught as prizes for our barracoons.
Have seen the nigger kings whose vanity
and greed turned wild black hides of Fellatah,
Mandingo, Ibo, Kru to gold for us.

And there was one—King Anthracite we named him—
fetish face beneath French parasols
of brass and orange velvet, impudent mouth
whose cups were carven skulls of enemies:

He'd honor us with drum and feast and conjo
and palm-oil-glistening wenches deft in love,
and for tin crowns that shone with paste,
red calico and German-silver trinkets

Would have the drums talk war and send
his warriors to burn the sleeping villages
and kill the sick and old and lead the young
in coffles to our factories.

Twenty years a trader, twenty years,
for there was wealth aplenty to be harvested
from those black fields, and I'd be trading still
but for the fevers melting down my bones.

III.

Shuttles in the rocking loom of history,
the dark ships move, the dark ships move,
their bright ironical names
like jests of kindness on a murderer's mouth;
plough through thrashing glister toward
fata morgana's lucent melting shore,
weave toward New World littorals that are
mirage and myth and actual shore.
Voyage through death,
                                    voyage whose chartings are unlove.
A charnel stench, effluvium of living death
spreads outward from the hold,
where the living and the dead, the horribly dying,
lie interlocked, lie foul with blood and excrement.

> *Deep in the festering hold thy father lies,*
> *the corpse of mercy rots with him,*
> *rats eat love's rotten gelid eyes.*

> *But, oh, the living look at you*
> *with human eyes whose suffering accuses you,*
> *whose hatred reaches through the swill of dark*
> *to strike you like a leper's claw.*

> *You cannot stare that hatred down*
> *or chain the fear that stalks the watches*
> *and breathes on you its fetid scorching breath;*
> *cannot kill the deep immortal human wish,*
> *the timeless will.*

"But for the storm that flung up barriers
of wind and wave, *The Amistad*, señores,
would have reached the port of Príncipe in two,
three days at most; but for the storm we should
have been prepared for what befell.
Swift as the puma's leap it came. There was
that interval of moonless calm filled only
with the water's and the rigging's usual sounds,
then sudden movement, blows and snarling cries
and they had fallen on us with machete
and marlinspike. It was as though the very
air, the night itself were striking us.

Exhausted by the rigors of the storm,
we were no match for them. Our men went down
before the murderous Africans. Our loyal
Celestino ran from below with gun
and lantern and I saw, before the cane-
knife's wounding flash, Cinquez,
that surly brute who calls himself a prince,
directing, urging on the ghastly work.
He hacked the poor mulatto down, and then
he turned on me. The decks were slippery
when daylight finally came. It sickens me
to think of what I saw, of how these apes
threw overboard the butchered bodies of
our men, true Christians all, like so much jetsam.
Enough, enough. The rest is quickly told:
Cinquez was forced to spare the two of us
you see to steer the ship to Africa,
and we like phantoms doomed to rove the sea
voyaged east by day and west by night,
deceiving them, hoping for rescue,
prisoners on our own vessel, till
at length we drifted to the shores of this
your land, America, where we were freed
from our unspeakable misery. Now we
demand, good sirs, the extradition of
Cinquez and his accomplices to La
Havana. And it distresses us to know
there are so many here who seem inclined
to justify the mutiny of these blacks.
We find it paradoxical indeed
that you whose wealth, whose tree of liberty
are rooted in the labor of your slaves
should suffer the august John Quincy Adams
to speak with so much passion of the right
of chattel slaves to kill their lawful masters
and with his Roman rhetoric weave a hero's
garland for Cinquez. I tell you that
we are determined to return to Cuba
with our slaves and there see justice done. Cinquez—
or let us say 'the Prince'—Cinquez shall die."

The deep immortal human wish,
the timeless will:

Cinquez its deathless primaveral image,
life that transfigures many lives.

Voyage through death
                    to life upon these shores.

Owen Dodson (1914-   )

Rag Doll and Summer Birds

(For Frank Harriott)

I

We sit in our cabin corners waiting for God
And the stove goes out,
The newspapers on the walls, telling of crimes,
Curl away from the walls.

We wait for the doctor five miles away,
And the child under the rag covers whispers
To the rag doll and dies;
We wait and our bellies roar a declamation,
Tears speak from our eyes,
Scream to our hands held to our eyes.

We sit in our cabin corners
And the Bible is in the wind,
The songs we sing darken in the night,
The oil goes lower,
The lamp grows darker,
This darkness is not a tender darkness
The last moth leaves to fly
To light anotherwhere.
In the blackness the stars are not enough!

We sit in our cabin corners and the cabins blow away.

II

The snow cannot melt too soon for the birds left behind.
The crumbs fall in the crevices of snow

And the birds taste winter in their throats,
Wonder where the warm seasons went.
Their wings do not know the directions
The other flocks are gone, the signs are covered with winter.
There are no signals . . . Directionless . . . Lost . . . Alone . . .

Why are the flowers on the trees so white?
Why are these flowers so cold?

Smoke is in the chimneys where warmth is,
The sky is low and dark and level in the barns,
The intricate cobwebs are thinner than branches:
They are not singing places, not resting places,
Hay has not the smell of their nests,
Their songs turn to ice in the air.

The dark stiff little compact spots you see on these white fields
are not shadows.

Counterpoint

(For Carl Van Vechten)

Terror does not belong to open day

Picnics on the beach, all along
The unmined water children play,
A merry-go-round begins a jingle song,
Horses churn up and down the peppermint poles,
Children reach for the brassy ring,
Children laugh while the platform rolls
Faster and faster while the horses sing:

merry-ro, merry-o,
this is the way your lives should go:
up and down and all around
listening to this merry sound.

Terror does not belong to open day

merry-ro, merry-ha,
snatch this ring and plant a star;

grow a field of magic light,
reap it on a winter night.

Terror does not belong to open day

Margaret Walker (1915-   )

For My People

For my people everywhere singing their slave songs repeatedly: their dirges and
their ditties and their blues and jubilees, praying their prayers nightly to an
unknown god, bending their knees humbly to an unseen power;

For my people lending their strength to the years, to the gone years and the
now years and the maybe years, washing ironing cooking scrubbing sewing
mending hoeing plowing digging planting pruning patching dragging along
never gaining never reaping never knowing and never understanding;

For my playmates in the clay and dust and sand of Alabama backyards playing
baptizing and preaching and doctor and jail and soldier and school and mama
and cooking and playhouse and concert and store and hair and Miss
Choomby and company;

For the cramped bewildered years we went to school to learn to know the reasons
why and the answers to and the people who and the places where and the
days when, in memory of the bitter hours when we discovered we were black
and poor and small and different and nobody cared and nobody wondered
and nobody understood;

For the boys and girls who grew in spite of these things to be man and woman,
to laugh and dance and sing and play and drink their wine and religion and
success, to marry their playmates and bear children and then die of con-
sumption and anemia and lynching;

For my people thronging 47th Street in Chicago and Lenox Avenue in New York
and Rampart Street in New Orleans, lost disinherited dispossessed and happy
people filling the cabarets and taverns and other people's pockets needing
bread and shoes and milk and land and money and something—something all
our own;

For my people walking blindly spreading joy, losing time being lazy, sleeping when hungry, shouting when burdened, drinking when hopeless, tied and shackled and tangled among ourselves by the unseen creatures who tower over us omnisciently and laugh;

For my people blundering and groping and floundering in the dark of churches and schools and clubs and societies, associations and councils and committees and conventions, distressed and disturbed and deceived and devoured by money-hungry glory-craving leeches, preyed on by facile force of state and fad and novelty, by false prophet and holy believer;

For my people standing staring trying to fashion a better way from confusion, from hypocrisy and misunderstanding, trying to fashion a world that will hold all the people, all the faces, all the adams and eves and their countless generations;

Let a new earth rise. Let another world be born. Let a bloody peace be written in the sky. Let a second generation full of courage issue forth; let a people loving freedom come to growth. Let a beauty full of healing and a strength of final clenching be the pulsing in our spirits and our blood. Let the martial songs be written, let the dirges disappear. Let a race of men now rise and take control.

Ann Petry (1911-   )

Like a Winding Sheet

He had planned to get up before Mae did and surprise her by fixing breakfast. Instead he went back to sleep and she got out of bed so quietly he didn't know she wasn't there beside him until he woke up and heard the queer soft gurgle of water running out of the sink in the bathroom.

He knew he ought to get up but instead he put his arms across his forehead to shut the afternoon sunlight out of his eyes, pulled his legs up close to his body, testing them to see if the ache was still in them.

Mae had finished in the bathroom. He could tell because she never closed the door when she was in there and now the sweet smell of talcum powder was drifting down the hall and into the bedroom. Then he heard her coming down the hall.

"Hi, babe," she said affectionately.

"Hum," he grunted, and moved his arms away from his head, opened one eye.

"It's a nice morning."

"Yeah," he rolled over and the sheet twisted around him, outlining his thighs, his chest. "You mean afternoon, don't ya?"

Mae looked at the twisted sheet and giggled. "Looks like a winding sheet," she said. "A shroud—." Laughter tangled with her words and she had to pause for a moment before she could continue. "You look like a huckleberry—in a winding sheet—"

"That's no way to talk. Early in the day like this," he protested.

He looked at his arms silhouetted against the white of the sheets. They were inky black by contrast and he had to smile in spite of himself and he lay there smiling and savouring the sweet sound of Mae's giggling.

"Early?" She pointed a finger at the alarm clock on the table near the bed, and giggled again. "It's almost four o'clock. And if you don't spring up out of there you're going to be late again."

"What do you mean 'again'?"

"Twice last week. Three times the week before. And once the week before and—"

"I can't get used to sleeping in the day time," he said fretfully. He pushed his legs out from under the covers experimentally. Some of the ache had gone out of them but they weren't really rested yet. "It's too light for good sleeping. And all that standing beats the hell out of my legs."

"After two years you oughtta be used to it" Mae said.

He watched her as she fixed her hair, powdered her face, slipping into a pair of blue denim overalls. She moved quickly and yet she didn't seem to hurry.

"You look like you'd had plenty of sleep," he said lazily. He had to get up but he kept putting the moment off, not wanting to move, yet he didn't dare let his legs go completely limp because if he did he'd go back to sleep. It was getting later and later but the thought of putting his weight on his legs kept him lying there.

When he finally got up he had to hurry and he gulped his breakfast so fast that he wondered if his stomach could possibly use food thrown at it at such a rate of speed. He was still wondering about it as he and Mae were putting their coats on in the hall.

Mae paused to look at the calendar. "It's the thirteenth," she said. Then a faint excitement in her voice. "Why it's Friday the thirteenth." She had one arm in her coat sleeve and she held it there while she stared at the calendar. "I oughtta stay home," she said. "I shouldn't go otta the house."

"Aw don't be a fool," he said. "To-day's payday. And payday is a good luck day everywhere, any way you look at it." And as she stood hesitating he said, "Aw, come on."

And he was late for work again because they spent fifteen minutes arguing before he could convince her she ought to go to work just the same. He had to talk persuasively, urging her gently and it took time. But he couldn't bring himself to talk to her roughly or threaten to strike her like a lot of men might have done. He wasn't made that way.

So when he reached the plant he was late and he had to wait to punch the time clock because the day shift workers were streaming out in long lines, in groups and bunches that impeded his progress.

Even now just starting his work-day his legs ached. He had to force himself to struggle past the out-going workers, punch the time clock, and get the little cart he pushed around all night because he kept toying with the idea of going home and getting back in bed.

He pushed the cart out on the concrete floor, thinking that if this was his plant he'd make a lot of changes in it. There were too many standing up jobs for one thing. He'd figure out some way most of 'em could be done sitting down and he'd put a lot more benches around. And this job he had—this job that forced him to walk ten hours a night, pushing this little cart, well, he'd turn it into a sittin-down job. One of those little trucks they used around railroad stations would be good for a job like this. Guys sat on a seat and the thing moved easily, taking up little room and turning in hardly any space at all, like on a dime.

He pushed the cart near the foreman. He never could remember to refer to her as the forelady even in his mind. It was funny to have a woman for a boss in a plant like this one.

She was sore about something. He could tell by the way her face was red and her eyes were half shut until they were slits. Probably been out late and didn't get enough sleep. He avoided looking at her and hurried a little, head down, as he passed her though he couldn't resist stealing a glance at her out of the corner of his eyes. He saw the edge of the light colored slacks she wore and the tip end of a big tan shoe.

"Hey, Johnson!" the woman said.

The machines had started full blast. The whirr and the grinding made the building shake, made it impossible to hear conversations. The men and women at the machines talked to each other but looking at them from just a little distance away they appeared to be simply moving their lips because you couldn't hear what they were saying. Yet the woman's voice cut across the machine sounds —harsh, angry.

He turned his head slowly. "Good Evenin', Mrs. Scott," he said and waited.

"You're late again."

"That's right. My legs were bothering me."

The woman's face grew redder, angrier looking. "Half this shift comes in late," she said. "And you're the worst one of all. You're always late. Whatsa matter with ya?"

"It's my leg," he said. "Somehow they don't ever get rested. I don't seem to get used to sleeping days. And I just can't get started."

"Excuses. You guys always got excuses," her anger grew and spread. "Every guy comes in here late always has an excuse. His wife's sick or his grandmother died or somebody in the family had to go to the hospital," she paused, drew a deep breath. "And the niggers are the worse. I don't care what's wrong with your legs. You get in here on time. I'm sick of you niggers—"

"You got the right to get mad," he interrupted softly. "You got the right to cuss me four ways to Sunday but I ain't letting nobody call me a nigger."

He stepped closer to her. His fists were doubled. His lips were drawn back in a thin narrow line. A vein in his forehead stood out swollen, thick.

And the woman backed away from him, not hurriedly but slowly—two, three steps back.

"Aw, forget it," she said. "I didn't mean nothing by it. It slipped out. It was a accident." The red of her face deepened until the small blood vessels in her cheeks were purple. "Go on and get to work," she urged. And she took three more slow backward steps.

He stood motionless for a moment and then turned away from the red lipstick on her mouth made him remember that the foreman was a woman. And he couldn't bring himself to hit a woman. He felt a curious tingling in his fingers and he looked down at his hands. They were clenched tight, hard, ready to smash some of those small purple veins in her face.

He pushed the cart ahead of him, walking slowly. When he turned his head, she was staring in his direction, mopping her forehead with a dark blue handkerchief. Their eyes met and then they both looked away.

He didn't glance in her direction again but moved past the long work benches, carefully collecting the finished parts, going slowly and steadily up and down, back and forth the length of the building and as he walked he forced himself to swallow his anger, get rid of it.

And he succeeded so that he was able to think about what had happened without getting upset about it. An hour went by but the tension stayed in his hands. They were clenched and knotted on the handles of the cart as though ready to aim a blow.

And he thought he should have hit her anyway, smacked her hard in the face, felt the soft flesh of her face give under the hardness of his hands. He tried to make his hands relax by offering them a description of what it would have been like to strike her because he had the queer feeling that his hands were not exactly a part of him any more—they had developed a separate life of their own over which he had no control. So he dwelt on the pleasure his hands would have felt—both of them cracking at her, first one and then the other. If he had done that his hands would have felt good now—relaxed, rested.

And he decided that even if he'd lost his job for it he should have let her have it and it would have been a long time, maybe the rest of her life before she called anybody else a nigger.

The only trouble was he couldn't hit a woman. A woman couldn't hit back the same way a man did. But it would have been a deeply satisfying thing to have cracked her narrow lips wide open with just one blow, beautifully timed and with all his weight in back of it. That way he would have gotten rid of all the energy and tension his anger had created in him. He kept remembering how his heart had started pumping blood so fast he had felt it tingle even in the tips of his fingers.

With the approach of night fatigue nibbled at him. The corners of his mouth dropped, the frown between his eyes deepened, his shoulders sagged; but his hands stayed tight and tense. As the hours dragged by he noticed that the women workers had started to snap and snarl at each other. He couldn't hear what they said because of the sound of the machines but he could see the quick lip movements that sent words tumbling from the sides of their mouths. They gestured irritably with their hands and scowled as their mouths moved.

Their violent jerky motions told him that it was getting close on to quitting time but somehow he felt that the night still stretched ahead of him, composed of endless hours of steady walking on his aching legs. When the whistle finally blew he went on pushing the cart, unable to believe that it had sounded. The whirring of the machines died away to a murmur and he knew then that he'd really heard the whistle. He stood still for a moment filled with a relief that made him sigh.

Then he moved briskly, putting the cart in the store room, hurrying to take his place in the line forming before the paymaster. That was another thing he'd change, he thought. He'd have the pay envelopes handed to the people right at their benches so there wouldn't be ten or fifteen minutes lost waiting for the pay. He always got home about fifteen minutes late on payday. They did it better in the plant where Mae worked, brought the money right to them at their benches.

He stuck his pay envelope in his pants' pocket and followed the line of workers heading for the subway in a slow moving stream. He glanced up at the sky. It was a nice night, the sky looked packed full to running over with stars. And he thought if he and Mae would go right to bed when they got home from work they'd catch a few hours of darkness for sleeping. But they never did. They fooled around—cooking and eating and listening to the radio and he always stayed in a big chair in the living room and went almost but not quite to sleep and when they finally got to bed it was five or six in the morning and daylight was already seeping around the edges of the sky.

He walked slowly, putting off the moment when he would have to plunge into the crowd hurring toward the subway. It was a long ride to Harlem and to-night the thought of it appalled him. He paused outside an all-night restaurant to kill time, so that some of the first rush of workers would be gone when he reached the subway.

The lights in the restaurant were brilliant, enticing. There was life and motion inside. And as he looked through the window he thought that everything within range of his eyes gleamed—the long imitation marble counter, the tall stools, the white porcelain topped tables and especially the big metal coffee urn right near the window. Steam issued from its top and a gas flame flickered under it—a lively, dancing, blue flame.

A lot of the workers from his shift—men and women—were lining up near the coffee urn. He watched them walk to the porcelain topped tables carrying steaming cups of coffee and he saw that just the smell of the coffee lessened the fatigue lines in their faces. After the first sip their faces softened, they smiled, they began to talk and laugh.

On a sudden impulse he shoved the door open and joined the line in front of the coffee urn. The line moved slowly. And as he stood there the smell of the coffee, the sound of the laughter and of the voices, helped dull the sharp ache in his legs.

He didn't pay any attention to the girl who was serving the coffee at the urn. He kept looking at the cups in the hands of the men who had been ahead of him. Each time a man stopped out of the line with one of the thick white cups the fragrant steam got in his nostrils. He saw that they walked carefully so as not to spill a single drop. There was a froth of bubbles at the top of each cup and he thought about how he would let the bubbles break against his lips before he actually took a big deep swallow.

Then it was his turn. "A cup of coffee," he said, just as he had heard the others say.

The girl looked past him, put her hands up to her head and gently lifted her hair away from the back of her neck, tossing her head back a little. "No more coffee for awhile," she said.

He wasn't certain he'd heard her correctly and he said, "What?" blankly.

"No more coffee for awhile," she repeated.

There was silence behind him and then uneasy movement. He thought some-one would say something, ask why or protest, but there was only silence and then a faint shuffling sound as though the men standing behind him had simultaneously shifted their weight from one foot to the other.

He looked at her without saying anything. He felt his hands begin to tingle and the tingling went all the way down to his finger tips so that he glanced down at them. They were clenched tight, hard, into fists. Then he looked at the girl again. What he wanted to do was hit her so hard that the scarlet lipstick on her mouth would smear and spread over her nose, her chin, out toward her cheeks; so hard that she would never toss her head again and refuse a man a cup of coffee because he was black.

He estimated the distance across the counter and reached forward, balancing his weight on the balls of his feet, ready to let the blow go. And then his hands fell back down to his sides because he forced himself to lower them, to unclench them and make them dangle loose. The effort took his breath away because his hands fought against him. But he couldn't hit her. He couldn't even now bring himself to hit a woman, not even this one, who had refused him a cup of coffee with a toss of her head. He kept seeing the gesture with which she had lifted the length of her blond hair from the back of her neck as expressive of her contempt for him.

When he went out the door he didn't look back. If he had he would have seen the flickering blue flame under the shiny coffee urn being extinguished. The line of men who had stood behind him lingered a moment to watch the people drinking coffee at the tables and then they left just as he had without having had the coffee they wanted so badly. The girl behind the counter poured water in the urn and swabbed it out and as she waited for the water to run out she lifted her hair gently from the back of her neck and tossed her head before she began making a fresh lot of coffee.

But he walked away without a backward look, his head down, his hands in his pockets, raging at himself and whatever it was inside of that had forced him to stand quiet and still when he wanted to strike out.

The subway was crowded and he had to stand. He tried grasping an overhead strap and his hands were too tense to grip it. So he moved near the train door and stood there swaying back and forth with the rocking of the train. The roar of the train beat inside his head, making it ache and throb, and the pain in his legs clawed up into his groin so that he seemed to be bursting with pain and he told himself that it was due to all that anger-born energy that had piled up in him and not been used and so it had spread through him like a poison—from his feet and legs all the way up to his head.

Mae was in the house before he was. He knew she was home before he put the key in the door of the apartment. The radio was going. She had it tuned up loud and she was singing along with it.

"Hello, Babe," she called out as soon as he opened the door.

He tried to say "hello" and it came out half a grunt and half sigh.

"You sure sound cheerful," she said.

She was in the bedroom and he went and leaned against the door jamb. The denim overalls she wore to work were carefully draped over the back of a chair by the bed. She was standing in front of the dresser, tying the sash of a yellow housecoat around her waist and chewing gum vigorously as she admired her reflection in the mirror over the dresser.

"What sa matter?" she said. "You get bawled out by the boss or somep'n?"

"Just tired," he said slowly. "For God's sake do you have to crack that gum like that?"

"You don't have to lissen to me," she said complacently. She patted a curl in place near the side of her head and then lifted her hair away from the back of her neck, ducking her head forward and then back.

He winced away from the gesture. "What you got to be always fooling with your hair for?" he protested.

"Say, what's the matter with you, anyway?" she turned away from the mirror to face him, put her hands on her hips. "You ain't been in the house two minutes and you're picking on me."

He didn't answer her because her eyes were angry and he didn't want to quarrel with her. They'd been married too long and got along too well and so he walked all the way into the room and sat down in the chair by the bed and stretched his legs out in front of him, putting his weight on the heels of his shoes, leaning way back in the chair, not saying anything.

"Lissen," she said sharply. "I've got to wear those overalls again tomorrow. You're going to get them all wrinkled up leaning against them like that."

He didn't move. He was too tired and his legs were throbbing now that he had sat down. Besides the overalls were already wrinkled and dirty, he thought. They couldn't help but be for she'd worn them all week. He leaned further back in the chair.

"Come on, get up," she ordered.

"Oh, what the hell," he said wearily and got up from the chair. "I'd just as soon live in a subway. There'd be just as much place to sit down."

He saw that her sense of humor was struggling with her anger. But her sense of humor won because she giggled.

"Aw, come on and eat," she said. There was a coaxing note in her voice. "You're nothing but a old hungry nigger trying to act tough and—" she paused to giggle and then continued, "You—"

He had always found her giggling pleasant and deliberately said things that might amuse her and then waited, listening for the delicate sound to emerge from her throat. This time he didn't even hear the giggle. He didn't let her finish what she was saying. She was standing close to him and that funny tingling started in his finger tips, went fast up his arms and sent his fist shooting straight for her face.

There was the smacking sound of soft flesh being struck by a hard object and it wasn't until she screamed that he realized he had hit her in the mouth—so hard that the dark red lipstick had blurred and spread over her full lips, reaching up toward the tip of her nose, down toward her chin, out toward her cheeks.

The knowledge that he had struck her seeped through him slowly and he was appalled but he couldn't drag his hands away from her face. He kept striking her and he thought with horror that something inside him was holding him, binding him to this act, wrapping and twisting about him so that he had to continue it. He had lost all control over his hands. And he groped for a phrase, a word, something to describe what this thing was like that was happening to him and he thought it was like being enmeshed in a winding sheet—that was it—like a winding sheet. And even as the thought formed in his mind his hands reached for her face again and yet again.

Richard Wright (1908-1960)

Bright and Morning Star

From Uncle Tom's Children

I

She stood with her black face some six inches from the moist windowpane and wondered when on earth would it ever stop raining. It might keep up like this all week, she thought. She heard rain droning upon the roof and high up in the wet sky her eyes followed the silent rush of a bright shaft of yellow that swung from the airplane beacon in far off Memphis. Momently she could see it cutting through the rainy dark; it would hover a second like a gleaming sword above her head, then vanish. She sighed, troubling, Johnny-Boys been trampin in this slop all day wid no decent shoes on his feet. . . . Through the window she could see the rich black earth sprawling outside in the night. There was more rain than the clay could soak up; pools stood everywhere. She yawned and mumbled: "Rains good n bad. It kin make seeds bus up thu the ground, er it kin bog things down lika watah-soaked coffin." Her hands were folded loosely over her stomach and the hot air of the kitchen traced a filmy vein of sweat on her forehead. From the cook stove came the soft singing of burning wood and now and then a throaty bubble rose from a pot of simmering greens.

"Shucks, Johnny-Boy coulda let somebody else do all tha runnin in the rain. Theres others betta fixed fer it than he is. But, naw! Johnny-Boy ain the one t trust nobody t do nothin. Hes gotta do it *all* hissef. . . ."

She glanced at a pile of damp clothes in a zinc tub. Waal, Ah bettah git t work. She turned, lifted a smoothing iron with a thick pad of cloth, touched a spit-wet finger to it with a quick, jerking motion: *smiiitz!* Yeah; its hot! Stooping, she took a blue work-shirt from the tub and shook it out. With a deft twist of her shoulders she caught the iron in her right hand; the fingers of her left hand took a piece of wax from a tin box and a frying sizzle came as she smeared the bottom. She was thinking of nothing now; her hands followed a life-long ritual of toil. Spreading a sleeve, she ran the hot iron to and fro until the wet cloth became stiff. She was deep in the midst of her work when a song rose up out of the far off days of her childhood and broke through half-parted lips:

> *Hes the Lily of the Valley, the Bright n Mawnin Star*
> *Hes the Fairest of Ten Thousan t ma soul . . .*

A gust of wind dashed rain against the window. Johnny-Boy oughta c mon home n eat his suppah. Aw, Lawd! Itd be fine ef Sug could eat wid us tonight! Itd be like ol times! Mabbe aftah all it wont be long fo he comes back. Tha lettah

Ah got from im last week said *Don give up hope*. . . . Yeah; we gotta live in hope. Then both of her sons, Sug and Johnny-Boy, would be back with her.

With an involuntary nervous gesture, she stopped and stood still, listening. But the only sound was the lulling fall of rain. Shucks, ain no usa me ackin this way, she thought. Ever time they gits ready to hol them meetings Ah gits jumpity. Ah been a lil scared ever since Sug went t jail. She heard the clock ticking and looked. Johnny-Boys a *hour* late! He sho must be havin a time doin all tha trampin, trampin thu the mud. . . . But her fear was a quiet one; it was more like an intense brooding than a fear; it was a sort of hugging of hated facts so closely that she could feel their grain, like letting cold water run over her hand from a faucet on a winter morning.

She ironed again, faster now, as if she felt the more she engaged her body in work the less she would think. But how could she forget Johnny-Boy out there on those wet fields rounding up white and black Communists for a meeting tomorrow? And that was just what Sug had been doing when the sheriff had caught him, beat him, and tried to make him tell who and where his comrades were. Po Sug! They sho musta beat the boy somethin awful! But, thank Gawd, he didnt talk! He ain no weaklin, Sug ain! Hes been lion-hearted all his life long.

That had happened a year ago. And now each time those meetings came around the old terror surged back. While shoving the iron a cluster of toiling days returned; days of washing and ironing to feed Johnny-Boy and Sug so they could do party work; days of carrying a hundred pounds of white folks' clothes upon her head across fields sometimes wet and sometimes dry. But in those days a hundred pounds was nothing to carry carefully balanced upon her head while stepping by instinct over the corn and cotton rows. The only time it had seemed heavy was when she had heard of Sug's arrest. She had been coming home one morning with a bundle upon her head, her hands swinging idly by her sides, walking slowly with her eyes in front of her, when Bob, Johnny-Boy's pal, had called from across the fields and had come and told her that the sheriff had got Sug. That morning the bundle had become heavier than she could ever remember.

And with each passing week now, though she spoke of it to no one, things were becoming heavier. The tubs of water and the smoothing iron and the bundles of clothes were becoming harder to lift, with her back aching so; and her work was taking longer, all because Sug was gone and she didn't know just when Johnny-Boy would be taken too. To ease the ache of anxiety that was swelling her heart, she hummed, then sang softly:

> *He walks wid me, He talks wid me*
> *He tells me Ahm His own.* . . .

Guiltily, she stopped and smiled. Looks like Ah jus cant seem t fergit them ol songs, no mattah how hard Ah tries. . . . She had learned them when she was a little girl living and working on a farm. Every Monday morning from the corn and cotton fields the slow strains had floated from her mother's lips, lonely and haunting; and later, as the years had filled with gall, she had learned their deep meaning. Long hours of scrubbing floors for a few cents a day had taught her who Jesus was, what a great boon it was to cling to Him, to be like Him and suffer without a mumbling word. She had poured the yearning of her life into the songs, feeling buoyed with a faith beyond this world. The figure of the Man nailed in agony to the Cross, His burial in a cold grave, His transfigured Resurrection, His being breath and clay, God and Man—all had focused her feelings upon an imagery which had swept her life into a wondrous vision.

But as she had grown older, a cold white mountain, the white folks and their laws, had swum into her vision and shattered her songs and their spell of peace. To her that white mountain was temptation, something to lure her from her Lord, a part of the world God had made in order that she might endure it and come through all the stronger, just as Christ had risen with greater glory from the tomb. The days crowded with trouble had enhanced her faith and she had grown to love hardship with a bitter pride; she had obeyed the laws of the white folks with a soft smile of secret knowing.

After her mother had been snatched up to heaven in a chariot of fire, the years had brought her a rough workingman and two black babies, Sug and Johnny-Boy, all three of whom she had wrapped in the charm and magic of her vision. Then she was tested by no less than God; her man died, a trial which she bore with the strength shed by the grace of her vision; finally even the memory of her man faded into the vision itself, leaving her with two black boys growing tall, slowly into manhood.

Then one day grief had come to her heart when Johnny-Boy and Sug had walked forth demanding their lives. She had sought to fill their eyes with her vision, but they would have none of it. And she had wept when they began to boast of the strength shed by a new and terrible vision.

But she had loved them, even as she loved them now; bleeding, her heart had followed them. She could have done no less, being an old woman in a strange world. And day by day her sons had ripped from her startled eyes her old vision, and image by image had given her a new one, different, but great and strong enough to fling her into the light of another grace. The wrongs and sufferings of black men had taken the place of Him nailed to the Cross; the meager beginnings of the party had become another Resurrection; and the hate of those who would destroy her new faith had quickened in her a hunger to feel how deeply her new strength went.

"Lawd, Johnny-Boy," she would sometimes say, "Ah jus wan them white folks t try t make me tell *who* is *in* the party n who *ain!* Ah jus wan em t try, Ahll show em somethin they never thought a black woman could have!"

But sometimes like tonight, while lost in the forgetfulness of work, the past and the present would become mixed in her; while toiling under a strange star for a new freedom the old songs would slip from her lips with their beguiling sweetness.

The iron was getting cold. She put more wood into the fire, stood again at the window and watched the yellow blade of light cut through the wet darkness. Johnny-Boy ain here yit . . . Then, before she was aware of it, she was still, listening for sounds. Under the drone of rain she heard the slosh of feet in mud. Tha ain Johnny-Boy. She knew his long, heavy footsteps in a million. She heard feet come on the porch. Some woman. . . . She heard bare knuckles knock three times, then once. Thas some of them comrades! She unbarred the door, cracked it a few inches, and flinched from the cold rush of damp wind.

"Whos tha?"

"Its me!"

"Who?"

"Me, Reva!"

She flung the door open.

"Lawd, chile, c mon in!"

She stepped to one side and a thin, blond-haired white girl ran through the door; as she slid the bolt she heard the girl gasping and shaking her wet clothes. Somethings wrong! Reva wouldna walked a mil t mah house in all this slop fer nothin! That gals stuck onto Johnny-Boy. Ah wondah ef anythin happened t im?

"Git on inter the kitchen, Reva, where its warm."

"Lawd, Ah sho is wet!"

"How yuh reckon yuhd be, in all tha rain?"

"Johnny-Boy ain here *yit?*" asked Reva.

"Naw! N ain no usa yuh worryin bout im. Jus yuh git them shoes off! Yuh wanna ketch yo deatha col?" She stood looking absently. Yeah; its somethin about the party er Johnny-Boy thas gone wrong. Lawd, Ah wondah ef her pa knows how she feels bout Johnny-Boy? "Honey, yuh hadn't oughta come out in sloppy weather like this."

"Ah had t come, An Sue."

She led Reva to the kitchen.

"Git them shoes off n git close t the stove so yuhll git dry!"

"An Sue, Ah got somethin t tell yuh . . ."

The words made her hold her breath. Ah bet its somethin bout Johnny-Boy! "Whut, honey?"

"The sheriff wuz by our house tonight. He come t see pa."

"Yeah?"

"He done got word from somewheres bout tha meetin tomorrow."

"Is it Johnny-Boy, Reva?"

"Aw, naw, An Sue! Ah ain hearda word bout im. Ain yuh seen im tonight?"

"He ain come home t eat yit."

"Where kin he be?"

"Lawd knows, chile."

"Somebodys gotta tell them comrades that meetings off," said Reva. "The sheriffs got men watchin our house. Ah had t slip out t git here widout em followin me."

"Reva?"

"Hunh?"

"Ahma ol woman n Ah wans yuh t tell me the truth."

"Whut, An Sue?"

"Yuh ain tryin t fool me, is yuh?"

"*Fool* yuh?"

"Bout Johnny-Boy?"

"Lawd, naw, An Sue!"

"Ef theres anythin wrong jus tell me, chile. Ah kin stan it."

She stood by the ironing board, her hands as usual folded loosely over her stomach, watching Reva pull off her water-clogged shoes. She was feeling that Johnny-Boy was already lost to her; she was feeling the pain that would come when she knew it for certain; and she was feeling that she would have to be brave and bear it. She was like a person caught in a swift current of water and knew where the water was sweeping her and did not want to go on but had to go on to the end.

"It ain nothin bout Johnny-Boy, An Sue," said Reva. "But we gotta do somethin er we'll all git inter trouble."

"How the sheriff know about tha meetin?"

"Thas whut pa wants t know."

"Somebody done turned Judas."

"Sho looks like it."

"Ah bet it wuz some of them new ones," she said.

"Its hard t tell," said Reva.

"Lissen, Reva, yuh oughta stay here n git dry, but yuh bettah git back n tell yo pa Johnny-Boy ain here n Ah don know when hes gonna show up. *Some*bodys gotta tell them comrades t stay erway from yo pas house."

She stood with her back to the window, looking at Reva's wide, blue eyes. Po critter! Gotta go back thu all tha slop! Though she felt sorry for Reva, not once did she think that it would not have to be done. Being a woman, Reva was not suspect; she would *have* to go. It was just as natural for Reva to go back through the cold rain as it was for her to iron night and day, or for Sug to be in jail. Right now, Johnny-Boy was out there on those dark fields trying to get home. Lawd, don let em git im tonight! In spite of herself her feelings became torn. She loved her son and, loving him, she loved what he was trying to do. Johnny-Boy was happiest when he was working for the party, and her love for him was for his happiness. She frowned, trying hard to fit something together in her feelings: for her to try to stop Johnny-Boy was to admit that all the toil of years meant nothing; and to let them go meant that sometime or other he would be caught, like Sug. In facing it this way she felt a little stunned, as though she had come suddenly upon a blank wall in the dark. But outside in the rain were people, white and black, whom she had known all her life. Those people depended upon Johnny-Boy, loved him and looked to him as a man and leader. Yeah; hes gotta keep on; he cant stop now. . . . She looked at Reva; she was crying and pulling her shoes back on with reluctant fingers.

"Whut yuh carryin on tha way fer, chile?"

"Yuh done los Sug, now yuh sendin Johnny-Boy . . ."

"Ah got t, honey."

She was glad she could say that. Reva believed in black folks and not for anything in the world would she falter before her. In Reva's trust and acceptance of her she had found her first feelings of humanity; Reva's love was her refuge from shame and degradation. If in the early days of her life the white mountain had driven her back from the earth, then in her last days Reva's love was drawing her toward it, like the beacon that swung through the night outside. She heard Reva sobbing.

"Hush, honey!"

"Mah brothers in jail too! Ma cries ever day . . ."

"Ah know, honey."

She helped Reva with her coat; her fingers felt the scant flesh of the girl's shoulders. She don git ernuff t eat, she thought. She slipped her arms around Reva's waist and held her close for a moment.

"Now, yuh stop that cryin."

"A-a-ah c-c-cant hep it. . . ."

"Everythingll be awright; Johnny-Boyll be back."

"Yuh think so?"

"Sho, chile. Cos he will."

Neither of them spoke again until they stood in the doorway. Outside they could hear water washing through the ruts of the street.

"Be sho n send Johnny-Boy t tell the folks t stay erway from pas house," said Reva.

"Ahll tell im. Don yuh worry."

"Good-bye!"

"Good-bye!"

Leaning against the door jamb, she shook her head slowly and watched Reva vanish through the falling rain.

II

She was back at her board, ironing, when she heard feet sucking in the mud of the back yard; feet she knew from long years of listening were Johnny-Boy's. But tonight, with all the rain and fear, his coming was like a leaving, was almost more than she could bear. Tears welled to her eyes and she blinked them away. She felt that he was coming so that she could give him up; to see him now was to say good-bye. But it was a good-bye she knew she could never say; they were not that way toward each other. All day long they could sit in the same room and not speak; she was his mother and he was her son. Most of the time a nod or a grunt would carry all the meaning that she wanted to convey to him, or he to her. She did not even turn her head when she heard him come stomping into the kitchen. She heard him pull up a chair, sit, sigh, and draw off his muddy shoes; they fell to the floor with heavy thuds. Soon the kitchen was full of the scent of his drying socks and his burning pipe. Tha boys hongry! She paused and looked at him over her shoulder; he was puffing at his pipe with his head tilted back and his feet propped on the edge of the stove; his eyelids drooped and his wet clothes steamed from the heat of the fire. Lawd, tha boy gits mo like his pa every day he lives, she mused, her lips breaking in a slow, faint smile. Hols tha pipe in his mouth just like his pa usta hol his. Wondah how they woulda got erlong ef his pa hada lived? They oughta liked each other, they so mucha like. She wished there could have been other children-besides Sug, so Johnny-Boy would not have to be so much alone. A man needs a woman by his side. . . . She thought of Reva; she liked Reva; the brightest glow her heart had ever known was when she had learned that Reva loved Johnny-Boy. But beyond Reva were cold white faces. Ef theys caught it means *death*. . . . She jerked around when she heard Johnny-Boy's pipe clatter to the floor. She saw him pick it up, smile sheepishly at her, and wag his head.

"Gawd, Ahm sleepy," he mumbled.

She got a pillow from her room and gave it to him.

"Here," she said.

"Hunh," he said, putting the pillow between his head and the back of the chair.

They were silent again. Yes, she would have to tell him to go back out into the cold rain and slop; maybe to get caught; maybe for the last time; she didn't know. But she would let him eat and get dry before telling him that the sheriff knew of the meeting to be held at Lem's tomorrow. And she would make him take a big dose of soda before he went out; soda always helped to stave off a cold. She looked at the clock. It was eleven. Theres time yit. Spreading a news-paper on the apron of the stove, she placed a heaping plate of greens upon it, a knife, a fork, a cup of coffee, a slab of cornbread, and a dish of peach cobbler.

"Yo suppahs ready," she said.

"Yeah," he said.

He did not move. She ironed again. Presently, she heard him eating. When she could no longer hear his knife tinkling against the edge of the plate, she knew he was through. It was almost twelve now. She would let him rest a little while longer before she told him. Till one er'clock, mabbe. Hes so tired. . . . She finished her ironing, put away the board, and stacked the clothes in her dresser drawer. She poured herself a cup of black coffee, drew up a chair, sat down and drank.

"Yuh almos dry," she said, not looking around.

"Yeah," he said, turning sharply to her.

The tone of voice in which she had spoken had let him know that more was coming. She drained her cup and waited a moment longer.

"Reva wuz here."

"Yeah?"

"She lef bout a hour ergo."

"Whut she say?"

"She said ol man Lem hada visit from the sheriff today."

"Bout the meetin?"

She saw him stare at the coals glowing red through the crevices of the stove and run his fingers nervously through his hair. She knew he was wondering how the sheriff had found out. In the silence he would ask a wordless question and in the silence she would answer wordlessly. Johnny-Boys too trustin, she thought. Hes trying t make the party big n hes takin in folks fastern he kin git t know em. You cant trust ever white man yuh meet. . . .

"Yuh know, Johnny-Boy, yuh been takin in a lotta them white folks lately . . ."

"Aw, ma!"

"But, Johnny-Boy . . ."

"Please, dont talk t me bout tha now, ma."

"Yuh ain t ol t lissen n learn, son," she said.

"Ah know whut yuh gonna say, ma. N yuh wrong. Yuh cant judge folks just by how yuh feel bout em n by how long yuh done knowed em. Ef we start that we wouldn't have *nobody* in the party. When folks pledge they word t be with us, then we gotta take em in. Wes too weak t be choosy."

He rose abruptly, rammed his hands into his pockets, and stood facing the window; she looked at his back in a long silence. She knew his faith; it was deep. He had always said that black men could not fight the rich bosses alone; a man could not fight with every hand against him. But he believes so hard hes blind, she thought. At odd times they had had these arguments before; always she would be pitting her feelings against the hard necessity of his thinking, and always she would lose. She shook her head. Po Johnny-Boy; he don know . . .

"But ain nona our folks tol, Johnny-Boy," she said.

"How yuh know?" he asked. His voice came low and with a tinge of anger. He still faced the window and now and then the yellow blade of light flicked across the sharp outline of his black face.

"Cause Ah know em," she said.

"*Any*body mighta tol," he said.

"It wuznt nona *our* folks," she said again.

She saw his hand sweep in a swift arc of disgust.

"*Our* folks! Ma, who in Gawds name is *our* folks?"

"The folks we wuz born n raised wid, son. The folks we *know!*"

"We cant make the party grow tha way, ma."

"It mighta been Booker," she said.

"Yuh don know."

". . . er Blattberg . . ."

"Fer Chrissakes!"

". . . er any of the fo-five others whut joined las week."

"Ma, yuh jus don wan me t go out tonight," he said.

"Yo ol ma wans yuh t be careful, son."

"Ma, when yuh start doubtin folks in the party, then there ain no end."

"Son, Ah knows ever black man n woman in this parta the county," she said, standing too. "Ah watched em grow up; Ah even heped birth n nurse some of em; Ah knows em *all* from way back. There ain none of em that *coulda* tol! The folks Ah know just don open they dos n ast death t walk in! Son, it wuz some of them *white* folks! Yuh just mark mah word n wait n see!"

"Why is it gotta be *white* folks?" he asked. "Ef they tol, then theys jus Judases, thas all."

"Son, look at whuts befo yuh."

He shook his head and sighed.

"Ma, Ah done tol yuh a hundred times. An cant see white n Ah cant see black," he said. "Ah sees rich men n Ah sees po men."

She picked up his dirty dishes and piled them in a pan. Out of the corners of her eyes she saw him sit and pull on his wet shoes. Hes goin! When she put the last dish away he was standing fully dressed, warming his hands over the stove. Just a few mo minutes now n hell be gone, like Sug, mabbe. Her throat tightened. This black mans fight takes *ever*thin! Looks like Gawd put us in this world just t beat us down!

"Keep this, ma," he said.

She saw a crumpled wad of money in his outstretched fingers.

"Naw, yuh keep it. Yuh might need it."

"It ain mine, ma. It berlongs t the party."

"But, Johnny-Boy, yuh might hafta go erway!"

"Ah kin make out."

"Don fergit yosef too much, son."

"Ef Ah don come back theyll need it."

He was looking at her face and she was looking at the money.

"Yuh keep tha," she said slowly. "Ahll give em the money."

"From where?"

"Ah got some."

"Where yuh git it from?"

She sighed.

"Ah been savin a dollah a week fer Sug ever since hes been in jail."

"Lawd, ma!"

She saw the look of puzzled love and wonder in his eyes. Clumsily, he put the money back into his pocket.

"Ahm gone," he said.

"Here; drink this glass of soda watah."

She watched him drink, then put the glass away.

"Waal," he said.

"Take the stuff outta yo pockets!"

She lifted the lid of the stove and he dumped all the papers from his pocket into the fire. She followed him to the door and made him turn round.

"Lawd, yuh tryin to maka revolution n yuh cant even keep yo coat buttoned." Her nimble fingers fastened his collar high around his throat. "There!"

He pulled the brim of his hat low over his eyes. She opened the door and with the suddenness of the cold gust of wind that struck her face, he was gone. She watched the black fields and the rain take him, her eyes burning. When the last faint footstep could no longer be heard, she closed the door, went to her bed, lay down, and pulled the cover over her while fully dressed. Her feelings coursed with the rhythm of the rain: Hes gone! Lawd, Ah *knows* hes gone! Her blood felt cold.

III

She was floating in a grey void somewhere between sleeping and dreaming and then suddenly she was wide awake, hearing and feeling in the same instant the thunder of the door crashing in and a cold wind filling the room. It was pitch black and she stared, resting on her elbows, her mouth open, not breathing, her ears full of the sound of tramping feet and booming voices. She knew at once: They lookin fer im! Then, filled with her will, she was on her feet, rigid, waiting, listening.

"The lamps burnin!"

"Yuh see her?"

"Naw!"

"Look in the kitchen!"

"Gee, this place smells like niggers!"

"Say, somebodys here er been here!"

"Yeah; theres fire in the stove!"

"Mabbe hes been here n gone?"

"Boy, look at these jars of jam!"

"Niggers make good jam!"

"Git some bread!"

"Heres some cornbread!"

"Say, lemme git some!"

"Take it easy! Theres plenty here!"

"Ahma take some of this stuff home!"

"Look, heres a pota greens!"

"N some hot cawffee!"

"Say, yuh guys! C mon! Cut it out! We didn't come here fer a feas!"

She walked slowly down the hall. They lookin fer im, but they ain got im yit! She stopped in the doorway, her gnarled, black hands as always folded over her stomach, but tight now, so tightly the veins bulged. The kitchen was crowded with white men in glistening raincoats. Though the lamp burned, their flashlights still glowed in red fists. Across her floor she saw the muddy tracks of their boots.

"Yuh white folks git outta mah house!"

There was a quick silence; every face turned toward her. She saw a sudden movement, but did not know what it meant until something hot and wet slammed her squarely in the face. She gasped, but did not move. Calmly, she wiped the warm, greasy liquor of greens from her eyes with her left hand. One of the white men had thrown a handful of greens out of the pot at her.

"How they taste, ol bitch?"

"Ah ast yuh t git outta mah house!"

She saw the sheriff detach himself from the crowd and walk toward her.

"Now, Anty . . ."

"White man, don yuh *Anty* me!"

"Yuh ain got the right sperit!"

"Sperit hell! Yuh git these men outta mah house!"

"Yuh ack like yuh don like it!"

"Naw, Ah don like it, n yuh knows dam waal Ah don!"

"What yuh gonna do about it?"

"Ahm telling yuh t git outta mah house!"

"Gittin sassy?"

"Ef telling yuh t git outta mah house is sass, then Ahm sassy!"

Her words came in a tense whisper; but beyond, back of them, she was watching, thinking, judging the men.

"Listen, Anty," the sheriff's voice came soft and low. "Ahm here t hep yuh. How come yuh wanna ack this way?"

"Yuh ain never heped yo *own* sef since yuh been born," she flared. "How kin the likes of yuh hep me?"

One of the white men came forward and stood directly in front of her.

"Lissen, nigger woman, yuh talkin t *white* men!"

"Ah don care who Ahm talkin t!"

"Yuhll wish some day yuh did!"

"Not t the likes of yuh!"

"Yuh need somebody t teach yuh how t be a good nigger!"

"*Yuh* cant teach it t me!"

"Yuh gonna change yo tune."

"Not longs mah bloods warm!"

"Don git smart now!"

"Yuh git outta mah house!"

"Spose we don go?" the sheriff asked.

They were crowded around her. She had not moved since she had taken her place in the doorway. She was thinking only of Johnny-Boy as she stood there giving and taking words; and she knew that they, too, were thinking of Johnny-Boy. She knew they wanted him, and her heart was daring them to take him from her.

"Spose we don go?" the sheriff asked again.

"Twenty of yuh runnin over one ol woman! Now, ain yuh white men glad yuh so brave?"

The sheriff grabbed her arm.

"C mon, now! Yuh don did ernuff sass fer one night. Wheres tha nigger son of yos?"

"Don yuh wished yuh knowed?"

"Yuh wanna git slapped?"

"Ah ain never seen one of yo kind that wuznt too low fer . . ."

The sheriff slapped her straight across her face with his open palm. She fell back against a wall and sank to her knees.

"Is tha whut white men do t nigger women?"

She rose slowly and stood again, not even touching the place that ached from his blow, her hands folded over her stomach.

"Ah ain never seen one of yo kind tha wuznt too low fer . . ."

He slapped her again; she reeled backward several feet and fell on her side.

"Is tha whut we too low t do?"

She stood before him again, dry-eyed, as though she had not been struck. Her lips were numb and her chin was wet with blood.

"Aw, let her go! Its the nigger we wan!" said one.

"Wheres that nigger son of yos?" the sheriff asked.

"Find im," she said.

"By Gawd, ef we hafta find im well kill im!"

"He wont be the only nigger yuh ever killed," she said.

She was consumed with a bitter pride. There was nothing on this earth, she felt then, that they could not do to her but that she could take. She stood on a narrow plot of ground from which she would die before she was pushed. And then it was, while standing there feeling warm blood seeping down her throat, that she gave up Johnny-Boy, gave him up to the white folks. She gave him up because they had come tramping into her heart demanding him, thinking they could get him by beating her, thinking they could scare her into making her tell where he was. She gave him up because she wanted them to know that they could not get what they wanted by bluffing and killing.

"Wheres this meetin gonna be?" the sheriff asked.

"Don yuh wish yuh knowed?"

"Ain there gonna be a meetin?"

"How come yuh astin me?"

"There *is* gonna be a meetin," said the sheriff.

"Is it?"

"Ah gotta great mind t choke it outta yuh!"

"Yuh so smart," she said.

"We ain playing wid yuh!"

"Did Ah say yuh wuz?"

"Tha nigger son of yos is erroun here somewheres n Ah aim to find im," said the sheriff. "Ef yuh tell us where he is n ef he talks, mabbe hell git off easy. But ef we hafta find im, well kill im! Ef we hafta find im, then yuh git a sheet t put over im in the mawnin, see? Git yuh a sheet, cause hes gonna be dead!"

"He wont be the only nigger yuh ever killed," she said again.

The sheriff walked past her. The other followed. Yuh didnt git whut yuh wanted! she thought exultingly. N yuh ain gonna *never* git it! Hotly, something arched in her to make them feel the intensity of her pride and freedom; her heart groped to turn the bitter hours of her life into words of a kind that would make them feel that she had taken all they had done to her in stride and could still take more. Her faith surged so strongly in her she was all but blinded. She walked behind them to the door, knotting and twisting her fingers. She saw them step to the muddy ground. Each whirl of the yellow beacon revealed glimpses of slanting rain. Her lips moved, then she shouted:

"Yuh didnt git whut yuh wanted! N yuh ain gonna nevah git it!"

The sheriff stopped and turned; his voice came low and hard.

"Now, by Gawd, thas ernuff outta yuh!"

"Ah know when Ah done said ernuff!"

"Aw, naw, yuh don!" he said. "Yuh don know when yuh done said ernuff, but Ahma teach yuh ternight!"

He was up the steps and across the porch with one bound. She backed into the hall, her eyes full on his face.

"Tell me when yuh gonna stop talkin!" he said, swinging his fist.

The blow caught her high on the cheek; her eyes went blank; she fell flat on her face. She felt the hard heel of his wet shoes coming into her temple and stomach.

"Lemme hear yuh talk some mo!"

She wanted to, but could not; pain numbed and choked her. She lay still and somewhere out of the grey void of unconsciousness she heard someone say: *Aw fer chrissakes leave her erlone, its the nigger we wan. . . .*

IV

She never knew how long she had lain huddled in the dark hallway. Her first returning feeling was of a nameless fear crowding the inside of her, then a deep pain spreading from her temple downward over her body. Her ears were filled with the drone of rain and she shuddered from the cold wind blowing through the door. She opened her eyes and at first saw nothing. As if she were imagining it, she knew she was half lying and half sitting in a corner against a wall. With difficulty she twisted her neck and what she saw made her hold her breath—a vast white blur was suspended directly above her. For a moment she could not tell if her fear was from the blur or if the blur was from her fear. Gradually the blur resolved itself into a huge white face that slowly filled her vision. She was stone still, conscious really of the effort to breathe, feeling somehow that she existed only by the mercy of that white face. She had seen it before; its fear had gripped her many times; it had for her the fear of all the white faces she had ever seen in her life. *Sue* . . . As from a great distance, she heard her name being called. She was regaining consciousness now, but the fear was coming with her. She looked into the face of a white man, wanting to scream out for him to go; yet accepting his presence because she felt she had to. Though some remote part of her mind was active, her limbs were powerless. It was as if an invisible knife had split her in two, leaving one half of her lying there helpless, while the other half shrank in dread from a forgotten but familiar enemy. *Sue its me Sue its me* . . . Then all at once the voice came clearly.

"Sue, its me! Its Booker!"

And she heard an answering voice speaking inside of her. Yeah, its Booker . . . The one whut just joined . . . She roused herself, struggling for full consciousness; and as she did so she transferred to the person of Booker the nameless fear she felt. It seemed that Booker towered above her as a challenge to her right to exist upon the earth.

"Yuh awright?"

She did not answer; she started violently to her feet and fell.

"Sue, yuh hurt!"

"Yeah," she breathed.

"Where they hit yuh?"

"Its mah head," she whispered.

She was speaking even though she did not want to; the fear that had hold of her compelled her.

"They beat yuh?"

"Yeah."

"Them bastards! Them Gawddam bastards!"

She heard him saying it over and over; then she felt herself being lifted.

"Naw!" she gasped.

"Ahma take yuh t the kitchen!"

"Put me down!"

"But yuh cant stay here like this!"

She shrank in his arms and pushed her hands against his body; when she was in the kitchen she freed herself, sank into a chair, and held tightly to its back. She looked wonderingly at Booker. There was nothing about him that should frighten her so, but even that did not ease her tension. She saw him go to the water bucket, wet his handkerchief, wring it, and offer it to her. Distrustfully, she stared at the damp cloth.

"Here; put this on yo fohead . . ."

"Naw!"

"C mon; itll make yuh feel bettah!"

She hesitated in confusion. What right had she to be afraid when someone was acting as kindly as this toward her? Reluctantly, she leaned forward and pressed the damp cloth to her head. It helped. With each passing minute she was catching hold of herself, yet wondering why she felt as she did.

"Whut happened?"

"Ah don know."

"Yuh feel bettah?"

"Yeah."

"Who all wuz here?"

"Ah don know," she said again.

"Yo head still hurt?"

"Yeah."

"Gee, Ahm sorry."

"Ahm awright," she sighed and buried her face in her hands.

She felt him touch her shoulder.

"Sue, Ah got some bad news fer yuh . . ."

She knew; she stiffened and grew cold. It had hapepned; she stared dry-eyed, with compressed lips.

"Its mah Johnny-Boy," she said.

"Yeah; Ahm awful sorry t hafta tell yuh this way. But Ah thought yuh oughta know . . ."

Her tension eased and a vacant place opened up inside of her. A voice whispered, Jesus, hep me!

"W-w-where is he?"

"They got im out t Foleys Woods tryin t make him tell who the others is."

"He ain gonna tell," she said. "They jus as waal kill im, cause he ain gonna nevah tell."

"Ah hope he don," said Booker. "But he didnt have a chance t tell the others. They grabbed im jus as he got t the woods."

Then all the horror of it flashed upon her; she saw flung out over the rainy countryside an array of shacks where white and black comrades were sleeping; in the morning they would be rising and going to Lem's; then they would be caught. And that meant terror, prison, and death. The comrades would have to be told; she would have to tell them; she could not entrust Johnny-Boy's work to another, and especially not to Booker as long as she felt toward him as she did. Gripping the bottom of the chair with both hands, she tried to rise; the room blurred and she swayed. She found herself resting in Booker's arms.

"Lemme go!"

"Sue, yuh too weak t walk!"

"Ah gotta tell em!" she said.

"Set down, Sue! Yuh hurt! Yuh sick!"

When seated, she looked at him helplessly.

"Sue, lissen! Johnny-Boys caught. Ahm here. Yuh tell me who they is n Ahll tell em."

She stared at the floor and did not answer. Yes; she was too weak to go. There was no way for her to tramp all those miles through the rain tonight. But should she tell Booker? If only she had somebody like Reva to talk to! She did not want to decide alone; she must make no mistake about this. She felt Booker's fingers pressing on her arm and it was as though the white mountain was pushing her to the edge of a sheer height: she again exclaimed inwardly. Jesus, hep me! Booker's white face was at her side, waiting. Would she be doing right to tell him? Suppose she did not tell and then the comrades were caught? She could not ever forgive herself for doing a thing like that. But maybe she was wrong; maybe her fear was what Johnny-Boy had always called "jus foolishness." She remembered his saying, Ma, we cant make the party grow ef we start doubtin everbody. . . .

"Tell me who they is, Sue, n Ahll tell em. Ah just joined n Ah don know who they is."

"Ah don know who they is," she said.

"Yuh *gotta* tell me who they is, Sue!"

"Ah tol yuh Ah don know!"

"Yuh *do* know! C mon! Set up n talk!"

"Naw!"

"Yuh wan em all t git *killed?*"

She shook her head and swallowed. Lawd, Ah don believe in this man!

"Lissen, Ahll call the names n yuh tell me which ones is in the party n which ones ain, see?"

"Naw!"

"Please, Sue!"

"Ah don know," she said.

"Sue, yuh ain doin right by em. Johnny-Boy wouldnt wan yuh t be this way. Hes out there holdin up his end. Les hol up ours . . ."

"Lawd, Ah don know . . ."

"Is yuh scared a me cause Ahm *white?* Johnny-Boy ain like tha. Don let all the work we done go fer nothin."

She gave up and bowed her head in her hands.

"Is it Johnson? Tell me, Sue?"

"Yeah," she whispered in horror; a mounting horror of feeling herself being undone.

"Is it Green?"

"Yeah."

"Murphy?"

"Lawd, Ah don know!"

"Yuh gotta tell me, Sue!"

"Mistah Booker, please leave me erlone . . ."

"Is it Murphy?"

She answered yes to the names of Johnny-Boy's comrades; she answered until he asked her no more. Then she thought, How he know the sheriffs men is watchin Lems house? She stood up and held onto her chair, feeling something sure and firm within her.

"How yuh know bout Lem?"

"Why . . . How Ah know?"

"Whut yuh doin here this tima night? How yuh know the sheriff got Johnny-Boy?"

"Sue, don yuh believe in me?"

She did not, but she could not answer. She stared at him until her lips hung open; she was searching deep within herself for certainty.

"You meet Reva?" she asked.

"Reva?"

"Yeah; Lems gal?"

"Oh, yeah. Sho, Ah met Reva."

"She tell yuh?"

She asked the question more of herself than of him; she longed to believe.

"Yeah," he said softly. "Ah reckon Ah oughta be goin t tell em now."

"Who?" she asked. "Tell *who?*"

The muscles of her body were stiff as she waited for his answer; she felt as though life depended upon it.

"The comrades," he said.

"Yeah," she sighed.

She did not know when he left; she was not looking or listening. She just suddenly saw the room empty and from her the thing that had made her fearful was gone.

V

For a space of time that seemed to her as long as she had been upon the earth, she sat huddled over the cold stove. One minute she would say to herself, They both gone now; Johnny-Boy n Sug . . . Mabbe Ahll never see em ergin. Then a surge of guilt would blot out her longing. "Lawd, Ah shouldna tol!" she mumbled. "But no man kin be so lowdown as to do a thing like that . . ." Several times she had an impulse to try to tell the comrades herself; she was feeling a little better now. But what good would that do? She had told Booker the names. He jus couldnt be a Judas to po folks like us . . . He *couldnt!*

"An Sue!"

Thas Reva! Her heart leaped with an anxious gladness. She rose without answering and limped down the dark hallway. Through the open door, against the background of rain, she saw Reva's face lit now and then to whiteness by the whirling beams of the beacon. She was about to call, but a thought checked her. Jesus, hep me! Ah gotta tell her bout Johnny-Boy . . . Lawd, Ah cant!

"An Sue, yuh there?"

"C mon in, chile!"

She caught Reva and held her close for a moment without speaking.

"Lawd, Ahm sho glad yuh here," she said at last.

"Ah thought somethin had happened t yuh," said Reva, pulling away. "Ah saw the do open . . . Pa told me to come back n stay wid yuh tonight . . ." Reva paused and started, "W-w-whuts the mattah?"

She was so full of having Reva with her that she did not understand what the question meant.

"Hunh?"

"Yo neck . . ."

"Aw, it ain nothin, chile. C mon in the kitchen."

"But theres blood on yo neck!"

"The sheriff wuz here . . ."

"Them fools! Whut they wanna bother yuh fer? Ah could kill em! So hep me Gawd, Ah could!"

"It ain nothin," she said.

She was wondering how to tell Reva about Johnny-Boy and Booker. Ahll wait a lil while longer, she thought. Now that Reva was here, her fear did not seem as awful as before.

"C mon, lemme fix yo head, An Sue. Yuh hurt."

They went to the kitchen. She sat silent while Reva dressed her scalp. She was feeling better now; in just a little while she would tell Reva. She felt the girl's finger pressing gently upon her head.

"Tha hurt?"

"A lil, chile."

"Yuh po thing."

"It ain nothin."

"Did Johnny-Boy come?"

She hesitated.

"Yeah."

"He done gone t tell the others?"

Reva's voice sounded so clear and confident that it mocked her. Lawd, Ah cant tell this chile . . .

"Yuh tol im, didnt yuh, An Sue?"

"Y-y-yeah . . ."

"Gee! Thas good! Ah tol pa he didnt hafta worry ef Johnny-Boy got the news. Mabbe thingsll come out awright."

"Ah hope . . ."

She could not go on; she had gone as far as she could. For the first time that night she began to cry.

"Hush, An Sue! Yuh awways been brave. Itll be awright!"

"Ain nothin awright, chile. The worls jus too much fer us, Ah reckon."

"Ef yuh cry that way itll make me cry."

She forced herself to stop. Naw; Ah cant carry on this way in fronta Reva . . . Right now she had a deep need for Reva to believe in her. She watched the girl get pine-knots from behind the stove, rekindle the fire, and put on the coffee pot.

"Yuh wan some cawffee?" Reva asked.

"Naw, honey."

"Aw, c mon, An Sue."

"Jusa lil, honey."

"Thas the way to be. Oh, say, Ah fergot," said Reva, measuring out spoonsful of coffee. "Pa tol me t tell yuh t watch out fer tha Booker man. Hes a stool."

She showed not one sign of outward movement or expression, but as the words fell from Reva's lips she went limp inside.

"Pa tol me soon as Ah got back home. He got word from town . . ."

She stopped listening. She felt as though she had been slapped to the extreme outer edge of life, into a cold darkness. She knew now what she had felt when she had looked up out of her fog of pain and had seen Booker. It was the image of all the white folks, and the fear that went with them, that she had seen and felt during her lifetime. And again, for the second time that night, something she had felt had come true. All she could say to herself was, Ah didnt like im! Gawd knows, Ah didnt! Ah tol Johnny-Boy it wuz some of them white folks . . .

"Here; drink yo cawffee . . ."

She took the cup; her fingers trembled, and the steaming liquid spilt onto her dress and leg.

"Ahm sorry, An Sue!"

Her leg was scalded, but the pain did not bother her.

"Its awright," she said.

"Wait; lemme put some lard on tha burn!"

"It don hurt."

"Yuh worried bout somethin."

"Naw, honey."

"Lemme fix yuh so mo cawffee."

"Ah don wan nothin now, Reva."

"Waal, buck up. Don be tha way . . ."

They were silent. She heard Reva drinking. No; she would not tell Reva; Reva was all she had left. But she had to do something, some way, somehow. She was undone too much as it was; and to tell Reva about Booker or Johnny-Boy was more than she was equal to; it would be too coldly shameful. She wanted to be alone and fight this thing out with herself.

"Go t bed, honey. Yuh tired."

"Naw; Ahm awright, An Sue."

She heard the bottom of Reva's empty cup clank against the top of the stove. Ah *got* t make her go t bed! Yes; Booker would tell the names of the comrades to the sheriff. If she could only stop him some way! That was the answer, the point, the star that grew bright in the morning of new hope. Soon, maybe half an hour from now, Booker would reach Foleys Woods. Hes boun t go the long way, cause he don know no short cut, she thought. Ah could wade the creek n beat im there. . . . But what would she do after that?

"Reva, honey, go t bed. Ahm awright. Yuh need res."

"Ah ain sleepy, An Sue."

"Ah knows whuts bes fer yuh, chile. Yuh tired n wet."

"Ah wanna stay up wid yuh."

She forced a smile and said:

"Ah don think they gonna hurt Johnny-Boy . . ."

"Fer *real*, An Sue?"

"Sho, honey."

"But Ah wanna wait up wid yuh."

"Thas mah job, honey. Thas whut a mas fer, t wait up fer her chullun."

"Good night, An Sue."

"Good night, honey."

She watched Reva pull up and leave the kitchen; presently she heard the shucks in the mattress whispering, and she knew that Reva had gone to bed. She was alone. Through the cracks of the stove she saw the fire dying to grey ashes; the room was growing cold again. The yellow beacon continued to flit past the window and the rain still drummed. Yes; she was alone; she had done this awful thing alone; she must find some way out, alone. Like touching a festering sore, she put her finger upon that moment when she had shouted her defiance to the sheriff, when she had shouted to feel her strength. She had lost Sug to save others; she had let Johnny-Boy go to save others; and then in a moment of weakness that came from too much strength she had lost all. If she had not shouted to the sheriff, she would have been strong enough to have resisted Booker; she would have been able to tell the comrades herself. Something tightened in her as she remembered and understood the fit of fear she had felt on coming to herself in the dark hallway. A part of her life she thought she had done away with forever had had hold of her then. She had thought the soft, warm past was over; she had thought that it did not mean much when now she sang: *"Hes the Lily of the Valley, the Bright n Mawnin Star"* . . . The days when she had sung that song were the days when she had not hoped for anything on this earth, the days when the cold mountain had driven her into the arms of Jesus. She had thought that Sug and Johnny-Boy had taught her to forget Him, to fix her hope upon the fight of black men for freedom. Through the gradual years she had believed and worked with them, had felt strength shed from the grace of their terrible vision. That grace had been upon her when she had let the sheriff slap her down; it had been upon her when she had risen time and again from the floor and faced him. But she had trapped herself with her own hunger; to water the long, dry thirst of her faith; her pride had made a bargain which her flesh could not keep. Her having told the names of Johnny-Boy's comrades was but an incident in a deeper horror. She stood up and looked at the floor while call and counter-call, loyalty and counter-loyalty struggled in her soul. Mired she was between two abandoned worlds, living, but dying without the strength of the grace that either gave. The clearer she felt it the fuller did something well up from the depths of her for release; the more urgent did she feel the need to fling into her black sky another star, another hope, one more terrible vision to give her the strength to live and act. Softly and restlessly she walked about the kitchen, feeling herself naked against the night, the rain, the world; and shamed whenever the thought of Reva's love crossed her mind. She lifted her empty hands and looked at her writhing fingers. Lawd, whut kin Ah do now? She could still wade the creek and get to Foleys Woods before Booker. And then what? How could she manage to see Johnny-Boy or Booker? Again she heard the sheriff's threatening voice: Git yuh a sheet, cause hes gonna be dead! The sheet! Thas it, the *sheet!* Her whole being leaped with will; the long years of her life bent toward a moment of focus, a point. Ah kin go wid mah sheet! Ahll be doin whut he said! Lawd Gawd in Heaven, Ahma go lika nigger woman wid mah windin sheet t git mah dead son! But then what? She stood straight and smiled grimly; she had in her heart the whole meaning of her life; her entire personality was poised on the brink of a total act. Ah know! Ah *know!* She thought of Johnny-Boy's gun in the dresser drawer. Ahll hide the gun in the sheet n go aftah Johnny-Boys body. . . . She tiptoed to her room, eased out the dresser drawer, and got a sheet. Reva was sleeping; the darkness was filled with her quiet breathing. She groped in the drawer and found the gun. She wound the gun in the sheet and held them both under her apron. Then she stole to the bedside and watched Reva. Lawd, hep her! But mabbe shes bettah off. This had t happen sometime . . . She n Johnny-Boy couldna been together in this here South . . . N Ah couldnt tell her about Booker. Itll come out awright n she wont nevah know. Reva's trust would never be shaken. She caught her breath as the shucks in the mattress rustled dryly; then all was quiet and she breathed easily again. She tiptoed to the door, down the hall, and stood on the porch. Above her the yellow beacon whirled through the rain. She went over muddy ground, mounted a slope, stopped and looked back at her house. The lamp glowed in her window, and the yellow beacon that swung every few seconds seemed to feed it with light. She turned and started across the fields, holding the gun and sheet tightly, thinking, Po Reva . . . Po critter . . . Shes fas ersleep . . .

VI

For the most part she walked with her eyes half shut, her lips tightly compressed, leaning her body against the wind and the driving rain, feeling the pistol in the sheet sagging cold and heavy in her fingers. Already she was getting wet; it seemed that her feet found every puddle of water that stood between the corn rows.

She came to the edge of the creek and paused, wondering at what point was it low. Taking the sheet from under her apron, she wrapped the gun in it so that her finger could be upon the trigger. Ahll cross here, she thought. At first she did not feel the water; her feet were already wet. But the water grew cold as it came up to her knees; she gasped when it reached her waist. Lawd, this creeks high! When she had passed the middle, she knew that she was out of danger. She came out of the water, climbed a grassy hill, walked on, turned a bend and saw the lights of autos gleaming ahead. Yeah; theys still there! She hurried with her head down. Wondah did Ah beat im here? Lawd, Ah *hope* so! A vivid image of Booker's white face hovered a moment before her eyes and a surging will rose up in her so hard and strong that it vanished. She was among the autos now. From nearby came the hoarse voices of the men.

"Hey, yuh!"

She stopped, nervously clutching the sheet. Two white men with shotguns came toward her.

"Whut in hell yuh doin out here?"

She did not answer.

"Didnt yuh hear somebody speak t yuh?"

"Ahm comin aftah mah son," she said humbly.

"Yo *son?*"

"Yessuh."

"What yo son doin out here?"

"The sheriffs got im."

"Holy Scott! Jim, its the niggers ma!"

"Whut yuh got there?" asked one.

"A sheet."

"A *sheet?*"

"Yessuh."

"Fer whut?"

"The sheriff tol me t bring a sheet t git his body."

"Waal, waal . . ."

"Now, ain tha somethin?"

The white men looked at each other.

"These niggers sho love one ernother," said one.

"N tha ain no lie," said the other.

"Take me t the sheriff," she begged.

"Yuh ain givin us *orders*, is yuh?"

"Nawsuh."

"Well take yuh when wes good n ready."

"Yessuh."

"So yuh wan his body?"

"Yessuh."

"Waal, he ain dead yit."

"They gonna kill im," she said.

"Ef he talks they wont."

"He ain gonna talk," she said.

"How yuh know?"

"Cause he ain."

"We got ways of makin niggers talk."

"Yuh ain got no way fer im."

"Yuh thinka lot of that black Red, don yuh?"

"Hes mah son."

"Why don yuh teach im some sense?"

"Hes mah son," she said again.

"Lissen, ol nigger woman, yuh stand there wid yo hair white. Yuh got bettah sense than t believe tha niggers kin make a revolution . . ."

"A black republic," said the other one, laughing.

"Take me t the sheriff," she begged.

"Yuh his ma," said one. "Yuh kin make im talk n tell whose in this thing wid im."

"He ain gonna talk," she said.

"Don yuh wan im t live?"

She did not answer.

"C mon, les take her t Bradley."

They grabbed her arms and she clutched hard at the sheet and gun; they led her toward the crowd in the woods. Her feelings were simple; Booker would not tell; she was there with the gun to see to that. The louder became the voices of the men the deeper became her feeling of wanting to right the mistake she had made; of wanting to fight her way back to solid ground. She would stall for time until Booker showed up. Oh, ef theyll only lemme git close t Johnny-Boy! As they led her near the crowd she saw white faces turning and looking at her and heard a rising clamor of voices.

"Whose tha?"

"A nigger woman!"

"Whut she doin out here?"

"This is his ma!" called one of the men.

"Whut she wans?"

"She brought a sheet t cover his body!"

"He ain dead yit!"

"They tryin t make im talk!"

"But he will be dead soon ef he don open up!"

"Say, look! The niggers ma brought a sheet t cover up his body!"

"Now, ain that sweet?"

"Mabbe she wans t hol a prayer meetin!"

"Did she git a preacher?"

"Say, go git Bradley!"

"O.K.!"

The crowd grew quiet. They looked at her curiously; she felt their cold eyes trying to detect some weakness in her. Humbly, she stood with the sheet covering the gun. She had already accepted all that they could do to her.

The sheriff came.

"So yuh brought yuh sheet, hunh?"

"Yessuh," she whispered.

"Looks like them slaps we gave yuh learned yuh some sense, didnt they?"

She did not answer.

"Yuh don need tha sheet. Yo son ain dead yit," he said, reaching toward her.

She backed away, her eyes wide.

"Naw!"

"Now, lissen, Anty!" he said. "There ain no use in yuh ackin a fool! Go in there n tell tha nigger son of yos t tell us whos in this wid im, see? Ah promise we wont kill im ef he talks. We'll let im git outta town."

"There ain nothin Ah kin tell im," she said.

"Yuh wan us t kill im?"

She did not answer. She saw someone lean toward the sheriff and whisper.

"Bring her erlong," the sheriff said.

They led her to a muddy clearing. The rain streamed down through the ghostly glare of the flashlights. As the men formed a semi-circle she saw Johnny-Boy lying in a trough of mud. He was tied with rope; he lay hunched and one side of his face rested in a pool of black water. His eyes were staring questioningly at her.

"Speak t im," said the sheriff.

If she could only tell him why she was here! But that was impossible; she was close to what she wanted and she stared straight before her with compressed lips.

"Say, nigger!" called the sheriff, kicking Johnny-Boy. "Heres yo ma!"

Johnny-Boy did not move or speak. The sheriff faced her again.

"Lissen, Anty," he said. "Yuh got mo say wid im than anybody. Tell im t talk n hava chance. Whut he wanna pertect the other niggers n white folks fer?"

She slid her finger about the trigger of the gun and looked stonily at the mud.

"Go t him," said the sheriff.

She did not move. Her heart was crying out to answer the amazed question in Johnny-Boy's eyes. But there was no way now.

"Waal, yuhre astin fer it. By Gawd, we gotta way to *make* yuh talk t im," he said, turning away. "Say, Tim, git one of them logs n turn that nigger upside-down n put his legs on it!"

A murmur of assent ran through the crowd. She bit her lips; she knew what that meant.

"Yuh wan yo nigger son crippled?" she heard the sheriff ask.

She did not answer. She saw them roll the log up; they lifted Johnny-Boy and laid him on his face and stomach, then they pulled his legs over the log. His kneecaps rested on the sheer top of the log's back and the toes of his shoes pointed groundward. So absorbed was she in watching that she felt that it was she who was being lifted and made ready for torture.

"Git a crowbar!" said the sheriff.

A tall, lank man got a crowbar from a nearby auto and stood over the log. His jaws worked slowly on a wad of tobacco.

"Now, its up t yuh, Anty," the sheriff said. "Tell the man whut t do!"

She looked into the rain. The sheriff turned.

"Mebbe she think wes playin. Ef she don say nothin, then break em at the kneecaps!"

"O.K., Sheriff!"

She stood waiting for Booker. Her legs felt weak; she wondered if she would be able to wait much longer. Over and over she said to herself, Ef he came now Ahd kill em both!

"She ain sayin nothin, Sheriff!"

"Waal, Gawddammit, let im have it!"

The crowbar came down and Johnny-Boy's body lunged in the mud and water. There was a scream. She swayed, holding tight to the gun and sheet.

"Hol im! Git the other leg!"

The crowbar fell again. There was another scream.

"Yuh break em?" asked the sheriff.

The tall man lifted Johnny-Boy's legs and let them drop limply again, dropping rearward from the kneecaps. Johnny-Boy's body lay still. His head rolled to one side and she could not see his face.

"Jus lika broke sparrow wing," said the man, laughing softly.

Then Johnny-Boy's face turned to her; he screamed.

"Go way, ma! Go way!"

It was the first time she had heard his voice since she had come out to the woods; she all but lost control of herself. She started violently forward, but the sheriff's arm checked her.

"Aw, naw! Yuh had yo chance!" He turned to Johnny-Boy. "She kin go ef yuh talk."

"Mistah, he ain gonna talk," she said.

"Go way, ma!" said Johnny-Boy.

"Shoot im! Don make im suffah so," she begged.

"He'll either talk or he'll never hear yuh ergin," the sheriff said. "Theres other things we kin do t im."

She said nothing.

"Whut yuh come here fer, ma?" Johnny-Boy sobbed.

"Ahm gonna split his eardrums," the sheriff said. "Ef yuh got anythin to say t im yuh bettah say it *now!*"

She closed her eyes. She heard the sheriff's feet sucking in mud. Ah could save im! She opened her eyes; there were shouts of eagerness from the crowd as it pushed in closer.

"Bus em, Sheriff!"

"Fix im so he cant hear!"

"He knows how t do it, too!"

"He busted a Jew boy tha way once!"

She saw the sheriff stoop over Johnny-Boy, place his flat palm over one ear and strike his fist against it with all his might. He placed his palm over the other ear and struck again. Johnny-Boy moaned, his head rolling from side to side, his eyes showing white amazement in a world without sound.

"Yuh wouldnt talk t im when yuh had the chance," said the sheriff. "Try n talk now."

She felt warm tears on her cheeks. She longed to shoot Johnny-Boy and let him go. But if she did that they would take the gun from her, and Booker would tell who the others were. Lawd, hep me! The men were talking loudly now, as though the main business was over. It seemed ages that she stood there watching Johnny-Boy roll and whimper in his world of silence.

"Say, Sheriff, heres somebody lookin fer yuh!"

"Who is it?"

"Ah don know!"

"Bring em in!"

She stiffened and looked around wildly, holding the gun tight. Is tha Booker? Then she held still, feeling that her excitement might betray her. Mabbe Ah kin shoot em both! Mabbe Ah kin shoot *twice!* The sheriff stood in front of her, waiting. The crowd parted and she saw Booker hurrying forward.

"Ah know em all, Sheriff!" he called.

He came full into the muddy clearing where Johnny-Boy lay.

"Yuh mean yuh got the names?"

"Sho! The ol nigger . . ."

She saw his lips hang open and silent when he saw her. She stepped forward and raised the sheet.

"Whut . . ."

She fired, once; then, without pausing, she turned, hearing them yell. She aimed at Johnny-Boy, but they had their arms around her, bearing her to the ground, clawing at the sheet in her hand. She glimpsed Booker lying sprawled in the mud, on his face, his hands stretched out before him; then a cluster of yelling men blotted him out. She lay without struggling, looking upward through the rain at the white faces above her. And she was suddenly at peace; they were not a white mountain now; they were not pushing her any longer to the edge of life. Its awright . . .

"She shot Booker!"

"She hada gun in the sheet!"

"She shot im right thu the head!"

"Whut she shoot im fer?"

"Kill the bitch!"

"Ah *thought* somethin wuz wrong bout her!"

"Ah wuz fer givin it t her from the firs!"

"Thas whut yuh git fer treatin a nigger nice!"

"Say, Bookers dead!"

She stopped looking into the white faces, stopped listening. She waited, giving up her life before they took it from her; she had done what she wanted. Ef only Johnny-Boy . . . She looked at him; he lay looking at her with tired eyes. Ef she could only tell im! But he lay already buried in a grave of silence.

"Whut yuh kill im fer, hunh?"

It was the sheriff's voice; she did not answer.

"Mabbe she wuz shootin at yuh, Sheriff?"

"Whut yuh kill im fer?"

She felt the sheriff's foot come into her side; she closed her eyes.

"Yuh black bitch!"

"Let her have it!"

"Yuh reckon she foun out bout Booker?"

"She mighta."

"Jesus Chris, whut yuh dummies *waitin* on!"

"Yeah; kill her!"

"Kill em *both!*"

"Let her know her nigger sons dead firs!"

She turned her head toward Johnny-Boy; he lay looking puzzled in a world beyond the reach of voices. At leas he cant hear, she thought.

"C mon, let im have it!"

She listened to hear what Johnny-Boy could not. They came, two of them, one right behind the other; so close together that they sounded like one shot. She did not look at Johnny-Boy now; she looked at the white faces of the men, hard and wet in the glare of the flashlights.

"Yuh hear tha, nigger woman?"

"Did tha surprise im? Hes in hell now wonderin whut hit im!"

"C mon! Give it t her, Sheriff!"

"Lemme shoot her, Sheriff! It wuz mah pal she shot!"

"Awright, Pete! Thas fair ernuff!"

She gave up as much of her life as she could before they took it from her. But the sound of the shot and the streak of fire that tore its way through her chest forced her to live again, intensely. She had not moved, save for the slight jarring impact of the bullet. She felt the heat of her own blood warming her cold, wet back. She yearned suddenly to talk. "Yuh didnt git whut yuh wanted! N yuh ain gonna nevah git it! Yuh didnt kill me; Ah come here by mahsef . . ." She felt rain falling into her wide-open, dimming eyes and heard faint voices. Her lips moved soundlessly. *Yuh didnt git yuh didnt yuh didnt* . . . Focused and pointed she was, buried in the depth of her star, swallowed in its peace and strength; and not feeling her flesh growing cold, cold as the rain that fell from the invisible sky upon the doomed living and the dead that never dies.

The Ethics of Living Jim Crow

(An Autobiographical Sketch)

I

My first lesson in how to live as a Negro came when I was quite small. We were living in Arkansas. Our house stood behind the railroad tracks. Its skimpy yard was paved with black cinders. Nothing green ever grew in that yard. The only touch of green we could see was far away, beyond the tracks, over where the white folks lived. But cinders were good enough for me and I never missed the green growing things. And anyhow cinders were fine weapons. You could always have a nice hot war with huge black cinders. All you had to do was crouch behind the brick pillars of a house with your hands full of gritty ammunition. And the first woolly black head you saw pop out from behind another row of pillars was your target. You tried your very best to knock it off. It was great fun.

I never fully realized the appalling disadvantages of a cinder environment .till one day the gang to which I belonged found itself engaged in a war with the white boys who lived beyond the tracks. As usual we laid down our cinder barrage, thinking that this would wipe the white boys out. But they replied with a steady bombardment of broken bottles. We doubled our cinder barrage, but they hid behind trees, hedges, and the sloping embankments of their lawns. Having no such fortifications, we retreated to the brick pillars of our homes. During the retreat a broken milk bottle caught me behind the ear, opening a deep gash which bled profusely. The sight of blood pouring over my face completely demoralized our ranks. My fellow-combatants left me standing paralyzed in the center of the yard, and scurried for their homes. A kind neighbor saw me and rushed me to a doctor, who took three stitches in my neck.

I sat brooding on my front steps, nursing my wound and waiting for my mother to come from work. I felt that a grave injustice had been done me. It was all right to throw cinders. The greatest harm a cinder could do was leave a bruise. But broken bottles were dangerous; they left you cut, bleeding, and helpless.

When night fell, my mother came from the white folks' kitchen. I raced down the street to meet her. I could just feel in my bones that she would understand. I knew she would tell me exactly what to do next time. I grabbed her hand and babbled out the whole story. She examined my wound, then slapped me.

"How come yuh didn't hide?" she asked me. "How come yuh awways fightin'?"

I was outraged, and bawled. Between sobs I told her that I didn't have any trees or hedges to hide behind. There wasn't a thing I could have used as a trench. And you couldn't throw very far when you were hiding behind the brick pillars of a house. She grabbed a barrel stave, dragged me home, stripped me naked, and beat me till I had a fever of one hundred and two. She would smack my rump with the stave, and, while the skin was still smarting, impart to me gems of Jim Crow wisdom. I was never to throw cinders any more. I was never to fight any more wars. I was never, never, under any conditions, to fight *white* folks again. And they were absolutely right in clouting me with the broken milk bottle. Didn't I know she was working hard every day in the hot kitchens of the white folks to make money to take care of me? When was I ever going to learn to be a good boy? She couldn't be bothered with my fights. She finished by telling me that I ought to be thankful to God as long as I lived that they didn't kill me.

All that night I was delirious and could not sleep. Each time I closed my eyes I saw monstrous white faces suspended from the ceiling, leering at me.

From that time on, the charm of my cinder yard was gone. The green trees, the trimmed hedges, the cropped lawns grew very meaningful, became a symbol. Even today when I think of white folks, the hard, sharp outlines of white houses surrounded by trees, lawns, and hedges are present somewhere in the background of my mind. Through the years they grew into an overreaching symbol of fear.

It was a long time before I came in close contact with white folks again. We moved from Arkansas to Mississippi. Here we had the good fortune not to live behind the railroad tracks, or close to white neighborhoods. We lived in the very heart of the local Black Belt. There were black churches and black preachers; there were black schools and black teachers; black groceries and black clerks. In fact, everything was so solidly black that for a long time I did not even think of white folks, save in remote and vague terms. But this could not last forever. As one grows older one eats more. One's clothing costs more. When I finished grammar school I had to go to work. My mother could no longer feed and clothe me on her cooking job.

There is but one place where a black boy who knows no trade can get a job, and that's where the houses and faces are white, where the trees, lawns, and hedges are green. My first job was with an optical company in Jackson, Mississippi. The morning I applied I stood straight and neat before the boss, answering all his questions with sharp yessirs and nosirs. I was very careful to pronounce my *sirs* distinctly, in order that he might know that I was polite, that I knew where I was, and that I knew he was a *white* man. I wanted that job badly.

He looked me over as though he were examining a prize poodle. He questioned me closely about my schooling, being particularly insistent about how much mathematics I had had. He seemed very pleased when I told him I had had two years of algebra.

"Boy, how would you like to try to learn something around here?" he asked me.

"I'd like it fine, sir," I said, happy. I had visions of "working my way up." Even Negroes have those visions.

"All right," he said. "Come on."

I followed him to the small factory.

"Pease," he said to a white man of about thirty-five, "this is Richard. He's going to work for us."

Pease looked at me and nodded.

I was then taken to a white boy of about seventeen.

"Morrie, this is Richard, who's going to work for us."

"Whut yuh sayin' there, boy!" Morrie boomed at me.

"Fine!" I answered.

The boss instructed these two to help me, teach me, give me jobs to do, and let me learn what I could in my spare time.

My wages were five dollars a week.

I worked hard, trying to please. For the first month I got along O.K. Both Pease and Morrie seemed to like me. But one thing was missing. And I kept thinking about it. I was not learning anything and nobody was volunteering to help me. Thinking they had forgotten that I was to learn something about the mechanics of grinding lenses, I asked Morrie one day to tell me about the work. He grew red.

"Whut yuh tryin' t' do, nigger, get smart?" he asked.

"Naw; I ain' tryin' t' git smart," I said.

"Well, don't, if yuh know whut's good for yuh!"

I was puzzled. Maybe he just doesn't want to help me, I thought. I went to Pease.

"Say, are yuh crazy, you black bastard?" Pease asked me, his gray eyes growing hard.

I spoke out, reminding him that the boss had said I was to be given a chance to learn something.

"Nigger, you think you're *white*, don't you?"

"Naw, sir!"

"Well, you're acting mighty like it!"

"But, Mr. Pease, the boss said . . ."

Pease shook his fist in my face.

"This is a *white* man's work around here, and you better watch yourself!"

From then on they changed toward me. They said goodmorning no more. When I was just a bit slow in performing some duty, I was called a lazy black son-of-a-bitch.

Once I thought of reporting all this to the boss. But the mere idea of what would happen to me if Pease and Morrie should learn that I had "snitched" stopped me. And after all the boss was a white man, too. What was the use?

The climax came at noon one summer day. Pease called me to his workbench. To get to him I had to go between two narrow benches and stand with my back against a wall.

"Yes, sir," I said.

"Richard, I want to ask you something," Pease began pleasantly, not looking up from his work.

"Yes, sir," I said again.

Morrie came over, blocking the narrow passage between the benches. He folded his arms, staring at me solemnly.

I looked from one to the other, sensing that something was coming.

"Yes, sir," I said for the third time.

Pease looked up and spoke very slowly.

"Richard, *Mr.* Morrie here tells me you called me *Pease.*"

I stiffened. A void seemed to open up in me. I knew this was the show-down.

He meant that I had failed to call him Mr. Pease. I looked at Morrie. He was gripping a steel bar in his hands. I opened my mouth to speak, to protest, to assure Pease that I had never called him simply *Pease,* and that I had never had any intentions of doing so, when Morrie grabbed me by the collar, ramming my head against the wall.

"Now, be careful, nigger!" snarled Morrie, baring his teeth. "*I* heard yuh call 'im *Pease!* 'N' if yuh say yuh didn't, yuh're callin' me a *lie,* see?" He waved the steel bar threateningly.

If I had said: No, sir, Mr. Pease, I never called you *Pease,* I would have been automatically calling Morrie a liar. And if I had said: Yes, sir, Mr. Pease, I called you *Pease,* I would have been pleading guilty to having uttered the worst insult that a Negro can utter to a southern white man. I stood hesitating, trying to frame a neutral reply.

"Richard, I asked you a question!" said Pease. Anger was creeping into his voice.

"I don't remember calling you *Pease,* Mr. Pease," I said cautiously. "And if I did, I sure didn't mean . . ."

"You black son-of-a-bitch! You called me *Pease,* then!" he spat, slapping me till I bent sideways over a bench. Morrie was on top of me, demanding:

"Didn't yuh call 'im *Pease?* If yuh say yuh didn't, I'll rip yo' gut string loose with this bar, yuh black granny dodger! Yuh can't cal a white man a lie 'n' git erway with it, you black son-of-a-bitch!"

I wilted. I begged them not to bother me. I knew what they wanted. They wanted me to leave.

"I'll leave," I promised. "I'll leave right *now.*"

They gave me a minute to get out of the factory. I was warned not to show up again, or tell the boss.

I went.

When I told the folks at home what had happened, they called me a fool.

They told me that I must never again attempt to exceed my boundaries. When you are working for white folks, they said, you got to "stay in your place" if you want to keep working. . . .

V

My next job was a hall-boy in a hotel. Here my Jim Crow education broadened and deepened. When the bell-boys were busy, I was often called to assist them. As many of the rooms in the hotel were occupied by prostitutes, I was constantly called to carry them liquor and cigarettes. These women were nude most of the time. They did not bother about clothing, even for bell-boys. When you went into their rooms, you were supposed to take their nakedness for granted, as though it startled you no more than a blue vase or a red rug. Your presence awoke in them no sense of shame, for you were not regarded as human. If they were alone, you could steal sidelong glimpses at them. But if they were receiving men, not a flicker of your eyelids could show. I remember one incident vividly. A new woman, a huge, snowy-skinned blonde, took a room on my floor. I was sent to wait upon her. She was in bed with a thick-set man; both were nude and uncovered. She said she wanted some liquor and slid out of bed and waddled across the floor to get her money from a dresser drawer. I watched her.

"Nigger, what in hell you looking at?" the white man asked me, raising himself upon his elbows.

"Nothing," I answered, looking miles deep into the blank wall of the room.

"Keep your eyes where they belong, if you want to be healthy!" he said.

"Yes, sir." . . .

VIII

One night, just as I was about to go home, I met one of the Negro maids. She lived in my direction, and we fell in to walk part of the way home together. As was passed the white night-watchman, he slapped the maid on her buttock. I turned around, amazed. The watchman looked at me with a long, hard, fixed-under stare. Suddenly he pulled his gun and asked:

"Nigger, don't yuh like it?"

I hesitated.

"I asked yuh don't yuh like it?" he asked again, stepping forward.

"Yes, sir," I mumbled.

"Talk like it, then!"

"Oh, yes, sir!" I said with as much heartiness as I could muster.

Outside, I walked ahead of the girl, ashamed to face her. She caught up with me and said:

"Don't be a fool! Yuh couldn't help it!"

This watchman boasted of having killed two Negroes in self-defense.

Yes, in spite of all this, the life of the hotel ran with an amazing smoothness.

It would have been impossible for a stranger to detect anything. The maids, the hall-boys, and the bell-boys were all smiles. They had to be.

IX

I had learned my Jim Crow lessons so thoroughly that I kept the hotel job till I left Jackson for Memphis. It so happened that while in Memphis I applied for a job at a branch of the optical company. I was hired. And for some reason, as long as I worked there, they never brought my past against me.

Here my Jim Crow education assumed quite a different form. It was no longer brutally cruel, but subtly cruel. Here I learned to lie, to steal, to dissemble. I learned to play that dual role which every Negro must play if he wants to eat and live.

For example, it was almost impossible to get a book to read. It was assumed that after a Negro had imbided what scanty schooling the state furnished he had no further need for books. I was always borrowing books from men on the job. One day I mustered enough courage to ask one of the men to let me get books from the library in his name. Surprisingly, he consented. I cannot help but think that he consented because he was a Roman Catholic and felt a vague sympathy for Negroes, being himself an object of hatred. Armed with a library card, I obtained books in the following manner: I would write a note to the librarian, saying: "Please let this nigger boy have the following books." I would then sign it with the white man's name. . . .

How do Negroes feel about the way they have to live? How do they discuss it when alone among themselves? I think this question can be answered in a single sentence. A friend of mine who ran an elevator once told me:

"Lawd, man! Ef it wuzn't fer them polices 'n' them ol' lynch-mobs, there wouldn't be nothin' but uproar down here!"

VII
The
Fifties
and
Sixties

Increased purchasing power, greater political power, a larger number
of black college-bred men and women—all these belonged to the black Americans
as the twentieth-century moved into the fifties. The militant spirit that had come
to characterize a majority of black Americans in the forties continued to grow in
the fifties as black people demanded all the rights and privileges belonging to the
American citizen. The demands were not new, but the time that black American
citizens were willing to grant for the fulfillment of their demands was shortened.
They demanded that discrimination, oppression, and second-class citizenship be
immediately abolished and that all the wrongs perpetrated against the black
people for centuries be immediately redressed. The spirit of the majority of
American's black citizens in the fifties was magnificently expressed by Mrs. Rosa
Parks when she took a seat in the "white" section of a Montgomery bus in 1955
and "made up her mind never to move again."

Mrs. Parks's action led to the Montgomery bus boycott, which captured the
imagination of the nation and brought Dr. Martin Luther King, Jr. to the forefront as America's most forceful, eloquent, and influential black leader since the
days of Booker T. Washington. The year before black Americans made up their
minds "never to move again," the Supreme Court had declared that separate educational facilities for black students were "inherently unequal" (*Brown v. Board
of Education*), and this decision by the highest court in the land had telling
ramifications in the years to follow. The court's decision, in fact, reached far
beyond public educational systems; for if separate educational facilities were
inherently unequal, then separate parks, museums, and libraries—all those facilities within the public domain—were open to attack by minority groups if these
facilities remained exclusively white. With the force of the law behind them, black
Americans marched forward to secure their just rights. Martin Luther King was
not the sole leader in this march; groups like the Congress of Racial Equality
(CORE) and the Student Non-Violent Coordinating Committee (SNCC) were
in the forefront of the struggle during the fifties; moreover, older groups like the
NAACP and the National Urban League stepped forward as champions in the
black liberation struggle of the fifties.

The work of Dr. King, of CORE, SNCC, the NAACP, and the Urban
League, however, is too well known to be detailed here. College students across
the nation, high school students in the north and the south, industrial workers,
black professionals, white ministers, church councils, and government officials
were all swept into action by the black man's struggles in the fifties. However, a
good number of those swept into action were not dedicated to the cause of
liberty and equality. White Citizens' Councils were formed throughout the South,
and a conservative reaction of phenomenal proportion began to build. The white
southern politician who wished to keep his office was virtually forced to oppose
the *Brown v. Board of Education* decision, and the old forces of violence against
the black American, the old myths and fears, were resurrected in an outpouring
of hatred and bitterness that was projected into every household in America and
throughout every nation in the world by the mass media.

When the sit-in movement got underway in the sixties, therefore, the lines of battle were fairly well drawn. On one hand stood white supremacy, conservatism, hatred, and fear; on the other stood black equality, radicalism, endurance, and love. The two forces met head-on at lunch counters, at theaters, at amusement parks, at swimming pools, in bus stations, and in the streets of large northern cities and small southern townships. Passive, unsmiling, well-dressed Americans (both black and white) jeered at, spat upon, mangled by police dogs, and shocked by electric cattle prods—these were the sights of the early sit-in movement. And the most striking aspects of the movement were the total commitment and courage of the young; America had become a young country with a young and charismatic president in office; the status quo and the old verities saw their alteration and death close at hand. A revolutionary consciousness, in short, had become the norm for the young in America, and the young were fast becoming the majority as the average age of the American population decreased.

The battle that was being waged by the young, by the black, and by the poor, however, was one against some of the greatest vested interests in America, against some of the oldest national customs, and against some of the most cherished formulas in the American *Weltanschauung*. Thus the opposition was massive and telling in its effect; Malcolm X, John Kennedy, Martin Luther King, Robert Kennedy, and countless others have been fatalities of the battle. And as the scale of violence has mounted against those of the new revolutionary consciousness, they have shifted their tactics, altered their strategies, and changed their ultimate goals. Nothing less than total revolution—a total change of the American social fabric—will suffice. Passive efforts and outgoing love in the manner of Thoreau and Gandhi yielded the bitter fruits of violence and death, and the violence, the deaths, have led to a demand for self-defense and outgoing, forceful resistance on the part of those of the revolutionary consciousness. In the case of the black American, the Harlem riot in the summer of 1964 and the Watts riot during the following summer marked a transitional stage; gradualism, passive resistance, and love became outmoded; the ideal of merging into the mainstream of American life became anathema; and the emergence of militant leaders bent on firm resistance, revolutionary action, and active self-defense became the order of the day. Malcolm X, Stokeley Carmichael, Ron Karenga, and Huey P. Newton all offer examples of the new type of leadership that has been endorsed by the black Americans, and the philosophy of black power has become the norm for a people bent on self-definition and a rejection of all those factors in American society that militate against such self-definition.

Predictably, the struggle of the black American during the last two decades has produced a rich and complex body of literature characterized by diverse philosophies, a variety of techniques, and the emergence of new and dynamic patterns of language. In the early fifties—when the ideal of the black American was still total integration into the mainstream of American life—we find the works of writers like Gwendolyn Brooks, James Baldwin, and Ralph Ellison appealing to a wide and diverse audience. Baldwin was quick to repudiate the "protest novel" as an immature and dehumanizing form in his essays "Everybody's Protest Novel" and "Many Thousands Gone"; and Ellison assured the broad audience that had enabled him to receive the National Book Award for *Invisible Man* that he was a complex American whose background included many strains. Gwendolyn Brooks, whose *Annie Allen* received a Pulitzer Prize, seemed bent on evoking a sense of shame and moral outrage in poems like "A Bronzeville Mother Loiters in Mississippi. Meanwhile, a Mississippi Mother Burns Bacon." An appeal to the moral sensibilities of the country at large and an attempt to become "American" writers rather than "black writers" seem to have characterized much of the work of the early fifties, and Baldwin's essays and his philosophy of love and understanding have made him one of the most telling artistic activists of the last two decades. *Notes of a Native Son*—like Ellison's *Shadow and Act* and Miss Brooks's *The Bean Eaters*—attempts to demonstrate to American society at large that the black American is truly an American citizen, a complex human being, and a loving individual who should be included in the entire life of the country.

J. Saunders Redding, LeRoi Jones, and William Melvin Kelley also made attempts in their early works to get away from the classification "black writer." Redding's novel, *Stranger and Alone,* takes as its protagonist a young black man who wishes to escape from the problems that being young and black in America occasion; and Kelley states in the introduction to his volume of short stories, *Dancers on the Shore,* that he does not hope to speak as a sociologist or an orator for the black race, but simply as a writer. Finally, LeRoi Jones, who is the father of the present-day black aesthetic, started his writing career as a beatnik poet writing in the manner of Allen Ginsberg and Jack Kerouac. Jones's first volume of poetry, *Preface to a Twenty Volume Suicide Note,* is filled with "beat" poetry, and his second volume, *The Dead Lecturer,* strives for the complexity, wit, and symbolism of the Pound-Eliot tradition. Jones's striving for polished, accomplished verse in the British and American tradition is paralleled by the struggle for ambiguity and imagistic profundity manifested by the early works of Conrad Kent Rivers and Mari Evans. And there can be little doubt that a novel like *The Grand Parade* by Julian Mayfield was designed for a "general American" audience.

None of what has been said, however, is designed to detract from the works mentioned; they reflect the milieu in which they were produced, and many of them stand as examples of consummate artistic endeavor. Moreover, there is an element in many of these early works by black writers of the fifties and sixties that serves to connect them with the best that has been thought and said in the black literary tradition. That element is the folk element. The title of one of Baldwin's essays, for example, is the title of a famous black spiritual; Ellison's

Invisible Man reflects the folk heritage of black cats' bones, High John de Conquer, and greasy greens from cover to cover; Redding's novel deals in highly descriptive terms with the Southern agrarian environment that served as the first environment of black Americans; Jones's work deals in laudatory terms with the African and American folk experiences of black people; and, in one of the best stories in his volume, Kelley explores the importance of the blues in black American life.

As the dream of moving into the mainstream of American life has been purged from the black psyche by conservative reactions and black counteractions, the folk element has become increasingly important in black literature. It is a long way from Baldwin's *Go Tell It on the Mountain* to his *Another Country*; the first deals with a religious folk heritage of passive endurance and fear; the second deals with the subversion, energy, and outgoing wrath that have been a part of the black literary tradition from the earliest folk song down to the latest poem by Don L. Lee. "Black," in short, or "blackness," has become another country in the works of black writers of the sixties, and these writers are intent on discovering the *sui generis* aspects of their country's history.

The process in which black writers are currently engaged is not a new one; the growth of nationalism has always been accompanied by a rediscovery and exaltation of the folk heritage. It is not surprising, therefore, that both LeRoi Jones and Ted Joans have sought to bring forth folk themes and folk forms in their writing; Joans has called his latest verses "jazz poems," and LeRoi Jones has exalted folk music, folk food, and the folk condition in his poems, essays, and dramas. And the same is true of poets like Don L. Lee, Larry Neal, and Etheridge Knight; all have sought to explicate the African, agrarian, and urban folk experiences of black Americans.

Spirituals, sermons, blues, jazz, tricksters, conversion experiences—all parts of the black folk heritage—have been taken up by today's black American writers; and they are being handled and lauded as the things of beauty they truly are. Moreover, new forms, techniques, and patterns of language are being formulated by the black writers of the present day—forms, techniques, and patterns of language that enable the writer to incorporate the folk experience into his work in a way that speaks directly and expressively to a black audience. Hence, we find Jones, Neal, and Lee attempting to capture the distinctive rhythms of the blues and the distinctive intonational patterns of the black preacher; and we find Ted Joans capturing the slow, cool rhythms of Charlie Parker, Pharoah Sanders, and Ornette Coleman. Writers like John Williams, Paule Marshall, John O. Killens, and Gwendolyn Brooks have turned to direct and telling statements of the value of the black folk heritage. Black writers, in short, have become intensely aware of the need to speak to a distinctive black audience, in a distinctive black language, about a distinctively beautiful experience—the experience of blackness.

And some of the most successful efforts at this type of expression have been in the form of the drama. Lorraine Hansberry, Ossie Davis, Lonnie Elder, and Ed Bullins are but a few of the names that must be mentioned in any discussion of the black literature of the fifties and sixties.

The tone of black writing has changed to one of pride and militancy; black writers realize with pride that blackness is not the evil entity that white civilization has labeled it, and they speak in bellicose voices to their brothers about the beauty of blackness and the necessity of resisting white cruelty with loaded guns and loaded words that will raise a proud nation of free black people. The desire to move into the mainstream is seldom expressed, for that movement simply means the obliteration of what is beautiful—one's blackness and one's accomplished folk heritage. Malcolm X is thus pointed to with pride by black writers. Malcolm refused to be engulfed by the mainstream and its yearnings; he molded standards that were fitting to black lives, and he remained intensely individualistic throughout his life. Malcolm, like so many of the black leaders and writers who have followed in his path, had "soul"—that energy and spirituality that proceed out of a distinctive folk heritage. The true spirituality of the black folk, their "soul," is what most black artists are attempting to capture today, and black critics like Addison Gayle, Hoyt Fuller, and J. Saunders Redding are essential to their work. For black critics, like black artists, have discovered the beauty of their heritage, and they are intent on defining new standards of excellence that will serve as guides to the distinctive artifacts that are being forged by today's black artists.

Reassessment, rejection, and *revival* are the terms that best sum up the literary output of the present generation of black writers. The present generation has reassessed traditional white American cultural products and standards, and it has found both the products and standards—in the words of LeRoi Jones— simply the reflections and projections of "tired white lives." Today's black writers, therefore, have rejected the dictates, products, and standards of white American culture; they have turned outward toward an emerging Africa and backward toward their own folk heritage in a search for meaning and value. Black writers of the present generation have found that a revival and exaltation, understanding, and appreciation of the soul life embodied in the folk heritage is the only way that a black writer can arrive at a firm sense of identity and speak meaningfully to his own people.

REFERENCES

Some of the most interesting critical statements about the black American literature of the past two decades have been made by black writers themselves. Baldwin, Ellison, Jones, Neal, Mayfield, and Lee have all made important statements about the task of the black artist. Some of these statements have been excerpted in Addison Gayle's *Black Expression* (1969), and others have appeared in periodicals like *Phylon, The Journal of Negro History, Negro Digest, Liberator, Freedomways,* and *The Journal of Black Poetry.* All these sources provide invaluable material for the student of recent black American literature, just as the pages of *Crisis* and *Opportunity* provide invaluable material for the student of early twentieth-century black American literature. The list of works below comprises only a brief, selected bibliography of some of the more helpful items dealing with recent black American literature.

Abramson, Doris E.: *Negro Playwrights in the American Theatre: 1925–1959,* Columbia University Press, New York, 1969.

Bone, Robert A.: *The Negro Novel in America,* Yale University Press, New Haven, 1958.

Bontemps, Arna: "The New Black Renaissance," *Negro Digest,* vol. XI November, 1961, pp. 52–58.

Brown, Sterling: "A Century of Negro Portraiture in American Literature," *Massachusetts Review,* Vol. VII, 1966, pp. 73–96.

Clarke, John Henrik: *Malcolm X, The Man and His Times,* Macmillan, New York, 1969.

Cook, Mercer, and Stephen Henderson: *The Militant Black Writer in Africa and the United States,* University of Wisconsin Press, Madison, 1969.

Eckman, Fern Marja: *The Furious Passage of James Baldwin,* J. B. Lippincott, New York, 1967.

Ellison, Ralph: "The World and the Jug," *Shadow and Act,* Random House, New York, 1953, pp. 115–148. (This is Ellison's answer to Irving Howe's comments on "Black Boys and Native Sons." Howe's essays can be found in his 1963 volume, *A World More Attractive.*)

Gayle, Addison: *Black Expression,* Weybright and Talley, New York, 1969.

Gross, Seymour L., and John Edward Hardy (eds.): *Images of the Negro in American Literature,* University of Chicago Press, Chicago, 1966. (The volume contains Leslie Fiedler's "The Blackness of Darkness: The Negro and the Development of American Gothic"; Marcus Klein's "Ralph Ellison's Invisible Man"; an interesting introduction by Gross; and several other helpful items.)

Hill, Herbert (ed.): *Anger and Beyond, The Negro Writer in the United States,* Harper & Row, New York, 1968. (This volume contains essays by Redding, Jones, Bontemps, and a fine introduction by Hill.)

Jones, LeRoi: "Myth of a Negro Literature," *Home,* William Morrow, New York, 1966, pp. 105–115. (This volume also contains "LeRoi Jones Talking" and "The Revolutionary Theatre," two essays that have helped to establish directions for present-day black writers.)

Killens, John O.: "The Black Writer Vis-à-Vis His Country," *Black Man's Burden,* Trident Press, New York, 1969, pp. 29–58.

Littlejohn, David: *Black on White, a Critical Survey of Writing by American Negroes,* Viking Press, New York, 1969.

Margolies, Edward: *Native Sons, a Critical Study of Twentieth-century Negro American Authors,* J. B. Lippincott, New York, 1969.

Mitchell, Lofton: *Black Drama: A History,* Hawthorne Books, New York, 1967.

James Baldwin (1924-   )

Many Thousands Gone

From Notes of a Native Son (1955)

It is only in his music, which Americans are able to admire because a protective sentimentality limits their understanding of it, that the Negro in America has been able to tell his story. It is a story which otherwise has yet to be told and which no American is prepared to hear. As is the inevitable result of things unsaid, we find ourselves until today oppressed with a dangerous and reverberating silence; and the story is told, compulsively, in symbols and signs, in hieroglyphics; it is revealed in Negro speech and in that of the white majority and in their different frames of reference. The ways in which the Negro has affected the American psychology are betrayed in our popular culture and in our morality; in our estrangement from him is the depth of our estrangement from ourselves. We cannot ask: what do we *really* feel about him—such a question merely opens the gates on chaos. What we really feel about him is involved with all that we feel about everything, about everyone, about ourselves.

The story of the Negro in America is the story of America—or, more precisely, it is the story of Americans. It is not a very pretty story: the story of a people is never very pretty. The Negro in America, gloomily referred to as that shadow which lies athwart our national life, is far more than that. He is a series of shadows, self-created, intertwining, which now we helplessly battle. One may say that the Negro in America does not really exist except in the darkness of our minds.

This is why his history and his progress, his relationship to all other Americans, has been kept in the social arena. He is a social and not a personal or a human problem; to think of him is to think of statistics, slums, rapes, injustices, remote violence; it is to be confronted with an endless cataloguing of losses, gains, skirmishes; it is to feel virtuous, outraged, helpless, as though his continuing status among us were somehow analogous to disease—cancer, perhaps, or tuberculosis—which must be checked, even though it cannot be cured. In this arena the black man acquires quite another aspect from that which he has in life. We do not know what to do with him in life; if he breaks our sociological and sentimental image of him we are panic-stricken and we feel ourselves betrayed. When he violates this image, therefore, he stands in the greatest danger (sensing which, we uneasily suspect that he is very often playing a part for our benefit); and, what is not always so apparent but is equally true, we are then in some danger ourselves—hence our retreat or our blind and immediate retaliation.

Our dehumanization of the Negro then is indivisible from our dehumanization of ourselves: the loss of our own identity is the price we pay for our annulment of his. Time and our own force act as our allies, creating an impossible, a fruitless tension between the traditional master and slave. Impossible and fruitless because, literal and visible as this tension has become, it has nothing to do with reality.

Time has made some changes in the Negro face. Nothing has succeeded in making it exactly like our own, though the general desire seems to be to make it blank if one cannot make it white. When it has become blank, the past as thoroughly washed from the black face as it has been from ours, our guilt will be finished—at least it will have ceased to be visible, which we imagine to be much the same thing. But, paradoxically, it is we who prevent this from happening; since it is we, who, every hour that we live, reinvest the black face with our guilt; and we do this—by a further paradox, no less ferocious—helplessly, passionately, out of an unrealized need to suffer absolution.

Today, to be sure, we know that the Negro is not biologically or mentally inferior; there is no truth in those rumors of his body odor or his incorrigible sexuality; or no more truth than can be easily explained or even defended by the social sciences. Yet, in our most recent war, his blood was segregated as was, for the most part, his person. Up to today we are set at a division, so that he may not marry our daughters or our sisters, nor may he—for the most part—eat at our tables or live in our houses. Moreover, those who do, do so at the grave expense of a double alienation: from their own people, whose fabled attributes they must either deny or, worse, cheapen and bring to market; from us, for we require of them, when we accept them, that they at once cease to be Negroes and yet not fail to remember what being a Negro means—to remember, that is, what it means to us. The threshold of insult is higher or lower, according to the people involved, from the bootblack in Atlanta to the celebrity in New York. One must travel very far, among saints with nothing to gain or outcasts with nothing to lose, to find a place where it does not matter—and perhaps a word or a gesture or simply a silence will testify that it matters even there.

For it means something to be a Negro, after all, as it means something to have been born in Ireland or in China, to live where one sees space and sky or to live where one sees nothing but rubble or nothing but high buildings. We cannot escape our origins, however hard we try, those origins which contain the key—could we but find it—to all that we later become. What it means to be a Negro is a good deal more than this essay can discover; what it means to be a Negro in America can perhaps be suggested by an examination of the myths we perpetuate about him.

Aunt Jemima and Uncle Tom are dead, their places taken by a group of amazingly well-adjusted young men and women, almost as dark, but ferociously literate, well-dressed and scrubbed, who are never laughed at, who are not likely ever to set foot in a cotton or tobacco field or in any but the most modern of kitchens. There are others who remain, in our odd idiom, "underprivileged"; some are bitter and these come to grief; some are unhappy, but, continually presented with the evidence of a better day soon to come, are speedily becoming less so. Most of them care nothing whatever about race. They want only their proper place in the sun and the right to be left alone, like any other citizen of the republic. We may all breathe more easily. Before, however, our joy at the demise of Aunt Jemima and Uncle Tom approaches the indecent, we had better ask whence they sprang, how they lived? Into what limbo have they vanished?

However inaccurate our portraits of them were, these portraits do suggest, not only the conditions, but the quality of their lives and the impact of this spectacle on our consciences. There was no one more forbearing than Aunt Jemima, no one stronger or more pious or more loyal or more wise; there was, at the same time, no one weaker or more faithless or more vicious and certainly no one more immoral. Uncle Tom, trustworthy and sexless, needed only to drop the title "Uncle" to become violent, crafty, and sullen, a menace to any white woman who passed by. They prepared our feast tables and our burial clothes; and, if we could boast that we understood them, it was far more to the point and far more true that they understood us. They were, moreover, the only people in the world who did; and not only did they know us better than we knew ourselves, but they knew us better than we knew them. This was the piquant flavoring to the national joke, it lay behind our uneasiness as it lay behind our benevolence: Aunt Jemima and Uncle Tom, our creations, at the last evaded us; they had a life—their own, perhaps a better life than ours—and they would never tell us what it was. At the point where we were driven most privately and painfully to conjecture what depths of contempt, what heights of indifference, what prodigies of resilience, what untamable superiority allowed them so vividly to endure, neither perishing nor rising up in a body to wipe us from the earth, the image perpetually shattered and the word failed. The black man in our midst carried murder in his heart, he wanted vengeance. We carried murder too, we wanted peace.

In our image of the Negro breathes the past we deny, not dead but living yet and powerful, the beast in our jungle of statistics. It is this which defeats us, which continues to defeat us, which lends to interracial cocktail parties their rattling, genteel, nervously smiling air: in any drawing room at such a gathering the beast may spring, filling the air with flying things and an unenlightened wailing. Wherever the problem touches there is confusion, there is danger. Wherever the Negro face appears a tension is created, the tension of a silence filled with things unutterable. It is a sentimental error, therefore, to believe that the past is dead; it means nothing to say that it is all forgotten, that the Negro himself has forgotten it. It is not a question of memory. Oedipus did not remember the thongs that bound his feet; nevertheless the marks they left testified to that doom toward which his feet were leading him. The man does not remember the hand that struck him, the darkness that frightened him, as a child; nevertheless, the hand and the darkness remain with him, indivisible from himself forever, part of the passion that drives him wherever he thinks to take flight.

The making of an American begins at that point where he himself rejects all other ties, any other history, and himself adopts the vesture of his adopted land. This problem has been faced by all Americans throughout our history—in a way it *is* our history—and it baffles the immigrant and sets on edge the second generation until today. In the case of the Negro the past was taken from him whether he would or no; yet to forswear it was meaningless and availed him nothing, since his shameful history was carried, quite literally, on his brow. Shameful; for he was heathen as well as black and would never have discovered the healing blood of Christ had not we braved the jungles to bring him these glad tidings. Shameful; for, since our role as missionary had not been wholly disinterested, it was necessary to recall the shame from which we had delivered him in order more easily to escape our own. As he accepted the alabaster Christ and the bloody cross—in the bearing of which he would find his redemption, as, indeed, to our outraged astonishment, he sometimes did—he must, henceforth, accept that image we then gave him of himself: having no other and standing, moreover, in danger of death should he fail to accept the dazzling light thus brought into such darkness. It is this quite simple dilemma that must be borne in mind if we wish to comprehend his psychology.

However we shift the light which beats so fiercely on his head, or *prove,* by victorious social analysis, how his lot has changed, how we have both improved, our uneasiness refuses to be exorcized. And nowhere is this more apparent than in our literature on the subject—"problem" literature when written by whites, "protest" literature when written by Negroes—and nothing is more striking than the tremendous disparity of tone between the two creations. *Kingsblood Royal* bears, for example, almost no kinship to *If He Hollers Let Him Go,* though the same reviewers praised them both for what were, at bottom, very much the same reasons. These reasons may be suggested, far too briefly but not at all unjustly, by observing that the presupposition is in both novels exactly the same: black is a terrible color with which to be born into the world.

Now the most powerful and celebrated statement we have yet had of what it means to be a Negro in America is unquestionably Richard Wright's *Native Son.* The feeling which prevailed at the time of its publication was that such a novel, bitter, uncompromising, shocking, gave proof, by its very existence, of what strides might be taken in a free democracy; and its indisputable success, proof that Americans were now able to look full in the face without flinching the dreadful facts. Americans, unhappily, have the most remarkable ability to alchemize all bitter truths into an innocuous but piquant confection and to transform their moral contradictions, or public discussion of such contradictions, into a proud decoration, such as are given for heroism on the field of battle. Such a book, we felt with pride, could never have been written before—which was true. Nor could it be written today. It bears already the aspect of a landmark; for Bigger and his brothers have undergone yet another metamorphosis; they have been accepted in baseball leagues and by colleges hitherto exclusive; and they have made a most favorable appearance on the national screen. We have yet to encounter, nevertheless, a report so indisputably authentic, or one that can begin to challenge this most significant novel.

It is, in a certain American tradition, the story of an unremarkable youth in battle with the force of circumstance; that force of circumstance which plays and which has played so important a part in the national fables of success or failure. In this case the force of circumstance is not poverty merely but color, a circumstance which cannot be overcome, against which the protagonist battles for his life and loses. It is, on the surface, remarkable that this book should have enjoyed among Americans the favor it did enjoy; no more remarkable, however, than that it should have been compared, exuberantly, to Dostoevsky, though placed a shade below Dos Passos, Dreiser, and Steinbeck; and when the book is examined, its impact does not seem remarkable at all, but becomes, on the contrary, perfectly logical and inevitable.

We cannot, to begin with, divorce this book from the specific social climate of that time: it was one of the last of those angry productions, encountered in the late twenties and all through the thirties, dealing with the inequities of the social structure of America. It was published one year before our entry into the last world war—which is to say, very few years after the dissolution of the WPA and the end of the New Deal and at a time when bread lines and soup kitchens and bloody industrial battles were bright in everyone's memory. The rigors of that unexpected time filled us not only with a genuinely bewildered and despairing idealism—so that, because there at least was *something* to fight for, young men went off to die in Spain—but also with a genuinely bewildered self-consciousness. The Negro, who had been during the magnificent twenties a passionate and delightful primitive, now became, as one of the things we were most self-conscious about, our most oppressed minority. In the thirties, swallowing Marx whole, we discovered the Worker and realized—I should think with some relief—that the aims of the Worker and the aims of the Negro were one. This theorem—to which we shall return—seems now to leave rather too much out of account; it became, nevertheless, one of the slogans of the "class struggle" and the gospel of the New Negro.

As for this New Negro, it was Wright who became his most eloquent spokesman; and his work, from its beginning, is most clearly committed to the social struggle. Leaving aside the considerable question of what relationship precisely the artist bears to the revolutionary, the reality of man as a social being is not his only reality and that artist is strangled who is forced to deal with human beings solely in social terms; and who has, moreover, as Wright had, the necessity thrust on him of being the representative of some thirteen million people. It is a false responsibility (since writers are not congressmen) and impossible, by its nature, of fulfillment. The unlucky shepherd soon finds that, so far from being able to feed the hungry sheep, he has lost the wherewithal for his own nourishment: having not been allowed—so fearful was his burden, so present his audience!—to recreate his own experience. Further, the militant men and women of the thirties were not, upon examination, significantly emancipated from their antecedents, however bitterly they might consider themselves estranged or however gallantly they struggled to build a better world. However they might extol Russia, their concept of a better world was quite helplessly American and betrayed a certain thinness of imagination, a suspect reliance on suspect and badly digested formulae, and a positively fretful romantic haste. Finally, the relationship of the Negro to the Worker cannot be summed up, nor even greatly illuminated, by saying that their aims are one. It is true only insofar as they both desire better working conditions and useful only insofar as they unite their strength as workers to achieve these ends. Further than this we cannot in honesty go.

In this climate Wright's voice first was heard and the struggle which promised for a time to shape his work and give it purpose also fixed it in an ever more unrewarding rage. Recording his days of anger he has also nevertheless recorded, as no Negro before him had ever done, that fantasy Americans hold in their minds when they speak of the Negro: that fantastic and fearful image which we have lived with since the first slave fell beneath the lash. This is the significance of *Native Son* and also, unhappily, its overwhelming limitation.

Native Son begins with the *Brring!* of an alarm clock in the squalid Chicago tenement where Bigger and his family live. Rats live there too, feeding off the garbage, and we first encounter Bigger in the act of killing one. One may consider that the entire book, from that harsh *Brring!* to Bigger's weak "Good-by" as the lawyer, Max, leaves him in the death cell, is an extension, with the roles inverted, of this chilling metaphor. Bigger's situation and Bigger himself exert on the mind the same sort of fascination. The premise of the book is, as I take it, clearly conveyed in these first pages: we are confronting a monster created by the American republic and we are, through being made to share his experience, to receive illumination as regards the manner of his life and to feel both pity and horror at his awful and inevitable doom. This is an arresting and potentially rich idea and we would be discussing a very different novel if Wright's execution had been more perceptive and if he had not attempted to redeem a symbolical monster in social terms.

One may object that it was precisely Wright's intention to create in Bigger a social symbol, revelatory of social disease and prophetic of disaster. I think, however, that it is this assumption which we ought to examine more carefully. Bigger has no discernible relationship to himself, to his own life, to his own people, nor to any other people—in this respect, perhaps, he is most American— and his force comes, not from his significance as a social (or anti-social) unit, but from his significance as the incarnation of a myth. It is remarkable that, though we follow him step by step from the tenement room to the death cell, we know as little about him when this journey is ended as we did when it began;

and, what is even more remarkable, we know almost as little about the social dynamic which we are to believe created him. Despite the details of slum life which we are given, I doubt that anyone who has thought about it, disengaging himself from sentimentality, can accept this most essential premise of the novel for a moment. Those Negroes who surround him, on the other hand, his hard-working mother, his ambitious sister, his poolroom cronies, Bessie, might be considered as far richer and far more subtle and accurate illustrations of the ways in which Negroes are controlled in our society and the complex techniques they have evolved for their survival. We are limited, however, to Bigger's view of them, part of a deliberate plan which might not have been disastrous if we were not also limited to Bigger's perceptions. What this means for the novel is that a necessary dimension has been cut away; this dimension being the relationship that Negroes bear to one another, that depth of involvement and unspoken recognition of shared experience which creates a way of life. What the novel reflects—and at no point interprets—is the isolation of the Negro within his own group and the resulting fury of impatient scorn. It is this which creates its climate of anarchy and unmotivated and unapprehended disaster; and it is this climate, common to most Negro protest novels, which has led us all to believe that in Negro life there exists no tradition, no field of manners, no possibility of ritual or intercourse, such as may, for example, sustain the Jew even after he has left his father's house. But the fact is not that the Negro has no tradition but that there has as yet arrived no sensibility sufficiently profound and tough to make this tradition articulate. For a tradition expresses, after all, nothing more than the long and painful experience of a people; it comes out of the battle waged to maintain their integrity or, to put it more simply, out of their struggle to survive. When we speak of the Jewish tradition we are speaking of centuries of exile and persecution, of the strength which endured and the sensibility which discovered in it the high possibility of the moral victory.

This sense of how Negroes live and how they have so long endured is hidden from us in part by the very speed of the Negro's public progress, a progress so heavy with complexity, so bewildering and kaleidoscopic, that he dare not pause to conjecture on the darkness which lies behind him; and by the nature of the American psychology which, in order to apprehend or be made able to accept it, must undergo a metamorphosis so profound as to be literally unthinkable and which there is no doubt we will resist until we are compelled to achieve our own identity by the rigors of a time that has yet to come. Bigger, in the meanwhile, and all his furious kin, serve only to whet the notorious national taste for the sensational and to reinforce all that we now find it necessary to believe. It is not Bigger whom we fear, since his appearance among us makes our victory certain. It is the others, who smile, who go to church, who give no cause for complaint, whom we sometimes consider with amusement, with pity, even with affection—and in whose faces we sometimes surprise the merest arrogant hint of hatred, the faintest, withdrawn, speculative shadow of contempt—who make us uneasy;

whom we cajole, threaten, flatter, fear; who to us remain unknown, though we are not (we feel with both relief and hostility and with bottomless confusion) unknown to them. It is out of our reaction to these hewers of wood and drawers of water that our image of Bigger was created.

It is this image, living yet, which we perpetually seek to evade with good works; and this image which makes of all our good works an intolerable mockery. The "nigger," black, benighted, brutal, consumed with hatred as we are consumed with guilt, cannot be thus blotted out. He stands at our shoulders when we give our maid her wages, it is his hand which we fear we are taking when struggling to communicate with the current "intelligent" Negro, his stench, as it were, which fills our mouths with salt as the monument is unveiled in honor of the latest Negro leader. Each generation has shouted behind him, *Nigger!* as he walked our streets; it is he whom we would rather our sisters did not marry; he is banished into the vast and wailing outer darkness whenever we speak of the "purity" of our women, of the "sanctity" of our homes, of "American" ideals. What is more, he knows it. He is indeed the "native son": he is the "nigger." Let us refrain from inquiring at the moment whether or not he actually exists; for we *believe* that he exists. Whenever we encounter him amongst us in the flesh, our faith is made perfect and his necessary and bloody end is executed with a mystical ferocity of joy.

But there is a complementary faith among the damned which involves their gathering of the stones with which those who walk in the light shall stone them; or there exists among the intolerably degraded the perverse and powerful desire to force into the arena of the actual those fantastic crimes of which they have been accused, achieving their vengeance and their own destruction through making the nightmare real. The American image of the Negro lives also in the Negro's heart; and when he has surrendered to this image life has no other possible reality. Then he, like the white enemy with whom he will be locked one day in mortal struggle, has no means save this of asserting his identity. This is why Bigger's murder of Mary can be referred to as an "act of creation" and why, once this murder has been committed, he can feel for the first time that he is living fully and deeply as a man was meant to live. And there is, I should think, no Negro living in America who has not felt, briefly or for long periods, with anguish sharp or dull, in varying degrees and to varying effect, simple, naked and unanswerable hatred; who has not wanted to smash any white face he may encounter in a day, to violate, out of motives of the cruelest vengeance, their women, to break the bodies of all white people and bring them low, as low as that dust into which he himself has been and is being trampled; no Negro, finally, who has not had to make his own precarious adjustment to the "nigger" who surrounds him and to the "nigger" in himself.

Yet the adjustment must be made—rather, it must be attempted, the tension perpetually sustained—for without this he has surrendered his birthright as a man no less than his birthright as a black man. The entire universe is then peopled only with his enemies, who are not only white men armed with rope and rifle, but his own far-flung and contemptible kinsmen. Their blackness is his degradation and it is their stupid and passive endurance which makes his end inevitable.

Bigger dreams of some black man who will weld all blacks together into a mighty fist, and feels, in relation to his family, that perhaps they had to live as they did precisely because none of them had ever done anything, right or wrong, which mattered very much. It is only he who, by an act of murder, has burst the dungeon cell. He has made it manifest that *he* lives and that his despised blood nourishes the passions of a man. He has forced his oppressors to see the fruit of that oppression: and he feels, when his family and his friends come to visit him in the death cell, that they should not be weeping or frightened, that they should be happy, *proud* that he has dared, through murder and now through his own imminent destruction, to redeem their anger and humiliation, that he has hurled into the spiritless obscurity of their lives the lamp of his passionate life and death. Henceforth, they may remember Bigger—who has died, as we may conclude, for them. But they do not feel this; they only know that he has murdered two women and precipitated a reign of terror; and that now he is to die in the electric chair. They therefore weep and are honestly frightened—for which Bigger despises them and wishes to "blot" them out. What is missing in his situation and in the representation of his psychology—which makes his situation false and his psychology incapable of development—is any revelatory apprehension of Bigger as one of the Negro's realities or as one of the Negro's roles. This failure is part of the previously noted failure to convey any sense of Negro life as a continuing and complex group reality. Bigger, who cannot function therefore as a reflection of the social illness, having, as it were, no society to reflect, likewise refuses to function on the loftier level of the Christ-symbol. His kinsmen are quite right to weep and be frightened, even to be appalled: for it is not his love for them or for himself which causes him to die, but his hatred and his self-hatred; he does not redeem the pains of a despised people, but reveals, on the contrary, nothing more than his own fierce bitterness at having been born one of them. In this also he is the "native son," his progress determinable by the speed with which the distance increases between himself and the auction-block and all that the auction-block implies. To have penetrated this phenomenon, this inward contention of love and hatred, blackness and whiteness, would have given him a stature more nearly human and an end more nearly tragic; and would have given us a document more profoundly and genuinely bitter and less harsh with an anger which is, on the one hand, exhibited and, on the other hand, denied.

Native Son finds itself at length so trapped by the American image of Negro life and by the American necessity to find the ray of hope that it cannot pursue its own implications. This is why Bigger must be at the last redeemed, to be received, if only by rhetoric, into that community of phantoms which is our tenaciously held ideal of the happy social life. It is the socially conscious whites who receive him—the Negroes being capable of no such objectivity—and we have, by way of illustration, that lamentable scene in which Jan, Mary's lover, forgives him for her murder; and, carrying the explicit burden of the novel, Max's long speech to the jury. This speech, which really ends the book, is one of the most desperate performances in American fiction. It is the question of Bigger's humanity which is at stake, the relationship in which he stands to all other Americans—and, by implication, to all people—and it is precisely this question which it cannot clarify, with which it cannot, in fact, come to any coherent terms. He is the monster created by the American republic, the present awful sum of generations of oppression; but to say that he is a monster is to fall into the trap of making him subhuman and he must, therefore, be made representative of a way of life which is real and human in precise ratio to the degree to which it seems to us monstrous and strange. It seems to me that this idea carries, implicitly, a most remarkable confession: that is, that Negro life is in fact as debased and impoverished as our theology claims; and, further, that the use to which Wright puts this idea can only proceed from the assumption—not entirely unsound—that Americans, who evade, so far as possible, all genuine experience, have therefore no way of assessing the experience of others and no way of establishing themselves in relation to any way of life which is not their own. The privacy or obscurity of Negro life makes that life capable, in our imaginations, of producing anything at all; and thus the idea of Bigger's monstrosity can be presented without fear of contradiction, since no American has the knowledge or authority to contest it and no Negro has the voice. It is an idea, which, in the framework of the novel, is dignified by the possibility it promptly affords of presenting Bigger as the herald of disaster, the danger signal of a more bitter time to come when not Bigger alone but all his kindred will rise, in the name of the many thousands who have perished in fire and flood and by rope and torture, to demand their rightful vengeance.

But it is not quite fair, it seems to me, to exploit the national innocence in this way. The idea of Bigger as a warning boomerangs not only because it is quite beyond the limit of probability that Negroes in America will ever achieve the means of wreaking vengeance upon the state but also because it cannot be said that they have any desire to do so. *Native Son* does not convey the altogether savage paradox of the American Negro's situation, of which the social reality which we prefer with such hopeful superficiality to study is but, as it were, the shadow. It is not simply the relationship of oppressed to oppressor, of master to slave, nor is it motivated merely by hatred; it is also, literally and morally, a *blood* relationship, perhaps the most profound reality of the American experience, and we cannot begin to unlock it until we accept how very much it contains of the force and anguish and terror of love.

Negroes are Americans and their destiny is the country's destiny. They have no other experience besides their experience on this continent and it is an experience which cannot be rejected, which yet remains to be embraced. If, as I believe, no American Negro exists who does not have his private Bigger Thomas living in the skull, then what most significantly fails to be illuminated here is the paradoxical adjustment which is perpetually made, the Negro being compelled to accept the fact that this dark and dangerous and unloved stranger is part of himself forever. Only this recognition sets him in any wise free and it is this, this necessary ability to contain and even, in the most honorable sense of the word, to *exploit* the "nigger," which lends to Negro life its high element of the ironic and which causes the most well-meaning of their American critics to make such exhilarating errors when attempting to understand them. To present Bigger as a warning is simply to reinforce the American guilt and fear concerning him, it is most forcefully to limit him to that previously mentioned social arena in which he has no human validity, it is simply to condemn him to death. For he has always been a warning, he represents the evil, the sin and suffering which we are compelled to reject. It is useless to say to the courtroom in which this heathen sits on trial that he is their responsibility, their creation, and his crimes are theirs; and that they ought, therefore, to allow him to live, to make articulate to himself behind the walls of prison the meaning of his existence. The meaning of his existence has already been most adequately expressed, nor does anyone wish, particularly not in the name of democracy, to think of it any more; as for the possibility of articulation, it is this possibility which above all others we most dread. Moreover, the courtroom, judge, jury, witnesses and spectators, recognize immediately that Bigger is their creation and they recognize this not only with hatred and fear and guilt and the resulting fury of self-righteousness but also with that morbid fullness of pride mixed with horror with which one regards the extent and power of one's wickedness. They know that death is his portion, that he runs to death; coming from darkness and dwelling in darkness, he must be, as often as he rises, banished, lest the entire planet be engulfed. And they know, finally, that they do not wish to forgive him and that he does not wish to be forgiven; that he dies, hating them, scorning that appeal which they cannot make to that irrecoverable humanity of his which cannot hear it; and that he *wants* to die because he glories in his hatred and prefers, like Lucifer, rather to rule in hell than serve in heaven.

For, bearing in mind the premise on which the life of such a man is based, *i.e.*, that black is the color of damnation, this is his only possible end. It is the only death which will allow him a kind of dignity or even, however horribly, a kind of beauty. To tell this story, no more than a single aspect of the story of the "nigger," is inevitably and richly to become involved with the force of life and legend, how each perpetually assumes the guise of the other, creating that dense, manysided and shifting reality which is the world we live in and the world we make. To tell his story is to begin to liberate us from his image and it is, for the first time, to clothe this phantom with flesh and blood, to deepen, by our understanding of him and his relationship to us, our understanding of ourselves and of all men.

But this is not the story which *Native Son* tells, for we find here merely, repeated in anger, the story which we have told in pride. Nor, since the implications of this anger are evaded, are we ever confronted with the actual or potential significance of our pride; which is why we fall, with such a positive glow of recognition, upon Max's long and bitter summing up. It is addressed to those among us of good will and it seems to say that, though there are whites and blacks among us who hate each other, we will not; there are those who are betrayed by greed, by guilt, by blood lust, but not we; we will set our faces against them and join hands and walk together into that dazzling future when there will be no white or black. This is the dream of all liberal men, a dream not at all dishonorable, but, nevertheless, a dream. For, let us join hands on this mountain as we may, the battle is elsewhere. It proceeds far from us in the heat and horror and pain of life itself where all men are betrayed by greed and guilt and blood lust and where no one's hands are clean. Our good will, from which we yet expect such power to transform us, is thin, passionless, strident: its roots, examined, lead us back to our forebears, whose assumption it was that the black man, to become truly human and acceptable, must first become like us. This assumption once accepted, the Negro in America can only acquiesce in the obliteration of his own personality, the distortion and debasement of his own experience, surrendering to those forces which reduce the person to anonymity and which make themselves manifest daily all over the darkening world.

Ralph Ellison (1914-   )

A Coupla Scalped Indians

From New World Writing (1956)

They had a small, loud-playing band and as we moved through the trees I could hear the notes of the horns bursting like bright metallic bubbles against the sky. It was a faraway and sparklike sound, shooting through the late afternoon quiet of the hill; very clear now and definitely music, band music. I was relieved. I had been hearing it for several minutes as we moved through the woods but the pain down there had made all my senses so deceptively sharp that I had decided that the sound was simply a musical ringing in my ears. But now I was doubly sure, for Buster stopped and looked at me, squinching up his eyes with his head cocked to one side. He was wearing a blue cloth headband with a turkey feather stuck over his ear, and I could see it flutter in the breeze.

"You hear what I hear, man?" he said.

"I *been* hearing it," I said.

"Damn! We better haul it outta these woods so we can see something. Why didn't you say something to a man?"

We moved again, hurrying along. Until suddenly we were out of the woods, standing at a point of the hill where the path dropped down to the town, our eyes searching. It was close to sundown and below me I could see the red clay of the path cutting through the woods and moving past a white, lightning-blasted tree to join the river road, and the narrow road shifting past Aunt Mackie's old shack and on, beyond the road and the shack, I could see the dull mysterious movement of the river. The horns were blasting brighter now, though still far away, sounding like somebody flipping bright handfuls of new small change against the sky. I listened and followed the river swiftly with my eyes as it wound through the trees and on past the buildings and houses of the town—until there, there at the farther edge of the town, past the tall smokestack and the great silver sphere of the gas storage tower, floated the tent, spread white and cloudlike with its bright ropes of fluttering flags.

That's when we started running. It was a dogtrotting Indian run, because we were both wearing packs and were tired from the test we had been taking in the woods and in Indian Lake. But now the bright blare of the horns made us forget our tiredness and pain and we bounded down the path like young goats in the twilight; our army-surplus mess kits and canteens rattling against us.

"We late, man," Buster said. "I told you we was gon' fool around and be late. But naw, you had to cook that damn sage hen with mud on him just like it says in the book. We coulda barbecued a damn elephant while we was waiting for a tough sucker like that to get done. . . ."

His voice grumbled on like a trombone with a big, fat, pot-shaped mute stuck in it and I ran on without answering. We had tried to take the cooking test by using a sage hen instead of a chicken because Buster said Indians didn't eat chicken. Se we'd taken time to flush a sage hen and kill him with a slingshot. Besides, he was the one who insisted that we try the running endurance test, the swimming test, *and* the cooking test all in one day. Sure it had taken time. I knew it would take time; especially with our having no Scout Master. We didn't even have a troop, only the Boy Scout's Handbook that Buster had found, and—as we'd figured—our hardest problem had been working out the tests for ourselves. He had no right to argue anyway, since he'd beaten me in all the tests—although I'd passed them too. And he was the one who insisted that we start taking them today, even though we were both still sore and wearing our bandages, and I was still carrying some of the catgut stitches around in me. I had wanted to wait a few days until I was healed but Mister Know-it-all Buster challenged me by saying that a real stud Indian could take the tests even right after the doctor had just finished sewing on him. So, since we were more interested in being *Indian* scouts than simply *boy* scouts, here I was running toward the spring carnival instead of being already there. I wondered how Buster knew so much about what an Indian would do, anyway. We certainly hadn't read anything about what the doctor had done to us. He'd probably made it up and I had let him urge me into going to the woods even though I had to slip out of the house. The doctor had told Miss Janey (she's the lady who takes care of me) to keep me quiet for a few days and she dead-aimed to do it. You would've thought from the way she carried on that she was the one who had the operation—only that's one kind of operation no woman ever gets to brag about.

Anyway, Buster and me had been in the woods and now we were plunging down the hill through the fast-falling dark to the carnival. I had begun to throb and the bandage was chafing but as we rounded a curve I could see the tent and the flares and the gathering crowd. There was a breeze coming up the hill against us now and I could almost smell that cotton candy, the hamburgers, and the kerosene smell of the flares. We stopped to rest and Buster stood very straight and pointed down below, making a big sweep with his arm like an Indian chief in the movies when he's up on a hill telling his braves and the Great Spirit that he's getting ready to attack a wagon train.

"Heap big . . . teepee . . . down yonder," he said in Indian talk. "Smoke signal say . . . Blackfeet . . . make . . . heap much . . . stink, buck-dancing in tennis shoes!"

"Ugh," I said, bowing my suddenly war-bonneted head, "ugh!"

Buster swept his arm from east to west, his face impassive, "Smoke medicine say . . . heap . . . *Big* stink! Hot toe jam!" He struck his palm with his fist and I looked at his puffed-out cheeks and giggled.

"Smoke medicine say you tell heap big lie," I said. "Let's get on down there."

We ran past some trees, Buster's canteen jangling. Around us it was quiet except for the roosting birds.

"Man," I said, "you making as much noise as a team of mules in full harness. Don't no Indian scout make all that racket when he runs."

"No scout-um now," he said. "Me go make heap much pow-wow at stinkydog carnival!"

"Yeah, but you'll get yourself scalped, making all that noise in the woods," I said. "Those other Indians don't give a damn 'bout no carnival—what does a carnival mean to them? They'll scalp the hell outta you!"

"Scalp?" he said, talking Colored now, "Hell, man—that damn doctor scalped me last week. Damn near took my whole head off!"

I almost fell with laughing. "Have mercy, Lord," I laughed, "we're just a coupla poor scalped Indians!"

We laughed. Buster stumbled about, grabbing a tree for support. The doctor had said that it would make us men and Buster had said, hell, he was a man already—what he wanted was to be an Indian. We hadn't thought about it making us scalped ones.

"You right, man," Buster said. "Since he done scalped so much of my head away I must be crazy as a fool. That's why I'm in such a hurry to get down yonder with the other crazy folks. I want to be right in the middle of 'em when they really start raising hell."

"Oh, you'll be there, Chief Baldhead," I said.

He looked at me blankly. "What you think ole Doc done with our scalps?"

"Made him a tripe stew, man."

"You nuts," Buster said, "he probably used 'em for fish bait."

"He did I'm going to sue him for one trillion, zillion dollars, cash," I said.

"Maybe he gave 'em to ole Aunt Mackie, man. I bet with them she could work up some out*rageous* spells!"

"Man," I said, suddenly shivering, "don't talk about that old woman, she's evil."

"Hell, everybody's so scared of her. I just wish she'd mess with me or my daddy, I'd fix her."

I said nothing—I was afraid. For though I had seen the old woman about town all my life she remained to me like the moon, mysterious in her very familiarity; and in the sound of her name there was terror:

Ho, Aunt Mackie, talker-with-spirits, prophetess-of-disaster, odd-dweller-alone in a riverside shack surrounded by sunflowers, morning-glories, and strange magical weeds (Yao, as Buster during our Indian phase, would have put it, Yao!); *Old Aunt Mackie, wizen-faced walker-with-a-stick, shrill-voiced ranter in the night, round-eyed malicious one, given to dramatic trances and fiery flights of rage; Aunt Mackie, preacher of wild sermons on the busy streets of the town, hot-voiced chaser of children, snuff-dipper, visionary; wearer of greasy headrags, wrinkled gingham aprons and old men's shoes; Aunt Mackie, nobody's sister but still Aunt Mackie to us all* (Ho, yao!); *teller of fortunes, concocter of powerful, body-rending spells* (Yao, Yao!); *Aunt Mackie, the remote one though always seen about us; night-consulted adviser to farmers on crops and cattle* (Yao!); *herb-healer, root-doctor, and town-confounding oracle to wildcat drillers seeking oil in the earth*—(Yaaaah-Ho!). It was all there in her name and before her name I shivered. Once uttered, for me the palaver was finished; I resigned it to Buster, the tough one.

Even some of the grown folks, both black and white, were afraid of Aunt Mackie, and all the kids except Buster. Buster lived on the outskirts of the town and was as unimpressed by Aunt Mackie as by the truant officers and others whom the rest of us regarded with awe. And because I was his buddy I was ashamed of my fear.

Usually I had extra courage when I was with him. Like the time two years before when we had gone into the woods with only our slingshots, a piece of fatback, and a skillet and had lived three days on the rabbits we killed and the wild berries we picked and the ears of corn we raided from farmers' fields. We slept each rolled in his quilt and in the night Buster had told bright stories of the world we'd find when we were grown-up and gone from hometown and family. I had no family, only Miss Janey, who took me after my mother died (I didn't know my father), so that getting away always appealed to me, and the coming time of which Buster liked to talk loomed in the darkness around me rich with pastel promise. And although we heard a bear go lumbering through the woods nearby and the eerie howling of a coyote in the dark, yes, and had been swept by the soft swift flight of an owl, Buster was unafraid and I had grown brave in the grace of his courage.

But to me Aunt Mackie was a threat of a different order, and I paid her the respect of fear.

"Listen to those horns," Buster said. And now the sound came through the trees like colored marbles glinting in the summer sun.

We ran again. And now keeping pace with Buster I felt good; for I meant to be there too, at the carnival; right in the middle of all that confusion and sweating and laughing and all the strange sights to see.

"Listen to 'em now, man," Buster said. "Those fools is starting to shout amazing grace on those horns. Let's step on the gas!"

The scene danced below us as we ran. Suddenly there was a towering Ferris wheel revolving slowly out of the dark, its red and blue lights glowing like drops of dew dazzling a big spider web when you see it in the early morning. And we heard the beckoning blare of the band now shot through with the small, insistent, buckshot voices of the barkers.

"Listen to that trombone, man," I said.

"Sounds like he's playing the dozens with the whole wide world."

"What's he saying, Buster?"

"He's saying. 'Ya'll's mamas don't wear 'em. Is strictly without 'em. Don't know nothing 'bout 'em. . . .'"

"Don't know about what, man?"

"Draw's, fool; he's talking 'bout draw's!"

"How you know, man?"

"I hear him talking, don't I?"

"Sure, but you been scalped, remember? You crazy. How he know about those peoples' mamas?" I said.

"Says he saw 'em with his great big ole eye."

"Damn! He must be a Peeping Tom. How about those other horns?"

"Now that there tuba's saying:

> "They don't play 'em, I know they don't.
> They don't play 'em, I know they won't.
> They just don't play no nasty dirty twelves. . . ."

"Man, you *are* a scalped-headed fool. How about that trumpet?"

"Him? That fool's a soldier, he's realy signifying. Saying,

> "So ya'll don't play 'em, hey?
> So ya'll *won't* play 'em, hey?
> Well pat your feet and clap your hands,
> 'Cause I'm going to play 'em to the promised land. . . .

"Man, the white folks know what that fool is signifying on that horn they'd run him clear on out the world. Trumpet's got a real *nasty* mouth."

"Why you call him a soldier, man?" I said.

" 'Cause he's slipping 'em in the twelves and choosing 'em, all at the same time. Talking 'bout they mamas and offering to fight 'em. Now he ain't like that ole clarinet; clarinet so sweet-talking he just *eases* you in the dozens."

"Say, Buster," I said, seriously now. "You know, we gotta stop cussing and playing the dozens if we're going to be boy scouts. Those white boys don't play that mess."

"You doggone right they don't," he said, the turkey feather vibrating above his ear. "Those guys can't take it, man. Besides, who wants to be just like them? Me, *I'm* gon' be a scout and play the twelves too! You have to, with some of these old jokers we know. You don't know what to say when they start easing you, you never have no peace. You have to outtalk 'em, outrun 'em, or outfight 'em and I don't aim to be running and fighting all the time. N'mind those white boys."

We moved on through the growing dark. Already I could see a few stars and suddenly there was the moon. It emerged bladelike from behind a thin veil of cloud, just as I heard a new sound and looked about me with quick uneasiness. Off to our left I heard a dog, a big one. I slowed, seeing the outlines of a picket fence and the odd-shaped shadows that lurked in Aunt Mackie's yard.

"What's the matter, man?" Buster said.

"Listen," I said. "That's Aunt Mackie's dog. Last year I was passing here and he sneaked up and bit me through the fence when I wasn't even thinking about him. . . ."

"Hush, man," Buster whispered, "I hear the sonofabitch back in there now. You leave him to me."

We moved by inches now, hearing the dog barking in the dark. Then we were going past and he was throwing his heavy body against the fence, straining at his chain. We hesitated, Buster's hand on my arm. I undid my heavy canteen belt and held it, suddenly light in my fingers. In my right I gripped the hatchet which I'd brought along.

"We'd better go back and take the other path," I whispered.

"Just stand still, man," Buster said.

The dog hit the fence again, barking hoarsely; and in the interval following the echoing crash I could hear the distant music of the band.

"Come on," I said, "let's go 'round."

"Hell, no! We're going straight! I ain't letting no damn dog scare me, Aunt Mackie or no Aunt Mackie. Come on!"

Trembling, I moved with him toward the roaring dog, then felt him stop again, and I could hear him removing his pack and taking out something wrapped in paper.

"Here," he said, "you take my stuff and come on."

I took his gear and went behind him, hearing his voice suddenly hot with fear and anger saying, "Here, you 'gator-mouthed egg-sucker, see how you like this sage hen," just as I tripped over the straps of his pack and went down. Then I was crawling frantically, trying to untangle myself and hearing the dog growling as he crunched something in his jaws. "Eat it, you buzzard," Buster was saying, "See if you tough as he is," as I tried to stand, stumbling and sending an old cooking range crashing in the dark. Part of the fence was gone and in my panic I had crawled into the yard. Now I could hear the dog bark threateningly and leap the length of his chain toward me, then back to the sage hen; toward me, a swift leaping form snatched backwards by the heavy chain, turning to mouth savagely on the mangled bird. Moving away I floundered over the stove and pieces of crating, against giant sunflower stalks, trying to get back to Buster when I saw the lighted window and realized that I had crawled to the very shack itself. That's when I pressed against the weathered-satin side of the shack and came erect. And there, framed by the window in the lamp-lit room, I saw the woman.

A brown naked woman, whose black hair hung beneath her shoulders. I could see the long graceful curve of her back as she moved in some sort of slow dance, bending forward and back; her arms and body moving as though gathering in something which I couldn't see but which she drew to her with pleasure; a young, girlish body with slender, well-rounded hips. *But who?* flashed through my mind as I heard Buster's *Hey, man; where'd you go? You done run out on me?* from back in the dark. And I willed to move, to hurry away—but in that instant she chose to pick up a glass from a wobbly old round white table and to drink, turning slowly as she stood with backward-tilted head, slowly turning in the lamp-light and drinking slowly as she turned, slowly; until I could see the full-faced glowing of her feminine form.

And I was frozen there, watching the uneven movement of her breasts beneath the glistening course of the liquid, spilling down her body in twin streams drawn by the easy tiding of her breathing. Then the glass came down and my knees flowed beneath me like water. The air seemed to explode soundlessly. I shook my head but she, the image, would not go away and I wanted suddenly to laugh wildly and to scream. For above the smooth shoulders of the girlish form I saw the wrinkled face of old Aunt Mackie.

Now I had never seen a naked woman before, only very little girls or once or twice a skinny one my own age, who looked like a boy with the boy part missing. And even though I'd seen a few calendar drawings they were not alive like this, nor images of someone you'd thought familiar through having seen them passing through the streets of the town; nor like this inconsistent, with wrinkled face mismatched with glowing form. So that mixed with my fear of punishment for peeping there was added the terror of her mystery. And yet I could not move away. I was fascinated, hearing the growling dog and feeling a warm pain grow beneath my bandage—along with the newly risen terror that this deceptive old woman could cause me to feel this way, that she could be so young beneath her old baggy clothes.

She was dancing again now, still unaware of my eyes, the lamplight playing on her body as she swayed and enfolded the air or invisible ghosts or whatever it was, within her arms. Each time she moved, her hair, which was black as night now that it was no longer hidden beneath a greasy headrag, swung heavily about her shoulders. And as she moved to the side I could see the gentle tossing of her breasts beneath her upraised arms. *It just can't be,* I thought, *it just can't* and moved closer, determined to see and to know. But I had forgotten the hatchet in my hand until it struck the side of the house and I saw her turn quickly toward the window, her face evil as she swayed. I was rigid as stone, hearing the growling dog mangling the bird and knowing that I should run even as she moved toward the window, her shadow flying before her, her hair now wild as snakes writhing on a dead tree during a springtime flood. Then I could hear Buster's hoarse-voiced, *Hey, man! where in hell are you?* even as she pointed at me and screamed, sending me moving backwards and I was aware of the sickle-bladed moon flying like a lightning flash as I fell, still gripping my hatchet, and struck my head in the dark.

When I started out of it someone was holding me and I lay in light and looked up to see her face above me. Then it all flooded swiftly back and I was aware again of the contrast between smooth body and wrinkled face and experienced a sudden warm yet painful thrill. She held me close. Her breath came to me, sweetly alcoholic as she mumbled something about, "Little devil, lips that touch wine shall never touch mine! That's what I told him, understand me? Never," she said loudly. "You understand?"

"Yes, ma'm. . . ."

"Never, never, NEVER!"

"No, ma'm." I said, seeing her study me with narrowed eyes.

"You young but you young'uns understand, devilish as you is. What you doing messing 'round in my yard?"

"I got lost," I said. "I was coming from taking some boy scout tests and I was trying to get by your dog."

"So that's what I heard," she said. "He bite you?"

"No, ma'm."

"Course not, he don't bite on the new moon. No, I think you come in my yard to spy on me."

"No, ma'm, I didn't," I said. "I just happened to see the light when I was stumbling around trying to find my way."

"You got a pretty big hatchet there," she said, looking down at my hand. "What you plan to do with it?"

"It's a kind of boy scout axe," I said. "I used it to come through the woods. . . ."

She looked at me dubiously, "So," she said, "you're a heavy hatchet man and you stopped to peep. Well, what I want to know is, is you a drinking man? Have your lips ever touched wine?"

"Wine? No, ma'm."

"So you ain't a drinking man, but do you belong to church?"

"Yes, ma'm."

"And have you been saved and ain't no backslider?"

"Yessum."

"Well," she said, pursing her lips, "I guess you can kiss me."

"MA'M?"

"That's what I said. You passed all the tests and you was peeping in my window. . . ."

She was holding me there on a cot, her arms around me as though I were a three-year-old, smiling like a girl. I could see her fine white teeth and the long hairs on her chin and it was like a bad dream. "You peeped," she said, "now you got to do the rest. I said kiss me, or I'll fix you. . . ."

I saw her face come close and felt her warm breath and closed my eyes, trying to force myself. *It's just like kissing some sweaty woman at church,* I told myself, *some friend of Miss Janey's.* But it didn't help and I could feel her drawing me and I found her lips with mine. It was dry and firm and winey and I could hear her sigh. "Again," she said, and once more my lips found hers. And suddenly she drew me to her and I could feel her breasts soft against me as once more she sighed.

"That was a nice boy," she said, her voice kind, and I opened my eyes. "That's enough now, you're both too young and too old, but you're brave. A regular lil' chocolate hero."

And now she moved and I realized for the first time that my hand had found its way to her breast. I moved it guiltily, my face flaming as she stood.

"You're a good brave boy," she said, looking at me from deep in her eyes, "but you forget what happened here tonight."

I sat up as she stood looking down upon me with a mysterious smile. And I could see her body up close now, in the dim yellow light; see the surprising silkiness of black hair mixed here and there with gray, and suddenly I was crying and hating myself for the compelling need. I looked at my hatchet lying on the floor now and wondered how she'd gotten me into the shack as the tears blurred my eyes.

"What's the matter, boy?" she said. And I had no words to answer.

"What's the matter, I say!"

"I'm hurting in my operation," I said desperately, knowing that my tears were too complicated to put into any words I knew.

"Operation? Where?"

I looked away.

"Where you hurting, boy?" she demanded.

I looked into her eyes and they seemed to flood through me, until reluctantly I pointed toward my pain.

"Open it, so's I can see," she said. "You know I'm a healer, don't you?"

I bowed my head, still hesitating.

"Well open it then. How'm I going to see with all those clothes on you?"

My face burned like fire now and the pain seemed to ease as a dampness grew beneath the bandage. But she would not be denied and I undid myself and saw a red stain on the gauze. I lay there ashamed to raise my eyes.

"Hmmmmmmmm," she said, "a fishing worm with a headache!" And I couldn't believe my ears. Then she was looking into my eyes and grinning.

"Pruned," she cackled in her high, old woman's voice, "pruned. Boy, you have been pruned. I'm a doctor but no tree surgeon—No, lay still a second."

She paused and I saw her hand come forward, three claw-like fingers taking me gently as she examined the bandage.

And I was both ashamed and angry and now I stared at her out of a quick resentment and a defiant pride. *I'm a man*, I said within myself. *Just the same I am a man!* But I could only stare at her face briefly as she looked at me with a gleam in her eyes. Then my eyes fell and I forced myself to look boldly at her now, very brown in the lamplight, with all the complicated apparatus within the globular curvatures of flesh and vessel exposed to my eyes. I was filled then with a deeper sense of the mystery of it too, for now it was as though the nakedness was nothing more than another veil; much like the old baggy dresses she always wore. Then across the curvature of her stomach I saw a long, puckered, crescent-shaped scar.

"How old are you, boy?" she said, her eyes suddenly round.

"Eleven," I said. And it was as though I had fired a shot.

"Eleven! Git out of here," she screamed, stumbling backwards, her eyes wide upon me as she felt for the glass on the table to drink. Then she snatched an old gray robe from a chair, fumbling for the tie cord which wasn't there. I moved, my eyes upon her as I knelt for my hatchet and felt the pain come sharp. Then I straightened, trying to arrange my knickers.

"You go now, you little rascal," she said. "Hurry and git out of here. And if I ever hear of you saying anything about me I'll fix your daddy and your mammy too. I'll fix 'em, you hear?"

"Yes, ma'm," I said, feeling that I had suddenly lost the courage of my manhood, now that my bandage was hidden and her secret body gone behind her old gray robe. But how could she fix my father when I didn't have one? Or my mother, when she was dead?

I moved, backing out of the door into the dark. Then she slammed the door and I saw the light grow intense in the window and there was her face looking out at me and I could not tell if she frowned or smiled but in the glow of the lamp the wrinkles were not there. I stumbled over the packs now and gathered them up, leaving.

This time the dog raised up, huge in the dark, his green eyes glowing as he gave me a low disinterested growl. *Buster really must have fixed you*, I thought, *But where'd he go?* Then I was past the fence into the road.

I wanted to run but was afraid of starting the pain again, and as I moved I kept seeing her as she'd appeared with her back turned toward me, the sweet undrunken movements that she made. It had been like someone dancing by herself and yet like praying without kneeling down. Then she had turned, exposing her familiar face. I moved faster now and suddenly all my senses seemed to sing alive. I heard a night bird's song, the lucid call of a quail arose. And from off to my right in the river there came the leap of a moon-mad fish and I could see the spray arch up and away. There was wisteria in the air and the scent of moonflowers. And now moving through the dark I recalled the warm, intriguing smell of her body and suddenly, with the shout of the carnival coming to me again, the whole thing became thin and dreamlike. The images flowed in my mind, became shadowy, no part was left to fit another. But still there was my pain and here was I, running through the dark toward the small, loud-playing band. It was real, I knew, and I stopped in the path and looked back, seeing the black outlines of the shack and the thin moon above. Behind the shack the hill arose with the shadowy woods and I knew the lake was still hidden there, reflecting the moon. All was real.

And for a moment I felt much older, as though I had lived swiftly long years into the future and had been as swiftly pushed back again. I tried to remember how it had been when I kissed her, but on my lips my tongue found only the faintest trace of wine. But for that it was gone, and I thought forever, except the memory of the scraggly hairs on her chin. Then I was again aware of the imperious calling of the horns and moved again toward the carnival. Where was that other scalped Indian, where had Buster gone?

Gwendolyn Brooks (1917-   )

A Bronzeville Mother Loiters in Mississippi.
Meanwhile, a Mississippi Mother Burns Bacon.

From The Bean Eaters (1959)

From the first it had been like a
Ballad. It had the beat inevitable. It had the blood.
A wildness cut up, and tied in little bunches,
Like the four-line stanzas of the ballads she had never quite
Understood—the ballads they had set her to, in school.

Herself: the milk-white maid, the "maid mild"
Of the ballad. Pursued
By the Dark Villain. Rescued by the Fine Prince.
The Happiness-Ever-After.
That was worth anything.
It was good to be a "maid mild."
That made the breath go fast.

Her bacon burned. She
Hastened to hide it in the step-on can, and
Drew more strips from the meat case. The eggs and sour-milk
        biscuits
Did well. She set out a jar
Of her new quince preserve.

. . . But there was a something about the matter of the Dark
        Villain.
He should have been older, perhaps.
The hacking down of a villain was more fun to think about
When his menace possessed undisputed breadth, undisputed height,
And a harsh kind of vice.
And best of all, when his history was cluttered
With the bones of many eaten knights and princesses.

The fun was disturbed, then all but nullified
When the Dark Villain was a blackish child
Of fourteen, with eyes still too young to be dirty,
And a mouth too young to have lost every reminder
Of its infant softness.

That boy must have been surprised! For
These were grown-ups. Grown-ups were supposed to be wise.
And the Fine Prince—and that other—so tall, so broad, so
Grown! Perhaps the boy had never guessed
That the trouble with grown-ups was that under the magnificent
        shell of adulthood, just under,
Waited the baby full of tantrums.
It occurred to her that there may have been something
Ridiculous in the picture of the Fine Prince
Rushing (rich with the breadth and height and
Mature solidness whose lack, in the Dark Villain, was impressing
        her,

Confronting her more and more as this first day after the trial
And acquittal wore on) rushing
With his heavy companion to hack down (unhorsed)
That little foe.
So much had happened, she could not remember now what that
          foe had done
Against her, or if anything had been done.
The one thing in the world that she did know and knew
With terrifying clarity was that her composition
Had disintegrated. That, although the pattern prevailed,
The breaks were everywhere. That she could think
Of no thread capable of the necessary
Sew-work.

She made the babies sit in their places at the table.
Then, before calling Him, she hurried
To the mirror with her comb and lipstick. It was necessary
To be more beautiful than ever.
The beautiful wife.
For sometimes she fancied he looked at her as though
Measuring her. As if he considered, Had she been worth It?
Had *she* been worth the blood, the cramped cries, the little
          stuttering bravado,
The gradual dulling of those Negro eyes,
The sudden, overwhelming *little-boyness* in that barn?
Whatever she might feel or half-feel, the lipstick necessity was
          something apart. He must never conclude
That she had not been worth It.

He sat down, the Fine Prince, and
Began buttering a biscuit. He looked at his hands.

He twisted in his chair, he scratched his nose.
He glanced again, almost secretly, at his hands.
More papers were in from the North, he mumbled. More meddling
          headlines.
With their pepper-words, "bestiality," and "barbarism," and
"Shocking."
The half-sneers he had mastered for the trial worked across
His sweet and pretty face.

What he'd like to do, he explained, was kill them all.
The time lost. The unwanted fame.

Still, it had been fun to show those intruders
A thing or two. To show that snappy-eyed mother,
That sassy, Northern, brown-black—

Nothing could stop Mississippi.
He knew that. Big Fella
Knew that.
And, what was so good, Mississippi knew that.
Nothing and nothing could stop Mississippi.
They could send in their petitions, and scar
Their newspapers with bleeding headlines. Their governors
Could appeal to Washington . . .

"What I want," the older baby said, "is 'lasses on my jam."
Whereupon the younger baby
Picked up the molasses pitcher and threw
The molasses in his brother's face. Instantly
The Fine Prince leaned across the table and slapped
The small and smiling criminal.

She did not speak. When the Hand
Came down and away, and she could look at her child,
At her baby-child,
She could think only of blood.
Surely her baby's cheek
Had disappeared, and in its place, surely,
Hung a heaviness, a lengthening red, a red that had no end.
She shook her head. It was not true, of course.
It was not true at all. The
Child's face was as always, the
Color of the paste in her paste-jar.

She left the table, to the tune of the children's lamentations, which
        were shriller
Than ever. She
Looked out of a window. She said not a word. *That*
Was one of the new Somethings—
The fear,
Tying her as with iron.

Suddenly she felt his hands upon her. He had followed her
To the window. The children were whimpering now.
Such bits of tots. And she, their mother,

Could not protect them. She looked at her shoulders, still
Gripped in the claim of his hands. She tried, but could not resist
    the idea
That a red ooze was seeping, spreading darkly, thickly, slowly,
Over her white shoulders, her own shoulders,
And over all of Earth and Mars.

He whispered something to her, did the Fine Prince, something
About love, something about love and night and intention.
She heard no hoof-beat of the horse and saw no flash of the
    shining steel.

He pulled her face around to meet
His, and there it was, close close,
For the first time in all those days and nights.
His mouth, wet and red,
So very, very, very red,
Closed over hers.

Then a sickness heaved within her. The courtroom Coca-Cola,
The courtroom beer and hate and sweat and drone,
Pushed like a wall against her. She wanted to bear it.
But his mouth would not go away and neither would the
Decapitated exclamation points in that Other Woman's eyes.

She did not scream.
She stood there.
But a hatred for him burst into glorious flower,
And its perfume enclasped them—big,
Bigger than all magnolias.

The last bleak news of the ballad.
The rest of the rugged music.
The last quatrain.

The Second Sermon on the Warpland

(For Walter Bradford)

From In the Mecca (1968)

1.

This is the urgency: Live!
and have your blooming in the noise of the whirlwind.

2.

Salve salvage in the spin.
Endorse the splendor splashes;
stylize the flawed utility;
prop a malign or failing light—
but know the whirlwind is our commonwealth.
Not the easy man, who rides above them all,
not the jumbo brigand,
not the pet bird of poets, that sweetest sonnet,
shall straddle the whirlwind.
Nevertheless, live.

3.

All about are the cold places,
all about are the pushmen and jeopardy, theft—
all about are the stormers and scramblers but
what must our Season be, which starts from Fear?
Live and go out.
Define and
medicate the whirlwind.

4.

The time
cracks into furious flower. Lifts its face
all unashamed. And sways in wicked grace.
Whose half-black hands assemble oranges
is tom-tom hearted
(goes in bearing oranges and boom).
And there are bells for orphans—
and red and shriek and sheen.
A garbageman is dignified
as any diplomat.
Big Bessie's feet hurt like nobody's business,
but she stands—bigly—under the unruly scrutiny, stands in the
        wild weed.

In the wild weed
she is a citizen,
and is a moment of highest quality; admirable.

It is lonesome, yes. For we are the last of the loud.
Nevertheless, live.

Conduct your blooming in the noise and whip of the whirlwind.

Dudley Randall (1914-   )

Ballad of Birmingham (1966)

(On the bombing of a church in Birmingham)

From Poem Counterpoem (1966)

"Mother dear, may I go downtown
Instead of out to play,
And march the streets of Birmingham
In the Freedom March today?"

"No, baby, no, you may not go,
For the dogs are fierce and wild,
And clubs and hoses, guns and jails
Aren't good for a little child."

"But, mother, I won't be alone.
More children will go with me,
And march the streets of Birmingham
To make our country free."

"No, baby, no, you may not go,
For I fear those guns will fire.
But you may go to church instead
And sing in the children's choir."

She's combed and brushed her night-dark hair,
And bathed rose petal sweet,
And drawn white gloves on her small brown hands,
And white shoes on her feet.

The mother smiled to know her child
Was in the sacred place,
But that smile was the last smile
To come upon her face.

For when she heard the explosion,
Her eyes grew wet and wild.
She raced through the streets of Birmingham
Calling for her child.

She clawed in bits of glass and brick,
Then lifted out a shoe.
"O, here's a shoe, but where's the foot,
And, baby, where are you?"

Primitives

From Cities Burning (1968)

Paintings with stiff
homuncules, flat in iron
draperies, with distorted
bodies against spaceless
landscapes.

Poems of old
poets in stiff
metres whose harsh
syllables
drag like
dogs with
crushed
backs.

We go back to
them, spurn difficult
grace and
symmetry,
paint tri-faced
monsters,
write lines that
do not sing, or
even croak, but that

bump,
jolt, and are hacked
off in the mid-
dle, as if by these dis-
tortions, this
magic, we can
exorcise
horror, which we
have seen and fear to
see again:

hate deified,
fears and
guilt conquering,
turning cities to
gas, powder and a
little rubble.

John O. Killens (1916-   )

God Bless America

From The California Quarterly (1952)

Joe's dark eyes searched frantically for Cleo as he marched with the other Negro soldiers up the long thoroughfare towards the boat. Women were running out to the line of march, crying and laughing and kissing the men good-by. But where the hell was Cleo?

Beside him Luke Robinson, big and fat, nibbled from a carton of Baby Ruth candy as he walked. But Joe's eyes kept traveling up and down the line of civilians on either side of the street. She would be along here somewhere; any second now she would come calmly out of the throng and walk alongside him till they reached the boat. Joe's mind made a picture of her, and she looked the same as last night when he left her. As he had walked away, with the brisk California night air biting into his warm body, he had turned for one last glimpse of her in the doorway, tiny and smiling and waving good-by.

They had spent last night sitting in the little two-by-four room where they had lived for three months with hardly enough space to move around. He had rented it and sent for her when he came to California and learned that his outfit was training for immediate shipment to Korea, and they had lived there fiercely and desperately, like they were trying to live a whole lifetime. But last night they had sat on the side of the big iron bed, making conversation, half-listening to a portable radio, acting like it was just any night. Play-acting like in the movies.

It was late in the evening when he asked her, "How's little Joey acting lately?"

She looked down at herself. "Oh, pal Joey is having himself a ball." She smiled, took Joe's hand, and placed it on her belly; and he felt movement and life. His and her life, and he was going away from it and from her, maybe forever.

Cleo said, "He's trying to tell you good-by, darling." And she sat very still and seemed to ponder over her own words. And then all of a sudden she burst into tears.

She was in his arms and her shoulders shook. "It isn't fair! Why can't they take the ones that aren't married?"

He hugged her tight, feeling a great fullness in his throat. "Come on now, stop crying, hon. Cut it out, will you? I'll be back home before little Joey sees daylight."

"You may never come back. They're killing a lot of our boys over there. Oh, Joe, Joe, why did they have to go and start another war?"

In a gruff voice he said, "Don't you go worrying about Big Joey. He'll take care of himself. You just take care of little Joey and Cleo. That's what you do."

"Don't take any chances, Joe. Don't be a hero!"

He forced himself to laugh, and hugged her tighter. "Don't you worry about the mule going blind."

She made herself stop crying and wiped her face. "But I don't understand, Joe. I don't understand what colored soldiers have to fight for—especially against other colored people."

"Honey," said Joe gently, "we got to fight like anybody else. We can't just sit on the sidelines."

But she just looked at him and shook her head.

"Look," he said, "when I get back I'm going to finish college. I'm going to be a lawyer. That's what I'm fighting for."

She kept shaking her head as if she didn't hear him. "I don't know, Joe. Maybe it's because we were brought up kind of different, you and I. My father died when I was four. My mother worked all her life in white folks' kitchens. I just did make it through high school. You had it a whole lot better than most Negro boys." She went over to the box of Kleenex and blew her nose.

"I don't see where that has a thing to do with it."

He stared at her, angry with her for being so obstinate. Couldn't she see any progress at all? Look at Jackie Robinson. Look at Ralph Bunche. Goddamn it! they'd been over it all before. What did she want him to do about it anyway? Become a deserter?

She stood up over him. "Can't see it, Joe—just can't see it! I want you here, Joe. Here with me where you belong. Don't leave me, Joe! Please——" She was crying now. "Joe, Joe, what're we going to do? Maybe it would be better to get rid of little Joey——" Her brown eyes were wide with terror. "No, Joe, No! I didn't mean that! I didn't mean it, darling! Don't know what I'm saying . . ."

She sat down beside him, bent over, her face in her hands. It was terrible for him, seeing her this way. He got up and walked from one side of the little room to the other. He thought about what the white captain from Hattiesburg, Mississippi, had said. "Men, we have a job to do. Our outfit is just as damn important as any outfit in the United States Army, white or colored. And we're working towards complete integration. It's a long, hard pull, but I guarantee you every soldier will be treated equally and without discrimination. Remember, we're fighting for the dignity of the individual." Luke Robinson had looked at the tall, lanky captain with an arrogant smile.

Joe stopped in front of Cleo and made himself speak calmly. "Look, hon, it isn't like it used to be at all. Why can't you take my word for it? They're integrating colored soldiers now. And anyhow, what the hell's the use of getting all heated up about it? I *got* to go. That's all there is to it."

He sat down beside her again. He wanted fiercely to believe that things were really changing for his kind of people. Make it easier for him—make it much easier for him and Cleo, if they both believed that colored soldiers had a stake in fighting the war in Korea. Cleo wiped her eyes and blew her nose, and they changed the subject, talked about the baby, suppose it turned out to be a girl, what would her name be? A little after midnight he kissed her good-night and walked back to the barracks.

The soldiers were marching in full field dress, with packs on their backs, duffle-bags on their shoulders, and carbines and rifles. As they approached the big white ship, there was talking and joke-cracking and nervous laughter. They were the leading Negro outfit, immediately following the last of the white troops. Even at route step there was a certain uniform cadence in the sound of their feet striking the asphalt road as they moved forward under the midday sun, through a long funnel of people and palm trees and shrubbery. But Joe hadn't spotted Cleo yet, and he was getting sick from worry. Had anything happened?

Luke Robinson, beside him, was talking and laughing and grumbling. "Boy, I'm telling you, these peoples is a bitch on wheels. Say, Office Willie, what you reckon I read in your Harlem paper last night?" Office Willie was his nickname for Joe because Joe was the company clerk—a high-school graduate, two years in college, something special. "I read where some of your folks' leaders called on the President and demanded that colored soldiers be allowed to fight at the front instead of in quartermaster. Ain't that a damn shame?"

Joe's eyes shifted distractedly from the line of people to Luke, and back to the people again.

"Percy Johnson can have my uniform any day in the week," said Luke. "He want to fight so bad. Them goddamn Koreans ain't done me nothing. I ain't mad with a living ass."

Joe liked Luke Robinson, only he was so damn sensitive on the color question. Many times Joe had told him to take the chip off his shoulder and be somebody. But he had no time for Luke now. Seeing the ship plainly, and the white troops getting aboard, he felt a growing fear. Fear that maybe he had passed Cleo and they hadn't seen each other for looking so damn hard. Fear that he wouldn't get to see her at all—never-ever again. Maybe she was ill, with no way to let him know, too sick to move. He thought of what she had said last night, about little Joey. Maybe . . .

And then he saw her, up ahead, waving at him, with the widest and prettiest and most confident smile anybody ever smiled. He was so goddamn glad he could hardly move his lips to smile or laugh or anything else.

She ran right up to him. "Hello, soldier boy, where you think you're going?"

"Damn," he said finally in as calm a voice as he could manage. "I thought for a while you had forgotten what day it was. Thought you had forgotten to come to my going-away party."

"Now, how do you sound?" She laughed at the funny look on his face, and told him he looked cute with dark glasses on, needing a shave and with the pack on his back. She seemed so cheerful, he couldn't believe she was the same person who had completely broken down last night. He felt the tears rush out of his eyes and spill down his face.

She pretended not to notice, and walked with him till they reached the last block. The women were not allowed to go any further. Looking at her, he wished somehow that she would cry, just a little bit anyhow. But she didn't cry at all. She reached up and kissed him quickly. "Good-by, darling, take care of yourself. Little Joey and I will write every day, beginning this afternoon." And then she was gone.

The last of the white soldiers were boarding the beautiful white ship, and a band on board was playing *God Bless America*. He felt a chill, like an electric current, pass across his slight shoulders, and he wasn't sure whether it was from *God Bless America* or from leaving Cleo behind. He hoped she could hear the music; maybe it would make her understand why Americans, no matter what their color, had to go and fight so many thousands of miles away from home.

They stopped in the middle of the block and stood waiting till the white regiment was all aboard. He wanted to look back for one last glimpse of Cleo, but he wouldn't let himself. Then they started again, marching toward the ship. And suddenly the band stopped playing *God Bless America* and jumped into another tune—*The Darktown Strutters' Ball* . . .

He didn't want to believe his ears. He looked up at the ship and saw some of the white soldiers on deck waving and smiling at the Negro soldiers, yelling "Yeah, Man!" and popping their fingers. A taste of gall crept up from his stomach into his mouth.

"Goddamn," he heard Luke say, "that's the kind of music I like." The husky soldier cut a little step. "I guess Mr. Charlie want us to jitterbug onto his pretty white boat. Equal treatment. . . . We ain't no soldiers, we're a bunch of goddamn clowns."

Joe felt an awful heat growing inside his collar. He hoped fiercely that Cleo was too far away to hear.

Luke grinned at him. "What's the matter, good kid? Mad about something? Damn—that's what I hate about you colored folks. Take that goddamn chip off your shoulder. They just trying to make you people feel at home. Don't you recognize the Negro national anthem when you hear it?"

Joe didn't answer. He just felt his anger mounting and he wished he could walk right out of the line and to hell with everything. But with *The Darktown Strutters' Ball* ringing in his ears, he put his head up, threw his shoulders back, and kept on marching towards the big white boat.

John A. Williams (1925-   )

Son in the Afternoon

From The Angry Black (1962)

It was hot. I tend to be a bitch when it's hot. I goosed the little Ford over Sepulveda Boulevard toward Santa Monica until I got stuck in the traffic that pours from L.A. into the surrounding towns. I'd had a very lousy day at the studio.

I was—still am—a writer and this studio had hired me to check scripts and films with Negroes in them to make sure the Negro moviegoer wouldn't be offended. The signs were already clear one day the whole of American industry would be racing pellmell to get a Negro, showcase a spade. I was kind of a pioneer. I'm a *Negro* writer, you see. The day had been tough because of a couple of verbs—slink and walk. One of those Hollywood hippies had done a script calling for a Negro waiter to slink away from the table where a dinner party was glaring at him. I said the waiter should walk, not slink, because later on he becomes a hero. The Hollywood hippie, who understood it all because he had some colored friends, said that it was essential to the plot that the waiter slink. I said you don't slink one minute and become a hero the next; there has to be some consistency. The Negro actor I was standing up for said nothing either way. He had played Uncle Tom roles so long that he had become Uncle Tom. But the director agreed with me.

Anyway . . . hear me out now. I was on my way to Santa Monica to pick up my mother, Nora. It was a long haul for such a hot day. I had planned a quiet evening: a nice shower, fresh clothes, and then I would have dinner at the Watkins and talk with some of the musicians on the scene for a quick taste before they cut to their gigs. After, I was going to the Pigalle down on Figueroa and catch Earl Grant at the organ, and still later, if nothing exciting happened, I'd pick up Scottie and make it to the Lighthouse on the Beach or to the Strollers and listen to some of the white boys play. I liked the long drive, especially while listening to Sleepy Stein's show on the radio. Later, much later of course, it would be home, back to Watts.

So you see, this picking up Nora was a little inconvenient. My mother was a maid for the Couchmans. Ronald Couchman was an architect, a good one I understood from Nora who has a fine sense for this sort of thing; you don't work in some hundred-odd houses during your life without getting some idea of the way a house should be laid out. Couchman's wife, Kay, was a playgirl who drove a white Jaguar from one party to another. My mother didn't like her too much; she didn't seem to care much for her son, Ronald, junior. There's something wrong with a parent who can't really love her own child, Nora thought. The Couchmans lived in a real fine residential section, of course. A number of actors lived nearby, character actors, not really big stars.

Somehow it is very funny. I mean that the maids and butlers knew everything about these people, and these people knew nothing at all about the help. Through Nora and her friends I knew who was laying whose wife; who had money and who *really* had money; I knew about the wild parties hours before the police, and who smoked marijuana, when, and where they got it.

To get to Couchman's driveway I had to go three blocks up one side of a palm-planted center strip and back down the other. The driveway bent gently, then swept back out of sight of the main road. The house, sheltered by slim palms, looked like a transplanted New England Colonial. I parked and walked to the kitchen door, skirting the growling Great Dane who was tied to a tree. That was the route to the kitchen door.

I don't like kitchen doors. Entering people's houses by them, I mean. I'd done this thing most of my life when I called at places where Nora worked to pick up the patched or worn sheets or the half-eaten roasts, the battered, tarnished silver—the fringe benefits of a housemaid. As a teen-ager I'd told Nora I was through with that crap; I was not going through anyone's kitchen door. She only laughed and said I'd learn. One day soon after, I called for her and without knocking walked right through the front door of this house and right on through the living room. I was almost out of the room when I saw feet behind the couch. I leaned over and there was Mr. Jorgensen and his wife making out like crazy. I guess they thought Nora had gone and it must have hit them sort of suddenly and they went at it like the hell-bomb was due to drop any minute. I've been that way too, mostly in the spring. Of course, when Mr. Jorgensen looked over his shoulder and saw me, you know what happened. I was thrown out and Nora right behind me. It was the middle of winter, the old man was sick and the coal bill three months overdue. Nora was right about those kitchen doors: I learned.

My mother saw me before I could ring the bell. She opened the door. "Hello," she said. She was breathing hard, like she'd been running or something. "Come in and sit down. I don't know *where* that Kay is. Little Ronald is sick and she's probably out gettin' drunk again." She left me then and trotted back through the house, I guess to be with Ronnie. I hated the combination of her white nylon uniform, her dark brown face and the wide streaks of gray in her hair. Nora had married this guy from Texas a few years after the old man had died. He was all right. He made out okay. Nora didn't have to work, but she just couldn't be still; she always had to be doing something. I suggested she quit work, but I had as much luck as her husband. I used to tease her about liking to be around those white folks. It would have been good for her to take an extended trip around the country visiting my brothers and sisters. Once she got to Philadelphia, she could go right out to the cemetery and sit awhile with the old man.

I walked through the Couchman home. I liked the library. I thought if I knew Couchman I'd like him. The room made me feel like that. I left it and went into the big living room. You could tell that Couchman had let his wife do that. Everything in it was fast, dart-like, with no sense of ease. But on the walls were several of Couchman's conceptions of buildings and homes. I guess he was a disciple of Wright. My mother walked rapidly through the room without looking at me and said, "Just be patient, Wendell. She should be here real soon."

"Yeah," I said, "with a snootful." I had turned back to the drawings when Ronnie scampered into the room, his face twisted with rage.

"Nora!" he tried to roar, perhaps the way he'd seen the parents of some of his friends roar at their maids. I'm quite sure Kay didn't shout at Nora, and I don't think Couchman would. But then no one shouts at Nora. "Nora, you come right back here this minute!" the little bastard shouted and stamped and pointed to a spot on the floor where Nora was supposed to come to roost. I have a nasty temper. Sometimes it lies dormant for ages and at other times, like when the weather is hot and nothing seems to be going right, it's bubbling and ready to explode. "Don't talk to *my* mother like that, you little—!" I said sharply, breaking off just before I cursed. I wanted him to be large enough for me to strike. "How'd you like for me to talk to *your* mother like that?"

The nine-year-old looked up at me in surprise and confusion. He hadn't expected me to say anything. I was just another piece of furniture. Tears rose in his eyes and spilled out onto his pale cheeks. He put his hands behind him, twisted them. He moved backwards, away from me. He looked at my mother with a "Nora, come help me" look. And sure enough, there was Nora, speeding back across the room, gathering the kid in her arms, tucking his robe together. I was too angry to feel hatred for myself.

Ronnie was the Couchman's only kid. Nora loved him. I suppose that was the trouble. Couchman was gone ten, twelve hours a day. Kay didn't stay around the house any longer than she had to. So Ronnie had only my mother. I think kids should have someone to love, and Nora wasn't a bad sort. But somehow when the six of us, her own children, were growing up we never had her. She was gone, out scuffling to get those crumbs to put into our mouths and shoes for our feet and praying for something to happen so that all the space in between would be taken care of. Nora's affection for us took the form of rushing out into the morning's five o'clock blackness to wake some silly bitch and get her coffee; took form in her trudging five miles home every night instead of taking the steetcar to save money to buy tablets for us, to use at school, we said. But the truth was that all of us liked to draw and we went through a writing tablet in a couple of hours every day. Can you imagine? There's not a goddamn artist among us. We never had the physical affection, the pat on the head, the quick, smiling kiss, the "gimmee a hug" routine. All of this Ronnie was getting.

Now he buried his little blond head in Nora's breast and sobbed. "There, there now," Nora said. "Don't you cry, Ronnie. Ol' Wendell is just jealous, and he hasn't much sense either. He didn't mean nuthin'."

I left the room. Nora had hit it of course, hit it and passed on. I looked back. It didn't look so incongruous, the white and black together, I mean. Ronnie was still sobbing. His head bobbed gently on Nora's shoulder. The only time I ever got that close to her was when she trapped me with a bearhug so she could whale the daylights out of me after I put a snowball through Mrs. Grant's window. I walked outside and lit a cigarette. When Ronnie was in the hospital the month before, Nora got me to run her way over to Hollywood every night to see him. I didn't like that worth a damn. All right, I'll admit it: it did upset me. All that affection I didn't get nor my brothers and sisters going to that little white boy who, without a doubt, when away from her called her the names he'd learned from adults. Can you imagine a nine-year-old kid calling Nora a "girl," "our girl?" I spat at the Great Dane. He snarled and then I bounced a rock off his fanny. "Lay down, you bastard," I muttered. It was a good thing he was tied up.

I heard the low cough of the Jaguar slapping against the road. The car was throttled down, and with a muted roar it swung into the driveway. The woman aimed it for me. I was evil enough not to move. I was tired of playing with these people. At the last moment, grinning, she swung the wheel over and braked. She bounded out of the car like a tennis player vaulting over a net.

"Hi," she said, tugging at her shorts.

"Hello."

"You're Nora's boy?"

"I'm Nora's son." Hell, I was as old as she was; besides, I can't stand "boy."

"Nora tells us you're working in Hollywood. Like it?"

"It's all right."

"You must be pretty talented."

We stood looking at each other while the dog whined for her attention. Kay had a nice body and it was well tanned. She was high, boy, was she high. Looking at her, I could feel myself going into my sexy bastard routine; sometimes I can swing it great. Maybe it all had to do with the business inside. Kay took off her sunglasses and took a good look at me. "Do you have a cigarette?"

I gave her one and lit it. "Nice tan," I said. Most white people I know think it's a great big deal if a Negro compliments them on their tans. It's a large laugh. You have all this volleyball about color and come summer you can't hold the white folks back from the beaches, anyplace where they can get some sun. And of course the blacker they get, the more pleased they are. Crazy. If there is ever a Negro revolt, it will come during the summer and Negroes will descend upon the beaches around the nation and paralyze the country. You can't conceal cattle prods and bombs and pistols and police dogs when you're showing your birthday suit to the sun.

"You like it?" she asked. She was pleased. She placed her arm next to mine. "Almost the same color," she said.

"Ronnie isn't feeling well," I said.

"Oh, the poor kid. I'm so glad we have Nora. She's such a charm. I'll run right in and look at him. Do have a drink in the bar. Fix me one too, will you?" Kay skipped inside and I went to the bar and poured out two strong drinks. I made hers stronger than mine. She was back soon. "Nora was trying to put him to sleep and she made me stay out." She giggled. She quickly tossed off her drink. "Another, please?" While I was fixing her drink she was saying how amazing it was for Nora to have such a talented son. What she was really saying was that it was amazing for a servant to have a son who was not also a servant. "Anything can happen in a democracy," I said. "Servants' sons drink with madames and so on."

"Oh, Nora isn't a servant," Kay said. "She's part of the family."

Yeah, I thought. Where and how many times had I heard *that* before?

In the ensuing silence, she started to admire her tan again. "You think it's pretty good, do you? You don't know how hard I worked to get it." I moved close to her and held her arm. I placed my other arm around her. She pretended not to see or feel it, but she wasn't trying to get away either. In fact she was pressing closer and the register in my brain that tells me at the precise moment when I'm in, went off. Kay was very high. I put both arms around her and she put both hers around me. When I kissed her, she responded completely.

"Mom!"

"Ronnie, come back to bed," I heard Nora shout from the other room. We could hear Ronnie running over the rug in the outer room. Kay tried to get away from me, push me to one side, because we could tell that Ronnie knew where to look for his Mom: he was running right for the bar, where we were. "Oh, please," she said, "don't let him see us." I wouldn't let her push me away. "Stop!" she hissed. "He'll *see* us!" We stopped struggling just for an instant, and we listened to the echoes of the word *see*. She gritted her teeth and renewed her efforts to get away.

Me? I had the scene laid right out. The kid breaks into the room, see, and sees his mother in this real wriggly clinch with this colored guy who's just shouted at him, see, and no matter how his mother explains it away, the kid has the image—the colored guy and his mother—for the rest of his life, see?

That's the way it happened. The kid's mother hissed under her breath, *"You're crazy!"* and she looked at me as though she were seeing me or something about me for the very first time. I'd released her as soon as Ronnie, romping into the bar, saw us and came to a full, open-mouthed halt. Kay went to him. He looked first at me, then at his mother. Kay turned to me, but she couldn't speak.

Outside in the living room my mother called, "Wendell, where are you? We can go now."

I started to move past Kay and Ronnie. I felt many things, but I made myself think mostly, *There you little bastard, there.*

My mother thrust her face inside the door and said, "Good-bye, Mrs. Couchman. See you tomorrow. 'Bye, Ronnie."

"Yes," Kay said, sort of stunned. "Tomorrow." She was reaching for Ronnie's hand as we left, but the kid was slapping her hand away. I hurried quickly after Nora, hating the long drive back to Watts.

Mari Evans

Status Symbol

From Poets of Today (1964)

i
Have Arrived
i am the
New Negro

                i
am the result of
President Lincoln
World War 1
and Paris
the
Red Ball Express
white drinking fountains
sitdowns and
sit-ins
Federal Troops
Marches on Washington
and
prayer meetings . . . .
today
They hired me
it
is a status
job . . . . .
along
with my papers
They
gave me my
Status Symbol . . .
the
key
to the
White
Locked
JOHN

I Am a Black Woman

From Negro Digest (September, 1969)

I am a black woman
the music of my song
some sweet arpeggio of tears
is written in a minor key
and I

can be heard humming in the night
Can be heard
                        humming
in the night

I saw my mate leap screaming to the sea
and I/with these hands/cupped the lifebreath
from my issue in the canebrake
I lost Nat's swinging body in a rain of tears
and heard my son scream all the way from Anzio
for Peace he never knew. . . . I
learned Da Nang and Pork Chop Hill
in anguish
Now my nostrils know the gas
and these trigger tire/d fingers
seek the softness in my warrior's beard

I
am a black woman
tall as a cypress
strong
beyond all definition still
defying place
and time
and circumstance
    assailed
        impervious
            indestructible
Look
    on me and be
renewed

Jay Saunders Redding (1906-   )

The Negro Writer and His Relationship to His Roots
From The Negro Writer and His Roots (1960)

I do not feel in the least controversial or argumentative about the announced subject. Indeed, I have touched upon it so often in one way or another that I long ago exhausted my store of arguments, and if I now revert to a kind of expressionistic way of talking, my excuse for it is patent. "The Negro Writer and his Relationship to his Roots" is the kind of subject which, if one talked directly on it for more than twenty minutes, he would have to talk at least a year. I shan't talk directly on it, and I shan't talk a year. An exhaustive treatment? Heaven forbid—or anything near it. Suggestive? Well, I can only hope.

And anyway, I realize now that my position here is that of the boy who, through native disability, cannot himself play but is perfectly willing to furnish the ball for others to play in exchange for the pleasure of watching the game.

Since my theme is that the American situation has complex and multifarious sources and that these sources sustain the emotional and intellectual life of American Negro writers, let me take as my starting point a classic oversimplification. This is that the meaning of American society and of the American situation to the Negro is summed up in such works as *Native Son, Invisible Man,* and the *Ordeal of Mansart,* and in two or three volumes of poetry, notably *Harlem Shadows, The Black Christ,* and *The Weary Blues,* and that the American Negro writer's entire spirit is represented by such writers as Richard Wright, Ralph Ellison and William Burghardt Du Bois—by realists, surrealists, and romantic idealists.

Please understand me. Wright, Ellison and Du Bois are not mendacious men, and they are doing what writers must always do. They are telling the truth as they see it, which happens to be largely what it is, and they are producing from the examined, or at least the observed causes, the predictable effects; and no one should blame them if the impression they give of the American situation is deplorable. They have been blamed, you know. But let those who blame these writers blame themselves for forgetting that fiction is fiction, and that no novel can pretend to be an exact photographic copy of a country or of the people in a country.

Moreover, dishonor, bigotry, hatred, degradation, injustice, arrogance and obscenity do flourish in American life, and especially in the prescribed and proscriptive American Negro life; and it is the right and the duty of the Negro writer to say so—to complain. He has cause. The temptation of the moral enthusiast is not only strong in him; it is inevitable. He never suspends social and moral judgment. Few actions and events that touch him as a man fail to set in motion his machinery as an artist. History is as personal to him as the woman he loves; and he is caught in the flux of its events, the currents of its opinion and the tides of its emotion; and he believes that the mood is weak which tolerates an impartial presentment of these, and that this weak mood cannot be indulged in a world where the consequences of the actions of a few men produce insupportable calamities for millions of humble folk. He is one of the humble folk. He forages in the cause of righteousness. He forgets that he is also one of Apollo's company.

On the one hand, the jungle; on the other, the resourceful hunter to clear it. The jungle, where lurk the beasts, nourishes the hunter. It is there that he has that sum of relationships that make him what he is. It is where he lives. It is precisely because the jungle is there and is terrible and dangerous that the Negro writer writes and lives at all.

But first, I suppose you must grant me, if only for the sake of this brief exposition, that the American Negro writer is not just an American with a dark skin. If he were, I take it, the theme of this conference would be mighty silly and the conference itself superfluous. This granted, you want to know what the frame of reference is, and about this I shall be dogmatic.

Neither the simplest nor the subtlest scrutiny reveals to an honest man that he has two utterly diverse kinds of experience, that of sense data and that of purpose. Psychology seems to have no difficulty establishing the natural gradation of impulse to purpose. In varying degrees, all our experiences are complications of physical processes.

Shifting from the dogmatic to the apologetic, I must eliminate from view a period of nearly three hundred years from 1619 to 1900. It was the period that saw the solid establishment here in America of a tradition of race relations and of the concepts that supported the tradition. It was a period that need not be rehearsed. Within the frame of reference thus established, let us look at a certain chain of events.

In 1902 came Thomas Dixon's *The Leopard's Spots*, and three years later *The Clansman*. Both were tremendously popular, and both were included in the repertoires of traveling theatrical companies; and I think it is significant—though we will only imply how—that even a colored company, The Lafayette Players, undertook an adaptation of *The Leopard's Spots*. In 1903 there was a race riot in New York. In 1906 race riots occurred in Georgia and Texas; in 1908 in Illinois. By this latter year, too, all the Southern states had disfranchised the Negro, and color caste was legalized or had legal status everywhere. The Negro's talent for monkeyshines had been exploited on the stage, and some of the music that accompanied the monkeyshines was created by James Weldon Johnson and his brother Rosamond. Meantime, in 1904, Thomas Nelson Page had written the one true canonical book of the law and the prophets, *The Negro, The Southerner's Problem*. And, most cogent fact of all, Booker Washington, having sworn on this bible of reactionism, had been made the undisputed leader of American Negroes because, as he had pledged to do, he advocated a race policy strictly in line with the tradition and the supporting concepts of race relations.

If there had been a time when this tradition seemed to promise the Negro a way out, that time was not now. He had been laughed at, tolerated, amusingly despaired of, but all his own efforts were vain. All the instruments of social progress—schools, churches, lodges—adopted by colored people were the subjects of ribald jokes and derisive laughter. "Mandy, has you studied yo' Greek?" "I'se sewing, Ma." "Go naked, Gal, Git Dat Greek!"

Any objective judgment of Booker Washington's basic notion must be that it was an extension of the old tradition framed in new terms. Under the impact of social change, the concept was modified to include the stereotype of the Negro as a happy peasant, a docile and satisfied laborer under the stern but kindly eye of the white boss, a creature who had a place and knew it and loved it and would keep it unless he got bad notions from somewhere. The once merely laughable coon had become now also the cheap farm grub or city laborer who could be righteously exploited for his own good and for the greater glory of America. By this addition to the concept, the Negro-white status quo, the condition of inferior-superior race and caste could be maintained in the face of profound changes in the general society.

What this meant to the Negro writer was that he must, if he wished an audience, adhere to the old forms and the acceptable patterns. It meant that he must create within the limitations of the concept, or that he must dissemble completely, or that he must ignore his racial kinship altogether and leave unsounded the profoundest depths of the peculiar experiences which were his by reason of that kinship. Some chose the first course; at least one—Dunbar—chose the second (as witness his sickly, sticky novels of white love life and his sad epithalamium to death); and a good many chose the third: Braithwaite's anthologies of magazine verse, James Weldon Johnson's contributions to the *Century Magazine*, and the writing of Alice Dunbar, Anne Spenser, and Angelina Grimke.

But given the whole web of circumstances—empirical, historic, psychological —these writers must have realized that they could not go on and that the damps and fevers, chills and blights, terrors and dangers of the jungle could not be ignored. They must have realized that, with a full tide of race-consciousness bearing in upon them, they could not go on forever denying their racehood and that to try to do this at all was a symptom of psychotic strain. Rather perish now than escape only to die of slow starvation.

What had happened was that Booker Washington, with the help of the historic situation and the old concepts, had so thoroughly captured the minds of white people that his was the only Negro voice that could be heard in the jungle. Negro schools needing help could get it only through Booker Washington. Negro social thought wanting a sounding board could have it only on Washington's say-so. Negro political action was weak and ineffective without his strength. Many Negro writers fell silent, and for the writer, silence is death.

Many, but not all. These were stubborn souls and courageous, and the frankly mad among them. There was the Boston *Guardian*, and the Chicago *Defender*, and the Atlanta University Pamphlets, and *The Souls of Black Folk*, and finally the *Crisis*; and this latter quickly developed a voice of multi-range and many tones. It roared like a lion and cooed like a dove and screamed like a monkey and laughed like a hyena. And always it protested. Always the sounds it made were the sounds of revolt in the jungle, and protestation and revolt were becoming—forgive me for changing my figure—powerful reagents in the social chemistry that produced the "new" Negro.

Other factors contributed to this generation too. The breath of academic scholarship was just beginning to blow hot and steadily enough to wither some of the myths about the Negro. The changes occurring with the onset of war in Europe sloughed off other emotional and intellectual accretions. The Negro might be a creature of "moral debate," but he was also something more. "I ain't a problem," a Negro character was made to say, "I's a person." And that person turned out to be a seeker after the realities in the American dream. When he was called upon to protect that dream with his blood, he asked questions and demanded answers. Whose dream was he protecting, he wanted to know, and why and wherefore? There followed such promises as only the less scrupulous politicians had made to him before. Then came the fighting and the dying, and finally came a thing called peace.

By this time, the Negro was already stirring massively along many fronts. He cracked Broadway wide open. The Garvey movement swept the country like wildfire. *Harlem Shadows, The Gift of Black Folk, Color, Fire in the Flint, The Autobiography of an Ex-coloured Man.* The writers of these and other works were declared to be irresponsible. A polemical offensive was launched against them, and against such non-artist writers as Philip Randolph, Theophilus Lewis, William Patterson, Angelo Herndon. They were accused of negativism; they were called un-American. Cultural nationalism raised its head and demanded that literature be patriotic, optimistic, positive, uncritical, like *Americans All,* and *American Ideals,* and *America is Promises,* and *It Takes a Heap O' Living,* which were all written and published in the period of which I speak. But democracy encourages criticism, and it is true that even negative criticism implies certain positive values like veracity, for instance, and these Negro writers had positive allegiances. Their sensibilities were violently irritated, but their faith and imaginations were wonderfully nourished by the very environment which they saw to be and depicted as being bad.

Fortunately there was more than faith and fat imagination in some of these works. There was also talent. Had this not been so, Negro writing would have come to nothing for perhaps another quarter century, for the ground would not have been plowed for the seeds of later talents. But Du Bois, Johnson, McKay, Fisher, Cullen, Hughes knew what they were about. Their work considerably furthered the interest of white writers and critics. Whatever else O'Neill, Rosenfeld, Connolley, Calverton and Heyward did, they gave validity to the notion that the Negro was material for serious literary treatment.

Beginning then and continuing into the forties, Negro writing had two distinct aspects. The first of these was arty, self-conscious, somewhat precious, experimental, and not truly concerned with the condition of man. Some of the "little reviews" printed a lot of nonsense by Negro writers, including the first chapter of a novel which was to be entirely constructed of elliptical sentences. Then there was *Cane:* sensibility, inwardness, but much of it for the purpose of being absorbed into the universal oneness. Nirvana. Oblivion. Transcendence over one's own personality through the practice of art for art's sake. The appropriate way of feeling and thinking growing out of a particular system of living. And so eventually Gurdjieff.

But the second aspect was more important. The pathos of man is that he hungers for personal fulfillment and for a sense of community with others. And these writers hungered. There is no American national character. There is only an American situation, and within this situation these writers sought to find themselves. They had always been alienated, not only because they were Negroes, but because democracy in America decisively separates the intellectual from everyone else. The intellectual in America is a radically alienated personality, the Negro in common with the white, and both were hungry and seeking, and some of the best of both found food and an identity in communism. But the identity was only partial and, the way things turned out, further emphasized their alienation. So— at least for the Negro writers among them—back into the American situation, the jungle where they could find themselves. A reflex of the natural gradation of impulse to purpose.

Surely this is the meaning of *Native Son.* "Bigger Thomas was not black all the time," his creator says. "He was white too, and there were literally millions of him. . . . Modern experiences were creating types of personalities whose existence ignored racial . . . lines." Identity. Community. Surely this is the meaning of *Invisible Man* and the poignant, pain-filled, pain-relieving humor of simple Jesse B. It is the meaning of *Go Tell It On The Mountain,* and it is explicitly the meaning of four brilliant essays in part three of a little book of essays called *Notes of a Native Son.* (How often that word "native" appears, and how meaningful its implications!) Let me quote a short, concluding passage from one of these essays.

"Since I no longer felt that I could stay in this cell forever, I was beginning to be able to make peace with it for a time. On the 27th . . . I went again to trial . . . . and the case . . . . was dismissed. The story of the *Drap De Lit, . . .* caused great merriment in the courtroom. . . . I was chilled by their merriment, even though it was meant to warm me. It could only remind me of the laughter I had often heard at home. . . . This laughter is the laughter of those who consider themselves to be at a safe remove from all the wretched, for whom the pain of living is not real. I had heard it so often in my native land that I had resolved to find a place where I would never hear it anymore. In some deep, black, stony and liberating way, my life, in my own eyes, began during that first year in Paris, when it was borne in on me that this laughter is universal and never can be stilled." Explicit.

The human condition, the discovery of self. Community. Identity. Surely this must be achieved before it can be seen that a particular identity has a relation to a common identity, commonly described as human. This is the ultimate that the honest writer seeks. He knows that the dilemmas, the perils, the likelihood of catastrophe in the human situation are real and that they have to do not only with whether men understand each other but with the quality of man himself. The writer's ultimate purpose is to use his gifts to develop man's awareness of himself so that he, man, can become a better instrument for living together with other men. This sense of identity is the root by which all honest creative effort is fed, and the writer's relation to it is the relation of the infant to the breast of the mother.

Conrad Kent Rivers (1933-1968)

Four Sheets to the Wind and a One-way Ticket to France, 1933

From These Black Bodies and This Sunburnt Face (1962)

As a Black Child I was a dreamer
I bought a red scarf and women told me how
Beautiful it looked.
Wandering through the heart of France
As France wandered through me.

In the evenings,
I would watch the funny people make love,
My youth allowed me the opportunity to hear
All those strange
Verbs conjugated in erotic affirmations,
I knew love at twelve.

When Selassie went before his peers and
Africa gained dignity
I read in two languages, not really caring
Which one belonged to me.

My mother lit a candle for King George,
My father went broke, we died.
When I felt blue, the champs understood,
And when it was crowded, the alley
Behind Harry's New York bar soothed my
Restless spirit.

I liked to watch the Bohemians gaze at the
Paintings along Gauguin's bewildered paradise.

Bracque once passed me in front of the Café Musique
I used to watch those sneaky professors examine
The populace,
American never quite fitted in, but they
Tried, so we smiled.

I guess the money was too much for my folks,
Hitler was such a prig and a scare, they caught
The last boat.
    I stayed.

Main street was never the same, I read Gide
And tried to
Translate Proust. (Now nothing is real except
French wine.)
For absurdity is reality, my loneliness unreal,

And I shall die an old Parisian, with much honor.

Africa

From These Black Bodies and This Sunburnt Face (1962)

They say you smile like a woman
When the sun comes to the end of her day.
For a while, the night-purple and blue
Veil of silence hovers over our universe,
Wither thou goest?

Surely some part of you
Blows a saddened dusky breeze across the sea,
Walks the streets of Harlem,
Lifts a veil of ignorance from our face
To remind us there was a homeland.

Where men remain alive
Not content to surrender their land.
Something stronger than a constitution
Brings in railroads and books
Where the forests and beasts once reigned
And the white man's God stands alone.

Watching dark and strong men build a new republic

Paule Marshall (1929-   )

Barbados

From Soul Clap Hands and Sing (1961)

Dawn, like the night which had preceded it, came from the sea. In a white mist tumbling like spume over the fishing boats leaving the island and the hunched, ghost shapes of the fishermen. In a white, wet wind breathing over the villages scattered amid the tall canes. The cabbage palms roused, their high headdresses solemnly saluting the wind, and along the white beach which ringed the island the casuarina trees began their moaning—a sound of women lamenting their dead within a cave.

The wind, smarting of the sea, threaded a wet skein through Mr. Watford's five hundred dwarf coconut trees and around his house at the edge of the grove. The house, Colonial American in design, seemed created by the mist—as if out of the dawn's formlessness had come, magically, the solid stone walls, the blind, broad windows and the portico of fat columns which embraced the main story. When the mist cleared, the house remained—pure, proud, a pristine white—disdaining the crude wooden houses in the villages outside its high gate.

It was not the dawn settling around his house which awakened Mr. Watford, but the call of his Barbary doves from their hutch in the yard. And it was more the feel of that sound than the sound itself. His hands had retained, from the many times a day he held the doves, the feel of their throats swelling with that murmurous, mournful note. He lay abed now, his hands—as cracked and callused as a cane cutter's—filled with the sound, and against the white sheet which flowed out to the white walls he appeared profoundly alone, yet secure in loneliness, contained. His face was fleshless and severe, his black skin sucked deep into the hollow of his jaw, while under a high brow, which was like a bastion raised against the world, his eyes were indrawn and pure. It was as if during all his seventy years, Mr. Watford had permitted nothing to sight which could have affected him.

He stood up, and his body, muscular but stripped of flesh, appeared to be absolved from time, still young. Yet each clenched gesture of his arms, of his lean shank as he dressed in a faded shirt and work pants, each vigilant, snapping motion of his head betrayed tension. Ruthlessly he spurred his body to perform like a younger man's. Savagely he denied the accumulated fatigue of the years. Only sometimes when he paused in his grove of coconut trees during the day, his eyes tearing and the breath torn from his lungs, did it seem that if he could find a place hidden from the world and himself he would give way to exhaustion and weep from weariness.

Dressed, he strode through the house, his step tense, his rough hand touching the furniture from Grand Rapids which crowded each room. For some reason,

Mr. Watford had never completed the house. Everywhere the walls were raw and unpainted, the furniture unarranged. In the drawing room with its coffered ceiling, he stood before his favorite piece, an old mantel clock which eked out the time. Reluctantly it whirred five and Mr. Watford nodded. His day had begun.

It was no different from all the days which made up the five years since his return to Barbados. Downstairs in the unfinished kitchen, he prepared his morning tea—tea with canned milk and fried bakes—and ate standing at the stove while lizards skittered over the unplastered walls. Then, belching and snuffling the way a child would, he put on a pith helmet, secured his pants legs with bicycle clasps and stepped into the yard. There he fed the doves, holding them so that their sound poured into his hands and laughing gently—but the laugh gave way to an irritable grunt as he saw the mongoose tracks under the hutch. He set the trap again.

The first heat had swept the island like a huge tidal wave when Mr. Watford, with that tense, headlong stride, entered the grove. He had planted the dwarf coconut trees because of their quick yield and because, with their stunted trunks, they always appeared young. Now as he worked, rearranging the complex of pipes which irrigated the land, stripping off the dead leaves, the trees were like cool, moving presences; the stiletto fronds wove a protective dome above him and slowly, as the day soared toward noon, his mind filled with the slivers of sunlight through the trees and the feel of earth in his hands, as it might have been filled with thoughts.

Except for a meal at noon, he remained in the grove until dusk surged up from the sea; then returning to the house, he bathed and dressed in a medical doctor's white uniform, turned on the lights in the parlor and opened the tall doors to the portico. Then the old women of the village on their way to church, the last hawkers caroling, "Fish, flying fish, a penny, my lady," the roistering saga-boys lugging their heavy steel drums to the crossroad where they would rehearse under the street lamp—all passing could glimpse Mr. Watford, stiff in his white uniform and with his head bent heavily over a Boston newspaper. The papers reached him weeks late but he read them anyway, giving a little savage chuckle at the thought that beyond his world that other world went its senseless way. As he read, the night sounds of the village welled into a joyous chorale against the sea's muffled cadence and the hollow, haunting music of the steel band. Soon the moths, lured in by the light, fought to die on the lamp, the beetles crashed drunkenly against the walls and the night—like a woman offering herself to him— became fragrant with the night-blooming cactus.

Even in America Mr. Watford had spent his evenings this way. Coming home from the hospital, where he worked in the boiler room, he would dress in his white uniform and read in the basement of the large rooming house he owned. He had lived closeted like this, detached, because America—despite the money and property he had slowly accumulated—had meant nothing to him. Each morning, walking to the hospital along the rutted Boston streets, through the smoky dawn light, he had known—although it had never been a thought—that his allegiance, his place, lay elsewhere. Neither had the few acquaintances he had made mattered. Nor the women he had occasionally kept as a younger man. After the first months their bodies would grow coarse to his hand and he would begin edging away. . . . So that he had felt no regret when, the year before his retirement, he resigned his job, liquidated his properties and, his fifty-year exile over, returned home.

The clock doled out eight and Mr. Watford folded the newspaper and brushed the burnt moths from the lamp base. His lips still shaped the last words he had read as he moved through the rooms, fastening the windows against the night air, which he had dreaded even as a boy. Something palpable but unseen was always, he believed, crouched in the night's dim recess, waiting to snare him. . . . Once in bed in his sealed room, Mr. Watford fell asleep quickly.

The next day was no different except that Mr. Goodman, the local shopkeeper, sent the boy for coconuts to sell at the racetrack and then came that evening to pay for them and to herald—although Mr. Watford did not know this—the coming of the girl.

That morning, taking his tea, Mr. Watford heard the careful tap of the mule's hoofs and looking out saw the wagon jolting through the dawn and the boy, still lax with sleep, swaying on the seat. He was perhaps eighteen and the muscles packed tightly beneath his lustrous black skin gave him a brooding strength. He came and stood outside the back door, his hands and lowered head performing the small, subtle rites of deference.

Mr. Watford's pleasure was full, for the gestures were those given only to a white man in his time. Yet the boy always nettled him. He sensed a natural arrogance like a pinpoint of light within his dark stare. The boy's stance exhumed a memory buried under the years. He remembered, staring at him, the time when he had worked as a yard boy for a white family, and had had to assume the same respectful pose while their flat, raw, Barbadian voices assailed him with orders. He remembered the muscles in his neck straining as he nodded deeply and a taste like alum on his tongue as he repeated the "Yes, please," as in a litany. But because of their whiteness and wealth, he had never dared hate them. Instead his rancor, like a boomerang, had rebounded, glancing past him to strike all the dark ones like himself, even his mother with her spindled arms and her stomach sagging with a child who was, invariably, dead at birth. He had been the only one of ten to live, the only one to escape. But he had never lost the sense of being pursued by the same dread presence which had claimed them. He had never lost the fear that if he lived too fully he would tire and death would quickly close the gap. His only defense had been a cautious life and work. He had been almost broken by work at the age of twenty when his parents died, leaving him enough money for the passage to America. Gladly had he fled the island. But nothing had mattered after his flight.

The boy's foot stirred the dust. He murmured, "Please, sir, Mr. Watford, Mr. Goodman at the shop send me to pick the coconut."

Mr. Watford's head snapped up. A caustic word flared, but died as he noticed a political button pinned to the boy's patched shirt with "Vote for the Barbados People's Party" printed boldly on it, and below that the motto of the party: "The Old Shall Pass." At this ludicrous touch (for what could this boy, with his splayed and shigoed feet and blunted mind, understand about politics?) he became suddenly nervous, angry. The button and its motto seemed, somehow, directed at him. He said roughly, "Well, come then. You can't pick any coconuts standing their looking foolish!"—and he led the way to the grove.

The coconuts, he knew, would sell well at the booths in the center of the track, where the poor were penned in like cattle. As the heat thickened and the betting grew desperate, they would clamor: "Man, how you selling the water coconuts?" and hacking off the tops they would pour rum into the water within the hollow centers, then tilt the coconuts to their heads so that the rum-sweetened water skimmed their tongues and trickled bright down their dark chins. Mr. Watford had stood among them at the track as a young man, as poor as they were, but proud. And he had always found something unutterably graceful and free in their gestures, something which had roused contradictory feelings in him: admiration, but just as strong, impatience at their easy ways, and shame. . . .

That night, as he sat in his white uniform reading, he heard Mr. Goodman's heavy step and went out and stood at the head of the stairs in a formal, proprietary pose. Mr. Goodman's face floated up into the light—the loose folds of flesh, the skin slick with sweat as if oiled, the eyes scribbled with veins and mottled, bold—as if each blemish there was a sin he proudly displayed or a scar which proved he had met life head-on. His body, unlike Mr. Watford's, was corpulent and, with the trousers caught up around his full crotch, openly concupiscent. He owned the one shop in the village which gave credit and a booth which sold coconuts at the race track, kept a wife and two outside women, drank a rum with each customer at his bar, regularly caned his fourteen children, who still followed him everywhere (even now they were waiting for him in the darkness beyond Mr. Watford's gate) and bet heavily at the races, and when he lost gave a loud hacking laugh which squeezed his body like a pain and left him gasping.

The laugh clutched him now as he flung his pendulous flesh into a chair and wheezed, "Watford, how? Man, I near lose house, shop, shirt and all at races today. I tell you, they got some horses from Trinidad in this meet that's making ours look like they running backwards. Be Jese, I wouldn't bet on a Bajan horse tomorrow if Christ heself was to give me the top. Those bitches might look good but they's nothing 'pon a track."

Mr. Watford, his back straight as the pillar he leaned against, his eyes unstained, his gaunt face planed by contempt, gave Mr. Goodman his cold, measured smile, thinking that the man would be dead soon, bloated with rice and rum—and somehow this made his own life more certain.

Sputtering with his amiable laughter, Mr. Goodman paid for the coconuts, but instead of leaving then as he usually did, he lingered, his eyes probing for a glimpse inside the house. Mr. Watford waited, his head snapping warily; then, impatient, he started toward the door and Mr. Goodman said, "I tell you, your coconut trees bearing fast enough even for dwarfs. You's lucky, man."

Ordinarily Mr. Watford would have waved both the man and his remark aside, but repelled more than usual tonight by Mr. Goodman's gross form and immodest laugh, he said—glad of the cold edge his slight American accent gave the words—"What luck got to do with it? I does care the trees properly and they bear, that's all. Luck! People, especially this bunch around here, is always looking to luck when the only answer is a little brains and plenty of hard work. . . ." Suddenly remembering the boy that morning and the political button, he added in loud disgust, "Look that half-foolish boy you does send here to pick the coconuts. Instead of him learning a trade and going to England where he might find work he's walking about with a political button. He and all in politics now! But that's the way with these down here. They'll do some of everything but work. They don't want work!" He gestured violently, almost dancing in anger. "They too busy spreeing."

The chair creaked as Mr. Goodman sketched a pained and gentle denial. "No, man," he said, "you wrong. Things is different to before. I mean to say, the young people nowadays is different to how we was. They not just sitting back and taking things no more. They not so frighten for the white people as we was. No, man. Now take that said same boy, for an example. I don't say he don't like a spree, but he's serious, you see him there. He's a member of this new Barbados People's Party. He wants to see his own color running the government. He wants to be able to make a living right here in Barbados instead of going to any cold England. And he's right!" Mr. Goodman paused at a vehement pitch, then shrugged heavily. "What the young people must do, nuh? They got to look to something . . ."

"Look to work!" And Mr. Watford thrust out a hand so that the horned knuckles caught the light.

"Yes, that's true—and it's up to we that got little something to give them work," Mr. Goodman said, and a sadness filtered among the dissipations in his eyes. "I mean to say we that got little something got to help out. In a manner of speaking, we's responsible . . ."

"Responsible!" The work circled Mr. Watford's head like a gnat and he wanted to reach up and haul it down, to squash it underfoot.

Mr. Goodman spread his hands; his breathing rumbled with a sigh. "Yes, in a manner of speaking. That's why, Watford man, you got to provide little work for some poor person down in here. Hire a servant at least! 'Cause I gon tell you something . . ." And he hitched forward his chair, his voice dropped to a wheeze. "People talking. Here you come back rich from big America and build a swell house and plant 'nough coconut trees and you still cleaning and cooking and thing like some woman. Man, it don't look good!" His face screwed in emphasis and he sat back. "Now, there's this girl, the daughter of a friend that just dead, and she need work bad enough. But I wouldn't like to see she working for these white people 'cause you know how those men will take advantage of she. And she'd make a good servant, man. Quiet and quick so, and nothing a-tall to feed and she can sleep anywhere about the place. And she don't have no boys always around her either. . . ." Still talking, Mr. Goodman eased from his chair and reached the stairs with surprising agility. "You need a servant," he whispered, leaning close to Mr. Watford as he passed. "It don't look good, man, people talking. I gon send she."

Mr. Watford was overcome by nausea. Not only from Mr. Goodman's smell—a stench of salt fish, rum and sweat—but from an outrage which was like a sediment in his stomach. For a long time he stood there almost kecking from disgust, until his clock struck eight, reminding him of the sanctuary within—and suddenly his cold laugh dismissed Mr. Goodman and his proposal. Hurrying in, he locked the doors and windows against the night air and, still laughing, he slept.

The next day, coming from the grove to prepare his noon meal, he saw her. She was standing in his driveway, her bare feet like strong dark roots amid the jagged stones, her face tilted toward the sun—and she might have been standing there always waiting for him. She seemed of the sun, of the earth. The folktale of creation might have been true with her: that along a riverbank a god had scooped up the earth—rich and black and warmed by the sun—and molded her poised head with its tufted braids and then with a whimsical touch crowned it with a sober brown felt hat which should have been worn by some stout English matron in a London suburb, had sculptured the passionless face and drawn a screen of gossamer across her eyes to hide the void behind. Beneath her bodice her small breasts were smooth at the crest. Below her waist her hips branched wide, the place prepared for its load of life. But it was the bold and sensual strength of her legs which completely unstrung Mr. Watford. He wanted to grab a hoe and drive her off.

"What it 'tis you want?" he called sharply.

"Mr. Goodman send me."

"Send you for what?" His voice was shrill in the glare.

She moved. Holding a caved-in valise and a pair of white sandals, her head weaving slightly as though she bore a pail of water there or a tray of mangoes, she glided over the stones as if they were smooth ground. Her bland expression did not change but her eyes, meeting his, held a vague trust. Pausing a few feet away, she curtsied deeply. "I's the new servant."

Only Mr. Watford's cold laugh saved him from anger. As always it raised him to a height where everything below appeared senseless and insignificant—

especially his people, whom the girl embodied. From this height, he could even be charitable. And thinking suddenly of how she had waited in the brutal sun since morning without taking shelter under the nearby tamarind tree, he said, not unkindly, "Well, girl, go back and tell Mr. Goodman for me that I don't need no servant."

"I can't go back."

"How you mean can't?" His head gave its angry snap.

"I'll get lashes," she said simply. "My mother say I must work the day and then if you don't wish me, I can come back. But I's not to leave till night falling, if not I get lashes."

He was shaken by her dispassion. So much so that his head dropped from its disdaining angle and his hands twitched with helplessness. Despite anything he might say or do, her fear of the whipping would keep her there until nightfall, the valise and shoes in hand. He felt his day with its order and quiet rhythms threatened by her intrusion—and suddenly waving her off as if she were an evil visitation, he hurried into the kitchen to prepare his meal.

But he paused, confused, in front of the stove, knowing that he could not cook and leave her hungry at the door, nor could he cook and serve her as though he were the servant.

"Yes, please."

They said nothing more. She entered the room with a firm step and an air almost of familiarity, placed her valise and shoes in a corner and went directly to the larder. For a time Mr. Watford stood by, his muscles flexing with anger and his eyes bounding ahead of her every move, until feeling foolish and frighteningly useless, he went out to feed his doves.

The meal was quickly done and as he ate he heard the dry slap of her feet behind him—a pleasant sound—and then silence. When he glanced back she was squatting in the doorway, the sunlight aslant the absurd hat and her face bent to a bowl she held in one palm. She ate slowly, thoughtfully, as if fixing the taste of each spoonful in her mind.

It was then that he decided to let her work the day and at nightfall to pay her a dollar and dismiss her. His decision held when he returned later from the grove and found tea awaiting him, and then through the supper she prepared. Afterward, dressed in his white uniform, he patiently waited out the day's end on the portico, his face setting into a grim mold. Then just as dusk etched the first dark line between the sea and sky, he took out a dollar and went downstairs.

She was not in the kitchen, but the table was set for his morning tea. Muttering at her persistence, he charged down the corridor, which ran the length of the basement, flinging open the doors to the damp, empty rooms on either side, and sending the lizards and the shadows long entrenched there scuttling to safety.

He found her in the small slanted room under the stoop, asleep on an old cot he kept there, her suitcase turned down beside the bed, and the shoes, dress and the ridiculous hat piled on top. A loose nightshift muted the outline of her body and hid her legs, so that she appeared suddenly defenseless, innocent, with a child's trust in her curled hand and in her deep breathing. Standing in the doorway, with his own breathing snarled and his eyes averted, Mr. Watford felt like an intruder. She had claimed the room. Quivering with frustration, he slowly turned away, vowing that in the morning he would shove the dollar at her and lead her like a cow out of his house. . . .

Dawn brought rain and a hot wind which set the leaves rattling and swiping at the air like distraught arms. Dressing in the dawn darkness, Mr. Watford again armed himself with the dollar and, with his shoulders at an uncompromising set, plunged downstairs. He descended into the warm smell of bakes and this smell, along with the thought that she had been up before him, made his hand knot with exasperation on the banister. The knot tightened as he saw her, dust swirling at her feet as she swept the corridor, her face bent solemn to the task. Shutting her out with a lifted hand, he shouted, "Don't bother sweeping. Here's a dollar. G'long back."

The broom paused and although she did not raise her head, he sensed her groping through the shadowy maze of her mind toward his voice. Behind the dollar which he waved in her face, her eyes slowly cleared. And, surprisingly, they held no fear. Only anticipation and a tenuous trust. It was as if she expected him to say something kind.

"G'long back!" His angry cry was a plea.

Like a small, starved flame, her trust and expectancy died and she said, almost with reproof, "The rain falling."

To confirm this, the wind set the rain stinging across the windows and he could say nothing, even though the words sputtered at his lips. It was useless. There was nothing inside her to comprehend that she was not wanted. His shoulders sagged under the weight of her ignorance, and with a futile gesture he swung away, the dollar hanging from his hand like a small sword gone limp.

She became as fixed and familiar a part of the house as the stones—and as silent. He paid her five dollars a week, gave her Mondays off and in the evenings, after a time, even allowed her to sit in the alcove off the parlor, while he read with his back to her, taking no more notice of her than he did the moths on the lamp.

But once, after many silent evenings together, he detected a sound apart from the night murmurs of the sea and village and the metallic tuning of the steel band, a low, almost inhuman cry of loneliness which chilled him. Frightened, he turned to find her leaning hesitantly toward him, her eyes dark with urgency, and her face tight with bewilderment and a growing anger. He started, not understanding, and her arm lifted to stay him. Eagerly she bent closer. But as she uttered the low cry again, as her fingers described her wish to talk, he jerked around, afraid that she would be foolish enough to speak and that once she did they would be brought close. He would be forced then to acknowledge something about her which he refused to grant; above all, he would be called upon to share a little of himself. Quickly he returned to his newspaper, rustling it to settle the air, and after a time he felt her slowly, bitterly, return to her silence. . . .

Like sand poured in a careful measure from the hand, the weeks flowed down to August and on the first Monday, August Bank holiday, Mr. Watford awoke to the sound of the excursion buses leaving the village for the annual outing, their backfire pelleting the dawn calm and the ancient motors protesting the overcrowding. Lying there, listening, he saw with disturbing clarity his mother dressed for an excursion—the white headtie wound above her dark face and her head poised like a dancer's under the heavy outing basket of food. That set of her head had haunted his years, reappearing in the girl as she walked toward him the first day. Aching with the memory, yet annoyed with himself for remembering, he went downstairs.

The girl had already left for the excursion, and although it was her day off, he felt vaguely betrayed by her eagerness to leave him. Somehow it suggested ingratitude. It was as if his doves were suddenly to refuse him their song or his trees their fruit, despite the care he gave them. Some vital past which shaped the simple mosaic of his life seemed suddenly missing. An alien silence curled like coal gas throughout the house. To escape it he remained in the grove all day and, upon his return to the house, dressed with more care than usual, putting on a fresh, starched uniform, and solemnly brushing his hair until it lay in a smooth bush above his brow. Leaning close to the mirror, but avoiding his eyes, he cleaned the white rheum at their corners, and afterward pried loose the dirt under his nails.

Unable to read his papers, he went out on the portico to escape the unnatural silence in the house, and stood with his hands clenched on the balustrade and his taut body straining forward. After a long wait he heard the buses return and voices in gay shreds upon the wind. Slowly his hands relaxed, as did his shoulders under the white uniform; for the first time that day his breathing was regular. She would soon come.

But she did not come and dusk bloomed into night, with a fragrant heat and a full moon which made the leaves glint as though touched with frost. The steel band at the crossroads began the lilting songs of sadness and seduction, and suddenly—like shades roused by the night and the music—images of the girl flitted before Mr. Watford's eyes. He saw her lost amid the carousings in the village, despoiled; he imagined someone like Mr. Goodman clasping her lewdly or tumbling her in the canebrake. His hand rose, trembling, to rid the air of her; he tried to summon his cold laugh. But, somehow, he could not dismiss her as he had always done with everyone else. Instead, he wanted to punish and protect her, to find and lead her back to the house.

As he leaned there, trying not to give way to the desire to go and find her, his fist striking the balustrade to deny his longing, he saw them. The girl first, with the moonlight like a silver patina on her skin, then the boy whom Mr. Goodman sent for the coconuts whose easy strength and the political button—"The Old Order Shall Pass"—had always mocked and challenged Mr. Watford. They were joined in a tender battle: the boy in a sport shirt riotous with color was reaching for the girl as he leaped and spun, weightless, to the music, while she fended him off with a gesture which was lovely in its promise of surrender. Her protests were little scattered bursts: "But, man, why don't you stop, nuh . . . ? But, you know, you getting on like a real-real idiot. . . ."

Each time she chided him he leaped higher and landed closer, until finally he eluded her arm and caught her by the waist. Boldly he pressed a leg between her tightly closed legs until they opened under the pressure. Their bodies cleaved into one whirling form and while he sang she laughed like a wanton, with her hat cocked over her ear. Dancing, the stones moiling underfoot, they claimed the night. More than the night. The steel band played for them alone. The trees were their frivolous companions, swaying as they swayed. The moon rode the sky because of them.

Mr. Watford, hidden by a dense shadow, felt the tendons which strung him together suddenly go limp; above all, an obscure belief which, like rare china, he had stored on a high shelf in his mind began to tilt. He sensed the familiar specter which hovered in the night reaching out to embrace him, just as the two in the yard were embracing. Utterly unstrung, incapable of either speech or action, he stumbled into the house, only to meet there an accusing silence from the clock, which had missed its eight o'clock winding, and his newspapers lying like ruined leaves over the floor.

He lay in bed in the white uniform, waiting for sleep to rescue him, his hands seeking the comforting sound of his doves. But sleep eluded him and instead of the doves, their throats tremulous with sound, his scarred hands filled with the shape of a woman he had once kept: her skin, which had been almost bruising in its softness; the buttocks and breasts spread under his hands to inspire both cruelty and tenderness. His hands closed to softly crush those forms, and the searing thrust of passion, which he had not felt for years, stabbed his dry groin. He imagined the two outside, their passion at a pitch by now, lying together behind the tamarind tree, or perhaps—and he sat up sharply—they had been bold enough to bring their lust into the house. Did he not smell their taint on the air? Restored suddenly, he rushed downstairs. As he reached the corridor, a thread of light beckoned him from her room and he dashed furiously toward it, rehearsing the angry words which would jar their bodies apart. He neared the door, glimpsed her through the small opening, and his step faltered; the words collapsed.

She was seated alone on the cot, tenderly holding the absurd felt hat in her lap, one leg tucked under her while the other trailed down. A white sandal, its strap broken, dangled from the foot and gently knocked the floor as she absently swung her leg. Her dress was twisted around her body—and pinned to the bodice, so that it gathered the cloth between her small breasts, was the political button the boy always wore. She was dreamily fingering it, her mouth shaped by a gentle, ironic smile and her eyes strangely acute and critical. What had transpired on the cot had not only, it seemed, twisted the dress around her, tumbled her hat and broken her sandal, but had also defined her and brought the blurred forms of life into focus for her. There was a woman's force in her aspect now, a tragic knowing and acceptance in her bent head, a hint about her of Cassandra watching the future wheel before her eyes.

Before those eyes which looked to another world, Mr. Watford's anger and strength failed him and he held to the wall for support. Unreasonably, he felt that she should assume some hushed and reverent pose, to bow as she had the day she had come. If he had known their names, he would have pleaded forgiveness for the sins he had committed against her and the others all his life, against himself. If he could have borne the thought, he would have confessed that it had been love, terrible in its demand, which he had always fled. And that love had been the reason for his return. If he had been honest, he would have whispered—his head bent and a hand shading his eyes—that unlike Mr. Goodman (whom he suddenly envied for his full life) and the boy with his political button (to whom he had lost the girl), he had not been willing to bear the weight of his own responsibility. . . . But all Mr. Watford could admit, clinging there to the wall, was, simply, that he wanted to live—and that the girl held life within her as surely as she held the hat in her hands. If he could prove himself better than the boy, he could win it. Only then, he dimly knew, would he shake off the pursuer which had given him no rest since birth. Hopefully, he staggered forward, his step cautious and contrite, his hands, quivering along the wall.

She did not see or hear him as he pushed the door wider. And for some time he stood there, his shoulders hunched in humility, his skin stripped away to reveal each flaw, his whole self offered in one outstretched hand. Still unaware of him, she swung her leg, and the dangling shoe struck a derisive note. Then, just as he had turned away that evening in the parlor when she had uttered her low call, she turned away now, refusing him.

Mr. Watford's body went slack and then stiffened ominously. He knew that he would have to wrest from her the strength needed to sustain him. Slamming the door, he cried, his voice cracked and strangled, "What you and him was doing in here? Tell me! I'll not have you bringing nastiness round here. Tell me!"

She did not start. Perhaps she had been aware of him all along and had expected his outburst. Or perhaps his demented eye and the desperation rising from him like a musk filled her with pity instead of fear. Whatever, her benign smile held and her eyes remained abstracted until his hand reached out to fling her back on the cot. Then, frowning, she stood up, wobbling a little on the broken shoe and holding the political button as if it was a new power which would steady and protect her. With a cruel flick of her arm she struck aside his hand, and, in a voice as cruel, halted him. "But you best move and don't come holding on to me, you nasty, pissy old man. That's all you is, despite yuh big house and fancy furnitures and yuh newspapers from America. You ain't people, Mr. Watford, you ain't people!" And with a look and a lift of her head which made her condemnation final, she placed the hat atop her braids, and turning aside picked up the valise which had always lain, packed, beside the cot—as if even on the first day she had known that this night would come and had been prepared against it. . . .

Mr. Watford did not see her leave, for a pain squeezed his heart dry and the driven blood was a bright, blinding cataract over his eyes. But his inner eye was suddenly clear. For the first time it gazed mutely upon the waste and pretense which had spanned his years. Flung there against the door by the girl's small blow, his body slowly crumpled under the weariness he had long denied. He sensed that dark but unsubstantial figure which roamed the nights searching for him wind him in its chill embrace. He struggled against it, his hands clutching the air with the spastic eloquence of a drowning man. He moaned—and the anguished sound reached beyond the room to fill the house. It escaped to the yard and his doves swelled their throats, moaning with him.

Addison Gayle (1932-   )

Cultural Strangulation: Black Literature and the White Aesthetic

From Negro Digest (July, 1969)

"This assumption that of all the hues of God, whiteness is inherently and obviously better than brownness or tan leads to curious acts. . . ."

W.E.B. Du Bois

The expected opposition to the concept of a "Black Aesthetic" was not long in coming. In separate reviews of *Black Fire,* an anthology edited by LeRoi Jones and Larry Neal, critics from the Saturday Review and The New York Review of Books presented the expected rebuttal. Agreeing with Ralph Ellison that sociology and art are incompatible mates, these critics, nevertheless, invoked the cliches of the social ideology of the "we shall overcome" years in their attempt to steer Blacks from "the path of literary fantasy and folly."

Their major thesis is simple: There is no Black aesthetic because there is no white aesthetic. The Kerner Commission Report to the contrary, America is not two societies but one. Therefore, Americans of all races, colors and creeds share a common cultural heredity. This is to say that there is one predominant culture—the American culture—with tributary national and ethnic streams flowing into the larger river. Literature, the most important by-product of this cultural monolith, knows no parochial boundaries. To speak of a Black literature, a Black aesthetic, or a Black state, is to engage in racial chauvinism, separatist bias, and Black fantasy.

The question of a white aesthetic, however, is academic. One has neither to talk about it nor define it. Most Americans, black and white, accept the existence of a "White Aesthetic" as naturally as they accept April 15th as the deadline for paying their income tax—with far less animosity towards the former than the latter. The white aesthetic, despite the academic critics, has always been with us: for long before Diotima pointed out the way to heavenly beauty to Socrates, the poets of biblical times were discussing beauty in terms of light and dark—the essential characteristics of a white and black aesthetic—and establishing the dichotomy of superior *vs.* inferior which would assume body and form in the 18th century. Therefore, more serious than a definition, is the problem of tracing the white aesthetic from its early origins and afterwards, outlining the various changes in the basic formula from culture to culture and from nation to nation. Such an undertaking would be more germane to a book than an essay; nevertheless, one may take a certain starting point and, using selective nations and cultures, make the critical point, while calling attention to the necessity of a more comprehensive study encompassing all of the nations and cultures of the world.

Let us propose Greece as the logical starting point, bearing in mind Will Durant's observation that "all of Western Civilization is but a footnote to Plato," and take Plato as the first writer to attempt a systematic aesthetic. Two documents by Plato, *The Symposium* and *The Republic*, reveal the twin components of Plato's aesthetic system.

In *The Symposium*, Plato divides the universe into spheres. In one sphere, the lower, one finds the forms of beauty; in the other, the higher, beauty, as Diotima tells Socrates, is absolute and supreme. In *The Republic*, Plato defines the poet as an imitator (a third-rate imitator—a point which modern critics have long since forgotten) who reflects the heavenly beauty in the earthly mirror. In other words, the poet recreates beauty as it exists in heaven; thus the poet, as Neo-Platonists from Aquinas to Coleridge have told us, is the custodian of beauty on earth.

However, Plato defines beauty only in ambiguous, mystical terms; leaving the problem of a more circumscribed, secular definition to philosophers, poets, and critics. During most of the history of the Western world, these aestheticians have been white; therefore, it is not surprising that, symbolically and literally, they have defined beauty in terms of whiteness. (An early contradiction to this tendency is the Marquis DeSade who inverted the symbols, making black beautiful, but demonic, and white pure, but sterile—the Marquis is considered by modern criticism to have been mentally deranged.)

The distinction between whiteness as beautiful (good) and blackness as ugly (evil) appears early in the literature of the middle ages—in the Morality Plays of England. Heavily influenced by both Platonism and Christianity, these plays set forth the distinctions which exist today. To be white was to be pure, good, universal, and beautiful; to be black was to be impure, evil, parochial, and ugly.

The characters and the plots of these plays followed this basic format. The villain is always evil, in most cases the devil; the protagonist, or hero, is always good, in most cases, angels or disciples. The plot then is simple; good (light) triumphs over the forces of evil (dark). As English literature became more sophisticated, the symbols were made to cover wider areas of the human and literary experience. To love was divine; to hate, evil. The fancied mistress of Petrarch was the purest of the pure; Grendel's mother, a creature from the "lower regions and marshes", is, like her son, a monster; the "bad" characters in Chaucer's *Canterbury Tales* tell dark stories; and the Satan of *Paradise Lost* must be vanquished by Gabriel, the angel of purity.

These ancients, as Swift might have called them, established their dichotomies as a result of the influences of Neo-Platonism and Christianity. Later, the symbols became internationalized. Robert Burton, in *The Anatomy of Melancholy*, writes of "dark despair" in the seventeenth century, and James Boswell describes melancholia, that state of mind common to intellectuals of the 17th and 18th centuries, as a dark, dreaded affliction which robbed men of their creative energies. This condition—dark despair or melancholia—was later popularized in what is referred to in English literature as its "dark period"—the period of the Grave Yard School of poets and the Gothic novels.

The symbols thus far were largely applied to conditions, although characters who symbolized evil influences were also dark. In the early stages of English literature, these characters were mythological and fictitious and not representative of people of specific racial or ethnic groups. In the 18th century English novel, however, the symbolism becomes ethnic and racial.

There were forerunners. As early as 1621, Shakespeare has Iago refer to Othello as that "old Black ram", attaching the mystical sexual characteristic to blackness which would become the motive for centuries of oppressive acts by white Americans. In *The Tempest*, Shakespeare's last play, Caliban, though not ostensibly black, is nevertheless a distant cousin of the colonial Friday in Daniel DeFoe's *Robinson Crusoe*.

Robinson Crusoe was published at a historically significant time. In the year 1719, the English had all but completed their colonization of Africa. The slave trade in America was on its way to becoming a booming industry; in Africa, Black people were enslaved mentally as well as physically by such strange bedfellows as criminals, businessmen, and Christians. In the social and political spheres, a rationale was needed, and help came from the artist—in this case, the novelist—in the form of *Robinson Crusoe*. In the novel, DeFoe brings together both Christian and Platonic symbolism, sharpening the dichotomy between light and dark on the one hand, while on the other establishing a criterion for the inferiority of Black people as opposed to the superiority of white.

One need only compare Crusoe with Friday to validate both of these statements. Crusoe is majestic, wise, white and a colonialist; Friday is savage, ignorant, black and a colonial. Therefore, Crusoe, the colonialist, has a double task. On the one hand he must transform the island (Africa—unproductive, barren, dead) into a little England (prosperous, life-giving, fertile), and he must recreate Friday in his own image, thus bringing him close to being an Englishman as possible. At the end of the novel, Crusoe has accomplished both undertakings; the island is a replica of "mother England"; and Friday has been transformed into a white man, now capable of immigrating to the land of the gods.

From such mystical artifacts has the literature and criticism of the Western world sprung; and based upon such narrow prejudices as those of DeFoe, the art of Black people throughout the world has been described as parochial and inferior. Friday was parochial and inferior until, having denounced his own culture, he assimilated another. Once this was done, symbolically, Friday underwent a change. To deal with him after the conversion was to deal with him in terms of a character who had been civilized and therefore had moved beyond racial parochialism.

However, DeFoe was merely a hack novelist, not a thinker. It was left to shrewder minds than his to apply the rules of the white aesthetic to the practical areas of the Black literary and social worlds, and no shrewder minds were at work on this problem than those of writers and critics in America. In America, the rationale for both slavery and the inferiority of Black art and culture was supplied boldly, without the trappings of 18th century symbolism.

In 1867, in a book entitled *Nojoque: A Question for a Continent*, Hinton Helper provided the vehicle for the cultural and social symbols of inferiority under which Blacks have labored in this country. Helper intended, as he states frankly in his preface, "to write the negro out of America." In the headings of the two major chapters of the book, the whole symbolic apparatus of the white aesthetic handed down from Plato to America is graphically revealed: the heading of one chapter reads: "Black: A Thing of Ugliness, Disease;" another heading reads: "White: A Thing of Life, Health, and Beauty."

Under the first heading, Helper argues that the color black "has always been associated with sinister things such as mourning, the devil, the darkness of night." Under the second, "White has always been associated with the light of day, divine transfiguration, the beneficent moon and stars . . . the fair complexion of romantic ladies, the costumes of Romans and angels, and the white of the American flag so beautifully combined with blue and red without ever a touch of the black that has been for the flag of pirates."

Such is the American critical ethic based upon centuries of distortion of the Platonic ideal. By not adequately defining beauty, and implying at least that this was the job of the poet, Plato laid the foundation for the white aesthetic as defined by Daniel DeFoe and Hinton Helper. However, the uses of that aesthetic to stifle and strangle the cultures of other nations is not to be attributed to Plato but, instead, to his hereditary brothers far from the Aegean. For Plato knew his poets. They were not, he surmised, a very trusting lot and, therefore, by adopting an ambiguous position on symbols, he limited their power in the realm of aesthetics. For Plato, there were two kinds of symbols: natural and proscriptive. Natural symbols corresponded to absolute beauty as created by God; proscriptive symbols, on the other hand, were symbols of beauty as proscribed by man, which is to say that certain symbols are said to mean such and such by man himself.

The irony of the trap in which the Black artist has found himself throughout history is apparent. Those symbols which govern his life and art are proscriptive ones, set down by minds as diseased as Hinton Helper's. In other words, beauty has been in the eyes of an earthly beholder who has stipulated that beauty conforms to such and such a definition. To return to Friday, DeFoe stipulated that civilized man was what Friday had to become, proscribed certain characteristics to the term "civilized", and presto, Friday, in order not to be regarded as a "savage under Western eyes," was forced to conform to this ideal. How well have the same stipulative definitions worked in the artistic sphere! Masterpieces are made at will by each new critic who argues that the subject of his doctoral dissertation is immortal. At one period of history, John Donne, according to the critic Samuel Johnson, is a second rate poet; at another period, according to the critic T. E. Eliot, he is one of the finest poets in the language. Dickens, argues Professor Ada Nisbet, is one of England's most representative novelists, while for F. R. Leavis, Dickens' work does not warrant him a place in *The Great Tradition*.

When Black literature is the subject, the verbiage reaches the height of the ridiculous. The good "Negro Novel", we are told by Robert Bone and Herbert Hill, is that novel in which the subject matter moves beyond the limitations of narrow parochialism. Form is the most important criterion of the work of art when Black literature is evaluated, whereas form, almost non-existent in Dostoyevskys *Crime and Punishment*, and totally chaotic in Kafka's *The Trial*, must take second place to the supremacy of thought and message.

Richard Wright, says Theodore Gross, is not a major American novelist; while Ralph Ellison, on the strength of one novel, is. LeRoi Jones is not a major poet, Ed Bullins not a major playwright, Baldwin incapable of handling the novel form—all because white critics have said so.

Behind the symbol is the object or vehicle, and behind the vehicle is the definition. It is the definition with which we are concerned, for the extent of the cultural strangulation of Black literature by white critics has been the extent to which they have been allowed to define the terms in which the Black artist will deal with his own experience. The career of Paul Laurence Dunbar is the most striking example. Having internalized the definitions handed him by the American society, Dunbar would rather not have written about the Black experience at all, and three of his novels and most of his poetry support this argument. However, when forced to do so by his white liberal mentors, among them was the powerful critic, William Dean Howells, Dunbar deals with Blacks in terms of buffoonery, idiocy and comedy.

Like so many Black writers, past and present, Dunbar was trapped by the definitions of other men, never capable of realizing until near the end of his life, that those definitions were not god-given, but man-given; and so circumscribed by tradition and culture that they were irrelevant to an evaluation of either his life or his art.

In a literary conflict involving Christianity, Zarathustra, Friedrich Nietzsche's iconoclast, calls for "a new table of the laws." In similar iconoclastic fashion, the proponents of a Black Aesthetic, the idol smashers of America, call for a set of rules by which Black literature and art is to be judged and evaluated. For the historic practice of bowing to other men's gods and definitions has produced a crisis of the highest magnitude, and brought us, culturally, to the limits of racial armegeddon. The trend must be reversed.

The acceptance of the phrase "Black is Beautiful" is the first step in the destruction of the old table of the laws and the construction of new ones, for the phrase flies in the face of the whole ethos of the white aesthetic. This step must be followed by serious scholarship and hard work; and Black critics must dig beneath the phrase and unearth the treasure of beauty lying deep in the untoured regions of the Black experience—regions where others, due to historical conditioning and cultural deprivation, cannot go.

William Melvin Kelly (1937-   )

Cry for Me

From Dancers on the Shore (1963)

This is about my Uncle Wallace, who most of you know by his last name—Bedlow—because that's all they ever put on his records. I only got one of his albums myself. It has a picture of him on it, sitting, holding his two guitars, wearing his white dinner jacket, his mouth wide open and his eyes squinted shut. The name of the album is: *Bedlow—Big Voice Crying in the Wilderness* and I got it in particular because it has the only two songs he sang that I really like: *Cotton Field Blues* and *John Henry*. Besides that, I don't much like folk songs or folk singers. But I liked Uncle Wallace all right.

I guess I should tell you about the first time I met Uncle Wallace; this was even before he was folk singing, or maybe before any of us *knew* it. We just knew he was a relative, my old man's brother, come North from the South.

That was in June of 1957. We went to Pennsylvania Station to meet him. He sent us a telegram; there wasn't enough time for him to write a letter because he told us later he only decided to come two days before he showed up.

So we went to the station, and the loud-speaker called out his train from down South. A *whole* bunch of colored people got off the train, all looking like somebody been keeping it a secret from them they been free for a hundred years, all bulgy-eyed and confused, carrying suitcases and shopping bags and boxes and little kids.

My old man was craning his neck, looking to find Uncle Wallace. None of us would-a recognized him because when my old man come North twenty years ago he didn't bring but one picture of Uncle Wallace and that was of him when he was about seven. But my old man been back South once and saw Uncle Wallace a man. He would recognize him all right.

But I heard my old man say to my mother, "Don't see him yet."

And then we did see him; we could not-a missed him because he come rumbling out the crowd—the size of a black Grant's Tomb with a white dinner jacket draped over it (he had the jacket even then, having won it in some kind-a contest driving piles, or cutting wood)—and punched my old man square in the chops so he flew back about twenty feet, knocking over this little redcap, and springing all the locks on the four suitcases he was carrying, scattering clothes in all directions like a flock of pigeons in Central Park you tossed a rock at.

My old man is about six-five and two-fifty and works in heavy construction and I ain't never seen anyone hit him, let alone knock him off his feet, and I thought sure he'd go nuts and get mad, but he didn't; he started to laugh, and Uncle Wallace stood over him and said: "How you doing, Little Brother? I see you ain't been keeping up your strength. Use to have more trouble with you when I was six." And he reached out his hand to my old man, who got up, and even though he was on his feet still looked like he was lying down because Uncle Wallace was at least a head taller.

My old man said, "Never could beat you, Wallace. Pa's the only man could." And I remember figuring how to be able to do that, my Grandpa Mance Bedlow must-a been close to eight feet tall and made of some kind of fireproof metal.

Then my old man turned to us and said: "I'd like you to meet my family. This is my wife, Irene." He pointed at my mother. "And this is Mance; we call him Little Brother." He pointed at my brother. "And this is my first born, Carlyle junior." And he pointed at me and I reached up my hand to Uncle Wallace before I realized he'd probably crush it. He took it, but didn't crush it at all, just squeezed it a little and smiled, looking down at me out tiny, red eyes in his black-moon face.

So we took Uncle Wallace home to the Bronx.

My old man got him a job with the same construction company he worked for and the foreman, he'd send them both up on the girders and give them enough work for eight men and they'd get it done, and then they'd come home and Uncle Wallace'd watch television until one and then go to sleep. He never seen it before and it knocked him out.

He hadn't seen anything of New York but our house and the building he and my old man was practically putting up singlehanded. That's why one Friday night, my old man said: "Carlyle, why don't you take old Wallace downtown and show him the city?"

I really didn't want to go; I mean, that's *nowhere* getting stuck with a man could be your father, but I went.

First I took him to Harlem near where we used to live and we said hello to some of my old friends who was standing in front of a bar, watching the girls swishing by in dresses where you could see everything, either because the dresses was so tight over what they should-a been covering, or because there wasn't no dress covering the other parts. I guess Uncle Wallace liked that pretty much because everybody was colored and where we live in the Bronx, everybody is Italian. So in Harlem, he must-a felt at home.

Then we went to Times Square. I don't think he liked that too much, too big and noisy for him, him being right out of a cotton field. I was about to take him home, but then I said: "Hey, Uncle Wallace, you ever seen a queer?"

He looked down at me. "What's that, Carlyle?"

I was about to laugh because I figured maybe he ain't seen a queer, but I would-a thought *everybody* knew what they was. But then I decided just to explain—I knew how strong he was, but hadn't been knowing him long enough to know how fast he got mad. So I just told him what a queer was.

He looked down at me blank and sort of stupid. "No stuff?"

"I wouldn't lie to you, Uncle Wallace." I took him by the arm. "Come on, I'll show you some queers."

That's why we went to Greenwich Village.

It was comical to see him looking at his first queer, who was as queer as a giraffe sitting on a bird's nest. Uncle Wallace just gaped like he seen a farmer hitch a chipmunk to a plow, then turned to me. "Well, I'll be lynched, Carlyle!"

After that we walked around past the handbag and sandal shops and the coffee houses and dug the queers and some girls in sort of black underwear, and then all of a sudden, he wasn't with me no more. I turned all the way around, a little scared because if he would-a got his-self lost, I'd never see him again. He was halfway back up the block, his head way above everybody else's like he was standing on a box, and a look on his face like he been knocked up side his head with a cast-iron Cadillac. I ran back up to him, but by the time I got to where he been standing, he was most down some steps leading into a cellar coffee shop called *The Lantern*. I called to him but he must-a not heard me over the singing that was coming from inside. He was already at the door and a cross-eyed little blond girl was telling him to put a dollar in the basket she was tending. So I followed him down, paid my dollar and caught up to him. "Hey, Uncle Wallace, what's the matter?"

He put his hand on my shoulder, grabbing it tight so I could hear the bones shift around. "Hush, boy." And then he turned to this little lit-up stage and there was this scrawny yellow Negro sitting on a stool playing the guitar and singing some folk song. He was wearing a green shirt open to his belly button, and a pair of tight back pants. What a queer!

The song he was singing was all about how life is tough—he looked like the toughest day he ever spent was when his boy friend didn't serve him breakfast in bed—and how when you're picking cotton, the sun seems to be as big as the whole sky. The last line was about how he'd pick all the cotton in the world and not plant no more and wouldn't have to work again and how he'd finally win out over the sun. When he finished, everybody snapped their fingers, which is what they do in the Village instead of clap.

Then he said: "And now, ladies and gentlemen, this next piece is another from the collection of Francis Mazer, a song he found during his 1948 trip through the South. A blues called *Wasn't That a Man.*" He struck a chord and started to sing: something about a Negro who swum a flooded, raging river with his two sons and his wife tied on his back. He sang it very fast so all the words ran together.

Uncle Wallace listened through one chorus, his eyes narrowing all the time until they about disappeared, and then he was moving, like a black battleship, and I grabbed his coat so he wouldn't make a fool of his-self in front of all them white folks, but then I just let him go. It was his business if he wanted to act like a nigger, and I couldn't stop him anyway. So I just stood there watching him walk in the dark between the little tables and looming out in the spotlight, burying the yellow Negro in his shadow.

Uncle Wallace reached out and put his hand around the neck of the guitar and the notes choked off. His hand must-a gone around the neck about three times.

The yellow Negro looked up at him, sort of shook. "I beg your pardon?"

"Brother, you better start begging somebody's pardon for what you doing to that song. You sings it all wrong."

Then a bald man in a shirt with the points of the collar all twisted and bent come up and patted Uncle Wallace on the back, hard. "Come on, buddy. Let's move out."

Uncle Wallace about-faced and looked way down at him. "Brother, next time you come up behind me and touch me, you'll find yourself peeping at me out of that guitar."

The bald man took a step back. Uncle Wallace looked at the yellow Negro again. "Now, look-a-here, colored brother, you can't sing my songs that way.

You sing them like I made them up or don't sing them at all. And if you *do* sing them your way, then you may just never sing again, ever." He was still holding the neck of the guitar.

"Your songs? You didn't write these songs," the yellow Negro said. "They grew up out of the Rural Southern Negro Culture."

"Go on, nigger! They grew up out-a me. That song you was just singing now, about the man and the river, I wrote that song about my very own Daddy."

A couple people in the audience started to sit up and listen. But that little yellow flit of a Negro didn't believe it. "I tell you, these songs were collected in 1948 by Francis Mazer, and there's no telling how long they've been sung. I heard the original tapes myself."

Uncle Wallace's eyes went blank for a second. Then he said: "What this Francis Mazer look like? He a little old gray-haired man with a game leg?"

That stopped the yellow Negro for a while. "Yessss." He held onto the word like he didn't want to let it out.

"Sure enough, I remember him. He was a mighty sweet old gentleman, told me all he wanted to do was put my songs on a little strip of plastic. I asked him if he meant to write *all* my songs on that small space. He said I got him wrong, that the machine he had with him would make a record of them. And I said for him to go on. I was playing a dance and the folks was happy and I sang from Friday night until the next afternoon, and that little gentleman stood by just putting them spools in his machine and smiling. And when I got done he give me thirty dollars, U.S. currency, and I went out and bought me some new strings and a plow too." Uncle Wallace stopped and shook his head. "Mighty sweet old gentleman. And you say his name was Mazer?"

"This has gone far enough!" The yellow Negro was real ticked off now, sort of cross like a chick. "Arthur, get him out of here." He was talking to the bald man.

Uncle Wallace looked at the bald man too, sort of menacing. Then he looked at the yellow Negro. "I don't want you singing my songs *at all*." Then he just walked away, out of the lights and it was like the sun come up on the yellow Negro all at once.

But the bald man wouldn't let it stop there and said: "Hey, you, mister, wait!" He was talking to Uncle Wallace, who didn't stop because (he told me later) he never in his life got called *Mister* by no white man, so he thought the bald man was talking to someone else.

The bald man run after him and was about to put his hand on his shoulder, but remembered what Uncle Wallace said before and hot-footed it around in front of him and started to talk, backing up. "I'm Arthur Friedlander. I own this place. If you're what you say you are, then I'd like you to sing some songs."

That stopped Uncle Wallace, who told me once he'd sing for anybody, even a president of a White Citizen's Council if he got asked. So he came to a halt

like a coal truck at a sudden red light and looked down on Mister Friedlander
and said: "You want me to sing?"

And Mister Friedlander said: "If you can. Sure, go on."

"But I ain't brung my guitars."

"He'll let you use his. Go on." He reached out sort of timid, like at a real
mean dog, and took Uncle Wallace's arm and started to lead him back to the
lights.

The yellow Negro, he didn't really want to give up his guitar, but I guess he
figured Mister Friedlander would fire him if he didn't, so he left it resting against
the stool and stormed off the stage.

Uncle Wallace and Mister Friedlander went up there and Uncle Wallace
picked up the guitar and ran his fingers over the strings. It looked like he was
holding a ukulele.

Mister Friedlander looked at the audience and said: *"The Lantern* takes
pleasure in presenting a new folk singer." He realized he didn't know Uncle
Wallace's name and turned around.

"Bedlow," Uncle Wallace said, sort-a shy.

"Bedlow," said Mister Friedlander to the audience.

A couple people giggled and a couple others snapped their fingers, but they
was joking. Uncle Wallace whacked the guitar again, and all of a sudden music
come out of it. I was surprised because way down deep I thought sure Uncle
Wallace was just a fool. He didn't play right off, though, just hit it a couple times
and started to talk:

"That song the other fellow was playing, I wrote that when my Daddy died,
for his funeral. That was 1947. It's all about how when I was a boy we had a
flood down home and where we was living got filled up with water. There was
only one safe, high spot in that country—an island in mid-river. But none of us
could swim but my Daddy, so he tied me and my brother on his back and my
Mama, she hung on and he swum the whole parcel of us over. So everybody
remembered that and when he was taken I made a song about it to sing over
his trench . . ." He hit another chord, but still didn't sing yet, just stopped.

"Say," he said, "anybody got another guitar?"

Some folks started mumbling about him being a fake and stalling and a
couple of them laughed. I was thinking maybe they was right.

A white boy with a beard come up with a guitar case and opened it and
reached over a guitar to Uncle Wallace and so now he had two guitars. I thought
he didn't like the yellow Negro's guitar, but he started to get them in the same
tune—hitting one and then the other. And when he judged they was all right,
he put one on his left knee, with his left hand around the neck like anybody
would hold a guitar, and then put the other one on his right knee and grabbed
the neck of that one with his right hand. His arms was way out and he looked
like he was about to fly away. Then he clamped his fingers down on the strings
of them both so hard and so fast they both sounded, not just a little noise, but a

loud chord like an organ in church, or two men playing guitars. Then he started to stamp his feet and clamp his fingers and you could hear the blues get going and then he was singing . . .

Well, not really, because the most you could say about his voice was that it was on key, and it was sure loud! It wasn't deep and hollow, or high and sweet. It didn't even sound like singing. In fact, I don't think anybody ever heard him sing or really listened to him. It wasn't a voice you heard or listened to; it was a voice you swallowed, because it always seemed to upset your stomach. I heard him sing lots of times and it was always the same: not hearing anything, but feeling kind of sick like you been drinking a gallon of wine, and the wine was fighting you inside, grabbing at your belly and twisting it around so you wanted to yell out, but didn't because you was scared the wine might take offense and tear you to pieces. And when he stopped and the grabbing stopped, you'd feel all weak and terrible like maybe you would feel if you gotten a date with a girl you thought might give you some tail and you been thinking about it all day in school and then you went out with her and when you took her home, her folks was out, and so she took you inside and you *did* get some tail and now that it was all over, you wished she'd run inside and not given you anything because then it wouldn't be all over now and you'd still have it to look forward to. But pretty soon he'd start singing again and everything would be like it was before, feeling sick, and wishing you was *still* sick when you didn't feel sick no more.

So that's the way it was that Friday in the Village; that's the way it always was. And the people was always the same. When he got through grabbing at them, no one snapped their fingers; no one ordered anything. The cooks come out the kitchen and the waitresses sat down with the customers. People come down the steps and paid their money and managed to get into a seat before he reached out and caught them, and when the seats was all gone—because nobody left—people kept coming until they was standing and sitting in the aisles, packed right to the doors, and even on the stage with him, nobody moving or making a sound, just getting sick in the stomach and hating it and loving it all at the same time.

So Uncle Wallace sang right until Saturday morning at four. And then we went home and I slept all day.

That was how we found out what Uncle Wallace was, or did. But for a while after he sang that Friday, he didn't sing no more. It was like before: Uncle Wallace going to work, him and my old man building their building, coming home and Uncle Wallace gassing himself on TV until one, then going to sleep.

But then the phone call came from Mister Friedlander and I answered it. He sounded real tired and said: "Hello? Is this the Bedlow residence? Do you have someone living with you or know of someone named Bedlow who sings folk songs?"

And when I answered the questions Yes, there was a silence and then I could hear sobbing on the other end of the line and through all the sobbing, him saying, "Thank God; Thank God," for about five minutes.

So at first I was about to hang up because I heard of guys calling up and cursing at women and all that mess, but then he said: "Who am I talking to?" I told him. "You were with that man who sang in my place four weeks ago? *The Lantern?* I'm Arthur Friedlander." So I said Hello, because I remembered him. He asked me what Uncle Wallace was to me and I told him.

"Carlyle," he said, "I've been trying to find your uncle for three weeks. I called Bedfords and Bradfords for the first two. It's like this, kid, every night a hundred people come into the place and ask for him and I have to say he isn't here and they get so mad they go away. He's ruining me! Where's your uncle now?"

I told him Uncle Wallace was at work.

"Listen, kid, there's a five in it for you if you can get him down here tonight by seven-thirty. And tell him I'll pay him thirty—no, make that fifty a week."

I said I could only *try* like I figured it might be hard to get Uncle Wallace to sing. Mister Friedlander give me his number and told me to call him back when I had an answer and hung up.

When Uncle Wallace come home, I said: "That man you sang for a month ago?—he wants you to come again . . . for money." I didn't have to add the money part because I could tell by his face, he was ready to go.

So I called back Mister Friedlander and told him we was coming. I said that to get Uncle Wallace to sing, which he hadn't wanted to do, I had to say Mister Friedlander was paying him seventy-five dollars a week.

Mister Friedlander didn't even seem surprised. He just said, "But you got him to come?"

"Yes, sir," I said.

"Good boy! I'm giving you ten dollars instead of five." Which is what I figured he'd do if I told him I had trouble.

When we turned the corner into *The Lantern's* block there was a riot going on, with a hundred people, maybe even a thousand there, not all Village people neither. A whole bunch of them was in suits, and fur coats and jewels. Man, if I been a pickpocket I could-a retired on what I could-a got there that night. And there was cops in their green cars with flashing lights going off and on, and on horses. Folks was pushing each other into the gutter and throwing punches. I looked up at Uncle Wallace and said: "Hey, we better split. We ain't got nothing to do with this, and you know how cops pick on colored folks."

"But I promised the man I'd sing, Carlyle," he said. But I could tell it wasn't that: he just wanted to sing, promise or no promise.

So we tried to sneak around behind all the rioting to get into *The Lantern*. And we most made it, but someone said: "Is that him?"

And someone answered: "Got to be."

I poked Uncle Wallace and said: "Now we really better get out-a here. These white folks think you done something."

"What?" he asked.

"I don't know, but we better get out-a here, *now*." And I grabbed his arm and started to pull him away, out-a there. I could tell he didn't want to go; he wanted to sing, but I figured I had to keep him out-a jail if I could.

Then someone started to yell at us to stop and I turned around to see how big they was and if there was more than we could handle, because either Uncle Wallace could flatten them or we could outrun them. But it was Mister Friedlander, chugging up the stairs, yelling.

We stopped.

He got to us and said, "What's wrong?"

"They think Uncle Wallace did something. He didn't do nothing. We just got here. We don't know nothing about this riot."

"Come inside. I'll explain," Mister Friedlander said. So we went down the stairs, and inside and he locked the door.

The place was jammed! There was more people there than that first Friday night.

Mister Friedlander said: "After you called, I put a sign in the window saying: *Bedlow here tonight.* Those people, they're here to see him. That's what the riot is." Then he asked me if I read that New York Sunday paper which weighs so much and ain't got no funnies. I told him No.

"Well, that Friday night your Uncle Wallace was here, there was a guy here from that paper. And the next Sunday he wrote an article—wait, I'll show you." So he ran behind the counter and come out with this page of a newspaper that he got magnified around forty times and pasted on cardboard. At the top of the page was this title: *Big Voice Crying in the Wilderness.*

The article under it was about Uncle Wallace. It told all about that other Friday night and said that Uncle Wallace was a voice speaking for all the colored folks and that to hear him was to understand the pain of discrimination and segregation and all that kind of stuff, which seemed like a lot of B-S to me because I didn't understand Uncle Wallace hardly myself; I didn't understand why he sang folk songs when he could sing rock-and-roll or jazz. So how the hell could he be *my* voice or the voice of anybody like me? But that's what this writer said anyway.

When I looked up from the story I must-a been frowning, or maybe looked like I didn't get it because Mister Friedlander grabbed me by the shoulders and shook me. "Don't you see? Your uncle is the hottest thing to hit New York since the Chicago Fire. He's a fad!"

And all the time he was telling me this, Uncle Wallace was standing by the window looking out at the people, not realizing this was all about him. That was when I started to dig something about him I never had before, and when I started to really like him and decided I'd have to look after him, even though he was old enough and big enough and smart enough to look after his-self: Uncle Wallace was innocent. To him you didn't sing for money, or for people even, but because you wanted to. And I guess the most important thing was that he wasn't some guy singing about love who never loved, or hard work who never worked hard because he done all that, loved women and picked cotton and plowed and chopped trees. And even though he was in show business, he wasn't at all like anybody else in it. He was more real somehow.

Anyway, I could say he was better that night than he was before, but that wouldn't be really honest because I didn't dig his music so I don't know if he was better or not. I think the people liked him better, but I can't be sure of *that* either because when he finished, they was in so much pain, they never snapped their fingers for him, just sat staring, sad and hurting like before.

After he sung three sets and was sitting back in the kitchen drinking gin and fruit juice, this man come in with Mister Friedlander. "Bedlow, this is A. V. Berger. He wants to speak to you a minute."

This Mister Berger was five feet tall—tops—but weighed close to three hundred pounds with black hair, straight and greasy. He was wearing a black wool suit—this was in midsummer now—with a vest and a scarf, which was black wool too. And the English this man spoke was fantabulous! I can only *try* to copy it. He hemmed and hawed a lot too so it sounded like:

"Mister Bedlow, (hem) I'm a concert producer. And (hem) I have been watching you perform. It seems quite likely that (hem) I can use you in a concert (hem) I'm staging at Carnegie Hall." He stopped there. I could see he was looking for Uncle Wallace to jump in the air and clap his hands. I knew what Carnegie Hall was, but I bet Uncle Wallace didn't. Mister Berger thought Uncle Wallace was playing it cagey.

"Mister Bedlow, (hem) I'm prepared to offer you a good price to appear in the show."

"What's it to be? A dance?" Uncle Wallace said. "Sure, I'll play for a dance. That's what I done down home."

"No, Mister Bedlow. You (hem) misunderstand. This will be a concert."

"Like what?" He turned to me. "Like what, Carlyle?"

"A concert, Uncle Wallace. That's when a whole lot of folks come and just sit and listen to you sing."

"You mean just like here?"

"No, Uncle Wallace. It's like a church." I was thinking about how the seats was arranged, but he didn't get me.

"But I don't sing church music, Carlyle. My songs is too dirty for church. They never let me sing in no church." He looked back at Mister Berger. "What kind-a church you running, mister, that they sing my kind-a songs in there?"

"(hem) I don't run a church, Mister Bedlow." Mister Berger looked sort-a bleak and confused.

"No, Uncle Wallace, it ain't in no church," I said. "It's in a big hall and they want you to sing for a couple thousand people."

"No stuff?"

"Yeah, sure," I said.

"That's (hem) right," said Mister Berger.

"Go on, Bedlow," chimed in Mister Friedlander.

So he did.

But that concert wasn't until October and Mister Berger asked him to appear in early July, so there was a lot of time in between, when Uncle Wallace was making all his records.

And there was that damn movie. It was about this plantation family and all their problems in the Civil War. It wasn't really such a bad movie, but Uncle Wallace made it worse. I mean, he was the best thing in it, but after he was on the screen you couldn't look at the movie no more.

The movie would be going on all right and then would come Uncle Wallace's scene. He be sitting on this log in raggedy clothes and they *even* had a bandana around his head. You know how they make movies about colored people in Hollywood; the slaves act like slavery was the best God-damn thing ever happened to them and all they did all day was sit around on logs and sing and love Old Master, instead of breaking their asses in his cotton field and waiting for the chance to run away or slit Old Master's throat wide open. But that wasn't the worst. Dig this! They made him sing *John Henry*. But it didn't matter. They didn't know Uncle Wallace. He started playing and singing and when he got through you had the feeling old John Henry wasn't no idiot after all. I mean, I heard some guy sing that song once and I said to myself: what an idiot this John Henry must-a been, killing his-self to beat a machine, when he could-a joined a union, like my old man's, and made twice the money and kept the machine out.

But when Uncle Wallace sang *John Henry* you didn't feel that way. You felt like old John Henry was trapped and he had to do what he did, like when a fellow says your Mama screws for syphilitic blind men, you got to hit him; you don't think about it; it don't even matter if he joking or not, you just got to hit him even if he beats all hell out-a you. Well, that's what Uncle Wallace did to you.

So when them white folks come back on the screen with their dumb problems, and started kissing it up, you could see they was cardboard; you could see they was acting and you got up and left out of there because you had to see real people again, and even when you got out in the street you sort-a felt like the people *out there* wasn't real neither, so what you did was go back in and stand in the lobby until the next showing when Uncle Wallace come on again for his two minutes and you'd go in and see him. Then you'd walk out again to the lobby. There was always a whole lot of folks out there waiting like you and not looking at you because you was as cardboardy to them as they was to you, and you'd wait for his two minutes again, and like that all day until you got too hungry to see.

After he made the movie he come back East and it was October and it was time for the concert at Carnegie Hall. And I guess you know what happened at the concert, but I'll tell it again and also some things I felt about it.

Mister Berger had-a told Uncle Wallace to play it cool and save his best until last, which meant that Uncle Wallace was to come out and sing a couple songs with only one guitar and then—bingo!—lay the two guitars on them. So they fixed me up in a tux and when the time come, I paraded out and give him the other guitar.

Uncle Wallace was tuning the second guitar when a voice come whispering up from the dark in the front row. "Hey, nigger, you the same one, ain't you."

Uncle Wallace squinted down, and there in the front row with all them rich white folks was this dark little Negro. There was a woman with him and a whole bunch of little kids, all shabby-looking, all their eyes shining like a row of white marbles.

"The same as what?" Uncle Wallace said.

And the voice come back. "The same fellow what played at a East Willson café in 1948."

"Yeah, I played there that year."

"There was one night in particular, when a cripple white man was taping you, and we all danced until the next day."

"Sure, it was!" Uncle Wallace snapped his fingers. "I remember you. You was with a *pretty* girl."

"You right, man. Here she is; my wife." He turned to the woman. "Honey, get up and meet Mister Bedlow." She did, and Uncle Wallace leaned over the edge of the stage and shook her hand. "Say, you know, I bought these big money seats because I wanted my kids to see you up close. Them is them." He pointed at the row of kids. "The oldest one, he's Bedlow. I named him after you because me and the wife wasn't getting on so good until that night." It was like they was all alone in that great big place, just those two down-home Negroes talking over old times. "And them others is Booker, Carver, Robeson, Robinson, and Bunche."

"Man, you do me proud. Pleased to meet you all. Say, you want to come up here and sit with me?"

"Now, you do *me* proud." So they all come up on stage like a row of ducks.

Then Uncle Wallace started to play and the littlest kid, that was Bunche— he was about three—he sat there for about one minute and then I saw him jump on his feet and start to do these wild little steps, just his feet moving like little pistons. Then the man got up and asked his wife to dance, and the next thing I knew, everybody was dancing—even me; I danced right out on stage—and all the rich white folks was on their feet in the aisles and their wives was hugging strangers, black and white, and taking off their jewelry and tossing it in the air and all the poor people was ignoring the jewelry, was dancing instead, and you could see everybody laughing like crazy and having the best old time ever. Colored folks was teaching white folks to dance, and white folks was dancing with colored folks and all the seats was empty and people was coming on stage to dance. Then the other singers backstage come out and started to back-up Uncle Wallace and we was all dancing, all of us, and over all the noise and laughing you could hear Uncle Wallace with his two guitars. You could hear him over the whole thing.

Then the air changed; you could feel it. It wasn't just air any more, it started to get sweet-tasting to breathe like perfume and the people started to run down the aisles toward the stage, and everybody on the stage started to dance in toward Uncle Wallace, and everybody, *everybody* in the whole place was sobbing and crying and tears was pouring down their cheeks and smearing their make-up and making their eyes red and big. I could hear Uncle Wallace singing louder than ever. The people was rushing toward him. They was all crying and smiling too like people busting into a trance in church and it seemed like everybody in the place was on stage trying to get near enough to touch him, grab his hand and shake it and hug him and kiss him even. And then the singing stopped.

I pushed my way through the crowd up to his chair. The first thing I seen was his two guitars all tore up and smashed and the strings busted. Uncle Wallace was sitting in his chair, slumped over, his face in his lap. And this was real strange; he looked like an old punctured black balloon, deflated and all. There wasn't a mark on him, but he was dead all right.

Mister Berger called in a whole bunch of doctors, but they just stood around shaking their heads. They couldn't figure out how he'd died. One of them said, "There isn't nothing wrong with him, except he's dead."

Now I know this'll sound lame to you, but I don't think anything killed him except maybe at that second, he'd done everything that he ever wanted to do; he'd taken all them people, and sung to them, and made them forget who they was, and what they come from, and remember only that they was people. So he'd seen all he wanted to see and there was no use going on with it. I mean, he'd made it. He got over.

It's kind of like that girl I was telling you about—the one who'd promised you some tail, and when you got it, you was sorry, because then you'd still have it to look forward to? Well, I think it's like that: getting tail and coming out of her house and there ain't nothing but pussycats and garbage cans in the street, and it's lonely and late and you wished you hadn't done it, but then you shrug and say to yourself: "Hell, man, you did, and that's it." And there ain't nothing to do but leave, because it's finished. But then there's something else. You're walking along and all at once you smile, and maybe even laugh, and you say: "Man, that was some *good* tail!" And it's a nice memory to walk home with.

Ted Joans (1928-   )

The Ubiquitous Lions

To O. Egbuna

From Black Pow-wow (1969)

There are four lions   at Trafalgar Square   stolen symbols
    that do not
bare any-kinda resemblance   to European royalty
These four lions   at Trafalgar Square   with whom European
    queens and
kings   try to identify   are African   and very very BLACK
The four lions at Trafalgar Square   sit regally/lazy/
    and cooly gaze
whilst mini-skirted tourists slide between their wide spread paws
although they have a hip sneer   across their majestic black jaws
These four lions at Trafalgar Square   bigger than young elephants
heavier than fourteen Rolls Royces   have nothing a-tall to do with
chalk-white kings or Europeans horses an auto roar imitates their
    black voices
These four black lions   of Africa   now sitting in London
    dreary town
lookout in four directions   at international tourists
    pose near or
around   for the photo shot   these lions DO NOT FROWN!
The four black lions   at Trafalgar Square   have heard and seen
white demonstrations/meeting & rally lost and won
they've witnessed white man's pro & con   white guilt & fears
Nearby stands the South African Building and closer still is
    a Hippy church
For U.S.A. Civil Rites   and Biafra white nigger crocodile shed tears
There are four lions   at Trafalgar Square   they are black   and
    like lions everywhere

on European buildings   pedestals and government seals
These black lions must be free   to attack imperialism and destroy
    that evil deal
Sic'em sic'em lions   git them   white devils who dared to identify
    with thy!

In Homage to Heavy Loaded Trane, J.C.

From Black Pow-wow (1969)

J.C. in these
sentences of three
read by
Stokely C. Allen G. & me
London summer '67
J.C. it said:
sheets of   sound
       MASCULINE MUSCLE MOODS   OF   BLUES
S   e   r   p
         e
           n
            t
             i
              n e   screams   of happiness
hot molted masses of marvelous messages
and HEAVY   anger
                  p
                    o
                    u
                      r
                       i
                        n
                         g
            forth   from   fiery   throats
of your thick reeds
spurting rhythms
all over
all under
and all around
J.C.
Mr. Trane
J.C.
John Coltrane

with pain
we read
three short English lines
of your dying
and we strain
J.C.
black people & me
to keep
from crying

Hoyt W. Fuller (1927-   )

The Role of the Negro Writer in an Era of Struggle

From Negro Digest (June, 1964)

The most successful polemicist of this generation is a bug-eyed, boy-sized Negro named James Baldwin who, despite it all, wants desperately to be known as a good novelist. In a decade, he has produced three novels, and while the most recent one, *Another Country,* was a bestseller, none of them has received the sort of critical praise the author would like for his fiction. On the other hand, Mr. Baldwin has published three collections of articles and essays which have gained for him the wildest critical acclaim ever accorded a Negro writer in this country. Two of these volumes, *Nobody Knows My Name* and *The Fire Next Time,* also have been bestsellers and the third, which, in fact, was his first published work of non-fiction, *Notes of A Native Son,* has been rushed into print again to capitalize on the author's sensational popularity.

Mr. Baldwin is quite pleased with the reception of his books, of course, both because it means the reading public is receiving his message and because it means financial independence for him. But he will readily admit that his personal ambition remains to be fulfilled: he wants to write novels which will draw from non-axe-grinding critics the lavish kudos his non-fiction already has earned.

Following publication of *Another Country* in 1962, Mr. Baldwin undertook a series of lectures and public appearances which took him to major literary centers across the country. His face and his statements became familiar in newspapers, magazines and journals. Then, in November, 1962, The New Yorker magazine published a long, rambling, extraordinarily searching essay by Mr. Baldwin which literally—as well as literarily—shook up the American reading public.

That essay, of course, is the meat of the book, *The Fire Next Time,* which was rushed into print a few weeks following the appearance of the magazine.

Suddenly, organizations and literary and social-conscious groups all over the country were clamoring for the writer's attention. Every newspaper and periodical of any significance whatever published news or reviews about him and his books, and Time magazine put him on its cover; the television networks brought him before their cameras, and it became a common sight to see the small, intensely alert figure with the great eloquent eyes solemnly setting forth his concept of the American failure and the American future on the nation's TV screens; he was interviewed and taped, and even recordings of him talking and reading became bestsellers; CORE beckoned, and he went, launching forth on a physically exhausting national tour to deliver his message in person, while bringing in badly needed funds for the vital work CORE is performing; and finally, the U. S. Attorney General called, and then came calling, and in a remarkable session which may have no parallel in history, the Negro writer who five years earlier was unknown to all but a few discerning readers was telling the man who then sat on the right hand side of the President of the United States that Negro Americans have reached the end of their endurance and that, hereafter, they would be in no mood to accept anything short of their full rights as citizens of this country. That done, the little black writer hied himself off to Puerto Rico and again took up his typewriter to finish his play, *Blues For Mr. Charlie*. He was, he explained, a writer, really, not a politician, and it is a writer's duty to write.

Nevertheless, in taking valuable time away from his work to become a civil rights activist, Mr. Baldwin demonstrated most dramatically what—for him, at any rate—is the black writer's role in this era of struggle. It is a role which many great writers of the past have played.

One such was Voltaire, the 18th century French dramatist and philosopher whose attacks on religious fanaticism and political injustice twice landed him in the Bastille, drove him into exile, and it has been said, helped to bring about the French Revolution.

Another was Thomas Paine, the American patriot, whose pamphlets fired his countrymen to action in our own Revolution. This is a role, then, which involves commitment of the writer to the noblest of human values, which demands of the writer as artist that he dedicate his skills to the proposition every man has the right to be free.

In pursuing such a role, the writer serves as disturber of that spurious peace which is arrived at through the degradation of *some* men; he seeks to move the uncommitted to positive action on the side of freedom; and he exhorts those who are numbed by oppression or blinded by bigotry to turn their eyes and their energies toward that which is true and just and which is both balm and sustenance for the human spirit.

It would seem that the black writer, himself a member of a group struggling to rise from the morass of degradation and apathy and near-despair, would find such a role tailored to his peculiar specifications.

Naturally, however, there are those who hold different views of the black writer's role in this—or any—era of struggle, particularly if that struggle is racial. In the chorus of general praise which has greeted the articles and declarations by James Baldwin, for instance, there have risen strident and discordant voices.

Lashing out at Mr. Baldwin in what masqueraded as a review of Richard Wright's posthumous novel, *Lawd Today*, ex-Life magazine correspondent Arthur Shay branded the writer an "Oedipal wreck" and cried: "Has *nothing* changed in the quarter century separating Wright and Baldwin? Doesn't 'the American dream' now include some Negroes?"

In an attack on the two Negro writers which bordered on hysteria, the critic expressed dubious sympathy for his black compatriots. "The American Negro has had an extraordinary run of bad luck in his literary spokesmen," Mr. Shay wrote, supremely ignorant of the fact that he spoke only for white people. "They go mute with rage, expatriating themselves from the theatre of their anguish, as Richard Wright did; they retire to some dark Olympus of the spirit, as James Baldwin is doing, and issue warnings like mail order seers."

Mr. Shay conveniently forgot that Richard Wright was in rather distinguished company in expatriating himself. Great and sensitive souls have been fleeing the American nightmare for generations, and they have included Henry James, Ezra Pound, T. S. Eliot, Gertrude Stein and Ernest Hemingway, to name a few. And even so narrow-visioned an observer as Mr. Shay ought to be able to discern by now that James Baldwin's warnings may have come just in time to deflect a national cataclysm: partly because of them, persons in authority from the White House down to community churches have been making an extra effort to put our national house in order. Mr. Baldwin never said the fire was inevitable.

What critics like Mr. Shay really find so hard to bear—apart from the indignity of having to listen to Negroes making demands rather than pleading for mercy—is the refusal of Negro writers to accept the crumbs of tokenism for the whole loaf of freedom. "Doesn't 'the American dream' now include *some* Negroes?" he asks, and the inference is, of course, that Negro writers ought to be celebrating the advances that have been made rather than endlessly complaining about remaining injustices. There are, after all, Marian Anderson and Ralph Bunche.

These critics consider writers like James Baldwin as dangerous, as well they should, although they rarely have the candor to state just what the writers are endangering. After taking a series of editorial potshots at Mr. Baldwin in his Chicago Tribune Magazine of Books column, World Almanac editor Harry Hansen admitted his "irritation" at the Negro writer although his reasons for discomfort were singularly unconvincing. Mr. Baldwin's "way of talking is doing the Negro writer some harm," he put it, displaying a sudden and touching concern for the welfare of Negro writers.

It remained for National Review editor William Buckley, the darling of the

Right-Wing, to state, as only the rapier-tongued Mr. Buckley can state, what was on all these critics' minds. "Baldwin is an eloquent menace," Mr. Buckley wrote in his syndicated column, going on to equate Mr. Baldwin's indictment of white American society with Adolf Hitler's indictment of the Weimar Republic and Karl Marx's indictment of capitalism. "We need to improve," Mr. Buckley conceded, speaking for the white race. "Simultaneously we need to reorder more generously our relationship with the Negro race, and to reject out of hand the preposterous and suicidal counsels of the Negroes' most inflamed spokesman."

It may not be too much to assume that Mr. Baldwin, had he read Mr. Buckley's assessment of him, would have been highly complimented. No self-respecting black man could desire the approval of a man who would express even his guilt in such racially patronizing terms.

And that, ultimately, states the problem and defines the protagonists. The problem concerns human freedom and dignity, and those who believe in it have joined battle with those who do not. It may be that some black writers being only human and therefore frail, can stand aside and pursue only their Muse. But in this era of struggle, as in all the others which have preceded it, such men are not easy to imagine.

LeRoi Jones (1934-   )

Preface to a Twenty Volume Suicide Note

(For Kellie Jones, born 16 May 1959)

From Preface to a Twenty Volume Suicide Note (1961)

Lately, I've become accustomed to the way
The ground opens up and envelopes me
Each time I go out to walk the dog.
Or the broad edged silly music the wind
Makes when I run for a bus . . .

Things have come to that.

And now, each night I count the stars,
And each night I get the same number.
And when they will not come to be counted,
I count the holes they leave.

Nobody sings anymore.

And then last night, I tiptoed up
To my daughter's room and heard her
Talking to someone, and when I opened
The door, there was no one there . . .
Only she on her knees, peeking into

Her own clasped hands.

I Substitute for the Dead Lecturer

From the Dead Lecturer (1964)

What is most precious, because
it is lost. What is lost,
because it is most
precious.

They have turned, and say that I am dying. That
I have thrown
my life
away. They
have left me alone, where
there is no one, nothing
save who I am. Not a note
nor a word.

        Cold air batters
the poor (and their minds
turn open
like sores). What kindness
What wealth
can I offer? Except
what is, for me,
ugliest. What is
for me, shadows, shrieking
phantoms. Except
they have need
of life. Flesh
at least,
        should be theirs.

The Lord has saved me
to do this. The Lord
has made me strong. I

am as I must have
myself. Against all
thought, all music, all
my soft loves.

For all these wan roads
I am pushed to follow, are
my own conceit. A simple muttering
elegance, slipped in my head
pressed on my soul, is my heart's
worth. And I am frightened
that the flame of my sickness
will burn off my face. And leave
the bones, my stewed black skull,
an empty cage of failure.

The Politics of Rich Painters

From the Dead Lecturer (1964)

is something like the rest
of our doubt, whatever slow thought
comes to rest, beneath the silence
of starving talk.
                    Just their fingers' prints
staining the cold glass, is sufficient
for commerce, and a proper ruling on
humanity. You know the pity
of democracy, that we must sit here
and listen to how he made his money.
Tho the catalogue of his possible ignorance
roars and extends through the room
like fire. "Love," becomes the pass,
the word taken intimately to combat
all the uses of language. So that learning
itself falls into disrepute.

2.

What they have gathered into themselves
in that short mean trip from mother's iron tit
to those faggot handmaidens of the french whore

who wades slowly in the narrows, waving her burnt out
torch. There are movies, and we have opinions. There are
regions of compromise so attractive, we daily long
to filthy our minds with their fame. And all the songs
of our handsome generation fall clanging like stones
in the empty darkness of their heads.

                        Couples, so beautiful
in the newspapers, marauders of cheap sentiment. So much *taste*
so little understanding, except some up and coming queer explain
cinema and politics while drowning a cigarette.

3.

They are more ignorant than the poor
tho they pride themselves with that accent. And
move easily in fake robes of egalitarianism. Meaning,
I will fuck you even if you don't like art. And are wounded
that you call their italian memories petit bourgeois.

                            Whose death
will be Malraux's? Or the names Senghor, Price, Baldwin
whispered across the same dramatic pancakes, to let each eyelash
    flutter
at the news of their horrible deaths. It is a cheap game
to patronize the dead, unless their deaths be accountable
to your own understanding. Which be nothing nothing
if not bank statements and serene trips to our ominous country-
    side.
Nothing, if not whining talk about handsome white men. Nothing
if not false glamourous and static. Except, I admit, your lives
are hideously real.

4.

The source of their art crumbles into legitimate history.
The whimpering pigment of a decadent economy, slashed into life
as Yeats' mad girl plummeting over the nut house wall, her broken
knee caps rattling in the weather, reminding us of lands
our antennae do not reach.
And there are people in these savage geographies
use your name in other contexts
think, perhaps, the title of your latest painting
another name for liar.

Black Art

Black Magic, Poetry 1961–1967

Poems are bullshit unless they are
teeth or trees or lemons piled
on a step. Or black ladies dying
of men leaving nickel hearts
beating them down. Fuck poems
and they are useful, wd they shoot
come at you, love what you are,
breathe like wrestlers, or shudder
strangely after pissing. We want live
words of the hip world live flesh &
coursing blood. Hearts Brains
Souls splintering fire. We want poems
like fists beating niggers out of Jocks
or dagger poems in the slimy bellies
of the owner-jews. Black poems to
smear on girdlemamma mulatto bitches
whose brains are red jelly stuck
between 'lizabeth taylor's toes. Stinking
Whores! We want "poems that kill."
Assassin poems, Poems that shoot
guns. Poems that wrestle cops into alleys
and take their weapons leaving them dead
with tongues pulled out and sent to Ireland. Knockoff
poems for dope selling wops or slick halfwhite
politicians Airplane poems, rrrrrrrrrrrrrrrr
rrrrrrrrrrrrrr . . . tuhtuhtuhtuhtuhtuhtuhtuhtuh
. . . rrrrrrrrrrrrrrrr . . . Setting fire and death to
whities ass. Look at the Liberal
Spokesman for the jews clutch his throat
& puke himself into eternity . . . rrrrrrrr
There's a negroleader pinned to
a bar stool in Sardi's eyeballs melting
in hot flame Another negroleader
on the steps of the white house one
kneeling between the sheriff's thighs
negotiating cooly for his people.
Agggh . . . stumbles across the room . . .
Put it on him, poem. Strip him naked
to the world! Another bad poem cracking
steel knuckles in a jewlady's mouth

Poem scream poison gas on beasts in green berets
Clean out the world for virtue and love,
Let there be no love poems written
until love can exist freely and
cleanly. Let Black People understand
that they are the lovers and the sons
of lovers and warriors and sons
of warriors Are poems & poets &
all the loveliness here in the world

We want a black poem. And a
Black World.
Let the world be a Black Poem
And Let All Black People Speak This Poem
Silently
or LOUD

Black People!

From Black Magic, Poetry 1961–1967

What about that bad short you saw last week
on Frelinghuysen, or those stoves and refrigerators, record players
in Sears, Bambergers, Klein's, Hahnes', Chase, and the smaller
    joosh
enterprises? What about that bad jewelry, on Washington Street,
    and
those couple of shops on Springfield? You know how to get it, you
    can
get it, no money down, no money never, money dont grow on
    trees no
way, only whitey's got it, makes it with a machine, to control you
you cant steal nothin from a white man, he's already stole it he
    owes
you anything you want, even his life. All the stores will open if
    you
will say the magic words. The magic words are: Up against the
    wall mother
fucker this is a stick up! Or: Smash the window at night (these
    are magic
actions) smash the windows daytime, anytime, together, let's
    smash the

window drag the shit from in there. No money down. No time to
  pay. Just
take what you want. The magic dance in the street. Run up and
  down Broad
Street niggers, take the shit you want. Take their lives if need
  be, but
get what you want what you need. Dance up and down the streets,
  turn all
the music up, run through the streets with music, beautiful radios
  on
Market Street, they are brought here especially for you. Our
  brothers
are moving all over, smashing at jellywhite faces. We must make
  our own
World, man, our own world, and we can not do this unless the
  white man
is dead. Let's get together and killhim my man, let's get to gather
  the fruit
of the sun, let's make a world we want black children to grow and
  learn in
do not let your children when they grow look in your face and
  curse you by
pitying your tomish ways.

Larry Neal (1937-   )

Love Song in Middle Passage

From Black Boogaloo (Notes on Black Liberation) (1969)

We plunge through time
and feel
the westward pull of death—
slave ships flank the shore,
across the veldt, songs,
moaning spirits and lonely rhythms;
voices plunge, screaming blood
in time's body
as
slick white knives slit black throats,
chew black brains, tearing their bodies

piece by piece, flesh-eating pirates.
and even though we be life itself
we must kill.

Sea-winds moan, one, Fulani warrior, breaks
a slave-runner's skull,
then kills his black self rather
than never see his land or children,
or hear the spirits of his ancestors
moving in the vibrations of the drum.

and even though we be life itself
we must kill.
must will death to white sea monsters
and their pale shit smelling philosophies.

Red glow of sea-death mornings.
and where will it end?
and who will end it?
our summits are endless
deep within
the soil-cosmos of our spirits.

and even though we be life
we must kill,
gouging out pale sea-water eyes,
crushing them and their generations,
spitting destruction upon their cities
which burn like plastic dreams;
blacks boogaloo through their cities shouting
and burning, hurling precise death-curses,
stone-cold killers bursting with revenge.
break through.
breaking through their time into our own.

even though we are the sun's song,
the roar, the surge, the rhythm and poetry;
the shocked sounds of saxophones, old men,
dancing children, and the women singing funky blues,
we must destroy
to live.

On the sea's horizon NcNamara scientists
with Ph.d.'s
lurk

twist bomb dials, manipulate Negro organizations.
contrive C.I.A. chaos, while drinking Emmett Till's
blood. (Welcome to Mississippi
                    land of sweet magnolias.)

We must become stone-cold killers,
panther-spirits, invisible men,
night specters: your uncle tom teeth brightly grin
or you scratch your stephin' fetchit head,
while thrusting the blade into the beast-heart,
and still grinning with your uncle tom grin,
say: "you de boss, boss, heh, heh, heh, heh,
              now try this for size, motherfucker!"

then expand,
sucking in the meaning of your discovery,
sucking in the liberated wonder of the cosmos,
expanding until the world is filled with
a vibrating black light.

Garvey's Ghost

(For Max Roach)

From Black Boogaloo (Notes on Black Liberation) (1969)

Look for me in the whirlwind
with you; in fire smeared faces
and burning black voices; the best
              that we would be
in the whirlwind's pain.
we spin, Africa's children, the sea
hard against our faces.

Look for me in the thunder rhythm
stabbing the flesh filled night; the best
that we would be in the best manner possible.
dance Spirits in time's womb and give
them strength.

Me in the whirlwind's thunder
with the weak ones crawling,
reaching to become that which we would be.
and were I in you and you in me; and were

we, my children, the grace of each other,
or those who speak some new music.
but where are our eyes? who has stolen
our voice? will the whirlwind be their doom?

nigger eyes in the wind and in the thunder,
red mouth niggers starkly bobbing out of the
sea. zombie faced ju-ju working niggers
cutting morbid fetish figures while crushing
the beast-skull; and singing, singing in the
whirlwind. the truth-bearing wind
knows no color especially. Knows only
truth and vengeance.

Jamaica rhythms are soft to feel
when you understand that quiet
moments are what a man also needs
below the surface of things;
yes under the face of things,
but these things you have never
really known or seen; a sea of your
own, your own green hope, your own
thing, your own sunlight.

None of these you have known;
but one continual cry is all,
one long historical moan
is all you have known
one continuous moan in the blues
kissed whirlwind

Malcolm X

Chapter Nineteen   1965

From the Autobiography of Malcolm X (1965)

I must be honest. Negroes—Afro-Americans—showed no inclination to rush to
the United Nations and demand justice for themselves here in America. I really
had known in advance that they wouldn't. The American white man has so
thoroughly brainwashed the black man to see himself as only a domestic "civil

rights" problem that it will probably take longer than I live before the Negro sees that the struggle of the American black man is international.

And I had known, too, that Negroes would not rush to follow me into the orthodox Islam which had given me the insight and perspective to see that the black men and white men truly could be brothers. America's Negroes—especially older Negroes—are too indelibly soaked in Christianity's double standard of oppression.

So, in the "public invited" meetings which I began holding each Sunday afternoon or evening in Harlem's well-known Audubon Ballroom, as I addressed predominantly non-Muslim Negro audiences, I did not immediately attempt to press the Islamic religion, but instead to embrace all who sat before me:

"—not Muslim, nor Christian, Catholic, nor Protestant . . . Baptist nor Methodist, Democrat nor Republican, Mason nor Elk! I mean the black people of America—and the black people all over this earth! Because it is as this collective mass of black people that we have been deprived not only of our civil rights, but even of our human rights, the right to human dignity. . . ."

On the streets, after my speeches, in the faces and the voices of the people I met—even those who would pump my hands and want my autograph—I would feel the wait-and-see attitude. I would feel—and I understood—their uncertainty about where I stood. Since the Civil War's "freedom," the black man has gone down so many fruitless paths. His leaders, very largely, had failed him. The religion of Christianity had failed him. The black man was scarred, he was cautious, he was apprehensive.

In understood it better now than I had before. In the Holy World, away from America's race problem, was the first time I ever had been able to think clearly about the basic divisions of white people in America, and how their attitudes and their motives related to, and affected Negroes. In my thirty-nine years on this earth, the Holy City of Mecca had been the first time I had ever stood before the Creator of All and felt like a complete human being.

In that peace of the Holy World—in fact, the very night I have mentioned when I lay awake surrounded by snoring brother pilgrims—my mind took me back to personal memories I would have thought were gone forever . . . as far back, even, as when I was just a little boy, eight or nine years old. Out behind our house, out in the country from Lansing, Michigan, there was an old, grassy "Hector's Hill," we called it—which may still be there. I remembered there in the Holy World how I used to lie on the top of Hector's Hill, and look up at the sky, at the clouds moving over me, and daydream, all kinds of things. And then, in a funny contrast of recollections, I remembered how years later, when I was in prison, I used to lie on my cell bunk—this would be especially when I was in solitary: what we convicts called "The Hole"—and I would picture myself talking to large crowds. I don't have any idea why such previsions came to me. But they did. To tell that to anyone then would have sounded crazy. Even I didn't have, myself, the slightest inkling. . . .

In Mecca, too, I had played back for myself the twelve years I had spent with Elijah Muhammad as if it were a motion picture. I guess it would be impossible for anyone ever to realize fully how complete was my belief in Elijah Muhammad. I believed in him not only as a leader in the ordinary *human* sense, but also I believed in him as a *divine* leader. I believed he had no human weaknesses or faults, and that, therefore, he could make no mistakes and that he could do no wrong. There on a Holy World hilltop, I realized how very dangerous it is for people to hold any human being in such esteem, especially to consider anyone some sort of "divinely guided" and "protected" person.

My thinking had been opened up wide in Mecca. In the long letters I wrote to friends, I tried to convey to them my new insights into the American black man's struggle and his problems, as well as the depths of my search for truth and justice.

"I've had enough of someone else's propaganda," I had written to these friends. "I'm for truth, no matter who tells it. I'm for justice, no matter who it is for or against. I'm a human being first and foremost, and as such I'm for whoever and whatever benefits humanity *as a whole.*"

Largely, the American white man's press refused to convey that I was now attempting to teach Negroes a new direction. With the 1964 "long, hot summer" steadily producing new incidents, I was constantly accused of "stirring up Negroes." Every time I had another radio or television microphone at my mouth, when I was asked about "stirring up Negroes" or "inciting violence," I'd get hot.

"It takes no one to stir up the sociological dynamite that stems from the unemployment, bad housing, and inferior education already in the ghettoes. This explosively criminal condition has existed for so long, it needs no fuse; it fuses itself; it spontaneously combusts from within itself. . . ."

They called me "the angriest Negro in America." I wouldn't deny that charge. I spoke exactly as I felt. "I *believe* in anger. The Bible says there is a *time* for anger." They called me "a teacher, a fomentor of violence." I would say point blank, "That is a lie. I'm not for wanton violence, I'm for justice. I feel that if white people were attacked by Negroes—if the forces of law prove unable, or inadequate, or reluctant to protect those whites from those Negroes—then those white people should protect and defend themselves from those Negroes, using arms if necessary. And I feel that when the law fails to protect Negroes from whites' attack, then those Negroes should use arms, if necessary, to defend themselves."

"Malcolm X Advocates Armed Negroes!"

What was wrong with that? I'll tell you what was wrong. I was a black man talking about physical defense against the white man. The white man can lynch and burn and bomb and beat Negroes—that's all right: "Have patience" . . . "The customs are entrenched" . . . "Things are getting better."

Well, I believe it's a crime for anyone who is being brutalized to continue to accept that brutality without doing something to defend himself. If that's how

"Christian" philosophy is interpreted, if that's what Gandhian philosophy teaches, well, then, I will call them criminal philosophies.

I tried in every speech I made to clarify my new position regarding white people—"I don't speak against the sincere, well-meaning, good white people. I have learned that there *are* some. I have learned that not all white people are racists. I am speaking against and my fight is against the white *racists*. I firmly believe that Negroes have the right to fight against these racists, by any means that are necessary."

But the white reporters kept wanting me linked with that word "violence." I doubt if I had one interview without having to deal with that accusation.

"I *am* for violence if non-violence means we continue postponing a solution to the American black man's problem—just to *avoid* violence. I don't go for non-violence if it also means a delayed solution. To me a delayed solution is a non-solution. Or I'll say it another way. If it must take violence to get the black man his human rights in this country. I'm *for* violence exactly as you know the Irish, the Poles, or Jews would be if they were flagrantly discriminated against. I am just as they would be in that case, and they would be for violence—no matter what the consequences, no matter who was hurt by the violence."

White society *hates* to hear anybody, especially a black man, talk about the crime the white man has perpetrated on the black man. I have always understood that's why I have been so frequently called "a revolutionist." It sounds as if *I* have done some crime! Well, it may be the American black man does need to become involved in a *real* revolution. The word for "revolution" in German is *Umwälzung*. What it means is a complete overturn—a complete change. The overthrow of King Farouk in Egypt and the succession of President Nasser is an example of a true revolution. It means the destroying of an old system, and its replacement with a new system. Another example is the Algerian revolution, led by Ben Bella; they threw out the French who had been there over 100 years. So how does anybody sound talking about the Negro in America waging some "revolution"? Yes, he is condemning a system—but he's not trying to overturn the system, or to destroy it. The Negro's so-called "revolt" is merely an asking to be *accepted* into the existing system! A *true* Negro revolt might entail, for instance, fighting for separate black states within this country—which several groups and individuals have advocated, long before Elijah Muhammad came along.

When the white man came into this country, he certainly wasn't demonstrating any "non-violence." In fact, the very man whose name symbolizes non-violence here today has stated:

"Our nation was born in genocide when it embraced the doctrine that the original American, the Indian, was an inferior race. Even before there were large numbers of Negroes on our shores, the scar of racial hatred had already disfigured colonial society. From the sixteenth century forward, blood flowed in battles over racial supremacy. We are perhaps the only nation which tried as a matter of national policy to wipe out its indigenous population. Moreover, we elevated that tragic experience into a noble crusade. Indeed, even today we have not permitted ourselves to reject or to feel remorse for this shameful episode. Our literature, our films, our drama, our folklore all exalt it. Our children are still taught to respect the violence which reduced a red-skinned people of an earlier culture into a few fragmented groups herded into impoverished reservations."

"Peaceful coexistence!" That's another one the white man has always been quick to cry. Fine! But what have been the deeds of the white man? During his entire advance through history, he has been waving the banner of Christianity . . . and carrying in his other hand the sword and the flintlock.

You can go right back to the very beginning of Christianity. Catholicism, the genesis of Christianity as we know it to be presently constituted, with its hierarchy, was conceived in Africa—by those whom the Christian church calls "The Desert Fathers." The Christian church became infected with racism when it entered white Europe. The Christian church returned to Africa under the banner of the Cross—conquering, killing, exploiting, pillaging, raping, bullying, beating—and teaching white supremacy. This is how the white man thrust himself into the position of leadership of the world—through the use of naked physical power. And he was totally inadequate spiritually. Mankind's history has proved from one era to another that the true criterion of leadership is spiritual. Men are attracted by spirit. By power, men are *forced*. Love is engendered by spirit. By power, anxieties are created.

I am in agreement one hundred per cent with those racists who say that no government laws ever can *force* brotherhood. The only true world solution today is governments guided by true religion—of the spirit. Here in race-torn America, I am convinced that the Islam religion is desperately needed, particularly by the American black man. The black man needs to reflect that he has been America's most fervent Christian—and where has it gotten him? In fact, in the white man's hands, in the white man's interpretation . . . where has Christianity brought this *world*?

It has brought the non-white two-thirds of the human population to rebellion. Two-thirds of the human population today is telling the one-third minority white man, "Get out!" And the white man is leaving. And as he leaves, we see the non-white peoples returning in a rush to their original religions, which had been labeled "pagan" by the conquering white man. Only one religion —Islam—had the power to stand and fight the white man's Christianity for a *thousand years!* Only Islam could keep white Christianity at bay.

The Africans are returning to Islam and other indigenous religions. The Asians are returning to being Hindus, Buddhists and Muslims.

As the Christian Crusade once went East, now the Islamic Crusade is going West. With the East—Asia—closed to Christianity, with Africa rapidly being converted to Islam, with Europe rapidly becoming un-Christian, generally today it is accepted that the "Christian" civilization of America—which is propping up the white race around the world—is Christianity's remaining strongest bastion.

Well, if *this* is so—if the so-called "Christianity" now being practiced in America displays the best that world Christianity has left to offer—no one in his right mind should need any much greater proof that very close at hand is the *end* of Christianity.

Are you aware that some Protestant theologians, in their writings, are using the phrase "post-Christian era"—and they mean *now?*

And what is the greatest single reason for this Christian church's failure? It is its failure to combat racism. It is the old "You sow, you reap" story. The Christian church sowed racism—blasphemously; now it reaps racism.

Sunday mornings in this year of grace 1965, imagine the "Christian conscience" of congregations guarded by deacons barring the door to black would-be worshipers, telling them "You can't enter *this* House of God!"

Tell me, if you can, a sadder irony than that St. Augustine, Florida—a city named for the black African saint who saved Catholicism from heresy—was recently the scene of bloody race riots.

I believe that God now is giving the world's so-called "Christian" white society its last opportunity to repent and atone for the crimes of exploiting and enslaving the world's non-white peoples. It is exactly as when God gave Pharaoh a chance to repent. But Pharaoh persisted in his refusal to give justice to those whom he oppressed. And, we know, God finally destroyed Pharaoh.

Is white America really sorry for her crimes against the black people? Does white America have the capacity to repent—and to atone? Does the capacity to repent, to atone, exist in a majority, in one-half, in even one-third of American white society?

Many black men, the victims—in fact most black men—would like to be able to forgive, to forget, the crimes.

But most American white people seem not to have it in them to make any serious atonement—to do justice to the black man.

Indeed, how *can* white society atone for enslaving, for raping, for unmanning, for otherwise brutalizing *millions* of human beings, for centuries? What atonement would the God of Justice demand for the robbery of the black people's labor, their lives, their true identities, their culture, their history—and even their human dignity?

A desegregated cup of coffee, a theater, public toilets—the whole range of hypocritical "integration"—these are not atonement.

After a while in America, I returned abroad—and this time, I spent eighteen weeks in the Middle East and Africa.

The world leaders with whom I had private audiences this time included President Gamal Abdel Nasser, of Egypt; President Julius K. Nyerere, of Tanzania; President Nnamoi Azikiwe, of Nigeria; Osagyefo Dr. Kwame Nkrumah, of Ghana; President Sekou Touré, of Guinea; President Jomo Kenyatta, of Kenya; and Prime Minister Dr. Milton Obote, of Uganda.

I also met with religious leaders—African, Arab, Asian, Muslim, and non-Muslim. And in all of these countries, I talked with Afro-Americans and whites of many professions and backgrounds.

An American white ambassador in one African country was Africa's most respected American ambassador: I'm glad to say that this was told to me by one ranking African leader. We talked for an entire afternoon. Based on what I had heard of him, I had to believe him when he told me that as long as he was on the African continent, he never thought in terms of race, that he dealt with human beings, never noticing their color. He said he was more aware of language differences than of color differences. He said that only when he returned to America would he become aware of color differences.

I told him, "What you are telling me is that it isn't the American white *man* who is a racist, but it's the American political, economic, and social *atmosphere* that automatically nourishes a racist psychology in the white man." He agreed.

We both agreed that American society makes it next to impossible for humans to meet in America and not be conscious of their color differences. And we both agreed that if racism could be removed, America could offer a society where rich and poor could truly live like human beings.

That discussion with the ambassador gave me a new insight—one which I like: that the white man is *not* inherently evil, but America's racist society influences him to act evilly. The society has produced and nourishes a psychology which brings out the lowest, most base part of human beings.

I had a totally different kind of talk with another white man I met in Africa—who, to me, personified exactly what the ambassador and I had discussed. Throughout my trip, I was of course aware that I was under constant surveillance. The agent was a particularly obvious and obnoxious one; I am not sure for what agency, as he never identified it, or I would say it. Anyway, this one finally got under my skin when I found I couldn't seem to eat a meal in the hotel without seeing him somewhere around watching me. You would have thought I was John Dillinger or somebody.

I just got up from my breakfast one morning and walked over to where he was and I told him I knew he was following me, and if he wanted to know anything, why didn't he ask me. He started to give me one of those too-lofty-to-descend-to-you attitudes. I told him then right to his face he was a fool, that he didn't know me, or what I stood for, so that made him one of those people who let somebody else do their thinking; and that no matter what job a man had, at least he ought to be able to think for himself. That stung him; he let me have it.

I was, to hear him tell it, anti-American, un-American, seditious, subversive, and probably Communist. I told him that what he said only proved how little he understood about me. I told him that the only thing the F.B.I., the C.I.A., or anybody else could ever find me guilty of, was being open-minded. I said I was seeking for the truth, and I was trying to weigh—objectively—everything on its own merit. I said what I was against was strait-jacketed thinking, and strait-jacketed societies. I said I respected every man's right to believe whatever his intelligence tells him is intellectually sound, and I expect everyone else to respect my right to believe likewise.

This super-sleuth then got off on my "Black Muslim" religious beliefs. I asked him hadn't his headquarters bothered to brief him—that my attitudes and beliefs were changed? I told him that the Islam I believed in now was the Islam which was taught in Mecca—that there was no God but Allah, and that Muhammad ibn Abdullah who lived in the Holy City of Mecca fourteen hundred years ago was the Last Messenger of Allah.

Almost from the first I had been guessing about something; and I took a chance—and I really shook up that "super-sleuth." From the consistent subjectivity in just about everything he asked and said, I had deduced something, and I told him, "You know, I think you're a Jew with an Anglicized name." His involuntary expression told me I'd hit the button. He asked me how I knew. I told him I'd had so much experience with how Jews would attack me that I usually could identify them. I told him all I held against the Jew was that so many Jews actually were hypocrites in their claim to be friends of the American black man, and it burned me up to be so often called "anti-Semitic" when I spoke things I knew to be the absolute truth about Jews. I told him that, yes, I gave the Jew credit for being among all other whites the most active, and the most vocal, financier, "leader" and "liberal" in the Negro civil rights movement. But I said at the same time I knew that the Jew played these roles for a very careful strategic reason: the more prejudice in America could be focused upon the Negro, then the more the white Gentiles' prejudice would keep diverted off the Jew. I said that to me, one proof that all the civil rights posturing of so many Jews wasn't sincere was that so often in the North the quickest segregationists were Jews themselves. Look at practically everything the black man is trying to "integrate" into for instance; if Jews are not the actual owners, or are not in controlling positions, then they have major stockholdings or they are otherwise in powerful leverage positions—and do they really sincerly exert these influences? No!

And an even clearer proof for me of how Jews truly regard Negroes, I said, was what invariably happened wherever a Negro moved into any white residential neighborhood that was thickly Jewish. Who would always lead the whites' exodus? The Jews! Generally in these situations, some whites stay put—you just notice who they are: they're Irish Catholics, they're Italians; they're rarely ever any Jews. And, ironically, the Jews themselves often still have trouble being "accepted."

Saying this, I know I'll hear "anti-Semitic" from every direction again. Oh, yes! But truth is truth.

Politics dominated the American scene while I was traveling abroad this time. In Cairo and again in Accra, the American press wire services reached me with trans-Atlantic calls, asking whom did I favor, Johnson—or Goldwater?

I said I felt that as far as the American black man was concerned they were both just about the same. I felt that it was for the black man only a question of Johnson, the fox, or Goldwater, the wolf.

"Conservatism" in America's politics means "Let's keep the niggers in their place." And "liberalism" means "Let's keep the *knee*-grows in their place—but tell them we'll treat them a little better; let's fool them more, with more promises." With these choices, I felt that the American black man only needed to choose which one to be eaten by, the "liberal" fox or the "conservative" wolf— because both of them would eat him.

I didn't go for Goldwater any more than for Johnson—except that in a wolf's den, I'd always know exactly where I stood; I'd watch the dangerous wolf closer than I would the smooth, sly fox. The wolf's very growling would keep me alert and fighting him to survive, whereas I *might* be lulled and fooled by the tricky fox. I'll give you an illustration of the fox. When the assassination in Dallas made Johnson President, who was the first person he called for? It was for his best friend, "Dicky"—Richard Russell of Georgia. Civil rights was "a moral issue," Johnson was declaring to everybody—while his best friend was the Southern racist who *led* the civil rights opposition. How would some sheriff sound, declaring himself so against bank robbery—and Jesse James his best friend?

Goldwater as a man, I respected for speaking out his true convictions—something rarely done in politics today. He wasn't whispering to racists and smiling at integrationists. I felt Goldwater wouldn't have risked his unpopular stand without conviction. He flatly told black men he wasn't for them—and there is this to consider: always, the black people have advanced further when they have seen they had to rise up against a system that they clearly saw was outright against them. Under the steady lullabys sung by foxy liberals, the Northern Negro became a beggar. But the Southern Negro, facing the honestly snarling white man, rose up to battle that white man for his freedom—long before it happened in the North.

Anyway, I didn't feel that Goldwater was any better for black men than Johnson, or vice-versa. I wasn't in the United States at election time, but if I had been, I wouldn't have put myself in the position of voting for either candidate for the Presidency, or of recommending to any black man to do so. It has turned out that it's Johnson in the White House—and black votes were a major factor in his winning as decisively as he wanted to. If it had been Goldwater, all I am saying is that the black people would at least have known they were dealing with an honestly growling wolf, rather than a fox who could have them half-digested before they even knew what was happening.

I kept having all kinds of troubles trying to develop the kind of Black Nationalist organization I wanted to build for the American Negro. Why Black Nationalism? Well, in the competitive American society, how can there ever be any white-black solidarity before there is first some black solidarity? If you will remember, in my childhood I had been exposed to the Black Nationalist teachings of Marcus Garvey—which, in fact, I had been told had led to my father's murder. Even when I was a follower of Elijah Muhammad, I had been strongly aware of how the Black Nationalist political, economic and social philosophies had the ability to instill within black men the racial dignity, the incentive, and the confidence that the black race needs today to get up off its knees, and to get on its feet, and get rid of its scars, and to take a stand for itself.

One of the major troubles that I was having in building the organization that I wanted—an all-black organization whose ultimate objective was to help create a society in which there could exist honest white-black brotherhood—was that my earlier public image, my old so-called "Black Muslim" image, kept blocking me. I was trying to gradually reshape that image. I was trying to turn a corner, into a new regard by the public, especially Negroes; I was no less angry than I had been, but at the same time the true brotherhood I had seen in the Holy World had influenced me to recognize that anger can blind human vision.

Every free moment I could find, I did a lot of talking to key people whom I knew around Harlem, and I made a lot of speeches, saying: "True Islam taught me that it takes *all* of the religious, political, economic, psychological, and racial ingredients, or characteristics, to make the Human Family and the Human Society complete.

"Since I learned the *truth* in Mecca, my dearest friends have come to include *all* kinds—some Christians, Jews, Buddhists, Hindus, agnostics, and even atheists! I have friends who are called capitalists, Socialists, and Communists! Some of my friends are moderates, conservatives, extremists—some are even Uncle Toms! My friends today are black, brown, red, yellow, and *white!*"

I said to Harlem street audiences that only when mankind would submit to the One God who created all—only then would mankind even approach the "peace" of which so much *talk* could be heard . . . but toward which so little *action* was seen.

I said that on the American racial level, we had to approach the black man's struggle against the white man's racism as a human problem, that we had to forget hypocritical politics and propaganda. I said that both races, as human beings, had the obligation, the responsibility, of helping to correct America's human problem. The well-meaning white people, I said, had to combat, actively and directly, the racism in other white people. And the black people had to build within themselves much greater awareness that along with equal rights there had to be the bearing of equal responsibilities.

I knew, better than most Negroes, how many white people truly wanted to see American racial problems solved. I knew that many whites were as frustrated as Negroes. I'll bet I got fifty letters some days from white people. The white people in meeting audiences would throng around me, asking me, after I had addressed them somewhere, "What *can* a sincere white person do?"

When I say that here now, it makes me think about that little co-ed I told you about, the one who flew from her New England college down to New York and came up to me in the Nation of Islam's restaurant in Harlem, and I told her that there was "nothing" she could do. I regret that I told her that. I wish that now I knew her name, or where I could telephone her, or write to her, and tell her what I tell white people now when they present themselves as being sincere, and ask me, one way or another, the same thing that she asked.

The first thing I tell them is that at least where my own particular Black Nationalist organization, the Organization of Afro-American Unity, is concerned, they can't *join* us. I have these very deep feelings that white people who want to join black organizations are really just taking the escapist way to salve their consciences. By visibly hovering near us, they are "proving" that they are "with us." But the hard truth is this *isn't* helping to solve America's racist problem. The Negroes aren't the racists. Where the really sincere white people have got to do their "proving" of themselves is not among the black *victims*, but out on the battle lines of where America's racism really *is*—and that's in their own home communities; America's racism is among their own fellow whites. That's where the sincere whites who really mean to accomplish something have got to work.

Aside from that, I mean nothing against any sincere whites when I say that as members of black organizations, generally whites' very presence subtly renders the black organization automatically less effective. Even the best white members will slow down the Negroes' discovery of what they need to do, and particularly of what they can do—for themselves, working by themselves, among their own kind, in their own communities.

I sure don't want to hurt anybody's feelings, but in fact I'll even go so far as to say that I never really trust the kind of white people who are always so anxious to hang around Negroes, or to hang around in Negro communities. I don't trust the kind of whites who love having Negroes always hanging around them. I don't know—this feeling may be a throwback to the years when I was hustling in Harlem and all of these red-faced, drunk whites in the afterhours clubs were always grabbing hold of some Negroes and talking about "I just want you to know you're just as good as I am—" And then they got back in their taxicabs and black limousines and went back downtown to the places where they lived and worked, where no blacks except servants had better get caught. But, anyway, I know that every time that whites join a black organization, you watch, pretty soon the blacks will be leaning on the whites to support it, and before you know it a black may be up front with a title, but the whites, because of their money, are the real controllers.

I tell sincere white people, "Work in conjunction with us—each of us working among our own kind." Let sincere white individuals find all other white people they can who feel as they do—and let them form their own all-white groups, to work trying to convert other white people who are thinking and acting so racist. Let sincere whites go and teach non-violence to white people!

We will completely respect our white co-workers. They will deserve every credit. We will give them every credit. We will meanwhile be working among our own kind, in our own black communities—showing and teaching black men in ways that only other black men can—that the black man has got to help himself. Working separately, the sincere white people and sincere black people actually will be working together.

In our mutual sincerity we might be able to show a road to the salvation of America's very soul. It can only be salvaged if human rights and dignity, in full, are extended to black men. Only such real, meaningful actions as those which are sincerely motivated from a deep sense of humanism and moral responsibility can get at the basic causes that produce the racial explosions in America today. Otherwise, the racial explosions are only going to grow worse. Certainly nothing is ever going to be solved by throwing upon me and other so-called black "extremists" and "demagogues" the blame for the racism that is in America.

Sometimes, I have dared to dream to myself that one day, history may even say that my voice—which disturbed the white man's smugness, and his arrogance, and his complacency—that my voice helped to save America from a grave, possibly even a fatal catastrophe.

The goal has always been the same, with the approaches to it as different as mine and Dr. Martin Luther King's non-violent marching, that dramatizes the brutality and the evil of the white man against defenseless blacks. And in the racial climate of this country today, it is anybody's guess which of the "extremes" in approach to the black man's problems might *personally* meet a fatal catastrophe first—"non-violent" Dr. King, or so-called "violent" me.

Anything I do today, I regard as urgent. No man is given but so much time to accomplish whatever is his life's work. My life in particular never has stayed fixed in one position for very long. You have seen how throughout my life, I have often known unexpected drastic changes.

I am only facing the facts when I know that any moment of any day, or any night, could bring me death. This is particularly true since the last trip that I made abroad. I have seen the nature of things that are happening, and I have heard things from sources which are reliable.

To speculate about dying doesn't disturb me as it might some people. I never have felt that I would live to become an old man. Even before I was a Muslim—when I was a hustler in the ghetto jungle, and then a criminal in prison, it always stayed on my mind that I would die a violent death. In fact, it runs in my family. My father and most of his brothers died by violence—my father because of what he believed in. To come right down to it, if I take the kind of things in which I believe, then add to that the kind of temperament that I have, plus the one hundred per cent dedication I have to whatever I believe in—these are ingredients which make it just about impossible for me to die of old age.

I have given to this book so much of whatever time I have because I feel, and I hope, that if I honestly and fully tell my life's account, read objectively it might prove to be a testimony of some social value.

I think that an objective reader may see how in the society to which I was exposed as a black youth here in America, for me to wind up in a prison was really just about inevitable. It happens to so many thousands of black youth.

I think that an objective reader may see how when I heard "The white man is the devil," when I played back what had been my own experiences, it was inevitable that I would respond positively; then the next twelve years of my life were devoted and dedicated to propagating that phrase among the black people.

I think, I hope, that the objective reader, in following my life—the life of only one ghetto-created Negro—may gain a better picture and understanding than he has previously had of the black ghettoes which are shaping the lives and the thinking of almost all of the 22 million Negroes who live in America.

Thicker each year in these ghettoes is the kind of teen-ager that I was— with the wrong kinds of heroes, and the wrong kinds of influences. I am not saying that all of them become the kind of parasite that I was. Fortunately, by far most do not. But still, the small fraction who do add up to an annual total of more and more costly, dangerous youthful criminals. The F.B.I. not long ago released a report of a shocking rise in crime each successive year since the end of World War II—ten to twelve per cent each year. The report did not say so in so many words, but I am saying that the majority of that crime increase is annually spawned in the black ghettoes which the American racist society permits to exist. In the 1964 "long, hot summer" riots in major cities across the United States, the socially disinherited black ghetto youth were always at the forefront.

In this year, 1965, I am certain that more—and worse—riots are going to erupt, in yet more cities, in spite of the conscience-salving Civil Rights Bill. The reason is that the *cause* of these riots, the racist malignancy in America, has been too long unattended.

I believe that it would be almost impossible to find anywhere in America a black man who has lived further down in the mud of human society than I have; or a black man who has been any more ignorant than I have been; or a black man who has suffered more anguish during his life than I have. But it is only after the deepest darkness that the greatest joy can come; it is only after slavery and prison that the sweetest appreciation of freedom can come.

For the freedom of my 22 million black brothers and sisters here in America, I do believe that I have fought the best that I knew how, and the best that I could, with the shortcomings that I have had. I know that my shortcomings are many.

My greatest lack has been, I believe, that I don't have the kind of academic education I wish I had been able to get—to have been a lawyer, perhaps. I do believe that I might have made a good lawyer. I have always loved verbal battle, and challenge. You can believe me that if I had the time right now, I would not be one bit ashamed to go back into any New York City public school and start where I left off at the ninth grade, and go on through a degree. Because I don't begin to be academically equipped for so many of the interests that I have. For instance, I love languages. I wish I were an accomplished linguist. I don't know anything more frustrating than to be around people talking something you can't understand. Especially when they are people who look just like you. In Africa, I heard original mother tongues, such as Hausa, and Swahili, being spoken, and there I was standing like some little boy, waiting for someone to tell me what had been said; I never will forget how ignorant I felt.

Aside from the basic African dialects, I would try to learn Chinese, because it looks as if Chinese will be the most powerful political language of the future. And already I have begun studying Arabic, which I think is going to be the most powerful spiritual language of the future.

I would just like to *study*. I mean ranging study, because I have a wide-open mind. I'm interested in almost any subject you can mention. I know this is the reason I have come to really like, as individuals, some of the hosts of radio or television panel programs I have been on, and to respect their minds—because even if they have been almost steadily in disagreement with me on the race issue, they still have kept their minds open and objective about the truths of things happening in this world. Irv Kupcinet in Chicago, and Barry Farber, Barry Gray and Mike Wallace in New York—people like them. They also let me see that they respected my mind—in a way I know they never realized. The way I knew was that often they would invite my opinion on subjects off the race issue. Sometimes, after the programs, we would sit around and talk about all kinds of things, current events and other things, for an hour or more. You see, most whites, even when they credit a Negro with some intelligence, will still feel that all he can talk about is the race issue; most whites never feel that Negroes can contribute anything to other areas of thought, and ideas. You just notice how rarely you will ever hear whites asking any Negroes what they think about the problem of world health, or the space race to land men on the moon.

Every morning when I wake up, now, I regard it as having another borrowed day. In any city, wherever I go, making speeches, holding meetings of my organization, or attending to other business, black men are watching every move I make, awaiting their chance to kill me. I have said publicly many times that I know that they have their orders. Anyone who chooses not to believe what I am saying doesn't know the Muslims in the Nation of Islam.

But I am also blessed with faithful followers who are, I believe, as dedicated to me as I once was to Mr. Elijah Muhammad. Those who would hunt a man need to remember that a jungle also contains those who hunt the hunters.

I know, too, that I could suddenly die at the hands of some white racists. Or I could die at the hands of some Negro hired by the white man. Or it could be some brainwashed Negro acting on his own idea that by eliminating me he would be helping out the white man, because I talk about the white man the way I do.

Anyway, now, each day I live as if I am already dead, and I tell you what I would like for you to do. When I *am* dead—I say it that way because from the things I *know*, I do not expect to live long enough to read this book in its finished form—I want you to just watch and see if I'm not right in what I say: that the white man, in his press, is going to identify me with "hate."

He will make use of me dead, as he has made use of me alive, as a convenient symbol of "hatred"—and that will help him to escape facing the truth that all I have been doing is holding up a mirror to reflect, to show, the history of unspeakable crimes that his race has committed against my race.

You watch. I will be labeled as, at best, an "irresponsible" black man. I have always felt about this accusation that the black "leader" whom white men consider to be "responsible" is invariably the black "leader" who never gets any results. You only get action as a black man if you are regarded by the white man as "irresponsible." In fact, this much I had learned when I was just a little boy. And since I have been some kind of a "leader" of black people here in the racist society of America, I have been more reassured each time the white man resisted me, or attacked me harder—because each time made me more certain that I was on the right track in the American black man's best interests. The racist white man's opposition automatically made me know that I did offer the black man something worthwhile.

Yes, I have cherished my "demagogue" role. I know that societies often have killed the people who have helped to change those societies. And if I can die having brought any light, having exposed any meaningful truth that will help to destroy the racist cancer that is malignant in the body of America—then, all of the credit is due to Allah. Only the mistakes have been mine.

Julian Mayfield (1928-   )

Into the Mainstream and Oblivion

From the American Negro Writer and His Roots (1960)

Recently an African student, long resident in this country, confessed to a group of his intimates that he did not trust the American Negro. "What will you do," he asked them, "in the unlikely event that the United States becomes involved in a colonial war in Africa?" The immediate answer was: "Man, we will shoot you down like dogs." The remark prompted general laughter, but, on reflection, it is not amusing.

The visiting student had sensed what his friends already took for granted: that the contemporary American Negro is faced with a most perplexing dilemma. He does not know who he is or where his loyalties belong. Moreover, he has every right to his confusion for he exists on a moving plateau that is rapidly shifting away from the candid oppression of the past toward—what? The future of the American Negro is most often depicted as an increasingly accelerated absorption into the mainstream of American life where, presumably, he will find happiness as a first-class citizen. This is perhaps the rosy view, but it already has validity insofar as it represents the attitude and aspiration of a majority of Negroes, especially those who are called leaders.

Unfortunately—and one cannot see how it could have been otherwise—the Negro writer has been unable to escape this confusion. The AMSAC writers' conference demonstrated that the Negro writer is having trouble squaring his art and his sense of reality with the American dream. He, too, finds himself wondering who he is, an American or what? And if finally the scholars convince him that he is indeed an American, he asks if this condition must be the extent of his vision. He is all too aware that in recent years a myth that was once accepted without question has shown signs of being discredited. This myth implied that if one could become a real American, he had achieved the best that world could offer.

The conference panel on social protest was especially interesting in regard to the advisability of the Negro's embracing the white American's literary values in exchange for those of his own that he now finds outmoded. Many of the speakers felt that social protest as we have known it, had outlived its usefulness. They knew, of course, that racial injustice still flourishes in our national life, but they felt that the moral climate has been established for the eventual breakdown of racism, and that they need not therefore employ their literary tools to attack it in the same old way, that is to say, directly and violently. To this participant it seemed that the younger writer was seeking a new way of defining himself. Grudgingly he admitted that his work in the past may have suffered artistically because of his preoccupation with the problem of being a Negro in the United States. Yet he seemed reluctant to leap head first into the nation's literary mainstream (a word that was heard repeatedly throughout the conference).

In this I believe the writers were being wiser than most of our church, civic, and political leaders, who are pushing with singular concentration toward one objective: integration. This is to be applauded and actively encouraged so long as integration is interpreted to mean the attainment of full citizenship rights in such areas as voting, housing, education, employment, and the like. But if, as the writers have reason to suspect, integration means completely identifying the Negro with the American image—that great-power face that the world knows and the Negro knows better—then the writer must not be judged too harshly for balking at the prospect.

Perhaps some of them had seen a recent film called *The Defiant Ones,* which attracted world-wide attention because of its graphic, symbolic depiction of American Negro-white relations. In the film a black convict and a white convict are chained to one another in a desperate bid for freedom. Each hates the other intensely, but both soon realize that if they are to find freedom they must co-operate for their mutual good. By the time their actual chains are removed, they have come to believe that they are bound together in a larger way—that their fates, their destinies, are intertwined—so much so that in the end, most re-markably (and, one hopes, not prophetically) the Negro foregoes his chance for freedom because his white comrade is too weak to escape.

The symbolism is obvious and, to one observer at least, disturbing in its implications. For it is not uncommon to hear nowadays that the American Negro and the white are forever bound together and must, perforce, pursue a common destiny. On the face of it this approach seems soundly based on common sense. Throughout his long, cruel history in this land, the Negro has been the most avid seeker of the American dream—most avid because for him its realization was often a matter of life and death. If he could but grasp the dream, he could walk in dignity without fear of the abuse heaped on him by a scornful white majority. So fervid has been his pursuit of the dream that in every war and regardless of the nature of the war, his leaders have offered up his sons, the strength of any race, saying, "Take our youth—take our youth and they will prove their worth as Americans."

But the dream has proved elusive, and there is reason to believe that for the Negro it never had a chance of realization. Now, because of a combination of international and domestic pressures, a social climate is being created wherein, at least in theory, he may win the trappings of freedom that other citizens already take for granted. One may suggest that during this period of transition the Negro would do well to consider if the best use of these trappings will be to align himself totally to the objectives of the dominant sections of the American nation. Just as an insurance company will not issue a policy without determining the life expectancy of the buyer, neither should the Negro—in this case the buyer—accept the policy before he determines if the company is solvent. If the dream he has chased for three centuries is now dying even for white Americans, he would be wise to consider alternative objectives. The urgency of our times demands a deeper and more critical approach from Negro leadership. This new approach is suggested by the Negro mother who, having lost one of her sons in the Korean adventures, was heard to remark: "I don't care if the army is inte-grated; next time I want to know what kind of war my boy is being taken to."

In the same sense the Negro writer is being gently nudged toward a rather vague thing called "the mainstream of American literature." This trend also would seem to be based on common sense. But before plunging into it he owes it to the future of his art to analyze the contents of the American mainstream to determine the full significance of his commitment to it. He may decide that, though the music is sweet, he would rather play in another orchestra. Or, to place himself in the position of the black convict in *The Defiant Ones*, he may decide that he need not necessarily share the fate of his white companion who, after all, proffers the hand of friendship a little late. The Negro writer may conclude that his best salvation lies in escaping the narrow national orbit—artistic, cultural and political—and soaring into the space of more universal experience.

What are the principal characteristics of the mainstream of American literature? To this observer they are apathy and either a reluctance or a fear of writing about anything that matters. William Barrett in *The New York Times* (May 10, 1959) asserts that power, vitality and energy have been abundant in recent American writing, but concedes that "the writers have lacked a center somewhere, they have been without great and central themes."

The phenomenon of our era is the seeming lack of concern shown by American creative writers for the great questions facing the peoples of the world. The most important of these, and the most obvious, is the madness of war. There are other great issues that challenge us, but the American writer has turned his back on them. He deals with the foibles of suburban living, the junior executive, dope addiction, homosexuality, incest and divorce.

I am not suggesting that anyone (least of all the present writer) should sit down with the grand purpose of writing a novel against war. But I do mean to imply that writers of the mainstream, reflecting the attitude of the American people generally, seem determined not to become involved in any of the genuine fury, turmoil, and passion of life; and it is only such involvement that makes life worth living. Where, for instance, is the humor that once characterized our national literature, and what has happened to the American's ability, indeed his proclivity, to laugh at himself? A stultifying respectability hangs over the land, and that is always a sign of decline, for it inhibits the flowering of new ideas that lead to progress and cultural regeneration. In short, the literary mainstream seems to be running dangerously shallow.

It would be pleasant to report that Negro writers have been unaffected by the current literary atmosphere, but it would not be candid. If the AMSAC conference demonstrated any one thing, it was that Negro writers generally are uncertain about the path they should explore in seeking to illuminate the life of man. I say "generally," for the individual writer charts his own course and follows or changes it at will. But it is interesting that there was evident so little unity of approach. One would have thought that Negro writers, representing a tragic and unique experience in our national history, would be bound together by a dominant theme in their work. But if this is the case, it was not obvious at the conference, and such a theme is difficult to detect in recent novels and plays.

The advantage of the Negro writer, the factor that may keep his work above the vacuity of the American mainstream, is that for him the façade of the American way of life is always transparent. He sings the national anthem *sotto voce* and has trouble reconciling the "dream" to the reality he knows. If he feels American at all, it is only when he is on foreign soil and, peculiarly enough, often finds himself defending that which he hated at home. He walks the streets of his nation an alien, and yet he feels no bond to the continent of his ancestors. He is indeed the man without a country. And yet this very detachment may give him the insight of the stranger in the house, placing him in a better position to illuminate contemporary American life as few writers of the mainstream can. This alienation should serve also to make him more sensitive to philosophical and artistic influences that originate beyond our national cultural boundaries.

Finally, if the situation I have described is real, a tragic future is indicated for the American Negro people. Unlike most of the colored peoples of the earth, he has no land and cannot realistically aspire to supremacy in the environment that has been his home for three centuries. In his most optimistic moods—and this period is one of them—the best he can hope for is submersion in what is euphemistically called the American melting pot. Despite the vigorous efforts of Negro leaders and the international pressures on the United States, it seems unlikely that this submersion will occur to any large degree within the foreseeable future. The likelihood is that the Negro people will continue for several decades to occupy, to a diminishing degree, the position of the unwanted child who, having been brought for a visit, must remain for the rest of his life. This is a hard conclusion to draw, but if it has validity, it is better recognized than ignored.

Don L. Lee (1942-   )

Back Again, Home

(Confessions of an ex-executive)

From Think Black (1967)

Pains of insecurity surround me;
    shined shoes,
    conservative suits,
    button down shirts with silk ties.
    bi-weekly payroll.

Ostracized, but not knowing why;
    executive haircut,
    clean shaved,
    "yes" instead of "yeah" and "no" instead of "naw",
    hours, nine to five. (after five he's alone)

"Doing an excellent job, keep it up;"
    promotion made—semi-monthly payroll,

very quiet—never talks,
budget balanced—saved the company money,
quality work—production tops.
He looks sick. (but there is a smile in his eyes)

He resigned, we wonder why;
let his hair grow—a mustache too,
out of a job—broke and hungry,
friends are coming back—bring food,
not quiet now—trying to speak,
what did he say?

"Back Again,

BLACK AGAIN,

Home."

Introduction

From Think Black (1967)

*I was born into slavery in Feb. of 1942. In the spring of that same year 110,000
persons of Japanese descent were placed in protective custody by the white
people of the United States. Two out of every three of these were American
citizens by birth; the other third were aliens forbidden by law to be citizens.
No charges had been filed against these people nor had any hearing been held.
The removal of these people was on racial or ancestral grounds only. World
War II, the war against racism; yet no Germans or other enemy aliens were
placed in protective custody. There should have been Japanese writers directing
their writings toward Japanese audiences.*

*Black. Poet. Black poet am I. This should leave little doubt in the minds
of anyone as to which is first. Black art is created from black forces that live
within the body. These forces can be lost at any time as in the case of Louis
Lomax, Frank Yerby and Ralph Ellison. Direct and meaningful contact with
black people will act as energizers for the black forces. Black art will elevate and
enlighten our people and lead them toward an awareness of self, i.e., their
blackness. It will show them mirrors. Beautiful symbols. And will aid in the
destruction of anything nasty and detrimental to our advancement as a people.
Black art is a reciprocal art. The black writer learns from his people and because
of his insight and "know how" he is able to give back his knowledge to the
people in a manner in which they can identify, learn and gain some type of
mental satisfaction, e.g., rage or happiness. We must destroy Faulkner, dick, jane*

and other perpetuators of evil. It's time for Du Bois, Nat Turner and Kwame Nkrumah. As Frantz Fanon points out: destroy the culture and you destroy the people. This must not happen. Black artists are culture stabilizers; bring back old values, and introducing new ones. Black art will talk to the people and with the will of the people stop the impending "protective custody."

```
America calling.
negroes.
can you dance?
play foot/baseball?
nanny?
cook?
needed now. negroes
who can entertain
ONLY.
others not
wanted.
(& are considered extremely dangerous.)
```

A Poem For Black Minds

From Black Pride (1968)

```
                 first. the color black/naturally
              beautiful canNot be mixed with whi
                  teness . . . . . . . . . . . . . . . must not
                                            it's
              mine. ours throughout black nights
                with guns watching . . . . . . . . them.
              we fucking/naturally. non . . . proper
              without thoughts of evil or insecure
              feelings. me. we. living. they existing.
              love can be a reality/thru blackness
              & other colors dark. watch negroes. whi
              te minds. enemies of black people. blew
                  their minds literally with whi
              te thoughts & images of western whi
              te woman. denying self. some see.
                  trying to come back
                                      to us.
                  ain't you glad you is/black?
                                      me too.
```

Assassination

From Don't Cry, Scream (1969)

it was wild.

the

bullet hit high.

      (the throat-neck)

& from everywhere:

    the motel, from under bushes and cars,
    from around corners and across streets,
    out of the garbage cans and from rat holes
    in the earth

they came running.

with

guns

drawn

they came running

toward the King—

      all of them

        fast and sure—

as if

the King

was going to fire back.

they came running,

fast and sure,

in the

wrong

direction.

Etheridge Knight (1933-   )

Hard Rock Returns to Prison from the Hospital for the Criminal Insane

From Poems from Prison (1968)

Hard Rock was "known not to take no shit
From nobody," and he had the scars to prove it:
Split purple lips, lumped ears, welts above
His yellow eyes, and one long scar that cut

Across his temple and plowed through a thick
Canopy of kinky hair.

The WORD was that Hard Rock wasn't a mean nigger
Anymore, that the doctors had bored a hole in his head,
Cut out part of his brain, and shot electricity
Through the rest. When they brought Hard Rock back,
Handcuffed and chained, he was turned loose,
Like a freshly gelded stallion, to try his new status.
And we all waited and watched, like indians at a corral,
To see if the WORD was true.

As we waited we wrapped ourselves in the cloak
Of his exploits: "Man, the last time, it took eight
Screws to put him in the Hole." "Yeah, remember when he
Smacked the captain with his dinner tray?" "He set
The record for time in the Hole—67 straight days!"
"Ol Hard Rock! man, that's one crazy nigger."
And then the jewel of a myth that Hard Rock had once bit
A screw on the thumb and poisoned him with syphilitic spit.

The testing came, to see if Hard Rock was really tame.
A hillbilly called him a black son of a bitch
And didn't lose his teeth, a screw who knew Hard Rock
From before shook him down and barked in his face.
And Hard Rock did *nothing*. Just grinned and looked silly,
His eyes empty like knot holes in a fence.

And even after we discovered that it took Hard Rock
Exactly 3 minutes to tell you his first name,
We told ourselves that he had just wised up,
Was being cool; but we could not fool ourselves for long,
And we turned away, our eyes on the ground. Crushed.
He had been our Destroyer, the doer of things
We dreamed of doing but could not bring ourselves to do,
The fears of years, like a biting whip,
Had cut grooves too deeply across our backs.

The Violent Space

(or When your sister sleeps around for money)

From Poems from Prison (1968)

Exchange in greed the ungraceful signs. Thrust
The thick notes between green apple breasts.

Then the shadow of the devil descends,
The violent space cries and angel eyes,
Large and dark, retreat in innocence and in ice.
(Run sister run—the Bugga man comes!)

The violent space cries silently,
Like you cried wide years ago
In another space, speckled by the sun
And the leaves of a green plum tree,
And you were stung
By a red wasp and we flew home.
(Run sister run—the Bugga man comes!)

Well, hell, lil sis, wasps still sting.
You are all of seventeen and as alone now
In your pain as you were with the sting
On your brow.
Well, shit, lil sis, here we are:
You and I and this poem.
And what should I do? should I squat
In the dust and make strange markings on the ground?
Shall I chant a spell to drive the demon away?
(Run sister run—the Bugga man comes!)

In the beginning you were the Virgin Mary,
And you are the Virgin Mary now.
But somewhere between Nazareth and Bethlehem
You lost your name in the nameless void.
O Mary don't you weep don't you moan
O Mary shake your butt to the violent juke,
Absorb the demon puke and watch the white eyes pop.
(Run sister run—the Bugga man comes!)

And what do I do. I boil my tears in a twisted spoon
And dance like an angel on the point of a needle.
I sit counting syllables like Midas gold.
I am not bold. I can not yet take hold of the demon
And lift his weight from your black belly,
So I grab the air and sing my song.
(But the air can not stand my singing long.)

It Was a Funky Deal

From Poems from Prison (1968)

It was a funky deal.
The only thing real was red,
Red blood around his red, red beard.

It was a funky deal.

In the beginning was the word,
And in the end the deed.
Judas did it to Jesus
For the same Herd. Same reason.
You made them mad, Malcolm. Same reason.

It was a funky deal.

You rocked too many boats, man.
Pulled too many coats, man.
Saw through the jive.
You reached the wild guys
Like me. You and Bird. (And that
Lil LeRoi cat.)

It was a funky deal.

Biographies

UP FROM SLAVERY

David Walker (1785–1830)

David Walker, the son of a free mother and a slave father, was born in Wilmington, North Carolina. As a free man, Walker traveled extensively in the South during his youth, and his travels combined with his reading convinced him that American slavery was the cruelest form of bondage that the world had ever seen. Walker moved to Boston sometime before 1827, and in Boston he wrote for *Freedom's Journal* and *Rights of All,* two abolitionist publications. In 1829, he brought out the first edition of his *Appeal,* and a second and third edition appeared in 1830. The work caused so much consternation that it was rumored a price had been placed on Walker's life by concerned southerners, and when the author was found dead outside his secondhand clothes shop in 1830, there were few who doubted that he had died a violent death.

Frederick Douglass (1817–1895)

Frederick Douglass was born as Frederick Augustus Washington Bailey on the eastern shore of Maryland. His mother, Harriet Bailey, was a slave on a neighboring plantation, and there were rumors that Douglass's father was his owner. As a slave, Douglass worked on Maryland plantations, in Baltimore as a young "house servant," and in Baltimore shipyards as a caulker. He made a daring and resourceful escape in 1838, and made his way to Massachusetts where he met Garrison and other abolitionists and became one of the foremost spokesmen of the abolitionist movement. In 1845 he published his *Narrative,* which unwittingly revealed his true identity and forced him to flee to England. During his life, Douglass lectured in Canada, England, Ireland, and Scotland. In 1847, he founded the *North Star,* a newspaper that he edited for seventeen years. Douglass quickly achieved prominence, and during his lifetime, he served as United States Secretary to Santo Domingo, as Marshal and Recorder of Deeds for the District of Columbia, and as United States Minister to Haiti. His *Narrative* was expanded in 1881 to the *Life and Times of Frederick Douglass,* and another edition appeared in 1893.

Booker Taliaferro Washington (1856–1915)

Born into slavery on James Burroughs's plantation at Hale's Ford, Franklin County, Virginia, Booker T. Washington was the son of Jane Ferguson, a slave cook. His father was believed to have been a white man from a neighboring plantation. After emancipation, Washington and his family moved to Malden, Virginia, and from there the young Washington made his way to Hampton Institute. After three years at Hampton, Washington taught for a time and then returned to his alma mater to take a position as director of Indian students and director of the night school. He began his life's work at Tuskegee in 1881, and he moved into the position of America's "black leader" as a result of his Atlanta address in 1895. The remainder of Washington's active life was dedicated to the uplifting of black Americans. He lectured, traveled, wrote, and solicited funds in an attempt to build a thriving institution at Tuskegee, Alabama. He was the founder of the National Negro Business League, and he received an honorary M.A. from Harvard University in 1896. A man respected by the crown heads of Europe and the outstanding philanthropists and political leaders of America, Washington wrote, in addition to *Up from Slavery: The Future of the American Negro* (1899); *Sowing and Reaping* (1900); *Character Building* (1902); *Working with the Hands* (1904); *Putting the Most into Life* (1906); *Frederick Douglass* (1907); *The Negro in Business* (1907); *The Story of the Negro* (1909); *My Larger Education* (1911); with R. E. Park, *The Man Farthest Down* (1912); and edited *Tuskegee and Its People* (1905).

William Edward Burghardt Du Bois (1868–1963)

W. E. B. Du Bois was born in Great Barrington, Massachusetts, and his ancestry included both French and Dutch strains. Du Bois, however, identified wholly with the black Americans. He received a Harvard Ph. D. in 1895 and did postgraduate work in Germany. His Harvard thesis was accepted as the first work in the *Harvard Historical Series*, and it was entitled "The Suppression of the African Slave Trade in America." Du Bois was the founder of the Niagara Movement along with William Monroe Trotter in 1905, and the movement grew into the National Association for the Advancement of Colored People by 1910. As the editor of the NAACP journal, *Crisis,* Du Bois exercised a commanding influence on the thought of black Americans (notably black intellectuals) for more than twenty years. During these years, he also served as a professor of economics and history at Atlanta University, and between 1932 and 1944, he headed the Sociology Department at Atlanta. Throughout his life, Du Bois was devoted to the cause of African liberation, and he was one of the leaders of the Pan-African Congresses of 1919, 1921, 1923, 1927, and 1945. In 1945, he acted as cochairman of the congress along with Kwame Nkrumah. Du Bois was an American radical until the 1940s, at which time he advocated pro-Soviet doctrines, and in 1961 he joined the Communist Party. In the following year, he settled in Ghana where he died in 1963. Du Bois was a prolific writer, and his works include many genres. His sociohistorical reflections include *The Souls of Black Folk* (1903), *Darkwater* (1920), and *The Gift of Black Folk* (1924). His novels include *The Quest of the Silver Fleece* (1911), *The Dark Princess* (1928), and *Black Flame* (a trilogy: 1958, 1959, 1961). In biography, there is *John Brown* (1909), and in history and sociology, there are, in addition to *The Suppression of the African Slave Trade* (1896):*The Philadelphia Negro* (1899); *The Negro* (1915); and *Black Reconstruction* (1935). His works against imperialism include: *Color and Democracy* (1945), *The World and Africa* (1947), and *In Battle for Peace* (1952). Du Bois's first attempt at an autobiography was entitled *Dusk of Dawn* (1940), and in 1968, *The Autobiography of W. E. B. Du Bois* appeared.

EARLY POETRY, FICTION, AND CRITICISM

Paul Laurence Dunbar (1872–1906)

Dunbar, the son of an escaped slave, was born in Dayton, Ohio, where he was the only black student in his high school. In high school, Dunbar was editor of the school newspaper and president of the literary society. After graduation, the only job that the young poet could find was as an elevator boy at a salary of four dollars a week. While working as an elevator boy, Dunbar wrote his first two volumes of verse: *Oak and Ivy* (1893) and *Majors and Minors* (1895). William Dean Howells championed the poet's cause in *Harper's Magazine*, and he went on to write an introduction for Dunbar's 1896 volume, *Lyrics of Lowly Life*. The poet's reputation was made. He went on to produce short stories, novels, and other volumes of verse; after 1898, his sole occupation was writing, though he worked for a time at the Library of Congress. Dunbar was not a healthy man, and he was forced to travel to Colorado for his health on a number of occasions; in 1906, he died of tuberculosis. His writings include, in addition to those mentioned: *Lyrics of the Hearthside* (1899), *Lyrics of Love and Laughter* (1903), and *Lyrics of Sunshine and Shadow* (1905). He produced a number of short stories, and his novels are: *The Uncalled* (1898), *The Love of Landry* (1900), *The Fanatics* (1901), and *The Sport of the Gods* (1902). His complete poems were published in 1913.

Charles Waddell Chesnutt (1858–1932)

The accomplishments of Chesnutt were sufficient to entitle the early prose writer to a centenary celebration in Cleveland in 1958. Chesnutt was born in Cleveland, and after spending the early part of his life as a school teacher and principal in North Carolina, he returned to his native city to study law and set up a legal stenography firm. He was admitted to the Ohio bar, and between 1895 and 1905 he practiced law and produced over fifty short stories and essays, a biography of Frederick Douglass, and three novels. In 1932, he received the Spingarn Medal from the NAACP. Chesnutt published two volumes of short stories: *The Conjure*

Woman (1899) and *The Wife of His Youth* (1899); and he wrote several novels: *The House behind the Cedars* (1900), *The Marrow of Tradition* (1901), and *The Colonel's Dream* (1905).

Fenton Johnson (1886–1958)

Johnson, as Arna Bontemps tells us, "was once a dapper boy who drove his own electric automobile around Chicago at the end of the first decade of this century." Johnson worked in Chicago as both a dramatic producer and as an editor of little magazines. During the early years of the century, he produced three volumes of rather poor romantic verse. In his later years, however, he responded to a bitterer muse and produced poems like "The Daily Grind" and "Tired." Out of his work with the Writers' Project of the WPA in Chicago came the posthumous *42 WPA Poems*. His writings include: *A Little Dreaming* (1913), *Visions of the Dusk* (1915), and *Songs of the Soil* (1916).

Benjamin Griffiths Brawley (1882–1939)

Brawley was born in Columbia, South Carolina, and by 1901, he had graduated from Morehouse College. He went on to receive another B.A. degree from the University of Chicago, and in 1908 he received an M.A. in English from Harvard. Brawley taught for a time at both Shaw and Howard universities before returning to his alma mater. He taught at Morehouse from 1912 to 1932. In 1933, he moved back to Howard as a professor of English literature. Though he was criticized strongly by Carter G. Woodson, Brawley was one of the first black historians to write on "non-Negro" topics: *A Short History of the English Drama* (1921) and *A History of the English Hymn* (1932). In addition to the invaluable *The Negro in Literature and Art* and *The Negro Genius* (1937), Brawley's works include: *A Short History of the American Negro* (1913); *Your Negro Neighbor* (1918); *Women of Achievement* (1919); *A Social History of the American Negro* (1921); *A New Survey of English Literature* (1925); and *Dr. Dillard of the Jeanes Fund* (1930).

James Weldon Johnson (1871–1938)

Johnson was born in Jacksonville, Florida; he was one of two talented sons born to James and Helen Johnson. Johnson received a B.A. degree from Atlanta University in 1894 and an M.A. degree from the same institution in 1904; he went on to study at Columbia University for a time, and he became the principal of the black high school in Jacksonville. He read law and was admitted to the Florida bar in 1897. At about this time, Johnson, who had early training in music, began writing songs along with his brother John Rosamond, and the two went off to New York to make their fortune. Though the Johnson brothers produced over two hundred songs—including the famous "Lift Every Voice and Sing"—they were not really successful. Johnson left Broadway to fill two foreign service posts in South America during Theodore Roosevelt's administration. In 1912, he published *The Autobiography of an Ex-Colored Man*, which received very little acclaim until it was reissued in 1927. Johnson's most dedicated social work began in 1916 when he became Field Secretary for the NAACP, a post he occupied until 1930. In 1938, he was killed in an automobile accident. The writings of James Weldon Johnson, one of the finest black American poets, include: *Fifty Years and Other Poems* (1917); *The Book of American Negro Poetry* (1922); *The Book of American Negro Spirituals* (1925); *The Second Book of American Negro Spirituals* (1926); *God's Trombones* (1927); *Black Manhattan* (1930); and *Along This Way* (1933), an autobiography. His works also include numerous dramatic and musical collaborations with his brother and several important works on the race problem.

THE RENAISSANCE OF THE TWENTIES

Alain Locke (1886–1954)

Locke was born and raised in Philadelphia. He graduated in philosophy from Harvard University (1907) and was the first Negro Rhodes Scholar. As a Rhodes Scholar, Locke studied at Oxford (1907–1910) and at the University of Berlin (1910–1911). He received his Ph.D. degree in philosophy from Harvard in 1918. For forty years, Locke taught at Howard University, and through his efforts as head of the philosophy department, students from all over the country were attracted to Howard. A brilliant man and a thorough scholar, Locke produced an amazing number of books and articles during his life. He wrote for *Opportunity* and for *Phylon,* and his most noted books include: *The New Negro* (1925); *Four Negro Poets* (1927); *Negro Art—Past and Present* (1936); and *The Negro and His Music* (1936). And Locke's materials provided the basis for Margaret Just Butcher's *The Negro in American Culture* (1956). Locke is best remembered, however, for his role as the interpreter of the Harlem Renaissance and for the inspiration and encouragement that he provided for black American artists throughout his life.

Countee Cullen (1903–1946)

Cullen was born in New York, and at the age of eleven, he became the foster son of Reverend Frederick Cullen, pastor of Salem Methodist Church in Harlem.

He graduated from De Witt Clinton High School and went on to New York University where he was elected to Phi Beta Kappa and published his first volume of poetry, *Color,* in 1925. Cullen won the Witter Bynner Prize for poetry in 1925, and by that year major American magazines were accepting his poems regularly. The young poet received an M.A. degree from Harvard University in 1926 and a Guggenheim fellowship for study in France during the same year. In 1934, he began a teaching career in the New York public schools, and he worked as a junior high school teacher for the rest of his life. Cullen's works include: *Copper Sun* (1927); *The Ballad of the Brown Girl* (1928); *The Black Christ and Other Poems* (1929); *One Way to Heaven,* a novel (1932); *The Medea and Some Poems* (1935); *The Lost Zoo* (1940); *My Nine Lives and How I Lost Them* (1942); and the posthumous volume, *On These I Stand* (1947).

Jean Toomer (1894–1967)

Toomer was born in Washington, D.C., and he was educated at the University of Wisconsin and the City College of New York. He began publishing his short stories, poems, and sketches in national magazines during the second decade of the century. In 1923, *Cane* was published, and Toomer became an immediate success among a small group of critics and intellectuals. The book, however, did not sell well, nor' did it receive the attention it so richly deserved. Toomer traveled in France during the twenties, and he spent a good part of his time in France and America attempting to get his work published. Presumably feeling that his racial identification militated against his career, Toomer denied his blackness. But he still could not find a publisher. He spent time in California, worked in Pennsylvania with the American Friends for whom he wrote at least one tract, and died in obscurity near Philadelphia in 1967.

Claude McKay (1889–1948)

McKay was born in Jamaica, British West Indies, and by the time he was twenty-three, he had published two volumes of poetry in West Indian dialect— *Songs of Jamaica* and *Constab Ballads,* both in 1912. In 1912, the poet came to America to study at Tuskegee, but finding the school's regimentation distasteful, he transferred to Kansas State College, where he studied from 1912 to 1914. In 1914, he went to New York and worked as a free-lance journalist often contributing to the radical periodical *Liberator;* in 1920, he published *Spring in New Hampshire,* a volume of verse that was followed by another—*Harlem Shadows*—in 1922. McKay was a cosmopolitan man who had lived in Russia, France, Spain, and Morocco. His novels reflect his experiences with the black migratory folk of the world, and the philosophy that he set forth in his fiction brought criticism from both liberal and left-wing intellectuals. In his later life,

McKay reverted to his early conservatism. He became a United States citizen in 1940, and in 1944 he was converted to the Catholic Church. From 1944 until his death, he worked with a Catholic bishop in Chicago. McKay's novels include: *Home to Harlem* (1928); *Banjo* (1929); and *Banana Bottom* (1933). He also published a volume of short stories, *Gingertown* (1932); an autobiography, *A Long Way from Home* (1937); and a study, *Harlem: Negro Metropolis* (1940). His *Selected Poems* were issued posthumously in 1953.

Rudolph Fisher (1897–1934)

Fisher was born in Washington, D.C., and after graduating from high school, he attended Brown University where he received a B.A. degree in 1919 and an M.A. degree in the following year. Fisher excelled in both biology and literature, and he was elected to three honor societies (including Phi Beta Kappa) while he was an undergraduate. After receiving his first graduate degree, Fisher taught biology for a year before entering Howard University's medical school. His internship was spent at Freedmen's Hospital in Washington, and afterward, Fisher went to work in New York. He was affiliated with the x-ray division of the department of health in New York, and it was in this job that he wrote the novels and short stories on which his fame rests. His novels are *The Walls of Jericho* (1928) and *The Conjure Man Dies* (1932), both mildly satirical works on the new black urban scene. His more notable stories include: "Blades of Steel," "City of Refuge," and "Ringtail."

Langston (James Mercer) Hughes (1902–1967)

Hughes was born in Joplin, Missouri. His mother and father separated when the poet was quite young, and his father, embittered by American racial discrimination, spent the remainder of his life in Mexico. Hughes was thus raised by his mother who was forced to move from city to city in search of suitable employment. The poet graduated from high school in Cleveland, and the summer following his graduation he wrote the famous "The Negro Speaks of Rivers." The poem attracted some attention, but it was only after Hughes had attended Columbia University (1921–1922) and traveled as a seaman to Africa and Europe that he won the *Opportunity* poetry prize (1925) and the Witter Bynner poetry award (1926). While working as a busboy in Washington, Hughes placed three of his poems beside Vachel Lindsay's plate and hastily retreated. The following day, Hughes found himself "discovered," and his literary career was launched. He received a scholarship to Lincoln University and graduated in 1929. In 1930, his first novel—*Not without Laughter*—appeared. Hughes continued to produce poetry, prose, drama, essays, and anthologies of merit until his death in 1967. A select list of his works would include under poetry: *The Weary Blues* (1926);

Fine Clothes to the Jew (1927); *The Dream Keeper* (1932); *Scottsboro Limited* (1932); *Shakespeare in Harlem* (1942); *Fields of Wonder* (1947); *One-way Ticket* (1948); *Montage of a Dream Deferred* (1951); *The Panther and the Lash* (1967).

His novels include: *Not without Laughter* (1930); *The Sweet Flypaper of Life* (1955); and *Tambourines to Glory* (1958).

His collections of short stories are: *The Ways of White Folks* (1934); *Laughing to Keep from Crying* (1952); and *Something in Common* (1963).

Hughes's dramas include: *Mulatto, Soul Gone Home, Little Ham, Simply Heavenly, Tambourines to Glory*—all collected by Webster Smalley as *Five Plays by Langston Hughes* (1963)—and *Street Scene*.

His humorous essays include: *Simple Speaks His Mind; Simple Takes a Wife; Simple's Uncle Sam; Simple Stakes a Claim;* and some of the finest pieces from these volumes in *The Best of Simple* (1961).

Hughes's autobiographical volumes are: *The Big Sea* (1940), and *I Wonder As I Wonder* (1956).

And his anthologies include: *The Poetry of the Negro* (1949, with Arna Bontemps); *The Book of Negro Folklore* (1958, with Arna Bontemps); *An African Treasury* (1960); *The Book of Negro Humor* (1966); and *The Best Short Stories by Negro Writers* (1967).

THE THIRTIES AND FORTIES

Arna Bontemps (1902–   )

Bontemps was born in Alexandria, Louisiana, but early in his life, his parents moved to California. Bontemps received his B.A. degree from the Pacific Union College of California in 1923, and he received an M.A. degree in library science from the University of Chicago. In 1926, he received the *Crisis* poetry prize, and in 1926 and 1927, he won the Alexander Pushkin Prize. He has continued to produce both prose and poetry up to the present day, and along his way, he has received both Guggenheim and Rosenwald fellowships. Starting in 1943, Bontemps worked as director of the Fisk University library. He has taught at Southern Illinois University, and he is currently serving as a lecturer in the Yale University department of English. His writings include: *God Sends Sunday* (1931) and *Black Thunder* (1936), both novels; *Golden Slippers, an Anthology of Poetry for Young People* (1941); *The Story of the Negro* (1948); *George Washington Carver* (1950); *Frederick Douglass: Slave, Fighter, Freeman* (1959); *100 Years of Negro Freedom* (1961); *American Negro Poetry* (1963); *Famous Negro*

Athletes (1964). Bontemps also collaborated with Langston Hughes and Jack Conroy on a number of Children's books, and he edited *The Book of Negro Folklore* and *The Poetry of the Negro* along with Langston Hughes. He has published one volume of poetry, *Personals* (1963).

Sterling Brown (1901–   )

Brown was born in Washington, D.C., and after finishing high school in Washington he graduated a member of Phi Beta Kappa from Williams College. He did graduate work at Harvard University and earned an M.A. degree in one year. He has worked as a professor of English since his graduation from Harvard, and he recently retired from the English department at Howard University, the school to which he dedicated most of his life. His first volume of poetry, *Southern Road,* was published in 1932, and since that year, he has proven one of the finest poets and critics among black American authors. His critical works include: *The Negro in American Fiction* (1937), and *Negro Poetry and Drama* (1937). He was one of the editors of the anthology *The Negro Caravan* first published in 1941 and recently reissued by the Arno Press. He has contributed a great number of critical articles to scholarly periodicals, and for a time, he wrote a regular literary column for *Opportunity*.

Melvin Tolson (1898–1966)

Tolson was born in Moberly, Missouri, and he was educated at Fisk University. He also studied at Lincoln and Columbia Universities. Tolson received several literary awards during his academic career, and a great part of his life was spent at things literary. He worked at Langston University in Oklahoma for a number of years, where he served as both a dramatic director and a debating coach. His first volume of poetry—*Rendezvous with America*—appeared in 1944, and one of the poems from that volume, "Dark Symphony," brought prizes and high praise for the author. *Libretto for the Republic of Liberia* (1953), which Tolson was commissioned to write, brought the author the title of "Poet Laureate of Liberia." Tolson's last volume, *Harlem Gallery* (1965), has received applause from some of the most notable critics of our day.

Robert Hayden (1913–   )

Hayden was born in Detroit, Michigan, and studied at Wayne State University. He then attended the University of Michigan for two years, where he held a teaching assistantship and in 1938 and 1942 won Avery Hopwood awards for poetry. In 1940, his first collection of poems—*Heartshape in the Dust*—was published, and in 1946, Hayden joined the faculty of Fisk University. In 1948, a volume of his poetry appeared under the title *The Lion and the Archer,* and in 1962, his volume *A Ballad of Remembrance* was published. In 1966, Hayden's *Selected Poems* appeared, and the following year *Kaleidoscope: Poems by American Negro Poets,* an anthology that Hayden edited, was issued. Hayden is currently serving as a visiting professor of English at the University of Michigan; his latest volume of poetry—*Words in the Mourning Time*—was published in 1970.

Owen Dodson (1914–   )

Dodson was born in Brooklyn, New York, and he graduated from Bates College a member of Phi Beta Kappa. He did graduate work at Yale University, and two of his verse plays, *Divine Comedy* and *Garden of Time,* were produced at Yale. Dodson collaborated with Countee Cullen on the play *The Third Fourth of July,* which was published by *Theatre Arts* in the summer of 1946, and a number of his plays have been produced by student groups throughout the country. Dodson has been on the faculty of the Howard University department of drama for a number of years, and in 1949 he took the Howard Players on a successful tour of Europe and Scandanavia. His awards include the Maxwell Anderson Verse Play Award, a Rosenwald fellowship, a Guggenheim fellowship, and an award for one of the best stories ("The Summer Fire," *Best Short Stories of the Paris Review,* 1961) from the *Paris Review.* Dodson's first volume of poetry, *Powerful Long Ladder,* appeared in 1946, and his novel, *Boy at the Window,* appeared in 1950. A new volume of poems, *The Confession Stone,* is forthcoming.

Margaret Walker (1915–   )

Margaret Walker was born in Birmingham, Alabama, and the fact that her father was a minister may help to explain the grace and beauty that she has managed to achieve in her poetry and prose. The author of "For My People" studied at Northwestern University and then went on to complete an M.A. degree at the University of Iowa; instead of the normal M.A. thesis, a collection of the poet's verse was accepted in fulfillment of the requirements for the degree. And continuing her creative work, the author produced the novel *Jubilee* (1966), which was accepted in lieu of a doctoral dissertation by the University of Iowa. She has received a number of awards during her career—including a Houghton Mifflin fellowship and a Rosenwald fellowship—and she has taught English at a number of southern colleges. The volume for which "For My People" provided the title poem won the Yale Younger Poets' Award in 1942, and it has recently been reissued by the Yale University Press. *Jubilee* has received international acclaim, and it has been translated into several languages.

Ann Lane Petry (1911–   )

Ann Petry was born in Old Saybrook, Connecticut. She came from a family whose members had traditionally been pharmacists, and Mrs. Petry was expected to carry on the tradition. When she graduated from high school in 1929, therefore, she enrolled in the College of Pharmacy at the University of Connecticut. She then went to work in her family's drugstore; her contacts and experiences there provided the material for some of her novels and short stories. In 1938, Mrs. Petry married and moved to New York where she worked as a reporter for the *People's Voice*. Her experiences in New York as a reporter gave her the true feel of the urban scene and enabled her to write with telling accuracy about the black American of the city. Her first published short story appeared in *Crisis* in 1943, and the story attracted the attention of the Houghton Mifflin Company. The company awarded Mrs. Petry a fellowship and published her first novel, *The Street*, in 1946. The novel won fame for its author, and her second novel, *Country Place*, appeared in 1947. Mrs. Petry's other works include: *Harriet Tubman: Conductor of the Underground Railroad* (1955); *The Drugstore Cat* (1949); *The Narrows* (1953); and *Tituba of Salem Village* (1964). Her story "Like a Winding Sheet" was named the best American short story for 1946.

Richard Wright (1908–1960)

Wright was born in Natchez, Mississippi. His grandparents had been slaves, and Wright himself worked in a number of positions associated with the lower echelons of black American life; he was a porter, a janitor, and a postal clerk before he was recognized as a writer. Wright published several short stories in the early thirties, and his greatest desire was always to become a noted writer. It was Wright's work with the Federal Writers' Project of the WPA that first gained him national recognition; out of the Chicago project came Wright's volume of short stories, *Uncle Tom's Children*, in 1938. The volume won Wright a $500 prize, and in the following year he won a Guggenheim fellowship and the Spingarn Medal of the NAACP. The publication of *Native Son* in 1940 secured Wright's place as a great literary artist. The hopeful treatment of Communism in the novel, however, is counteracted by *The God That Failed* (1944), which details the author's disenchantment with the Communist Party. Wright traveled widely during his lifetime, and the last years of his life were spent as an expatriate in Paris. His other works include: *12 Million Black Voices* (1941), a pictorial history; *Black Boy* (1945), an autobiography; *The Outsider* (1953); *Savage Holiday* (1954); *Black Power* (1954), reflections on a visit to the Gold Coast; *The Color Curtain* (1956), a report on the Bandung Conference; *White Man Listen!* (1957), originally lectures given in Europe from 1950 through 1956; *Pagan Spain* (1957), a report on a visit to Spain; *The Long Dream* (1958); a volume of short stories published posthumously under the title *Eight Men* (1961); and a posthumously published novel, *Lawd Today* (1963).

THE FIFTIES AND SIXTIES

James Baldwin (1924–   )

Baldwin was born in Harlem and educated in the schools of New York City. When he first began writing, Baldwin was working as a waiter in Greenwich Village, but a Rosenwald Fellowship aided his creative efforts. The author traveled to Europe where his first novel, *Go Tell It on the Mountain,* was finished in 1953. *Go Tell It on the Mountain,* along with *Notes of a Native Son* (1955) and *Giovanni's Room* (1956), established Baldwin's reputation as a writer. Since 1956, Baldwin has published essays, a three-act play, a volume of short stories, and two novels. His works include: *Nobody Knows My Name* (essays, 1961); *Another Country* (novel, 1962); *The Fire Next Time* (essays, 1963); *Blues for Mr. Charlie* (drama, 1964); *Going to Meet the Man* (short stories, 1965); and *Tell Me How Long the Train's Been Gone* (novel, 1968).

Ralph Ellison (1914–   )

Ellison was born in Oklahoma City, and he exhibits great pride in having descended from the colorful stock of Oklahoma freedmen. His background includes time spent at Tuskegee Institute and a period of artistic endeavor in New York City. Ellison studied music and sculpture in New York, and he worked for a time as a jazz trumpeter. The author's honors and awards are numerous, and he has lectured or been employed at many American colleges and universities. In addition to *Invisible Man* (novel, 1952), which won the National Book Award, and *Shadow and Act* (a collection of essays, 1954), Ellison has published parts of a second novel in various literary journals. The story included here appeared in *New World Writing* in 1956.

Gwendolyn Brooks (1917–   )

Miss Brooks, who was born in Topeka, Kansas, spent most of her childhood in Chicago. She has been the winner of a Guggenheim Fellowship, prizes from the Midwestern Writers' Conference, and the Pulitzer Prize for poetry (1950). Her poems have appeared in a number of magazines including *Harpers Magazine, Poetry, Common Ground,* and the *Yale Review.* She is one of the most distinguished black American poets now living. Miss Brooks's volumes of poetry include: *A Street in Bronzeville* (1945); *Annie Allen* (1949, for which she won the Pulitzer Prize); *Bronzeville Boys and Girls* (1956); *The Bean Eaters* (1959); *In the Mecca* (1968); and *Riot* (1969). She has also published a novel, *Maud Martha,* which appeared in 1953.

Dudley Randall (1914–   )

Randall was born in Washington, D.C. He received a B.A. degree from Wayne State University in 1949, and in 1951, he received an M.A. degree from the University of Michigan. The writer has received several awards for poetry, and he is the general editor of Broadside Press, which he founded in 1965. In addition to his own poems, Randall has produced translations of French, Latin, and Russian poetry, and his short stories and articles have appeared in a number of periodicals. His works include: *Poem Counterpoem* (a volume of poetry along with Margaret Danner, 1966); *Cities Burning* (poetry, 1968); and *For Malcolm* (an anthology of poems dedicated to Malcolm X edited with Margaret Burroughs, 1967).

John O. Killens (1916–   )

Killens was born in Macon, Georgia. He has attended Edward Waters College, Morris Brown College, Howard University, Terrell Law School, Columbia University, and New York University. In 1936, he joined the staff of the National Labor Relations Board, and he served with the board until 1942. In 1942, Killens became a member of the United States armed services. During World War II, the author served in the Pacific and suffered the indignities of a racist military establishment. Since his return to the National Labor Relations Board in 1946, Killens has led an exciting and productive life. He has served as chairman of the Writers Committee of the American Society of African Culture; he has received numerous awards and honors; he has written for television and the movies; and he has travelled extensively in West Africa. Killens has also served in several academic posts including writer-in-residence at Fisk University. His major literary works include: *Youngblood* (a novel, 1954); *And Then We Heard the Thunder* (novel, 1963); *Black Man's Burden* (a collection of essays, 1965); and *'Sippi* (a novel, 1967).

John A. Williams (1925–   )

Williams was born in Jackson, Mississippi, but spent a good part of his childhood in Syracuse, New York. He served in the armed forces during World War II, and after the war he entered Syracuse University. Williams left the university before he had finished the requirements for a B.A. degree and began a life that has included many jobs and diverse locales. He has traveled in Europe, Africa, Spain, and throughout the United States. He has been, at times, a writer, a publisher, and a critic. He is currently working with *Amistad Magazine* and lecturing at the City College of New York. His novels include: *The Angry Ones* (1960); *Night Song* (1961); *Sissie* (1963); *The Man Who Cried I Am* (1967); and *Sons of Darkness, Sons of Light* (1969). His works of history and social criticism include: *Africa, Her History, Lands and People* (1962); *This Is My Country Too* (1965, reflections on his travels in the United States); and *Beyond the Angry Black* (1966).

Mari Evans

Mari Evans is a native of Toledo, Ohio. She was a John Hay Whitney Fellow during 1965–1966. Her work as a poet has been used on record albums, several television specials, two off-Broadway productions, and in over thirty textbooks and anthologies, including Italian, German, Swedish, British, French, and Dutch works. Presently writer-in-residence at Indiana-Purdue University, Indianapolis, she is also producer/director of a weekly half-hour television series "The Black Experience."

Jay Saunders Redding (1906–   )

Redding was born in Wilmington, Delaware, and he was a Phi Beta Kappa graduate of Brown University, the school at which he earned both the B.A. and the M.A. degrees. After studying Elizabethan drama at Columbia University, Redding began a teaching career at Morehouse College. He worked for a number of years at Hampton Institute and is currently teaching at Cornell University. Redding, who has received both a Rockerfeller Foundation Fellowship and a Guggenheim Fellowship, has produced fiction, historical studies, and at least one important volume of literary criticism. His most important works include: *To Make a Poet Black* (1939, a critical study of black American poetry); *No Day of Triumph* (1942, an autobiography); *Stranger and Alone* (1950, a novel); *They Came in Chains: Americans from Africa* (1950, history); *The Lonesome Road: The Story of the Negro's Part in America* (1958); *On Being Negro in America* (1962, social criticism); and *The Negro* (1967).

Conrad Kent Rivers (1933–1968)

Rivers was born in Atlantic City, New Jersey. A good part of his life, however, was spent in Chicago. His poems appeared in *Antioch Review* and in *Kenyon Review*, and he published two volumes of poetry during the course of his tragically brief life—*Perchance to Dream, Othello* (1959), and *These Black Bodies and This Sunburnt Face* (1962).

Paule Marshall (1929–   )

Paule Marshall was born in Brooklyn, New York; her parents were from Barbados, and at the age of nine the writer traveled to her parents' country. The literary result of this trip was a volume of youthful poetry. The author is a graduate of Brooklyn College and a member of Phi Beta Kappa. Since leaving Brooklyn College, she has worked as a librarian, a reporter, and a writer, traveling to various parts of the world on her assignments. Her works include: *Brown Girl, Brownstones* (1959, a novel); *Soul Clap Hands and Sing* (1961, a collection of short stories); and *Chosen Place: The Timeless People* (1970, a novel).

Addison Gayle (1932–   )

Gayle was born in Newport News, Virginia. He attended high school in Newport News and went on to the City College of New York, where he took a B.A. degree in English literature. Gayle received an M.A. degree in English from the University of California at Los Angeles in 1966 and returned to New York to begin a teaching career at City College. He is currently employed as an Assistant Professor at Baruch College, which is a division of the City University of New York. Gayle's critical articles have appeared in *Rights and Reviews, Negro History Bulletin, Negro Digest*, the *C.L.A. Journal*, the *Journal of Human Relations*, and the *Journal of Negro History*. He is the editor of *Black Expression* (1969), a volume of critical statements by black writers and artists. Three new books, including a biography of Paul Laurence Dunbar, are scheduled to appear in 1971.

William Melvin Kelley (1937–   )

Kelley was born in New York City. After receiving secondary education at Fieldson School, he attended Harvard University, where he studied creative writing and received several creative writing awards. He has been a John Hay Whitney fellow, and he has served as author-in-residence at the State University College at Genesco. His short stories and articles have appeared in *Esquire, Saturday Review*, and *Negro Digest*. His novels include: *A Different Drummer* (1962); *A Drop of Patience* (1965); and *Dem* (1967). A volume of his short stories, *Dancers on the Shore*, appeared in 1964, and a new novel, *Dunfords Travels Everywheres* (1970).

Ted Joans (1928–   )

Joans was born in Cairo, Illinois. He received a B.A. degree in fine arts from Indiana University in 1951, and since that time has traveled throughout the world and worked as both a painter and a jazz trumpeter. Like LeRoi Jones, Ted Joans was part of the beatnik upsurge of the fifties, and his poems and paintings were pointed to as consummate examples of "beat" art. Joans's poems have appeared in several anthologies, but his first volume of verse, *Black Pow-Wow*, was not published until 1969. The poet is currently engaged in writing an autobiography (*Spadework: An Autobiography of a Hipster*) and a novel (*Niggers from Outer Space*).

Hoyt W. Fuller (1927–   )

Fuller was born in Atlanta, Georgia. He was reared in Detroit, Michigan, where he attended Wayne State University and earned his B.A. degree. After doing graduate work at Wayne, Fuller began a job as feature editor for the *Michigan Chronicle*. He has worked as an associate editor for *Ebony*, and in 1959 he worked in Africa as a corespondent for the Dutch newspaper *Haagse Post*. When he returned from Africa, Fuller worked for a time with *Collier's* Encyclopedia. In 1961, Johnson publications gave him the task of reviving the *Negro Digest,* which had not appeared since 1951. In 1965, Fuller spent a year in Africa as a John Hay Whitney Fellow, and he is now editor of *Black World* (formerly *Negro Digest*), for which he writes a regular review column. Fuller's short stories and articles have appeared in the *New Yorker, New Republic, Midstream, Critic,* and *Southwest Review*.

LeRoi Jones (1934–   )

Jones, who is perhaps the most important black writer of his age, was born in Newark, New Jersey. He received a B.A. degree from Howard University and did graduate work at Columbia University. After serving in the Air Force for four years (an experience which he describes vividly in one section of his novel), Jones was awarded a John Hay Whitney Fellowship in 1961. He has also received a Guggenheim Fellowship, and his play *Dutchman* was awarded an Obie for the best off-Broadway play of 1964. Jones's works include many genres, and they show a range of achievement that has scarcely been equalled by any other American writer of the fifties and sixties. His volumes of poetry include: *Preface to a Twenty-volume Suicide Note* (1961); *The Dead Lecturer* (1964); *Sabotage* (1963); *Target Study* (1965); and *Black Art* (1966)—the last three included in *Black Magic*, published in 1969. His dramas include: *Dutchman* (1964); *The Slave* (1964); *Baptism* (1967); *The Toilet* (1967); *Slave Ship* (1967); and *Arm Yourself, or Harm Yourself* (1967). He has produced one novel, *The System of Dante's Hell* (1966), and a collection of short stories, *Tales* (1967). Jones's volumes of criticism include *Blues People* (1963) and *Black Music* (1967), and he has published one collection of essays, *Home* (1966). His anthologies include: *The Moderns* (1963); *Four Young Lady Poets* (1964); and *Black Fire* (1968, along with Larry Neal).

Larry Neal (1937–)

Neal was born in Atlanta, Georgia, and reared in Philadelphia, Pennsylvania. He has served as arts editor for *Liberator,* and he is a contributing editor for *The Journal of Black Poetry.* Neal has also served as editor of *The Cricket,* a magazine of black music, and he has published poems and articles in *Freedomways, Negro Digest, Soulbook,* and *Black Dialogue.* His first volume of poetry, *Black Boogaloo,* appeared in 1969. Neal served as coeditor along with LeRoi Jones of *Black Fire,* an anthology of recent black American writings.

Malcolm X (1925–1965)

Malcolm X was born in Omaha, Nebraska; his father, Reverend Earl Little, was West Indian, and he was an organizer for Marcus Garvey's Universal Negro Improvement Association. Malcolm's childhood, therefore, was a transient one, and it was one in which the lesson of violence was learned early: the late black leader saw his father die at the hands of white terrorists. It was Malcolm's role as a Muslim leader that earned him fame, admiration, and respect. The leader was committed to the ideas of Elijah Muhammed for a number of years, and he worked as a preacher, organizer, and second in command until 1964. In 1964, after visits to Mecca and Africa, Malcolm established his own group dedicated to black liberation—the Organization of Afro-American Unity. In February of 1965, Malcolm X was assassinated in a Harlem ballroom while conducting a political meeting. His life story was set down with the assistance of Alex Haley in *The Autobiography of Malcolm X* (1964). "1965" is the last chapter of Malcolm's autobiography.

Julian Mayfield (1928–)

Mayfield was born in Greer, South Carolina, and spent a good part of his childhood in Washington, D.C. After service in the army, he returned to the United States, where he studied at Lincoln University in Pennsylvania. He has worked at a host of jobs during his lifetime, but his major achievements have been artistic ones. Mayfield has written essays, drama, and fiction, and he has worked as both a drama critic and an actor. Mayfield's major literary works are his three novels: *The Hit* (1957); *The Long Night* (1958); and *The Grand Parade* (1961). The essay that appears in this volume was published by the American Society of African Culture in a collection of essays entitled *The American Negro Writer and His Roots* (1960), the same volume that contains Redding's "The Negro Writer and His Relationship to His Roots."

Don L. Lee (1942–   )

Lee was reared in Detroit, Michigan, and educated in Chicago. He has worked as a staff member of the Museum of African-American History and as a teacher of Afro-American literature at Columbia College in Chicago; he has also served as poet-in-residence at Cornell University. Lee's poems have appeared in *Negro Digest* and *The Journal of Black Poetry,* and his volumes of poetry include: *Think Black* (1967); *Black Pride* (1968); *Don't Cry, Scream* (1969); and *We Walk the Way of the New World* (1970).

Etheridge Knight (1933–   )

Knight was born in Corinth, Mississippi. He served for a time in the United States Army, and he was wounded in Korea. In 1960, he was sentenced to Indiana State Prison where he began writing the poems and short stories that have established his reputation as one of the most promising black writers of the present day. Knight's poems and short stories have appeared in *Negro Digest, The Journal of Black Poetry, The Lakeshore Outlook,* and *Prison Magazine.* His works were also included in the anthologies *For Malcolm* and *Potere Negro,* and his first volume of poetry—*Poems from Prison*—was published in 1968. Knight is currently working on a novel, and his *Lettere dalla Prigione* was published in Italy in 1968.

175